ADA
Language
and Methodology

Prentice-Hall International
Series in Computer Science

C.A.R. Hoare, Series Editor

BACKHOUSE, R.C., *Program Construction and Verification*
BACKHOUSE, R.C., *Syntax of Programming Languages, Theory and Practice*
DE BAKKER, J.W., *Mathematical Theory of Program Correctness*
BJØRNER, D., and JONES, C.B., *Formal Specification and Software Development*
BORNAT, R., *Programming from First Principles*
CLARK, K.L., and McCABE, F.G., *micro-PROLOG: Programming in Logic*
DROMEY, R.G., *How to Solve it by Computer*
DUNCAN, F., *Microprocessor Programming and Software Development*
ELDER, J., *Construction of Data Processing Software*
GOLDSCHLAGER, L., and LISTER, A., *Computer Science: A Modern Introduction*
HAYES, I., (Ed.), *Specification Case Studies*
HEHNER, E.C.R., *The Logic of Programming*
HENDERSON, P., *Functional Programming: Application and Implementation*
HOARE, C.A.R., *Communicating Sequential Processes*
HOARE, C.A.R., and SHEPHERDSON, J.C., *Mathematical Logic and Programming Languages*
INMOS LTD., *Occam Programming Manual*
JACKSON M.A., *System Development*
JOHNSTON, H., *Learning to Program*
JONES, C.B., *Systematic Software Development Using VDM*
JOSEPH, M., PRASAD, V.R., and NATARAJAN, N., *A Multiprocessor Operating System*
LEW. A., *Computer Science: A Mathematical Introduction*
MacCALLUM, I., *Pascal for the Apple*
MacCALLUM, I., *UCSD Pascal for the IBM PC*
MARTIN, J.J., *Data Types and Data Structures*
POMBERGER, G., *Software Engineering and Modula-2*
REYNOLDS, J.C., *The Craft of Programming*
SLOMAN, M., and KRAMER, J., *Distributed Systems and Computer Networks*
TENNENT, R.D., *Principles of Programming Languages*
WATT, D.A., WICHMANN, B.A., and FINDLAY, W., *Ada: Language and Methodology*
WELSH, J., and ELDER, J., *Introduction to Pascal, 2nd Edition*
WELSH, J., ELDER, J., and BUSTARD, D., *Sequential Program Structures*
WELSH, J., and HAY, A., *A Model Implementation of Standard Pascal*
WELSH, J., McKEAG, M., *Structured System Programming*

A D A
Language and Methodology

David A. Watt
University of Glasgow, UK

Brian A. Wichmann
National Physical Laboratory, Teddington, Middlesex, UK

William Findlay
University of Glasgow, UK

Prentice/Hall International

Englewood Cliffs, New Jersey London Mexico New Delhi
Rio de Janeiro Singapore Sydney Tokyo Toronto

Library of Congress Cataloging-in-Publication Data

Watt, David A. (David Anthony)
Ada, language and methodology.

Bibliography: p.
Includes index.
1. Ada (Computer program language) I. Wichmann, Brian A. II. Findlay, William, *1947-* III. Title.
QA76.73.A35W38 1987 005.13'3 86-18696
ISBN 0-13-004078-9 (pbk.)
ISBN 0-13-004086-X (disk)

British Library Cataloguing in Publication Data

Watt, David A.
Ada: language and methodology.
1. Ada (Computer program language)
I. Title II. Wichmann, Brian A.
III. Findlay, William, *1947* -
005.13'3 QA76.73.A15

ISBN 0-13-004078-9

Prentice-Hall Inc., *Englewood Cliffs, New Jersey*
Prentice-Hall International (UK) Ltd, *London*
Prentice-Hall of Australia Pty Ltd, *Sydney*
Prentice-Hall Canada Inc., *Toronto*
Prentice-Hall Hispanoamericana S.A., *Mexico*
Prentice-Hall of India Private Ltd, *New Delhi*
Prentice-Hall of Japan Inc., *Tokyo*
Prentice-Hall of Southeast Asia Pte Ltd, Singapore
Editora Prentice-Hall do Brasil Ltda, *Rio de Janeiro*

Printed and bound in Great Britain for Prentice-Hall International (UK) Ltd., 66 Wood Lane End, Hemel Hempstead, Hertfordshire, HP2 4RG at the University Press, Cambridge.

3 4 5 90 89 88

ISBN 0-13-004078-9

Ada is a registered trade mark of the
US Government Ada Joint Program Office

The supplementary disk (see enclosed order form) has been prepared by Brian Wichmann using Microtext. The PC DOS version of Microtext was provided by Transdata Limited, Microelectronic Systems Division, 11 South Street, Havant, Hampshire PO9 1BU, England. Microtext is the copyright of Transdata Limited and the National Physical Laboratory.

Contents

Foreword

'I enjoyed reading the Algol 60 report; it taught me a lot about programming.' This is the comment of a data processing manager of a major motor manufacturing company, who had no conceivable prospect of ever using the language to program a computer. It is a most perceptive comment, because it describes an important goal in the design of a new programming language: that it should be an aid in specification, description, and design of programs, as well as in the construction of reliable code.

This was one of the main aims in the design of the language which was later given the name Ada. As a result, the language incorporates many excellent structural features which have proved their value in many precursor languages such as Pascal and Pascal Plus.

The combination of many complex features into a single language has led to an unfortunate delay in availability of production-quality implementations. But the long wait is coming to an end, and one can now look forward to a rapid and widespread improvement in programming practice, both from those who use the language and from those who study its concepts and structures.

I hope that this book will contribute directly to these ideals, which have inspired many of the other books in the same series. It continues the tradition of the series in that it describes how the language can be used as the target of a sound programming methodology, embracing the full life cycle of a programming project. It explains not just the features and details of the language, but also their purpose and method of effective use.

The complexities and difficulties are not glossed over; they are explained within the appropriate context, with hints on how to avoid any consequent problems. I hope the book will be useful, both to those who have the privilege or obligation to use the language, and to those who have the interest and curiosity to understand and appreciate its rationale.

C. A. R. Hoare

Preface

As its title suggests, this book has two aims. The first is to introduce the reader to the programming language Ada. The second is to place programming and the Ada language in perspective as part of the larger process of software development. We emphasize systematic techniques for designing large programs ('structured design') as well as techniques for implementing program modules ('structured programming').

Ada was designed to be suitable for a wide class of applications, in particular those requiring the construction and maintenance of large programs. In our experience, Ada is also well suited to teaching a variety of software engineering techniques, many of which cannot be convincingly demonstrated in earlier languages. Certainly, the reader of this book should learn more than just another language: Ada is a tool, not an end in itself.

The book is aimed at professional programmers and students with at least a year's experience of programming in a high-level language. Some familiarity with the fundamental concepts of programming is assumed, but we do not assume familiarity with methodologies such as structured programming and structured design. Much of the material in the book has been tested in courses at Glasgow University — on Ada itself, on software development and on concurrent programming. If the book is used to teach Ada as a *first* language, it should be supplemented by additional material on the elements of programming. (However, we advise novices to learn Pascal before attempting to learn Ada.)

Content

The book is divided into four parts.

Part I (*Programming in the Small*) covers a subset of Ada comparable with many other programming languages: scalar and composite data types, control structures, subprograms and parameters. Most readers will find Part I straightforward, but it should be studied carefully, since the Ada concepts and terminology introduced here are an essential foundation for understanding the more advanced features of the language. Moreover, Chapter 5 introduces the methodology of structured programming, which is used throughout the book.

Part II (*Programming in the Large*) is perhaps the most important of the book. Its title deliberately contrasts with that of Part I. Part II introduces the features of Ada that make it suitable for construction of large programs: packages, exceptions, separate compilation and the program library. Taken together, these features allow programs to be constructed from robust reusable modules. The methodology of structured design is introduced in Chapter 16. On completing Part II, the reader should be able to undertake substantial projects in Ada.

Part III (*Advanced Data Types*) completes our treatment of the data types of Ada: access types, discriminants, numeric types, and the role of types in programming.

Finally, Part IV (*Advanced Program Structures*) completes our treatment of the program structures of Ada: operator definitions and overloading, generics, tasks, portability and machine-dependent programming. Tasks, like packages, are extremely important in Ada; they allow for the modular construction of concurrent and real-time programs.

Examples and case studies

Numerous examples are provided to illustrate the use of the programming language. Most have been tested on a computer. An important feature of the book is a series of case studies, designed to illustrate the methodologies of structured programming and structured design and their relationship to Ada. Case studies may be found in Chapters 13, 16, and 25. The last chapter is indeed given over entirely to a case study sketching the design and implementation of a large system, demonstrating the use of Ada for both programming-in-the-small and programming-in-the-large.

Exercises

Most chapters are followed by exercises, designed to provide experience in using the features covered by the chapter. If possible the programs should be run on a computer. Sample solutions to selected exercises are provided.

Use of the book

The book is intended to be read more or less sequentially. Some topics could be skipped at a first reading and are so marked in the text. We have not written a work of reference, although we hope that by means of the index the reader will be able to find information on specific topics. Nor have we attempted to cover all the more obscure and subtle interactions between language features. For information on points not covered by this book the reader must consult the official Ada reference definition [Ada 1983]. Another useful reference is the Ada Rationale [Ada 1979], which explains in detail the design of (an earlier version of) Ada. The bibliography lists a number of other works that complement this book. These are important if the more specialized areas of Ada and system design are to be fully understood.

Computer-aided instruction

A floppy disk containing a computer-aided instruction course is available as a supplement to the book. This will run on any IBM PC compatible computer. The course is arranged in modules, one module per chapter of the book. On the completion of each module, an assessment is made of the reader's progress, indicating whether his or her level of understanding is sufficient to advance to the next module. Hence this supplement will be of substantial value to readers teaching themselves Ada.

The computer-aided instruction disk can be ordered from the publishers, using the enclosed order form.

Acknowledgments

We are very happy to acknowledge the detailed and incisive reviews of earlier versions of the text by the Prentice-Hall referees, which we found extremely valuable. We are also grateful to Jan Madey, Helen Watt and Val Wichmann, who read parts of the manuscript for us. Finally, we would like to thank Henry Hirschberg of Prentice-Hall for his patience in waiting for a manuscript that was as overdue as the first Ada compilers; and Helen Martin and Robert Chaundy for seeing the book through to publication.

Appendices B and C have been reproduced from [Ada 1983] with permission of the Ada Joint Program Office, U. S. Department of Defense.

The computer-aided instruction course was produced using **Microtext** and was implemented by Gary Allman of Transdata Ltd.

The book was typeset in the Computing Science Department of Glasgow University. We are grateful to all those colleagues who made this possible, in particular Malcolm Atkinson, Tom Baxter, Robert Fee, Dennis Gilles, Naveed Khan, John Livingstone, Nick Nei and Zdravko Podoloski. We used Donald Knuth's excellent TEX typesetting system and Leslie Lamport's LATEX package.

David Watt
Brian Wichmann
Bill Findlay

PART I

Programming in the Small

1

Introduction to Ada

1.1. Background

The programming of electronic digital computers has a short history, dating only from the late 1940s. At an early stage two major fields of programming activity emerged. The first was scientific numerical computation, which includes applications such as trajectory calculations, analysis of experimental results, aircraft design and weather forecasting. The second field was commercial data processing, which includes business applications such as invoicing, payrolls and stock control. These two fields were dominated by the high-level programming languages FORTRAN and COBOL, respectively.

By the mid-1960s it was apparent that neither FORTRAN nor COBOL was suitable for use outside its own original application area. Computer applications were by then diverging rapidly, into areas such as database management, artificial intelligence, telecommunications, word processing, instrumentation and control. This trend was accelerated in the 1970s by the appearance of microprocessors that not only made existing applications still more attractive but also made feasible many new applications in areas such as aerospace and consumer goods.

The expansion of application areas has been paralleled by an equally dramatic expansion of specially-tailored programming languages. There have been various attempts to bring order out of this chaos by designing a single *general-purpose* language suitable for all applications, including software such as compilers and operating systems. None of the earlier general-purpose languages, such as PL/I or Algol 68, ever matched the success of FORTRAN or COBOL. Perhaps the most successful language of this period was Pascal. Pascal is not a truly general-purpose language (lacking in particular any capability for concurrent and real-time programming), but with its nicely designed control structures and data structures it proved well suited to a wide range of applications, and it gained rapidly in popularity during the 1970s.

In 1976 the U. S. Department of Defense (DoD) carried out a survey of high-level languages used for writing the software of their computer systems, and they found that at least 450 different languages were in use. Not one of these, however, was considered suitable for adoption as a standard language for writing DoD software. As a result of this discovery, the DoD commissioned an ambitious project to design not only a new general-purpose high-level programming language, using the latest ideas in language design, but also a standard programming support environment. Future suppliers of computer systems to the DoD would be required to standardize on the new language and its support environment, thus allowing DoD programmers to be familiar with only one language and only one system for creating, editing, compiling, testing and documenting programs. In this way they expected to reduce, and eventually eliminate, fragmentation of their programmers' efforts among a multiplicity of languages and support systems, and thus to make significant savings on their software expenditure.

The new language was completed in 1979, and revised during 1980–82, by a team led by Jean Ichbiah. This new language built on the success of Pascal and its descendants. It was named *Ada*, after Augusta Ada Byron, Countess Lovelace (1815–1852), who was the world's first programmer and a collaborator of Charles Babbage. Ada has since been adopted as a standard programming language not only by the DoD but also by several other major national and international organizations.

1.2. The programming language Ada

Ada is a *high-level* programming language. In other words, it is a notation that is intended to be natural and convenient for writing and reading computer programs. Ada is a blend of mathematical notation with English words and phrases that are used with precise meanings. In this respect it is similar to other high-level languages such as those already mentioned; and quite different from *low-level* machine languages and assembly languages, which require programs to be written in terms of the instruction sets and registers of specific computers. Low-level language programs tend to be much more difficult to write, to debug and to understand than equivalent high-level language programs. Moreover, they are specific to the computers for which they were written, so they cannot be transferred to dissimilar computers. Thus low-level language programs are both more costly and less valuable than equivalent high-level language programs. The usual advantage claimed for writing programs in low-level languages is efficiency, but in practice this is rarely important enough to justify their extra cost.

Before being executed an Ada program must first be translated into machine language. We need some terminology to distinguish the three programs involved here: the *Ada compiler* is a program that accepts a *source program* (expressed in Ada) and translates it into an equivalent *object program* (expressed in machine language). The object program may then be executed immediately. More likely, it will be stored in a *program library*; this allows it to be executed as often as desired, without compiling the Ada source program every time.

An Ada program library can contain not only complete programs but also *subprograms* (procedures and functions) and *packages*. These are portions of programs that can be written, compiled and tested separately. This idea allows well-tested and generally useful subprograms and packages to be incorporated in several programs. We shall see how to write subprograms and packages in Part II, but we shall be *using* certain standard packages and subprograms right from the start.

Like any language, Ada has *syntax* and *semantics*. The syntax of Ada is a set of rules for writing down well-formed Ada constructs such as expressions, statements, declarations, subprograms and packages. Its semantics is a set of rules defining the meaning or effect of each well-formed Ada construct. In common with other programming languages, Ada's syntax and semantics are rigidly defined. An Ada source program will be successfully compiled only if it adheres to the language's syntax rules.

In this book the syntax rules of Ada are expressed by *syntax diagrams*. Each syntax diagram defines the syntax of a single construct. A complete set of syntax diagrams for the whole Ada language may be found in Appendix A. In the text we shall sometimes reproduce these in a simplified form, but more usually you will be referred to the appendix.

Two simple syntax diagrams may be seen in Figure 1.1 and Figure 1.2. We shall use these to illustrate how syntax diagrams are interpreted. Identifiers are used in Ada as names for programs and various entities within programs. Consider the syntax diagram headed 'identifier' in Figure 1.1. Choose any path from the diagram's entrance to its exit, following the direction of the arrows, and note everything you pass on the way. One possibility is the sequence 'letter letter letter digit'. From the syntax diagram headed 'digit', in Figure 1.2, it is easy to see that a digit is any one of the characters `0`, `1`, `2`, `3`, `4`, `5`, `6`, `7`, `8` or `9`. The syntax diagram headed 'letter' is not shown, but as you might expect it defines a letter to be one of `A`, `a`, `B`, `b`, ..., `Z` or `z`. Thus `Top1` and `ABS0` are examples of identifiers. Other examples are `A`, `pi`, `X1`, `V_1_a` and `Oxygen_flow_rate`. On the other hand, `1st_Char` and `_X` are *not* identifiers, since the syntax diagram 'identifier' requires every identifier to start with a letter. Nor are `Denom__or`, `V8.1` and `CostIn$`. (*Exercise*: verify these examples.)

1.3. A simple Ada program

In this chapter we set the scene by means of a very simple example.

Example 1.1 *A first complete Ada program*

The line numbers on the left below are not part of the Ada program — they are present only to facilitate the explanation that follows.

```
1    -- Program Show_Time_of_Day reads the number of
2    -- seconds since midnight, and writes the time
3    -- of day in the form H:M:S, using the 24-hour clock.
```

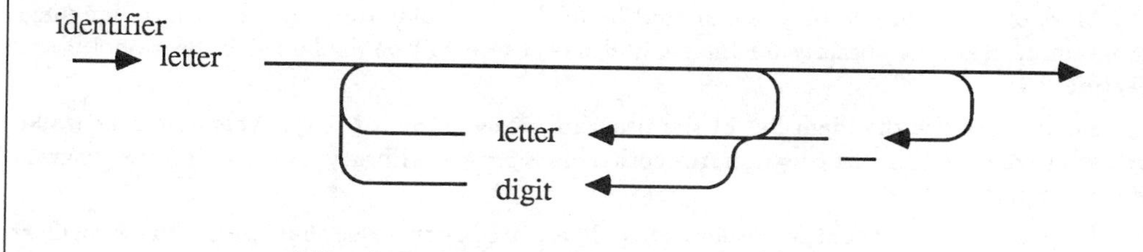

Fig. 1.1 Syntax diagram for identifiers

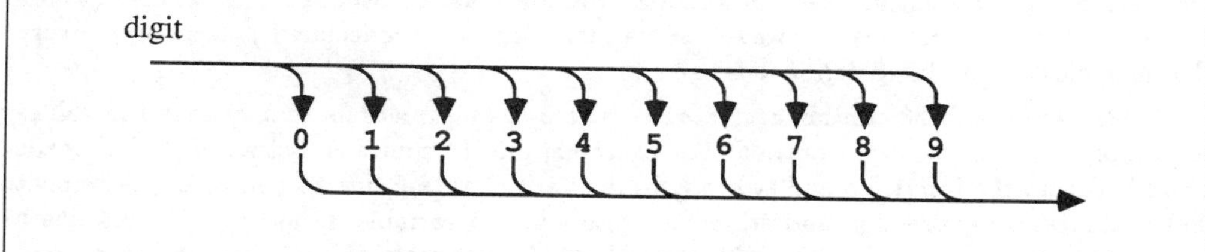

Fig. 1.2 Syntax diagram for digits

```
4   with Text_IO;  use Text_IO;
5   procedure Show_Time_of_Day is
6       package Int_IO is new Integer_IO (Integer);  use Int_IO;
7       Secs_per_Min : constant Integer := 60;
8       Mins_per_Hr  : constant Integer := 60;
9       Secs_per_Hr  : constant Integer
10                       := Secs_per_Min * Mins_per_Hr;
11      Time         : Integer;
12      H, M, S      : Integer;
13  begin
14      Get (Time);                       -- secs. since midnight
15      H := Time / Secs_per_Hr;          -- hours since midnight
16      Time := Time rem Secs_per_Hr;     -- secs. since last hour
17      M := Time / Secs_per_Min;         -- mins. since last hour
18      S := Time rem Secs_per_Min;       -- secs. since last min.
19      Put ("Time of day is    ");
20      Put (H);  Put (':');
21      Put (M);  Put (':');
22      Put (S);
23      New_Line;
24  end Show_Time_of_Day;
```

Given the integer 54450 as input data, the program's output might look like this:

```
Time of day is       15:    7:   30
```

□ *End of Example 1.1*

Most of this example program should be fairly self-explanatory to a high-level language programmer (except possibly for lines 4 and 6 — these will be explained in Section 1.9 and Section 2.3).

Line 5 specifies the identifier of the program, `Show_Time_of_Day`. This identifier would be used to distinguish this program from others in a program library. An Ada (main) program is usually a *procedure*.

Lines 6 through 12 contain *declarations*. These are instructions that specify the identifiers and properties of various entities to be used in the Ada program. For example, line 7 declares `Secs_per_Min` to be an `Integer` constant whose value is 60; and line 11 declares `Time` to be an `Integer` variable. In Ada terminology, obeying a declaration is called *elaborating* that declaration. Every identifier used in an Ada program *must* be declared somewhere. (There are no implicit declarations. However, some identifiers are predeclared.) Moreover, every identifier must be declared *before* it is used.

Lines 14 through 23 contain *statements*. These are instructions that change the values of variables or perform input-output. For example, line 14 contains a statement that reads a number from the input file and stores it in the variable `Time`; line 15 contains a statement that evaluates an expression and stores the result in the variable `H`; and line 22 contains a statement that writes out the value of the variable `S`. In Ada terminology, obeying a statement is called *executing* that statement.

The symbols **begin** and **end** (lines 13 and 24) bracket the statements of the program. The bracketed statements are executed in exactly the sequence in which they are written. It is good practice (but not obligatory) for the final **end** to be followed by the program's identifier.

Note carefully the punctuation of the program. Every declaration, every statement and the program as a whole is terminated by a semicolon. This rule is necessary because declarations and statements may be written several to a line, or they may continue from one line to the next. The declarations are collected together in the *declarative part*, and segregated from the statements. The syntax of Ada programs is shown, in a highly simplified form, in Figure 1.3.

We now look at the elementary features of Ada in more detail.

1.4. Lexicon

The lexicon of Ada consists of various symbols that may classified as literals, identifiers, reserved words and delimiters.

Literals are used to denote constant values of various types, for example:

```
0    1    60    1_000_000          (integer literals)
0.0    3.14158                     (real literals)
'H'    ':'    ' '                  (character literals)
"Time of day is "    "???"         (string literals)
```

Identifiers are names given to constants, variables, types, subprograms, packages and other entities in Ada programs. We have already seen some examples of legal (and illegal) identifiers, in Section 1.2. Corresponding upper- and lower-case letters are equivalent (except in character and string literals), so `put_line`, `Put_Line` and `PUT_LINE` are all the same identifier (but not `PutLine` — the underscore is significant).

Reserved words are certain English words that are used for specific purposes in the Ada language. Because of this they must not be chosen as identifiers, although they all conform to the syntax of Ada identifiers — hence the description 'reserved'. Some examples of reserved words are:

procedure **begin** **end** **constant** **use** **is**

all of which occurred in Example 1.1. There are over 60 reserved words in Ada; they are listed in full in Appendix A. Corresponding upper- and lower-case letters are equivalent in reserved words, as in identifiers. In order to help you recognize the reserved words, in this book we adopt the *convention* of writing reserved words in lower case and identifiers in upper or mixed case.

The *delimiters* include the following punctuation symbols, brackets, operators and other special symbols:

```
,    ;    :    .    '
(    )    <<    >>
**    *    /    +    -    &    =    /=    <    <=    >=    >
:=    ..    |    =>    <>
```

Each delimiter consists of one or two characters.

A summary of the lexicon of Ada may be found in Appendix A.

1.5. Comments, layout and style

Comments may be incorporated within a source program to explain it to a human reader; they are ignored by the compiler. In Ada a comment is introduced by the two-character combination '--' and continues up to the end of the same line. Thus a comment may either follow some symbols on the same line (as in lines 14 through 18 of Example 1.1) or occupy a complete line by itself (as in lines 1 through 3 of Example 1.1). If commentary is to continue over several lines, each line must start with '--'.

Each literal, identifier, reserved word and delimiter must be contained entirely within one line and (apart from character and string literals) must not contain any embedded spaces. Consecutive identifiers, reserved words and numeric literals on the same line must be separated by spacing. This rule is essential to distinguish the following, quite different, statements:

```
A := C and Y;                    A := CandY;
```

Otherwise spacing may be used freely to enhance the readability of a program.

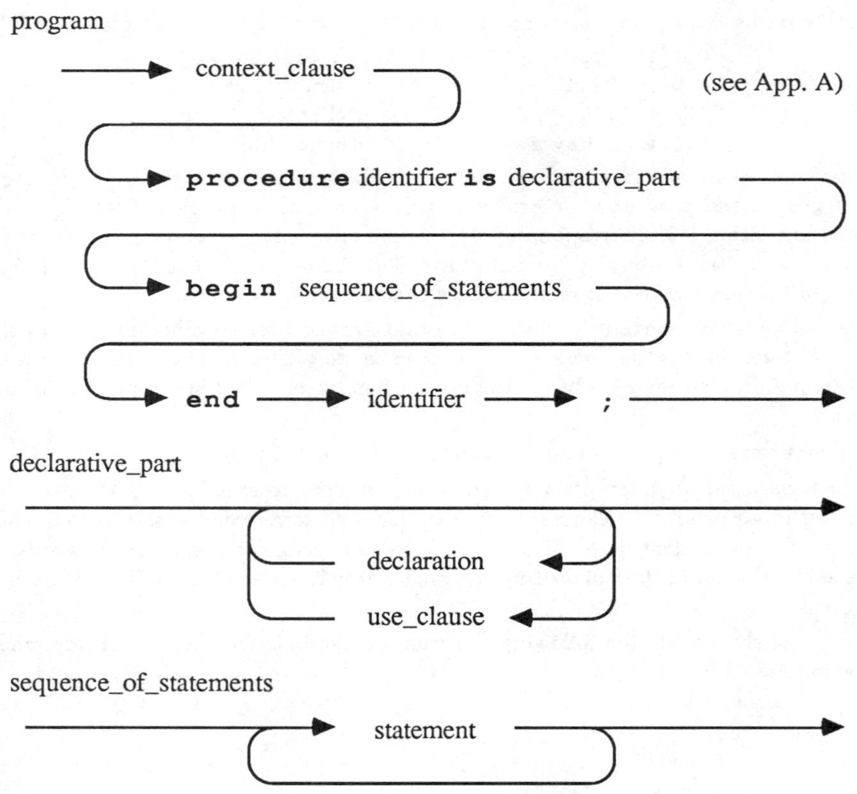

Fig. 1.3 Syntax of Ada programs (simplified)

This leads on to the topic of *programming style*. Most useful programs are read not only by their authors but also by other programmers. Each reader needs to be able to see easily how a program works, perhaps to locate and correct errors or to make changes. A badly styled program is unpleasant reading, even for its own author. These factors make it highly desirable to write programs with a view to readability. In particular:

- Use comments freely to describe the function of a program, and to explain how each part works.
- Choose identifiers to be as descriptive as possible. Use nouns for constants and variables (e.g. `Secs_per_Min`, `Time`), and verbs for procedures (e.g. `Show_Time_of_Day`, `Get`, `Put`). Avoid cryptic identifiers (e.g. `I`, `J`, `K`) and vague general terms (e.g. `Data`, `Value`, `Compute`). Finally, make use of both upper- and lower-case letters, if available (but be consistent!).
- Make the program layout reflect its syntactic structure, as in Example 1.1. Write declarations and statements one per line, and *indent* them relative to the words **procedure**, **begin** and **end**. Later we shall come across more constructs for which indentation is desirable.

We shall use this programming style consistently throughout this book, and we recommend it to you. Of course, programming style is of no concern to the Ada compiler; it is for the benefit of human readers only.

1.6. Data types

In Ada, every data object has a *type*. A type is characterized by a set of values together with the operations that may be performed on these values.

In Ada each type is named by an identifier; examples are `Integer`, `Boolean` and `Character`. The `Integer` type consists of the whole numbers (within certain limits) together with the familiar arithmetic operations of addition, subtraction, multiplication and so on. The `Boolean` type consists of the truth values, `False` and `True`, together with the logical operations such as **or** and **and**. The values of the `Character` type are single characters.

Ada is a *strongly-typed* language. This means that every data object (constant or variable) has a fixed type, and must be used only with operations applicable to that type. For example, `Integer` objects may be used as operands in additions or subtractions, whereas `Boolean` or `Character` objects may not. Any attempt to use a data object with an inapplicable operation will be detected by the Ada compiler as a *type error*.

This feature of Ada is a valuable aid to programmers, for experience with strongly-typed languages has shown that type checking in the compiler detects many programming errors that would otherwise show up only on executing the program, or not at all. As a very simple example, a programmer might carelessly write '`C:=0;`' instead of the intended '`C:='0';`' (where `C` is a `Character` variable). The Ada compiler will immediately flag this as a type error. In the absence of type checking this kind of error, buried in the middle of a large program, might escape detection for a long time.

Sometimes it *is* necessary to convert a value from one type to another. Ada does allow this, but such conversions must always be *explicit*. This rules out accidental type conversions.

The types mentioned in this section are only some of the types of Ada. There are other predefined types, and furthermore the programmer can define new types as required in a particular program. The types of Ada can be classified in various ways. For example, two broad classes are ***scalar types*** (whose values are indivisible, such as numbers, characters or truth values) and ***composite types*** (arrays and records, whose values are composed of several simpler values). The type classification is important because it underlies the type rules; for example, there are certain operations applicable to scalar values but not to composite values. The type classification is summarized diagrammatically in Figure 20.1, which you might like to preview. Much of it will be familiar if you already know a language like Pascal. In the rest of this book we shall treat the predefined types and the type classes one at a time, showing how each fits into the overall scheme.

1.7. Object declarations

When we talk about data, we distinguish between constants and variables. A ***constant*** is a data object whose value, once fixed, never changes. Examples are the number of hours in a day and the ratio of the circumference of a circle to its diameter. A ***variable*** is a data object whose value may change. Examples are today's date, your bank balance, and the population of the world.

A constant may be denoted by a literal, for example 24 for the number of hours in a day. Often, however, it is preferable to give a name to an important constant. For example, physicists use the name *c* for the speed of light. This makes physical formulae easier to write and to read than would be the case if they wrote down its literal value every time. Moreover, if they obtain a more accurate measurement of the speed of light, they do not need to modify all the formulae. In programming there are similar advantages to using named constants, hence the declarations of `Secs_per_Min`, `Mins_per_Hr` and `Secs_per_Hr` in Example 1.1.

In Ada constants and variables are declared by means of ***object declarations***. The syntax of object declarations is shown in simplified form in Figure 1.4. Every object declaration introduces one or more identifiers and specifies their type. Each identifier becomes the name of a separate object. The reserved word `constant` obviously indicates that the declared identifiers are constants rather than variables.

Example 1.1 contains several examples of constant declarations. Elaborating the decla-

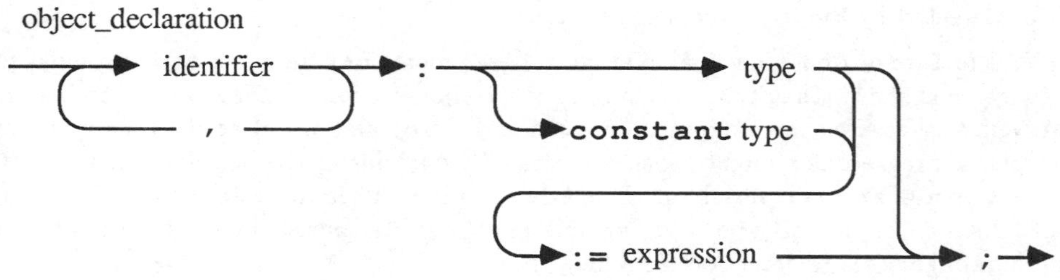

Fig. 1.4 Syntax of object declarations (simplified)

ration on line 7 introduces the identifier `Secs_per_Min` to denote a constant of type `Integer`, whose value will be 60. The slightly more complicated declaration starting on line 9 likewise introduces `Secs_per_Hr` to denote a constant of type `Integer`, but this time the value of the constant is given by an *expression*, '`Secs_per_Min * Mins_per_Hr`', whose value turns out to be 3600. This value could have been written into the declaration, as follows:

```
Secs_per_Hr : constant Integer := 3600;
```

but it is preferable to show explicitly any dependence of one constant on others.

The simplest form of variable declaration is illustrated in Example 1.1. Line 11 declares a variable, `Time`, of type `Integer`, and line 12 declares three variables, `H`, `M` and `S`, also of type `Integer`. These declarations do not initialize the variables. We say that such variables initially have ***undefined*** values. Using an undefined value in a computation makes the effect of the computation unpredictable: a common programming error.

Sometimes we wish to initialize a variable when its declaration is elaborated. For example:

```
Pay : Integer := Hours_Worked * Hourly_Rate;
```

Here `Pay` is declared to be a variable of type `Integer`, initialized to the value of the expression '`Hours_Worked * Hourly_Rate`'. (This assumes that `Hours_Worked` and `Hourly_Rate` have already been declared and given values; they could be either constants or variables.)

1.8. Expressions and assignment statements

Expressions occur in assignment statements, in object declarations and in many other Ada constructs.

An expression is a rule or formula for computing a value. Expressions in Ada are composed of operands (such as objects and literals), operators and parentheses. Ada has the following set of operators:

Dyadic operators	*Monadic operators*	*Precedence*
`**`	`abs` `not`	highest
`*` `/` `mod` `rem`		
`+` `-` `&`	`+` `-`	
`=` `/=` `<` `<=` `>=` `>`		
`and` `or` `xor`		lowest

Some operators have higher precedence than others. For example, the expression `I+J/K` is interpreted as `I+(J/K)` rather than as `(I+J)/K`. When operators of the same precedence are used together, they associate to the left. Thus `I/J*K` is interpreted as `(I/J)*K` rather than as `I/(J*K)`. Explicit parentheses may always be used to override these precedence and association rules if desired.

The ***assignment statement*** is used to change the value of a variable. There are several examples in Example 1.1, on lines 15 through 18. See the syntax diagram 'assignment_statement' in Appendix A. The symbol '`:=`' is pronounced 'becomes equal to'. When the assignment statement is executed, the expression on the right of '`:=`' is evaluated, then its value is assigned to the variable on the left.

Every expression in Ada has a unique type that can be deduced by the compiler. Ada has the general rule that the types of the variable and expression in an assignment statement must match exactly; this guarantees that the variable will be assigned a value of the correct type when the assignment statement is executed. There are no exceptions to this rule. On the other hand, the assignment statement is very general in that it may be used to assign values of *any* type. (There is a single exception, which we shall not meet until Chapter 13.) Similar rules apply to object declarations containing the symbol ':='.

One last point before we leave the topic of expressions. A *static expression* is an expression whose value can be predicted without actually executing the program. In Example 1.1, 60 is obviously a static expression, but so too is 'Secs_per_Min * Mins_per_Hr', whose value will be 3600. 'Time / Secs_per_Hr' is not a static expression, since one its operands is the variable Time. Static expressions can be evaluated by the Ada compiler, but non-static expressions can be evaluated only when the program is executed. The expressions in object declarations (even constant declarations) need not be static expressions, although frequently they will be. Later, however, we shall come across certain contexts where Ada *requires* an expression to be static.

1.9. Text input-output

Input-output devices such as VDUs, teletypes and printers have the common property that data is transmitted in the form of *text* (lines of characters).

Unlike most high-level languages, Ada has no special language features for handling text input-output. Instead the necessary facilities are provided by a package called Text_IO. This is an example of a standard package of the kind mentioned in Section 1.2. It is available to every program that starts with the following *with clause*:

```
with Text_IO;
```

(Any program that depends on library packages or subprograms must say so explicitly in a with clause. With clauses will be explained more fully in Chapter 16.)

Text_IO contains several subprograms for performing text input-output operations, including the following basic operations:

- Get(X); — reads a single character, or a string of characters, and stores it in the variable X.
- Put(*X*); — writes the value of the expression *X*, which may be a single character or a string of characters.
- Skip_Line; — skips the remainder of the current line of input.
- New_Line; — forces subsequent output to be written on a fresh line.

To make use of these subprograms it is convenient to insert a *use clause*:

```
use Text_IO;
```

immediately after the corresponding with clause. Without this use clause, statements like:

```
Put (S);  New_Line;
```

would have to be written down less concisely as:

```
Text_IO.Put (S);  Text_IO.New_Line;
```

This point will be explained in Chapter 13.

Unless otherwise specified, input operations like `Get` and `Skip_Line` are applied to a ***standard input file***, and output operations like `Put` and `New_Line` are applied to a ***standard output file***. For example, the standard input might well be text typed on a VDU keyboard and the standard output might be text displayed on the VDU screen. All the input-output operations in Example 1.1 are applied to the standard input and output. For example, the statement '`Put(':');`' writes a single character (a colon), and the statement on line 19 writes a string of characters, both to the standard output.

It is possible to read and write not only characters and strings but also numbers and literals of other types. That, however, requires additional declarations such as the declaration on line 6 of Example 1.1. We shall describe these extra facilities as they arise, starting in Chapter 2.

Finally, let us re-iterate that `Text_IO` is merely a library package and that the facilities it provides are ***not*** built into the Ada language. Many Ada programs ('embedded systems' such as aircraft landing systems) will not require text input-output and therefore will not use `Text_IO`.

1.10. Errors and exceptions

All programmers are fallible, and various kinds of error can crop up in an Ada program. We distinguish carefully between errors detected during compilation of the program and those that arise during its execution.

Syntactic errors are errors of form, such as an identifier containing an invalid character, or a missing or misplaced symbol. ***Type errors*** are violations of the type rules, as described in Section 1.6. ***Declarative errors*** include the use of an identifier in a manner inconsistent with its declaration, the use of an identifier that has not been declared at all, or a double declaration of an identifier. Syntactic errors, type errors and declarative errors will all be detected and reported by the Ada compiler. A source program containing any of these errors will fail to compile, since its meaning could not safely be deduced by the compiler.

A program that adheres to these rules and is successfully compiled might still fail to behave in the manner intended. For example, the program might attempt some impossible operation such as division by zero or reading nonexistent data from a file. The effect is to ***raise an exception***. Unless anticipated, raising an exception causes the execution of the program to terminate immediately. (A good Ada system will then produce diagnostic information to assist in diagnosing the cause of the exception.) There are several kinds of exceptions, each of which has an identifier. For example, division by zero raises the exception named `Numeric_Error`, and attempting to read data past the end of a file raises the exception named `End_Error`. We shall discuss the various exceptions as they arise, and in Chapter 14 we shall see how they can be anticipated.

It is possible for a program to behave in an unpredictable fashion without actually raising an exception. A common example of this has already been mentioned: using the value of an uninitialized variable. Such a program is called simply an ***erroneous program***. Their unpredictability makes these errors the most troublesome of all.

2

The `Integer` Data Type

2.1. Integer data

Integers are used in programming principally for counting purposes. For example the number of items in a list, the size of a population, and a sum of money (expressed in cents or similar units) are all integers. These examples involve *natural* numbers (zero or more), but negative numbers are useful too. For example a bank balance might be represented by a positive integer (if in credit) or a negative integer (if overdrawn).

2.2. Type `Integer`: values and operations

We have already met the type `Integer`. Its values are positive and negative whole numbers:

$\ldots, -3, -2, -1, 0, +1, +2, +3, \ldots$

Hardware properties (word size and integer representation) influence the range of `Integer` values that can be efficiently represented in a given computer. Some programs might need to know the minimum and maximum values of this range. In Ada they are available as `Integer'First` and `Integer'Last` respectively. These are *attributes* of the `Integer` type, and they are available to every Ada program. These particular attributes are constants, although their actual values are implementation-dependent. (This means that their values vary from one Ada implementation to another.) Figure 2.1 gives some typical values of these attributes.

(There are other integer types in Ada in addition to the standard type `Integer`. Some implementations provide a type `Short_Integer`, containing a narrower range of values but

Integer representation	`Integer'First`	`Integer'Last`
16 bits, 2's complement	-32768	+32767
16 bits, 1's complement	-32767	+32767
32 bits, 2's complement	2147483648	+2147483647
32 bits, 1's complement	-2147483647	+2147483647

Fig. 2.1 Typical values of `Integer` attributes

requiring less storage space, and/or a type Long_Integer, containing a wider range of values but requiring more storage space. These types, if provided, have their own attributes such as Short_Integer'First and Short_Integer'Last.)

We have already seen *integer literals*, which are used in Ada for writing down integer values. Integer literals are usually written in the conventional decimal notation, and underscores may be used to break up long numbers. Thus 1_999_999 is equivalent to 1999999 but easier to read.

Chapter 1 contained several examples of object declarations introducing constants and variables of type Integer. A variable declared as follows:

```
I : Integer;
```

may be given any value in the range Integer'First through Integer'Last. Often, however, we want to restrict an Integer variable to a narrower range of values. In Example 1.1 the variable M is used to contain the number of complete minutes since the last hour. M will be an Integer variable, but we also know that its value cannot sensibly be less than 0 nor greater than the value of Mins_per_Hr-1 (i.e., 59). We could state this explicitly by inserting the *range constraint*:

```
range 0 .. Mins_per_Hr - 1
```

immediately after its type in the declaration of M. Any attempt now to give M a value outside its declared range will raise the exception Constraint_Error. This could happen, for example, if there were some programming error in the way the value of M is computed, or if the values used in its computation were themselves invalid. In any case, the exception would immediately highlight a situation that needs attention. In the absence of the range constraint, a nonsensical value like -1 or 60 *could* be placed in M without any warning. Experience has shown that range checks detect many programming errors that would otherwise go unnoticed, so it is sensible to use range constraints wherever appropriate. To make full use of range constraints in Example 1.1, we must replace its object declarations by the following:

```
Secs_per_Min : constant Integer := 60;
Mins_per_Hr  : constant Integer := 60;
Hrs_per_Day  : constant Integer := 24;
Secs_per_Hr  : constant Integer
               := Secs_per_Min * Mins_per_Hr;
Secs_per_Day : constant Integer
               := Secs_per_Hr * Hrs_per_Day;
Time : Integer range 0 .. Secs_per_Day - 1;
H    : Integer range 0 .. Hrs_per_Day - 1;
M    : Integer range 0 .. Mins_per_Hr - 1;
S    : Integer range 0 .. Secs_per_Min - 1;
```

The attributes Integer'First and Integer'Last may be used in range constraints, for example:

```
Count : Integer range 0 .. Integer'Last;
```

This declaration states that the value of Count will never be negative, but may be as large as the Integer representation will allow. During elaboration of an object declaration, the first expression in any range constraint is evaluated to give the minimum value of the declared object(s), and the second expression is evaluated to give their maximum value. These expressions are not necessarily static expressions.

The following operators are available for use in `Integer` expressions. Their operand(s) must be of type `Integer`, and the result is also of type `Integer`.

Dyadic operators		*Monadic operators*	
`+`	addition	`+`	identity
`-`	subtraction	`-`	negation
`*`	multiplication	`abs`	absolute value
`/`	division with truncation		
`rem`	remainder on division		
`mod`	modulo		
`**`	exponentiation		

The monadic operator `abs` yields the absolute value (or magnitude) of its operand. For example, '`abs I`' yields +5 if the value of `I` is either +5 or −5.

The operation `I**J` yields the result of raising `I` to the power `J`, where the value of `J` must be nonnegative (in order to guarantee that the result is an integer). For example, `I**2` yields the square of `I`.

The 'division operators' `/`, `rem` and `mod` are fairly straightforward when no negative operands are involved. For example, `11/5` has the value 2; '`11 rem 5`' and '`11 mod 5`' both have the value 1. The operator `/` always yields a result truncated, if necessary, towards zero. In general:

`(-I)/J` = `-(I/J)` = `I/(-J)`

The operators `rem` and `mod` always yield results smaller in magnitude than their right operands. They are interchangeable unless their operands have opposite signs. The difference is that `rem` always takes its sign from its *left* operand, whereas `mod` always takes its sign from its *right* operand. They are defined by:

`I rem J` = `I - (I/J)*J`

`I mod J` = `I - J*`*n* for some integer *n* such that `abs (I mod J)` < `abs J` and such that `I mod J` has the same sign as `J`

The following table illustrates the effect of the three division operators with various combinations of positive and negative operands:

I	J	I / J	I rem J	I mod J
+9	+4	+2	+1	+1
−9	+4	−2	−1	+3
+9	−4	−2	+1	−3
−9	−4	+2	−1	−1

There are several examples of the use of the division operators in Example 1.1. Suppose that the value read into `Time` is 36090. Then the statement '`H := Time / Secs_per_Hr;`' computes 36090 / 3600 which is 10, and assigns that value to `H`. The next statement '`Time := Time rem Secs_per_Hr;`' computes 36090 `rem` 3600 which is 90, and assigns that to `Time`. In this example the operator `rem` could be replaced by `mod`, without making any difference, since the values involved are always nonnegative. In practice, the division operators are rarely used with negative operands.

If the right operand of a division operator is zero, the exception `Numeric_Error` is raised. The same exception is raised if any of the `Integer` operations yields a result outside the `Integer` range, i.e., `Integer'First` through `Integer'Last`. This situation is frequently described as *overflow.* You must therefore formulate your Integer expressions with care when large numbers are likely to be involved. For example, the following two expressions:

```
I**2 - J**2                (I+J) * (I-J)
```

are mathematically equivalent, but the first expression is much more likely to overflow than the second.

Exceeding the Integer range is not just a hypothetical possibility, as illustrated by the harmless-looking program of Example 1.1. The user might supply as input the integer 55010, expecting the output 'Time of day is 15:16:50'. But on a 16-bit computer (see Figure 2.1) 55010 is greater than Integer'Last, so the statement 'Get(Time);' would raise an exception.

Example 2.1 *Integer expressions*

Let us write a statement that computes the value of the polynomial:

$$y = Ax^3 + Bx^2 + Cx + D$$

given that A, B, C, D, X and Y have been declared as Integer variables.

The 'obvious' solution is a straightforward transcription of the above equation:

```
Y := A*X**3 + B*X**2 + C*X + D;
```

However, since X**2 is computed by multiplying X by itself and X**3 is computed by multiplying X by itself twice, this solution requires six multiplications in all. A more efficient solution using nested multiplication requires only three multiplications:

```
Y := ((A*X + B)*X + C)*X + D;
```

□ *End of Example 2.1*

2.3. Type Integer: input-output

Text input-output is concerned with the input and output of lines of characters, so the *basic* Get and Put subprograms provided by the standard package Text_IO introduced in Chapter 1 work only for single characters and strings of characters. Yet there is also a need for the input and output of numbers in textual form.

The textual representation of a number (a sequence of characters such as +1049, which is convenient for humans) is quite different from its representation inside the computer (typically a pattern of binary digits such as 0000010000011001, which is more efficient for computer arithmetic). A number read from a text must be converted from its textual to its internal representation, and a number written out to a text must be converted from its internal to its textual representation.

Within the package Text_IO there is a facility called Integer_IO that provides for text input-output of integers with the necessary changes of representation. Line 6 of Example 1.1 shows how to declare your intention to use this facility. The first part of line 6:

```
package Int_IO is new Integer_IO (Integer);
```

in effect creates a new package, named Int_IO (any identifier could be chosen). Int_IO provides subprograms for input-output of values of the Integer type (as opposed to some other integer type, such as `Long_Integer`). The use clause '`use Int_IO;`' then allows convenient reference to these subprograms:

`Get(I);` reads an integer literal (optionally signed), converts it into its internal representation, and assigns it to the `Integer` variable `I`.

`Put(`*I*`);` converts the value of the `Integer` expression *I* to its textual representation as an integer literal, and writes that out.

These subprograms have the same identifiers as the subprograms used for input-output of characters, but you should always be aware that they are fundamentally more complicated operations, and that they are made available only by declarations and use clauses such as those cited above. Examples of their use can be found in Example 1.1.

When `Get` is used to read an integer, any leading spaces are skipped, and reading may continue from one line of the input text to another until a non-space character is found. If what follows does not conform to the syntax of an integer literal, the input data is taken to be invalid and the exception `Data_Error` is raised. Figure 2.2 illustrates the effect of `Get` in various situations.

When `Put` is used to write out an integer literal, the latter is normally written in decimal, signed only if negative, with no leading zeros, and possibly with some leading spaces. The total number of characters written (including leading spaces) is fixed by the implementation,

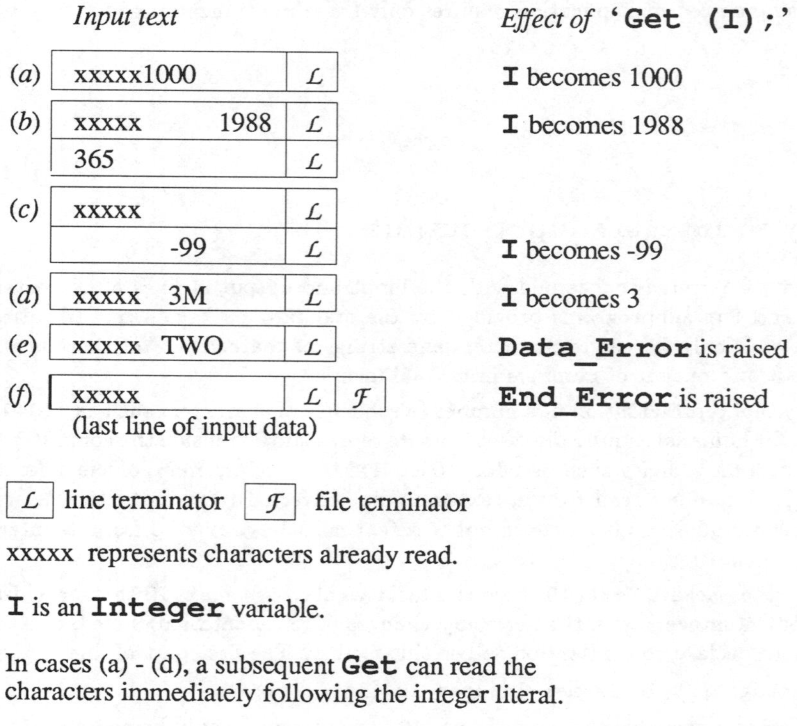
Input text
Effect of 'Get (I);'
(a) xxxxx1000 L
I becomes 1000
(b) xxxxx 1988 L
365 L
I becomes 1988
(c) xxxxx L
-99 L
I becomes -99
(d) xxxxx 3M L
I becomes 3
(e) xxxxx TWO L
Data_Error is raised
(f) xxxxx L F
(last line of input data)
End_Error is raised
L line terminator
F file terminator
xxxxx represents characters already read.
I is an Integer variable.
In cases (a) - (d), a subsequent Get can read the characters immediately following the integer literal.

Fig. 2.2 Effect of `Get` used to read an integer

and is just sufficient to write *any* value of the type Integer.

Often it is desirable to specify explicitly how many characters are to be written. This can be done by calling Put with a Width parameter, which specifies the *minimum* number of characters to be written. For example, the statement:

```
Put (GNP, Width=>12);
```

(where GNP is an Integer variable) writes the value of GNP as an integer literal in a field of (at least) 12 character positions. The following table illustrates the effect of Put in various cases. (◇ indicates a single space. It is assumed that the default Width is 6.)

Value of *I*	*Output from* Put(*I*);	*Output from* Put(*I*,Width=>4);	*Output from* Put(*I*,Width=>1);
0	◇◇◇◇◇0	◇◇◇0	0
+21	◇◇◇◇21	◇◇21	21
+6789	◇◇6789	6789	6789
-12345	-12345	-12345	-12345

Note that the Width parameter is ignored if it specifies a field too narrow for the integer literal. In particular, a Width parameter of 1 guarantees no leading spaces.

Let us summarize what is necessary to obtain text input-output facilities. A program that is to perform *any* text input-output should be headed by:

```
with Text_IO;  use Text_IO;
```

Any program (or part of a program) that is to perform text input-output of Integer values should *in addition* include the following in its declarative part:

```
package Int_IO is new Integer_IO (Integer); use Int_IO;
```

For the present you should treat this as a magic formula to be reproduced whenever required. Exactly how it works will be explained in Chapter 22.

Example 2.2 *Integer input-output*

```
-- Program Compute_Tax computes a taxpayer's income-tax bill,
-- given his/her income and number of dependents.  It assumes
-- a fixed personal tax allowance of $5000, plus an allowance
-- of $2000 per dependent, and it assumes that tax is
-- computed at 30% of income less allowances.

with Text_IO;  use Text_IO;

procedure Compute_Tax is

   package Int_IO is new Integer_IO (Integer); use Int_IO;

   Tax_Rate             : constant Integer := 30;      -- %
   Personal_Allowance   : constant Integer := 5000;    -- $
   Dependent_Allowance  : constant Integer := 2000;    -- $
   Income, Taxable_Income, Tax : Integer;              -- $
   Nr_Dependents : Integer range 0 .. Integer'Last;

begin
   Get (Income);
   Get (Nr_Dependents);
```

```
    Taxable_Income := Income - Personal_Allowance -
                        Nr_Dependents * Dependent_Allowance;
    Tax := Taxable_Income * Tax_Rate / 100;
    Put ("$");  Put (Income, Width => 5);
    Put ("  gross income");  New_Line;
    Put ("$");  Put (Taxable_Income, Width => 5);
    Put ("  taxable income");  New_Line;
    Put ("$");  Put (Tax, Width => 5);
    Put ("  tax due");  New_Line;
    Put ("$");  Put (Income - Tax, Width => 5);
    Put ("  net income");  New_Line;
end Compute_Tax;
```

Given the following input data:

```
24205  2
```

this program would write the following output:

```
$24205  gross income
$15205  taxable income
$ 4561  tax due
$19644  net income
```

□ *End of Example 2.2*

Exercises 2

2.1. Consider a vending machine that accepts 25-, 10-, 5- and 1-cent coins. You are given as input (1) the total amount inserted into the machine, and (2) the price of the item selected (both in cents). Write a program to determine the minimum number of coins to be dispensed in change.

2.2. Write a program that reads the current GMT time of day (in hours and minutes, using the 24-hour clock), and that outputs the current time of day in New York (5 hours behind GMT) and Tokyo (9 hours ahead of GMT).

3

The Boolean Data Type

3.1. Conditions

In order to build programs significantly more complex than the examples we have seen so far, we need to be able to write down *conditions* to control the course of the computation. A condition may be used to decide whether certain statements are to be executed or skipped. Alternatively, a condition may be used to decide whether the repetition of certain statements is to be continued or terminated. If a condition is satisfied its value is said to be ***true***, otherwise its value is said to be *false*. These ***truth values*** and certain operations on them are the subject of *Boolean algebra*.

Consider, for example, the statement 'the number of days in year Y is 366 if Y is a leap year, or 365 otherwise'. Here 'Y is a leap year' is an example of a condition. Its value of course depends on the value of Y.

3.2. Type Boolean: values and operations

In Ada, the two truth values are the (only) values of the Boolean type. They are denoted by the identifiers True and False.

Here are some examples of Boolean object declarations:

```
This_is_Leap_Year : Boolean;

Pressure_is_High, Alarm_on : Boolean := False;

AD : constant Boolean := True;
```

Here This_is_Leap_Year is declared to be a Boolean variable; Pressure_is_High and Alarm_on are declared to be Boolean variables and both are initialized to False; and AD is declared to be a Boolean constant, with value True.

Here are examples of Boolean assignment statements:

```
Pressure_is_High := True;
Alarm_on := Pressure_is_High;
```

The simplest way to compute a Boolean value is by a *relation*, in which two values of the same type are compared. Thus we may compare two Integer values, or two Character values, or indeed two Boolean values. (Comparing a Character value with an Integer value would be meaningless, and is is a type error.) The following *relational operators* are available for such purposes:

Relational operators	
=	is equal to
/=	is not equal to
<	is less than
<=	is less than or equal to
>=	is greater than or equal to
>	is greater than

The type rules for the relational operators are strict in that only values of the same type may be compared. On the other hand, the relational operators = and /= may be used to compare values of (almost) *any* type. The other relational operators are not quite so general, but they may be used to compare values of any *scalar* type. (Preview Figure 20.1.)

The relational operators have lower precedence than the arithmetic operators. Thus the expression 'I**2+J**2>K**2' is interpreted as '(I**2+J**2) > (K**2)'.

Conditions of any desired complexity can be composed from Boolean objects and relations by using the *logical operators* and, or, xor and not. These operators take Boolean operands (not is monadic, the others are dyadic), and yield a Boolean result. It is convenient to summarize each logical operator by a *truth table*, which shows the result of applying the logical operator to every possible combination of operand values. The truth tables for and, or, xor and not are given in Figure 3.1. Note that or is inclusive-or and xor is exclusive-or.

The Ada syntax does not allow extended relations like 'X=Y=Z'. To express a condition like this, we must we test the relations 'X=Y' and 'Y=Z' separately, and then test whether both are True:

```
X = Y and Y = Z
```

The logical operators and, or and xor have lower precedence than the relational operators, so this expression is equivalent to '(X = Y) and (Y = Z)'.

Example 3.1   *Boolean expressions*

For many centuries a year was counted as a leap year simply if it was a multiple of 4. This rule is expressed in Ada as:

```
Year : Integer;
Is_Leap_Year : Boolean;
...
Is_Leap_Year := Year mod 4 = 0;
```

A	B	A and B	A or B	A xor B	not B
False	False	False	False	False	True
False	True	False	True	True	False
True	False	False	True	True	
True	True	True	True	False	

Fig. 3.1   Truth tables for and, or, xor and not

In 1582 this rule was refined so that the multiples of 100 were no longer counted as leap years unless they were also multiples of 400; thus 1700, 1800 and 1900 were *not* leap years, but 2000 will be. This refined rule may be expressed in two different ways:

```
Is_Leap_Year :=
        Year mod 4 = 0 and (Year mod 100 /= 0 or Year mod 400 = 0);
Is_Leap_Year :=
        (Year mod 4 = 0 and Year mod 100 /= 0) or Year mod 400 = 0;
```

(*Exercise*: construct truth tables to verify that both of these solutions are correct.)

□ *End of Example 3.1*

When a mixture of the operators and, or and xor is used in the same Boolean expression, parentheses must always be used to indicate the desired grouping, as illustrated by Example 3.1. Expressions like the following:

```
A and B and C          A or B or C
```

are legal, because there is no doubt about their meaning. However, expressions like:

```
A or B and C          A and B or C
```

are illegal: parentheses are required to make their meaning clear.

Apart from the simple relations already discussed, there is another kind of relation, using the special ***membership operator*** in (or its converse, not in) to test whether a given value lies within a given range of values or not.

Example 3.2 *Membership operators*

```
Age                 : Integer range 0 .. 150;
School_Leaving_Age  : Integer := 15;
Retirement_Age      : Integer := 65;
Of_Working_Age      : Boolean;
...
Of_Working_Age := Age in School_Leaving_Age .. Retirement_Age-1;
```

This statement assigns True to Of_Working_Age if and only if Age is within the range School_Leaving_Age through Retirement_Age-1 *inclusive*. Thus it is equivalent to (but neater than):

```
Of_Working_Age := Age>=School_Leaving_Age and Age<=Retirement_Age-1;
```

□ *End of Example 3.2*

The right operand of in (or not in) is a *range* of values, which must both be of the same type as its left operand. The operator not in, as you might expect, yields the opposite result to in, so the following are equivalent:

```
I not in L .. M          not (I in L .. M)
```

4

Fundamental Control Structures

4.1. Selective and repetitive execution

The most fundamental control structures of programming are ***selection*** and ***repetition*** (or ***iteration***). These form the subject of this chapter.

Selective execution is illustrated by the flowcharts of Figure 4.1. Flowchart (a) shows a situation where some action, A, is to be performed only if some condition, C, is satisfied. Flowchart (b) shows a situation where action A1 is to be performed if condition C is satisfied, otherwise action A2 is to be performed. Flowchart (a) may be seen to be just a special case of flowchart (b).

Repetitive execution is illustrated by the flowchart of Figure 4.2. This shows a situation where action A is to be performed repeatedly as long as condition C is satisfied. For obvious reasons a repetitive structure is also called a ***loop***.

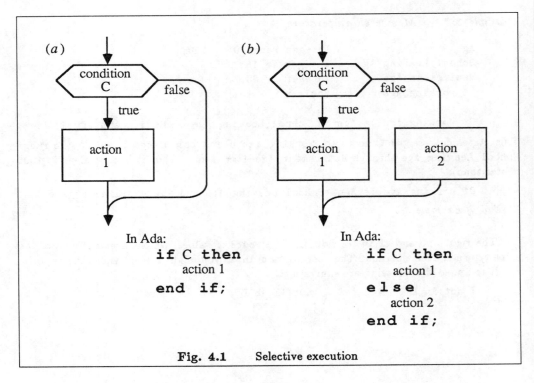

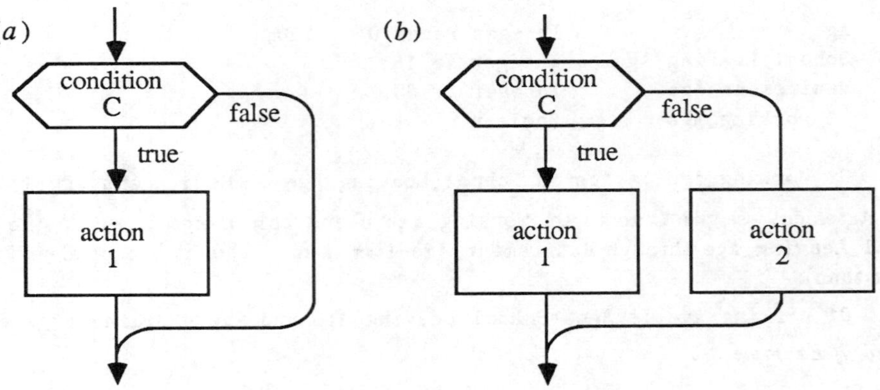

In Ada:

```
if C then
   action 1
end if;
```

In Ada:

```
if C then
   action 1
else
   action 2
end if;
```

Fig. 4.1 Selective execution

In low-level languages, and even in some of the older 'high-level' languages, it is necessary to specify the order of execution in terms of primitive test and jump instructions. In modern high-level languages such as Ada, however, there are statement forms that correspond exactly to the flowcharts of Figure 4.1 and Figure 4.2. These are the *if statement* and the *while loop statement*. These statements allow the programmer to specify selective and repetitive execution without having to think in terms of flowcharts or in terms of primitive tests and jumps. For that reason they are called *control structures*; they are a basis of the discipline of *structured programming*.

A word of caution. In this book we use flowcharts for one purpose only: to define the semantics of Ada's control structures. We do not recommend (conventional) flowcharts as a tool for *writing* programs, since they are too low-level. It is better to think in terms of the higher-level control structures themselves.

4.2. If statements

Figure 4.1 shows the Ada if statements corresponding to the two flowcharts for selective execution.

Example 4.1 *Simple if statements*

Example 2.2 is unrealistic in that the tax calculation:

```
Taxable_Income := Income - Personal_Allowance -
```

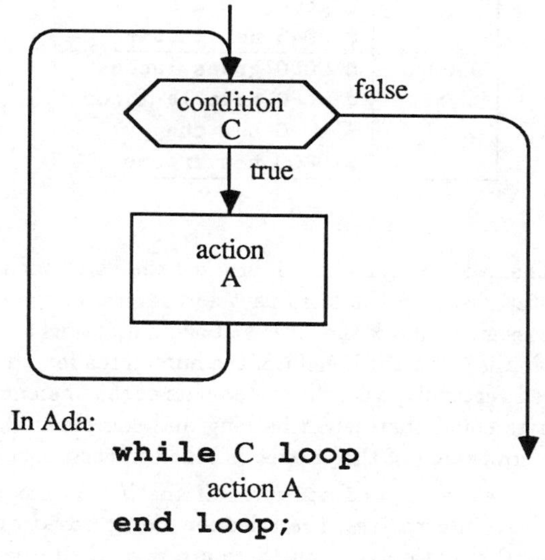

Fig. 4.2 Repetitive execution

```
                         Nr_Dependents * Dependent_Allowance;
Tax := Taxable_Income * Tax_Rate / 100;
```

would result in a negative tax bill if the allowances exceed the income. It would be more realistic in this situation to set the tax bill to zero. This could be done as follows:

```
Taxable_Income := Income - Personal_Allowance -
                         Nr_Dependents * Dependent_Allowance;
Tax := Taxable_Income * Tax_Rate / 100;
if Tax < 0 then
   Tax := 0;
end if;
```

These statements apply the tax formula even when it can be anticipated that Tax will be zero or negative, namely when Taxable_Income itself is zero or negative. The following would be more natural (and also more efficient):

```
Taxable_Income := Income - Personal_Allowance -
                         Nr_Dependents * Dependent_Allowance;
if Taxable_Income > 0 then
   Tax := Taxable_Income * Tax_Rate / 100;
else
   Tax := 0;
   Taxable_Income := 0;
end if;
```

Assuming that these statements are substituted for the two assignment statements in Example 2.2, here are some examples of input and output from the modified program:

Input	*Output*
24205 2	$24205 gross income $15205 taxable income $ 4560 tax due $19645 net income
9000 6	$ 9000 gross income $ 0 taxable income $ 0 tax due $ 9000 net income

□ *End of Example 4.1*

The symbols if, then, else and end if bracket the components of the if statement. There may be several statements in the then part and several in the else part. The symbol end if is therefore necessary to mark the extent of the if statement unambiguously. That is for the benefit of the compiler. For the benefit of the human reader, the symbols if, else and end if should be aligned vertically, with the statements of the then and else parts indented. The then and else parts could themselves be long and complicated, so this indentation is needed to show clearly how much of the text is included in each part of the if statement.

The 'if ... then ... else ... end if' form of the if statement allows a program to select one action from two alternatives, the selection being based on the value of a single condition. A more general situation is when there are *several* alternative actions, each with an associated condition that must be satisfied before that one action is selected. This situation is illustrated by the flowchart of Figure 4.3. If condition C1 is satisfied, action A1 alone is performed; otherwise if condition C2 is satisfied, action A2 alone is performed; and so on. There may be a 'default' action, A0, that is to be performed if none of the conditions is satisfied. Selection like this from several alternatives is achieved in Ada by a *cascaded* if statement. See Appendix A for the complete syntax of if statements.

Example 4.2 *A cascaded if statement*

```
if Score < 50 then
   Grade := 'F';
elsif Score < 60 then
   Grade := 'C';
elsif Score < 70 then
   Grade := 'B';
else
   Grade := 'A';
end if;
```

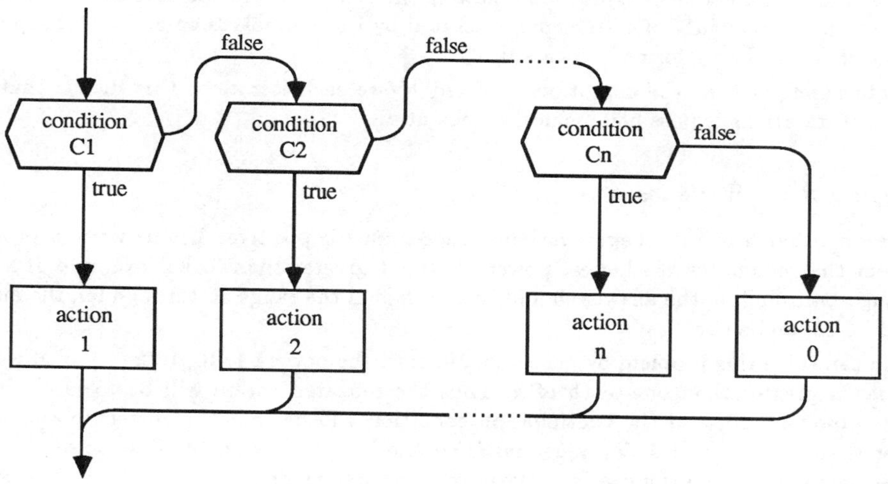

In Ada:

```
if C1 then
      action 1
elsif C2 then
      action 2
   ...
elsif Cn then
      action n
else
      action 0
end  if;
```

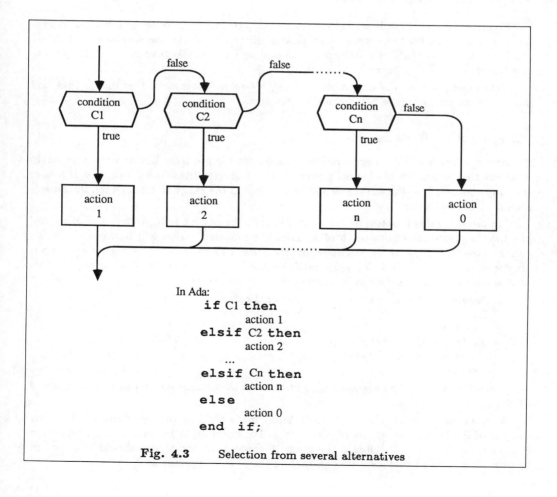

Fig. 4.3 Selection from several alternatives

□ *End of Example 4.2*

In a cascaded if statement, the first condition is preceded by `if`, and all the subsequent conditions (there may be any number of these) are preceded by the symbol `elsif`. These conditions are evaluated in textual order until one is found to be `True`, and only the statement sequence immediately following that one is executed. If all the conditions evaluate to `False`, only the statement sequence following `else` is executed (or no action is taken if the `else` part is absent).

The order of evaluation of the conditions is not critical if the conditions are mutually exclusive. Example 4.2, however, illustrates a situation where the order *is* critical. If the condition `Score < 70` were evaluated first, for example, *any* value of `Score` less than 70 would result in the statement '`Grade := 'B';`' being executed.

4.3. While loop statements

Figure 4.2 shows the Ada while loop statement corresponding to the flowchart for repetitive execution. The `Boolean` expression following the symbol `while` specifies the continuation condition, and a sequence of statements bracketed by the symbols `loop` and `end loop` specifies the action to be performed repeatedly.

Note carefully that the condition is tested *before* each iteration; this means that any number of iterations is possible, including none at all.

Example 4.3 *While loops*

Assume that `N` is an `Integer` variable whose value is positive. Let us write a program fragment that computes the largest power of 10 not greater than `N`. For example, if `N` is in the range 1 through 9, the answer should be 1; if `N` is in the range 10 through 99, the answer should be 10; and so on.

We can solve this problem by generating in turn the powers 1, 10, 100, ..., until we find one that is greater than one-tenth of `N`. Thus the repeated action will be to multiply the current power by 10, and the continuation condition will be that the current power is not greater than one-tenth of `N`. We must *initialize* the loop by taking the first power, 1. This analysis leads to the following Ada declaration and statements:

```
Power : Integer range 1 .. Integer'Last;
...
Power := 1;
while Power <= N/10 loop
   Power := 10 * Power;
end loop;
```

(*Exercise:* modify the program fragment to avoid the unnecessary repeated evaluation of `N/10`.)

A slight variation on this problem is to compute the 'integer logarithm' of `N` — the number of the largest power not greater than `N`. For example, if `N` is in the range 1 through 9, the answer should be 0; if `N` is in the range 10 through 99, the answer should be 1; and so on. We adapt the original solution by counting the powers, starting at 0:

```
Power : Integer range 1 .. Integer'Last;
Log   : Integer range 0 .. Integer'Last;
...
Power := 1;
Log := 0;
while Power <= N/10 loop     -- Power = 10**Log
   Power := 10 * Power;
   Log := Log + 1;
end loop;
```

In this solution Power and Log are always updated together in such a way that Power equals 10**Log whenever the while condition is tested, as noted by the comment.

(*Exercise:* check both program fragments by manual tracing, with various values of N.)

□ *End of Example 4.3*

Example 4.4 *Reading numbers with an endmarker*

Suppose that a list of integers is supplied as input data, the end of the list being marked by a specific value, say −999. Let us write a program that computes the sum of these integers (excluding the endmarker).

Clearly this program must contain a loop. The repeated action must include reading an integer and adding an integer to a partial sum. The continuation condition must be that the integer just read is *not* the endmarker. Thus within the loop we must add an integer to the partial sum *before* reading the next integer, and the loop must be initialized not only by setting the partial sum to zero but also by reading the first integer. This also ensures that the continuation condition can be evaluated on the first iteration.

```
with Text_IO;  use Text_IO;
procedure Sum_to_Endmarker is
   package Int_IO is new Integer_IO (Integer);  use Int_IO;
   Endmarker : constant Integer := -999;
   Summand   : Integer;
   Sum       : Integer := 0;
begin
   Get (Summand);
   while Summand /= Endmarker loop
      Sum := Sum + Summand;
      Get (Summand);
   end loop;
   Put ("Total: ");  Put (Sum);  New_Line;
end Sum_to_Endmarker;
```

(*Exercise:* trace program Sum_to_Endmarker with the input data 7 5 0 8 99 -999.)

□ *End of Example 4.4*

It is essential that the repeated statements of a while loop influence the value of the while condition, otherwise the repetition might never terminate. In Example 4.3, the repeated statements increase the value of Power, so the condition 'Power < N/10' must eventually be False. In Example 4.4 the repeated statements read some input data, so repetition must eventually cease. (Of course, if the input data is exhausted before an endmarker is read, the exception End_Error will be raised.)

4.4. Nested control structures

The syntax of Ada allows any sequence of statements to be placed after the symbol loop in a loop statement, or after then or else in an if statement. The sequence may include statements that are themselves if statements or while loops, and are said to be *nested* within the enclosing statement. Indeed, statements can be nested within one another to any depth. This makes it possible to build control structures of any desired complexity.

Example 4.5 *Nested if statements*

Assume the variable declarations:

```
Month : Integer range 1 .. 12;
Year  : Integer range 1582..3999;
Month_Size : Integer range 28 .. 31;
```

Let us write a statement that assigns to Month_Size the number of days in the month represented by the current values of Month and Year.

There are three cases here: February has 28 or 29 days; April, June, September and November each have 30 days; and all the other months have 31 days. These cases can be handled by a statement with the structure 'if ... then ... elsif ... then ... else ... end if'. Within the February case, we must distinguish between a leap year and an ordinary year. This can be done using a statement with the structure 'if ... then ... else ... end if', nested within the outer if statement.

```
if Month = 2 then
   if Year mod 4 = 0 and
         (Year mod 100 /= 0 or Year mod 400 = 0) then
      Month_Size := 29;
   else
      Month_Size := 28;
   end if;
elsif Month = 4 or Month = 6 or Month = 9 or Month = 11 then
   Month_Size := 30;
else
   Month_Size := 31;
end if;
```

□ *End of Example 4.5*

Example 4.6 *Nested loops*

Let us write a program that reads a list of nonnegative integers and outputs them in the form of a histogram. Each positive integer is to be represented by a row of that number of asterisks. Zeros are to be written numerically. Any negative integer is to be treated as an endmarker.

This program will have an outer loop similar to that of Example 4.4, only the processing of each integer will be more complicated. This processing will involve an if statement, since we have to treat zero and positive integers differently.

The treatment of a positive integer N itself requires a loop, since N asterisks are to be written. We can do this by writing a single asterisk repeatedly, exactly N times. We need an auxiliary variable to count the iterations.

This analysis leads to the following solution:

```
with Text_IO;  use Text_IO;
procedure Make_Histogram is
   package Int_IO is new Integer_IO (Integer);  use Int_IO;
   Number, Asterisk_Count : Integer;
begin
   Get (Number);
   while Number >= 0 loop
      if Number = 0 then
         -- output zero numerically --
         Put ('0');
      else
         -- output a row of Number asterisks --
         Put (' ');
         Asterisk_Count := 0;
         while Asterisk_Count < Number loop
            Put ('*');
            Asterisk_Count := Asterisk_Count + 1;
         end loop;
      end if;
      New_Line;
      Get (Number);
   end loop;
end Make_Histogram;
```

□ *End of Example 4.6*

The preceding two examples should convince you of the value of indentation to highlight the structure of a program with nested statements. For example, if you are reading a program and you come across a `while`, you will want to see clearly where the corresponding `end loop` is. If the program is properly indented, all you need do is to look down the page for an `end loop` vertically aligned with the `while`.

We are now developing relatively complicated programs. The logical analysis at the start of Example 4.6 has hinted at a methodical approach to writing such programs. Methodical programming is a major theme of this book, and it is the subject of Chapter 5.

4.5. Short-circuit control forms

(This section may be omitted on a first reading.)

Expressions containing **and** or **or** have the peculiar property that the value of the expression can often be predicted before all its operands have been evaluated. Consider, for example, the expression '`A and B`'; if `A` is `False`, the value of '`A and B`' must be `False`, regardless of the value of `B` (unless evaluation of `B` raises an exception). Similarly, the value of '`A or B`' will be `True` if `A` is `True`.

It is often argued that evaluation of the right operand should be skipped in these circumstances. This is called ***short-circuit evaluation.*** The arguments are: (a) short-circuit evaluation is more efficient; and (b) it permits greater flexibility in forming expressions where the right operand might raise an exception if not skipped. However, short-circuit evaluation would make **and** and **or** different from all the other operators and would lose their mathematical properties of associativity and commutativity. For these reasons, Ada's rule is that both the operands of any dyadic operator are always evaluated (and not necessarily in the order in which they appear).

Nevertheless, Ada does allow the programmer to opt for short-circuit evaluation *explicitly*, by using special forms of **and** and **or**; these are the ***short-circuit control forms*** **and then** and **or else**.

Example 4.7 Short-circuit control forms

Suppose a student fails to graduate if he or she completes fewer than 36 courses, or fails to achieve a minimum average score over these courses. We might attempt to express this as follows:

```
if Nr_Courses < 36 or
      Total_Score/Nr_Courses < Pass_Score then
   Put ("fail");
else
   Put ("pass");
end if;
```

However, both operands of **or** are evaluated even if the first turns out to be `True`, so the division will raise the exception `Numeric_Error` if `Nr_Courses` is zero.

The simplest solution is to replace **or** by the short-circuit control form **or else**:

```
if Nr_Courses < 36 or else
      Total_Score/Nr_Courses < Pass_Score then
   Put ("fail");
else
   Put ("pass");
end if;
```

Now if the relation `Nr_Courses < 36` is found to be `True`, the **if** condition as a whole is immediately taken to be `True`.

□ *End of Example 4.7*

The value of the expression '`A or else B`' is `True` (and `B` is skipped) if `A` is `True`, otherwise the expression has the same value as `B`. The value of the expression '`A and then B`' is `False` (and `B` is skipped) if `A` is `False`, otherwise it has the same value as `B`.

Exercises 4

4.1. Modify the program of Example 1.1 to output the time of day in terms of the 12-hour clock (e.g., `12:7:30 AM` rather than `0:7:30`, `1:7:30 AM` rather than `1:7:30`, `12:7:30 PM` rather than `12:7:30`, and `1:7:30 PM` rather than `13:7:30`.)

4.2. Write programs to read a list of nonnegative integers and output their maximum: (a) when the list is terminated by a negative integer; (b) when the list is preceded by a count of the number of integers in the list.

4.3. A cargo consisting of many separate items of differing weights is to be flown to its destination in a single aircraft, first-come first-served. Write a program to determine how many trips are required, and the total payload on each trip, given as input the maximum payload of the aircraft, followed by the weights of the individual items of cargo (all rounded to the nearest kilogram), terminated by a negative integer.

5

Methodical Programming

5.1. Aspects of methodical programming

The title of this book emphasizes that its aim is to present not just the details of the programming language Ada but also a coherent methodology for developing high-quality Ada programs. Now that we have presented enough of the programming language to write nontrivial programs, this chapter introduces the methodology.

There are several criteria of quality in programs, including *correctness*, *efficiency* and *modifiability*. All are important, but correctness is of primary importance. Sometimes it might be necessary to sacrifice modifiability for increased efficiency, or *vice versa*, but correctness cannot be sacrificed in any circumstances.

In this chapter we start by examining the methods by which we can check whether a program is correct or not. Then we present a technique suitable for systematically constructing high-quality programs: stepwise refinement. We integrate these techniques into a methodology whose aim is make it easier to develop programs that are *already correct*, or nearly so, when completed. This methodology has proved vastly superior to the older approach of *ad hoc* program construction followed (inevitably) by a painful and interminable period of debugging.

This chapter is only an introduction to programming methodology. In later chapters we present more advanced aspects of the methodology as we introduce the powerful Ada features that support them: subprograms, packages and tasks.

5.2. Program testing

A program is *correct* only if, for every possible input, it generates the required output and terminates normally. If, for any input, the program generates the wrong output, or fails to terminate, or terminates abnormally (by raising an exception), then it is incorrect. What inputs the program must accept, and what the corresponding outputs should be, must be judged against the specification to which the program was written in the first place.

How can we check whether a program is correct or not? The most common approach is *testing*, which consists of executing the program with one or more sets of input data and comparing the actual outputs with the expected outputs. An alternative approach is *verification*, which consists of proving the correctness of the program by logical reasoning. Both approaches are useful and they complement each other well. Testing is described briefly in this section. Unfortunately verification is too big a topic to introduce in this book: see [Dijkstra 1976] or [Gries 1981] for a full treatment.

Although testing is a routine matter for programmers, it is important to be aware that a nontrivial program can never be *proved* correct by testing (although it might be proved incorrect, by demonstrating an error). This might seem surprising, but even a program that has behaved perfectly in a large number of tests might fail on some input that has not yet been tried. Most nontrivial programs have an infinite number of possible inputs and therefore cannot be tested exhaustively. Thus the aim of testing is the limited one of raising our degree of confidence in the program, by checking that it performs to specification on a variety of carefully chosen and realistic inputs. The crucial problem is the selection of test cases. Here we describe two approaches to this problem: black-box testing and white-box testing.

Black-box testing

Black-box testing (or *functional testing*) is so called because the program is treated as a 'black box' and tested against its specification, without regard for the way the program is implemented. This approach allows the test cases to be selected before the program is written, and indeed to be selected by someone other than the programmer. This is highly advantageous because programmers (like everyone else) tend to be reluctant to accept that their own work is fallible, and are therefore unlikely to test it as thoroughly as they ought.

One principle of black-box testing is to study the specification and identify all distinct equivalence classes in input or output. An *equivalence class* is a subset of the possible values that are likely to be treated equivalently to one another. Then devise one or more test cases so that each equivalence class is covered at least once. The assumption here is that any one value in an equivalence class is just as likely to expose a bug as any other. Consider, for example, a program whose inputs are a *month* and a *year* and whose output is to be the number of days in that month. For the input *month* there are three equivalence classes, the long months, the medium-length months, and the short month (February); for the input *year* there are only two relevant equivalence classes, leap years and non-leap years; for the output there are four equivalence classes, 28, 29, 30 and 31. All these equivalence classes can be covered by four test cases: for example January 1983 (output 31), February 1983 (output 28), February 1984 (output 29) and April 1986 (output 30).

When an equivalence class is a *range* of values, we should choose not only a 'typical' value from the range but also the 'boundary' values from the ends of the range. Consider, for example, a program that performs a tax calculation, where there are three tax bands with different tax rates: up to \$10000; \$10001 through \$30000; and above \$30000. Then three test cases are needed to cover 'typical' values, for example with inputs \$5000, \$21000 and \$38000; and five more test cases are needed to cover 'boundary' values, with inputs \$0, \$10000, \$10001, \$30000 and \$30001. The reasoning behind the concentration on boundary values is that errors are more likely there: it is very easy to write a relation like `Income<10000` when it should be `Income<=10000`.

These simple techniques ensure that all interesting values of each individual input are tried, but they do not ensure that all interesting *combinations* of inputs are tried. Suppose, for example, that the calendar were altered to make February in a leap year have *30* days. Then the simple techniques discussed above would require only *three* test cases: for example, January 1983 (output 31), February 1983 (output 28) and April 1984 (output 30). Yet February in a leap year is still an interesting combination of inputs, likely to be covered by special logic in the program, even if the corresponding output happens to be the same as the third test case.

White-box testing

White-box testing (or *structural testing*) is the converse of black-box testing and involves testing the internal logic of the program. The aim is to ensure that every statement in the program is exercised at least once and that every condition has been both true and false on different occasions. (In other words, white-box testing ensures that every branch of the program's flowchart is followed at least once.) In terms of Ada's fundamental control structures, the test cases should be designed to ensure the following. In each *if statement*, both the `then` alternative and the `else` alternative must be exercised. If `else` is absent, nevertheless this dummy alternative must be exercised (since it is possible that omitting the `else` alternative was a programming error). In a cascaded if statement, all the `then` alternatives must be exercised. A *while loop* should be exercised with zero, one and several iterations.

For example, consider program `Make_Histogram` of Example 4.6. The following test cases suffice for white-box testing:

- the sequence -1;
- the sequence 5 -1;
- the sequence 1 0 21 -1.

These three test cases ensure zero, one and several iterations of the outer while loop, respectively. The integer 0 ensures that the `then` alternative of the if statement is exercised, and the positive integers ensure that its `else` alternative is exercised. The integer 1 and the larger integers ensure one and several iterations of the inner while loop, respectively. (The program logic makes it impossible to achieve zero iterations of this loop.)

It is also necessary to check each expression in the program to ensure that it represents the right formula. `Integer` expressions should be tested especially for possible overflow and for incorrect use of the division operators. (For example, the expression `N div 5` is discontinuous between 4 and 5, between 9 and 10, and so on; this is a potential source of errors.) `Boolean` expressions containing logical operators or short-circuit control forms should be tested with all relevant combinations of `False` and `True` operands. For example, the expression '`Married and Nr_Children < 2`' should be tested with all four combinations of `Married` being `False` or `True` and `Nr_Children` being less than or not less than 2.

Summary

We recommend a blend of black-box and white-box testing. A set of black-box test cases should be devised before the program is written. Afterwards, any further test cases necessary to satisfy the aims of white-box testing should be added.

A thorough approach such as this is likely to lead to a large number of test cases for all but the simplest programs. Moreover, every test output must be compared carefully with the expected output. It is essential to plan the testing phase to make it as efficient as possible. An excellent idea is to prepare, in advance of testing, the expected output for each test case, and to have this *automatically* compared with the actual test output. (Some sophisticated software tools are available that accurately report differences between two texts.) This eliminates a particularly tedious chore.

All the above observations, about the efficacy of testing and about the selection of test cases, apply whether the testing is to be done by hand or by computer. Hand-testing is useful in that it shows the individual steps as well as the final output, and thus might provide more insight into the working of the program. It also has the advantage of being applicable to program *fragments*, a fact that we shall soon exploit. Computer testing is indispensable, however, since hand-testing is error-prone and impossibly tedious when many steps are involved.

For a much more thorough treatment of software testing, see for example [Myers 1979].

5.3. Programming by stepwise refinement

Many people think that programming is easy. It is indeed easy to produce incorrect, inefficient and difficult-to-modify programs! However, the experience of three decades has shown that writing ***high-quality*** software is difficult.

The reason is perhaps the diversity of skills a programmer needs. An ideal programmer is versatile, creative, logical and persistent; capable of meticulous attention to detail, yet always aware of the overall picture. Paragons such as this are in short supply. The vast majority of programmers are wise to make things as simple for themselves as possible. In particular, a systematic method of work should be adopted. The method chosen matters less than its consistent application, but in this book we advocate a method that is both simple and effective: ***stepwise refinement.***

The basic idea of stepwise refinement is as follows. Given a complex problem, such as designing a program, split it up into a number of (more or less) independent subproblems. If we can assume that each subproblem is solvable, we have an outline solution to the problem. Now turn to the subproblems and solve each separately. If a subproblem is trivial, write down its final solution directly. If not, solve the subproblem by applying stepwise refinement to it in turn. This generates a number of smaller subproblems. Proceed in this fashion until all subproblems have been completely solved.

Splitting a problem into subproblems is called ***refinement.*** It is important to note that, when we generate a new set of subproblems, we content ourselves with stating ***what*** each subproblem is; we delay any decision on ***how*** the subproblem is to be solved until later, when the subproblems can be solved one at a time. That is why the method is called ***stepwise*** refinement.

Example 5.1 *Stepwise refinement*

Let us develop a program to solve the quadratic equation:

$$Ax^2 + Bx + C = 0$$

where A, B and C are all integers, A being nonzero. The program is to simplify the solution as much as possible without using real arithmetic. Here are some examples of inputs and corresponding outputs:

Input			*Output*
A	*B*	*C*	
2	5	1	`x = -5+-sqrt(17) / 4`
1	2	−2	`x = -1+-sqrt(3)`
−4	0	1	`x = +-1 / 2`
1	2	1	`x = -1`
2	0	0	`x = 0`
1	0	7	`x = +-sqrt(-7)`

Program outline

The solution to the quadratic equation is given by the formula:

$$x = \frac{-B \pm \sqrt{(B^2 - 4AC)}}{2A}$$

It may be seen that the solution contains three parts that can be computed immediately: the fixed part of the numerator (-B), the discriminant ($B^2 - 4AC$) and the denominator ($2A$). Having computed these we can simplify by making the denominator positive and then by eliminating any common factors. Further simplifications will directly affect the output, so we postpone consideration of them until later.

These observations lead to the following outline solution:

```
procedure Solve_Quadratic_Equation is
   declarations;
begin
   read A, B and C;
   compute the fixed part of the numerator, the discriminant and the denominator;
   make the denominator positive;
   eliminate any common factors;
   write the solution;
end Solve_Quadratic_Equation;
```

The '*declarations*' must include declarations of the `Integer` variables `A`, `B` and `C`.

The above is intended to be a self-explanatory outline of the program. Bold text is already formalized in terms of Ada; normal text informally describes something that will later be refined into Ada. For example, '*write the solution*' represents an action that will later be refined into Ada statements. For the moment it does not matter what these statements will be — any correct implementation will be satisfactory.

Refinement of '*compute the fixed part of the numerator, ...*'

We must introduce `Integer` variables to contain the fixed part of the numerator, the discriminant and the denominator. Let us call them `Num`, `Discrim` and `Denom` respectively. With these we can refine directly into Ada:

```
Num := - B;
Discrim := B**2 - 4 * A * C;
Denom := 2 * A;
```

Refinement of '*make the denominator positive*'

If the denominator is negative, we must negate both it and the fixed part of the numerator. (The discriminant is not affected.)

```
if Denom < 0 then
   Denom := - Denom;
   Num := - Num;
end if;
```

Refinement of '*eliminate any common factors*'

This can be done by dividing the fixed part of the numerator, the square root of the discriminant and the denominator by their highest common factor. A simple way to find this highest common factor is to examine positive integers from `abs Denom` downwards, stopping as soon as a common factor is found. (We know that `Denom` will be nonzero, since `A` is nonzero.) To test whether an integer is a factor of the square root of `Discrim`, without actually computing the square root, we can test whether the square of the integer is a factor of `Discrim`.

```
HCF := abs Denom;
while HCF > 1 and then not (
          HCF is a factor of Num and
          HCF is a factor of Denom and
          HCF**2 is a factor of Discrim ) loop
   HCF := HCF - 1;
end loop;
if HCF > 1 then
   divide Num and Denom by HCF, and Discrim by HCF**2;
end if;
```

We must remember to declare the `Integer` variable `HCF`.

This refinement is not expressed entirely in Ada, so further refinements will be needed. These are very straightforward, however, so we postpone them until later.

Refinement of '*write the solution*'

At this stage we must take into account further simplifications. The denominator may be omitted if it is 1. The fixed part of the numerator and the discriminant may each be omitted if it is zero. We must take care, however: if both are zero we must not omit them both! This analysis leads to the following refinement:

```
Put ("x = ");
write the fixed part of the numerator, unless
   it is zero and the discriminant is nonzero;
write the discriminant part, unless it is zero;
write the denominator part, unless it is 1;
New_Line;
```

This refinement has introduced three actions that remain to be refined into Ada. We now consider these one by one.

Refinement of '*write the fixed part of the numerator, ...*'

This is straightforward:

```
if not (Num = 0 and Discrim /= 0) then
   Put (Num, Width => 1);
end if;
```

Refinement of '*write the denominator part unless it is 1*'

This is also straightforward:

```
if Denom /= 1 then
   Put (" / ");  Put (Denom, Width => 1);
end if;
```

Refinement of '*write the discriminant part unless it is zero*'

If the discriminant is zero, nothing is to be written. If the discriminant is nonzero, we are interested in whether it is a perfect square, for if so we can compute and write its square root as an integer.

```
if Discrim /= 0 then
   Put ("+-");
   determine whether Discrim is a perfect square;
   if Discrim is a perfect square then
      Put (square root of Discrim);
   else
      Put ("sqrt("); Put (Discrim, Width => 1); Put (")");
   end if;
end if;
```

Refinement of '*determine whether* `Discrim` *is a perfect square*'

This can be done by making an `Integer` variable `S` take values 1, 2, ..., until its square equals (or exceeds) the value of `Discrim`:

```
S := 1;
while S**2 < Discrim loop
   S := S + 1;
end loop;
```

Now the condition '`Discrim` *is a perfect square*' is easily refined to '`Discrim = S**2`', and the expression '*square root of* `Discrim`' is refined simply to `S`.

Refinement of '*read* `A`, `B` *and* `C`'

```
Get (A);  Get (B);  Get (C);
```

This and the previous refinements involving input-output require us to incorporate the usual with clause for `Text_IO` and the usual declaration for `Integer_IO`.

Completed program

Substituting all these refinements into the program outline, together with a few remaining minor refinements, we obtain the following complete Ada program:

```
with Text_IO;  use Text_IO;
procedure Solve_Quadratic_Equation is
   package Int_IO is new Integer_IO (Integer);  use Int_IO;
   A, B, C : Integer;
   Num, Discrim, Denom : Integer;
   HCF, S : Integer range 0 .. Integer'Last;
begin
   Get (A);  Get (B);  Get (C);
   -- compute the fixed part of the numerator,
   --     the discriminant and the denominator --
   Num := - B;
   Discrim := B**2 - 4 * A * C;
   Denom := 2 * A;
   -- make the denominator positive --
   if Denom < 0 then
      Denom := - Denom;
      Num := - Num;
   end if;
   -- eliminate any common factors --
   HCF := abs Denom;
   while HCF > 1 and then not (
         Num mod HCF = 0 and
         Denom mod HCF = 0 and
         Discrim mod HCF**2 = 0 ) loop
      HCF := HCF - 1;
   end loop;
   if HCF > 1 then
      Num := Num / HCF;
      Denom := Denom / HCF;
      Discrim := Discrim / HCF**2;
   end if;
   -- write the solution --
   Put ("x = ");
   -- write the fixed part of the numerator, unless
   --     it is zero and the discriminant is nonzero --
   if not (Num = 0 and Discrim /= 0) then
      Put (Num, Width => 1);
   end if;
   -- write the discriminant part unless it is zero --
   if Discrim /= 0 then
      Put ("+-");
      -- compute the square root of Discrim --
      S := 1;
```

```
        while S**2 < Discrim loop
           S := S + 1;
        end loop;
        if Discrim = S**2 then  -- perfect square
           Put (S);
        else
           Put ("sqrt("); Put (Discrim, Width => 1); Put (")");
        end if;
     end if;
     -- write the denominator part unless it is 1 --
     if Denom /= 1 then
        Put (" / ");  Put (Denom, Width => 1);
     end if;
     New_Line;
  end Solve_Quadratic_Equation;
```

Note the use of comments in this example. The title of each refinement has been carried forward as a comment preceding the refined text. Thus a reader can see the outline of the program by reading the comments and skipping the details that follow them. The comments serve to explain what is being done by each part of the program.

□ *End of Example 5.1*

How do we choose a refinement? Part of the answer is that, like many things, it gets easier with practice. Many problems lead to similar structures. The skilled programmer soon recognizes these structures in the specification, enabling suitable refinements to be written down very quickly.

A more adequate answer is that *any* action can be refined either as a sequence of actions, or as a selection between alternative actions, or as a repetition of actions. Usually the choice is obvious, but care is necessary because an inappropriate choice might lead to difficulties. For example, consider a program that reads some input, performs some computation and writes some results. The following refinement seems obvious:

read input;
compute results;
write results;

but this implies that *all* the input is read (and stored) before the computation phase begins and that *all* the results are computed (and stored) before the writing phase ends. In some cases this is perfectly appropriate. In other cases it is not, for example if the input is a sequence of items that are to be processed individually.

When deciding whether a refinement should be sequential, selective or repetitive, it is often helpful to take into account the structure of the input that is to be accepted or of the output that is to be generated. Refer back to Example 5.1. The refinement of '*write the solution*' had to take into account two alternative possibilities, the solution being zero or nonzero, so the refinement had the form of an if statement. Within the nonzero case, the output consisted of three distinct parts, so the nonzero case was refined to a sequence of three steps. Where the input or output is a sequence of similar items, the refinement to perform the input or output will be a loop.

Good refinements have the following desirable properties:

- *Modularity.* A program is said to be modular if its various components are relatively independent of one another. Choose refinements where the subproblems interact as little as possible. This reduces the complexity of the refinements to be done later. In Example 5.1, the components '***make the denominator positive***', '***eliminate any common factors***' and '***write the solution***' of the program outline were relatively independent of one another, in that each of them should operate correctly even in the absence of the others. To see this, imagine that '***make the denominator positive***', or '***eliminate any common factors***', or even both, were removed from the program; the solution written would still be correct, although not completely simplified. Of course, these components were not entirely independent of one another, since they used the common variables `Num`, `Discrim` and `Denom`.
- *Localization.* A program displays good localization if related parts of the program are close to one another in the program text. This improves readability by reducing the amount of text that has to be scanned to see how related parts connect together. Program `Solve_Quadratic_Equation` displays reasonable localization in that all the output is grouped in one part of the program, under the comment 'write the solution'; however it could be criticized on the grounds that part of the computation proper (testing whether `Discrim` is a perfect square) has been placed right in the middle of the output part.
- *Consistency.* When refining similar things, choose similar refinements. In Example 5.1, all the refinements of '... ***is a factor of*** ...' were done using the operator `mod`. In any of them the operator `rem` could have been used instead, but the inconsistency would have left the reader wondering, needlessly, whether there was some subtle reason for the difference. If there is good reason to vary from a pattern, provide an explanation in a comment.
- *Delayed decisions.* Choose refinements that incorporate only those design decisions that cannot be postponed. This avoids committing the design prematurely to specific implementation ideas, makes it easier to modify the design later, and postpones minor details which might be distracting. In Example 5.1, questions like how to determine whether a integer is a perfect square, or how to decide whether one integer is a factor of another, were postponed until the very last stage of the design.
- *Simplicity.* The human mind is capable of outstanding feats of intuition and insight, but is severely limited in the number of facts or relationships that it can process simultaneously. So avoid overreaching yourself: choose refinements with only a few components. Do not try to introduce too much detail too soon. Indeed it is a major advantage of stepwise refinement that it allows progress to be made without introducing too many new details at each step.

Every programmer finds, occasionally, that ideas stop flowing and a difficult (sub)problem blocks all further progress. When this happens, suspect that an inappropriate earlier design decision has set you an impossible task. If the design seems sound, look for a solution by someone else to this or a similar problem. If all else fails, you might try solving a simplified version of the problem, then generalizing your solution.

Neither stepwise refinement nor any other method of program development, of course, can guarantee that the resulting program is correct. Testing or verification might demonstrate faults in the completed program. Then it is necessary to track down all incorrect refinements, and to correct these refinements and consequent refinements. Merely 'patching' the source program is not recommended because it makes the source program inconsistent with its design record.

Working right through the refinement process and only then testing the completed program is not the best mode of development, however. A much better idea is to check the correctness of each individual refinement as soon as it is written down. Thus a faulty refinement can be corrected immediately. This avoids wasting time in further refinement of something that is incorrect to start with. Moreover, a program is likely to be checked more thoroughly if its components are checked individually.

Of course, computer testing of incompletely refined program fragments is not possible. However, hand testing and verification are both possible here. Indeed, an individual refinement is usually quite short and simple, and it is in these very circumstances that hand testing and verification are practicable.

Example 5.2 *Stepwise checking*

We illustrate this idea by showing how the program outline and refinements of Example 5.1 could have been checked individually. Imagine that the checks are being done immediately after writing down the outline or refinement.

Let us first check the outline of program `Solve_Quadratic_Equation` by hand testing with some of the test cases cited in Example 5.1. Here are the results in tabular form, showing the expected values of `A`, `B`, `C`, the fixed part of the numerator, the discriminant and the denominator after each step:

	A	B	C	*num.*	*discr.*	*denom.*
`Get(A); Get(B); Get(C);`	2	5	1	?	?	?
compute num., discr. and denom.	2	5	1	-5	17	4
make the denom. positive	2	5	1	-5	17	4
eliminate any common factors	2	5	1	-5	17	4
write the solution	writes: `x = -5+-sqrt(17) / 4`					
`Get(A); Get(B); Get(C);`	1	2	-2	?	?	?
compute num., discr. and denom.	1	2	-2	-2	12	2
make the denom. positive	1	2	-2	-2	12	2
eliminate any common factors	1	2	-2	-1	3	1
write the solution	writes: `x = -1+-sqrt(3)`					
`Get(A); Get(B); Get(C);`	-4	0	1	?	?	?
compute num., discr. and denom.	-4	0	1	0	16	-8
make the denom. positive	-4	0	1	0	16	8
eliminate any common factors	-4	0	1	0	1	2
write the solution	writes: `x = +-1 / 2`					

(*Exercise*: devise a complete set of black-box test cases for this program, and hand-test the program outline using them.)

Let us now hand-test the refinement of '***eliminate any common factors***'. This contains a while loop and an if statement. We should choose test cases that ensure zero, one and several iterations of the loop, and ensure that the if condition is both `True` and `False`. These requirements are met by the following test cases:

	Num	Discrim	Denom	HCF
initially	2	0	2	?
`HCF := abs Denom;`	2	0	2	2
`while HCF>1 and then not (...)`	condition is `False`			
`if HCF>1`	condition is `True`			
divide `Num` *and* `Denom` *by* `HCF`, ...	1	0	1	2
initially	1	-3	2	?
`HCF := abs Denom;`	1	-3	2	2
`while HCF>1 and then not (...)`	condition is `True`			
`HCF := HCF-1;`	1	-3	2	1
`while HCF>1 and then not (...)`	condition is `False`			
`if HCF>1`	condition is `False`			
initially	2	-12	4	?
`HCF := abs Denom;`	2	-12	4	4
`while HCF>1 and then not (...)`	condition is `True`			
`HCF := HCF-1;`	2	-12	4	3
`while HCF>1 and then not (...)`	condition is `True`			
`HCF := HCF-1;`	2	-12	4	2
`while HCF>1 and then not (...)`	condition is `False`			
`if HCF>1`	condition is `True`			
divide `Num` *and* `Denom` *by* `HCF`, ...	1	-3	2	2

Note that these three test cases, although sufficient to exercise every 'statement' in the refinement, are not sufficient to exercise every possible combination of truth values for the four relations in the while condition. (*Exercise*: devise additional test cases to exercise every possible combination, and hand-test the refinement with them.)

In a similar manner we can hand-test (or verify) the remaining refinements of the program.

□ *End of Example 5.2*

Example 5.2 illustrates the checking of the program outline and of individual refinements. This checking can and should be done as soon as each outline or refinement is written down. This is when the outline or refinement is freshest in your mind, and therefore when it is easiest to locate and correct faults. If you conscientiously and systematically check your refinements in this way as you go along, then there is no reason why the completed program should not be substantially correct even before it is subjected to computer testing. Another good reason for checking each outline or refinement immediately is that it forces you to be clear about what each unrefined action is supposed to do.

Exercises 5

5.1. Write the three programs discussed as examples of black-box testing in Section 5.2. For each of your programs, are the test cases given in Section 5.2 sufficient to satisfy the aims of white-box testing? If not, devise further test cases that are needed.

5.2. A bank maintains a file of *account records*, one for each account. Each account record consists of an account number (a 6-digit integer) and the current balance of that account (an integer, negative if the account is overdrawn). The bank generates a set of ***transaction records*** over each accounting period. Each transaction record consists of an account number, the amount of the transaction (an integer, positive for a credit, negative for a debit), and the date (year, month, day). All these records have been sorted together in such a way that each account record is immediately followed by all the transaction records for the same account. The whole lot is terminated by a dummy account record with an account number of 0.

Write a program to read the sorted records and produce a printed bank statement for each account. Each statement must be headed by the account number and must list each transaction on a separate line. For each transaction, the date, the amount of the transaction (unsigned) and the updated balance (unsigned) must be printed. Credit and debit transaction amounts must be aligned in separate columns. An overdrawn (negative) balance must be indicated by the word 'overdrawn'.

For example, the input:

```
123456   +1000
123456    +200   87  3  1
123456    -500   87  3  3
123456    +100   87  3 10
297600     -12
297600     +10   87  3 11
000000
```

contains details of two accounts.

5.3. Air pollution counts (integers in the range 0 through 100) have been measured for several consecutive days. These counts are supplied as input data, terminated by a negative integer. Write a program to find ***peaks*** in the pollution counts, in other words counts that exceed the counts of the previous and following days. For each peak the program must output the number of the day on which it occurred (counting from 1) and the count on that day. The total number of peaks found, and the total number of measurements, must also be output. How will your program treat the first and last days?

5.4. Write an interactive program to play a game of Nim against a human opponent.

The rules of Nim are as follows. The first player lays down some number of matchsticks (at least 4). Starting with the second player, the players move alternately. A move consists of removing 1, 2 or 3 matchsticks. The player who removes the last matchstick(s) wins the game.

The program should allow the human opponent to choose the initial number of matchsticks. On each turn it should output the number of matchsticks it wishes to remove, and also the number remaining; it should then prompt the opponent for a reply and read it.

Here is a sample dialog, with the human opponent's replies distinguished:

```
How many matchsticks shall we start with? 8
I remove 3.   Number remaining: 5.   Your move? 1
I remove 2.   Number remaining: 2.   Your move? 2
Congratulations, you win.
```

6

The Character Data Type

6.1. Character data and character sets

Characters have a special importance as the most common medium of communication between humans and computers. Computer character sets are quite limited. Moreover, several incompatible character sets are in use, hindering the transfer of textual data between different computers.

The most widely used character set is that defined by ISO (the International Standards Organization). This character set is a standard for data communications, and a *de facto* standard for mini- and micro-computers. It consists of 128 characters, of which 95 are ***graphic characters***, i.e., characters that can be printed or displayed. The others are ***control characters***, which are used as format effectors on printers and displays, for control of data communications, and so on. The ISO character set allows for some variation from one country to another (e.g., in the choice of currency symbol). In this book we use the American version, *ASCII*, which is shown in Figure 6.1.

All Ada programs may assume that their text input-output is in terms of the ISO character set. If a different character set is normally used on your computer, the standard package `Text_IO` will carry out any necessary character code conversions behind the scenes.

6.2. Type `Character`: values and operations

The values of the standard data type `Character` are the 128 characters of the ISO character set. Here we shall concern ourselves only with the 95 graphic characters, which include the space character. A graphic character is denoted in a program by enclosing it in quotes, for example `'A'`, `'a'`, `'7'`, `'+'`, `' '` (the space character), and `'''` (the quote character itself).

Here are some examples of declarations of `Character` constants and variables:

```
Space   : constant Character := ' ';
Query   : constant Character := '?';
Initial : Character;
Ch      : Character := Space;
```

There is an ordering on the ISO characters that is defined by their positions in the ISO character table (Figure 6.1). For the upper-case letters, and separately for the lower-case letters, the ISO ordering corresponds to the usual alphabetic ordering: the letter A comes before the letter B, which in turn comes before the letter C, and so on. In Ada we may compare two `Character` values using any of the relational operators. Thus the relation

`Initial<='D'` is `True` if the value of `Initial` is `'A'`, `'B'`, `'C'` or `'D'`; it is `False` if its value is any other upper-case letter. (You must consult the ISO character table to determine the result if the value of `Initial` is not an upper-case letter.) The expression:

```
('a' <= Ch) and (Ch <= 'z')
```

is `True` if and only if the value of `Ch` is a lower-case letter.

The ordering of the characters makes it sensible to think in terms of *ranges* of characters. For example, the above expression can be written more concisely using a membership operator:

```
Ch in 'a' .. 'z'
```

We can also use range constraints in `Character` object declarations, for example:

```
Capital : Character range 'A' .. 'Z';
```

Any attempt to give `Capital` a value outside the specified range will raise the exception `Constraint_Error`.

Example 6.1 *Simple character handling*

The following program fragment reads a person's forename and surname (in that order), and writes the surname followed by the initial letter of the forename. It allows for spaces

	0	1	2	3	4	5	6	7
0	*NUL*	*SOH*	*STX*	*ETX*	*EOT*	*ENQ*	*ACK*	*BEL*
8	*BS*	*HT*	*LF*	*VT*	*FF*	*CR*	*SO*	*SI*
16	*DLE*	*DC1*	*DC2*	*DC3*	*DC4*	*NAK*	*SYN*	*ETB*
24	*CAN*	*EM*	*SUB*	*ESC*	*FS*	*GS*	*RS*	*US*
32	*SP*	!	"	#	$	%	&	'
40	(	)	*	+	,	-	.	/
48	0	1	2	3	4	5	6	7
56	8	9	:	;	<	=	>	?
64	@	A	B	C	D	E	F	G
72	H	I	J	K	L	M	N	O
80	P	Q	R	S	T	U	V	W
88	X	Y	Z	[	\	]	^	_
96	`	a	b	c	d	e	f	g
104	h	i	j	k	l	m	n	o
112	p	q	r	s	t	u	v	w
120	x	y	z	{	|	}	~	*DEL*

The control characters are named in italics.
SP denotes the space character (position number 32).
The position number (internal code) of each character is the sum of its row and column numbers in the table.

Fig. 6.1 The ASCII variant of the ISO character set

before the forename, and it assumes that the forename and surname are followed by space(s). It checks that the initial is a capital letter. The declarations of Space, Initial and Ch given above are assumed.

```
-- skip any spaces before the forename --
while Ch = Space loop
   Get (Ch);
end loop;
-- note the initial and check it is a capital letter --
Initial := Ch;
if Initial not in 'A'..'Z' then
   Put ("WARNING: initial is not a capital letter");
   New_Line;
end if;
-- skip the rest of the forename --
while Ch /= Space loop
   Get (Ch);
end loop;
-- skip spaces between the names --
while Ch = Space loop
   Get (Ch);
end loop;
-- read and write the surname --
while Ch /= Space loop
   Put (Ch);  Get (Ch);
end loop;
-- write the initial --
Put (Space);  Put (Initial);  Put ('.');  New_Line;
```

□ *End of Example 6.1*

Two important attributes of the Character type are Character'Pos and Character'Val. These are functions that convert between Character values and their *position numbers* in the ISO character table (see Figure 6.1). For example, the upper-case letters 'A', 'B', ..., 'Z' have the consecutive position numbers 65, 66, ..., 90. Specifically:

Character'Pos(*C*) yields the position number of the character *C*.

Character'Val(*I*) yields the character whose position number is *I* (or raises the exception Constraint_Error if no such character exists).

Thus the expression:

```
Character'Val (Character'Pos('A') + N - 1)
```

yields the N'th upper-case letter of the alphabet, provided that N has a value in the range 1 through 26.

Style

The expression cited above could be simplified to `Character'Val(N+64)`, which yields the same result, but the use of the obscure literal 64 makes its meaning much less clear. Likewise, a relation like '`Ch in '!'..'/'`' can only be understood by reference to the ISO character table; unlike the relation '`Ch in 'A'..'Z'`' it has no intuitive significance. Generally speaking, it is bad practice for programs to assume detailed knowledge about the ordering and position numbers of the ISO characters. However, it *is* reasonable to exploit the following properties of the ISO character set:

- the digits `'0'`, `'1'`, ..., `'9'` are numerically ordered and have consecutive position numbers;
- the upper-case letters `'A'`, `'B'`, ..., `'Z'` are alphabetically ordered and have consecutive position numbers;
- the lower-case letters `'a'`, `'b'`, ..., `'z'` are alphabetically ordered and have consecutive position numbers.

(Note, however, that there is one commonly used character set — EBCDIC — in which the letters do *not* have consecutive position numbers.)

Some programs have no choice but to assume detailed knowledge of the ISO character table. In these cases explanatory comments should be used, for example:

```
Ch : Character range ' ' .. '"';     -- ISO-DEPENDENT
      -- Ch will range over the graphic characters only.
```

Example 6.2 *Edited numerical output*

Assume N contains a nonnegative integer number. We wish to write this number with commas every three positions (e.g., 1,234,567 or 75,000 or 144 or 0).

To solve this problem, we could write the number one decimal digit at a time, starting with the most significant digit. We write a comma whenever the number of digits still to be written is a positive multiple of 3. To generate the digits in the desired order, we can repeatedly split the residue of the number into its leading digit and remainder:

```
initialize Residue to N;
while Residue still has digits to be written loop
    split Residue into its leading digit and remainder;
    write the leading digit;
    if Residue has a positive multiple of 3 digits then
        write a comma;
    end if;
end loop;
```

Clearly we must know the number of (significant) digits in Residue. To refine '*split* Residue *into its leading digit and remainder*' we must also know the corresponding power of 10. Note that we need not compute these afresh on every repetition. Completing the refinements we arrive at the following declarations and statements:

```
Residue, Power  : Integer range 0 .. Integer'Last;
Nr_Digits       : Integer range 0 .. Integer'Last;
Next_Digit      : Integer range 0 .. 9;
Zero_Pos        : constant Integer := Character'Pos('0');
```

```
...
Residue := N;
Power := 1;  Nr_Digits := 1;
while Power <= Residue/10 loop
   Power := 10 * Power;  Nr_Digits := Nr_Digits + 1;
end loop;
while Nr_Digits > 0 loop
   -- Nr_Digits = number of decimal digits in Residue,
   -- Power = 10 ** (Nr_Digits-1).
   Next_Digit := Residue / Power;
   Residue := Residue mod Power;
   Nr_Digits := Nr_Digits - 1;  Power := Power / 10;
   Put (Character'Val (Next_Digit + Zero_Pos));
   if Nr_Digits > 0 and Nr_Digits mod 3 = 0 then
      Put (',');
   end if;
end loop;
```

Next_Digit is assigned an integer in the range 0 through 9, which we wish to convert to the corresponding character in the range '0' through '9'. The required position number is obtained by adding Character'Pos('0') to Next_Digit, since the digits have consecutive position numbers.

□ *End of Example 6.2*

6.3. Type Character: input-output

We have already seen some simple examples of the use of Get and Put to read and write single characters. Now we present a fuller (but still somewhat simplified) picture of the structure of text files. We also introduce some more facilities from the standard package Text_IO.

A *text file* consists of zero or more *lines*, each of which consists of zero or more graphic characters. The number of characters may vary from one line to another. In order to understand the Get and Put operations in detail, it is useful to consider each line as being terminated by a *line terminator*, and the text file as a whole as being terminated by a *file terminator*, as illustrated in Figure 6.2. In an actual character file each terminator might be represented by one or more control characters, or by some other means. What is important is that we can write Ada programs that process text files without making any assumptions about the representation of these terminators.

Suppose that the text file of Figure 6.2 is the standard input file. The reading position is initially at the beginning of the first line. Repeated execution of the statement 'Get(Ch);' (where Ch is a Character variable) successively sets Ch to 'P', 'A', 'R', 'I', 'S', 'I', 'N', ' ', 'T', 'H', 'E', 'S', 'P', 'R', 'I', 'N', 'G', '-', 'T', 'I', 'M', and finally 'E'. In other words, Get ignores line terminators. The reading position is always just beyond the latest character read. Executing 'Get(Ch);' when the last character has already been read would raise End_Error.

In order to test whether the entire text file has been read, we use the Boolean function `End_of_File`, which returns the value `True` if the reading position is at the file terminator, or at the last line terminator (Figure 6.2).

We often need some means of testing whether the whole of the current line has been read. This is provided by the Boolean function `End_of_Line`, which returns `True` when the reading position is at a line terminator (Figure 6.2).

Finally, the effect of executing '`Skip_Line;`' is to skip past the next line terminator — Figure 6.2.

Example 6.3   *A scheme for line-by-line processing*

Text files are often processed one line at a time. For each line, we process the data on that line, then call `Skip_Line` to move on to the next line. This is repeated as long as `End_of_File` returns `False`:

```
perform start-of-input processing;
while not End_of_File loop
    read and process the data on the current line;
    Skip_Line;
end loop;
perform end-of-input processing;
```

□ *End of Example 6.3*

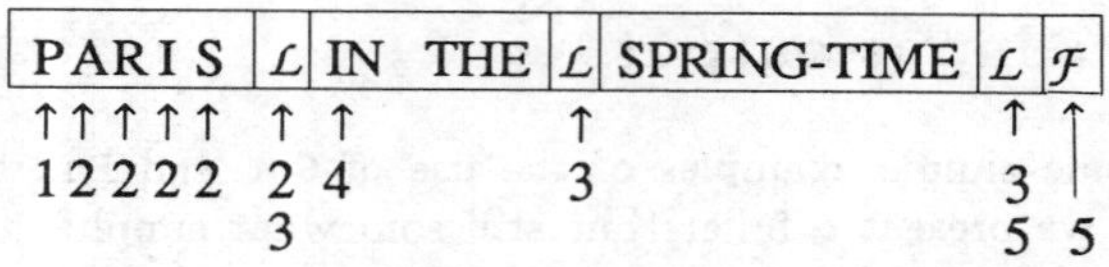

$\mathcal{L}$ line terminator $\mathcal{F}$ file terminator

Key:

1 initial reading position.
2 reading positions after reading consecutive characters from line 1.
3 reading positions in which `End_of_Line` returns `True`.
4 reading positions after `Skip_Line` in positions 1 or 2.
5 reading positions in which `End_of_File` returns `True`.

This text file when printed or displayed would look like this:

PARIS
IN THE
SPRING-TIME

Fig. 6.2   **Text file structure**

Two different examples of this scheme follow. Each illustrates a common theme in text file processing, which can easily be adapted to more complicated programs.

Example 6.4 *Copying a text file*

The following program transcribes text from input to output:

```
with Text_IO;  use Text_IO;
procedure Copy is
   Ch : Character;
begin
   while not End_of_File loop
      -- transcribe one line from input to output --
      while not End_of_Line loop
         Get (Ch);  Put (Ch);
      end loop;
      New_Line;
      Skip_Line;
   end loop;
end Copy;
```

☐ *End of Example 6.4*

Example 6.5 *Reading numbers up to end of file*

The following program sums integers (one per line of input) up to the end of the input file:

```
with Text_IO;  use Text_IO;
procedure Sum_to_End_of_File is
   package Int_IO is new Integer_IO (Integer);  use Int_IO;
   Summand : Integer;
   Sum : Integer := 0;
begin
   while not End_of_File loop
      -- read a number and add it to Sum --
      Get (Summand);
      Sum := Sum + Summand;
      Skip_Line;
   end loop;
   Put ("Total: ");  Put (Sum);  New_Line;
end Sum_to_End_of_File;
```

☐ *End of Example 6.5*

As illustrated by Example 6.5, `End_of_File` can be used for detecting the end of a list of data items such as numbers, provided that the data items are presented one per line and '`Skip_Line;`' is executed after reading each data item. Figure 6.3 illustrates possible input to program `Sum_to_End_of_File`. After reading each number, the reading position is just beyond the last character of the number. The statement '`Skip_Line;`' cannot be omitted since it is possible that the last number might be followed by space(s).

Exercises 6

6.1. A mailing list is supplied as input. Each line of the mailing list contains one person's name and address, e.g.:

```
Hugh McShuggle/13 Loch Road/Bonny Doon/Scotland
```

Write a program to read the mailing list and output the names and addresses, taking a new line at each oblique. Successive addresses are to be separated by two blank lines.

6.2. Write a program that mimics a simple calculator. The input data is a series of integers separated by operation symbols (+, -, *, /), and terminated by =, e.g., 3+7*12=. The program is to compute the result of the calculation, 1080 in this case. The operations are to be performed strictly left-to-right: * and / have no precedence over + and -.

6.3. An integer N in the range 0 through $10^D - 1$ is given as input.

(a) Write a program to output the value of N as a literal of exactly D decimal digits, including leading zeros (e.g., 1988 or 0012 or 0000, in the case that D is 4).

(b) Modify your program so that leading zeroes are replaced by asterisks, as in computer-printed checks (e.g., **12).

(c) Modify your program to read the value of N without using `Integer_IO`; instead read and evaluate the literal one character at a time. The literal may be preceded by any number of spaces and line terminators; reading must cease after the first nonnumeric character has been read.

6.4. Write a program that reads natural-language text (consisting of words separated by

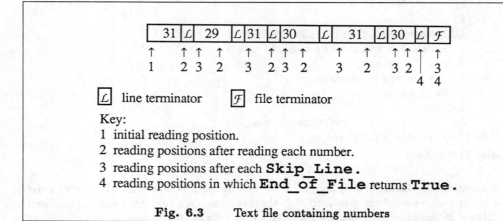

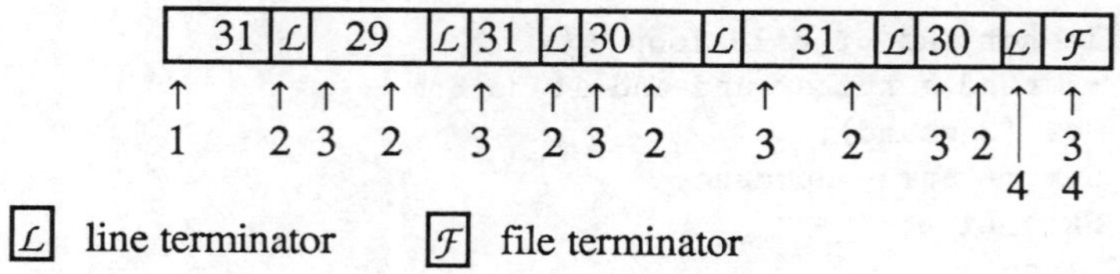

Key:
1 initial reading position.
2 reading positions after reading each number.
3 reading positions after each **Skip_Line**.
4 reading positions in which **End_of_File** returns **True**.

Fig. 6.3 Text file containing numbers

spaces, line terminators and punctuation) and outputs each word on a separate line. Treat each sequence of letters as a word.

6.5. Write a program that reads natural-language text (as in the previous exercise) and computes the average number of letters per word and the average number of words per sentence in the text. (These averages are quite good measures of the obscurity of a text!) How will you detect the end of a sentence?

7

Discrete Types

7.1. Enumeration types and type declarations

So far we have looked in detail at three of Ada's data types: `Integer`, whose values are whole numbers; `Boolean`, whose values are `False` and `True`; and `Character`, whose values are characters. Often the programmer needs a wider choice of data types than this, for example to model the days of the week, or the months of the year, or the states of a traffic light. A list of potentially useful data types could be extended indefinitely, and it would be unreasonable to expect Ada to provide all of them. Instead Ada provides a means for the programmer to declare new data types to suit the particular application.

Suppose, for example, we wish to declare some variables whose values represent days of the week. We could declare them as follows:

```
Today, Tomorrow : Integer range 0 .. 6;
```

where it is understood that 0 represents Sunday, 1 represents Monday, and so on. Then we could write statements like '`Today := 5;`'. A disadvantage of this is the necessity to remember what each integer represents. By introducing the constant declarations:

```
Sunday    : constant Integer := 0;
Monday    : constant Integer := 1;
Tuesday   : constant Integer := 2;
Wednesday : constant Integer := 3;
Thursday  : constant Integer := 4;
Friday    : constant Integer := 5;
Saturday  : constant Integer := 6;
```

we could replace '`Today := 5;`' by the more natural '`Today := Friday;`'. This solution is an improvement, but still not entirely satisfactory. The seven constant declarations are tedious to write. Moreover, statements like '`Today := 5;`' or even '`if Today mod 3 = 0 then ...`' cannot be faulted, although they violate the spirit of type checking.

The use of integers to represent the days of the week is the best solution available in most programming languages, but Ada is more powerful. It allows us to declare a new data type for the purpose:

```
type Days is (Sunday, Monday, Tuesday,
              Wednesday, Thursday, Friday, Saturday);
```

This is an example of a *type declaration*. It introduces `Days` as the name of a new data type with seven distinct values. It also introduces `Sunday`, `Monday`, and so on, as names for these values. (They are called *enumeration literals*.) The parenthesized list of identifiers:

```
(Sunday,Monday,Tuesday,Wednesday,Thursday,Friday,Saturday)
```

is an example of an ***enumeration type definition***, so called because the new type is defined by enumerating its values.

A simplified syntax of type declarations is shown in Figure 7.1. Type declarations are not restricted to enumeration types; we shall meet other kinds of type declaration in later chapters.

Following a type declaration, we can use the new type name to declare constants and variables of the new type, for example:

```
Today, Tomorrow : Days;
Pay_Day : constant Days := Friday;
```

We can also write down statements like 'Today := Friday;'. Now, however, 'Today := 5;' is a type error since 5 is not a value of the type Days; so too is the expression Today+1, since the value of Today is not an integer.

The following are examples of type declarations for the other data types mentioned in the first paragraph:

```
type Months is
      (Jan,Feb,Mar,Apr,May,Jun,Jul,Aug,Sep,Oct,Nov,Dec);
type Traffic_Lights is (Red, Amber, Green);
```

It may now be seen that Integer, Boolean and Character are just predeclared type names. (They are *not* reserved words.) Indeed, roughly speaking:

```
type Boolean is (False, True);
```

although this type declaration does not convey the special properties of the Boolean type, for example its connection with if statements. Nevertheless it shows that Boolean is an enumeration type, and that False and True are enumeration literals. Character is also an enumeration type, only its literals are character literals rather than identifiers.

7.2. Discrete types and their properties

All the data types we have described so far — Integer, Boolean, Character, and enumeration types declared in type declarations — are collectively called ***discrete types***, because each has a discrete and totally ordered set of values. Consequently the discrete types have a number of attributes and operations in common that are not shared by the other data types of Ada (such as real types and composite types). At this point you should preview Figure 20.1 to see the relationship of discrete types to the other type classes of Ada.

- The ordering on the values of each discrete type allows us to use any of the relational operators to compare two values of the same type. Similarly, we can use the membership operators in and not in to test whether a given value lies within a range

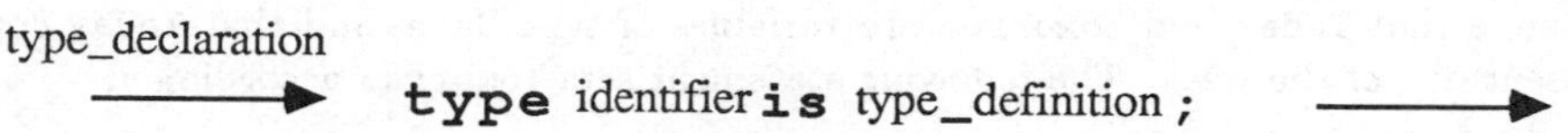
type_declaration
type identifier is type_definition ;

Fig. 7.1 Syntax of type declarations (simplified)

of values of the same type. We have already seen examples of such relations for the types Integer and Character. The ordering of the values of an enumeration type is defined by their order in the enumeration type definition. In the type Days, for example, Sunday comes before Monday, which in turn comes before Tuesday, and so on. Thus the relation 'Today > Thursday' is True if Today's value is Friday or Saturday, otherwise it is False. Note in particular that the relation 'Saturday < Sunday' is False. The relation 'Tomorrow in Monday .. Friday' is True if and only if Tomorrow's value is in the range Monday through Friday.

- Each discrete type T has a unique *first* value and a unique *last* value. These are given by the constant attributes T'First and T'Last respectively. For example, Months'First is Jan and Months'Last is Dec.
- Each value of a given discrete type (except the first value) has a unique *predecessor* and each value (except the last) has a unique *successor*. Each discrete type T correspondingly has two function attributes T'Pred and T'Succ. For example:

Integer'Pred(7)	= 6	Integer'Succ(7)	= 8
Character'Pred('E')	= 'D'	Character'Succ('E')	= 'F'
Months'Pred(Sep)	= Aug	Months'Succ(Sep)	= Oct

  Months'Pred(Jan) or Months'Succ(Dec) would raise the Constraint_Error exception. Clearly, Integer'Pred(I) is equivalent to I-1 and Integer'Succ(I) is equivalent to I+1.
- The values of any discrete type have consecutive *position numbers*. In particular, the values of an enumeration type have position numbers 0, 1, 2, ..., in the order of their enumeration. Each discrete type T has a function attribute T'Pos that converts a value of type T into its position number, and an inverse function attribute T'Val that converts a position number into the corresponding value of type T. For example:

Integer'Pos(7)	= 7	Integer'Val(7)	= 7
Character'Pos('A')	= 65	Character'Val(65)	= 'A'
Months'Pos(Jan)	= 0	Months'Val(0)	= Jan
Months'Pos(Feb)	= 1	Months'Val(1)	= Feb

  and so on. Months'Val(12) or Months'Val(-1) would raise the exception Constraint_Error since no value of the Months type has position number 12 or -1.

The following relationships hold among these attributes, where X and Y are of any discrete type T, and I is of type Integer:

```
          X < Y  =  T'Pos(X) < T'Pos(Y)
      T'Pred(X)  =  T'Val(T'Pos(X)-1)
      T'Succ(X)  =  T'Val(T'Pos(X)+1)
 T'Val(T'Pos(X)) =  X
 T'Pos(T'Val(I)) =  I                       (if T'Val(I) exists)
```

Example 7.1 *Using the* Succ *attribute*

Assume that Today and Tomorrow are variables of type Days, and that Today contains the present day of the week. The following statement sets Tomorrow accordingly:

```
if Today = Days'Last then
   Tomorrow := Days'First;
else
```

```
        Tomorrow := Days'Succ(Today);
    end if;
```

□ *End of Example 7.1*

Example 7.2 *Using the* `Pos` *and* `Val` *attributes*

Assuming that `Day` and `N` are variables of types `Days` and `Integer` respectively, the following statement advances the value of `Day` by `N` days:

```
    Day := Days'Val ((Days'Pos (Day) + N) mod 7);
```

The solution requires the use of modulo 7 arithmetic. Integer operations cannot be applied to `Day` itself, since its value is not an integer. Therefore the `Pos` attribute is used to convert its value to an integer, and the `Val` attribute is used to convert the numeric result back to a value of the `Days` type.

□ *End of Example 7.2*

7.3. Subtypes and subtype declarations

We have seen that *type* is a fixed property of every value and every object in an Ada program, and that each type is characterized by a set of values and by a set of operations that may be performed on these values. In the case of the type `Character`, for example, the values are the ISO characters and the operations are assignment, equality and ordering relations, `Succ`, `Pred`, `Pos`, `Val` and so on. These operations may be applied to *any* `Character` object(s), and a `Character` object (if declared without any range constraint) can take *any* `Character` value.

A `Character` object declared *with* a range constraint, for example:

```
    Initial : Character range 'A' .. 'Z';
```

has a restriction placed on the set of values it may take, but no restriction on the operations that may be applied to it. Thus it is correct to state that `Initial`'s *type* is `Character`, because we may apply any `Character` operation to it; but its properties are more completely described by the phrase:

```
    Character range 'A' .. 'Z'
```

It is convenient to have a term for this more complete description; it is called the object's *subtype*.

A subtype of a type `T` is characterized by the same operations as the type `T` but by a *subset* of the values of `T`. This subset is specified by a ***constraint***. We have already met ***range constraints***, which may be applied to objects of any scalar type; an example of a range constraint is '`range 'A'..'Z'`' above. Later we shall meet other kinds of constraints.

In the simplified syntax diagram for object declarations (Figure 1.4), each occurrence of 'type' should have been 'subtype_indication'. A ***subtype indication*** consists of a type name (such as `Integer` or `Character` or `Days`) optionally followed by a suitable constraint.

A program can often be made more readable if we give a name to a subtype, by means of a ***subtype declaration***. For example:

```
subtype Letters is Character range 'A' .. 'Z';

subtype Scores is Integer range 0 .. 100;

subtype Weekdays is Days range Monday .. Friday;
```

Subsequent declarations may use these subtype names, for example:

```
Initial : Letters;

My_Score : Scores;

Work_Day : Weekdays;
```

Here `Letters` is used as an abbreviation for the subtype indication '`Character range 'A'..'Z'`'.

See the syntax diagrams 'subtype_indication' and 'subtype_declaration' in Appendix A. Note that the constraint is optional, so that in the declaration:

```
I : Integer;
```

`Integer` on its own is a subtype indication; it may be regarded as equivalent to '`Integer range Integer'First .. Integer'Last`', where the constraint is rather weak! Likewise we may write:

```
subtype Logical is Boolean;
```

and thereafter declare objects with subtype `Logical`; the effect is as if these objects were declared directly as `Boolean`. Note also that we may specify a subtype of a subtype, as in:

```
subtype Passing_Scores is Scores range 50 .. 100;
```

`Passing_Scores` is considered to be a subtype of `Integer`.

There are two predefined subtypes that are often useful:

```
subtype Natural is Integer range 0 .. Integer'Last;
subtype Positive is Integer range 1 .. Integer'Last;
```

The `Natural` values are nonnegative integers, and the `Positive` values are positive integers.

We have already met the membership operators `in` and `not in` used with a range as their right operand, as in the relations:

```
Ch in 'A' .. 'Z'                Day not in Monday .. Friday
```

(where `Ch` is of type `Character` and `Day` is of type `Days`). A membership operator may alternatively be followed by any subtype indication, so these examples could be written as:

```
Ch in Letters                Day not in Weekdays
```

Likewise the relation '`I > 0`' could alternatively be expressed as '`I in Positive`'.

7.4. Input-output for enumeration types

Ada allows for text input and output of values of any enumeration type. Enumeration values are represented in the input or output text (as in the source program) by their identifiers. The necessary conversions between the textual and internal representations are performed by a facility called `Enumeration_IO` within the standard package `Text_IO`. By including a 'magic formula' like the following:

```
package T_IO is new Enumeration_IO (T);  use T_IO;
```

within a declarative part, we gain access to the following procedures for input-output of values of the enumeration type `T`:

`Get(X);` reads an identifier and assigns the corresponding value of type `T` to the variable `X` (or raises the exception `Data_Error` if the identifier is not a literal of type `T`).

`Put(X);` writes the identifier corresponding to the value of *X*, which is of type `T`.

The `Get` procedure will skip any spaces or line terminators preceding the identifier. It does not distinguish between corresponding upper- and lower-case letters. Figure 7.2 illustrates the effect of `Get` in various situations.

The `Put` procedure writes the identifier in upper case by default, but we can request lower case by including the parameter '`Set => Lower_Case`'. There is also an optional `Width` parameter, which specifies the minimum number of characters to be written; any extra spaces necessary to achieve this field width *follow* the identifier in the output text. (Compare this behavior with the `Put` procedure of `Integer_IO`, Section 2.3; in that case the extra spaces *precede* the number. The rationale is that a column of numbers will be aligned on the right, whereas a column of identifiers will be aligned on the left, as customary.) In the absence of

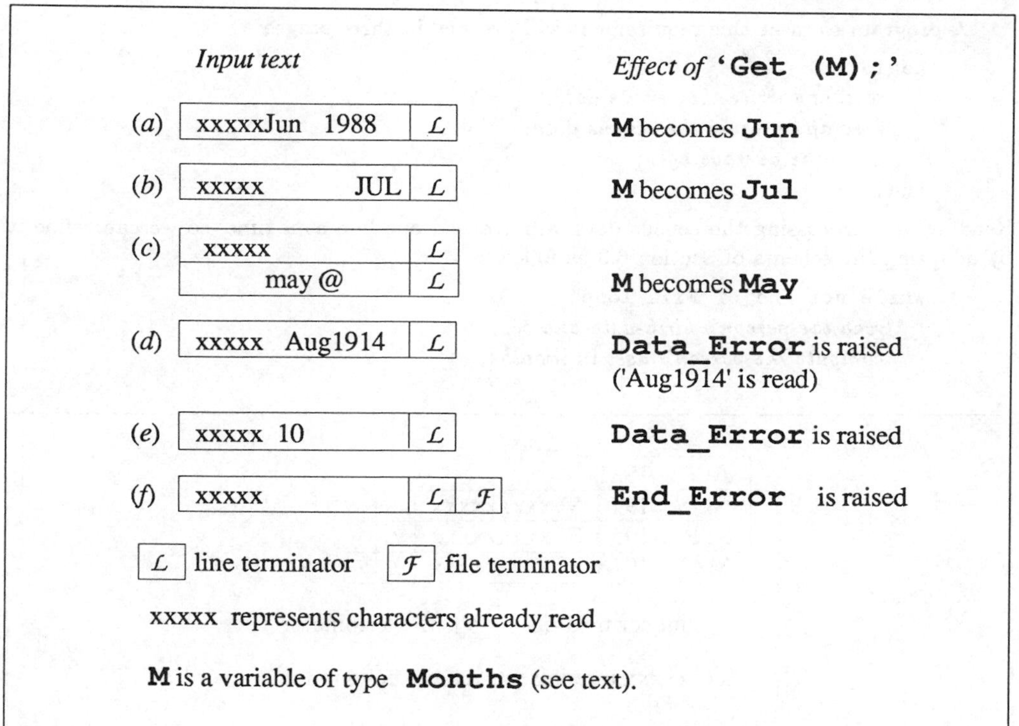
Input text
Effect of 'Get (M);'
(a) xxxxxJun 1988 L
M becomes Jun
(b) xxxxx JUL L
M becomes Jul
(c) xxxxx L
may @ L
M becomes May
(d) xxxxx Aug1914 L
Data_Error is raised
('Aug1914' is read)
(e) xxxxx 10 L
Data_Error is raised
(f) xxxxx L F
End_Error is raised
L line terminator
F file terminator
xxxxx represents characters already read
M is a variable of type Months (see text).

Fig. 7.2 Enumeration input

a `Width` parameter no leading or trailing spaces are written. Here are some illustrations of the effect of `Put`, assuming that `D` is of type `Days` (◇ indicates a single space):

Value of `D`	*Output from* `Put(D);`	*Output from* `Put(D,Width=>8);`	*Output from* `Put(D,Set=>Lower_Case);`
`Monday`	`MONDAY`	`MONDAY◇◇`	`monday`
`Thursday`	`THURSDAY`	`THURSDAY`	`thursday`
`Wednesday`	`WEDNESDAY`	`WEDNESDAY`	`wednesday`

Example 7.3 *Enumeration input-output*

Data taken from a census are provided as one line of text per person, in the following fixed format:

Columns 1–3:	month of birth (3 letters: `JAN/FEB/MAR/etc.`)
Columns 5–8:	year of birth (integer)
Column 10:	sex (`M/F`)
Columns 12–end:	other data of no concern here

(All other columns are blank.) Data for a number of persons are preceded by a single line containing the census month and year in columns 1–8, in the same format as above. Figure 7.3 shows a (very small) example of this data.

A program is required to read and analyze this data and to write the average ages, in months, of the males and of the females (separately). The census date is also to be written.

A program to meet this requirement will proceed in three stages:

begin
    read and write the census date;
    read and process the census data;
    write the average ages;
end;

Reading and processing the census data will proceed one line at a time, so we can refine it by adapting the schema of Section 6.3 as follows:

while not `End_of_File` **loop**
    read the person's birth-date and sex;
    compute the person's age, in months;

```
APR  1981 [L]
NOV  1946 M xxxxxxxxx [L]
SEP  1950 F xxxxxxxxx [L]
MAY  1978 F xxxxxxxxx [L][F]
```

[L] line terminator [F] file terminator

xxxxxxxxx represents data to be ignored.

Fig. 7.3 Example of census data (see text)

```
      update the male or female count and age total;
      Skip_Line;  -- skips the other data on the current line
   end loop;
```

This assumes that the male and female counts and age totals have been initialized to zero. These initializations can conveniently be included in their declarations.

The specification ensures that there will be spaces between the month, year, sex and other data. Moreover, the specified textual representations for months (JAN, FEB, etc.) and for sexes (M and F) happen to conform to Ada's syntax for identifiers. Thus the program can take advantage of Integer_IO and Enumeration_IO, provided that it uses appropriate enumeration type definitions for the months and for the sexes.

Completing the refinement we may arrive at the following program:

```
with Text_IO;  use Text_IO;
procedure Compute_Mean_Ages is
   type Months is
         (JAN,FEB,MAR,APR,MAY,JUN,JUL,AUG,SEP,OCT,NOV,DEC);
   type Sexes is (M, F);
   package Int_IO is new Integer_IO (Integer);
   package Month_IO is new Enumeration_IO (Months);
   package Sex_IO is new Enumeration_IO (Sexes);
   use Int_IO, Month_IO, Sex_IO;
   subtype Years is Integer range 1801 .. 2199;
   Census_Month, Birth_Month : Months;
   Census_Year, Birth_Year : Years;
   Sex : Sexes;
   Age : Natural;
   M_Count, F_Count : Natural := 0;
   M_Age_Total, F_Age_Total : Natural := 0;
begin
   -- read and write the census date --
   Get (Census_Month);  Get (Census_Year);  Skip_Line;
   Put (Census_Month, Width => 4);
   Put (Census_Year, Width => 4);
   New_Line (2);     -- writes 2 line terminators
   -- read and process the census data --
   while not End_of_File loop
      -- read the person's birth-date and sex --
      Get (Birth_Month);  Get (Birth_Year);  Get (Sex);
      -- compute the person's age, in months --
      Age := 12 * (Census_Year - Birth_Year)
            + Months'Pos (Census_Month) - Months'Pos (Birth_Month);
      -- update the male or female count and age total --
      if Sex = M then  -- male
         M_Count := M_Count + 1;
         M_Age_Total := M_Age_Total + Age;
      else  -- female
```

```
            F_Count := F_Count + 1;
            F_Age_Total := F_Age_Total + Age;
         end if;
         Skip_Line;  -- skips the other data on this line
      end loop;
      -- write the average ages --
      Put ("Average male age: ");
      Put (M_Age_Total/M_Count, Width => 4);
      Put (" months."); New_Line;
      Put ("Average female age: ");
      Put (F_Age_Total/F_Count, Width => 4);
      Put (" months."); New_Line;
   end Compute_Mean_Ages;
```

□ *End of Example 7.3*

Note finally that since `Boolean` is an enumeration type, `Boolean` input-output can be achieved using `Enumeration_IO`.

Exercises 7

7.1. Given the following variables representing a date:

```
Day : Integer range 1 .. 31;  Month : Months;  Year : Positive;
```

write statements to do the following: (a) output the date in the style illustrated by `1988 FEBRUARY 29`; (b) output the date in the style illustrated by `2/29/88`; (c) update the variables to the following day's date.

7.2. Write a program that reads from each line of input the name of a chemical element, and outputs that name followed by the atomic number and chemical symbol of that element. For example, given the input:

```
hydrogen
carbon
```

the program should output:

```
hydrogen  1 H
carbon   12 C
```

(*Hint*: declare two enumerations types, one for the symbols and one for the names of the elements, enumerated in the order of their atomic numbers.)

8

Further Control Structures

8.1. What further control structures are needed?

The theoretical answer to the question posed above is: none. It can be proved that every algorithm (i.e., every flowchart) can be programmed using an appropriate combination of the if statements and while loop statements described in Chapter 4. Nevertheless, Ada as a practical language provides additional control structures that are more natural in many situations. The most important of these are the *case statement*, which helps with many-way selection, and the *for loop statement*, which is convenient with loops in which the number of iterations is known in advance. These two control structures are introduced here because they are closely associated with the discrete types discussed in the preceding chapter, in much the same way that if statements and while loops are closely associated with the `Boolean` type.

We often need to write down loops that are less restrictive than the fundamental while loops and for loops. For example, we might need freedom in positioning the test for loop termination. We might even want two or more such tests at different positions. To meet these needs Ada provides generalized loops and exits. These are covered later in this chapter.

This chapter also ties up a couple of loose ends. *Blocks* are introduced as a means to place declarations close to where they are actually needed. And we conclude our treatment of control flow by describing the *goto statement*, which is unruly and rarely useful anyway.

8.2. Case statements

The if statement allows a program to select one of *two* actions, depending on the value of a `Boolean` expression. The *case statement* allows a program to select one of *several* actions, depending on the value of an expression of some discrete type. This possibility is illustrated by the flowchart of Figure 8.1. The following example illustrates the use of case statements.

Example 8.1 *A case statement*

```
type Days is (Sunday, Monday, Tuesday,
              Wednesday, Thursday, Friday, Saturday);
Today : Days;
Today_Hours : Natural range 0 .. 24;
Total_Hours : Natural range 0 .. 168;
Hourly_Rate, Pay : Natural;
...
case Today is
```

```
        when Monday =>
           Total_Hours := Todays_Hours;
        when Tuesday .. Thursday =>
           Total_Hours := Total_Hours + Todays_Hours;
        when Friday =>
           Total_Hours := Total_Hours + Todays_Hours;
           Pay := Total_Hours * Hourly_Rate;
        when Saturday | Sunday =>
           null;
     end case;
```

This case statement contains four alternatives, of which exactly one will be executed. The first alternative will be selected if the value of `Today` is `Monday`; the second alternative if its value is in the range `Tuesday` through `Thursday`; the third alternative if its value is `Friday`; and the fourth alternative if its value is `Saturday` or `Sunday`.

□ *End of Example 8.1*

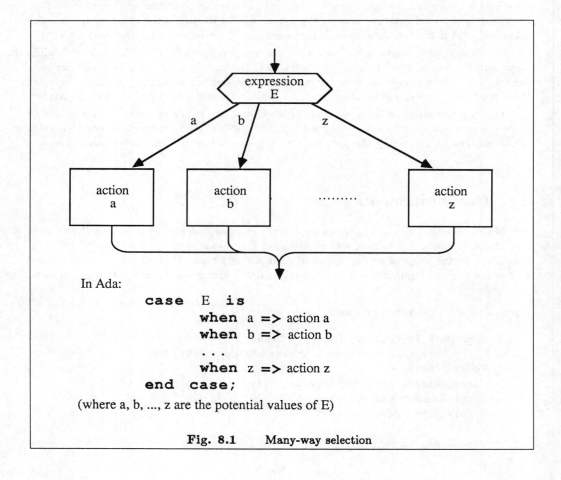

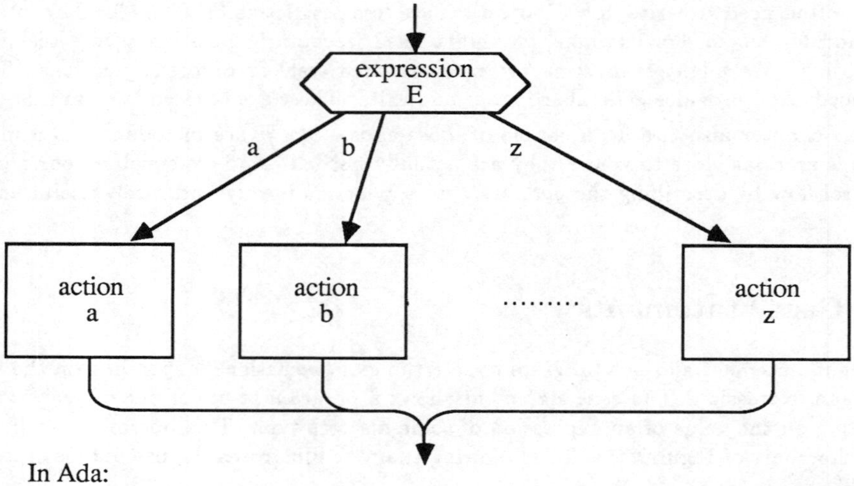

In Ada:

```
case E is
      when a => action a
      when b => action b
      . . .
      when z => action z
end case;
```

(where a, b, ..., z are the potential values of E)

Fig. 8.1 Many-way selection

The case statement contains (between the reserved words `case` and `is`) an expression that is evaluated to select *one* of the case statement's alternatives for execution. Each alternative is a sequence of statements that is preceded by a list of *choices* (enclosed between the symbols `when` and '`=>`') specifying some of the potential values of the case expression. Ada requires every potential value of the case expression to be specified in one, and only one, of the case statement's choices. (The order in which they are specified is immaterial.) Thus execution of the case statement always causes exactly one of its alternatives to be selected for execution.

In Example 8.1 the case expression is `Today`, and it may be seen that each of its seven potential values is specified in exactly one choice.

Various forms of notation may be used between `when` and '`=>`' to list potential values of the case expression. There may be a single choice, as in each of the first three alternatives above. More generally there may be a list of choices, separated by the delimiter '`|`', as in the fourth alternative above. Each choice may specify either a single value, such as `Monday` in the first alternative, or a range of consecutive values, such as '`Tuesday .. Thursday`' in the second alternative. The latter choice is equivalent to the list of choices '`Tuesday | Wednesday | Thursday`'.

The choice `others` may be used to stand for all values not previously specified. (It is restricted to the last alternative of a case statement.) Thus the list of choices '`Saturday | Sunday`' in the last alternative of Example 8.1 could be replaced by `others`.

See the syntax diagrams 'case_statement' and 'choice' in Appendix A. Since the compiler must check that every potential value of a case expression is specified by exactly one choice in the case statement, all expressions used in choices must be static expressions. Note that a case statement in which `others` appears as a choice guarantees at least that no potential value is omitted. (On the other hand, using `others` makes it impossible for the compiler to detect the accidental omission of a choice from another alternative.)

One last point about Example 8.1. The fourth alternative contains only a *null statement*, which does nothing at all. Every sequence of statements in Ada must contain at least one statement, even if only a null statement.

Example 8.2 Roman numerals

A classical Roman numeral is composed of letters having the following values: I is 1, V is 5, X is 10, L is 50, C is 100, D is 500, and M is 1000. Thus MDCCCCLXXXVIII stands for 1988. The letters must be arranged in descending order of rank. (For the sake of simplicity, combinations such as IV for 4 will not be considered here.)

Let us develop a program fragment that will read a Roman numeral, terminated by a space, and place its value in a variable `Value`. A `Boolean` variable `Valid` is to be set `False` if an invalid character is found or if the letters are out of sequence.

The characters must be read one by one until a space is read. Each letter must be converted into its individual value (if it has one), and this must be added to `Value` (unless it exceeds the previous letter's value). The conversion can conveniently be done by a case statement.

```
Value  : Natural := 0;
Valid  : Boolean := True;
Letter : Character;
Letter_Value, Prev_Letter_Value : Positive range 1 .. 1000;
```

```
...
Prev_Letter_Value := 1000;
Get (Letter);
while Letter /= ' ' loop
   case Letter is
      when 'I' =>  Letter_Value := 1;
      when 'V' =>  Letter_Value := 5;
      when 'X' =>  Letter_Value := 10;
      when 'L' =>  Letter_Value := 50;
      when 'C' =>  Letter_Value := 100;
      when 'D' =>  Letter_Value := 500;
      when 'M' =>  Letter_Value := 1000;
      when others =>  Valid := False;
   end case;
   if Valid then
      if Letter_Value > Prev_Letter_Value then
         Valid := False;
      else
         Value := Value + Letter_Value;
         Prev_Letter_Value := Letter_Value;
      end if;
   end if;
   Get (Letter);
end loop;
```

The case statement here is preferable to the equivalent cascaded if statement:

```
if      Letter = 'I'  then  Letter_Value := 1;
elsif   Letter = 'V'  then  Letter_Value := 5;
elsif   Letter = 'X'  then  Letter_Value := 10;
elsif   Letter = 'L'  then  Letter_Value := 50;
elsif   Letter = 'C'  then  Letter_Value := 100;
elsif   Letter = 'D'  then  Letter_Value := 500;
elsif   Letter = 'M'  then  Letter_Value := 1000;
else Valid := False;
end if;
```

The case statement is more lucid, and the value of Letter is tested only once rather than several times.

□ *End of Example 8.2*

8.3. For loop statements

The while loop is simple yet powerful. It is well suited to situations where the number of iterations cannot be predicted in advance. An example of such a loop is one that reads input data until the input is exhausted.

Loops where the number of iterations *is* known in advance are very common. Such loops use variables to count the iterations. They can easily be programmed using while loops, the while condition being framed in such a way as to become `False` when the required number of iterations has been reached. Because such loops are very common Ada provides a special construct, the ***for loop statement***, as a more natural notation.

Example 8.3 A while loop and a for loop

Consider the part of Example 4.6 that was to output a row of `Number` asterisks. The solution using a while loop was as follows:

```
Asterisk_Count := 0;
while Asterisk_Count < Number loop
   Put ('*');
   Asterisk_Count := Asterisk_Count + 1;
end loop;
```

Because the number of iterations is known in advance (`Number`), a for loop would have been a neater solution:

```
for Asterisk_Count in 1 .. Number loop
   Put ('*');
end loop;
```

The iteration rule '`for Asterisk_Count in 1 .. Number`' has the following meaning: repeatedly execute the statements between `loop` and `end loop` with `Asterisk_Count` taking consecutive values from 1 through `Number`. If `Number` is zero (or negative), there are no iterations.

The for loop solution is equivalent to the while loop in all but one important respect: `Asterisk_Count` is *not* to be declared in an object declaration. Rather, the for loop itself implicitly declares `Asterisk_Count`. Its subtype is '`Integer range 1 .. Number`'.

□ *End of Example 8.3*

The construct bracketed by `loop` and `end loop` is called a ***basic loop***. The identifier following `for` is called a ***loop parameter***. The loop parameter's declaration, initialization, testing and updating are all performed automatically. Ada imposes the following restrictions on loop parameters.

- No reference to the loop parameter is allowed outside the basic loop.
- The loop parameter is effectively a constant within the basic loop. Thus its value may be used but not changed by the statements of the basic loop. This rule prevents these statements from interfering with the counting of iterations.

The syntax of for loops is shown in Figure 8.2. The subtype of the loop parameter is deduced from the range of values that it is to receive. The syntax diagram shows that this range is specified, in general, by a ***discrete range***, which may be written in various ways. For example, given the following subtype declaration:

```
subtype This_Century is Integer range 1900 .. 1999;
```

the following iteration rules are all equivalent:

```
for Year in 1900 .. 1999
```

```
for Year in Integer range 1900 ..  1999
for Year in This_Century
```

Every discrete range specifies a range of values of some discrete type.

The lower and upper bounds of this range are specified by expressions, which are not necessarily static. In Example 8.3, the upper bound of the range was specified by the variable `Number`. Thus a loop parameter's range of values is not necessarily known until execution-time. Moreover, it is possible for the lower bound to exceed the upper bound, in which case there are zero iterations of the for loop.

In each of our examples so far, the discrete range (and hence the loop parameter) has been of type `Integer`. The following examples illustrate that a loop parameter may be of any discrete type.

Example 8.4 A for loop ranging over an enumeration

The following program reads input data consisting of the population and area of each state of the USA, and writes the name, population, area and population density of each state followed by the same for the whole USA.

```
with Text_IO;  use Text_IO;
procedure Tabulate_State_Statistics is
   type USA is (AL,AK,AZ,AR,CA,CO,CT,DE,DC,FL,GA,HI,ID,IL,IND,IA,KS,
                KY,LA,ME,MD,MA,MI,MN,MS,MO,MT,NE,NV,NH,NJ,NM,NY,NC,
                ND,OH,OK,ORE,PA,RI,SC,SD,TN,TX,UT,VT,VA,WA,WV,WI,WY);
   package Int_IO   is new Integer_IO (Integer);  use Int_IO;
   package State_IO is new Enumeration_IO (USA);  use State_IO;
   State_Pop, Total_Pop   : Natural;
   State_Area, Total_Area : Natural;
   W : constant Integer := 15;  -- output column width
begin
   Total_Pop := 0;  Total_Area := 0;
   for State in USA loop
      Get (State_Pop);  Get (State_Area);
      Put (State, Width => W);
```

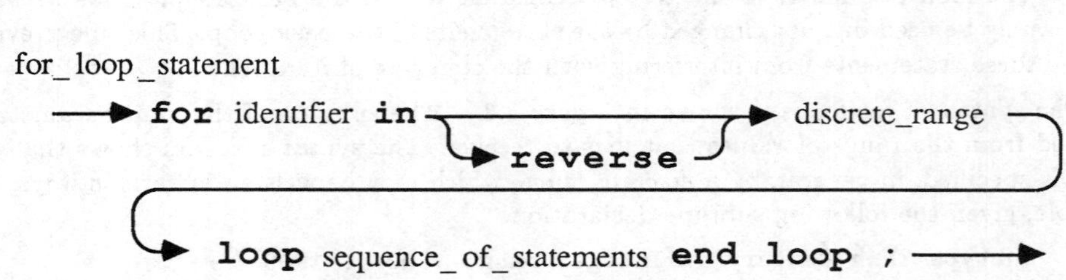

Fig. 8.2 Syntax of for loops

```
            Put (State_Pop, Width => W);
            Put (State_Area, Width => W);
            Put (State_Pop/State_Area, Width => W);
            New_Line;
            Total_Pop := Total_Pop + State_Pop;
            Total_Area := Total_Area + State_Area;
         end loop;
         Put ("USA Total       ");  -- width = W
         Put (Total_Pop, Width => W);
         Put (Total_Area, Width => W);
         Put (Total_Pop/Total_Area, Width => W);
         New_Line;
      end Tabulate_State_Statistics;
```

In the iteration rule '**for** State **in** USA', the discrete range is simply USA and stands for the entire range of values of the type USA. The iteration rule could equivalently (but less clearly) have been written as '**for** State **in** USA **range** AL .. WY' or '**for** State **in** AL .. WY'. Thus the loop parameter State receives in turn the values AL, AK, AZ, ..., WI and WY.

(*Exercise:* why were the standard 2-letter abbreviations IN and OR not chosen for the states Indiana and Oregon?)

□ *End of Example 8.4*

Example 8.5 *Counting in reverse*

The following for loop writes the upper-case alphabet *in reverse*:

```
   for Letter in reverse Character range 'A' .. 'Z' loop
      Put (Letter);
   end loop;
```

(Simply omitting **reverse** would cause the alphabet to be written in the usual order.)

□ *End of Example 8.5*

As illustrated by Example 8.5, the reserved word **reverse** in a for loop causes the loop parameter to receive its sequence of values in *descending* order rather than the usual ascending order.

8.4. Loops and exits

Refer back to the while-loop flowchart in Figure 4.2. An important property of this flowchart is that the while condition is tested at the *beginning* of each iteration. This property permits the number of iterations to be zero, if the condition is initially False, but also requires the condition to have a defined value initially.

Sometimes it is necessary to write down loops with a more general structure, in which the exit (loop termination) condition is tested in the *middle* of the loop. This is illustrated by Figure 8.3, which also shows the Ada notation corresponding to the flowchart. Such a structure reduces to a while loop in the special case that the action A1 is null. Another interesting special case is when the action A2 is null, for then the exit condition is tested at the *end* of the loop, so at least one complete iteration is guaranteed.

This loop structure can usefully be generalized even further. There may be *any* number of exit points inside the loop, rather than just one. Furthermore, an exit point may be embedded within an inner construct such as an if statement or case statement or even a nested loop.

All these possibilities are easily expressed in Ada by means of *exit statements*. The simplest form:

```
exit;
```

immediately and unconditionally terminates the smallest enclosing loop. The conditional form:

```
exit when C;
```

terminates the loop only if the condition C is satisfied.

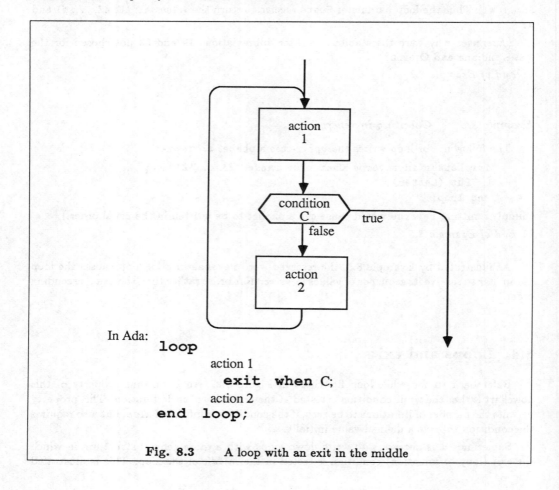

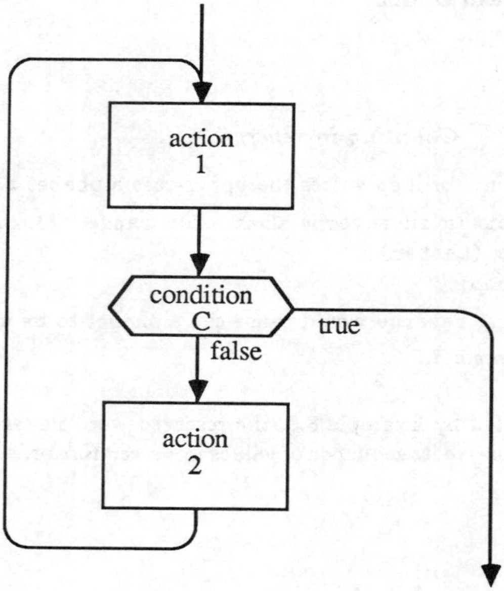

In Ada:

```
loop
    action 1
    exit when C;
    action 2
end loop;
```

Fig. 8.3 A loop with an exit in the middle

Example 8.6 *A loop with an exit in the middle*

Reading input data up to a value designated as an endmarker was illustrated by Example 4.4, where a solution using a while loop was given. Here is a solution using a basic loop and an exit:

```
begin
   loop
      Get (Summand);
      exit when Summand = Endmarker;
      Sum := Sum + Summand;
   end loop;
   Put ("Total: "); Put (Sum); New_Line;
end Sum_to_Endmarker;
```

This is a situation in which the loop termination condition cannot sensibly be tested until one of the repeated statements has been executed. The natural structure is a loop with an exit in the middle. This is preferable to a while loop because the latter requires duplication of the statement before the exit.

□ *End of Example 8.6*

Example 8.6 illustrates a *basic loop* with no preceding iteration rule. The statements inside such a basic loop are repeated indefinitely, unless and until the repetition is terminated by execution of an exit statement (or by some other means such as raising an exception).

Exit statements may also be placed inside ordinary while loops and for loops, as illustrated by the next example.

Example 8.7 *A for loop with an exit*

The input to the program of Example 8.4 must consist of exactly 51 pairs of numbers. In practice it is possible that due to data preparation errors there may be omissions or excess data. Let us modify the program: (a) to expect one pair of numbers per line; (b) to detect any shortage of lines of input (without raising the exception End_Error); and (c) to detect any excess of lines of input (rather than just ignoring the excess).

To satisfy (a), we must insert Skip_Line; after the two Get statements. Then we can use End_of_File tests to satisfy (b) and (c). The statements of program Tabulate_State_Statistics are modified as follows:

```
begin
   Total_Pop := 0;  Total_Area := 0;
   for State in USA loop
      if End_of_File then
         Put ("ERROR: input data incomplete"); New_Line;
         exit;
      end if;
      Get (State_Pop); Get (State_Area); Skip_Line;
      write State, State_Pop, State_Area, etc.;
      update Total_Pop and Total_Area;
   end loop;
```

```
      write Total_Pop and Total_Area;
      if not End_of_File then
         Put ("ERROR: input data excess");  New_Line;
      end if;
   end Tabulate_State_Statistics;
```

End_of_File is tested before attempting to read each pair of numbers. If it is True, indicating that some input data is missing, the exit statement is executed to force immediate termination of the for loop. This avoids attempting to read nonexistent input data.

□ *End of Example 8.7*

An exit statement inside a for loop might cause termination of the loop before the loop parameter has received its complete sequence of values. Similarly, an exit statement inside a while loop might cause termination before the while condition has turned False. Such usage of the exit statement could be misleading to the reader and therefore is appropriate only in abnormal situations. Thus in Example 8.7 the program expects one line of input data for each state, and shortage of input data is treated as abnormal.

Each exit statement we have seen so far terminates (implicitly) the ***smallest*** enclosing loop. That can be made explicit, if desired, by giving the loop a name and citing the loop name in each exit statement within the loop. (See the syntax diagrams 'loop_statement' and 'exit_statement' in Appendix A. Note that a named loop must have its loop name repeated after end loop.) For instance, here is the loop of Example 8.6 modified so that the exit statement explicitly names the loop it terminates:

```
   Read_and_Sum:
   loop
      Get (Summand);
      exit Read_and_Sum when Summand = Endmarker;
      Sum := Sum + Summand;
   end loop Read_and_Sum;
```

Naming the loop explicitly is not particularly useful in this very small example, but it is likely to enhance the readability of a larger loop.

Consider a program that contains one loop nested within another. Suppose that we want an exit point for the ***outer*** loop inside the ***inner*** loop. To achieve the desired effect, the outer loop ***must*** be named and the outer loop name must be given in the exit statement.

Example 8.8 Exit from a nested loop

Let us further modify the program of Example 8.4 and Example 8.7 to repeat the whole process (reading and writing a complete set of state data) for each of the census years 1901, 1911, 1921, ..., 1981.

```
   begin
      Decade_Loop:
      for Decade in 190 .. 198 loop
         New_Page;
         Put ("Year: ");  Put (10 * Decade + 1, Width => 4);
         New_Line (2);
         Total_Pop := 0;  Total_Area := 0;
```

```
      State_Loop:
      for State in USA loop
         if End_of_File then
            Put ("ERROR: input data incomplete");  New_Line;
            exit Decade_Loop;
         end if;
         Get (State_Pop);  Get (State_Area);  Skip_Line;
         write State, State_Pop, State_Area, etc.;
         update Total_Pop and Total_Area;
      end loop State_Loop;
      write Total_Pop and Total_Area;
   end loop Decade_Loop;
   if not End_of_File then
      Put ("ERROR: input data excess");  New_Line;
   end if;
end Tabulate_State_Statistics;
```

The statement exit Decade_Loop; explicitly names the loop that it terminates. If it were written simply as exit; then only State_Loop would be terminated.

□ *End of Example 8.8*

8.5. Blocks

It is undesirable to group all declarations together at the head of the program, as we have done up to now: this conflicts with the principle of localization. One way to avoid this is the ***block***, which is a self-contained group of declarations and statements, bracketed by the reserved words **declare**, **begin** and **end**. A block is itself a statement and so may be placed among other statements. Using a block we can place declarations (e.g., those of auxiliary variables) close to where they are actually needed.

Example 8.9 Swapping

The following swaps the values of the Integer variables M and N, if necessary to ensure that the smaller value is in M:

```
if M > N then
   declare
      M_Copy : Integer := M;
   begin
      M := N;
      N := M_Copy;
   end;
end if;
```

The variable M_Copy is declared inside the block because it is for local use only. This avoids cluttering the declarations at the head of the program.

□ *End of Example 8.9*

See the syntax diagram 'block' in Appendix A. Note the similarity of blocks to complete programs. Note also that blocks may be named in the same way as loops. Indeed, a for loop is like a block inside which the control variable is implicitly declared and updated.

A block is self-contained in the sense that the declarations placed inside the block are effective only inside the block. In the example, no reference to `M_Copy` would be legal (or sensible) outside the block. `M_Copy` is said to be *local* to the block.

8.6. Goto statements

(This section may be omitted on a first reading.)

A *goto statement* is a means of forcing a direct jump from one part of a program to another. Goto statements are really a hangover from earlier programming languages with inadequate control structures. As we have seen, Ada provides a rich set of control structures for expressing selective execution (if and case statements) and repetition (while loops, for loops, basic loops and exits). Thus the use of goto statements in Ada programs should be very rare indeed, with the possible exception of programs transcribed into Ada from other languages.

A goto statement has the general form `goto L;` and its effect is to jump directly to the statement with the *label* L. The latter statement must be prefixed by <<L>>. (This notation is designed to make labels very conspicuous, so that the reader of the program will be made aware of the presence of irregular jumps.)

Any statement may be labeled, but there are severe restrictions on the positioning of goto statements referring to a given label. No goto statement may cause a jump *into* any construct (such as an if or case statement or a loop) from outside, nor from one alternative of an if or case statement to another. Such jumps would have consequences hard to predict! However, it is legal to jump from one statement to another in the same sequence, or to jump out of a control structure.

Note that loop names and block names are *not* labels. In Example 8.8, '`goto State_Loop;`' would be illegal.

Style

Experience has shown that excessive use of goto statements makes a program difficult to understand and to check. Consider the following program fragments:

(a)
```
if X > Y then goto L1;
Min := X;
goto L2;
<<L1>>
Min := Y;
<<L2>>
Put (Min);
```

(b)
```
if X > Y then
    Min := Y;
else
    Min := X;
end if;
Put (Min);
```

(c)
```
<<L1>>
if R < N then goto L2;
R := R - N;
goto L1;
<<L2>>
Put (R);
```

(d)
```
while R >= N loop
   R := R - N;
end loop;
Put (R);
```

Program fragment (a) has the same effect as (b), and (c) the same effect as (d), but which are the easier to understand?

Part of the difficulty of goto statements is that their appearance alone does not suggest their effect. For example, the statement '`goto L1;`' in (a) jumps *forwards*, and thus causes statements to be skipped, whereas the same statement in (c) jumps *backwards*, and thus causes statements to be repeated. Moreover, (a) and (c) cannot properly be understood in isolation, for there could be other jumps to L1 or L2 from elsewhere in the program.

Exercises 8

8.1. Write a program that counts the number of letters (upper and lower case together), the number of digits and the number of punctuation marks in its input data.

8.2. Details taken from an employee's monthly payslips are supplied as input data. For each of the months January through December, the employee's gross pay, tax deduction and social security deduction are supplied (all integers). Write a program to read these and output the employee's total gross pay, total tax and social security deductions, and total net pay.

8.3. A word (one of 'addition', 'subtraction' or 'multiplication') and an integer N are supplied as input data. Write a program to read these and output an addition, subtraction or multiplication table for all combinations of integers 1 through N.

8.4. The minimum and maximum temperatures at some place have been recorded over a number of consecutive days. Write a program that reads the temperatures (supplied in the form of a pair of integers per line, one line for each day) and plots them down the screen or page, allowing for negative temperatures.

8.5. The following program fragments might well have been mechanically transcribed from FORTRAN to Ada. Rewrite them to use only proper control structures. This exercise should convince you that it is better to write programs that are well-structured in the first place!

(a)

```
P := 0;
<<L1>>
if B = 0 then
   goto L3;
end if;
if B mod 2 = 0 then
   goto L2;
end if;
P := P+A;
<<L2>>
A := A*2;
B := B/2;
goto L1;
<<L3>>
Product := P;
```

(b)

```
<<L1>>
Get (N);
if N < 0 then
   goto L4;
end if;
if N = 0 then
   goto L1;
end if;
<<L2>>
if N <= 1 then
   goto L3;
end if;
Put ('-');
N := N-1;
goto L2;
<<L3>>
Put ('+');
goto L1;
<<L4>>
null;
```

9

The `Float` Data Type

9.1. Real numbers and real arithmetic

Real numbers arise from the measurement of quantities such as distances, time intervals, weights and probabilities. Such quantities have the property of being continuously variable — even in a finite interval (such as the range of probabilities 0.0 through 1.0) there are infinitely many real numbers.

Only a limited number of digits can be used in the representation of real numbers in a digital computer, so approximation is forced on us. Given a fixed number of digits, there are two alternative ways of representing real numbers. We shall illustrate these in the case of a hypothetical computer in which numbers are represented in decimal.

- *Fixed-point representation.* We choose a fixed position for the decimal point. Suppose the computer can store five-digit numbers. If we choose to fix the point between the third and fourth digits, then the following nonnegative numbers can be represented exactly:

  000.00, 000.01, 000.02, 000.03, ..., 999.98, 999.99

- *Floating-point representation.* Only the most significant digits of each number are stored, together with a *scale factor* that represents the position of the decimal point relative to the stored digits. If the computer can store a four-digit mantissa that ranges from .1000 through .9999 and a scale factor that ranges from −9 through +9, then the following nonnegative numbers can be represented exactly:

  $.0000,$
  $.1000\times10^{-9}, .1001\times10^{-9}, .1002\times10^{-9}, \ldots, .9998\times10^{-9}, .9999\times10^{-9},$
  $.1000\times10^{-8}, .1001\times10^{-8}, .1002\times10^{-8}, \ldots, .9998\times10^{-8}, .9999\times10^{-8},$
  $\ldots,$
  $.1000\times10^{+8}, .1001\times10^{+8}, .1002\times10^{+8}, \ldots, .9998\times10^{+8}, .9999\times10^{+8},$
  $.1000\times10^{+9}, .1001\times10^{+9}, .1002\times10^{+9}, \ldots, .9998\times10^{+9}, .9999\times10^{+9}$

  The floating-point representation is so called because the decimal point 'floats' relative to the stored digits.

Fixed-point arithmetic is similar to integer arithmetic. Floating-point arithmetic is more complicated, because of the varying scale factors, and requires either special hardware (which is unavailable in many small computers) or software interpretation (which is very slow).

Fixed point is adequate for most 'commercial' applications, where the real numbers are typically sums of money or weights and measures, and is also used in certain real-time applications. On the other hand, floating point provides a much wider range of magnitudes (.0000000001 through 999900000 in the example above) and is therefore much preferable in 'scientific' applications where the real numbers might be distances ranging from atomic to galactic, or time intervals ranging from picoseconds to eons.

As a general-purpose language, Ada provides for both fixed point and floating point. These topics will be described fully in Chapter 19. In this chapter we shall concentrate on floating point, since it is simpler from the programmer's point of view (there is no need to specify the position of the point) and since Ada provides a standard data type, `Float`, for this purpose.

The use of floating point sets a number of traps for the unwary programmer. We shall illustrate these in the case of a four-decimal-digit mantissa and a one-decimal-digit scale factor.

- *Representational error.* Most real numbers cannot be represented exactly. For example, 386.473 would have to be represented by either $.3864 \times 10^{+3}$ (if truncated) or $.3865 \times 10^{+3}$ (if rounded). Moreover, irrational numbers such as π and e cannot be represented exactly in any computer, however precise.
- *Computational error.* Arithmetic operations tend to compound any errors in their operands, since intermediate results might have to be rounded or truncated. For example, if we divide 1.0 by 3.0 and then multiply by 3.0, we get the result 0.9999 rather than 1.0, since the intermediate result is represented by $.3333 \times 10^{0}$. Or if we add 0.0004 to 1.0 and then subtract 1.0, we get the result zero! (On the other hand, if we subtract 1.0 from 1.0 first and then add 0.0004, we get the expected result 0.0004.)

Most computers use a binary floating-point representation rather than decimal. The same principles apply, however, except for the additional problem that many decimal fractions, such as 0.9, are recurring fractions in binary and therefore subject to representational error.

Representational and computational errors depend on the degree of precision provided by the computer. Users must ensure that the computer is capable of processing their real data with sufficient precision. This might not seem to be a serious problem when the computer provides seven digits precision and the original data is accurate to only three digits, but computational errors tend to accumulate in highly iterative programs.

9.2. Type `Float`: values and operations

The values of Ada's predefined type `Float` are positive and negative floating-point numbers as described in the preceding section. The precision and range of scale factors vary from one computer to another, but `Float` has various attributes which allow a program to determine these. `Float'Digits` provides the number of *decimal* digits of precision in values of the type. `Float'Small` and `Float'Large` provide the smallest and largest *positive* values of the type. `Float'Epsilon` provides the difference between 1.0 and the next distinct value above 1.0. Some typical values of these attributes are given in Figure 9.1. Finally, like all scalar types (see Figure 20.1) `Float` has attributes `First` and `Last` that provide its minimum and maximum values. Other `Float` attributes are listed in Appendix B.

An implementation may predefine additional floating-point types, `Short_Float` and `Long_Float`, and a program can declare new floating-point types. These all have the same set of attributes as `Float`, but possibly with different values.

Each *real literal* has a decimal point with at least one digit on each side of it. It may also have a decimal scale factor preceded by the letter `e` or `E`, which stands for 'times ten to the power of'; this is convenient for writing down very large and very small values. As in integer literals, underscores may be used to break up long numbers. Here are some examples:

```
0.0     1.5     386_473.0     3.141_592_65
3.86473e5     3.0e+8     0.1234E-20
```

See the syntax diagram 'numeric_literal' in Appendix A; a real literal is distinguished from an integer literal by the presence of a point.

Here are some examples of **Float** object declarations:

```
Km_per_Mile : constant Float := 1.6093;

X, Y : Float;

Prob : Float range 0.0 .. 1.0;
```

Note that **Float** may be followed by a range constraint in which both bounds are **Float** expressions (not necessarily static). Indeed this is an example of a subtype indication, so we may also write:

```
subtype Probability is Float range 0.0 .. 1.0;
Prob : Probability;
```

The subtype **Probability** has its own attributes, for example **Probability'First** is 0.0 and **Probability'Last** is 1.0.

The following operators are available for use in **Float** expressions.

Dyadic operators		*Monadic operators*	
+	addition	+	identity
-	subtraction	-	negation
*	multiplication	**abs**	absolute value
/	division		
**	exponentiation		

The right operand of ** must be integer, since exponentiation in Ada is defined to be equivalent to repeated multiplication (followed by reciprocation if the exponent is negative). Otherwise all operands must be of type **Float**.

Division by zero, or any operation whose result is greater in magnitude than **Float'Large** (*overflow*), might raise the exception **Numeric_Error**. An operation whose result is smaller in magnitude than **Float'Small** (*underflow*) does not raise an exception but might yield the result zero.

Floating-point representation	32-bit (24-bit mantissa)	64-bit (56-bit mantissa)
Float 'Digits	7	16
Float 'Small	2^{-97}	2^{-225}
Float 'Large	2^{96} approx.	2^{224} approx.
Float 'Epsilon	2^{-23}	2^{-55}

Fig. 9.1 Typical values of some **Float** attributes

Example 9.1 *Floating-point arithmetic*

Here are some examples of **Float** object declarations and assignment statements:

```
Pi : constant Float := 3.141_592_65;
Radius, Circumference : Float range 0.0 .. Float'Large;
Area : Float range 0.0 .. Float'Large;
...
Circumference := 2.0 * Pi * Radius;
Area := Pi * Radius**2;
```

□ *End of Example 9.1*

The relational operators =, /=, <, <=, >= and > may be used to compare two **Float** values, and the membership operators **in** and **not in** may be used to test a **Float** value for membership in a range of **Float** values.

Example 9.2 *Floating-point relations*

The following program fragment determines in which quadrant of the *xy* plane the point with coordinates **X** and **Y** lies:

```
Quadrant : Integer range 1 .. 4;
...
if X > 0.0 then
   if Y > 0.0 then Quadrant := 1; else Quadrant := 4; end if;
else
   if Y > 0.0 then Quadrant := 2; else Quadrant := 3; end if;
end if;
```

The following statement determines whether the same point lies inside the rectangle bounded by the lines $x = A$, $x = B$, $y = C$, and $y = D$ (where $A \leq B$ and $C \leq D$):

```
Inside := X in A .. B and Y in C .. D;
```

□ *End of Example 9.2*

Ada does not permit **Integer** values to be used directly in **Float** expressions, nor does it allow direct comparison between values of these two types. For example, the expression **2*Pi*Radius** contains a type error. If it is desired to use an **Integer** value in a **Float** expression, it must first be ***explicitly*** converted into the corresponding **Float** value, using the type name **Float** as a conversion function. For example, **Float(7)** yields the **Float** value 7.0. The following program fragment computes the mean of a set of **N** real numbers whose sum has already been computed:

```
Sum, Mean : Float;
N : Natural;
...
Mean := Sum / Float (N);
```

Conversion from a **Float** value to an **Integer** value is also allowed. This conversion uses the type name **Integer** as a conversion function; the **Float** value supplied is ***rounded*** to the nearest integer. For example, the following program fragment performs a compound interest calculation, rounding the result to the nearest cent:

```
Sum, Interest : Integer;      -- in cents
Rate          : Float;        -- monthly rate of interest
Period        : Natural;      -- in months
...
Interest := Integer (Sum * ((1.0+Rate)**Period - 1.0));
```

Alternatively we could write:

```
subtype Money is Integer;  -- in cents
Sum, Interest : Money;
...
Interest := Money (Sum * ((1.0+Rate)**Period - 1.0));
```

9.3. Type Float: input-output

The standard package `Text_IO` contains a facility called `Float_IO` that provides for input and output of real literals with conversion to or from their internal floating-point representation. To use this for input-output of `Float` values, include the following 'magic formula' among your declarations:

```
package Real_IO is new Float_IO (Float);  use Real_IO;
```

This creates a new package, with identifier `Real_IO` (any identifier would do), which provides the following subprograms for input-output of `Float` values:

`Get(F);` reads a real literal (optionally signed), converts it into its internal representation, and assigns it to the `Float` variable `F`.

`Put(`*F*`);` converts the value of the `Float` expression *F* to its textual representation as a real literal and writes that out.

By default, `Put` writes the real literal with a mantissa of `Float'Digits` decimal digits, with one digit before the decimal point, and with a signed decimal scale factor; the whole lot is preceded by a minus sign if negative, and possibly some leading spaces.

The format can be controlled by an appropriate combination of the optional `Fore`, `Aft` and `Exp` parameters. The `Fore` parameter specifies the number of character positions before the decimal point (including leading spaces and any sign) — the default is 2. The `Aft` parameter specifies the number of character positions (all digits) after the decimal point — the default is `Float'Digits-1`. The `Exp` parameter specifies the number of character positions for the scale factor — the default is 3. If `Exp` is zero then no scale factor is written at all.

The following examples illustrate the effect of `Put` in various cases, assuming that `Float'Digits` is 4 (◇ indicates a single space):

Value of F	*Output from* Put(F);	*Output from* Put(F,Aft=>2);	*Output from* Put(F,Fore=>4, Aft=>2,Exp=>0);
0.0	◇0.000e+00	◇0.00e+00	◇◇◇0.00
+98.7	◇9.870e+01	◇9.87e+01	◇◇98.70
-0.0005	-5.000e-04	-5.00e-04	◇◇-0.00
345840.0	◇3.458e+05	◇3.46e+05	345840.00

9.4. Programming with floating-point data

In this section we demonstrate by examples some of the subtle programming problems that arise from the use of floating-point arithmetic.

Example 9.3 *Testing for approximate equality*

Suppose we are to test whether a triangle is right-angled, given that the Float variables A, B and C contain the lengths of the sides of the triangle, and given that side C is the longest. Using a Boolean variable Right_Angled, the following is a direct transcription of Pythagoras' Law:

```
Right_Angled := A**2 + B**2 = C**2;
```

Comparing two Float values for equality or inequality is allowed in Ada, but the result is unlikely to be meaningful, since representational and computational errors make it unlikely that two computed values will be exactly equal even when they should be. The test is better expressed like this:

```
Right_Angled := abs ((A**2 + B**2)/C**2 - 1.0) < 1.0e-4;
```

This version tests whether A**2 + B**2 and C**2 are equal ***to within 4 significant figures.*** In general, expected errors in the values of A, B and C should be taken into account in choosing the tolerance factor.

□ *End of Example 9.3*

Example 9.4 *Tabulation of a real function*

The following is a possible outline of a program that tabulates the position of a moving object over a period of 5 seconds, at intervals of one-twelfth of a second. (The details of the position calculation are omitted since they are not the point of this example.)

```
with Text_IO;  use Text_IO;
procedure Tabulate_Position is
   package Real_IO is new Float_IO (Float);  use Real_IO;
   Finish_Time  : constant Float := 5.0;
   Interval     : constant Float := 1.0/12.0;
   Time         : Float := 0.0;
begin
   while Time < Finish_Time loop
      Time := Time + Interval;
      Put (Time);
      compute and write the position of the projectile;
      New_Line;
   end loop;
end Tabulate_Position;
```

A problem with this program is that the stored value of Interval will be only an approximation to 1/12, and as this approximate value is repeatedly added to Time, cumulative computational errors will make the value of Time drift further and further from what you might expect. Worse still, if the represented value of `Interval` is even slightly smaller than 1/12, then `Time` will still be less than 5 after the expected 60 iterations have been completed. (On our hypothetical four-digit decimal computer, for example, the stored value of `Interval` would be $.8333\times10^{-1}$; after 60 iterations, `Time` would be $.4984\times10^{+1}$ instead of $.5000\times10^{+1}$, so an extra iteration would take place.)

The mistake in the program is its use of a `Float` variable for counting. The program can be improved by using an `Integer` variable instead, and computing `Time` afresh in each iteration, thus avoiding ***cumulative*** computational error. We rewrite the statements of the program as follows:

```
begin
   for Count in 1 .. Integer (Finish_Time/Interval) loop
      Time := Float (Count) * Interval;
      Put (Time);
      compute and write the position of the projectile;
      New_Line;
   end loop;
end Tabulate_Position;
```

Even in this version the values of `Time` are not exact. (In our four-digit decimal computer, for example, its first value will be 0.08333 rather than 0.083333....)

□ *End of Example 9.4*

Fortunately, computational errors are amenable to mathematical analysis. For many common computations, such as roots of polynomials, trigonometric functions and matrix arithmetic, sophisticated algorithms have been developed and analyzed that keep computational errors to a minimum. In a 'scientific' computer installation the local Ada program library should provide packages of accurate algorithms for use by any programmer who needs them.

Exercises 9

9.1. Write a program that computes the square root of a positive real number, X. Use Newton's method: if E is an estimate of $\sqrt{X}$, then a better estimate is the mean of E and X/E. Initialize E to any positive value, then repeatedly replace E by a better estimate using the formula above, stopping when the square of E is sufficiently close to X.

9.2. Given the lengths of the sides of a triangle, A, B and C, write a program to determine the area of the triangle. (If S is half the perimeter of the triangle, its area is given by $\sqrt{[S(S-A)(S-B)(S-C)]}$. No triangle with sides A, B and C exists if this product is negative.) Use the square-root algorithm from the previous exercise.

9.3. A rough graph of a polynomial can be plotted on a text output device, like this:

```
Graph of    y = 4.0*x**3 - 24.0*x**2 + 42.0*x + 0.0
y interval:  2.0

 0.0+
 0.5|                    +
 1.0|                             +
 1.5|                             +
 2.0|                          +
 2.5|                       +
 3.0|                       +
 3.5|                             +
 4.0|                                         +
```

The position of the plotted point in each line is obtained by dividing the function value by the *y* interval (2.0 above) and rounding the result to the nearest integer.

Write a program that reads the coefficients of a cubic polynomial, the first and last values of *x*, and the *x* and *y* intervals, and that plots a rough graph of the polynomial as above. Your program may ignore out-of-range *y* values.

10

Arrays and Strings

10.1. Use of arrays in programming

In this and the following chapter we show how to define data structures in Ada. So far we have worked exclusively with *scalar types* — a scalar object is a single item of data, such as a number, a truth value or a character. Now we examine *composite types* — a composite object consists of several simpler objects, its *components*. Composite types are used to define data structures. At this point you should preview Ada's type classification shown in Figure 20.1.

An *array* is a composite object consisting of a fixed number of components, all of the same type. Individual components of an array can be referenced by *indexing*. Arrays are familiar to all programmers; indeed in many programming languages they are the only composite objects provided. They are used for a variety of purposes, including: *lists* or *sequences* of items; *vectors* and *matrices*; *tabular data*; *strings* (which can be represented by arrays of characters); and *sets* (which can be represented by arrays of truth values).

10.2. Array values and operations

In Ada an array object is declared by an object declaration that specifies an *array type* for the declared object(s).

Consider an election contested by four candidates, numbered 1 through 4. To count the votes cast for each candidate we shall use an array, `Vote_Count`, with components `Vote_Count(1)`, `Vote_Count(2)`, `Vote_Count(3)` and `Vote_Count(4)`. A candidate number (1, 2, 3 or 4) is used as an *index* for each component of the array `Vote_Count`. The following statement adds one vote for candidate `C` (where `C` is a variable of type `Integer`):

```
Vote_Count(C) := Vote_Count(C) + 1;
```

The object declaration for `Vote_Count` would be:

```
Vote_Count : array (Integer range 1 .. 4) of Natural;
```

Here the phrase starting **array** is an *array type definition*. The discrete range '`Integer range 1..4`' between parentheses specifies that the array will have `Integer` indices in the range 1 through 4. The phrase '**of** `Natural`' specifies that each component of the array will be of subtype `Natural`. Alternatively:

```
subtype Candidates is Integer range 1 .. 4;
Vote_Count : array (Candidates) of Natural;
```

This object declaration is equivalent but preferable, since the subtype name `Candidates` here suggests the meaning of the index. Moreover, the same subtype name can be used to declare variables, like `C`, intended to index `Vote_Count`.

In general, an array type definition may be used in an object declaration to declare an array object. (It replaces the usual subtype indication — see the syntax diagram 'object_declaration' in Appendix A.) The array type definition specifies the following:

- The *index type and range*. The only restriction here is that the index type must be *discrete*. (Thus Ada is much more flexible than most languages, which restrict array indices to integers.) The index type and range are specified by a discrete range (see Section 8.3 and Appendix A) between parentheses following the reserved word array.
- The *component subtype*. This is specified by a subtype indication after the reserved word of. Every array has the property that all its components share the same subtype. There is no restriction on the choice of the component subtype.

These points are illustrated by the following further examples:

```
type Months is (Jan,Feb,Mar,Apr,May,Jun,Jul,Aug,Sep,Oct,Nov,Dec);

type Lines is array (1 .. 80) of Character;

Char_Count   : array (Character) of Natural;
Letter_Count : array (Character range 'A' .. 'Z') of Natural;

Month_Size : array (Months) of Integer range 28 .. 31;

Monthly_Rainfall : array (Months) of Float;
Yearly_Rainfall  : array (1900 .. 1999) of Float;

Wettest_Month : array (1900 .. 1999) of Months;

Line   : Lines;
Screen : array (1 .. 24) of Lines;
```

Here Char_Count has one component, of subtype Natural, for each ISO character; Letter_Count has one component for each upper-case letter; Month_Size has one component, of type Integer, for each of the twelve values of type Months; and so on. The second type declaration declares Lines to be the name of an array type. Line is declared to be a variable of type Lines, thus an array of 80 characters. Screen has 24 components, each of type Lines; thus each component of Screen is itself an array of 80 characters. Note that (1..24) is an allowable abbreviation for '(Integer range 1..24)'.

Ada provides a convenient notation, the *array aggregate*, for constructing an array value. We simply list all the individual component values, for example:

```
Month_Size := (31, 28, 31, 30, 31, 30, 31, 31, 30, 31, 30, 31);

Vote_Count := (0, 0, 0, 0);
```

These examples illustrate the *positional* notation for array aggregates; the component values are listed in index order. The alternative is the *named* notation, in which the index values (or ranges thereof) are associated explicitly with the component values:

```
Month_Size := (Feb => 28, Apr|Jun|Sep|Nov => 30,
                          Jan|Mar|May|Jul|Aug|Oct|Dec => 31);

Vote_Count := (1..4 => 0);
```

The named notation has several advantages: it is more explicit; component values can be listed in any convenient order; and components with identical values may be grouped together using the symbol '|'. In the first example the components with indices Apr, Jun, Sep and Nov are all given the value 30. In the second example the components with indices 1 through 4 are all given the value 0. See the syntax diagram 'aggregate' in Appendix A. Note that each

'=>' is preceded by a list of *choices*, similar to what may precede '=>' in each alternative of a case statement (see Section 8.2). In particular, any *discrete range* may be used in named notation to specify a range of index values when the corresponding components are to receive identical values, so the following aggregates are all equivalent:

```
(1..4 => 0)
(Candidates => 0)
(Candidates range 1..4 => 0)
```

The syntax diagram shows that the choice `others` may also be used, similarly to the case statement; however its use in array aggregates is restricted to certain contexts, so it is probably best to avoid it. Note that positional and named notation may not be mixed in an aggregate.

Array aggregates are particularly useful for initializing array variables on declaration and for declaring constant arrays, for example:

```
Vote_Count : array (Candidates) of Natural
                := (Candidates => 0);

Month_Size : constant array (Months) of Integer
                := (Feb => 28,
                    Mar|Jun|Sep|Nov => 30,
                    Jan|Mar|May|Jul|Aug|Oct|Dec => 31);
```

In our examples of array aggregates all the index values and component values have been literals, but that is not obligatory. Index values may be given by any *static* expressions of the index type. Component values can be given by *any* expressions of the component type. For example:

```
N : Integer := ...;
Powers_of_N : constant array (0 .. 4) of Integer
                  := (1, N, N**2, N**3, N**4);
```

We have already seen that an individual component of an array can be referred to by writing an index between parentheses after the array name. The index can be given by any expression of the array's index type, for example:

```
Letter_Count(Ch)       Month_Size(Apr)       Yearly_Rainfall(Year+1)
Line(X)                Screen(Y)             Screen(Y)(X)
```

where `Ch` is of type `Character`, and `Year`, `Y` and `X` are of type `Integer`. The above are all examples of *indexed components* (see Figure 10.1). Note that the indexed component `Screen(Y)` is itself the name of an array, of type `Lines`. Therefore it may be further indexed as in `Screen(Y)(X)`, the resulting component being of type `Character`. `Screen` could be used

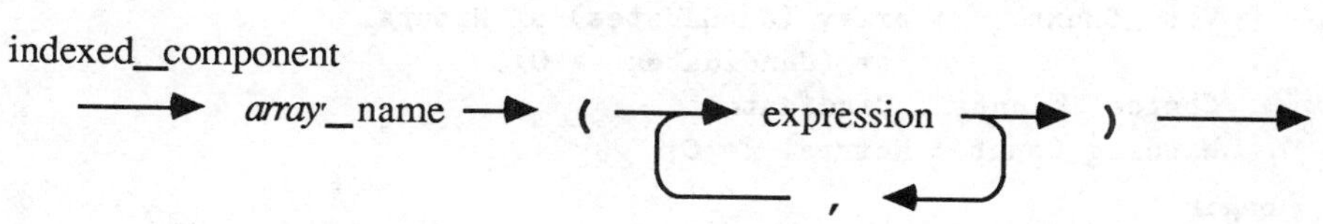

Fig. 10.1 Syntax of indexed components

to store the array of characters visible on an ordinary VDU screen; then `Screen(Y)` would represent the line of characters on row `Y` of the screen, and `Screen(Y)(X)` would represent the character in column `X` of row `Y`.

In an indexed component, the index expression must be an expression of the named array's index type. When evaluated, moreover, its value must be within the array's index range, otherwise the exception `Constraint_Error` is raised. This happens if, for example, we refer to `Line(X)` when `X` is outside the range 1 through 80.

If the array being indexed is a constant, the indexed component is itself a constant. Thus the above declaration of `Month_Size` as a constant array would make the statement '`Month_Size(Feb) := 29;`' illegal. If the array is a variable, on the other hand, the indexed component is itself a variable and can be used on either side of an assignment statement.

We have already seen a few examples of array assignment statements. Here is another:

```
Line := Screen(Y);
```

Both sides are of the same type (`Lines`), thus satisfying the general type rule for assignment statements. The statement's effect is to copy all 80 characters of `Screen(Y)` into `Line`.

Example 10.1 *Vote counting*

Let us develop a complete program for counting the votes and finding the winner of a 4-candidate election. The winner is simply to be the candidate with most votes. (Ties are to be neglected.) Each voter's choice of candidate is recorded as a single line of input containing a candidate number (1 through 4).

This problem requires all the votes to be counted before the winner can be determined. After that, the results can be written. This ordering is reflected by the following outline solution:

```
begin
    read and count the votes;
    determine the candidate with most votes;
    write the vote-counts and the winner;
end;
```

To count the votes for each candidate we need an array, `Vote_Count`, with one component for each candidate. Finding the winner then amounts to finding the maximum component value in `Vote_Count`. These considerations lead to the following complete program:

```
with Text_IO;  use Text_IO;
procedure Conduct_Election is

    package Int_IO is new Integer_IO (Integer);  use Int_IO;

    subtype Candidates is Integer range 1 .. 4;
    Vote_Count     : array (Candidates) of Natural
                        := (Candidates => 0);
    Choice, Winner : Candidates;
    Winning_Count  : Natural := 0;

begin
    -- read and count the votes --
    while not End_of_File loop
```

```
         Get (Choice);  Skip_Line;
         Vote_Count(Choice) := Vote_Count(Choice) + 1;
      end loop;
      -- determine the candidate with most votes --
      for Candidate in Candidates loop
         if Vote_Count(Candidate) > Winning_Count then
            Winning_Count := Vote_Count(Candidate);
            Winner := Candidate;
         end if;
      end loop;
      -- write the vote-counts and the winner --
      Put (" Candidate     Votes");  New_Line;
      for Candidate in Candidates loop
         Put (Candidate, Width => 10);
         Put (Vote_Count(Candidate), Width => 10);
         New_Line;
      end loop;
      New_Line;
      Put ("Winner is candidate ");  Put (Winner, Width => 1);
      New_Line;
   end Conduct_Election;
```

This solution assumes that the input is error-free. If the input contains an invalid candidate number, the `Get` statement will raise the exception `Data_Error`. Declaring `Choice` with type `Integer` would merely postpone the exception: the statement that updates `Vote_Count(Choice)` would raise `Constraint_Error`.

(*Exercise*: modify the program so that it treats invalid candidate numbers on input as 'spoiled ballots', to be counted separately. Further modify it so that, in the event of a tie, it writes the numbers of all tying candidates.)

□ *End of Example 10.1*

Every array type or array object `A` has the following attributes. `A'First` and `A'Last` are the values of the lower and upper bounds, respectively, of `A`'s index range. `A'Length` is the number of components of `A`. `First`, `Last` and `Length` are all constant attributes. Finally, `A'Range` represents the range '`A'First .. A'Last`'. This is useful for declaring variables that will be used to index `A`, including loop parameters. For example:

```
Month_Size'First    = Jan
Month_Size'Last     = Dec
Month_Size'Length   = 12
Screen'First        = 1
Screen'Last         = 24
Screen(Y)'First     = 1
Screen(Y)'Last      = 80
```

Example 10.2 *Array linear search*

Linear search involves examining a given list of 'items', one at a time, to find the first item that matches a given 'target'. The items and the target could, for example, be numbers or characters.

Suppose we are given:

```
List   : array ( Index range ... ) of Items;
Target : Items;
```

where Items and Index are (sub)type names declared elsewhere. For the present, we assume that Items is scalar. The index range of List need not be known explicitly, since it can be deduced from the attributes List'First and List'Last.

We introduce a variable, Pos, to index successive components of List and finally to record the index of the matching item (if any); and a Boolean variable, Matched, to record the success or failure of the search:

```
Matched : Boolean;
Pos     : Index range List'Range;
...
Pos := List'First;
loop
   if List(Pos) = Target then
      Matched := True;  exit;
   elsif Pos = List'Last then
      Matched := False;  exit;
   else
      Pos := Index'Succ(Pos);
   end if;
end loop;
```

Care is needed to ensure that Pos does not go outside the index range of List, for that would raise the exception Constraint_Error; hence the check that Pos is not yet equal to List'Last *before* incrementing Pos.

(*Exercise*: modify the program fragment to allow for the possibility that List'First exceeds List'Last. This is allowed in Ada — if an array's lower bound exceeds its upper bound, the array is assumed to have zero components.)

□ *End of Example 10.2*

Note the use of the array attributes in Example 10.2: significant processing of an array can be performed with no explicit knowledge of its index bounds. We recommend this style of programming even when the array's bounds are known, since it makes the program more readable and more flexible: it reduces the number of modifications needed if the array's bounds are changed.

Example 10.3 *Exchange sort*

Consider again the list of items of Example 10.2. Suppose we wish to rearrange the list into ascending order.

One simple method is *exchange sort*. The minimum item is found and exchanged with the first item in the list. Thereafter the first item is ignored and the process is repeated with the remainder of the list; and so on.

The following declarations and statements implement exchange sort:

```
Min_Pos  : Index range List'Range;
Min_Item : Items;
...
for First_Pos in List'First .. Index'Pred(List'Last) loop
   -- find the minimum of List(First_Pos..List'Last) --
   Min_Pos := First_Pos;  Min_Item := List(Min_Pos);
   for Pos in Index'Succ(First_Pos) .. List'Last loop
      if List(Pos) < Min_Item then
         Min_Pos := Pos; Min_Item := List(Min_Pos);
      end if;
   end loop;
   -- exchange the minimum item with List(First_Pos) --
   List(Min_Pos) := List(First_Pos);
   List(First_Pos) := Min_Item;
end loop;
```

□ *End of Example 10.3*

Style

Consider the following little example:

```
subtype Years is Integer range 1900 .. 1999;
Rain, Sun, Temp : array (Years) of Float;
Yr : Integer;  Year1, Year2 : Integer;
...
Yr := Year1;
Put (Rain(Yr));  Put (Sun(Yr));  Put (Temp(Yr));
```

Three run-time index range checks are required, because no information is available to the compiler about the possible range of values of Yr. Suppose now that we replace the declaration of Yr by:

```
Yr : Years;
```

Then the assignment to Yr requires a run-time range check but the three index range checks become unnecessary, since the compiler now knows that Yr cannot possibly take any value outside the index range of the three arrays. The reduced number of run-time checks makes the object program smaller and faster. And in the following statement:

```
for Yr in Years range Year1 .. Year2 loop
   Put (Rain(Yr));  Put (Sun(Yr));  Put (Temp(Yr));
end loop;
```

the run-time range check on Yr will be done only once rather than repeatedly. (Even that check would be avoided if Year1 and Year2 were also declared with subtype Years.)

The moral of all this is that when declaring a variable that is to be used for indexing an array you should, if possible, declare it with the same subtype as the array index. This practice tends to make programs more efficient and more secure.

10.3. Multi-dimensional arrays

All the examples so far have illustrated ***one-dimensional*** arrays, which are arrays with a single index. Arrays with more than one index are called ***multi-dimensional*** arrays. For each index of a multi-dimensional array, the array type definition includes one discrete range to specify the type and range of that index. Any number of dimensions is allowed.

Here are two examples of declarations of multi-dimensional arrays:

```
Population : array (States, 1900 .. 1999) of Natural;
Book : array (1 .. Nr_Pages,
              1 .. Page_Depth,
              1 .. Page_Width) of Character;
```

`Population` is two-dimensional, and `Book` is three-dimensional. (Here we have assumed that `States` is a suitably declared type name, and that `Nr_Pages`, `Page_Depth` and `Page_Width` are suitably declared integers.)

When indexing a multi-dimensional array it is necessary to supply a sequence of indices, one index for each dimension. Thus `Population(State,Year)` could represent the population of state `State` in year `Year`; and `Book(P,L,C)` could represent the character in column `C` of line `L` of page `P` of a book.

Ada makes a clear distinction between a multi-dimensional array and an array of arrays. The array `Screen` declared earlier is an array whose components happen to be arrays of characters; this allows us to refer to any of the following:

```
Screen            -- the whole screenful of characters
Screen(Y)         -- row Y of the screen
Screen(Y)(X)      -- column X of row Y of the screen
```

If instead `Screen` is declared as follows:

```
Screen : array (1 .. 24, 1 .. 80) of Character;
```

then `Screen` is a two-dimensional array, and must therefore be indexed by exactly two indices. This allows us to refer to the following:

```
Screen            -- the whole screenful of characters
Screen(Y,X)       -- column X of row Y of the screen
```

We cannot, however, write a statement like '`Line := Screen(Y);`' since in this case `Screen(Y)` has the wrong number of indices.

Array aggregates can be used to construct multi-dimensional array values. A two-dimensional array aggregate is written down as an aggregate whose component values are themselves given by one-dimensional array aggregates, and similarly for arrays of higher dimensionality. For example:

```
Screen := (10|15 => (21..60 => '*', 1..20|61..80 => ' '),
           11..14 => (21|60 => '*', 1..20|22..59|61..80 => ' '),
           1..9|16..24 => (1..80 => ' '));
```

Here `Screen` is made to contain a centered rectangle of asterisks on a blank background. Note that this statement is valid whether `Screen` is declared as a two-dimensional array or as an array of arrays — array aggregates are written the same way in both cases.

The array attributes `First`, `Last`, `Length` and `Range`, if applied to a multi-dimensional array, refer to the *first* (outermost) dimension of the array. Thus, for example, `Book'Length` has the value Nr_Pages. By appending '(2)' to any of these attributes, however, we obtain the relevant attribute of the second dimension, and similarly for other dimensions. Thus Book'Length(1) also has the value Nr_Pages, Book'Length(2) has the value Page_Depth, and Book'Length(3) has the value Page_Width.

The following program fragment prints the entire contents of Book:

```
for P in Book'Range(1) loop
   Put (P, Width => Page_Width);  New_Line (2);
   for L in Book'Range(2) loop
      for C in Book'Range(3) loop
         Put (Book(Page_Nr,L,C));
      end loop;
      New_Line;
   end loop;
   New_Page;
end loop;
```

10.4. Unconstrained array types

Recall the array type declaration:

```
type Lines is array (1 .. 80) of Character;
```

The type name Lines can now be used in several object declarations. All the declared arrays would be identical in shape, consisting of Character components indexed from 1 through 80. This type declaration, and all the object declarations of Section 10.2, featured what are known as *constrained* array type definitions. All array objects declared with the same constrained array type definition have identical index ranges.

Suppose we are writing a program that deals in vectors and matrices. It would be convenient to write down type declarations for vectors (one-dimensional arrays with Float components and Integer indices) and matrices (two-dimensional arrays with Float components and Integer indices). We might try:

```
type Vector is array (1 .. N) of Float;
type Matrix is array (1 .. P, 1 .. Q) of Float;
```

But then every array declared with type Vector would have the same number of components (N). Likewise every variable declared with type Matrix would have the same number of rows (P) and the same number of columns (Q). Vector and Matrix cannot be used to declare vectors and matrices of various sizes. The problem is that constrained array type definitions specify rigidly the range as well as the type of each index.

We can solve this problem by declaring Vector and Matrix with *unconstrained* array type definitions, which specify the type *but not the range* of each index. For example:

```
type Vector is array (Integer range <>) of Float;
type Matrix is array (Integer range <>,
                      Integer range <>) of Float;
```

Here the phrase 'range <>' stands for an unspecified range.

An unconstrained array type name cannot be used on its own in an array *variable* declaration, since every array variable must have its index range specified on declaration. An appropriate *index constraint* must therefore be inserted after the unconstrained array type name in each variable declaration. For example:

```
V : Vector (1 .. N);
W : Vector (1 .. 10);
A, B : Matrix (1 .. P, 1 .. Q);
```

declares an N-element vector, V, a 10-element vector, W, and two P × Q matrices, A and B. We have actually met index constraints already; the parenthesized part of a constrained array type definition is just an index constraint.

An index constraint is not essential in an array *constant* declaration, however, provided that the index range of the constant array can be deduced from the index range of the initializing value. For example:

```
Zero : constant Vector := (1..M => 0.0);
```

declares a constant of type Vector with index range 1 through M.

Vector(1..10) is a *subtype* of the unconstrained array type Vector. The type Vector includes all one-dimensional arrays with Float components and Integer index. The subtype Vector(1..10) includes only those Vector values whose index range is 1 through 10. An unconstrained array type name followed by an index constraint is an example of a subtype indication. (See the syntax diagram 'subtype_indication' in Appendix A.) Thus we can write declarations like:

```
subtype Vector10 is Vector (1 .. 10);
W : Vector10;
```

Summarizing, to declare an array variable we may include any of the following in its object declaration:

- a constrained array type definition (as in both declarations of Screen above); or
- a constrained array type name or array subtype name (as in the declaration of Line in Section 10.2, or the latter declaration of W above); or
- an unconstrained array type name followed by a suitable index constraint (as in the declarations of V, A and B above).

Study the syntax diagram 'array_type_definition' in Appendix A. The path through 'index_constraint' defines the syntax of a constrained array type definition; the other path defines the syntax of an unconstrained array type definition. An example of the use of unconstrained array types will be given in the next section.

All array objects declared with the same type name (such as Vector) are considered to be of the same type. This means, for example, that it is legal to assign a Vector object to a Vector variable even if their index ranges differ. Ada does require, however, that they have the same number of components, otherwise the assignment raises the exception Constraint_Error. For example, consider the following declarations and assignment statements:

```
W : Vector10;                -- W has subtype Vector (1..10)
X : Vector (0 .. 9);
Y : Vector (0 .. 10);
```

- 'W := X;' assigns X(0) to W(1), X(1) to W(2), and so on.

- '`X := W;`' has the opposite effect.
- '`Y := X;`' raises the exception `Constraint_Error`.
- '`X := Y;`' raises the exception `Constraint_Error`.

In the case of assigning multi-dimensional arrays, the two arrays must have the same number of components in each dimension, that is to say they must be similar in size and shape.

It is also possible to compare any two arrays of the same type, using the relational operators `=` and `/=`. This is allowed even if they have different numbers of components, although in that case they are always considered to be unequal. Thus the relation '`W = X`' evaluates to `True` if and only if `W(0)` equals `X(1)`, `W(1)` equals `X(2)`, and so on. The relation '`W = V`' always evaluates to `False`, unless `N` happens to be 10.

(You may have noticed a slight inconsistency in Ada: array type definitions may be used directly in object declarations, whereas enumeration type definitions may be used only in type declarations. The *general* rule in Ada is that every type used in a program must be given a name in a type declaration. The direct use of an array type definition in an object declaration is, in fact, the *only* exception to this general rule.)

10.5. Dynamic arrays

If all the bounds of an array object are given by static expressions, the array is called a *static array*. If any bound is not static, the array is called a *dynamic array*. A static array's size and shape are known at compile-time, whereas a dynamic array's size and shape are not determined until run-time. For example, the `Vector` objects `W`, `X` and `Y` declared in the previous section are certainly static arrays. The `Matrix` objects `A` and `B` are dynamic arrays if either `P` or `Q` is a variable (or a constant whose value has been given by a non-static expression).

All expressions occurring in an index constraint in an array declaration are evaluated at the time when the declaration is elaborated. Thus the number of components of each array object is fixed once its declaration is elaborated. For example, the number of components of `A` does not change even if `P` is a variable that is subsequently assigned a new value.

The idea of dynamic arrays is quite straightforward and often very useful, but their use in practical programming has certain implications that we shall bring out by an example.

Example 10.4 *Matrix multiplication*

Let us develop a program to perform a general matrix multiplication — to compute the matrix product $C = AB$, where A is an $M \times N$ matrix, B is an $N \times P$ matrix, and C is an $M \times P$ matrix. The input is to consist of:

- the values of M, N and P in that order;
- the elements of A in row order;
- the elements of B in row order.

The output is to be the elements of C in the usual rectangular layout.

The sequence of steps seems straightforward:

```
begin
   read M, N and P;
   read matrix A;
   read matrix B;
   make C the matrix product of A and B;
   write matrix C;
end;
```

Closer inspection reveals a problem: where do we declare A, B and C? They will be dynamic arrays, their bounds depending on the variables M, N and P. Therefore their declarations cannot be elaborated until the values of M, N and P are known. Thus their declarations must somehow be inserted between '*read* M, N *and* P' and '*read matrix* A'. Since Ada does not permit statements and declarations to be mixed, we must introduce a block, as follows:

```
begin
   read M, N and P;
   declare
      declarations of A, B and C;
   begin
      read matrix A;
      read matrix B;
      make C the matrix product of A and B;
      write matrix C;
   end;
end;
```

Now that we have a satisfactory program structure, we can complete the refinement as follows:

```
with Text_IO;  use Text_IO;
procedure Multiply_Matrices is

   package Int_IO  is new Integer_IO (Integer);  use Int_IO;
   package Real_IO is new Float_IO (Float);      use Real_IO;
   M, N, P : Positive;
begin
   Get (M);  Get (N);  Get (P);
   declare
      type Matrix is array (Integer range <>,
                            Integer range <>) of Float;
      A : Matrix (1 .. M, 1 .. N);
      B : Matrix (1 .. N, 1 .. P);
      C : Matrix (1 .. M, 1 .. P);
   begin
      -- read matrix A --
      for I in 1 .. M loop
         for J in 1 .. N loop
            Get (A(I,J));
         end loop;
      end loop;
```

```
      -- read matrix B --
      for I in 1 .. N loop
         for J in 1 .. P loop
            Get (B(I,J));
         end loop;
      end loop;
      -- make C the matrix product of A and B --
      for I in 1 .. M loop
         for J in 1 .. P loop
            C(I,J) := 0.0;
            for K in 1 .. N loop
               C(I,J) := C(I,J) + A(I,K)*B(K,J);
            end loop;
         end loop;
      end loop;
      -- write matrix C --
      for I in 1 .. M loop
         for J in 1 .. P loop
            Put (C(I,J));
         end loop;
         New_Line;
      end loop;
   end;
end Multiply_Matrices;
```

□ *End of Example 10.4*

10.6. The String data type

Arrays of characters, or ***strings***, are particularly useful for representing words and text. Ada recognizes their practical importance by providing a predefined type String, which is declared as follows:

```
type String is array (Positive range <>) of Character;
```

Thus String is an unconstrained array type. As such it is subject to the rules described in Section 10.4. For example, String must be followed by an index constraint when used in a variable declaration (or as the component type in an array type definition), but not necessarily in a constant declaration:

```
This_Book : constant String := "Ada: Language and Methodology";
Title : String (1 .. 29) := This_Book;
Author : array (1 .. 3) of String (1 .. 10);
```

Here This_Book is declared to be a constant whose value is a 29-character string; Title is declared to be a String variable of 29 characters, initialized with the value of This_Book; and Author is declared to be an array of 3 components, each of which is a string of 10 characters.

We have already met ***string literals***. Each string literal is a sequence of zero or more graphic characters enclosed between string brackets ("). If a string literal is itself to contain string brackets, each string bracket must be doubled to avoid confusion with the closing string bracket, for example:

```
"""Hamlet"""            -- an 8-character string literal
```

A string literal is just a special notation for writing down a character array value. The example above is equivalent to (but much briefer than) the following positional array aggregate:

```
('"', 'H', 'a', 'm', 'l', 'e', 't', '"')
```

Since strings are arrays, all the general array operations including indexing are available for strings also; they have the same meanings, and the same rules apply. In particular, a `String` value must have exactly the same length (i.e. the same number of character components) as a `String` variable to which it is to be assigned. Thus the following statements are all *illegal*:

```
Author(1) := "Watt";
Author(2) := "Wichmann";
Author(3) := "Findlay";
```

It is conventional to pad out a string with blanks to make it up to the desired length:

```
Author(1) := "Watt      ";  -- exactly 10 characters
Author(2) := "Wichmann  ";
Author(3) := "Findlay   ";
```

We now introduce some operations that are particularly useful for strings, although none is restricted to strings alone.

The well-known alphabetical ordering of words can be generalized to a *lexicographic ordering* of strings. In Ada any two strings may be compared using the relational operators =, /=, <, <=, >= and >. For example, the relation '`Word < "catfish"`' is `True` if the value of `Word` is `"boar"`, `"carp"` or `"cat"`, but `False` if its value is `"catfish"`, `"cow"` or `"dog"`. Two strings of different lengths are always unequal, and a string is always greater than any of its prefixes, including the empty string `""`. Note that the ordering of strings in Ada is based on the underlying ordering of the (ISO) character set, so it is *not* the same as conventional dictionary order.

(The relational operators = and /= may be used to compare *any* two arrays of the same type. The relational operators <, <=, >= and > may be used for lexicographic comparison of any two *one-dimensional* arrays of the same type, provided that their component types are discrete.)

Example 10.5 *String comparisons*

Example 10.2 and Example 10.3 illustrated searching and sorting in a list of 'items', where the (sub)type of the items, `Items`, was not specified. If `Items` is declared as follows:

```
subtype Items is String (1 .. N);
```

then `Target` is a string of `N` characters, and `List` is an array of similar strings. Both examples will still work without modification. In particular, the exchange sort will sort the strings in `List` into lexicographic order: the 'minimum item' that is located and exchanged within the main loop will be the string which should come first in lexicographic order.

□ *End of Example 10.5*

A useful operation on strings is *concatenation*, whereby two strings are joined end-to-end to form a single longer string. This is achieved in Ada using the concatenation operator & (which has the same precedence as + and -). For example, "cat"&"fish" yields the string "catfish". Concatenation is also allowed with one or two Character operands. For example, "ham"&'s' yields the string "hams", 's'&"ham" yields "sham", and 'I'&'Q' yields "IQ". In each case the result is of type String.

(The operator & can similarly be used with any *one-dimensional* arrays.)

Indexing may be used to refer to individual characters of a string. It is often useful to be able to refer to *substrings* of a string, for example to refer to individual words within a string such as This_Book. This is possible in Ada using a *slice*, which is like an indexed component except that the index expression is replaced by a *discrete range*. For example, This_Book(1..3) refers to the substring of This_Book consisting of the characters with indices 1 through 3; thus its value is "Ada". With a string *variable*, a slice can be used to *alter* part of the string selectively. For example, after executing the following:

```
Word : String (1 .. 9) := "elocution";
...
Word(2..3) := "xe";
```

the value of Word would be "execution".

(Slicing is allowed for any *one-dimensional* array.)

Example 10.6 String slicing and concatenation

Assume the declarations:

```
subtype Names is String (1 .. 20);
Full_Name, Abbrev_Name : Names;
```

and assume that Full_Name contains a person's full name in the form of one or more fore-names followed by a surname, the names being separated by spaces. It is desired to place in Abbrev_Name the surname followed by a comma followed by the initial letters of all the fore-names, each initial preceded by a space and followed by a period. For example, 'Augusta Ada Byron' should be abbreviated to 'Byron, A. A.'. The abbreviated name is to be left-justified in Abbrev_Name. The full name is not necessarily left-justified.

Here is an outline solution to this problem:

```
begin
    find the start and finish of the surname within Full_Name;
    copy the surname, followed by a comma, into Abbrev_Name;
    find each initial within Full_Name and append
        a space, the initial and a period to Abbrev_Name;
    pad Abbrev_Name with spaces;
end;
```

The step '*find the start and finish of the surname* ...' can be implemented by searching Full_Name from right to left.

The step '*copy the surname* ...' can be implemented by taking the substring of Full_Name that contains the surname, concatenating a comma, and assigning the result to a left-justified substring of Abbrev_Name. Note that the bounds of the target substring must be computed exactly in advance, in order to ensure that the string being assigned has exactly the same length as the target substring.

The step '*find each initial ...*' can be implemented by searching the part of Full_Name preceding the surname. An initial is identified as a non-space character preceded by a space (or at the leftmost end of Full_Name). Care must be taken not to add more initials to Abbrev_Name than there is room for.

```
Abbreviate_Name:
declare
   Space : constant Character := ' ';
   Surname_Start, Surname_Finish,
   Abbrev_Length, Surname_Length : Positive range Names'Range;
begin
   -- find the start and finish of the surname --
   Surname_Finish := Full_Name'Last;
   while Full_Name(Surname_Finish) = Space loop
      Surname_Finish := Surname_Finish - 1;
   end loop;
   Surname_Start := Surname_Finish;
   while Full_Name(Surname_Start-1) /= Space loop
      Surname_Start := Surname_Start - 1;
   end loop;
   -- copy the surname and a comma into Abbrev_Name --
   Surname_Length := Surname_Finish - Surname_Start + 1;
   Abbrev_Length := Surname_Length + 1;
   Abbrev_Name(1..Abbrev_Length) :=
         Full_Name(Surname_Start..Surname_Finish) & ',';
   -- find and append each initial --
   for I in 1 .. Surname_Start - 2 loop
      if Full_Name(I) /= Space and
            (I = 1 or else Full_Name(I-1) = Space) then
            -- Full_Name(I) is an initial
         if Abbrev_Length+3 <= Abbrev_Name'Last then
            Abbrev_Length := Abbrev_Length + 3;
            Abbrev_Name(Abbrev_Length-2..Abbrev_Length)
                  := Space & Full_Name(I) & '.';
         else
            exit;  -- no more initials will fit
         end if;
      end if;
   end loop;
   -- pad Abbrev_Name with spaces --
   for I in Abbrev_Length + 1 .. Abbrev_Name'Last loop
      Abbrev_Name(I) := Space;
   end loop;
end Abbreviate_Name;
```

□ *End of Example 10.6*

10.7. Type String: input-output

Various subprograms for text input-output of strings are provided by the standard package `Text_IO`, but we shall mention only the simplest here.

`Get(S);` reads characters into all components of the `String` variable `S`.

`Put(`*S*`);` writes all characters of the value of the `String` expression *S*.

'`Get(S);`' is defined in terms of the `Get` subprogram for individual characters:

```
for I in S'Range loop
   Get (S(I));
end loop;
```

Thus it is possible for line terminators to be skipped during the reading of characters into `S`. '`Put(`*S*`);`' is similarly defined in terms of the `Put` subprogram for individual characters.

Example 10.7 *String input-output*

Suppose that the standard input contains a person's full name in the first 20 columns of each line, followed by other data of no concern here. The name is in the format described in Example 10.6. The following program will read this input and write each person's name in the abbreviated form:

```
with Text_IO;  use Text_IO;
procedure Abbreviate_All_Names is
   subtype Names is String (1 .. 20);
   Full_Name, Abbrev_Name : Names;
begin
   while not End_of_File loop
      Get (Full_Name);  Skip_Line;
      Abbreviate_Name:
      abbreviate Full_Name to Abbrev_Name, as above;
      Put (Abbrev_Name);  New_Line;
   end loop;
end Abbreviate_All_Names;
```

□ *End of Example 10.7*

10.8. Boolean arrays

(This section may be skipped on a first reading.)

Arrays with `Boolean` components are useful to represent ***sets*** of values of the same (discrete) type. For example, given the type declaration:

```
type Month_Sets is array (Months) of Boolean;
```

we can declare objects of type `Month_Sets` to represent sets of months:

```
Vacation : constant Month_Sets
```

```
              := (Jul..Sep => True, Jan..Jun|Oct..Dec => False);
    Sunny : Month_Sets;
```

Vacation represents the set whose members are the months July through September only. Sunny could at different times represent different subsets of the months (depending on which of its components were set to True).

The logical operators and, or, xor and not may be applied not only to Boolean operands but also to one-dimensional Boolean *array* operands. Both operands of and, or and xor must be of the same type and must have the same number of components. In all cases the operation is performed on a component-by-component basis and the result is an array of the same type and size as the operand(s).

Thus, for example, the expression 'not Vacation' yields the following result, of type Month_Sets:

```
    (Jul..Sep => False, Jan..Jun|Oct..Dec => True)
```

The expression 'Vacation and Sunny' yields a result of type Month_Sets whose component values are computed by applying and to corresponding components of Vacation and Sunny.

Observe that not computes a set complement, and corresponds to set intersection, or corresponds to set union, and xor corresponds to symmetric difference.

Example 10.8 Set manipulation

Suppose the seats in an aircraft are numbered 01 through 90. A seat reservation program will need to handle various sets of seats, for example the set of window seats, the set of seats in smoking areas, the set of seats currently reserved, and so on. Thus the following declarations will be useful:

```
subtype Seats is Integer range 01 .. 90;
type Seat_Sets is array (Seats) of Boolean;
At_Window : constant Seat_Sets
              := (01|06|07|12|13|18|19|24|25|30|
                  31|36|37|42|43|48|49|54|55|60|
                  61|66|67|72|73|78|79|84|85|90 => True,
                  02..05|08..11|14..17|20..23|26..29|
                  32..35|38..41|44..47|50..53|56..59|
                  62..65|68..71|74..77|80..83|86..89 => False);
Smoking    : constant Seat_Sets
              := (01..60 => False, 61..90 => True);
Reserved   : Seat_Sets
              := (Seats => False);
```

The following block will list all currently unreserved non-smoking window seats:

```
declare
   Suitable : Seat_Sets
              := (not Reserved) and (not Smoking) and At_Window;
begin
   for Seat_Nr in Seats loop
      if Suitable(Seat_Nr) then
         Put (Seat_Nr);  New_Line;
```

```
        end if;
    end loop;
end;
```

□ *End of Example 10.8*

Exercises 10

10.1. Write a program that determines the frequency of each letter of the alphabet in a text supplied as input data, expressing each letter's frequency as a percentage of the total number of letters in the text. Treat corresponding upper- and lower-case letters as equivalent.

10.2. The heights of a group of people are provided as input data. Write a program that computes their mean, median and standard deviation, and that also determines how many heights are within one standard deviation of the mean, how many are between one and two standard deviations of the mean, and how many are outside this range. The standard deviation of a set of N numbers is given by:

$$\sqrt{[\mathit{sum\ of\ squares}/N - \mathit{mean}^2]}$$

The median is obtained by arranging the numbers into order and taking either the middle number (if N is odd) or the mean of the middle two numbers (if N is even).

10.3. Write a program that reads English-language text and counts all occurrences of the words 'he', 'she' and 'it'.

10.4. A dealership keeps a record of all its car sales in the form of a text file, with each line having the following fixed format:

Columns 1–8:	license plate number (left-justified)
Columns 9–20:	make (left-justified)
Columns 21–28:	sale date

The date is in the format '*yy/mm/dd*', where *yy*, *mm* and *dd* are the 2-digit year, month and day numbers. Write a program that will read such data and output the details of all cars of make 'Renault' sold from August 1987 through January 1989 (*Hint*: treat the dates as 8-character strings, and use string comparisons.)

10.5. Each line of input data contains a person's full name, with the surname prefixed by an asterisk. (Unlike Example 10.6, do not assume that the surname is the last name.) For example:

```
Abu Ja'far Mohammed ibn Musa *Al'Khowarizmi
*Chu Shih-Chieh
*Halayudha
Blaise *Pascal
```

Write a program that reads the names and outputs each name with the surname first, followed by a comma and all the other names. For example:

```
Al'Khowarizmi, Abu Ja'far Mohammed ibn Musa
```

```
Chu, Shih-Chieh
Halayudha
Pascal, Blaise
```

10.6. A class of students has taken an examination consisting of 4 papers. The following data have been prepared: (1) the number of students in the class; (2) a list of the students' names, each name on a separate line (none longer than 20 characters); (3) a list of the students' scores in paper 1, in the same order as their names, followed by similar lists for papers 2 through 4. Write a program to read these and output the scores in a tabular format, with one row for each student and one column for each paper. Each student's name and total score are also to be output in the table. At the foot of the table, the average score for each paper and the average total score are to be output under the corresponding columns.

Then modify your program to sort the students into lexicographic order. How would you sort them instead by their total scores?

11

Records

11.1. Use of records in programming

We have seen that an array is a composite object consisting of a fixed number of components, all of the same subtype, where each component is referenced by indexing. Powerful and useful as arrays are, alone they are not adequate for representing complicated data structures.

A common need is for a composite object having several related components possibly of *different* subtypes. A simple example of this is a *date*, which consists of a day, a month and a year. A more complicated example is the information that might be held in a person's record in a population registry office, typically including the person's surname, forename, date of birth, sex and marital status. Such composite objects are called ***records***. The components of a record are referenced not by indexing (which would not make sense, for a record's components are nonhomogeneous) but by name: each component of a given record type must have a distinct name.

Record types, like array types, are classified as composite types. Preview Figure 20.1.

Gathering together a collection of objects as components of a record has the following advantages: (a) the relationship of the objects to one another is explicitly stated, and (b) we can choose either to manipulate the record as a single object or to manipulate its components individually, as circumstances dictate.

11.2. Record values and operations

If we wish to declare objects with a given record structure, we must define this structure using a ***record type definition***, that specifies the identifier and subtype of each component of the record, all enclosed between the reserved words `record` and `end record`. See the simplified syntax diagram 'record_type_definition' in Figure 11.1.

Every record type definition must be incorporated in a type declaration. This gives the record type a name, which is subsequently used to declare all objects of the corresponding record structure.

Example 11.1 *Dates*

The following type declarations introduce `Dates` as the name of a new record type with components `Day`, `Month` and `Year` of appropriate types:

```
type Months is (Jan,Feb,Mar,Apr,May,Jun,Jul,Aug,Sep,Oct,Nov,Dec);
type Dates is
```

```
record
    Day   : Positive range 1 .. 31;
    Month : Months;
    Year  : Integer range 1801 .. 2099;
end record;
```

Armed with the declaration of `Dates`, we can now easily declare objects that will represent dates:

```
Today, Tomorrow : Dates;
Lunar_Landing   : constant Dates := (11, Jul, 1969);
```

The latter declaration illustrates a *record aggregate*, which is discussed below.

□ *End of Example 11.1*

Example 11.2 *Personal records*

The following type declarations introduce `Person_Details` as the name of a record type for personal records (as described in Section 11.1). The type declarations of Example 11.1 are assumed.

```
subtype Names is String (1 .. 12);
type Sexes is (Male,Female);
type Marital_Statuses is (Single,Married,Divorced,Widowed);
type Person_Details is
    record
        Surname, Forename : Names;
        Birthdate         : Dates;
        Sex               : Sexes;
        Status            : Marital_Statuses;
    end record;
```

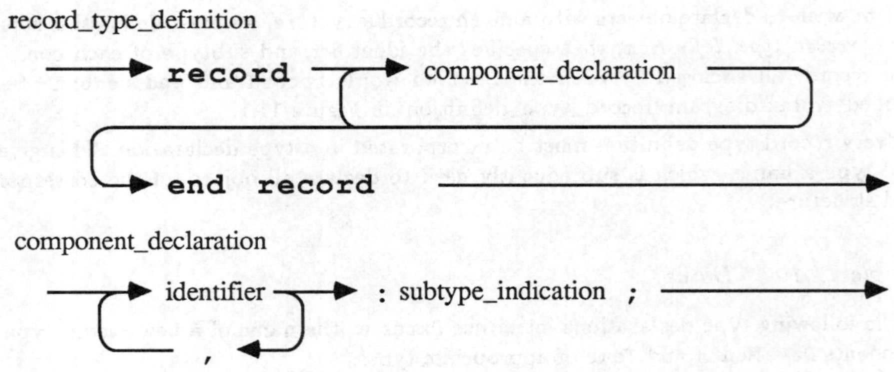

Fig. 11.1 Syntax of record type definitions (simplified)

```
New_Born : Person_Details;
Me       : constant Person_Details
           := ("Watt         ", "David        ",
               (5, Nov, 1946), Male, Married);
```

□ *End of Example 11.2*

Record aggregates are similar to array aggregates (Section 10.2) in that both positional and named notation are available (but may not be mixed). When writing a record aggregate using named notation, however, component identifiers are used in place of index values. Moreover, only components of the same type may be grouped together. The following statements are equivalent:

```
Today := (1, Jan, 1987);
Today := (Month=>Jan, Day=>1, Year=>1987);
```

The advantage of the named notation is that it needs no modification if the order of the record components is changed.

The declaration of `Me` in Example 11.2 illustrates a record aggregate in which the component `Birth_Date` is itself given a value by a record aggregate.

To refer to an individual component of a record we use a *selected component*, in which the record name is followed by a period and the identifier of the desired record component. For example, `Today.Month` refers to the component `Month` of the record `Today`. `Today.Month` is a variable, since `Today` is a variable. On the other hand, `Lunar_Landing.Year` is a constant — with value 1969 — since `Lunar_Landing` is itself a constant.

Notice that both the record name and the component identifier must always be given in selected components. A record component identifier can never be used in isolation (except in record aggregates) because of the possibility of ambiguity. For example, in the statement '`Put(Year);`' the identifier `Year` could be referring to the third component of any of the declared `Dates` objects. We must write '`Put(Today.Year);`' or '`Put(Tomorrow.Year);`' or whatever is required. The advantages of this strict rule are: (a) selected components are easily identified; and (b) choosing an identifier for a record component does not preclude choosing the same identifier for a different purpose — there is no possibility of ambiguity.

Example 11.3 Manipulation of dates

Assuming the declarations of Example 11.1 and assuming that `Today` contains an appropriate value, the following block sets `Tomorrow` accordingly:

```
begin
   if Today.Day < the number of days in Today.Month then
      Tomorrow := (Today.Day + 1, Today.Month, Today.Year);
   elsif Today.Month < Months'Last then
      Tomorrow := (1, Months'Succ(Today.Month), Today.Year);
   else
      Tomorrow := (1, Months'First, Today.Year + 1);
   end if;
end;
```

□ *End of Example 11.3*

A record object may be assigned to a record variable of the same type, for example:

```
New_Born.Birth_Date := Today;
```

This single assignment statement is equivalent to:

```
New_Born.Birth_Date.Day   := Today.Day;
New_Born.Birth_Date.Month := Today.Month;
New_Born.Birth_Date.Year  := Today.Year;
```

but is more concise and lucid.

Record objects of the same type may also be compared, using the relational operators = and /= only. For example, the relation 'Me.Birth_Date = Lunar_Landing' is False. The relation 'Today = (1,Jan,1987)' is True if and only if the current value of Today represents the first day of 1987.

The possibility of assigning and comparing complete records illustrates well the benefits of grouping related objects as components of records.

11.3. Data structures

A *data structure* is an collection of data items organized in such a way as to reflect their inter-relationships. Arrays and records are the basic building blocks of data structures. Since Ada imposes no arbitrary restriction on the types of array or record components, the components may themselves be scalar, arrays or records. This allows us to define data structures of any complexity required by the problem at hand.

A thorough treatment of data structures is beyond the scope of this book. Here we shall illustrate some simple data structures that are both common and useful. Some more complex data structures will be illustrated in Chapter 17.

Consider the record type Person_Details of Example 11.2. Each object of this type has a component Birth_Date that is itself a record, of type Dates. Thus records of type Person_Details have a hierarchical structure. Since the selected component Me.Birth_Date is itself a record name, we may select a component from it, such as Me.Birth_Date.Year. In this manner we may manipulate a data structure at any desired level of detail.

Tables and *directories* are often represented by arrays with one component for each entry. If each entry consists of several data items, then the array components will themselves be records.

Example 11.4 A personal telephone directory

Each entry in a personal telephone directory might consist of a name (of a person or organization), and a telephone number. We can describe this structure by the following type declaration:

```
type Directory_Entries is
      record
         Name   : String (1 .. 20);
         Number : String (1 .. 12);
      end record;
```

where we have assumed that the name is 20 characters long and the number is 12 characters long. We can represent a collection of directory entries by an array, `List`, of such records. The problem with this is that the number of directory entries is likely to vary, as entries are inserted or deleted, so how many components should we give the array on declaration? A reasonable compromise is to choose a maximum size for the directory, `Max_Size` say, and to use a variable, `Size`, to keep track of the *current* number of entries. Now `List` and `Size` *together* represent the directory, so rather than leaving them as two separate variables we should wrap them up as a record, `Directory`:

```
Max_Size : constant Positive := 25;  -- arbitrary limit
type Entry_Lists is
      array (Positive range <>) of Directory_Entries;
type Directories is
      record
         Size : Natural range 0 .. Max_Size;
         List : Entry_Lists (1 .. Max_Size);
      end record;
Directory : Directories;
```

Since the selected component `Directory.List` is itself an array, we can refer to a single component of that array by indexing, for example `Directory.List(I)`. Now this component is itself a record, so we can select any of its components, for example `Name`, by writing `Directory.List(I).Name`. Finally, since this component is itself an array (of characters), we can refer to any of *its* components by indexing, for example `Directory.List(I).Name(1)`.

Let us adopt the convention that the components of `Directory.List` with indices 1 through `Directory.Size` contain real directory entries, the remaining components being unused. Thus the following statement is sufficient to initialize the directory to be empty:

```
-- make the directory empty --
Directory.Size := 0;
```

The following statements append a new entry, with name `New_Name` and telephone number `New_Number`, to the directory:

```
-- append (New_Name, New_Number) to the directory --
Directory.Size := Directory.Size + 1;
Directory.List(Directory.Size) := (New_Name, New_Number);
```

(This assumes that there is room for the new entry.)

Let us now develop a piece of program to find the telephone number corresponding to a given name `Given_Name`. The corresponding number, if found, is to be assigned to a variable `Corr_Number`.

To keep the example simple, let us use linear search on the array `Directory.List`. (A more efficient search method would be preferable, especially if the directory were larger.) We can adapt the linear search of Example 10.2. Here, however, the list to be searched is only part of the array, and we must take into account the possibility that this list is empty.

```
-- find the number corresponding to Given_Name --
if Directory.Size = 0 then
   Name_Found := False;
else
   declare
```

```
            Pos : Positive range Directory.List'Range := 1;
        begin
            loop
                if Directory.List(Pos).Name = Given_Name then
                    Name_Found := True;
                    Corr_Number := Directory.List(Pos).Number;
                    exit;
                elsif Pos = Directory.Size then
                    Name_Found := False;
                    exit;
                else
                    Pos := Pos + 1;
                end if;
            end loop;
        end;
    end if;
```

□ *End of Example 11.4*

11.4. Renaming declarations

(This section may be omitted on a first reading.)

When processing a complicated data structure, we often find that a part of the program concentrates on one component of the data structure. Inside the loop of Example 11.4, for example, the component `Directory.List(Pos)` is being processed and there are several references to it. In such circumstances writing out the name of that component in full every time we wish to refer to it might be tedious and might reduce the clarity of the program.

Ada allows an identifier to be declared as a synonym for any object by means of a *renaming declaration.* Referring to Example 11.2:

```
My_Name : Names
          renames Me.Surname;
```

would allow `Me.Surname` to be abbreviated to `My_Name`, and therefore `Me.Surname(1)` to be abbreviated to `My_Name(1)`, and so on. Since `Me` and therefore its component `Me.Surname` are constants, `My_Name` is also a constant.

Example 11.5 Directory search again

Let us revise the directory search of Example 11.4 by introducing `This_Entry` as a synonym for `Directory.List(Pos)`. This will allow us to abbreviate references to components of `Directory.List(Pos)`.

The problem remains of where to insert the necessary renaming declaration. Placing it immediately after the declaration of `Pos` would be useless, for then `This_Entry` would be made a synonym for `Directory.List(1)`. The renaming declaration must be placed at a point where `Pos` already has the value used in references to `Directory.List(Pos)`; this point has to be inside the loop. Since we cannot mix declarations with statements, we must introduce a block inside the loop, as follows:

```
   ...
      loop
         declare
            This_Entry : Directory_Entries
                           renames Directory.List(Pos);
         begin
            if This_Entry.Name = Given_Name then
               Name_Found := True;
               Corr_Number := This_Entry.Number;
               exit;
            elsif Pos = Directory.Size then
               Name_Found := False;
               exit;
            else
               Pos := Pos + 1;
            end if;
         end;
      end loop;
   ...
```

□ *End of Example 11.5*

Exercises 11

11.1. Write a program that reads and classifies a poker hand of five cards. Each card is identified by a ***suit*** (club, heart, diamond or spade) and a ***rank*** (two, three, four, five, six, seven, eight, nine, ten, jack, queen, king or ace), and should be represented by a record. A poker hand is classified as plain, a pair, a double pair, a three-of-a-kind, a straight, a flush, a four-of-a-kind, a full-house or a straight flush. (A ***pair*** contains two cards of the same rank; likewise a ***three-*** or ***four-of-a-kind*** contains three or four cards of the same rank. A ***full-house*** contains both a three-of-a-kind and a pair. A ***flush*** means all five cards have the same suit. A ***straight*** means all five cards have consecutive ranks.)

11.2. Telephone directory entries like those described in Example 11.4 are supplied as input data. Each line contains one entry: a 20-character name followed by a 12-character number. Write a program to read these entries and output them in pages and columns. The number of entries per column and the number of columns per page are also given as input data (before the directory entries). You may assume that the entries are supplied already in alphabetic order. On output, the entries must be arranged in order ***down*** the columns. On the last page, the columns must be of approximately equal depth. Each page should have a header that indicates the first and last names on that page. Do ***not*** assume any arbitrary limit on the total number of entries.

12

Subprograms

12.1. Program units, functions and procedures

The topics covered so far — data types, type and object declarations, statements and control structures — have been concerned with the fine details of programming in Ada. We now describe the larger building blocks of the language — components that can be compiled and tested separately and that can be stored in program libraries for later use. These components are called ***program units***. The program units of Ada are ***subprograms***, ***packages*** and ***tasks***. Subprograms are introduced in this chapter. Packages will be introduced in Chapter 13, and tasks in Chapter 23.

Subprograms are found in every high-level programming language, in one form or another. In Ada there are two kinds of subprograms: functions and procedures. A ***function*** is a program unit that computes a ***result***, which is used immediately in an expression. Examples are the functions `End_of_File` and `End_of_Line` provided by the standard package `Text_IO`, and the function attributes `Succ`, `Pred`, `Val` and so on. A ***procedure*** is a program unit that produces some ***effect*** such as changing the value of a variable or performing input-output. Examples are the procedures `Get`, `Put` and `New_Line` provided by `Text_IO`. Subprograms may be provided with ***parameters***, which determine the values or variables on which they are to operate.

The effect of each subprogram is defined by a self-contained set of declarations and statements, called the ***body*** of the subprogram. This is obeyed when the subprogram is called, after which the program continues execution at the point of call.

The main program is itself a subprogram. All the programs we have seen so far have in fact been parameterless procedures.

Every Ada program library will contain standard subprograms that are widely useful. Each program library is also likely to contain subprograms useful to particular groups of programmers. For example, 'scientific' programmers are likely to be provided with mathematical functions that compute sines, cosines, square roots and so on. The program library thus avoids much duplication of effort, and makes sophisticated algorithms devised by experts readily available even to inexperienced programmers.

12.2. Functions

Imagine a function, `Alphabetic`, that takes a character and tests whether it is a letter or not. Then `Alphabetic('Q')` and `Alphabetic(Initial)` are examples of ***function calls***. (Here we are assuming that `Initial` is an object of type `Character`.) The expression between parentheses is called an ***actual parameter***, and the function will operate on the ***value*** of this actual parameter. In these function calls the parameter is of type `Character`, and the result is of type `Boolean`.

As another example, we could introduce a function `GCD` to compute the greatest common divisor of two given positive integers, and use it in function calls like `GCD(N+1,72)`. This function's two parameters and its result would all be of subtype `Positive`.

Function calls may be written with any number of actual parameters; see the syntax diagram 'function_call' in Appendix A.

For each function we must specify its name and its result subtype (the subtype of the result that it is to compute). Most functions will have one or more parameters, and each parameter also has a name and a subtype. All these must be specified in a *function declaration.*

Example 12.1 Function declarations

Here are declarations of the functions `Alphabetic` and `GCD` mentioned above:

```
function Alphabetic (Ch : Character)  return Boolean;
function GCD (Number1, Number2 : Positive)
     return Positive;
```

□ *End of Example 12.1*

The name of the function follows the reserved word `function`. Its result type is specified after the reserved word `return`. Between these and enclosed in parentheses we write any *parameter specifications*. Each of these specifies the names of one or more parameters and their subtype.

The function `Alphabetic` has one parameter, whose type is `Character` and whose name is `Ch`. The name `Ch` will allow us to refer to the parameter from inside the function body without referring to any particular actual parameter. For this reason `Ch` is called a *formal parameter* of the function.

The function `GCD` has two formal parameters, `Number1` and `Number2`, both of subtype `Positive`. (Thus their type is `Integer`, but they are constrained to be positive integers.)

Note that function declarations such as those of Example 12.1 contain all the information that the programmer needs to know to write down legal function calls (and all that the compiler needs to know to check them). A function declaration does not, however, specify *how* the function result is computed. For that we must also write a corresponding *function body*, that provides the statements to compute the function result from the parameter(s).

Example 12.2 A function body

The following is a possible body for the function `Alphabetic` of Example 12.1:

```
function Alphabetic (Ch : Character) return Boolean  is
begin
   return  Ch in 'A' .. 'Z' or Ch in 'a' .. 'z';
end Alphabetic;
```

□ *End of Example 12.2*

The function body has a heading that matches the corresponding function declaration. The reserved word **is** indicates that details of how the function is implemented follow. Example 12.2 is extremely simple, in that the function body contains a single statement, a *return statement*. In a function body a return statement serves two purposes: (a) it terminates the execution of the function body; and (b) the expression following the reserved word **return** is evaluated to determine the function result.

Consider, for example, evaluating the function call `Alphabetic(Initial)`. First the formal parameter `Ch` is given the value of the corresponding actual parameter, `Initial`. Suppose this value is `'?'`. Then the statement(s) between **begin** and **end** are executed. The return statement's expression evaluates to `False`, so the function call has produced the result `False`. If the value of the actual parameter had been `'Q'`, the result would have been `True`.

More generally, a function body may contain several statements and possibly also some internal declarations.

Example 12.3 *A function body with local variables*

The function `GCD` declared in Example 12.1 can be implemented in several ways. Here is one possibility:

```
function GCD (Number1, Number2 : Positive)
      return Positive  is
   M : Positive := Number1;
   N : Positive := Number2;
   R : Natural;
begin
   loop
      R := M mod N;
      if R = 0 then
         return N;
      end if;
      M := N;  N := R;
   end loop;
end GCD;
```

This function body contains declarations that introduce `M`, `N` and `R` as variables to be used within the function body. `M` and `N` are initialized to the values of the formal parameters `Number1` and `Number2` respectively. The function result here is computed by a loop that uses `M`, `N` and `R` to implement Euclid's algorithm. Eventually the return statement will be executed, when `M` is an exact multiple of `N`, leaving the final value of `N` as the function result.

□ *End of Example 12.3*

There may be one or more return statements in a function body. (Note that the statement preceding the **end** of the function body is not necessarily a return statement.) Each must contain an expression of the function's result type. It is essential that one of these return statements be executed eventually. When that happens, the expression after **return** is evaluated to determine the function result, and execution of the function body terminates immediately. The value must be in the result *subtype*, otherwise the exception `Constraint_Error` is raised.

Any identifiers introduced by declarations within a body are for use only within the body. They are *local* to the body in the same way that identifiers introduced within a block are local to the block. Any reference to a local identifier outside the body is an error (since it would be meaningless) and will be rejected by the Ada compiler.

The formal parameters Number1 and Number2 of Example 12.3 are *not* variables, so they cannot be updated. Euclid's algorithm requires the two numbers to be repeatedly replaced by other numbers, until one number is found to be a multiple of the other, so our GCD function body first copies the two numbers into local variables, which may be updated as required.

There are no restrictions on the result type of a function, nor on the types of its parameters. In particular, any of these may be composite.

Example 12.4 Functions with composite parameters and results

This example shows two functions suitable for handling complex numbers represented by records. The functions are incorporated in a program that reads two complex numbers, A and B, and writes the magnitude of their sum.

```
with Sqrt;
with Text_IO;  use Text_IO;
procedure Demonstrate_Complex is
   package Real_IO is new Float_IO (Float);  use Real_IO;
   type Complex is
         record
            Re, Im : Float;   -- real part, imaginary part
         end record;
   A, B : Complex;
   function Sum (C1, C2 : Complex)  return Complex  is
   begin
      return (Re => C1.Re+C2.Re, Im => C1.Im+C2.Im);
   end Sum;
   function Magnitude (C : Complex)  return Float  is
   begin
      return Sqrt (C.Re**2 + C.Im**2);
   end Magnitude;
begin
   Get (A.Re);  Get (A.Im);    -- read A as a pair of reals
   Get (B.Re);  Get (B.Im);    -- read B as a pair of reals
   Put (Magnitude (Sum (A,B)));  New_Line;
end Demonstrate_Complex;
```

Note that the return statement in the Sum function body contains an expression that is a Complex record aggregate.

This program assumes that the program library contains another function, Sqrt, with a Float result and a single Float parameter. Sqrt is named in a with clause at the head of the program and is called by the Magnitude function body.

The function call Sum(A,B) has two Complex actual parameters and is itself a Complex expression. Therefore it is a legitimate actual parameter for the function Magnitude, which expects a `Complex` actual parameter and returns a `Float` result. In the second last line of the program, this result is passed directly to `Put` for output.

□ *End of Example 12.4*

12.3. Procedures

A function must return a single result. If we want to write a subprogram with several results, or no results at all, we resort to a *procedure*.

A procedure call stands on its own as a statement. We have written many procedure calls already, calling the procedures provided by `Text_IO`. For example, the statement '`New_Line;`' calls the procedure `New_Line` with no parameters, and the statement '`Put('?');`' calls the procedure `Put` with one actual parameter. See the syntax diagram 'subprogram_call' in Appendix A.

As with functions, we distinguish between a procedure declaration and a procedure body. The *procedure declaration* specifies the procedure's name and the names and subtypes of its formal parameters. The *procedure body* duplicates the information of the procedure declaration and also contains the local declarations and statements that implement the procedure.

Example 12.5 *A procedure declaration and body*

Here is a suitable declaration for a procedure that is to write a given number of spaces:

```
procedure Put_Spaces (Nr_Spaces : Natural);
```

This procedure could be called by statements like:

```
Put_Spaces (10);      Put_Spaces (N-1);
```

Here is a possible body for this procedure:

```
procedure Put_Spaces (Nr_Spaces : Natural)  is
begin
   for Count in 1 .. Nr_Spaces loop
      Put (' ');
   end loop;
end Put_Spaces;
```

□ *End of Example 12.5*

In a function body, return statements serve to determine the function result as well as to end execution of the function body. In a procedure body the first role is not needed, so any return statement must not contain an expression. Moreover, there is an implicit return immediately before the final end of each procedure body. Many procedure bodies (including Example 12.5) will contain no return statement at all. See the syntax diagram 'return_statement' in Appendix A.

12.4. Subprogram declarations and subprogram bodies

We have seen that a new subprogram (whether a function or a procedure) is introduced by a subprogram declaration and a subprogram body. Since the subprogram body duplicates all the information from the subprogram declaration, the declaration may often be omitted, as in Example 12.4. When written separately, subprogram declarations are placed among the other declarations in a declarative part. Subprogram bodies, however, must follow all the type and object declarations in a declarative part, again as illustrated by Example 12.4. See the syntax diagrams 'subprogram_declaration', 'subprogram_body' and 'declarative_part' in Appendix A.

If a program contains several large subprograms, it is a good idea to write their declarations and bodies separately. This allows the declarations to be grouped together with the other (type and object) declarations of the program, making it easier for a reader to skip the details of the subprogram bodies.

There are some situations where it is essential to write down subprogram declarations separately. We shall come across these later.

Before going on to study parameters in more detail, let us summarize the basic call-and-return mechanism for subprograms. The effect of calling a subprogram is as follows (neglecting the handling of any parameters):

(1) The declarations of the subprogram body are elaborated.

(2) The statements of the body are executed.

(3) On execution of a return statement, or on reaching the final end of the body, the subprogram call is completed and control returns to the calling (sub)program.

In the case of a function, execution of a return statement also determines the function result. If the final end of the function body is reached, the function result is undefined and the exception `Program_Error` is raised.

This call-and-return mechanism is the only way to enter or leave a subprogram body (except that control can leave the body through an exception — this possibility will be covered in Chapter 14). In particular, no goto statement may jump into a subprogram body, nor may any goto statement or exit statement jump out.

On return from a subprogram, all formal parameters and objects declared within the subprogram cease to exist. (Thus memory occupied by them is released for other purposes.)

12.5. Parameters

In the following three subsections, we explain three kinds, or *modes*, of subprogram parameters provided by Ada. These are `in` parameters, `out` parameters, and `in out` parameters, respectively. They differ in the way that data flows into or out of the subprogram.

In parameters

Every subprogram we have seen so far has shown parameters being used to supply values to the subprogram. Such parameters are called `in` parameters, because they pass values *into* the subprogram.

The mechanism for in parameters is as follows. Each formal in parameter acts as a *local constant* whose value is provided by the corresponding actual parameter (which must, therefore, be an expression of the same type as the formal parameter). Thus in Example 12.4, the in parameter `C` of function `Magnitude` acts as a local `Complex` constant. In the function call '`Magnitude(Sum(A,B))`', the value of `C` is determined by evaluating the `Complex` actual parameter '`Sum(A,B)`'.

Formal parameters may be specified explicitly as in parameters by placing the reserved word in after the colon in their parameter specification. This word is optional, however, so the following procedure declarations are equivalent:

```
procedure Put_Spaces (Nr_Spaces : Natural);
procedure Put_Spaces (Nr_Spaces : in Natural);
```

Out parameters

It is also possible to specify parameters that are to be used to get values *out* of a procedure and stored in variables, where they can be retained for later use. Such parameters are called out parameters, and they are specified by placing the reserved word out immediately after the colon in their parameter specification. With such parameters we can write procedures that have several results.

Example 12.6 `Out` *parameters*

Assuming the type declarations:

```
type Months is (Jan,Feb,Mar,Apr,May,Jun,Jul,Aug,Sep,Oct,Nov,Dec);
type Monthly_Stats is array (Months) of Integer;
```

the following procedure computes the minimum and maximum values stored in an array of type `Monthly_Stats`:

```
procedure Max_Min
            (Stats    : in Monthly_Stats;
             Min, Max : out Integer) is
begin
   Min := Stats(Jan);  Max := Stats(Jan);
   for Month in Feb .. Dec loop
      if Stats(Month) < Min then
         Min := Stats(Month);
      elsif Stats(Month) > Max then
         Max := Stats(Month);
      end if;
   end loop;
end Max_Min;
```

Given the object declarations:

```
Rainfall   : Monthly_Stats;
High, Low  : Integer;
```

we could write the procedure call:

```
Max_Min (Rainfall, Low, High);
```

The in parameter `Stats` would receive the value of the corresponding actual parameter `Rainfall`. The body of `Max_Min` is executed, and the final values of the out parameters `Min` and `Max` are passed out to the corresponding actual parameters, the variables `Low` and `High` respectively.

□ *End of Example 12.6*

Example 12.7 *Another* out *parameter*

Example 12.4 can be improved by introducing a procedure to read a complex number represented by a pair of real literals. Since the complex number, once read, must be passed *out* of the procedure to a variable of the program, the procedure needs an out parameter of type `Complex`.

```
procedure Get_Complex (C : out Complex)  is
begin
   Get (C.Re);  Get (C.Im);
end Get_Complex;
```

The statements of program `Demonstrate_Complex` can now be cleaned up as follows:

```
begin
   Get_Complex (A);  Get_Complex (B);
   Put (Magnitude (Sum (A,B)));  New_Line;
end Demonstrate_Complex;
```

(It is paradoxical that a procedure that performs input of data will communicate the data through an out parameter, whereas a procedure that performs output of data will communicate the data through an in parameter!)

□ *End of Example 12.7*

The mechanism for out parameters is as follows. Each formal out parameter acts as a ***local variable*** of the procedure, initially undefined. Any value assigned to it during the execution of the procedure body will be passed out to the corresponding actual parameter (which must, therefore, be a ***variable*** of the same type as the formal parameter).

In out parameters

An in parameter allows a value to be passed into a procedure and an out parameter allows a value to be passed out. Sometimes we wish to have a procedure *update* a variable supplied as an actual parameter, in other words to pass its value into the procedure, alter it, and pass the altered value back out of the procedure. For such a purpose we use an in out parameter, which is specified by placing in out after the colon in the parameter specification.

Example 12.8 In out *parameters*

Here is a very simple procedure with an in out parameter:

```
procedure Increment (Count : in out Integer)  is
begin
   Count := Count + 1;
```

```
end Increment;
```

We could call this procedure as follows:

```
Vote_Count : array (Candidates) of Natural;
C : Candidates;
...
Increment (Vote_Count(C));
```

`Vote_Count(C)` is a variable of subtype `Natural`, so its *type* (`Integer`) matches the type of the formal parameter `Count`.

□ *End of Example 12.8*

The mechanism for **in out** parameters is as follows. Each formal **in out** parameter acts as a *local variable* of the procedure. On entry to the procedure body, this local variable's value is the value of the corresponding actual parameter. Any new value assigned to it during the execution of the procedure body will be passed out to the corresponding actual parameter. As for an **out** parameter, the actual parameter must be a variable of the same type as the formal parameter.

Parameters of functions

Note that the preceding description of **out** and **in out** parameters has referred exclusively to procedures. Functions in Ada are restricted to having **in** parameters only. There is a good reason for this: a function with an **out** or **in out** parameter would, when called, change the value of some nonlocal variable. Such a phenomenon is called a *side-effect*. The use of side-effects in functions tends to make programs harder to understand.

Actually, it *is* possible for an Ada function to have side-effects, by altering nonlocal variables directly, or by performing input-output. Usually this is bad programming practice. Consider, for example:

```
function Next_Integer  return Integer  is
   I : Integer;
begin
   Get (I);
   return I;
end Next_Integer;
```

Evaluating the expression '`Next_Integer - Next_Integer`' causes two integers to be read, but the value of the expression depends on the order in which the two operands are evaluated. (Ada does not allow you to assume the operands are evaluated in any particular order.)

This little example also illustrates a function with no parameters. Parameterless functions are uncommon in well-structured programs, but they do have uses. Two examples are the functions `End_of_File` and `End_of_Line` provided by `Text_IO`. A parameterless function or procedure will have no formal part in its declaration and body, and calls on it will have no actual parameters. A parameterless function call occurring in an expression is therefore not easy to distinguish from a reference to a data object, so beware.

Array parameters and results

Before we leave the topic of parameters, we must look at a special feature of array (and string) parameters. Whereas every array *object* must be declared with an index constraint, which specifies all its index bounds, an array *formal parameter* may be specified in a parameter specification with an unconstrained array type. In this case the array formal parameter's index bounds are taken from the corresponding array actual parameter. This rule makes it possible to write subprograms that operate flexibly on array parameters with different index ranges.

Example 12.9 *String parameters*

Here is a procedure with two String parameters, one in parameter and one out parameter. It transcribes the first string into the second with all lower-case letters replaced by the corresponding upper-case letters.

```
procedure Change_to_Upper_Case
            (S : in String;
             T : out String)  is
   function Upper_Case (Ch : Character)
         return Character  is
   begin
      if Ch in 'a' .. 'z' then
         return Character'Val (Character'Pos (Ch) +
                  Character'Pos ('A') - Character'Pos ('a'));
      else
         return Ch;
      end if;
   end Upper_Case;
begin
   if S'Length /= T'Length then
      Put ("ERROR: strings have different lengths");
   else
      for Offset in 0 .. S'Length - 1 loop
         T(T'First+Offset) := Upper_Case (S(S'First+Offset));
      end loop;
   end if;
end Change_to_Upper_Case;
```

Now consider:

```
Word, ID : String (1 .. 12);
Line     : String (1 .. 100);
L, U     : Positive range Line'Range;
...
Change_to_Upper_Case (Word, ID);
Change_to_Upper_Case (Line(L..U), ID);
```

In the first procedure call, S receives its index bounds from Word, for example S'Length is 12; T receives its index bounds from ID, so T'Length is also 12. In the second procedure call, S'Length has the value of L-U+1, and T'Length again has the value 12.

□ *End of Example 12.9*

As noted in Section 10.2, the array attributes `First`, `Last`, `Length` and `Range` make it easy to process an array without explicit knowledge of its index bounds, so unconstrained array parameters do not present any new programming problems. Indeed, these attributes should be used even in cases where the index bounds are known, since they make the subprogram more flexible.

It is also possible to write a function whose result is of an unconstrained array type.

Example 12.10 *A string-valued function*

Here is a function whose result is of the unconstrained array type `String`:

```
subtype Digits is Positive range 1 .. 9;
function Verbal (D : Digits) return String  is
begin
   case D is
      when 1 =>  return "one";
      when 2 =>  return "two";
      when 3 =>  return "three";
      when 4 =>  return "four";
      when 5 =>  return "five";
      when 6 =>  return "six";
      when 7 =>  return "seven";
      when 8 =>  return "eight";
      when 9 =>  return "nine";
   end case;
end Verbal;
```

The type of the result is `String`, but its *subtype* could be `String(1..3)`, `String(1..4)` or `String(1..5)`, depending on the value of the actual parameter. After the following declaration, `Seven` will have subtype `String(1..5)`:

```
Seven : constant String := Verbal (7);
```

The following statement writes the value of `Digit` as a word:

```
Put (Verbal (Digit));
```

Note that it would be hazardous to assign the result of a function call such as '`Verbal (Digit)`' to a variable, since the length of the result is rather unpredictable; the exception `Constraint_Error` would be raised if the length of the result did not exactly match the declared length of the `String` variable. This is a general problem with functions of unconstrained array type.

□ *End of Example 12.10*

Summary of parameter rules

Let us summarize the rules of correspondence between actual and formal parameters:

- In a subprogram call, there must be one actual parameter for each formal parameter, and the actual parameters are paired off with the formal parameters by position. (This requirement will be relaxed in Section 12.10.)

- Each actual parameter A must be of the same type as the corresponding formal parameter F (but not necessarily of the same subtype). If F is an in parameter, F acts as a local constant, and A may be any expression of the required type; otherwise F acts as a local variable, and A must be a variable name.
- If F is an in parameter, F allows the value of A to be fetched but not updated. The expression A is evaluated before entry to the subprogram, and its value must satisfy any constraint implied by the subtype of F.
- If F is an out parameter, F permits the value of A to be updated. The variable A is identified before entry to the subprogram. The value of F on return from the subprogram must satisfy any constraint implied by the subtype of A.
- If F is an in out parameter, F permits the value of A to be both fetched and updated. The variable A is identified before entry to the subprogram. Its value at that point must satisfy any constraint implied by the subtype of F. Moreover, the value of F on return from the subprogram must satisfy any constraint implied by the subtype of A.

If any of these constraints is not satisfied, the exception Constraint_Error is raised by the subprogram call.

Parameter mechanisms

(This subsection may be omitted on a first reading.)

The wording of the last three rules above is not meant to imply any particular mechanism for implementing parameters. Indeed two distinct mechanisms are possible:

- *Copy mechanism.* The value of an in or in out parameter could be copied in on entry to the subprogram, and the value of an out or in out parameter could be copied out on return.
- *Reference mechanism.* The address of the actual parameter could be passed to the subprogram, allowing all inspections and updates on the formal parameter to be performed immediately on the actual parameter. No value copying would take place on entry or return.

Ada in fact mandates the copy mechanism for scalar parameters, but the compiler is free to choose either mechanism for composite parameters (arrays or records). Thus it is possible for a particular Ada program to have different effects depending on the parameter mechanism chosen by the compiler. Since this is highly undesirable, any such program is defined to be erroneous.

Example 12.11 *Aliasing*

Recall the procedure Change_to_Upper_Case of Example 12.9. Consider the following call:

```
Word : String (1 .. 6) := "banana";
...
Change_to_Upper_Case (Word, Word);
```

What is the value of the formal parameter S immediately before return from the procedure? (We could display that value by inserting 'Put(S);' at the end of the procedure body.)

- If the compiler chooses the copy mechanism for both parameters, the value is "banana", as we would expect.
- If the compiler chooses the reference mechanism, the value is "BANANA". The reason for this surprising effect is that all changes to `T` affect `Word` *immediately* (since `T` is implemented as a reference to `Word`), and fetching the value of `S` is equivalent to fetching the current value of `Word` (since `S` is implemented as a reference to `Word`).

□ *End of Example 12.11*

The phenomenon illustrated by Example 12.11 is known as ***aliasing***. Aliasing occurs when the same variable occurs as an actual parameter twice in the same procedure call (unless these are both in parameters). Another cause of aliasing is when a variable that occurs as an actual parameter in a procedure call is also accessed directly by the corresponding procedure body. The term 'aliasing' is appropriate because in each case the same variable is masquerading under two different names.

12.6. The virtues of subprograms

Many programmers view subprograms as little more than a useful tool for avoiding duplication of statements. This view grossly underestimates the benefits to be gained by using subprograms. Here is a summary of them.

- A subprogram can be called without knowledge of ***how*** it works; the user of the subprogram can concentrate attention on ***what*** the subprogram does. Conversely, the subprogram can be read and understood without regard for ***why*** it is used. This separation of concerns is called ***abstraction***, and is a powerful intellectual tool in coping with complex problems.
- Subprograms can be used to build a program from small self-contained parts, with each subprogram having a single purpose. The construction of a large program is simplified by the possibility of writing and testing each subprogram separately. (As we shall see later, subprograms can often be ***compiled*** separately too.)
- Subprograms give names to pieces of program. By a judicious choice of names for subprograms (and other entities like objects and types), we can make a program read almost like prose. Choosing a suitable name for a subprogram is made easier if the subprogram has a single, simply described, purpose.
- A subprogram may be called from several different places, with different actual parameters if desired. This avoids tedious (and error-prone) duplication of program text.
- It is easy to replace one version of a subprogram body by another. As long as the subprogram ***declaration*** is unchanged, the rest of the program need not be changed either.

Example 12.12 ***Illustrating the virtues of subprograms***

A program for reading and multiplying two matrices was given as Example 10.5. This program was monolithic. Figure 12.1 shows (in outline) a different version of the same program, this time conveniently broken down into subprograms.

The original version cannot be read without at once plunging into the details of matrix manipulation. The improved version can be read without concern for these details, by skipping the subprogram bodies and studying only the declarations and statements of the main program. The brevity of the main program and the well-chosen subprogram identifiers make the program outline immediately clear. The reader who *is* interested in the details of matrix manipulation can study the subprogram bodies individually, without concern for the way these subprograms are used.

(*Exercise*: (a) Fill in the program details omitted from Figure 12.1. (b) Modify both versions of program `Multiply_Matrices` to write matrices `A` and `B` as well as their matrix product. Modifications like this illustrate the flexibility provided by the use of subprograms, and convincingly justify the use of subprograms even in programs where they are called only once.)

□ *End of Example 12.12*

The pragma Inline

Following our guidelines on when to introduce new subprograms often leads to subprograms that are very short, containing as few as one or two statements. Several of the examples in this chapter have been like that. In such cases the time overhead associated with the subprogram call and return might exceed the time required to obey the subprogram body itself; it is then tempting to 'optimize' the program by eliminating the subprogram and expanding each subprogram call in place. For example, one could eliminate the function `Sum` of Example 12.4 by replacing the function call `Sum(A,B)` by:

```
(Re => A.Re+B.Re, Im => A.Im+B.Im)
```

Such manual 'optimizations' are error-prone, and they rarely make the program run appreciably faster. Even if the subprogram is called very frequently, program clarity has been sacrificed for a modest efficiency gain. Fortunately, Ada makes this choice unnecessary: it is possible to keep the subprogram but, by means of a suitable pragma, to request that the *compiler* expand each subprogram call in place.

A ***pragma*** is a means for the programmer to convey information to the compiler, for example a request to suspend or resume the source program listing, or a request to optimize some part of the program. Generally, pragmas have no effect on the *meaning* of a program, and they might even be ignored by the compiler. A pragma starts with the reserved word `pragma` and is terminated by a semicolon. Different pragmas have different placement rules, and we shall introduce them as they arise. A complete list of predefined pragmas may be found in Appendix C.

In Example 12.4, we could request that the subprograms `Sum` and `Magnitude` be expanded in place simply by adding the pragma:

```
pragma Inline (Sum, Magnitude);
```

after the subprograms.

In general, the pragma `Inline` may list the names of one or more subprograms, and it must be placed in the same declarative part as the named subprograms and after their declarations.

```
with Text_IO; use Text_IO;
procedure Multiply_Matrices is
  ...
  M,N,P : Positive;
begin
  Get (M); Get (N); Get (P);
  declare
    type Matrix is ... ;
    procedure Get_Matrix (M:out Matrix) ;
    procedure Put_Matrix (M:in  Matrix) ;
    function Matrix_Product
      (M1,M2:Matrix) return Matrix;
    A:Matrix (1..M,1..N);
    B:Matrix (1..N,1..P);
    C:Matrix (1..M,1..P);
    procedure Get_Matrix
        (M : out Matrix)  is
    begin
      for I in M'Range(1) loop
        for J in M'Range(2) loop
          Get (M(I,J));
        end loop;
      end loop;
    end Get_Matrix;
    procedure Put_Matrix
        (M : in Matrix) is
    begin
      ...
    end Put_Matrix;
    function Matrix_Product
      (M1,M2:Matrix) return Matrix is
      P : Matrix (...,...);
    begin
      ... return P;
    end Matrix_Product;
  begin
    Get_Matrix (A);
    Get_Matrix (B);
    C := Matrix_Product (A, B);
    Put_Matrix (C);
  end;
end Multiply_Matrices;
```

(a) (b) (c)

Dotted lines show where the identifiers are not directly visible.

(a) Scope of **M**, global.
(b) Scope of `Matrix`.
(c) Scope of `Get_Matrix`.

Fig. 12.1 Visibility rules for blocks and subprograms

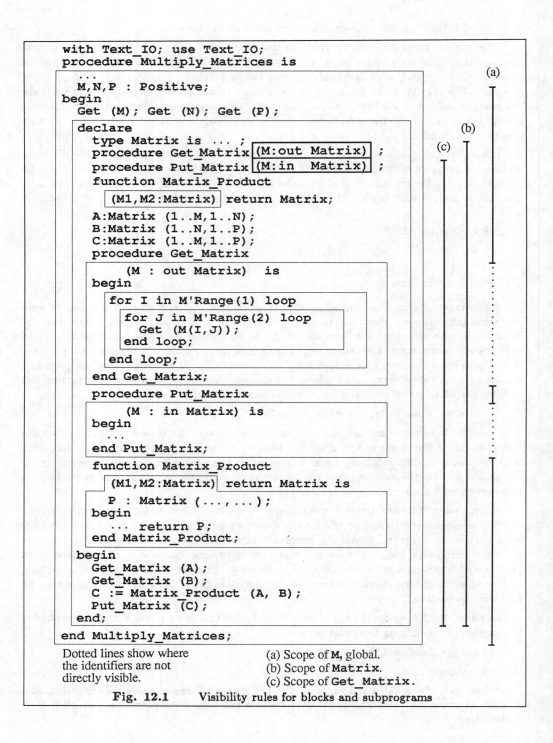

12.7. Visibility rules for blocks and subprograms

We have seen already that identifiers declared within a block or subprogram body are *local*, in that they are declared for use only within the block or body. On the other hand, identifiers declared outside a block or body may, in general, be used inside as well. It is necessary now to examine these issues more closely.

The rules concerning the declaration and use of identifiers in Ada are known as the *visibility rules*. They are so called because they define where in a program each identifier is *visible* (available for use) and where it is *invisible* (unavailable for use). Any program that violates the visibility rules will be rejected by the Ada compiler. In their entirety the visibility rules are complicated, since they cover a variety of diverse constructs. Here we shall summarize the visibility rules only as they apply to subprogram bodies, blocks and for loops, which are collectively described as *declarative regions*. The main program itself is a subprogram body and therefore a declarative region.

These declarative regions can be nested one within another in an Ada program. This is so because a subprogram body can appear in the declarative part of a body or block, and a block or for loop can appear among the statements of any declarative region. The nesting is clear if we box in each declarative region as illustrated by Figure 12.1. To simplify the following discussion, we make the box enclosing each subprogram body exclude the subprogram name.

The *scope* of an identifier is part of the declarative region in which it is declared: it extends from just *after* the identifier's declaration up to the end of the enclosing declarative region. In Figure 12.1, the scope of the identifier `Matrix` is the whole of the block apart from its own declaration; the scope of the identifier `Put_Matrix` extends from after its declaration (*not its body*) to the end of the block.

Armed with the definition of scope, we can now state the basic visibility rules.

- *No identifier is visible outside its scope.* In Figure 12.1, the identifiers `Matrix`, `Get_Matrix`, `Put_Matrix`, `Matrix_Product`, `A`, `B` and `C` are declared within the block and are therefore invisible outside the block.

  Note that the definition of scope implies that every identifier must be declared before use. In Figure 12.1, therefore, the declaration of `Matrix` could not placed any later.

- *No identifier may be declared twice in the same declarative region.* If two objects were declared with the same identifier in the same declarative region, it would be impossible to distinguish between them. (There are certain exceptions to this rule, but we shall ignore these until Chapter 21.)

  Any identifier may, on the other hand, be declared in two disjoint declarative regions or in nested declarative regions (such as `M` and `P` in Figure 12.1).

- *Each identifier is potentially visible throughout its scope, but if the same identifier is declared in a declarative region nested within this scope, then the outer declaration is hidden throughout the scope of the inner declaration.* Thus the `Positive` variable identifier `P` is visible throughout its scope, except inside the body of `Matrix_Product` where `P` is redeclared as a `Matrix` variable identifier. Every occurrence of `P` within `Matrix_Product` refers to the local `Matrix` variable, whereas all other occurrences of `P` in the program refer to the global `Positive` variable. The outer declaration of `P` is said to be *hidden* by the inner declaration because the inner declaration prevents the global `P` from being directly visible within the body of `Matrix_Product`. The other example of hiding in Figure 12.1 is the introduction of `M` as a formal parameter of

Get_Matrix (and of Put_Matrix); this hides the global Positive variable identifier M within the subprogram body.

An entity whose identifier is hidden can always be referred to, however, by prefixing its identifier with the name of the declarative region in which it is declared. Thus Get_Matrix and Put_Matrix could refer to the global Positive variable M by the notation Multiply_Matrices.M.

These rules apply to all identifiers. That includes block identifiers, loop identifiers and labels. For the purposes of the visibility rules, labels are considered to be declared just before the **begin** of the innermost enclosing block or body.

This discussion has, for ease of presentation, over-simplified the visibility rules of Ada. Some identifiers may be used only in restricted contexts. For example, a record type's component identifiers may be used only in selected components (after a period) or in aggregates of that record type. Such identifiers are not directly visible even within their scope; they become directly visible only in suitable contexts.

It is reasonable to ask what useful purpose is served by these visibility rules, which are quite complicated (and the complete set is more so). The fundamental justification is that they help to make bodies, blocks and for loops self-contained. A programmer can write one of these, choosing any suitable identifiers for locally declared entities, without worrying about unintended clashes with identifiers declared in other parts of the same program. The special rules for record component identifiers ensure that they can always be chosen freely; a record component identifier may be the same as the identifier of an object (for example) declared in the same declarative region.

Although the visibility rules allow considerable freedom in the choice of identifiers in different parts of a program, that freedom should be used with restraint, since using the same identifier indiscriminately for a variety of purposes tends to make a program difficult to understand.

Each data object exists (i.e. occupies memory) only during the execution of the declarative region in which it is declared. This portion of the program's execution time is called the *lifetime* of the object. This rule, which permits economical use of memory, is directly related to the rule that the object's identifier is visible only inside that same declarative region.

12.8. Case Study I: sorting

We now present a case study of program development showing how subprograms can be introduced naturally during stepwise refinement.

Requirement

A list of names is supplied as input data, one name per line. The names are in no particular order. A program is required that will read all the names and write them in lexicographic order. The following assumptions are permitted: (a) there are no more than 100 names; (b) no name is longer than 20 characters.

Solution

As usual, we start by designing a program outline, then we successively refine it to develop a completed program.

Program outline

This is a *sorting* problem. Of the many sorting techniques that have been devised, we shall illustrate one of the simplest, called *insertion sort*. The names are kept in an ordered list. Each time a name is read, it is inserted immediately in its correct position in the list. When all the names have been read and inserted, it is necessary only to write the names in listed order. This analysis leads to the following program outline.

```
procedure Sort_Names is
    global declarations;
begin
    make the list empty;
    while there are still names to be read loop
        read a name;
        insert this name in its correct position in the list;
    end loop;
    write all the names in listed order;
end Sort_Names;
```

The program outline contains six actions to be refined into Ada. Of these, three are concerned with the representation of the list of names: '*make the list empty*', '*insert this name ...*', and '*write all the names in listed order*'. If we choose a specific representation for the list now and refine these actions in place, the effect will be to clutter the program with the details of the list representation, details that are irrelevant to the outline structure of the program. Rather than doing so, let us introduce the following procedures to handle the details of list manipulation:

```
type Names is ...;
procedure Make_List_Empty;
procedure Insert (New_Name : in Names);
procedure Write_All_Names;
```

The details of the type `Names` can be postponed that for the time being. These declarations must be included in '*global declarations*'.

Refinement of '*make the list empty*'

This will be a simple procedure call:

```
Make_List_Empty;
```

Refinement of '*insert this name in its correct position in the list*'

Assume that a variable `Current_Name`, of type `Names`, will be declared to contain the name that is to be inserted:

```
Insert (Current_Name);
```

Refinement of '*write all the names in listed order*'

Again, a simple procedure call:

```
Write_All_Names;
```

Representation of the list

Before we can refine any of the procedures we have introduced, we must choose a suitable representation for the list. Given the assumption that no more than 100 names will be input, one possibility is to use an array with space for 100 names. We also need to keep track of the actual number of names in the list. So we add to '*global declarations*':

```
Max_Size : constant Positive := 100;
List     : array (Positive range 1 .. Max_Size) of Names;
Size     : Natural range 0 .. Max_Size;
```

(Alternatively, `Size` and `List` could be grouped together as a record.)

We can now refine the three procedures by writing down their bodies, at least in outline.

Refinement of `Make_List_Empty`

This is trivial:

```
procedure Make_List_Empty is
begin
   Size := 0;
end Make_List_Empty;
```

Refinement of `Insert`

In general, the new name will be inserted in some intermediate position in the list. This will require the name already stored in that position, and those in subsequent positions, to be shifted up to make room for the new name. The refinement must also be capable of dealing with the following boundary situations: inserting a name at the end of the list; inserting a name at the beginning of the list; or inserting a name in an empty list.

Since `List` has room for only `Max_Size` names, it is essential to check whether `List` is already full before attempting to insert a new name. This leads to the following refinement:

```
procedure Insert (New_Name : in Names)  is
   New_Pos : Positive range 1 .. Max_Size;
begin
   if Size < Max_Size then
      find the insertion position, New_Pos, for New_Name;
      shift up the names in positions New_Pos through Size;
      List(New_Pos) := New_Name;
      Size := Size + 1;
   else
      warn that New_Name cannot be inserted;
   end if;
end Insert;
```

Refinement of Write_All_Names

The body of this procedure is a simple loop:

```
procedure Write_All_Names is
begin
   for Pos in 1 .. Size loop
      write the name in List(Pos)
   end loop;
end Write_All_Names;
```

Refinement of '*find the insertion position,* New_Pos, *for* Name'

This can be done by linear search, comparing Name in turn with List(1), List(2) and so on, until a name is found that should *follow* Name in lexicographic order; New_Pos must then be set to the position of this name in List. If no such name is found, the search must stop with New_Pos set to Size+1, indicating that Name will be inserted at the end of the list. The details are shown below, in the completed program.

Refinement of '*shift up the names in positions* New_Pos *through* Size'

This must take into account the possibility, already mentioned, that the value of New_Pos is Size+1.

```
for Pos in reverse New_Pos .. Size loop
   List(Pos+1) := List(Pos);
end loop;
```

Representation of names

At this stage we must decide on a representation for names, by means of a suitable type declaration for the identifier Names. The requirement in procedure Insert to compare names lexicographically suggests the use of strings, and the assumption that no name is longer than 20 characters leads us to add the following to '*global declarations*':

```
subtype Names is String (1 .. 20);
```

Refinement of '*read a name*'

Simply refining this to 'Get (Current_Name);' is not good enough here, since this statement will always read exactly 20 characters and will therefore malfunction if any name is supplied on a line shorter than that. So we must resort to reading the characters of the name one at a time, stopping if a line terminator is encountered. Since this involves details irrelevant to the rest of the program, let us refine this using a new procedure, Get_Name:

```
Get_Name (Current_Name);   Skip_Line;
```

The body of Get_Name is quite straightforward: see the completed program, below.

Refinement of '*write the name in* List(Pos)'

This could be refined simply as:

```
Put (List(Pos));  New_Line;
```

but we prefer to introduce a procedure Put_Name which is a natural counterpart to Get_Name. Thus the refinement is:

```
Put_Name (List(Pos));  New_Line;
```

The body of Put_Name is very simple — see below.

Refinement of '*there are still names to be read*'

Since the refinement of '*read a name*' reads a complete line of input, we can use the end-of-file test here:

```
not End_of_File
```

Completed program

After completing a few minor refinements, and adding essential details like a with clause for Text_IO, we arrive at the following program:

```
with Text_IO;  use Text_IO;
procedure Sort_Names is
   subtype Names is String (1 .. 20);
   Current_Name : Names;
   procedure Get_Name (Name : out Names);
   procedure Put_Name (Name : in Names);
   procedure Make_List_Empty;
   procedure Insert (New_Name : in Names);
   procedure Write_All_Names;
   -- Representation of the list of names --
   Max_Size : constant Positive := 100;
   List     : array (Positive range 1 .. Max_Size) of Names;
   Size     : Natural range 0 .. Max_Size;
   procedure Make_List_Empty is
   begin
      Size := 0;
   end Make_List_Empty;
   procedure Insert (New_Name : in Names)  is
      New_Pos : Positive range 1 .. Max_Size;
   begin
      if Size < Max_Size then
         -- find the insertion position for New_Name --
         New_Pos := 1;
         while New_Pos <= Size and then
               New_Name > List(New_Pos) loop
```

```
            New_Pos := New_Pos + 1;
          end loop;
          -- shift up the names in succeeding positions --
          for Pos in reverse New_Pos .. Size loop
            List(Pos+1) := List(Pos);
          end loop;
          List(New_Pos) := New_Name;
          Size := Size + 1;
        else
          Put ("WARNING: no room for ");
          Put_Name (New_Name);  New_Line (2);
        end if;
      end Insert;

   procedure Write_All_Names is
   begin
      for Pos in 1 .. Size loop
         Put_Name (List(Pos));  New_Line;
      end loop;
   end Write_All_Names;

   procedure Get_Name (Name : out Names)  is
   begin
      for Col in Name'Range loop
         if End_of_Line then
            Name(Col) := ' ';
         else
            Get (Name(Col));
         end if;
      end loop;
   end Get_Name;

   procedure Put_Name (Name : in Names)  is
   begin
      Put (Name);
   end Put_Name;

begin
   Make_List_Empty;
   while not End_of_File loop
      Get_Name (Current_Name);  Skip_Line;
      Insert (Current_Name);
   end loop;
   Write_All_Names;
end Sort_Names;
```

Observations

This program illustrates the fact that subprograms can make an important contribution towards achieving the goals of modularity, localization and simplicity expounded in Chapter 5. Each part of the program is short and easy to understand, much more so than a monolithic program would be. For example, the statements of the program body can be read and understood without any knowledge of the representation chosen for the list. Notice how much these statements resemble the original program outline.

The procedures `Make_List_Empty`, `Insert` and `Write_All_Names` are not completely self-contained — they interact with one another through the global objects `Max_Size`, `List` and `Size`. These objects and procedures form a ***cluster*** because of their mutual dependence. Any change in the representation of the list might require all three procedures to be modified accordingly, but will not affect the rest of the program. Thus the program has been written in such a way that the cluster is logically self-contained, although the individual procedures are not.

The procedures `Get_Name` and `Put_Name` also form a natural cluster. We have emphasized the clusters by appropriate layout. The structure of the program is imperfect, however, since the clusters are only informal. There is nothing in the visibility rules to prevent some other part of the program from accessing the objects `Max_Size`, `List` and `Size` directly, thus destroying the self-contained nature of their cluster. In Chapter 13 we shall see how clusters like these can be made completely self-contained, as ***packages***.

12.9. Recursion

Subprograms can be used to build hierarchical programs, in which higher-level subprograms call lower-level subprograms, which in turn call still lower-level subprograms, and so on. It is also possible for a subprogram to call itself. Such a subprogram is said to be ***recursive***. Recursive subprograms allow very elegant solutions to a certain class of programming problems. We illustrate this idea with a pair of examples.

Example 12.13 *The factorial function*

The *factorial* of a nonnegative integer N is written $N!$ and is defined by:

$$N! = \begin{cases} 1 & \text{if } N \leq 1 \\ N \times (N-1)! & \text{otherwise} \end{cases}$$

This is a recursive form of definition, and it can be transcribed directly into an Ada function body:

```
function Factorial (N : Natural)  return Positive  is
begin
   if N <= 1 then
      return 1;
   else
      return N * Factorial (N-1);
   end if;
```

```
end Factorial;
```

To demonstrate that this function will indeed yield a result, let us compute `Factorial(3)` by hand. With `N` equal to 3, the function body requires the computation of `3*Factorial(2)`, so `Factorial` calls itself. With `N` equal to 2, the function body requires the computation of `2*Factorial(1)`, so `Factorial` calls itself again. But this time `N` is 1, so the function returns the result 1 directly. Now the recursion 'unwinds': `2*Factorial(1)` is found to be 2, and then `3*Factorial(2)` is found to be 6.

□ *End of Example 12.13*

Of course, the function `Factorial` could easily be programmed using a loop rather than recursion. Moreover, the loop version is likely to be more efficient since it avoids the overheads associated with subprogram calls and returns. Nevertheless, there are certain computations that are 'naturally' recursive, in the sense that they are difficult to program without recursion. The second example illustrates such a computation.

Example 12.14 The Quicksort algorithm

The insertion sort method illustrated by Case Study I is rather inefficient for long lists. (If the number of items in the list is doubled, the number of steps is quadrupled!)

The *Quicksort* algorithm is much more efficient and is also rather elegant. Consider an unordered list of integers, for example:

33 14 99 3 67 51 80 32 19 7

We pick up the first integer — call it the *pivot* — and then rearrange the list into three parts: (1) a sublist containing all the integers smaller than the pivot; followed by (2) the pivot itself; followed by (3) a sublist containing all the integers larger than the pivot:

[14 3 32 19 7] 33 [99 67 51 80]

The problem has now been reduced to sorting the two sublists, shown bracketed above. This 'divide-and-conquer' strategy is highly effective.

Let us write an Ada subprogram that uses the Quicksort algorithm to sort a list of type `Item_Lists`. The necessary declarations are:

```
type Item_Lists is array (Integer range <>) of Items;
procedure Sort (List : in out Item_Lists);
```

The body of `Sort` will be refined along the following lines:

```
procedure Sort (List : in out Item_Lists) is
   Pivot     : Items;
   Pivot_Pos : Integer range List'Range;
begin
   if List'Length > 1 then
      Pivot := List(List'First);
      rearrange List so that Pivot follows all lesser items and precedes
         all greater items, and set Pivot_Pos to the new position of Pivot;
      sort the sublist List(List'First .. Pivot_Pos-1);
      sort the sublist List(Pivot_Pos+1 .. List'Last);
   end if;
end Sort;
```

Note that Sort has been programmed to do nothing when there is only one item in the list (or none), for then there is no sorting to be done.

How do we refine '*sort the sublist* ...'? Since sorting a sublist is analogous to sorting the original list, simply a recursive call of Sort will do the trick. So the last two unrefined actions are refined to:

```
Sort (List(List'First .. Pivot_Pos-1));
Sort (List(Pivot_Pos+1 .. List'Last));
```

The remaining refinement requires no special programming technique. (*Exercise*: complete it.)

□ *End of Example 12.14*

We can identify general principles underlying the proper use of recursive subprograms:

- A recursive subprogram must, in at least one degenerate case, perform its function without calling itself. In Factorial, the degenerate case is when N is 1. In Sort, the degenerate case is when the (sub)list to be sorted has only one item (or none).
- A recursive subprogram must call itself only in such a way as to approach a degenerate case (to ensure that the subprogram does not call itself forever). Factorial calls itself with a parameter that is positive but smaller than before, so it has moved closer to the case where its parameter is 1. Sort calls itself with a sublist parameter shorter than the original.

12.10. Named parameters and defaults

All the function and procedure calls we have seen so far in this chapter have used the conventional *positional* notation for the actual parameters, whereby the actual parameters are listed in the same order as the corresponding formal parameters. Ada also allows each actual parameter to be preceded by the name of the corresponding formal parameter. This is called the *named* notation. The advantage of named notation is that the order in which the actual parameters are written becomes irrelevant. This is particularly convenient when the subprogram concerned has a long list of parameters. Moreover, the use of named notation can make the subprogram call more readable. We illustrate this idea with an example.

Example 12.15 *Named parameters*

Consider a procedure with the following declaration:

```
procedure Substitute
            (Target, Replacement : in String;
             Subject             : in out String);
   -- Edits the string Subject by replacing the first
   -- substring matching Target by the string Replacement.
```

A typical call on this procedure, written in positional notation, would be:

```
Substitute (S1, S2, Line);
```

where S1, S2 and Line are all String variables. This procedure call does not itself give any indication of which parameter is which, so the reader must consult the procedure declaration to understand the procedure call. Moreover, the positional notation is error-prone in this example; the programmer could write the actual parameters in the wrong order without receiving any warning from the compiler, since all the actual parameters are String variables.

Using named parameters, the call could be written thus:

```
Substitute (Target => S1, Replacement => S2, Subject => Line);
```

This notation is more readable and less error-prone. The actual parameters can also be written in a different order:

```
Substitute (Subject => Line, Target => S1, Replacement => S2);
```

without any effect on the meaning.

Positional and named parameters may be mixed in one call, if desired, provided that all the positional parameters come first:

```
Substitute (S1, S2, Subject => Line);
```

□ *End of Example 12.15*

Defaults

Another useful device concerns an **in** parameter that takes one particular value more commonly than any other. The common value can be made a *default* value for the **in** parameter, and subprogram calls can then be abbreviated by omitting that parameter altogether if the default value is satisfactory. A default value is specified in an **in** parameter specification in exactly the same way that an initial value is specified in a variable declaration.

Example 12.16 Default parameters

The procedure of the previous example might commonly be used to *delete* the first occurrence of a target string in a subject string, in which case the replacement string would be empty. We could make the empty string the default value for Replacement:

```
procedure Substitute
          (Target      : in String;
           Replacement : in String := "";
           Subject     : in out String);
```

Now the procedure call:

```
Substitute (Target => S1, Subject => Line);
```

has the effect of calling Substitute with Replacement defaulted to the empty string. The same call may be written as:

```
Substitute (S1, Subject => Line);
```

but note that all actual parameters following the defaulted parameter *must* be named.

□ *End of Example 12.16*

A parameter's default value may be specified by any expression. It is important to note that this expression is evaluated at the time of *call* of the subprogram (not at the time of elaboration of its declaration). This point is particularly relevant if the expression contains a variable.

The subprograms of `Text_IO` make extensive use of defaults. We shall take a closer look at them in Section 15.5.

Exercises 12

12.1. Implement the `Square_Root` function used in Example 12.4. Use Newton's method (see Exercises 9 for the algorithm.)

12.2. Implement procedures with the following declarations:

```
procedure Get_Vector (V : out Vector);
procedure Put_Vector (V : in Vector);
```

which respectively read and write a sequence of `V'Length` real numbers. (See Section 10.4 for the declaration of `Vector`.)

12.3. Given the following procedure declaration:

```
procedure Get_Word (Word : out String);
```

write the corresponding procedure body. The procedure is to read a single word from the input file, passing back the word through the parameter `Word`. For the purpose of this exercise, consider a 'word' to be any sequence of nonspace characters followed by a space or line terminator. Your procedure should skip any spaces or line terminators preceding the word. The word should be padded with spaces, or truncated, as necessary according to the length of `Word`.

12.4. Write functions that accept a parameter of type `Matrix` and determine: (a) whether the matrix is symmetric; (b) whether the matrix is lower-triangular (i.e. every element above the main diagonal is zero). In each case the result should be `False` if the matrix is not square.

12.5. Write functions that accept a `String` parameter and return: (a) its reverse; (b) the same string stripped of leading and trailing spaces.

12.6. Write a procedure that, given two records of type `Person_Details` (see Example 11.2), determines whether the two persons may legally marry, and if so updates the records accordingly.

12.7. Assume that the total interest payable on a bank loan is the product of the amount of the loan, the loan period in months, and the monthly interest rate; the capital and interest are paid off in equal monthly instalments over the period of the loan. Write a function that computes the monthly repayment, given the amount of the loan, the loan period in months and the monthly interest rate. Include your function in a program that reads the monthly interest rate and tabulates the monthly repayments for loans of \$100, \$200, ..., \$1000 and for loan periods of 3, 6, ..., 24 months.

12.8. Given the declarations:

```
subtype Sub_Million is Positive range 1 .. 999_999;
procedure Put_in_Words (N : Sub_Million);
```

write a body for `Put_in_Words` that writes the value of `N` in *words*. For example, 715023 should be written as 'seven hundred fifteen thousand twenty three'.

12.9. Write a procedure that outputs a calendar for any specified year between 1901 and 2099. (*Note*: the first day of 1901 was a Tuesday.) For example, a 1987 calendar might start as follows:

```
              JANUARY   1987

Su    Mo    Tu    We    Th    Fr    Sa
                         1     2     3
 4     5     6     7     8     9    10
11    12    13    14    15    16    17
18    19    20    21    22    23    24
25    26    27    28    29    30    31
```

12.10. Sometimes it is useful to be able to print 'banner headlines', in letters much larger than usual. For example, 'PROGRAM' might be printed as:

```
PPPP   RRRR    OOO    GGG   RRRR     A    M   M
P   P  R   R  O   O  G      R   R   A A   MM MM
PPPP   RRRR   O   O  G GGG  RRRR   A   A  M M M
P      R  R   O   O  G   G  R  R   AAAAA  M   M
P      R   R   OOO    GGGG  R   R  A   A  M   M
```

Design a complete set of letters for banner headlines. Write and test a procedure that accepts a `String` parameter and prints the string as a banner headline. (*Hint*: for each letter, represent its two-dimensional image by a array of five 5-character strings.)

12.11. Write and test a pair of functions that convert a Roman numeral (stored in a string) into its corresponding value, and *vice versa*.

12.12. Modify the calculator program of Exercises 6 to allow parenthesized subexpressions. For example, '`83+(7*12)=`' should be allowed, and should give the answer 167. (*Hint*: make the part of the program that reads and evaluates the expression into a function; then make the function call itself recursively on encountering a '`(`'.)

PART II

Programming in the Large

13

Packages

13.1. Clusters and packages

We saw in Chapter 12 that it is easy to find a good name for a subprogram if it encapsulates a single, readily understandable operation. We also saw that the methodical use of subprograms often leads us to form *clusters* — collections of types and objects, and subprograms to work on them. Using the language features we have seen so far, a program's conceptual division into clusters cannot be fully exploited. By means of comments and layout conventions we can suggest the clustering to a reader, but this does not provide the high level of compiler-checked security found in the rest of the language. To be specific, the following difficulties remain.

- The syntax of a declarative part (see Appendix A) forces us to separate declarations and bodies. Hence, in a program with more than one cluster, each cluster must be split into two parts: (1) its type, object and subprogram declarations; and (2) its subprogram bodies. The clusters must then be merged. This requires care. More importantly, it conflicts with the principle of localization, by preventing us from grouping the components of a cluster as closely as we would like.
- If a program is built by merging previously-written clusters there might be a clash of identifiers between them. Because of this problem clusters are much less convenient than we would wish as 'kits of parts' from which programs could be assembled.
- Some of the components of a cluster are of purely local significance, not being part of the interface between the cluster and the rest of the program. For example, an object might be intended for use only within the subprograms of a cluster. (An example is the pair of variables `List` and `Size` in Case Study I.) The visibility rules cannot be used to make such objects visible only inside the cluster. This makes the cluster susceptible to interference from outside and is a serious breach of the principle of modularity.
- Copying clusters physically into a source program leads to a large, monolithic program text. It is cluttered with the internal detail of the clusters and is cumbersome to develop. The entire text must be recompiled if a change is made to any part of it. Several programmers working together on such a program would find it hard to coordinate the changes each needed to make.

The larger the program and the more clusters it contains, the more troublesome these difficulties become. Ada was designed with the construction of large programs in mind. For that reason it provides a powerful means to declare and to use clusters of data and subprograms. This is the *package* feature. With packages at our disposal we can exploit the structural advantages of clustering to the full.

The title of this part of the book is 'Programming in the Large', for here we deal with the techniques that are essential to the methodical development of large programs. Do not be misled by this into believing that these techniques are useful *only* in large, complicated programs. Even small programs can benefit from their application, and especially from the careful use of packages. In fact, packages are probably Ada's most important single contribution to the repertoire of the typical programmer.

If you would like an impression of how packages are used, scan through Case Study II in Section 13.5 before tackling the descriptive material in the following two sections. You will probably not be able to understand the case study fully at this stage, but it might whet your appetite for what is to come.

13.2. Packages in Ada

An Ada package differs from an informal cluster in being declared as a named ***program unit***. A program unit is a subprogram, package or task. (Tasks are treated in Chapter 23.) Thus packages, like subprograms, are formally recognized as building blocks for an Ada program.

A package has two distinct parts — its ***declaration*** and its ***body***. The package declaration declares the types, objects and subprograms that the package makes available. We say that the identifiers declared in a package declaration are ***exported*** by the package. Only those components declared in the package declaration are visible from outside the package. Hence packages are an important aid to modularity.

Simple packages

When a package contains no statements it is fully defined by the type and object declarations in the package declaration. A body is not needed. Such a data package establishes a set of declarations that can be used throughout the scope of the package. By incorporating the same package in several programs, consistency of identifier usage is automatically enforced.

A package containing only data objects is somewhat similar to a record, but allows us to include constant components as well as variables. Unlike a record, however, a data package is not itself an object; for example it cannot be assigned or passed as a parameter. (A package of variable objects only is analogous to the `COMMON` block of FORTRAN, but is much less error-prone.)

Example 13.1 A data package

The following package declares some variables and constants that might be used in several modules of a telecommunications system.

```
package Modem_Data is
    Byte_Count : Natural;
    Sending    : constant Natural := 0;
    Receiving  : constant Natural := 1;
    Idle       : constant Natural := 2;
    Status     : Natural range Sending .. Idle := Idle;
```

```
    Buffer      : String (1 .. 512);
  end Modem_Data;
```

☐ *End of Example 13.1*

Identifiers declared in a package declaration have the same scope as they would enjoy if declared outside the package but in the same textual position in the program. In other words, each identifier's scope extends from just after its declaration to the end of the scope of the package itself. If the declaration is an object declaration, the declared object comes into existence when the declaration is elaborated, and it ceases to exist at the end of the block or subprogram that contains the package. So putting object declarations inside a package has no effect on the *lifetime* of the declared objects, but it does affect their *visibility*.

Inside a package a component is known simply by its identifier. For example, see the references to `Sending` and `Idle` in the declaration of the `Status` component of `Modem_Data`. An exported component is referred to *outside* the package by giving both the package name and the component's identifier, separated by a period. For example, the variable `Status` declared within the `Modem_Data` package of Example 13.1 is known outside the package as `Modem_Data.Status`. Similarly, we can refer to a typical character of the `Buffer` component as `Modem_Data.Buffer(I)`. As these examples show, components of packages become visible outside the package only when they are qualified by the name of the package containing them, using selected component notation similar to that used for records. (Since packages can be nested within packages, this might involve several levels of qualification.) Thus components of two or more packages can be named uniquely, even if their identifiers happen to clash.

The selected component notation is clumsy when there is no clash of identifiers, so Ada provides the *use clause* to allow an abbreviated notation. For example, if the clause:

```
use Modem_Data;
```

follows the declaration of `Modem_Data`, the components of the package become *directly visible*. Then we can refer simply to `Status`, `Buffer`, and so on, without qualification. See the syntax diagram 'use_clause' in Appendix A.

If two packages named in use clauses do have components with clashing identifiers, these components are not made directly visible by the use clauses. To avoid ambiguity, the full selected component notation is required for these components. Suppose that a package called `Data_Comms` also exports an object called `Buffer`. After:

```
use Modem_Data;  use Data_Comms;
```

we can write simply `Status` to refer to `Modem_Data.Status`, but the `Buffer` components must still be named as `Modem_Data.Buffer` and `Data_Comms.Buffer`.

Use clauses have been appearing in our programs since Chapter 1, in order to abbreviate the names of subprograms exported by the `Text_IO` package. Without our old friend, '`use Text_IO;`', we would need to write things like '`Text_IO.Put(X);`' and '`Text_IO.New_Line;`' — a considerable inconvenience.

When a program-defined type is widely used in a program, or in several related programs, it is often convenient to declare it within a package, perhaps with some useful constants of the new type.

Example 13.2 *A packaged type definition*

```
package Complex_Definitions is
```

```
        type Complex is
              record
                 Re, Im : Float;
              end record;
        I : constant Complex := (Re => 0.0, Im => 1.0);
     end Complex_Definitions;
```

Having declared this package, we can now use it to declare objects of type Complex, both constants and variables:

```
     use Complex_Definitions;
     Impedance : Complex;
     Unity     : constant Complex := (1.0, 0.0);
     J         : Complex  renames I;
```

□ *End of Example 13.2*

Package bodies

In most cases a package declaration must be followed by a corresponding *package body*. This supplies implementation details that are of no concern to the user of the package. There is an analogy between subprogram declarations and bodies on the one hand and package declarations and bodies on the other.

Elaboration of a package body causes its internal declarations to be elaborated in turn. Each identifier declared in a package body has a scope that extends from just after its declaration to the end of the package body. Thus the visibility of identifiers declared within a package body is restricted to the package body itself. Unlike identifiers declared in the package declaration, those declared in the body of a package are *not* exported. Outside the package body they are quite invisible. This protects them from external interference (or even inspection).

Packages exporting program units

When a package exports a subprogram, the package declaration contains the subprogram's declaration only. A package body is also needed, and it contains the corresponding subprogram body. Exported packages and tasks are treated analogously.

The declaration of an exported subprogram, given in the package declaration, describes a facility that the package makes available. The subprogram body, given in the package body, defines the steps the subprogram must take to implement that facility. Thus the declaration of facilities (in the package declaration) is kept apart from their implementation (in the package body).

Example 13.3 A package of subprograms

A collection of mathematical functions can be written in Ada as a package exporting only subprograms. Here is one that exports a sine function and a cosine function. The package declaration contains only subprogram declarations for the functions Sin and Cos.

```
     package Math_Functions is
```

```
     function Sin (X : Float) return Float;
     function Cos (X : Float) return Float;
  end Math_Functions;
```

Here is the corresponding package body. It contains the bodies of the exported functions, as well as declarations that are local to the package body.

```
  package body Math_Functions is
     Pi : constant Float := 3.1415927;
     type Coefficients is array (Natural range <>) of Float;
     function Polynomial (C : Coefficients; X : Float)
           return Float is
     begin
        compute C(0) + C(1)*X + C(2)*X**2 + C(3)*X**3 + ...;
     end Polynomial;
     function Sin (X : Float) return Float is
        Sin_Terms : constant Coefficients := ... ;
     begin
        calculate sin X, using Polynomial (Sin_Terms, X);
     end Sin;
     function Cos (X : Float) return Float is
        Cos_Terms : constant Coefficients := ... ;
     begin
        calculate cos X, using Polynomial (Cos_Terms, X);
     end Cos;
  end Math_Functions;
```

The type Coefficients, the object Pi and the function Polynomial are all declared inside the package body. Therefore they can be used in the body but are invisible outside.

The functions in the Math_Functions package could be invoked as follows:

```
  Amplitude, Phi : Float;
  ...
  Amplitude := Math_Functions.Sin (Phi+0.5);
```

Alternatively we could make them directly visible by a use clause:

```
  use Math_Functions;
  Amplitude, Phi : Float;
  ...
  Amplitude := Sin (Phi+0.5);
```

□ *End of Example 13.3*

Package initialization

Sometimes we wish to initialize a package. For example, a variable might have to be initialized, or some storage allocated, or a file opened, before the package can be used properly. In simple cases variables can be initialized in their declarations, but that is not always sufficient. To allow arbitrary initializations we use a package body with a statement part. The statement part is executed *once*, as part of the elaboration of the package body, immediately after elaborating any local declarations of the body.

Example 13.4 *Package initialization*

The following data package is declared inside a procedure that takes as parameter a claimant's benefit record, `Claimant`. The statements of the procedure expect all components of the package to have a value, but the component `Benefit_Due` is computed according to rules that cannot be represented as a single Ada expression. Consequently it cannot be initialized in the package declaration.

```
package Benefit_Data is
   subtype Money is Natural;
   Limit : constant Money := 600;
   Rate  : constant Money := 25;
   Benefit_Due : Money;
end Benefit_Data;
```

To set up the value of `Benefit_Due` the package body consists of a statement part that uses the `Weeks_Worked` component of `Claimant`. Each time the procedure containing this package is called, `Claimant` will have a different value and the package body will be elaborated to initialize `Benefit_Due` accordingly.

```
package body Benefit_Data is
   Total : Money := Claimant.Weeks_Worked * Rate;
begin
   if Total > Limit then
      Benefit_Due := Limit;
   else
      Benefit_Due := Total;
   end if;
end Benefit_Data;
```

□ *End of Example 13.4*

Renaming declarations for packages and package components

An alternative to use clauses for abbreviating names is provided by the *renaming declaration*, already introduced in Section 11.4. Unlike a use clause, a renaming declaration affects just one identifier, so a separate renaming declaration is needed for each name to be abbreviated. On the other hand, renaming operates equally well whether identifier clashes are present or not. For example:

```
subtype Buffers is String (1 .. 512);
Modem_Buffer : Buffers  renames Modem_Data.Buffer;
Comms_Buffer : Buffers  renames Data_Comms.Buffer;
```

Another possibility is simply to abbreviate the package name itself by renaming, for example:

```
package MD  renames Modem_Data;
package DC  renames Data_Comms;
```

and then refer to `MD.Buffer` or `DC.Buffer`.

It is possible to use renaming declarations to give alternative names to subprograms as well as data objects. For example, if we wanted to write a program to compare the accuracy of two Sin functions — one from Math_Functions and one exported by a package called Trig_Functions, we might write renaming declarations such as the following:

```
function SinM (X : Float) return Float
                renames Math_Functions.Sin;
function SinT (X : Float) return Float
                renames Trig_Functions.Sin;
```

When renaming a subprogram different formal parameter names can be specified, also different default values, and so on. We shall not go deeply into this topic here; if you want more information, consult [Ada 1983]. See the syntax diagram 'renaming_declaration' in Appendix A.

There is no renaming declaration for types, but subtype declarations provide essentially the same facility.

13.3. Abstract data structures

The fundamental principle on which structured programming rests is *abstraction*. All the other guidelines we have suggested, such as modularity and localization, can be derived from it. There is a tendency to think of abstraction as something difficult and confusing — perhaps abstract paintings come to mind! This is a pity, because the idea is really quite simple.

Taken literally, abstraction means 'drawing away from'. In programming, where the difficulty is to keep in mind *what* we are trying to achieve rather than *how* we intend to achieve it, abstraction implies a drawing away from implementation details, the better to concentrate on application concepts. These concepts might be far from simple, but that is the result of applying computers to difficult problems and cannot be blamed on abstraction itself. On the contrary, once we acknowledge our limited mental capacities, abstraction remains as our only hope of success.

We are already using a number of powerful abstractions, merely as a consequence of programming in a high-level language rather than machine language or assembly language. One of the most important is the idea of a data type, which abstracts from the machine-oriented view of data as comprising bits, bytes and words. Another is the idea of a control structure, which abstracts from machine features like condition codes and jump instructions. Note that these abstractions provide us with much of the convenience and security that Ada has to offer.

Within Ada itself the facility to declare subprograms with parameters allows us to abstract an algorithm from the particular data values and variables on which it is to operate. The principle of abstraction is also reflected in Ada by the division of a package into declaration and body. The declaration is concerned with presenting an abstraction for use in the rest of the program, whereas the body is concerned with its implementation. In accordance with the principle, the declaration and body are kept physically as well as logically separate. (There is even provision in Ada to abstract from the *types* of operands. This is the *generic* facility, to be described in Chapter 22.)

Of more immediate relevance is the following idea. Just as Ada allows us to abstract from low-level machine details, if we want to achieve an understandable and modular program we should try to abstract as much as possible from the characteristics of the Ada language itself. In particular, the data structures on which our programs operate should be conceived in terms of the properties that make them suitable for the application, and not in terms of particular Ada types. The standard package `Text_IO` is a good example of this. Text files are defined by the operations that can be applied to them, such as `New_Line`, `Put` and `Get`; the implementation of text files in terms of buffer areas and file control blocks is completely hidden. This frees us from the burden of coping with these details, for the very good reason that they are irrelevant to the problem on hand.

We can exploit the same idea ourselves. Whenever we invent a data structure we should take care to formulate it cleanly in terms of (a) data objects that carry the information content of the structure, and (b) subprograms that operate on these data objects. By declaring the data objects within a package we insulate the rest of the program from the details of the data structure. Its important properties, the *abstract* ones, are made accessible through the interface given by the package declaration. Such a package implements an *abstract data structure* and the exported subprograms provide the *primitive operations* upon it.

Example 13.5 *Implementing an abstract data structure*

The complex number is a simple example of an abstract data structure, with well-known primitive operations (those of complex arithmetic). We can extend our package `Complex_Definitions` from Example 13.2 to a package that exports subprograms for these operations.

```
package Complex_Arithmetic is
   type Complex is
      record
         Re, Im : Float;
      end record;
   I : constant Complex := (Re => 0.0, Im => 1.0);
   function Sum  (C1, C2 : Complex) return Complex;
   function Diff (C1, C2 : Complex) return Complex;
   other subprogram declarations;
end Complex_Arithmetic;

package body Complex_Arithmetic is
   function Sum  (C1, C2 : Complex) return Complex is
   begin
      return (Re => C1.Re+C2.Re, Im => C1.Im+C2.Im);
   end Sum;
   function Diff (C1, C2 : Complex) return Complex is
   begin
      return (Re => C1.Re-C2.Re, Im => C1.Im-C2.Im);
   end Diff;
   other subprogram bodies;

end Complex_Arithmetic;
```

Having declared this package we can now declare `Complex` objects and operate upon them using the subprograms provided:

Drozdek

To: All Advisors
From: Tom Keagy
Subject: Spring Preregistration
Date: October 21, 1988

1.) Preregistration for the spring semester of 1989 will begin Thursday, November 3 and end Monday, November 14. Before that time you should review the files of your advisees and begin to prepare for your session with them. The progress sheet should be updated each semester and any other comments or agreements about the student's program should be documented in writing and placed in the file.

2.) Ms. Ann Gyurisin from the Advising Center has agreed to be available to answer any questions you may have about the advising process on Wednesday, October 26 at 12:30 p.m. The session, which will be in the fourth floor faculty lounge, will be conducted informally.

3.) Professor Loch has designed convenient progress sheets for mathematics and computer science majors who have entered the university under the new core requirements. They are available in the departmental office.

4.) Until more complete data is made available (which is supposed to be soon), a copy of the most up-to-date information regarding core courses, majors in other disciplines, etc. that I have will be available in a notebook on the file cabinets in the departmental office. Please do not take the document from that room.

```
use Complex_Arithmetic;
A, B : Complex;
Unity : constant Complex := (1.0, 0.0);
...
B := Sum (Unity, (Re => -A.Im, Im => -A.Re));
```

□ *End of Example 13.5*

In the case of complex numbers the abstract data objects have a traditional representation (as real and imaginary parts) that can reasonably be accessible to the user of the package. By exporting the `Complex` type we allowed access to its definition in terms of the `Re` and `Im` components. This enabled us to write the record aggregate `(1.0,0.0)` to construct a `Complex` value, and the notation `A.Im` to access the imaginary part of `A`.

In the case of a less well-established structure the principle of abstraction suggests that it would be better to make a clear distinction between the structure's conceptual definition (in terms of the primitive operations) and its implementation (in terms of Ada data types). This separation makes the rest of the program independent of the implementation, greatly increasing its modularity. It follows that components of an abstract data structure should be accessible *only* through the primitive operations. Unauthorized access (access other than through the appropriate primitives) can be prevented by declaring the data components in the package body and exporting only the subprograms that implement the primitive operations. In other words, we force the program to respect the abstraction by *encapsulating* the implementation of the data structure within the package.

Example 13.6 An encapsulated variable

The following is based on Example 11.4. It illustrates the use of a package to encapsulate an abstract data structure, namely a telephone directory defined by the primitive operations `Insert_Entry` and `Lookup_Entry`. Here is the package declaration:

```
package Directory_Service is
   subtype Names   is String (1 .. 20);
   subtype Numbers is String (1 .. 12);
   procedure Insert_Entry
            (New_Name   : in Names;
             New_Number : in Numbers);
   procedure Lookup_Entry
            (Given_Name  : in Names;
             Name_Found  : out Boolean;
             Corr_Number : out Numbers);
end Directory_Service;
```

The following package body is a possible implementation:

```
package body Directory_Service is
   type Directory_Entries is
         record
            Name : Names;
            Number : Numbers;
         end record;
```

```
   Max_Size : constant Positive := 25;  -- arbitrary limit
   type Entry_Lists is
         array (Positive range <>) of Directory_Entries;
   type Directories is
         record
            Size : Natural range 0 .. Max_Size;
            List : Entry_Lists (1 .. Max_Size);
         end record;
   Directory : Directories;
   procedure Insert_Entry
               (New_Name   : in Names;
                New_Number : in Numbers) is
   begin
      insert (New_Name, New_Number) in Directory;
   end Insert_Entry;
   procedure Lookup_Entry
               (Given_Name  : in Names;
                Name_Found  : out Boolean;
                Corr_Number : out Numbers) is
   begin
      locate Given_Name in Directory, setting
         Name_Found and Corr_Number accordingly;
   end Lookup_Entry;
begin  -- initialization
   Directory.Size := 0;
end Directory_Service;
```

(The coding of the bodies of Insert_Entry and Lookup_Entry would be similar to Example 11.4.) The following program fragment illustrates the use of Directory_Service:

```
use Directory_Service;
Client : Names;  Num : Numbers;  Found : Boolean;
...
Insert_Entry (Client, "041-339 8855");
...
Lookup_Entry (Client, Found, Num);
if Found then
   Put (Client);  Put (" has number ");  Put (Num);
else
   Put (Client);  Put (" not in directory");
end if;
```

Directory_Service illustrates the benefits of abstraction. The user of Directory_Service is concerned only with the net effect of the two exported operations, Insert_Entry and Lookup_Entry, and is therefore able to ignore their implementation. The implementation illustrated above is in fact very crude; however, it can be changed by modifying the package body, without affecting either the package declaration or the rest of the program. We shall see this done in Example 17.3.

Directory_Service also illustrates all the main features of a package body. The body uses identifiers declared in the package declaration, it declares its own hidden types, constants and variables, and it has a statement part to initialize the package. Note that the package body has full access to everything declared either in the package declaration or in the body itself.

□ *End of Example 13.6*

13.4. Abstract data types

In Section 13.3 we saw that packages support a quite abstract view of data structures. However we now face a dilemma. We have seen how to make a package export a data type (such as Complex) that can be used to declare as many objects of the type as we need. But the internal details of the type (such as the Re and Im components of Complex) are exported as well. If we want to hide those details we must hide the type itself, by declaring it within the package body. But then we can declare objects of the type only within the package body, such as the encapsulated variable Directory in Example 13.6.

Consider the package Complex_Arithmetic in Example 13.5. This was based on the traditional representation of a complex number in terms of its *real* and *imaginary* parts, and this representation was made available to users of the package. However, scientists and engineers also use a definition in terms of a complex number's *magnitude* and *phase*, and this is more convenient for some purposes. We should be able to write our package so that the type Complex can be defined in either way, without requiring modifications to programs that use it. (The program fragment at the end of Example 13.5 contains several dependencies on the definition of Complex; it would therefore need several changes if the definition were changed.)

The package Directory_Service of Example 13.6 suffers from the converse problem. In this example we were able to hide completely the definition of the Directories type, by including it in the package body. Unfortunately, this meant that the type name itself was invisible outside the package. Consequently it was impossible to have more than one Directories variable.

It seems that we must choose between revealing everything about a type by exporting it, or revealing nothing by hiding it. This is too inflexible. We need a way of exporting a type name from a package without exporting its definition as well. With this facility we could use packages to encapsulate entire types, not just single variables. This need is met in Ada by *private types*.

Private types

A private type is declared in the package declaration, using the reserved word private in place of the normal type definition. A full declaration of the type is provided later, in the *private part* of the package declaration. This is a sequence of declarations, introduced by the reserved word private, where all the hidden details of private types are given. The declarations that precede the reserved word private constitute the *visible part* of the package declaration. See the syntax diagram 'package_declaration' in Appendix A.

Example 13.7 *Declaring and using a private type*

We can use a private type to amend our package `Complex_Arithmetic` from Example 13.5 so that the definition of the `Complex` type is hidden. Since this makes the real and imaginary components of a `Complex` object invisible (in fact, they might not even be represented directly), we must provide functions to return the real and imaginary parts of a given `Complex` value. We also need a function to construct a `Complex` value from its real and imaginary parts. (To be perfectly thorough, we should also declare similar functions that work in terms of magnitude and phase instead. As they involve no new principle, we shall omit them here.)

```
package Complex_Arithmetic is
    type Complex is private;
    I : constant Complex;
    function Real (C : Complex) return Float;
    function Imag (C : Complex) return Float;
    function Complex_Value (Real, Imag : Float) return Complex;
    function Sum  (C1, C2 : Complex) return Complex;
    function Diff (C1, C2 : Complex) return Complex;
    other subprogram declarations;
private
    implementation details
end Complex_Arithmetic;
```

This incomplete package declaration is all that its user needs to know about a package defining a private type. The declarations following the reserved word `private`, which have been omitted above, are needed by the compiler to allocate storage properly for `Complex` objects, but form no part of the logical interface between the package and the rest of the program. The programmer who writes the package body, on the other hand, does need to know what the private part contains.

Note that we had to alter the declaration of the constant `I`. Since it is to be exported along with `Complex`, it is declared in the visible part of the package declaration. But there the definition of `Complex` is unavailable, so it is impossible to write a `Complex` expression to initialize the constant. Instead we must declare it as a *deferred constant*, stating merely that it *is* a constant and has type `Complex`. The constant declaration must be completed in the package's private part, after the full declaration of the private type.

Here is one possible version of the declarations missing from the private part:

```
type Complex is
        record
           Re, Im : Float;
        end record;
I : constant Complex := (Re => 0.0, Im => 1.0);
```

Alternatively, if we chose to work in terms of magnitude and phase, the private declarations might look like this:

```
Pi : constant Float := 3.1415927;
type Complex is
        record
           Mag : Float;
```

```
            Ph : Float range 0.0 .. 2.0*Pi;
         end record;
      I : constant Complex := (Mag => 1.0, Ph => Pi/2.0);
```

Assuming that we chose the representation in terms of real and imaginary parts, we would write the package body as follows:

```
package body Complex_Arithmetic is
   function Real (C : Complex) return Float is
   begin
      return C.Re;
   end Real;

   function Imag (C : Complex) return Float is
   begin
      return C.Im;
   end Imag;

   function Complex_Value (Real, Imag : Float)
         return Complex is
   begin
      return (Re => Real, Im => Imag);
   end Complex_Value;

   function Sum  (C1, C2 : Complex) return Complex is
   begin
      return (Re => C1.Re+C2.Re, Im => C1.Im+C2.Im);
   end Sum;

   function Diff (C1, C2 : Complex) return Complex is
   begin
      return (Re => C1.Re-C2.Re, Im => C1.Im-C2.Im);
   end Diff;

   other subprogram bodies;

end Complex_Arithmetic;
```

With either version of the package we can now declare and manipulate Complex objects as follows:

```
use Complex_Arithmetic;
A, B : Complex;
Unity : constant Complex := Complex_Value (1.0, 0.0);
...
B := Sum (Unity, Complex_Value (-Imag (A), -Real (A)));
```

This is a less convenient notation than Example 13.5 provided, but that is a small price to pay for the increased modularity.

□ *End of Example 13.7*

As illustrated by Example 13.7, a private type does not altogether lack properties. In fact the following operations apply to any private type, even outside its defining package:

- An object of a private type can be passed as a parameter to a subprogram.
- A value of a private type can be returned as the result of a function.

- A value of a private type can be assigned to an object of the same type. This allows initializing an object in its declaration, whether it be a variable or a constant.
- The relational operators `=` and `/=` can be applied to values of a private type. These operations work on the private type as if its definition were visible. For example, if the private type is defined as `Integer` then an integer comparison takes place, and if it is defined as a record type (like `Complex`) then a record comparison takes place. It follows that a private type must be defined in terms of types for which equality comparisons are available. (As we shall see later, there are some types — the limited types — for which this is not the case.)

The only other operations available on a private type are subprograms exported from the same package as the private type itself. Further operations can be defined subsequently, outside the package, but these would have no access to the private type's hidden representation.

Limited private types

In the case of our `Complex` type the properties of private types seemed ideal. In particular, the pairwise comparison of components that takes place when comparing records or arrays does provide a valid test of mathematical equality for complex numbers. Unfortunately, this is not always true of abstract data structures. It can happen that the language-defined relational operators do not give the desired result. This is because comparing the data objects that represent the abstract values might not be sufficient to determine equality or inequality. It might be necessary to take other factors into account as well. For example, we might want to consider two tables to be equal if they contain the same entries, ignoring the order in which they appear. A simple array comparison is not sufficient, because it indicates equality only if the two arrays have equal components in corresponding positions. Using an array comparison would give misleading results. Sometimes testing for equality is not even a meaningful operation for the abstract structure. In cases like these, assignment, which is the pairwise *copying* of components, can also be inadequate or meaningless. It seems that we additionally need a more restrictive class of types than the private types.

In Ada we can limit a private type even further, so that assignment and equality comparisons are not allowed. This is done by declaring it as a *limited private type*, using the pair of reserved words `limited private` as the type definition. Limited private types are declared and used just like private types, but values of limited private types cannot be assigned or compared.

Example 13.8 ***Declaring and using a limited private type***

We now amend the `Directory_Service` package from Example 13.6 to allow any number of different directories to be declared, by exporting the `Directories` type. If we made it a private type it would be possible to assign or compare `Directories` variables. In general this would not be meaningful, so we export it as a limited private type instead. (*Exercise*: Can you think of ways to implement type `Directories` in which assignment or comparison of directories (a) *would*, and (b) *would not*, give sensible results?)

```
package Multi_Directory_Service is
   subtype Names   is String (1 .. 20);
```

```
   subtype Numbers is String (1 .. 12);
   type Directories is limited private;
   procedure Insert_Entry
                (New_Name   : in Names;
                 New_Number : in Numbers;
                 Directory  : in out Directories);
   procedure Lookup_Entry
                (Given_Name  : in Names;
                 Name_Found  : out Boolean;
                 Corr_Number : out Numbers;
                 Directory   : in Directories);
private
   type Directory_Entries is
        record
           Name : Names;
           Number : Numbers;
        end record;
   Max_Size : constant Positive := 25;  -- arbitrary limit
   type Entry_Lists is
        array (Positive range <>) of Directory_Entries;
   type Directories is
        record
           Size : Natural range 0 .. Max_Size := 0;
           List : Entry_Lists (1 .. Max_Size);
        end record;
end Multi_Directory_Service;

package body Multi_Directory_Service is
   procedure Insert_Entry
                (New_Name   : in Names;
                 New_Number : in Numbers;
                 Directory  : in out Directories) is
   begin
      insert (New_Name, New_Number) in Directory;
   end Insert_Entry;
   procedure Lookup_Entry
                (Given_Name  : in Names;
                 Name_Found  : out Boolean;
                 Corr_Number : out Numbers;
                 Directory   : in Directories) is
   begin
      locate Given_Name in Directory, setting
           Name_Found and Corr_Number accordingly;
   end Lookup_Entry;
end Multi_Directory_Service;
```

Some changes are apparent in this version. Now that we allow for several directories, the procedures Insert_Entry and Lookup_Entry each needs an additional parameter indicating which directory to work on. For the same reason we can no longer use the body's statement part to initialize the directory. Instead, every directory is separately initialized as a result of the default initial value we have specified for the `Size` component of the `Directories` type. (Actually, we could have done this in the original version too.)

Note also that the private part contains, as well as the definition of the private type itself, any declarations that support the private type and are not themselves to be be exported (even as private types). These declarations are visible only in the private part and in the package body.

Here is a program fragment that illustrates the use of this package by declaring and operating on two directories:

```
use Multi_Directory_Service;
Personal_Directory, Business_Directory : Directories;
Client : Names;  Num : Numbers;  Found : Boolean;
...
Insert_Entry (Client, "041-339 8855", Business_Directory);
Lookup_Entry (Client, Found, Num, Personal_Directory);
```

□ *End of Example 13.8*

Several important consequences follow from the unavailability of assignment for values of limited private types:

- A variable of a limited private type cannot be initialized in its declaration outside the package that exports the type.
- A constant of a limited private type can be declared only within the package that exports the type.
- No default value can be specified for a subprogram parameter of a limited private type.

As an aid to memory, note that these are precisely the constructs in which the symbol `:=` occurs.

These rules hold even if the limited private type happens to be defined in terms of a type for which assignment and equality are available. For instance, objects of the `Directories` type are actually records containing arrays of records. Within the body of `Multi_Directory_Service` this fact is known, and they could be assigned or compared if desired. Outside the package the definition is invisible and the restrictions on limited private types apply instead.

Objects of limited private types can still be passed as parameters, and a value of a limited private type may be returned as a function result. Thus it *is* possible to copy or compare values of limited private types, but only if the package exporting the limited private type provides these facilities as exported subprograms. For example, if desired we could augment `Multi_Directory_Service` to export:

```
procedure Copy_Directory
              (Original : in Directories;
               Copy     : out Directories);
```

(*Exercise*: modify the package accordingly.)

13.5. Case Study II: a sorting package

In Case Study I, Section 12.8, we developed a program to sort a list of names, using subprograms as our primary means of structuring. We now rework this case study to illustrate the use of packages.

Our sorting program contains two clusters, each a natural candidate for conversion to a package. The first copes with reading and writing names. We shall make this into the package `Name_IO`, exporting the procedures `Get_Name` and `Put_Name`. The second cluster is responsible for maintaining a data structure into which we insert names in any order, and from which we retrieve them in lexicographic order.

Case Study I contains a procedure, `Write_All_Names`, that not only fetches names from the sorted list but also writes them out directly. In the context of Case Study I that was a reasonable design, since the requirement stated that the sorted names were to be written out. However, converting the sorting cluster to a sorting package makes that design less appropriate. A package (like a subprogram) should provide its facilities in as general a way as possible, thus ensuring that it will be widely useful in many different programs. Some programs that need to sort names will want to use the sorted names as input to further processing steps. In these programs it is not appropriate to write the names directly. It is better to have a procedure, say `Extract`, that is complementary to `Insert` and allows names to be retrieved on demand. Each call of `Extract` will pass back the next name in lexicographic order. To position `Extract` at the beginning of the list we introduce a further procedure, `Prepare_Extraction`. Together these procedures allow repeated scans of the sorted names. Our sorting package, which we call `Sort_Service`, exports the procedures `Make_List_Empty`, `Insert`, `Prepare_Extraction` and `Extract`. It hides within its body the variables `List` and `Size` (which are used to implement the sorting algorithm) and `Extracted` (which indicates how many names have already been retrieved).

These changes not only generalize the sorting cluster, they also make the program more modular. `Write_All_Names` established an intimate connection between the sorting cluster and the input-output cluster. The new design removes this connection. We shall refine the action 'write all the names in listed order', in the program outline, to a loop that repeatedly calls `Extract` and `Put_Name`.

How is the main program to know when all the names have been retrieved from the list? In Case Study I `Write_All_Names`, being part of the sorting cluster, had access to the variable `Size` that held the number of names in the list. `Sort_Service` hides `Size`, the corresponding component of the package, because it is part of an encapsulated data structure. To export `Size` would violate the integrity of `Sort_Service`, for `Size` could then be changed in an uncontrolled way outside the package, thereby corrupting the data structure. We could make the size of the list available by exporting an `Integer` function that returns the current value of `Size`. This would not endanger `Size` itself, but would require users of the package to count names in and out. Instead we prefer to export a `Boolean` function, `All_Extracted`. The value returned by this function is `True` only when the last name in the sorted list has already been retrieved by `Extract`. We now have our program:

```
with Text_IO;  use Text_IO;
procedure Sort_Names is
   subtype Names is String (1 .. 20);
   Current_Name : Names;
```

```
package Sort_Service is
   procedure Make_List_Empty;
   procedure Insert (New_Name : in Names);
   procedure Prepare_Extraction;
   procedure Extract (Old_Name : out Names);
   function All_Extracted  return Boolean;
end Sort_Service;

package Name_IO is
   procedure Get_Name (Name : out Names);
   procedure Put_Name (Name : in Names);
end Name_IO;

use Sort_Service, Name_IO;

package body Sort_Service is
   Max_Size          : constant Positive := 100;
   List              : array (Positive range 1 .. Max_Size) of Names;
   Size, Extracted : Natural range 0 .. Max_Size;

   procedure Make_List_Empty is
   begin
      Size := 0;
   end Make_List_Empty;

   procedure Insert (New_Name : in Names) is
   begin
      insert New_Name in its correct position in the list;
   end Insert;

   procedure Prepare_Extraction is
   begin
      Extracted := 0;
   end Prepare_Extraction;

   procedure Extract (Old_Name : out Names) is
   begin
      Extracted := Extracted + 1;
      Old_Name := List(Extracted);
   end Extract;

   function All_Extracted  return Boolean is
   begin
      return (Extracted = Size);
   end All_Extracted;
end Sort_Service;

package body Name_IO is

   procedure Get_Name (Name : out Names) is
   begin
      read Name from a single line of input;
   end Get_Name;

   procedure Put_Name (Name : in Names) is
```

```
            begin
               Put (Name);
            end Put_Name;

         end Name_IO;

      begin
         Make_List_Empty;
         while not End_of_File loop
            Get_Name (Current_Name);  Skip_Line;
            Insert (Current_Name);
         end loop;
         Prepare_Extraction;
         while not All_Extracted loop
            Extract (Current_Name);
            Put_Name (Current_Name);  New_Line;
         end loop;
      end Sort_Names;
```

(The bodies of `Insert` and `Get_Name` are exactly as in Case Study I.)

Several features of this program merit comment. Firstly, the method of sorting is now encapsulated in the body of `Sort_Service`. If we wanted to change to a more efficient technique, the body of `Sort_Service` could be changed in complete confidence that no other part of the program would be affected. (*Exercise*: replace the insertion sort by Quicksort, described in Example 12.14. Delay actual sorting until `Prepare_Extraction` is called.)

The package `Name_IO` also achieves an important abstraction. Only in its body is the external format of the data taken into account. We could change that external format, and modify the body of `Name_IO` accordingly, without affecting the rest of the program. For example, we might change the data format so that each name consisted of several forenames followed by a surname. This can be accommodated without difficulty by altering `Get_Name` to pass back a string in which it has moved the forenames after the surname, and by altering `Put_Name` to move them back again before output.

Robustness

The author of any software that is intended to be of general utility must face the issue of how to deal with malfunctions. Setting aside the question of malfunction in the underlying computer system, two broad categories of problem seem to arise.

Problems of the first category are caused by misusing the software. In the case of `Sort_Service`, for example, it is wrong to call `Extract` if the previous call had passed back the last name in the list. It is the responsibility of the user of `Sort_Service` to check the value returned by `All_Extracted` and to avoid calling `Extract` when it is `True`. If this is not done, `Extract` will malfunction in some way that depends on the implementation of the procedure.

Problems of the second category arise when the software encounters an internal limitation that makes it impossible to carry out some operation, even when that operation was validly requested. An example of this occurs in `Sort_Service`, when `Insert` is called more than `Max_Size` times. Eventually the array `List` becomes full and it is impossible to insert another name. When this problem arises `Insert` writes an error message to the current output file, warning the eventual user of the output that something went wrong. However there is no way for the calling program to detect the error, or recover from it. In this particular program, which is very simple, the error message is probably adequate; but if Sort_Service is to be of truly general usefulness an error message is quite inadequate.

How can we do better? One possibility would be to export Max_Size from the package. It would then be the caller's responsibility to count the names as it inserts them and refrain from making too many calls. A powerful argument against this is that to export Max_Size would violate the principle of abstraction. (For example, it is quite possible to program the body of Sort_Service in such a way that it has *no* Max_Size, as we shall see in Example 17.3.) Alternatively, Sort_Service could instead export a Boolean function, say Insertion_Possible, that must be checked before each call of Insert. Or Insert could have a Boolean out parameter whose value would have to be checked after each call of Insert.

None of these suggestions leads to an attractive structure for the calling program, which gets cluttered with statements to ensure that Sort_Service will not malfunction. This clutter represents a compromise of the modularity we hoped to gain by introducing a package in the first place. What we need now is some way in which Sort_Service can inform a caller that an internal limit of the package has been reached, without the caller having to allow for this explicitly on each call. Such a mechanism would also be useful in dealing with malfunctions of the first category. We shall see in Chapter 14 that the *exception* feature of Ada provides just such a facility.

13.6. Visibility rules for packages

Here we summarize the visibility rules as they apply to identifiers declared within packages. This section should be regarded as an addendum to Section 12.7.

A package declaration and body *together* constitute a declarative region in the sense of Section 12.7. This is illustrated in Figure 13.1 and Figure 13.2.

Consider a package P and an identifier I declared within P. The scope of I is defined below.

- If I is declared in the *visible part* of P's declaration, the scope of I extends from just after its declaration to the end of the scope of P itself. Thus identifiers exported by a package are unlike identifiers local to a block or subprogram, in that their scope transcends the declarative region in which they are declared.
- If I is declared in the *private part* of P's declaration, the scope of I extends from just after its declaration to the end of the package declaration, and also extends over the whole of the corresponding package body.
- If I is declared in the *body* of P, the scope of I extends from just after its declaration to the end of the package body.

In the second and third cases, I is completely invisible outside P. In the first case, I is not in general *directly visible* outside P; it is referred to by the selected component notation P.I. However, the use clause '**use** P;' makes I directly visible throughout the scope of the use clause, *except*:

```
with Text_IO; use Text_IO;
procedure Sort_Names is
   subtype Names is ...;
   Current_Name : Names;
   package Sort_Service is
      ...
      procedure Insert
         (New_Name:Names) ;
      ...
      end Sort_Service;
      ...
      use Sort_Service;
      package body Sort_Service is
      ...
      List : ...;
      ...
      procedure Insert
         (New_Name:Names) is
         ...
      begin
      ...
      end Insert;
      ...
   end Sort_Service;
   ...
begin
   ...
   Insert (Current_Name);
   ...
end Sort_Names;
```

Dotted lines show where the identifiers are not directly visible, and therefore must be qualified.

(a) Scope of **Names**.
(b) Scope of **Insert**.
(c) Scope of **List**.

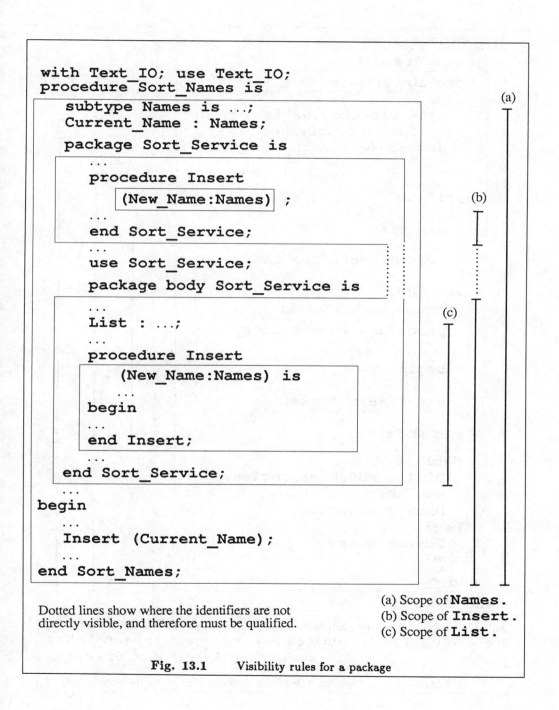

Fig. 13.1 Visibility rules for a package

```
procedure P is
  procedure Q is
    package MDS is
      ...
      type Directories is
          limited private;
      procedure Insert_Entry
            ... ;
      ...
    private
      ...
      Max_Size : ...;
      ...
      type Directories is
          ...;
    end MDS;
    package body MDS is
      procedure Insert_Entry
            ... is
      begin
        ...
      end Insert_Entry;
      ...
    end MDS;
    declare
      Dir1 : MDS.Directories;
      use MDS;
      Dir2 : Directories;
    begin
      Insert_Entry (...);
    end;
  end Q;
end P;
```

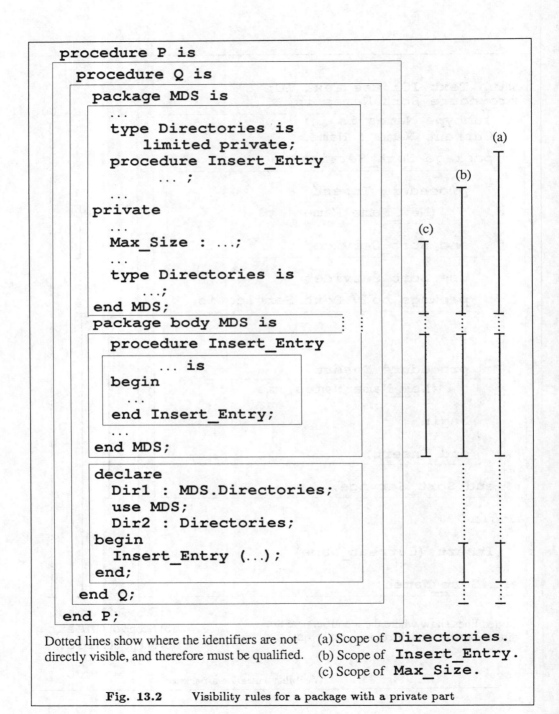

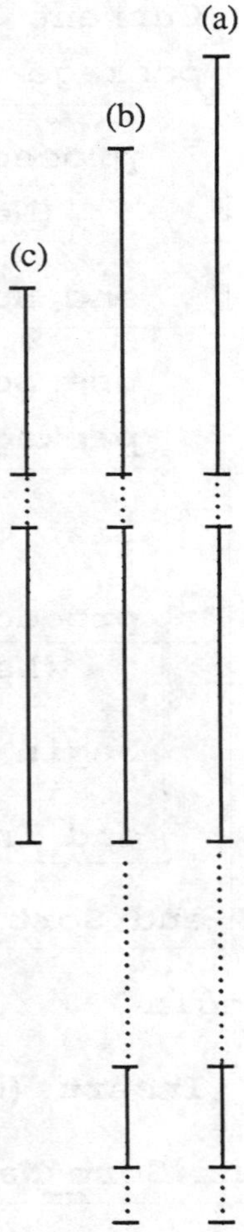

Dotted lines show where the identifiers are not directly visible, and therefore must be qualified.

(a) Scope of `Directories`.
(b) Scope of `Insert_Entry`.
(c) Scope of `Max_Size`.

Fig. 13.2 **Visibility rules for a package with a private part**

- within the scope of any ordinary declaration of `I` (i.e., where an identifier `I` would be visible in the absence of any use clauses); *or*
- within the scope of another use clause '`use Q;`' where the package `Q` also exports an identifier `I`.

Figure 13.1 illustrates these rules as they apply to Case Study II. Figure 13.2 does likewise for a program containing the package `Multi_Directory_Service` (abbreviated here to `MDS`) of Example 13.8. Notice that the *first* declaration of `Directories`, in the visible part of `MDS`, is the one that counts.

Some of the consequences of the rules concerning identifier clashes introduced by use clauses are illustrated by Figure 13.3. Notice that '`use A, B;`' does not make either `Y` directly visible, because of the potential ambiguity; also that the ordinary declaration of `Z` hides the `Z` exported by `B` (the same would be true even if `Z` had been declared in an outer scope).

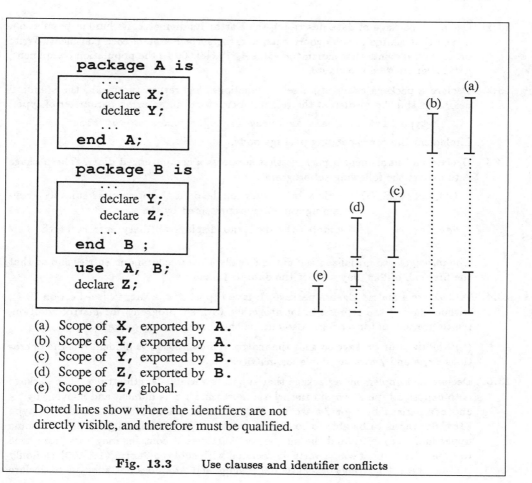

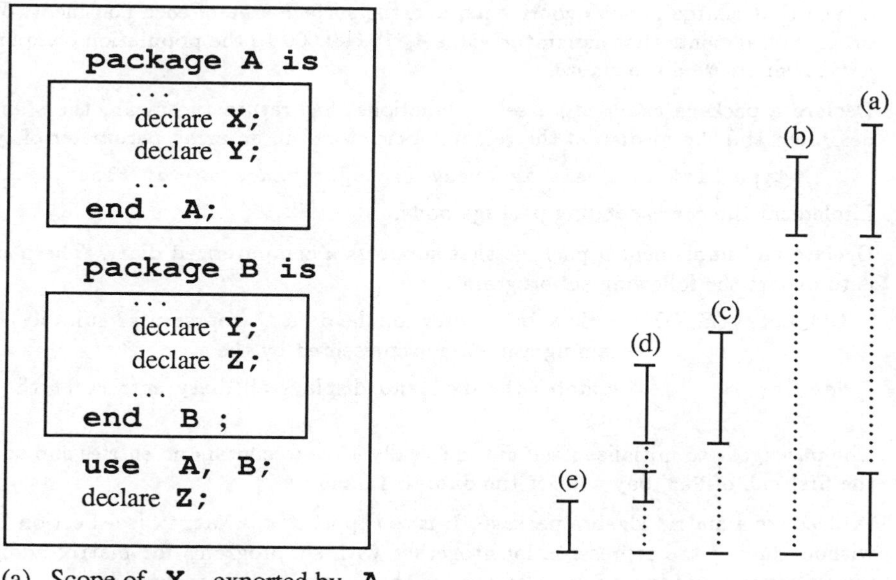

(a) Scope of **X,** exported by **A.**
(b) Scope of **Y,** exported by **A.**
(c) Scope of **Y,** exported by **B.**
(d) Scope of **Z,** exported by **B.**
(e) Scope of **Z,** global.

Dotted lines show where the identifiers are not directly visible, and therefore must be qualified.

Fig. 13.3 Use clauses and identifier conflicts

Style

The rules concerning identifier clashes introduced by use clauses are distinctly tricky! If we have two packages that export entities with the same identifiers, a program that names both packages in use clauses is likely to be difficult to read, indeed it could be downright misleading. The same applies to a program containing a package that exports an entity with the same identifier as an entity declared outside the package.

It is a good idea to choose highly specific identifiers for the identifiers exported by a package. This reduces the probability of clashes with identifiers exported by other packages or declared elsewhere. (For this reason the identifiers `Status` and `Buffer` exported by `Modem_Data` (Example 13.1) might reasonably be criticized, as they are quite likely to be chosen as identifiers for other purposes.)

Exercises 13

13.1. Declare a package of data describing the Earth: its diameter, its human population, a type that enumerates its continents, and the surface area of each continent. Write program fragments that assign the value 4,415,000,000 to the population component, ***without*** and ***with*** a use clause.

13.2. Declare a package exporting a set of functions that return the mean, the standard deviation and the median of the real numbers stored in an array parameter of type:

```
type List_of_Reals is array (Integer range <>) of Float;
```

Implement the corresponding package body.

13.3. Declare and implement a package that supports a computerized diary. The package is to export the following subprograms:

`Add_Entry(`S`,`D`);` adds a diary entry for the date D (represented suitably), containing a message represented by the string S.

`New_Day;` updates the date and displays all diary entries for the new day.

The package is to initialize itself automatically so as to contain no entries and so that the first call of `New_Day` will set the date to 1 January.

13.4. (a) Declare a matrix algebra package. It is to export a type `Matrix` (see Section 10.4), without hiding the representation, together with subprograms for matrix addition, multiplication and inversion. Also outline the corresponding package body.

(b) Modify your package so that the matrix representation *is* hidden, but the operations `:=`, `=` and `/=` are available for matrices.

13.5. Declare and implement a package that supports variable-length strings. The package is to export a type `Flex_String` whose representation is hidden, and copying by `:=` and comparison by `=` or `/=` are *not* to be allowed. A variable declared with type `Flex_String` is to be able to contain character strings of any length from 0 to some upper limit (say 100), and the number of characters it contains may vary from time to time. (By comparison, a variable declared with subtype `String(1..100)` can only contain character strings of length 100 *exactly*; and Ada does not allow us to declare variables with the unconstrained array type `String`.) The package is to export the following operations:

`Length(`*X*`)` is a function that returns the *current* length of the `Flex_String` value *X*.

`Flex(`*S*`)` is a function that converts the `String` value *S* to the corresponding `Flex_String` value.

`Append(`*X*`,Y);` appends the `Flex_String` value *X* to the `Flex_String` variable `Y`.

(*Hint*: represent a `Flex_String` value by a fixed-length string of 100 characters together with a count of the actual number of characters stored in it.)

What changes would be needed to your package declaration and body if `:=`, `=` and `/=` *were* to be allowed, to ensure that they produce the correct results?

13.6. Write a program, using `Directory_Service` (Example 13.6), that interactively accepts and responds to directory enquiries and additions.

14

Exceptions

14.1. Introduction

A hallmark of high-quality software is ***robustness.*** Robust software not only performs correctly when used normally, but also performs reasonably when misused. Robustness can be achieved by ***defensive programming***, that is to say, by anticipating and allowing for misuse. Naturally, there is a limit to what can be achieved; for instance, a program cannot completely protect itself from hardware malfunction or operating system faults.

Each module in a modular program is written to a specification that includes stated preconditions (assumptions that the module may make about its inputs) and stated postconditions (conditions that must hold after execution of the module). If the module is written correctly, and its inputs do satisfy its preconditions, then the module will perform actions to satisfy its postconditions. What happens if the preconditions are ***not*** satisfied? In Ada, some preconditions are a consequence of the type rules or are imposed by subtype constraints. For example, a subprogram with a `Natural` formal parameter can never be called with a `Character` actual parameter (because of the type rules); and a call in which the actual parameter is negative will fail because of the range constraint. Many preconditions cannot be expressed directly in Ada, however. For example, a subprogram might expect a sorted array as a parameter. If the array is not in fact sorted, then the call will not fail but the subprogram will not work correctly. In such circumstances, it should not return as if it ***had*** worked correctly. The Ada exception mechanism is designed to handle such situations so that robustness can be achieved at reasonable cost.

Handling error situations in an adequate manner is very difficult. Nevertheless, we must recognize that good error handling is essential in many applications. For instance, air traffic control, aircraft navigation, industrial control and patient monitoring systems all need to perform their functions with extremely high reliability. If such a system detects a hardware or software error, it would be unacceptable for the system simply to halt (even with a suitable diagnostic message). Somehow the system must ***recover*** and continue running. In a telephone exchange control program, for example, the inability to connect a single call would be acceptable, but termination of the control program itself (which would stop all calls) would be unacceptable; hence the system design must allow the current call to be aborted without affecting the integrity of the system as a whole. The Ada exception mechanism is designed to make such error recovery feasible.

Consider the example of a data communications system. The lowest level of software deals with the communications hardware and, consequently, will detect any hardware malfunction. Some malfunctions can be handled at this level by retransmitting a message. In other cases such recovery is not possible, so the error must be signaled to higher levels of the software. It is likely that only the very highest levels of the software can take the necessary remedial action if the basic message transmission subsystem fails. For example, the form of remedial action is likely to depend upon the type or priority of the message involved.

How are we to program the reporting and handling of error situations? The problem is an interaction between the lower and higher levels of a system. An obvious technique is to provide each subprogram with a `Boolean` out parameter that indicates success or failure. Such parameters must be present at all levels of the software, so there is a danger of the program being dominated by error-handling code, spoiling the simplicity of the normal case. Ada's exception mechanism allows the handling of exceptional situations to be separated from the normal case.

The basic idea of the exception mechanism is very simple:

- An *exception* is essentially a named signal. Exceptions are declared like all other entities in Ada.
- An exception can be *raised*, signaling that an exceptional situation has occurred. This can happen either implicitly (if a language rule is broken) or explicitly if a *raise statement* is executed.
- Any computation that raises an exception is terminated, and control passes to a suitable *exception handler*, if one is provided.

Example 14.1 A simple example of exception handling

Let us return to program `Tabulate_State_Stats`, Example 8.4. This program reads and tabulates certain data for each of the states of the USA. It is not at all robust: for example it will fail if data for any states are missing. The solution in Example 8.7 was to test for `End_of_File` inside the for loop and exit if it is found to be `True`. This change undoubtedly makes the program more robust, but it also distracts the reader's attention from the normal case.

An alternative solution is to allow the program to attempt to read the missing data, raising the exception `End_Error`, but to provide a handler for `End_Error` that allows the program to terminate gracefully:

```
begin
   Total_Pop := 0;  Total_Area := 0;
   for State in USA loop
      Get (State_Pop);  Get (State_Area);  Skip_Line;
      write State, State_Pop, State_Area, etc.;
      update Total_Pop and Total_Area;
   end loop;
   write Total_Pop and Total_Area;
   if not End_of_File then
      Put ("ERROR: input data excess");  New_Line;
   end if;
exception
   when End_Error =>
      Put ("ERROR: input data incomplete");  New_Line;
end Tabulate_State_Stats;
```

Note that this version is actually *more* robust than the version with the conditional exit, which still relies on the data supplied for each state being complete; this version will terminate gracefully if *any* data are omitted. Furthermore, this version can easily be made to cope with garbled data, for example nonnumeric data. On attempting to read such data, `Get` will raise the exception `Data_Error`. The program can be made to produce a helpful message in this eventuality, simply by adding an exception handler for `Data_Error`:

```
when Data_Error =>
    Put ("ERROR: input data invalid");  New_Line;
```

It would be far more difficult to modify the original version to allow for garbled data.

□ *End of Example 14.1*

14.2. Exception declarations

Errors detected by the program itself can be signaled by means of program-defined exceptions. Such exceptions must be declared, for example:

```
Transmission_Error : exception;
Connection_Failed  : exception;
```

Exceptions must be declared in a scope that is wide enough to allow use of the identifier both for raising the exception and for providing handlers. The predefined exceptions, such as `Constraint_Error` and `Numeric_Error`, can be used anywhere. Some other exceptions, such as `End_Error` and `Data_Error`, are declared in the package `Text_IO`.

Example 14.2 Signaling misuse of a package by exceptions

The package `Sort_Service` of Case Study II has two important limitations. Firstly, it cannot cater for sorting of more than 100 names. Secondly, it malfunctions if `Extract` is called when all names have already been retrieved from the list. Clearly, the subprograms of the package cannot perform correctly if they are misused. Such misuses can be signaled by exceptions declared in the package declaration:

```
package Sort_Service is
   procedure Make_List_Empty;
   procedure Insert (New_Name : in Names);
   procedure Prepare_Extraction;
   procedure Extract (Old_Name : out Names);
   function All_Extracted  return Boolean;
   List_Full, List_Empty : exception;
end Sort_Service;
```

The simplicity of the subprograms in the package is preserved — they have not been complicated by any additional parameters — but now it is possible for them to signal misuse. This in turn (as we shall see) allows the user of the package to recover from errors.

□ *End of Example 14.2*

Exceptions can be renamed in much the same way as other entities. This can be useful to abbreviate long exception names. For example:

```
Full : exception  renames Sort_Service.List_Full;
```

14.3. Raise statements

A *raise statement* raises an exception explicitly. An example of a raise statement is:

```
raise Transmission_Error;
```

A raise statement is effectively a jump out of the current context to an exception handler. When an exception is explicitly raised, therefore, it is important that any data structures used by the handler should be in a self-consistent state.

Example 14.3 Raising an exception on a misuse of a package

Let us continue with the sorting package of Case Study II and Example 14.2. Having declared the exceptions in the package declaration, it is necessary to modify the package body to raise the exceptions where appropriate.

The exception List_Full must be raised when Insert is called with the list already full:

```
procedure Insert (New_Name : in Names) is
   New_Pos : Positive range 1 .. Max_Size;
begin
   if Size < Max_Size then
      find the insertion position, New_Pos, for New_Name;
      shift up the names in positions New_Pos through Size;
      List(New_Pos) := New_Name;
      Size := Size + 1;
   else
      raise List_Full;
   end if;
end Insert;
```

Here the statements that wrote a warning message have been replaced by a raise statement. No other change is necessary since, even when the list is full, Insert leaves the encapsulated data structure in a self-consistent state. Hence continued use of the package is possible even after the exception has been raised.

The exception List_Empty must be raised if Extract is called with no names remaining to be retrieved. We insert the following before the other statements of Extract:

```
if Extracted = Size then
   raise List_Empty;
end if;
```

These two exceptions are logically different. An abstract specification of the sorting package might not mention any limitation on the list size. Thus it is not really a programming error if the list becomes full and the List_Full exception is raised. On the other hand, to attempt to retrieve a name that does not exist clearly *is* a programming error. However, the principle of defensive programming requires that the programmer of Extract should not neglect the possibility of misuse. Raising List_Empty ensures that the misuse does not go unnoticed by the user of the package.

□ *End of Example 14.3*

14.4. Exception handlers

Handlers for exceptions are placed just before the final **end** of a subprogram body, package body, or block (or task body — see Chapter 23). These constructs we shall collectively call *units*. When a unit fails because of an exception, then an appropriate exception handler may be executed. Since there are many potential exceptions with perhaps different handlers, the handlers are grouped together by means of a construct similar to a case statement. See the syntax diagrams 'exception_handler', 'block', 'subprogram_body' and 'package_body' in Appendix A.

Consider, again, the message communications system that was introduced in Section 14.1; a typical unit might have the following exception handling part inserted before the final end of the unit:

```
exception
   when Transmission_Error =>
      Log_Error;
      Retransmit (Current_Message);
   when others =>
      Reboot_System;
```

Here we have two handlers. The first handler is for the single exception `Transmission_Error`; this simply logs the error and retransmits the message. The `others` choice in the exception part has the same meaning as in a case statement: it covers *all* exceptions not explicitly named.

The statements within a handler are not restricted in any way. They can call procedures, which themselves might raise exceptions. As with all recovery mechanisms, these possibilities need care if an endless cycle of attempted recovery is to be avoided when a malfunction persists.

The execution of a handler can be completed in one of three ways:

- by executing a return statement;
- by executing a raise statement; or
- by reaching the end of the handler.

In all cases, the handler is regarded as completing the execution of the enclosing unit. Consequently, an exception handler placed inside a function body *must* finally execute a return statement defining the function result — or execute a further raise statement. The resulting flow of control is illustrated in Figure 14.1.

As the syntax diagram in Appendix A shows, a raise statement need not contain an exception name. The statement '`raise;`' may appear only within an exception handler, and its effect is to re-raise the same exception that caused entry to the handler.

Example 14.4 A local handler

The package `Complex_Arithmetic` of Example 13.7 could be augmented with a function to calculate the magnitude of a `Complex` value. Such a function might be:

```
function Magnitude (C : Complex) return Float is
begin
   return Square_Root (C.Re**2 + C.Im**2);
```

```
end Magnitude;
```

Unfortunately, this simple implementation has a defect. The expression in the return statement could overflow even if its result is in range (e.g., when `C.Re` is large but `C.Im` is zero). This could be avoided by a more cautious (but awkward) implementation. The best compromise is to use the simple implementation, and resort to the cautious implementation only when forced to it, by providing an exception handler for `Numeric_Error`:

```
function Magnitude (C : Complex) return Float is
begin
   return Square_Root (C.Re**2 + C.Im**2);
exception
   when Numeric_Error =>
      declare
         R : constant Float := abs C.Re;
         I : constant Float := abs C.Im;
      begin
         if R > I then
            return R * Square_Root (1.0 + (I/R)**2);
         else
            return I * Square_Root (1.0 + (R/I)**2);
         end if;
      end;
end Magnitude;
```

The handler itself uses the cautious approach, so the correct value is returned by the function even in cases where the simple implementation fails. Of course, the cautious implementation could have been used in the main body, but the method given above is more efficient in the normal case where the simple implementation works. (Also, the main body above is easier to understand and could act as a logical specification of the function.)

□ *End of Example 14.4*

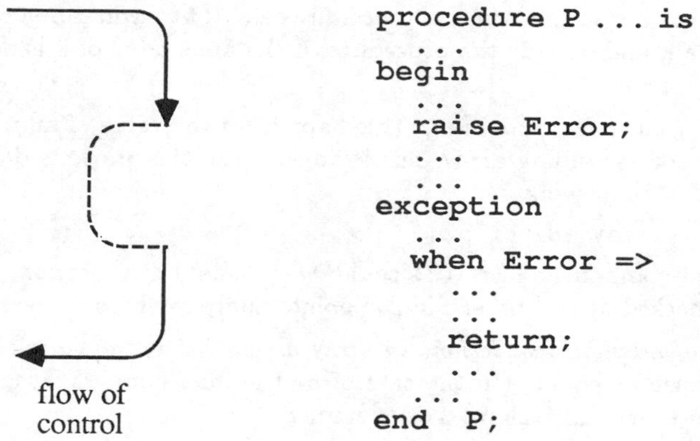

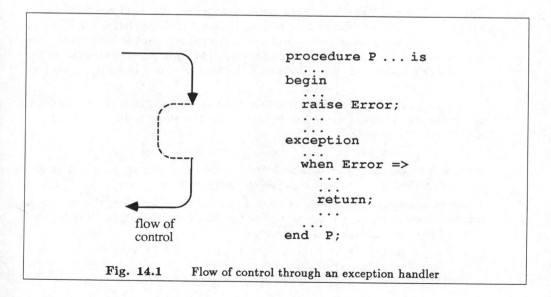

Fig. 14.1 Flow of control through an exception handler

14.5. The predefined exceptions

Breaking a language rule during the execution of a program will raise a predefined exception. These exceptions are noted in the appropriate chapters of this book. They are also summarized below.

The exception Constraint_Error

As the name suggests, this exception is raised when some constraint is violated. Some of the possible causes are summarized below.

- *Violation of a range constraint.* This can happen during an assignment, if the object being assigned to has a range constraint that is not satisfied by the value being assigned. For example, after the declarations:

  ```
  subtype S is T range M .. N;
  I : S;  J : T;
  ```

  the assignment 'I := J;' will raise Constraint_Error if the current value of J is not in the range M through N. This can be seen most clearly if we view the assignment statement as equivalent to:

  ```
  if J in M .. N then
     I := J;
  else
     raise Constraint_Error;
  end if;
  ```

  A range constraint can also be violated by passing a parameter. Consider, for example:

  ```
  procedure P (F : in S);
  procedure Q (F : out T);
  ```

  The procedure call 'P(J);' will raise Constraint_Error if the current value of J is not in the range of the subtype S. Note in particular that the exception will be raised before the call, and *outside* the procedure, since it is the call that has failed rather than the procedure body. Likewise the procedure call 'Q(I);' will raise Constraint_Error after the call, and outside the procedure, if the final value of F is not in the subtype of I.

- *Violation of an index constraint.* This happens if the value of an index expression is not in the corresponding array index range. Take the previous declarations of S, I and J, and the following:

  ```
  A : array (S) of ...;
  ```

  An indexed component like A(J) could raise Constraint_Error, so the value of J must be checked at run-time. Similar points apply to slices.

- *Violation of a length restriction.* In array assignments, the length of the two arrays involved must be equal. (In the case of multi-dimensional arrays, the lengths must be equal in every dimension.) For example:

  ```
  type Vector is array (Integer range <>) of Float;
  V : Vector (...);
  W : Vector (...);
  ```

Then the array assignment 'V := W;' may be viewed as equivalent to:

```
if V'Length = W'Length then
   V := W;
else
   raise Constraint_Error;
end if;
```

On the other hand, if V and W were declared with the same subtype, the length check would be unnecessary. Similar considerations apply in assignment to or from a slice.

Other ways of raising Constraint_Error will be mentioned in later chapters.

The exception Numeric_Error

An arithmetic operation might yield a result outside the range of numbers of the type concerned. If this overflow were not detected, the result would be meaningless. An Ada implementation is required to detect such overflow, or division by zero, and raise the exception Numeric_Error. We defer detailed consideration of this exception until Chapter 19.

The exception Storage_Error

The storage required for an Ada program consists of two quite separate parts: storage for the object-program instructions (and literals), and storage for the data objects. The former is fixed, and the program will not run at all unless sufficient storage is available. The storage required for data objects is quite different: in general, it is not possible to predict how much is needed before the program is executed. For example, the size of an array could depend upon the program's inputs, as could the depth of subprogram calls.

An Ada implementation might allocate a fixed amount of storage for running a program. If this storage becomes exhausted, the exception Storage_Error is raised. The most likely causes are entering a block or subprogram, elaborating a declaration, or evaluating an allocator (see Chapter 17).

It might seem impossible to handle this particular exception because the handler itself would require storage. Fortunately, the raising of an exception in itself never requires extra storage, as we shall see later.

The exception Program_Error

An erroneous program is one whose effect is deliberately not defined by Ada. For example, a program is erroneous if it uses an undefined value in an expression; or if its effect depends on a particular order of evaluation of the operands of a dyadic operator; or if its effect depends on a particular mechanism for passing parameters. An implementation that detects such an error *may* raise Program_Error at the point of the error. The necessary checks might be extremely difficult, however, so no Ada implementation is obliged to provide them. Thus no program should rely on having such an error signaled by Program_Error. However, Program_Error is certainly raised if the final end of a function body is reached and no return statement has defined the function result.

The exception Tasking_Error

This predefined exception will be described in Chapter 23.

Example 14.5 Defensive programming

The recursive function named after Ackermann has been used as a benchmark to measure the efficiency of the subprogram calling mechanism of a number of languages and compilers [Wichmann 1976].

Each activation of the function requires additional storage and, since the function is deeply recursive, storage can be exhausted very rapidly. In many non-Ada systems, exhaustion of storage prevents normal termination of the program. Storage exhaustion can be anticipated in an Ada program, however, by providing a handler for Storage_Error.

```
with Text_IO;  use Text_IO;
procedure Test_Ackermann is
   package Int_IO is new Integer_IO (Integer);  use Int_IO;
   Result, Nr_Calls, I : Positive;
   function Ackermann (N, M : Natural) return Positive is
   begin
      if N = 0 then
         return M + 1;
      elsif M = 0 then
         return Ackermann (N - 1, 1);
      else
         return Ackermann (N - 1, Ackermann (N, M - 1));
      end if;
   end Ackermann;
begin
   I := 1;
   while 4**(I-1) < Integer'Last/512 loop
      Put ("Ackermann(3,");  Put (I, Width => 1);  Put (")");
      Result := Ackermann (3, I);
      Put (Result, Width => 8);
      Nr_Calls := (128 * 4**I - 120 * 2**I + 9*I + 37) / 3;
      Put (Nr_Calls, Width => 15);  Put (" calls");  New_Line;
      if Result /= 8 * 2**I - 3 then
         Put ("WARNING: wrong result!");  New_Line;
      end if;
      I := I + 1;
   end loop;
exception
   when Storage_Error =>
      Put ("ERROR: storage space exceeded");  New_Line;
end Test_Ackermann;
```

The program tabulates the values of Ackermann(3,I), and checks these values using a known formula. It also writes out the number of recursive calls of Ackermann using a known formula.

Note that the number of calls could be very large. However, the main loop checks that I is not too big, so overflow is not possible. In principle, we could have used the Numeric_Error exception for the same purpose, but this would be poor practice when the condition is so easily anticipated. On the other hand, it is impossible to determine in advance how far the recursion can proceed before storage is exhausted, so the use of Storage_Error is reasonable.

Handling the Storage_Error exception will not itself need additional storage. This is because the handler is in the main program Test_Ackermann, so the storage used by all the activations of the function will be released before the handler is executed.

□ *End of Example 14.5*

14.6. Finding the handler

The three basic constituents of the exception mechanism have now been described: exception declarations, the raising of exceptions, and exception handlers. It remains to describe how the appropriate exception handler is found once an exception has been raised, especially if the handler is not in the unit in which the exception was raised. In general, finding the handler for an exception proceeds in a number of steps as follows. Suppose that an exception E has been raised in a unit U.

- If E was raised by a *statement* of U, and if U contains a handler for E, then this handler is executed and completes the execution of U. (This was the situation in Example 14.4.)
- If U contains no handler for E, or if E was raised during the elaboration of a *declaration* of U, then U has failed. In that case, the exception is *propagated* to the point of 'call' of U. This means that, in effect, the 'call' of U raises E. The process of finding an exception handler is now repeated.

For the purposes of this explanation: if U is a block, it can be considered to be 'called' at the point where it occurs in the program; or if U is a package (or task) body, its initialization part can be considered to be 'called' when the body is elaborated.

Consider a system constructed from a number of units on different levels, as in Figure 14.2. (The boxes represent units, and the arrows represent calls.) The lower-level units have no knowledge of the higher-level ones. A low-level unit might raise an exception, say E. The higher-level units presumably know the identity of E (e.g., if it is exported by a package). What happens if a statement of Send_Block raises E? Any of the callers of Send_Block might wish to handle this exception (i.e., Send_Message, Receive_Message, or Comms_Control). It is the sequence of active units leading to the call of Send_Block that determines the handler that is executed. If Comms_Control calls Receive_Message which calls Send_Block, and a statement of Send_Block raises E, then there are four possibilities:

- If a handler for E exists in Send_Block: this handler replaces the execution of the remaining statements of Send_Block.
- If no handler for E exists in Send_Block but there is one in Receive_Message: the execution of Send_Block is terminated and E is propagated to Receive_Message, where the handler is executed and replaces the remaining statements of Receive_Message.

- If there is no handler for E in either Send_Block or Receive_Message, but there is one in Comms_Control: both Send_Block and Receive_Message are terminated and the exception is propagated to Comms_Control, where the handler is executed and replaces the remaining statements of Comms_Control.

- If there is no handler for E in any of Send_Block, Receive_Message or Comms_Control, and if Comms_Control is the main program: the whole system fails.

An exception can be raised during the execution of a handler. In such circumstances, the handler is not re-executed, but instead the exception is propagated to the calling unit. In Example 14.4, it is possible that the return statement in the handler will itself raise Numeric_Error. The exception is then raised at the point where the function Magnitude was called. This is perfectly appropriate, since it indicates that the magnitude really is too large to be represented, rather than that the body of the function is in error.

Finding a handler always releases storage when Storage_Error is raised. If the exception is raised during the execution of a statement, this must be by attempting to enter a block, or to call a subprogram, or some other action that requires additional storage. That attempt will be abandoned when the handler is executed, even if it is a local handler. If Storage_Error is raised during the elaboration of a declarative part, then the storage already allocated for the declared objects will be released, since the exception is propagated outside the unit containing this declarative part.

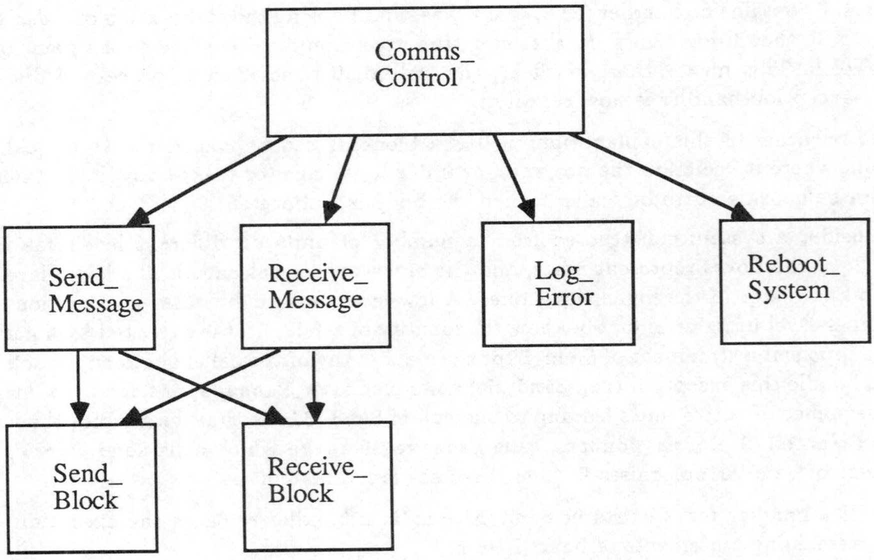

Fig. 14.2 Structure diagram of a message communication system

Example 14.6 OIS: Recovery by means of a nonlocal handler

This example, and many subsequent ones, are parts of an office information system (OIS) that will be developed as a case study in Chapter 25.

A procedure is required to read names from a file and to display them, sorted, on a screen. The package `Sort_Service` of Example 14.2 is to be used for sorting. In the event that there are too many names for `Sort_Service` to sort, the names are to be displayed in their original order.

The following declarations are to be assumed:

```
type Names is ...;
procedure Reset_Names;
   -- Resets reading to the beginning of the names file.
procedure Get_Name (Name : out Names);
   -- Reads the next name from the names file.
function End_of_Names  return Boolean;
   -- Returns True iff no more names remain to be read.
procedure Display (Name : in Names);
   -- Displays the name on the screen.
```

Here is a possible solution:

```
procedure Display_Names is
   Current_Name : Names;
   use Sort_Service;
begin
   Make_List_Empty;
   Reset_Names;
   while not End_of_Names loop
      Get_Name (Current_Name);
      Insert (Current_Name);
   end loop;
   -- display sorted names --
   Prepare_Extraction;
   while not All_Extracted loop
      Extract (Current_Name);
      Display (Current_Name);
   end loop;
exception
   when List_Full =>
      -- display unsorted names --
      Reset_Names;
      while not End_of_Names loop
         Get_Name (Current_Name);
         Display (Current_Name);
      end loop;
end Display_Names;
```

In this example, the call of the procedure `Insert` could raise the exception `List_Full`. This exception is then propagated to `Display_Names` where the handler for `List_Full` will be executed.

□ *End of Example 14.6*

Example 14.7 OIS: Handling a break-in

The office information system is designed for use by a single operator using a VDU. A facility is to be provided for terminating a command, job, or other lengthy activity. This is done by depressing a special 'break-in' key on the VDU keyboard.

How are we to implement this facility in Ada? A forced abandonment of a critical operation could leave data structures or files in an inconsistent state. Hence the point of termination must be controlled. On the other hand, if the reaction to the break-in is programmed explicitly at every level of the software, the logic of the normal (non-interrupted) operations will be obscured. An exception allows the break-in mechanism to be programmed in a modular fashion.

The declaration of this exception needs to be very wide in scope. Several different levels of the software will need to provide handlers. For example, it might be a complete command (such as 'print') that is terminated, or just a single function within the editor. Let us assume that the system includes a package, `Globals`, containing the global types and constants of the system. The exception should be declared there:

```
package Globals is
   ...
   Break_in : exception;
   ...
end Globals;
```

The details of the communication between the keyboard and the system components will be described in Chapter 25. For now, it is sufficient to note that all keyboard input will be channeled through a system component called the ***keyboard driver***. Normally, when the keyboard driver is called it will fetch a character or line typed by the operator. However, if the 'break-in' key has been depressed then the keyboard driver will ignore the requested operation and raise the exception `Break_in` instead. Suppose that the 'break-in' key corresponds to the ASCII control character *ETX*. The keyboard driver will then contain something like the following:

```
if Char = ASCII.ETX then
   raise Break_in;
end if;
```

(The standard package `ASCII` contains identifiers for all the ASCII control characters). This implies that every unit that calls the keyboard driver, either directly or indirectly, must either contain a handler for `Break_in` or be prepared to be terminated by propagation of the exception.

Consider, for example, a function within the editor that displays all lines containing a particular sequence of characters. The recovery after a `Break_in` might be to restore the previous editing position:

```
procedure Display_Lines_Containing (Target : in String) is
   Original_Position : Line_Number := Editing_Position;
begin
   set Editing_Position to each line containing Target, and display that line;
exception
   when Break_in =>
      Editing_Position := Original_Position;
```

```
end Display_Lines_Containing;
```

In more complicated situations, it might be necessary to provide handlers for the exception at several levels, and to make the lower-level handlers re-raise the exception. The purpose of the lower-level handlers would be to ensure the consistency of internal data structures (such as the current editor position above).

□ *End of Example 14.7*

Style

Exceptions (like goto statements) are very easy to misuse. They should be used with caution, especially as they are likely to be unfamiliar to most programmers. The following guidelines seem sensible:

- Do not use exceptions if an alternative approach leads to a cleaner and simpler solution.
- Use exceptions only for rare events in which some loss of information (caused by propagation of the exception) is acceptable.
- Anticipate possible misuses of each program component. Test for them, and use an exception to signal a detected misuse.

14.7. Suppressing exceptions

(This section may be omitted on a first reading.)

We have seen that run-time checks make an important contribution to the security of running Ada programs. Unfortunately, these checks can be quite expensive, in terms of both time and space. Some computers have special hardware or special instructions for index range checks, but few (if any) directly support all the run-time checks of Ada.

It is often possible to reduce the number of run-time checks, by programming in such a way that the compiler can verify that language rules are not being violated. For instance, almost every index expression should be clearly within the corresponding index range, and thus need not be checked.

When the cost of run-time checks is unacceptable, the programmer can use the pragma `Suppress` to suppress them selectively. This can be dangerous, because if a language rule is violated when the corresponding run-time checks have been suppressed, the program's behavior will become unpredictable. Nevertheless, it happens often enough in practice that a program with run-time checks is too large to fit into a limited memory or is too slow to meet a time constraint. The suppression of run-time checks for such reasons must, however, be regarded as a desperate measure.

The pragma `Suppress` must be inserted in the declarative part of the unit for which the suppression is required. Its simplest form is:

```
pragma Suppress (check_identifier);
```

For each predefined exception there are one or more kinds of check that might raise the exception. The *check_*identifier is the name of the check to be suppressed.

The checks corresponding to `Constraint_Error` are as follows:

- `Range_Check` corresponds to the check that a value satisfies a range constraint.
- `Index_Check` corresponds to the check that an index constraint is satisfied by an index expression, or by an array actual parameter (where the corresponding formal parameter is constrained).
- `Length_Check` corresponds to the check that the number of components in an array assignment or other array operation is correct (see Chapter 10).
- `Access_Check` is associated with access types (see Chapter 17).
- `Discriminant_Check` corresponds to the check that a discriminant constraint is satisfied (see Chapter 18).

The checks corresponding to `Numeric_Error` are as follows:

- `Division_Check` corresponds to the check that the right operand of `/`, `rem`, or `mod` is nonzero.
- `Overflow_Check` corresponds to the check that a computed value is not outside the range handled by the machine.

There is only one check corresponding to `Storage_Error`, namely `Storage_Check`.

There is only one check corresponding to `Program_Error`, namely `Elaboration_Check`.

It is possible to limit suppression of checks to operations associated with a single named object, or to operations associated with objects of a single named type. For example, if `A` is the name of an array object, or the name of an array type, then

```
pragma Suppress (Index_Check, On => A);
```

requests suppression of index checks only on the array object `A`, or only on arrays of type `A` (respectively).

It is important to note that there is no *obligation* on the compiler to suppress any checks. On machines with hardware index checks, for example, suppression of `Index_Check` might be prohibitively expensive or even impossible. Moreover, if a unit in which checks have been suppressed 'calls' a unit that has been compiled with checks, then an exception might be propagated into the calling unit anyway. An implementor might even decide not to implement the suppression of `Storage_Check` because continuing execution would be catastrophic.

Example 14.8 Suppressing exceptions

Consider the matrix multiplication function from Example 12.11:

```
function Matrix_Product (M1, M2 : Matrix)
      return Matrix is
   P : Matrix (M1'Range(1), M2'Range(2));
begin
   for I in P'Range(1) loop
      for J in P'Range(2) loop
         P(I,J) := 0.0;
         for K in M1'Range(2) loop
            P(I,J) := P(I,J) + M1(I,K) * M2(K,J);
```

```
            end loop;
         end loop;
      end loop;
      return P;
   end Matrix_Product;
```

This function is not robust: it just assumes that `M1'Range(2)` is identical to `M2'Range(1)`. Within the innermost loop the compiler will generate a time-consuming check on the value of `K` in `M2(K,J)`. However, a single test that `M1'Range(2)` is identical to `M2'Range(1)` would suffice. This test can be placed *outside* the loops, and then the repeated index checks can safely be suppressed.

```
function Matrix_Product (M1, M2 : Matrix)
      return Matrix is
   P : Matrix (M1'Range(1), M2'Range(2));
   pragma Suppress (Index_Check);
begin
   if not (M1'First(2) = M2'First(1) and
           M1'Last(2) = M2'Last(1)) then
      raise Constraint_Error;
   end if;
   for I in P'Range(1) loop
      ...
   end loop;
   return P;
end Matrix_Product;
```

□ *End of Example 14.8*

This kind of hand optimization requires substantial care. Each operation that could require a check must be analyzed to ensure that the check is in fact unnecessary.

Exercises 14

14.1. In Example 14.1, if an exception handler for `Data_Error` is placed beside the handler for `End_Error`, the program will react to garbled input data by writing a message and then simply stopping. It would be preferable instead to continue reading and processing the data for the remaining states. The message should also give the name of the state whose data was garbled. Modify the program accordingly.

14.2. In the example at the beginning of Section 14.4, what happens if `Reboot_System` raises `Transmission_Error`?

14.3. Given the declarations:

```
type Item_Lists is array (Integer range <>) of Items;
Not_Sorted : exception;

procedure Search
         (List : in Item_Lists;
```

```
Target : in Items;
Matched : out Boolean;
Pos : out Integer);
```

write a body for `Search` that uses binary search to locate the value of `Target` in the array `List`, which is supposed to be ordered. `Search` is to raise `Not_Sorted` if it detects that `List` is not in fact ordered.

14.4. In a compiler written in Ada, would it be reasonable to raise an exception on detecting that the source program is invalid?

15

Input-Output

15.1. Input-output and files

In this chapter we shall see how to use text files other than the standard input and standard output. We shall also see how to use binary (non-text) files. The latter are important because, when a set of data is not intended for preparation or inspection by the human user, time and space can be saved by storing the data on a machine-readable medium in its internal (binary) representation, thus avoiding the cost of converting the data to or from a textual representation. (These conversions are called ***formatting.***)

It is helpful to take a somewhat abstract view of the sets of data read and written by programs. We define a ***file*** to be a data structure that is not internal to any particular program. This very general definition:

- allows for both text files and binary files;
- allows for a variety of file structures, such as sequential or direct;
- is independent of the medium on which the data is recorded, so a program is decoupled (as far as possible) from the peculiarities of each medium.

Input-output tends to be one of the most complicated features of a programming system. This is a consequence of the diversity of possible file structures, the diversity of possible input-output operations, the diversity of media, and the diversity of things that can go wrong! In the case of text files, there is also a diversity of possible formatting conventions.

The most common 'solution' to this problem has been to build special input-output features into programming languages. For example, FORTRAN, COBOL and PL/I all have special declarations for files and special statements for input-output operations. Pascal integrates files into its type structure, and provides standard procedures for input-output operations; but these procedures are irregular in the number, types and even syntax of their parameters. In such languages input-output is a built-in anomaly. Additional input-output operations or additional file structures cannot be provided simply by writing appropriate library software; instead the programming language itself must be extended and its compiler modified. (This does happen in practice, but the resulting language extensions are nonstandard and inhibit program portability if used.)

Ada's solution is preferable. There are no special language features for input-output. Instead, all input-output is provided by a group of standard packages, whose declarations are written entirely in Ada itself. Each package may be invoked simply by nominating it in the program's context clause. Input-output operations are achieved by ordinary subprogram calls. If an operation goes wrong, an appropriate exception is propagated by the subprogram. Thus the language is not complicated by special features that have to be learned and understood by programmers; and the scheme is readily extendible by addition of further packages to provide alternative input-output facilities, without any change to the language itself.

The definition of files given above is more general than the structures actually provided by the standard input-output packages. Three file structures are provided, each supported by a standard package. In all cases, a file is viewed as an ordered set of *elements.*

- `Text_IO` supports *text input-output.* The elements of a text file are pages, lines and characters, which must be read or written in sequence.
- `Sequential_IO` supports *sequential input-output.* The elements of a sequential file are all of the same (any) type. They must be read or written in sequence, starting at the first element of the file.
- `Direct_IO` supports *direct input-output.* The elements of a direct file are all of the same (any) type. They may be read and written in any order, by specifying the index of each element to be read or written.

There is no change of representation when the elements of a sequential or direct file are read or written.

Section 15.3 is an introduction to sequential input-output, and Section 15.4 to direct input-output. Section 15.5 consolidates and extends what we have already learned about text input-output. In each section we shall concentrate on the most important features of the input-output packages and on typical program schemes for using them. Space prevents us from describing every last detail. If necessary you should consult [Ada 1983] for full details.

15.2. External files and file objects

Each file in a system will have its own unique, permanent, *filename.* Each operating system has its own rules for how filenames may be constructed. The system must maintain some kind of *catalog* to record the filename, physical location, access permissions, etc., of each file. Some systems allow only disk and tape files to be named. Modern systems extend their naming convention to *all* files, including transitory files associated with input-output devices like VDUs and printers.

Each input-output operation must somehow identify the file on which the operation is to be performed. Now it would be very undesirable to use the filename itself for this purpose, since that would imply searching the catalog on every single input-output operation. Instead, the usual convention is to associate each file that is being read or written by a program with a *file object* (sometimes called a *file descriptor*) that is local to the program. In order to avoid any confusion between files and file objects, we shall henceforth use the term *external file* to refer to the data structure that is external to the program.

An association between an external file and an internal file object is established by the operation of *opening* the file. The association is terminated by the converse operation of *closing* the file. Parameters to the *open* operation include a file object and the filename of an external file. The filename is used to search the catalog and thus determine the physical location of the file, check any access permissions, etc., and relevant information obtained from the catalog is stored in the file object. Other input-output operations (such as reading and writing) can then supply this file object as a parameter, and no further references to the filename or catalog are necessary.

15.3. Sequential input-output

A program that is to perform sequential input-output must nominate the standard package Sequential_IO in its context clause. Sequential_IO is actually what is called a *generic* package: it can be used to instantiate a distinct copy of itself for each required element type. The following 'magic formula' (actually a *generic instantiation*):

```
package SIO is new Sequential_IO (ELEM);
```

instantiates a package that supports sequential input-output of elements of type ELEM. This can best be understood by studying the instantiated package. Here it is (with some details omitted):

```
package SIO is
   type File_Type is limited private;
   type File_Mode is (In_File, Out_File);
   -- File management --
   procedure Create      (File   : in out File_Type;
                           Mode   : in File_Mode := Out_File;
                           Name   : in String := "";
                           Form   : in String := "");
   procedure Open        (File   : in out File_Type;
                           Mode   : in File_Mode;
                           Name   : in String;
                           Form   : in String := "");
   procedure Close       (File   : in out File_Type);
   procedure Delete      (File   : in out File_Type);
   procedure Reset       (File   : in out File_Type;
                           Mode   : in File_Mode);
   -- Input and output operations --
   procedure Read        (File   : in File_Type;
                           Item   : out ELEM);
   procedure Write       (File   : in File_Type;
                           Item   : in ELEM);
   function End_of_File (File   : in File_Type)
                        return Boolean;
   exception declarations (see Section 15.6);
private
   implementation details
end SIO;
```

SIO.File_Type is used to declare file objects that can be associated with sequential external files whose elements are of type ELEM. Note particularly that SIO.File_Type is limited private, so only the operations exported by SIO are available for objects of this type. In particular, :=, = and /= are not defined for file objects. The available operations are SIO.Create, SIO.Open, SIO.Close, and so on.

As usual, we can avoid the selected component notation by means of a use clause (but not if two copies of Sequential_IO have been instantiated).

The external file associated with a SIO.File_Type object is viewed as a sequence of elements of type ELEM. Elements can be read or written only in strict sequence, starting from the first element of the file. Each file has a *current mode*. `Read` and `End_of_File` are permitted only if the current mode is `In_File`; `Write` is permitted only if the current mode is `Out_File`.

Here are brief descriptions of the operations of `Sequential_IO`:

`Create(F,`*M*`,`*N*`);`	creates a sequential external file with filename *N*, and associates it with file object `F` in mode *M*. If *N* is the empty string (the default case), the file is anonymous and temporary. (The `Form` parameter is implementation-defined, and optional anyway, so we shall ignore it here.)
`Open(F,`*M*`,`*N*`);`	opens the sequential external file whose filename is *N*, and associates it with the file object `F` in mode *M*.
`Close(F);`	dissociates `F` from its external file.
`Delete(F);`	deletes the external file associated with `F`.
`Reset(F,`*M*`);`	resets the file object `F` so that input-output, in mode *M*, is restarted at the first element of the external file.
`Read(F,X);`	reads the next element of `F` into the variable `X`.
`Write(F,`*X*`);`	writes the value *X* to the next element of `F`.
`End_of_File(F)`	returns `True` if and only if no more elements can be read from `F`.

Example 15.1 *Sequential file update*

A bank maintains a record of each account, including the account number (a unique 8-digit integer), the customer's name and address (20- and 60-character strings), and the current balance of the account (in cents, possibly negative). Every transaction is recorded. A transaction record consists of the account number, an indication of whether it is a credit or debit transaction, the amount of the credit or debit (in cents), and the date. A program is to be designed that uses the transaction records to update the account records. For the purposes of this example, assume that we are restricted to using sequential files only.

An efficient solution is as follows. The accounts are held in a sequential file, ordered by account number. The transaction records are accumulated in a (sequential) transactions file. At the end of each day, a program is run that uses the day's transactions file and the old accounts file to produce a new, updated, accounts file. The latter then becomes the old accounts file for the next day's run. The algorithm is as follows:

1. *Sort* the transactions by account number.
2. *Merge* the sorted transactions with the old accounts file. That is to say, read the sorted transactions file and the accounts file simultaneously, keeping in step by matching the account numbers, and use all the transactions on each account (which will be consecutive) to update the account record and write it to the new accounts file.

The program is to be a procedure with three parameters, the filenames of the transactions file, the old accounts file and new accounts files.

The obvious decomposition of this problem is into the sort phase and the merge phase. Let us implement these as procedures, with parameters identifying the files involved. The main program can perform all the necessary creation, opening and closing of files, so the lower-level procedures can work on file objects only. We assume the following global package:

```
package Account_Details is
   subtype Account_Numbers is Integer range 0 .. 99999999;
   subtype Money is Integer;  -- cents
   type Dates is ...;
   type Accounts is
         record
            Acc_No  : Account_Numbers;
            Name    : String (1 .. 20);
            Address : String (1 .. 60);
            Balance : Money;
         end record;
   type Transactions is
         record
            Acc_No  : Account_Numbers;
            Credit  : Boolean;
            Amount  : Money range 1 .. Money'Last;
            Date    : Dates;
         end record;
end Account_Details;
```

Our first-level solution is:

```
with Sequential_IO;
with Account_Details;  use Account_Details;
procedure Update_Accounts_by_Batch
            (Trans_Filename,
             Old_Acc_Filename, New_Acc_Filename : in String) is
   package TIO is new Sequential_IO (Transactions);
   package AIO is new Sequential_IO (Accounts);
   Unsorted_Trans_File, Sorted_Trans_File : TIO.File_Type;
   Old_Acc_File, New_Acc_File : AIO.File_Type;
   procedure Sort_Transactions
               (Unsorted_File, Sorted_File : in TIO.File_Type) is
   begin
      sort Unsorted_File to produce Sorted_File;
   end Sort_Transactions;
   procedure Merge_Transactions
               (Trans_File : in TIO.File_Type;
                Old_Acc_File, New_Acc_File : in AIO.File_Type) is
   begin
      merge Trans_File with Old_Acc_File to produce New_Acc_File;
   end Merge_Transactions;
begin
   TIO.Open (Unsorted_Trans_File, TIO.In_File, Trans_Filename);
   TIO.Create (Sorted_Trans_File, TIO.Out_File);
         -- temporary file for the sorted transactions
   Sort_Transactions (Unsorted_Trans_File, Sorted_Trans_File);
   TIO.Close (Unsorted_Trans_File);
```

```
      TIO.Reset (Sorted_Trans_File, TIO.In_File);
      AIO.Open (Old_Acc_File, AIO.In_File, Old_Acc_Filename);
      AIO.Open (New_Acc_File, AIO.Out_File, New_Acc_Filename);
      Merge_Transactions
         (Sorted_Trans_File, Old_Acc_File, New_Acc_File);
      TIO.Close (Sorted_Trans_File);
      AIO.Close (Old_Acc_File);
      AIO.Close (New_Acc_File);
   end Update_Accounts_by_Batch;
```

Note that we are consistently using the selected component notation to avoid possible confusion between the types and subprograms exported by TIO and those exported by AIO.

Now we turn to the implementation of Merge_Transactions. In general, there could be any number of transactions (including zero) corresponding to each account record. There could also, conceivably, be transactions that do not have the same account number as any account record. We shall use a procedure:

```
   procedure Report (Erroneous_Trans : in Transactions);
```

to display a suitable warning message.

Several algorithms have been devised for merging. The one we shall adopt is a loop that updates exactly one account record per iteration. This updating requires all transactions corresponding to that account to be read (and all previously-encountered transactions with smaller account numbers to be rejected):

```
   procedure Merge_Transactions
               (Trans_File : in TIO.File_Type;
                Old_Acc_File, New_Acc_File : in AIO.File_Type) is
      Account : Accounts;
   begin
      while not AIO.End_of_File (Old_Acc_File) loop
         AIO.Read (Old_Acc_File, Account);
         read and reject all transactions whose
            account numbers are less than Account.Acc_No;
         read all transactions whose account numbers equal
            Account.Acc_No and use them to update Account;
         AIO.Write (New_Acc_File, Account);
      end loop;
      read and reject all remaining transactions;
   end Merge_Transactions;
```

Care must be taken over the reading of transactions. For example, '*read all transactions whose account numbers equal* Account.Acc_No ...' inevitably results in reading (or attempting to read) one transaction with a greater account number. The same is true of the preceding step '*read and reject all transitions whose ...*'. In general, therefore, the reading of transactions must always be one transaction ahead. To set the ball rolling, the very first transaction must be read *before* entry to the main loop. There is a problem at the end of the transactions file, where it is impossible to read ahead. So we introduce a pair of variables, Trans and Trans_Acc_No. Trans will contain the last transaction read (if any). Trans_Acc_No normally will contain a copy of Trans.Acc_No, but will be artificially set to a large number when the end of the transactions file has already been reached. We introduce a local procedure, Read_Next_Trans, to ensure that these variables are updated properly. These refinements lead to the following completed version of Merge_Transactions:

```
procedure Merge_Transactions
            (Trans_File : in TIO.File_Type;
             Old_Acc_File, New_Acc_File : in AIO.File_Type) is
   Account      : Accounts;
   Trans        : Transactions;
   Trans_Acc_No : Integer;
   Large_Acc_No : constant Integer := Account_Numbers'Last + 1;
   procedure Read_Next_Trans is
   begin
      if TIO.End_of_File (Trans_File) then
         Trans_Acc_No := Large_Acc_No;
      else
         TIO.Read (Trans_File, Trans);
         Trans_Acc_No := Trans.Acc_No;
      end if;
   end Read_Next_Trans;
   procedure Perform_Transaction
               (Trans   : in Transactions;
                Account : in Accounts) is
   begin
      if Trans.Credit then
         Account.Balance := Account.Balance + Trans.Amount;
      else
         Account.Balance := Account.Balance - Trans.Amount;
      end if;
   end Perform_Transaction;
begin
   Read_Next_Trans;
   while not AIO.End_of_File (Old_Acc_File) loop
      AIO.Read (Old_Acc_File, Account);
      while Trans_Acc_No < Account.Acc_No loop
         Report (Trans);
         Read_Next_Trans;
      end loop;
      while Trans_Acc_No = Account.Acc_No loop
         Perform_Transaction (Trans, Account);
         Read_Next_Trans;
      end loop;
      AIO.Write (New_Acc_File, Account);
   end loop;
   while Trans_Acc_No < Large_Acc_No loop
      Report (Trans);
      Read_Next_Trans;
   end loop;
end Merge_Transactions;
```

In practice the implementation would be more elaborate, with error handling and so on.

The implementation of Sort_Transactions is omitted here for space reasons. (See Exercises 15).

□ *End of Example 15.1*

Example 15.1 illustrates a classical use of sequential files in data processing. Example 15.2 in the next section illustrates a more modern and more efficient solution to the same problem.

15.4. Direct input-output

Direct input-output is possible on storage media such as disks that can be addressed at random. A direct file is like a large array that resides in backing store.

A program that is to perform direct input-output must nominate the standard package Direct_IO in its context clause. Like Sequential_IO, Direct_IO is a generic package that must be instantiated for each required element type. The generic instantiation:

```
package DIO is new Direct_IO (ELEM);
```

instantiates a package that supports direct input-output of elements of type ELEM. This can best be understood by studying the instantiated package. Here it is (with some details omitted):

```
package DIO is
   type File_Type is limited private;
   type File_Mode is (In_File, InOut_File, Out_File);

   type Count is range 0 .. implementation-defined;
   subtype Positive_Count is Count range 1 .. Count'Last;

   -- File management --
   procedure Create     (File   : in out File_Type;
                         Mode   : in File_Mode := InOut_File;
                         Name   : in String := "";
                         Form   : in String := "");
   procedure Open       (File   : in out File_Type;
                         Mode   : in File_Mode;
                         Name   : in String;
                         Form   : in String := "");
   procedure Close      (File   : in out File_Type);
   procedure Delete     (File   : in out File_Type);
   function Size        (File   : in File_Type)
                        return Count;

   -- Input and output operations --
   procedure Read       (File   : in File_Type;
                         Item   : out ELEM;
                         From   : in Positive_Count);
   procedure Write      (File   : in File_Type;
                         Item   : in ELEM;
```

```
                                  To      : in Positive_Count);
      exception declarations (see Section 15.6);
   private
      implementation details
   end DIO;
```

DIO.File_Type is used to declare file objects that can be associated with direct external files whose elements are of type ELEM. Note that DIO.File_Type is limited private, so only the operations exported by DIO are available for objects of this type.

An external file associated with a DIO.File_Type object is viewed as an array of elements of type ELEM. An element can be read or written by giving its *index*, an integer of the subtype DIO.Positive_Count.

We now briefly describe the operations of Direct_IO. Create, Open, Close and Delete are analogous to the corresponding operations of Sequential_IO (see Section 15.3). The only difference here is a third possible value for the mode, namely InOut_File; this mode allows both reading and writing of the direct file. The other operations have the following meanings:

Size(F)	returns the current size of the external file associated with F, i.e., the index of its last element, or zero. Note that the current size of a direct external file may be changed by writing to an element anywhere beyond the previous last element.
Read(F,X,*I*);	reads the *I*'th element of F into the variable X.
Write(F,*X*,*I*);	writes the value *X* to the *I*'th element of F.

Example 15.2 Direct file update

The program of Example 15.1 can be improved by storing the account records in a direct file rather than a sequential file. It is only necessary to structure the accounts file in such a way that the index of an account record can be determined efficiently from its account number. Then it is no longer necessary to accumulate a batch of transactions for later sorting and merging; instead each transaction can be performed immediately.

The simplest possible structure is to use the account number itself as an index into the accounts file:

```
with Direct_IO;
with Account_Details;  use Account_Details;
procedure Update_Accounts_Interactively
            (Acc_Filename : in String) is
   package AIO is new Direct_IO (Accounts);
   Acc_File : AIO.File_Type;
   Trans : Transactions;
   procedure Get_Transaction (Trans : out Transactions) is
   begin
      read one transaction from standard input;
   end Get_Transaction;
   procedure Perform_Transaction
```

```
                  (Trans   : in Transactions;
                   Account : in Accounts) is
      begin
         as before
      end Perform_Transaction;

      procedure Update_Account
                  (Trans    : in Transactions;
                   Acc_File : in AIO.File_Type) is
         Account : Accounts;
         Acc_Index : constant AIO.Positive_Count
               := AIO.Positive_Count (Trans.Acc_No);
      begin
         AIO.Read (Acc_File, Account, Acc_Index);
         Perform_Transaction (Trans, Account);
         AIO.Write (Acc_File, Account, Acc_Index);
      end Update_Account;

   begin
      AIO.Open (Acc_File, AIO.InOut_File, Acc_Filename);
      loop
         ...
         Get_Transaction (Trans);
         Update_Account (Trans, Acc_File);
         ...
      end loop;
      AIO.Close (Acc_File);
   end Update_Accounts_Interactively;
```

This file structure is impractical, however, since the accounts file will be very sparse. (For example, one of the digits of an account number is likely to be a check digit.) A more realistic solution, allowing the accounts file to be just large enough to store the accounts that actually exist, is suggested in Exercises 15.

A possible implementation of `Get_Transaction` will be given in Example 15.5.

□ *End of Example 15.2*

15.5. Text input-output

In Section 6.3 we described a text file as a two-dimensional structure of lines and characters. Actually, that description was over-simplified, although it is an adequate model for many purposes. In this section we shall describe the text file structure in full detail, and take a closer look at the standard package `Text_IO`.

A text file is a three-dimensional structure of pages, lines and columns:

- a text file is a sequence of (one or more) pages;
- a page is a sequence of (one or more) lines;

- a line is a sequence of (zero or more) columns, each of which contains a single graphic character.

It is also possible to view a text file as a one-dimensional structure, if we consider each line to be followed by a ***line terminator***, each page to be followed by a ***page terminator***, and the last page to be followed by a ***file terminator***. From this point of view, a text file is like an ordinary sequential file whose elements are graphic characters, line terminators, page terminators, and a file terminator. Figure 15.1 illustrates both ways of viewing the same text file.

The nature of these terminators is not defined by `Text_IO`. Each might be represented by a control character, by a combination of control characters, or by some other means. The user of `Text_IO` simply calls the appropriate subprograms to generate terminators or to

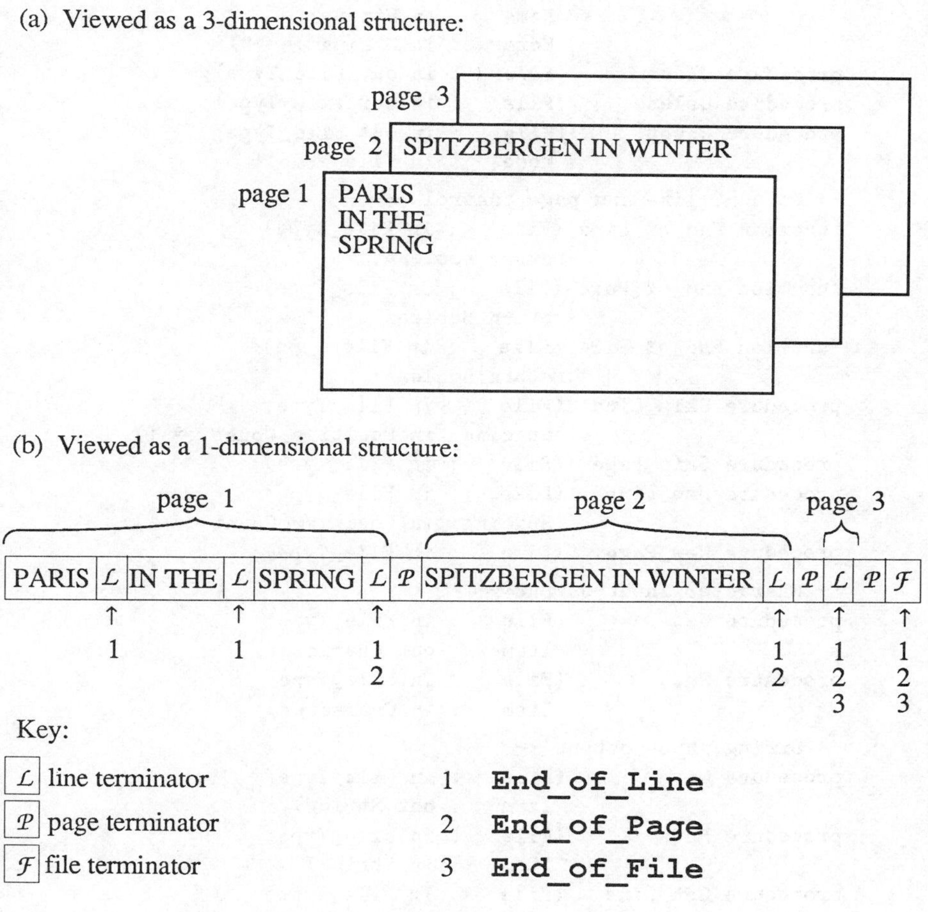

Fig. 15.1 Structure of a text file

detect their presence.

Here is the package declaration of Text_IO (some details omitted):

```
package Text_IO is
   type File_Type is limited private;
   type File_Mode is (In_File, Out_File);
   type Count is range 0 .. implementation-defined;
   subtype Positive_Count is Count range 1 .. Count'Last;
   -- File management --
   procedure Create     (File   : in out File_Type;
                         Mode   : in File_Mode := Out_File;
                         Name   : in String := "";
                         Form   : in String := "");
   procedure Open       (File   : in out File_Type;
                         Mode   : in File_Mode;
                         Name   : in String;
                         Form   : in String := "");
   procedure Close      (File   : in out File_Type);
   procedure Delete     (File   : in out File_Type);
   procedure Reset      (File   : in out File_Type;
                         Mode   : in File_Mode);
   -- Column, line and page control --
   function End_of_Line (File   : in File_Type)
                        return Boolean;
   function End_of_Page (File   : in File_Type)
                        return Boolean;
   function End_of_File (File   : in File_Type)
                        return Boolean;
   procedure Skip_Line  (File   : in File_Type;
                         Spacing: in Positive_Count := 1);
   procedure Skip_Page  (File   : in File_Type);
   procedure New_Line   (File   : in File_Type;
                         Spacing: in Positive_Count := 1);
   procedure New_Page   (File   : in File_Type);
   -- Character input-output --
   procedure Get        (File   : in File_Type;
                         Item   : out Character);
   procedure Put        (File   : in File_Type;
                         Item   : in Character);
   -- String input-output --
   procedure Get        (File   : in File_Type;
                         Item   : out String);
   procedure Put        (File   : in File_Type;
                         Item   : in String);
   procedure Get_Line   (File   : in File_Type;
                         Item   : out String;
                         Last   : out Natural);
```

```
    procedure Put_Line    (File    : in File_Type;
                           Item    : in String);
    declaration of the generic package Enumeration_IO;
    declaration of the generic package Integer_IO;
    declaration of the generic package Float_IO;
    declaration of the generic package Fixed_IO;
    exception declarations (see Section 15.6);
private
    implementation details
end Text_IO;
```

Although not shown here, most subprograms in Text_IO may be called without a file parameter. In the cases of End_of_Line, End_of_Page, End_of_File, Skip_Line, Skip_Page, Get and Get_Line, the standard input file is assumed by default; in the cases of New_Line, New_Page, Put and Put_Line, the standard output file is assumed by default.

The operations concerned with *file management*, namely Create, Open, Close, Delete and Reset, are similar to the corresponding procedures in Sequential_IO (see Section 15.3), with the following qualifications:

- 'Open(F,In_File,...);' and 'Reset(F,In_File);' set the reading position to the first element of F, i.e., the first character (if any) of line 1 of page 1.
- 'Create(F,Out_File,...);', 'Open(F,Out_File,...);' and 'Reset(F,Out_File);' set the writing position to the first character of line 1 of page 1 of F.
- 'Close(F);' appends a file terminator to F, having previously called 'New_Page(F);' unless the current page is already terminated. Thus Close ensures that F has a proper text file structure before actually closing it.

Here are brief explanations of the operations concerned with *column, line and page control*:

End_of_Line(F) returns True if no more characters remain to be read from the current line of F (i.e., if the reading position is at a line terminator, or at the file terminator).

End_of_Page(F) returns True if no more lines remain to be read from the current page of F (i.e., if the reading position is at the last line terminator of a page, or at the file terminator).

End_of_File(F) returns True if no more pages remain to be read from F (i.e., if the reading position is at the file terminator, or at the last line terminator of the file).

Skip_Line(F); skips the rest of the current line of F (i.e., advances the reading position beyond the next line terminator, and beyond a page terminator if one immediately follows that line terminator). 'Skip_Line(F,*N*);' does the same, *N* times.

Skip_Page(F); skips the rest of the current page of F (i.e., advances the reading position just beyond the next page terminator).

New_Line(F); appends a line terminator to F. 'New_Line(F,*N*);' does the same, *N* times.

`New_Page(F);` appends a page terminator to `F`, preceded by a line terminator if the current line is not already terminated. Thus `New_Page` ensures that the current page has a proper structure before starting a new page.

The '`End_of_`' and '`Skip_`' operations are allowed only when `F` is in mode `In_File`; the '`New_`' operations are allowed only when `F` is in mode `Out_File`.

Here are brief explanations of the operations concerned with *character input-output*:

`Get(F,C);` reads the next graphic character from `F` into the `Character` variable `C`, having skipped any preceding line and page terminators.

`Put(F,`*C*`);` appends the graphic character *C* to `F`.

Here are brief explanations of the operations concerned with *string input-output*:

`Get(F,S);` performs a `Get` operation from `F` for each character of the `String` variable `S`. Note that the input string might straddle line and page terminators.

`Put(F,`*S*`);` performs a `Put` operation to `F` for each character of the string *S*.

`Get_Line(F,S,L);` reads successive characters from `F` into successive components of the `String` variable `S`. Reading stops when a line terminator is encountered, in which case `Skip_Line` is called; or earlier, when all components of `S` have been read into. In both cases, `L` is set to the index of the last component of `S` read into.

`Put_Line(F,`*S*`);` is equivalent to '`Put(F,`*S*`); New_Line(F);`'.

Example 15.3 ***A scheme for page-by-page processing***

In Example 6.3 we presented a scheme for line-by-line processing of an input text file. That scheme simply ignored the page structure of the input file (but otherwise was perfectly satisfactory). Here is a generalization of the scheme that takes into account the page structure of the input text file `F`:

```
prepare to read from F;
perform start-of-file processing;
while not End_of_File (F) loop
   perform start-of-page processing;
   while not End_of_Page (F) loop
      read and process the data on one line of F;
         -- at this point End_of_Line(F) should be True
      if not End_of_Page (F) then
         Skip_Line (F);
      end if;
   end loop;
   perform end-of-page processing;
   Skip_Page (F);
end loop;
perform end-of-file processing;
```

Note that it is essential to test `End_of_Page` before calling `Skip_Line`. When `End_of_Page` is `True`, an immediate `Skip_Line` would skip the following line terminator *and* page terminator, prematurely going on to the next page. '*Prepare to read from* F' could be Open(F,In_File,...) or Reset(F,In_File).

□ *End of Example 15.3*

Example 15.4 *String input-output*

Here is a concise way to copy a text file line-by-line, ignoring its page structure. It is assumed that no line is longer than 120 characters.

```
with Text_IO;  use Text_IO;
procedure Copy_Lines
            (Source_Filename, Dest_Filename : in String) is
   SF, DF : File_Type;
   Max_Line_Length : constant Natural := 120;
   Line_Text       : String (1 .. Max_Line_Length);
   Line_Length     : Natural range 0 .. Max_Line_Length;
begin
   Open (SF, In_File, Source_Filename);
   Open (DF, Out_File, Dest_Filename);
   while not End_of_File (SF) loop
      Get_Line (SF, Line_Text, Line_Length);
      Put_Line (DF, Line_Text(1..Line_Length));
   end loop;
end Copy_Lines;
```

□ *End of Example 15.4*

Enumeration input-output

Input-output of enumeration literals is provided by a generic package declared within Text_IO, namely Enumeration_IO.

The generic instantiation:

```
package ENUM_IO is new Text_IO.Enumeration_IO (ENUM);
```

instantiates a copy of the package Enumeration_IO suitable for text input-output of values of the enumeration type ENUM. The instantiated package looks like this (with some details omitted):

```
package ENUM_IO is
   procedure Get (File    : in File_Type;
                  Item    : out ENUM);
   procedure Put (File    : in File_Type;
                  Item    : in ENUM;
                  Width   : in Field := 0;
                  Set     : in Type_Set := Upper_Case);
end ENUM_IO;
```

where the following declarations are in Text_IO proper (but were omitted from the outline above for the sake of simplicity):

```
subtype Field is Integer range 0 .. implementation-defined;
type Type_Set is (Lower_Case, Upper_Case);
```

Here are brief explanations of the operations of `Enumeration_IO`:

`Get(F,E);` reads an enumeration literal from `F`. It first skips spaces, tabs, line and page terminators; then reads a sequence of characters that conforms to the syntax of an enumeration literal; then sets `E` to the corresponding value of type `ENUM`. The case of the letters is not significant.

`Put(F,`*E*`,`*W*`,`*S*`);` appends to `F` the characters of the enumeration literal corresponding to the value of *E*. If the literal occupies fewer than *W* columns, trailing spaces are appended to make up the difference. The letters are written in the case specified by *S*.

Integer input-output

Input-output of integer literals is provided by a generic package declared within `Text_IO`, namely `Integer_IO`.

The generic instantiation:

```
package INT_IO is new Integer_IO (INT);
```

instantiates a copy of the package `Integer_IO` suitable for text input-output of values of the integer type `INT` (which could be, for example, `Integer` or `Long_Integer`). The instantiated package looks like this (with some details omitted):

```
package INT_IO is
   procedure Get (File   : in File_Type;
                  Item   : out INT;
                  Width  : in Field := 0);
   procedure Put (File   : in File_Type;
                  Item   : in INT;
                  Width  : in Field := INT'Width;
                  Base   : in Number_Base := 10);
end INT_IO;
```

where the following declarations are to be found in `Text_IO`:

```
subtype Field is Integer range 0 .. implementation-defined;
subtype Number_Base is Integer range 2 .. 16;
```

and where `INT'Width` is the maximum number of characters in any `INT` literal.

Here are brief explanations of the operations of `Integer_IO`:

`Get(F,I,`*W*`);` reads an integer literal from `F`. If *W* is *zero*: it first skips spaces, tabs, line and page terminators; then reads a sequence of characters that conforms to the syntax of an integer literal; then sets `I` to the corresponding value of type `INT`. If *W* is *nonzero*: exactly *W* characters are read, including leading blanks and tabs (unless a line terminator is encountered first).

`Put(F,`*I*`,`*W*`,`*B*`);` writes an integer literal corresponding to the value of *I*. If the literal occupies fewer than *W* columns, *leading* spaces are written to make up the difference. If *B* is 10 (the default), an ordinary decimal literal is written, otherwise a based literal with base *B* is written.

The only really new feature here is the use of the `Width` parameter of `Get` to achieve fixed-format input.

Real input-output

Input-output of real literals is provided by two generic packages declared within `Text_IO`, namely `Float_IO` and `Fixed_IO`. These are broadly similar to `Integer_IO`, but we shall not discuss their details here, as that would drag in issues to be covered later, in Chapter 19.

Example 15.5 Fixed-format input

Typically, the transactions of Example 15.1 would be keyed in a fixed format, i.e., each item of data occupying fixed columns, as follows:

Columns 1–8:	account number.
Column 9:	'C' for a credit, 'D' for a debit.
Columns 10–16:	amount (in cents).
Columns 17–20:	year.
Columns 21–22:	month (1–12).
Columns 23–24:	day of month.

All numeric fields are right-justified. A debit transaction of $365 on account 33988559, dated 29 February 1984, would be input as 33988559D003650019840229.

Since consecutive numeric fields are not separated by spaces, care must be taken to read them as separate integers. The following procedure will read a single line from the standard input and return a record of the type `Transactions` declared in Example 15.1.

```
procedure Get_Transaction (Trans : out Transactions) is
   package Int_IO is new Integer_IO (Integer);  use Int_IO;
   Credit_Flag : Character;
begin
   Get (Trans.Acc_No, Width => 8);
   Get (Credit_Flag);
   case Credit_Flag is
      when 'C'      =>  Trans.Credit := True;
      when 'D'      =>  Trans.Credit := False;
      when others   =>  Skip_Line;  raise Data_Error;
   end case;
   Get (Trans.Amount, Width => 7);
   Get (Trans.Date.Year, Width => 4);
   Get (Trans.Date.Month, Width => 2);
   Get (Trans.Date.Day, Width => 2);
   Skip_Line;
end Get_Transaction;
```

□ *End of Example 15.5*

15.6. Input-output exceptions

A troublesome feature of input-output is the variety of things that can go wrong, for example attempting an impossible input or output operation, attempting to open a nonexistent file, or even malfunction of the hardware. All the input-output packages react to such an error by raising an appropriate exception. A program can anticipate and handle such errors by including appropriate exception handlers.

Most of the possible errors are common to all the standard input-output packages, so the exception declarations are collected into a single standard library package:

```
package IO_Exceptions is
    Status_Error : exception;
    Mode_Error   : exception;
    Name_Error   : exception;
    Use_Error    : exception;
    Device_Error : exception;
    End_Error    : exception;
    Data_Error   : exception;
    Layout_Error : exception;
end IO_Exceptions;
```

`Sequential_IO`, `Direct_IO` and `Text_IO` all contain renaming declarations for each of these, for example:

```
    Status_Error : exception
                        renames IO_Exceptions.Status_Error;
    Mode_Error   : exception
                        renames IO_Exceptions.Mode_Error;
```

so a program using `Sequential_IO`, `Direct_IO` or `Text_IO` need not refer explicitly to the package `IO_Exceptions`.

Here we shall briefly describe the circumstances under which each exception can be raised. If more than error arises at the same time, the first-named exception is the one that is raised.

`Status_Error` — is raised by operating on a file that is not open, or by attempting to open a file that is already open.

`Mode_Error` — is raised by attempting an operation inconsistent with the file's current mode.

`Name_Error` — is raised by `Create` or `Open` if the filename parameter is ill-formed.

`Use_Error` — is raised by attempting an operation that is impossible because of a property of the external file, for example writing to a read-only file.

`Device_Error` — is raised if the underlying hardware fails.

`End_Error` — is raised by attempting to read beyond the end of a file.

`Data_Error` — is raised in the enumeration and numeric input-output packages of `Text_IO` by attempting a `Get` when the input literal is not of the expected type, or its value is out of range. The same exception might also be raised in `Sequential_IO` or `Direct_IO` if the external file's elements are not of the required type.

`Layout_Error` is raised in `Text_IO` if any output operation cannot succeed because of a limitation on the number of columns per line or on the number of lines per page.

Example 15.5 illustrates a subprogram that might propagate an input-output exception. `Get_Transaction` contains a number of calls to `Get` to read integers from fixed fields. If any of the fields contains data that is not an integer literal, right-justified, or if the value of the integer literal is out of range, then `Get` raises `Data_Error`, which is in turn propagated by `Get_Transaction`. For consistency, `Get_Transaction` explicitly raises the same exception if column 9 contains any character other than 'C' or 'D'.

An example of using exception handlers to recover from input-output errors has already been given, see Example 14.1.

Exercises 15

15.1. Write a procedure that copies one sequential file to another. The two filenames are to be parameters. Assume that the first file contains elements of type `Items`, and that the second file does not already exist.

15.2. The heights of a group of people are provided in a sequential file named `HEIGHTS`, whose elements are of type `Float`. Write a procedure that computes their mean, median and standard deviation, and that also determines how many heights are within one standard deviation of the mean, how many are between one and two standard deviations of the mean, and how many are outside this range. (This is similar to a problem in Exercises 10, where definitions of 'median' and 'standard deviation' may be found. In this exercise, do not use an array to store the heights; the file may be read as often as desired.)

15.3. Implement the `Sort_Transactions` procedure of Example 15.1, (a) assuming that the number of transactions is small enough to be sorted in main memory; (b) using an 'external sort' algorithm [Knuth 1973].

15.4. Here is a more realistic file structure for the program of Example 15.2. Use a *pair* of direct files. The account records themselves are stored in the first file (in no particular order). Each element in the second file contains an account number and the index of

File 1

1	2	3	4	5	6
27371217 0	42925657 .... +50445	97732228 .... +4000	33988559 .... -99995	94287154 .... -7650	43113387 0

File 2

27371217 1	33988559 4	42925657 2	43113387 6	94287154 5	97732228 3

Fig. 15.2 A direct file with an indirect index

the corresponding account record in the first file. The elements in the second file are ordered by account number. See Figure 15.2. Modify the program along these lines, using the declaration:

```
procedure Update_Accounts_Interactively
                    (Acc_1_Filename, Acc_2_Filename : in String);
```

Use binary search to match an account number in the second file.

15.5. Write a procedure, with declaration:

```
procedure Concatenate
                    (Source_Filenames, Dest_Filename : in String);
```

that interprets `Source_Filenames` as a sequence of one or more filenames separated by ampersands, e.g., `"Part1&Part2&Appendix"`. The procedure is to write the concatenation of these text files to the existing file whose filename is `Dest_Filename`.

16

Program Design and Construction

16.1. Software development

Large programs

In previous chapters we have been concerned with the methodical use of Ada in designing and implementing relatively small programs. These are programs of a few hundred lines of source text, which an experienced programmer could expect to complete in a week or two. Our advice to you has been uncompromising: using the technique of stepwise refinement think carefully about your design, invent suitable abstractions, strive for a modular and readable program, and test and document it systematically. We believe that this approach will enable you to write programs that are correct, modifiable and efficient. The effort consumed by debugging, historically excessive, is kept under control by letting fewer errors creep into a program to start with, instead of weeding them out after the damage has been done.

So far, so good. Now we turn to the much more difficult problem of ***programming in the large***, where we attempt to design and construct programs, or systems of programs, containing many thousands of lines of source text. The difficulties that we encounter when programming in the small are magnified enormously when working in the large.

Very large programs must be written as a team effort, if they are to be completed in a reasonable amount of time. To the programming problem, therefore, is added the management problem of coordinating several (or many) programmers. At the extreme, a few systems containing millions of lines have been written. Their construction remains at the boundary of the possible.

Our aim in this chapter is much more modest. We discuss the design and construction of programs that are large, but not too large for individual programmers to tackle. Therefore we do not discuss the vital issues of project organization and management. From time to time, however, we shall point out features of Ada that are particularly relevant to team programming. (For many profound and witty insights into these topics, see [Brooks 1975].)

Large programs are disproportionately harder to write than small programs. This is because interactions between the parts of a program tend to vary as the square of its length, rather than linearly. For example, a 5000-line program would probably take much more effort than ten programs of 500 lines. It is clear that some discipline must be adopted to limit this explosive increase in difficulty if large programs are ever to written successfully. Ideally, the difficulty of writing a large program would vary linearly with its length, or as nearly so as possible. Small programs developed by stepwise refinement of the program text have essentially this linear property, but textual refinement on its own is not an adequate approach to programming in the large. (However, it remains an essential tactic for coping with the components of a large program, once these have been defined by other means.)

To be honest, we cannot recommend any approach to the design and implementation of large programs as confidently as we recommend textual refinement for programming in the small. Moreover, it is difficult to give a convincing example of the method we do recommend, if only because it would have to be a program comparable in length with this entire chapter! Bear with us then, as we briefly survey approaches to a methodology for programming in the large. We can do no more than give you an impression of the ideas that seem to us the most important, referring you to the literature for further details. In particular, our treatment of the subject is based on the work of Yourdon and Constantine. Their book on structured design [Yourdon 1978] is essential reading for anyone undertaking a large programming project.

The software life cycle

Software development starts with an idea in the mind of a potential *customer*, and ends (hopefully) with a computer solution satisfying the customer's requirement. Programming forms only a part of the effort that brings such a project to a successful conclusion. It is widely accepted that a *life cycle* applies to the development of any nontrivial software system. This cycle has the following stages:

- *Systems analysis and requirements definition.* A precise customer requirement is developed. The difficulty here is discovering exactly what the customer requires, especially if the latter is unfamiliar with the capabilities of computers and is unaccustomed to expressing a requirement with the necessary precision. Often a feasibility study is undertaken to check that the proposed system will be cost-effective.

- *System design.* The requirement has been stated in the customer's terms and must now be expressed in programmers' terms. In general a system of programs (or program components) will be needed. Each of these must be specified by detailing its inputs and outputs.

- *Program design.* Given its input-output specification, each program is designed down to the level of modules.

- *Program construction and testing.* The modules are written, tested and assembled.

- *Maintenance.* Since the customer requirement is always subject to change, the programs might later need to be modified. Changes will also be needed to correct errors discovered by the user. If the changes are radical, modifying the programs might be impractical; then the programs are obsolete, and the whole cycle begins again.

Only the last three steps constitute what we call *programming*.

The larger the project, the greater the importance assumed by systems analysis, requirements definition and system design. Indeed they can account for much of the effort put into a project. The analysis and design of large systems is a vast subject in its own right and not one we can do justice in this book. For a modern treatment, compatible with our recommendations on program design, see [Gane 1979] or [DeMarco 1979].

The maintenance phase of most software projects is much the most prolonged. It can be very costly unless great care has been taken to design the software with a view to ease of maintenance. For this reason we stress modifiability, along with correctness, as a primary criterion of good program design.

System documentation

The ***documentation*** of a software system consists of those supporting specifications and descriptions that are written for use before, during and after its development. Adequate documentation is essential both for the maintenance programmer and for the user. A system that is inadequately documented or whose actual behavior differs from its documentation is almost worthless in practice.

The principal forms of documentation are as follows.

- The ***customer requirement*** has already been mentioned. This is the document agreed between the customer and the systems analyst. It describes the system to be developed, in the customer's terms.
- The ***external specification*** is a precise definition of the system as a whole, expressed in terms of its inputs and outputs. This document is written by the systems analyst and used by the system designer. In general a system contains several programs (or program components), and the system designer produces an external specification for each of them in turn.
- The ***internal specification*** of a program (or program component) is a document written by the programmer who implements it, for the benefit of the programmer who must later maintain it. It should include a complete program outline and refinement history, with explanations for important design decisions, and summarized by a structure diagram. Most importantly it must include the source program itself, since only the source program is fully authoritative. This is why we have stressed the importance of good programming style — the maintenance programmer should not have to waste time trying to decipher an unreadable source text.
- The ***user manual*** is the document that the users of the system will need. It must define precisely what each program does, what inputs it accepts (including fine details such as layout, where appropriate), and what outputs are produced. The user manual should also cover what happens when incorrect input is supplied. If a program has known faults, it is honest and helpful to state what they are and under what circumstances they show up. It might also be appropriate to include some indication of time and memory requirements for running each program, and instructions for running it under the operating system.

All items of documentation should be clearly written, complete, unambiguous, accurate, timely and up-to-date. Writing documentation to this standard is as difficult as programming and should be undertaken with equal care. It is worth noting that many of the ideas that lead to readable programs also help in writing readable prose. The principles of modularity, localization, consistency and simplicity are particularly relevant.

16.2. Structured design

Data flow

On completion of systems analysis we have a requirement, stated in the customer's terms, and the external specification of a system to meet those requirements. In general, a suite of several programs will be necessary, and these programs will interact with several sets of data. Once the system designer has determined what data is initially available, and what must be generated by the system, the external specification for each program of the suite can be stated by detailing its inputs and outputs.

Suppose that we are asked to write one of these programs, given its external specification. What if the program is too large to be tackled by the methods of programming in the small? Our approach will be to decompose the program into several modules, each of a more manageable size. If a module turns out to be too big, it can be decomposed in the same way. This strategy is well known as 'divide and conquer'.

To be more precise about this, a *module* is a program construct that has a name and a well-defined boundary. In Ada several constructs qualify as modules: subprograms, packages and tasks. In this chapter we shall seldom concern ourselves with program components that are smaller than complete modules.

Perhaps you are wondering how this approach differs from stepwise refinement. Previously we have used stepwise refinement to derive the flow of *control* through the *statements* of a program. We now focus on the flow of *data* between the *modules* of a program. Just like control flow, data flow can be determined first in outline, then successively refined until an implementation becomes 'obvious'. This is essentially what is done to produce the system design and hence the program specifications, except that the system designer treats whole programs as basic operations. We on the other hand must decompose a program into modules, decompose the latter into smaller modules, and so on. As we shall see in the next section, Ada makes no fundamental distinction between a program and a module, so we shall speak only in terms of modules from now on.

It appears to be the case that in successful systems each module performs some identifiable transformation of specific inputs, thereby producing specific outputs. At that level of abstraction, the techniques used within a module to realize the transformation are not relevant. The modules can be treated as 'black box' components, and the design merely states the transformations they perform and the data flowing between them. Our methodology is based on this observation.

It is often convenient to display the data flow structure of a program in the form of a diagram. The traditional 'system flowchart' depicts program modules as boxes; the flow of data through the system is also shown, special shapes being used to distinguish input-output devices such as visual displays, line printers, keyboards, disks and tapes. The modern equivalent, the *data flow diagram*, abstracts from this mass of detail just the barest essentials: the *transforms* and the *data flows* between them.

The modular structure of a program (i.e., the assignment of its transforms to a set of modules) is *not* shown on its data flow diagram. Nor is the flow of control between modules depicted. Instead all transforms can be regarded as being active at once. The only sequencing constraint implied by a data flow diagram is the obvious one that a transform using a data item must wait until that data item reaches it.

As an example, Figure 16.1(1) is the data flow diagram for a program to meet the requirement of Case Study I or II. The input is a text file of names in any order, and the output is to be a text file containing the same names, lexicographically ordered.

Each input or output text (which forms an interface between the program and the outside world) is shown in the data flow diagram as a double square, suggesting a document. Each transform is shown as a circle or rounded rectangle. Each data flow is indicated by a labeled arrow directed from the producer of the data to its receiver.

In Figure 16.1(1), input text flows into 'get names', a transform that extracts a name from each line of the input text. The names flow on to 'sort names internally'. Note that the list of names, being purely an internal matter for 'sort names internally', does not appear in the diagram. 'Sort names internally' outputs names in lexicographic order. The names flow on to 'put names', which outputs a text with one name per line.

Imagine a data flow diagram pulsing as an invisible heart pumps data around it. At each pulse some transform must receive an input or produce an output, but they need not all do so. Indeed some transforms might need several pulses before accumulating enough input to start work, and more pulses before producing any output. The transform 'sort names internally' in Figure 16.1(1) has both properties: it must receive at least two names before it can start to sort them, and it must receive them all before it starts to output them in lexicographic order.

Data flow diagrams are deliberately unspecific about the data flows. The inputs and outputs of each transform are stated purely in terms of their information content. The data flow diagram does *not* specify input-output media, file names or formats, record layouts, or data representations. (There *is* a place for such specifications: in the program's ***data dictionary***, a separate document that describes each data item to an appropriate level of detail [Gane 1979].)

It might seem that data flow diagrams are so abstract as to be of little use either as

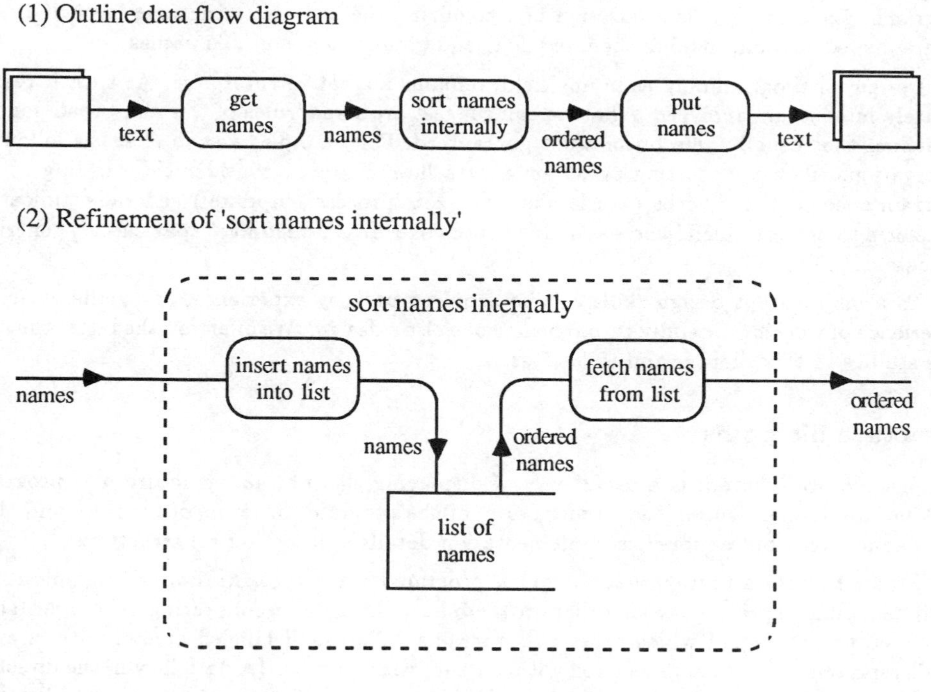

Fig. 16.1 Data flow diagrams for `Sort_Names`

a design tool or as documentation. In fact it is precisely because the data flow diagram is highly abstract that it complements stepwise refinement of the program text so well. The latter is essentially concerned with the systematic management of a great many detailed design decisions. The data flow diagram, by contrast, suppresses these details and so exposes the essential structure. At the start of a project, when you first grapple with the design of a program, it can be difficult to see the relationships between the various aspects you must consider. The data flow diagram provides a framework within which you can set ideas, without tempting you to express yourself in terms of a particular implementation. There is a converse problem during implementation and maintenance: it can be hard to perceive the overall structure of a large program if you have access only to its textual details. A data flow diagram displays the 'big picture'.

Just as we can develop a program text by stepwise refinement, so too we can refine a data flow diagram. Each transform in a top-level diagram can be refined to show its internal data flows. The resulting hierarchy of data flow diagrams vividly depicts the evolving abstractions on which the design of the program is based.

In Figure 16.1(2) we give one possible refinement for the transform 'sort names internally'. The open-ended rectangle appearing at the center of this diagram represents a *data store* — a repository of data items that may be either permanent (like a database) or temporary (like a local variable of a subprogram). In this example, the data store is the list of names being sorted.

Splitting up a program into a set of transforms and data flows is the first step in program design. This can be regarded as an extension of system design into the domain of individual programs. Essentially, it is a question of recognizing the abstract structures implicit in the program specification, making them explicit, and giving them suitable names.

Design, in programming as in any field, remains a creative enterprise. As such it resists a purely intellectual analysis. What we can suggest are some 'rules of thumb', broad general guidelines that usually help but are not guaranteed. For example, we can offer the following observation. To get a starting point for a data flow diagram, consider the wording of the program specification. Verbs (words like 'analyze', 'process', 'update') generally indicate a transform to be performed, whereas nouns (words like 'data', 'readings', 'pay check') generally indicate data flows.

To a large extent design skills can be acquired only by experience, or by the vicarious experience of working carefully through someone else's design. We offer you the latter through case studies in this chapter and thereafter.

Structure diagrams

A structure diagram is a useful way of displaying the internal structure of a program. A structure diagram shows the 'architecture' of the program, in terms of modules and their interconnections, but suppresses implementation details such as control structures.

Figure 16.2 is a structure diagram of the program `Multiply_Matrices` of Example 12.11. Each rectangle represents a subprogram module. The arrows connecting rectangles show which subprograms call which other subprograms. The small labeled arrows with circular heads represent data flows associated with the subprogram calls. (A data flow in the direction of the call corresponds to an `in` parameter in Ada, and a data flow in the opposite direction corresponds to an `out` parameter or function result.)

Further conventions are needed to display the structural characteristics of more complicated programs. A thick arrow originating inside one module and pointing *inside* a second module indicates a direct reference to a variable local to the second module. Data flows associated with the reference are shown by small labeled arrows, in the same manner as data flows associated with a call. See Figure 16.3(a), which is a structure diagram of the program `Sort_Names` of Case Study I. The subprograms `Make_List_Empty`, `Insert` and `Write_All_Names` all contain direct references to the variables that represent the list of names (i.e., `List` and `Size`), which are local to the main-program module `Sort_Names`. They suggest a messy design, and indeed we have already stressed its defects.

The improved version of this program in Case Study II has quite a different structure: the list of names is now local to the package module `Sort_Service` rather than local to `Sort_Names`. This structure is displayed in Figure 16.3(b). The box with curved ends represents a data module — in this case the list of names — data that is not local to any subprogram. (This corresponds to a data store in a data flow diagram.) Arrows pointing to the curved box represent direct references to the data object; data flows associated with these references are also shown. Each large rectangle represents the boundary of a package module. Note that the boundary of `Sort_Service` reveals the subprograms `Make_List_Empty`, `Insert`, and so on (so that they may be called outside the package), but hides the data object representing the list of names itself.

Designing modules

Assume that we have a data flow diagram. The next step is to design a structure diagram displaying the modular structure of the program and the interconnections between the modules. This amounts to deciding how the transforms that appear in the data flow diagrams will be realized in terms of modules. We can realize several transforms with one, general module; or we can realize one transform by one module; or we can use several modules to realize one transform. In practice all three groupings are useful.

Many authors have proposed criteria for making these decisions. The 'Jackson technique' [Jackson 1974] is one perspective on the problem: the idea is to base the structure of the program on the structure of its data. If the input and output have similar structures (as in

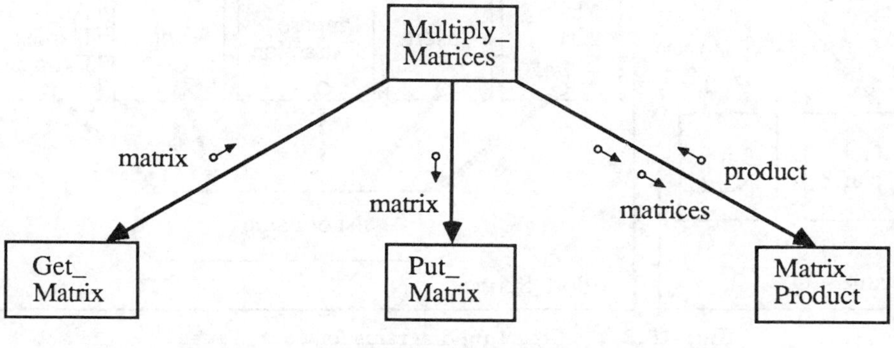

Fig. 16.2 Structure diagram for `Multiply_Matrices`

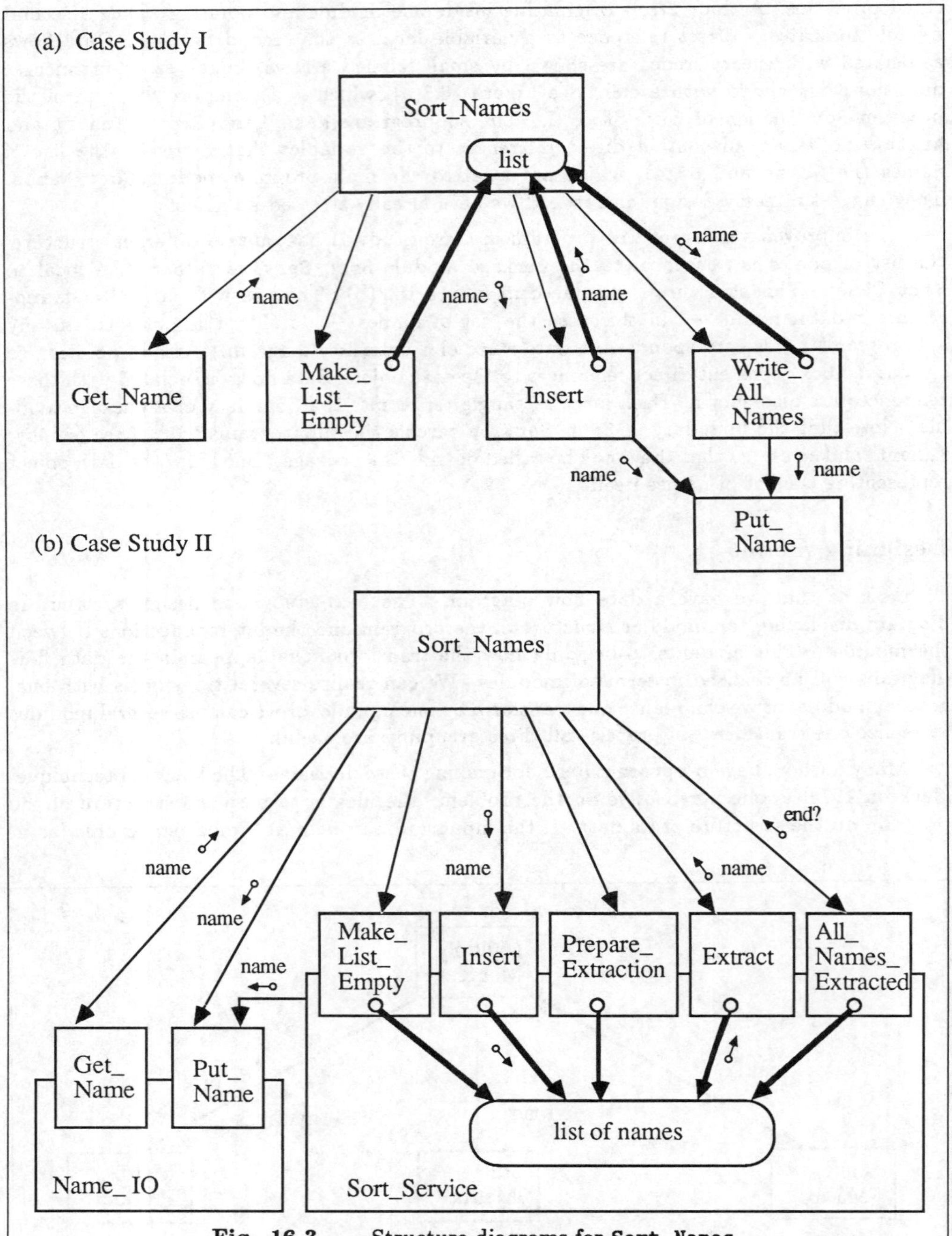

Fig. 16.3 Structure diagrams for `Sort_Names`

many simple data-processing programs) then the program structure follows directly; otherwise there is a 'structure clash' and the program has to be broken down into components that resolve the structure clash.

A more recent methodology is 'object-oriented design'. Here the idea is to study the requirement systematically in order to identify 'objects' (data structures) and operations on these objects, and then to design the program in terms of packages that encapsulate these objects and their operations.

We shall combine these ideas with the approach of Yourdon and Constantine [Yourdon 1978]. Observing that the quality of a design is related to the ease with which the program can be implemented, tested and modified, Yourdon and Constantine suggest that the program should be composed of modules that are small, implementable individually, testable individually, modifiable individually, and that bear a simple relationship to some aspect of the application. Now these criteria are somewhat subjective and difficult to define, so Yourdon and Constantine propose two technical criteria that can be defined more precisely. These criteria are ***coupling*** and ***cohesion***.

Coupling is concerned with interconnections between modules. In a structure diagram, the arrows represent some (but not all) of these interconnections. A module `A` is said to be ***tightly coupled*** to another module `B` if it has many dependencies on `B`, or if any of these dependencies are complex. `A` is ***loosely coupled*** to `B` if it has few, simple dependencies on `B`. In general, all else being equal, a loosely coupled design is preferable to a tightly coupled design. Of course coupling cannot be avoided altogether: the modules of a program must cooperate in some way! The more tightly modules are coupled, however, the more difficult they will be to implement, test and modify individually.

A loose form of coupling occurs when one module calls another. Each data flow that accompanies the call tightens the coupling a little, for now both modules must agree on the type and direction of the data flow. This form of coupling is called ***normal coupling***, for it occurs in every nontrivial program and is relatively harmless.

If one module contains a direct reference to any entity (e.g., data object or type) that is declared in another module, then the modules are coupled to each other by that reference: a change to the second module might well cause the first module to fail. How tight this coupling is, however, depends on the nature of the reference. We shall discuss references to types, constants and variables.

If the entity referred to is a ***type*** or a ***constant***, and moreover is referred to only by its name, `X`, then the coupling is loose: the details of the declaration of `X` can be changed without affecting the module that refers to it. On the other hand, if the referring module uses information gleaned from the declaration of `X` then the coupling is tighter: the declaration of `X` cannot be changed without affecting the referring module. Consider, for example, the type `Names` in Case Study II (not shown in Figure 16.3(b)). Although `Sort_Service` uses `Names` to declare various parameters and objects, its only assumption about the declaration of `Names` is that assignment and the relational operators are valid for this type. This is loose coupling. On the other hand, `Name_IO` does assume complete information about the declaration of `Names`. This is tighter coupling. If a module simply refers to the name of a constant declared in another module, that is loose coupling. But if it makes any assumption about the constant's ***value***, that would be tighter coupling.

We shall use broken arrows in structure diagrams to represent references to constants and types. Such an arrow ending at the edge of a box indicates a reference to the constant or type by name only; an arrow pointing into the box indicates some assumption about the constant's or type's declaration.

This discussion has important implications for packages that define and export types. A package that exports a visibly defined type permits other modules to be quite tightly coupled to it; a package that exports a private type permits only looser coupling; and a package that exports a limited private type permits only very loose coupling, since only the type name and operations exported by the package are available to the referring modules.

Likewise, when a *variable* is declared in one module and referred to by another module, the more information that is assumed about the variable's structure by the referring module, the tighter the coupling. However, references to nonlocal variables are fundamentally different from references to nonlocal constants and types. When two or more modules refer to a common variable, they *all* become tightly coupled to one another, as well as to the module where the variable is declared. There is a potential data flow from every one of these modules to every other one, through the common variable, so the modules must all depend on common assumptions about how the variable is updated. This is called ***common-environment coupling***. A typical example of common-environment coupling occurs in Figure 16.3(a). Three of the subprograms are tightly coupled to one another and to the main-program module through their common references to the list of names. Worse still, there is nothing (other than discipline on the programmer's part) to prevent *all* the modules becoming coupled in this way, whether by accident or by design.

The issue of common-environment coupling is closely related to the visibility rules of the programming language. Languages like BASIC *force* all variables to be global and thus positively encourage common-environment coupling. In languages like PL/I and Pascal, the situation is better because variables declared within a module are not accessible outside that module; but there is nothing to prevent any module from referring to variables declared in an enclosing module, regardless of the designer's intentions. This can happen in Ada too, but Ada offers the alternative of packages, which allow access to a common group of variables to be suitably restricted. In Figure 16.3(b), all the subprograms of the `Sort_Service` package are tightly coupled to one another through their common access to the list of names. This coupling is inevitable. However, no possibility exists for the coupling to extend to any other part of the program. Further, the `Sort_Service` module *as a whole* is only loosely coupled to the rest of the program.

Unlike coupling, ***cohesion*** is a property of an individual module. A module is said to be ***strongly cohesive*** if it is responsible for a single function. A module that is responsible for two or more distinct functions is said to be ***weakly cohesive***. A weakly cohesive module could probably be split into two or more modules, each of which would be smaller, simpler, and therefore easier to implement, test and modify. A few examples should clarify this.

Each of the subprograms in Figure 16.2 and Figure 16.3(b) is responsible for a single function — `Get_Name` for input of names, `Insert` for insertion of names into the list, and so on; therefore they are strongly cohesive. Most of the subprograms in Figure 16.3(a) are also strongly cohesive; but `Write_All_Names` is responsible for two functions, extracting names from the list and output of names. These functions are related only in the sense that they happen to be interleaved in time. This is a rather weak form of cohesion. As a further example, suppose that we 'simplify' the package `Sort_Service` by combining the functions of the two subprograms `Make_List_Empty` and `Prepare_Extraction` into a single subprogram, `Initialize_List`, and replace the calls to these two subprograms by a single call to `Initialize_List`. The new subprogram possesses a very weak form of cohesion, since it performs two unrelated functions. This lack of cohesion has a practical consequence: it is no longer possible for a program incorporating `Sort_Service` to traverse the same list of names more than once.

Now consider how we can assess the cohesion of a package module, as opposed to the cohesion of individual subprogram modules within the package. (This issue is not treated in [Yourdon 1978].) Just as a subprogram module is strongly cohesive if it supports a single function, so a package module is strongly cohesive if it supports a single *abstraction*. This could be an abstract data structure, such as the directory supported by `Directory_Service` in Example 13.6, or the list of names supported by `Sort_Service` in Case Study II. Alternatively it could be an abstract data type, such as the type `Directories` exported by `Multi_Directory_Service` in Example 13.8. Each of these packages provides all and only the resources needed to support its own abstraction; therefore each package is strongly cohesive. A package that groups together a collection of loosely related data or subprograms (such as `Math_Functions` in Example 13.3) exhibits a weaker but still useful degree of cohesion. The difference here is that the grouping is convenient rather than essential. As a last example, a package that exported a `Sin` function, a definition of a data type called `Complex`, and a collection of constants for metric conversion, would exhibit very weak cohesion.

A good rule of thumb is that the function of a cohesive module can be described succinctly in a single sentence: 'module `M` does A'. If you are forced to describe your module's function in terms such as 'module `M` does A if C', or 'module `M` does A and B', or worse still 'module `M` does A followed by B', that is a likely indication of weak cohesion.

Incidentally, cohesion is a good criterion for judging complete programs too. Some of the 'utility' programs provided by certain vendors are notoriously difficult to use, precisely because they provide a rag-bag of assorted functions.

It is time to summarize our approach to program modularity. A good design is one in which the program is composed of modules that are small and easy to implement, test and modify individually. This is achieved by minimizing the degree of coupling between modules and maximizing the cohesion of individual modules. Where tight coupling in a group of modules cannot be avoided, it is likely that they ought to be formally grouped in a package: internal coupling in a package is more manageable than coupling between separate modules.

[Yourdon 1978] describes techniques ('transform analysis' and 'transaction analysis') for deriving a program's structure diagram, more or less systematically, from its data flow diagram. The essence of these techniques is that they lead to a design with the following characteristics: (a) each transform of the data flow diagram is usually embodied in a single module; and (b) these transform modules are subordinated to 'coordinate modules' that serve only to control the sequencing of calls on the transform modules and the flow of data between them.

For example, compare the data flow diagram of program `Sort_Names` (Figure 16.1) and its structure diagram (Figure 16.3(b)). Each transform appears as a single module in the structure diagram:

Transform	*Module*
get names	`Get_Name`
put names	`Put_Name`
insert names into list	`Insert`
fetch names from list	`Extract`

These modules are coordinated by the main-program module, `Sort_Names`, which controls the sequencing, the flow of data from `Get_Name` to `Insert` and the flow of data from `Extract` to `Put_Name`. (*Exercise*: consider how the coupling and cohesion of the design would be affected by alternative ways of achieving these data flows; for example if `Get_Name` called `Insert`, or *vice versa*, or if these two subprograms communicated directly through a global variable.) The remaining modules are concerned with initialization (`Make_List_Empty` and `Prepare_Extraction`) or with termination (`All_Extracted`). They do not correspond to anything in the data flow diagram, precisely because data flow diagrams are not concerned with such issues. This illustrates the fact that the structure diagram cannot in general be derived automatically from the data flow diagram. However, the data flow diagram serves as a guide to the design, in that for every transform and for every data flow there must be a corresponding feature in the structure diagram.

Program construction and testing

Let us now consider how we can exploit a well structured design to implement and test the modules of a program individually. The advantages should be evident. Modules can conveniently be assigned to the individual programmers of a team; and a large program is far more likely to be tested thoroughly if the modules from which it is composed can be tested individually as well as together.

The traditional modular programming strategy is to implement and test the modules *independently*, followed by a final integration phase when the complete program is assembled from its components. This strategy has important defects:

- Design and interface errors tend not to be discovered until the integration phase, late in the project, when they are most costly to correct.
- An elaborate testing environment must be devised for every single module, so that it can be tested independently of its neighbors in the structure diagram.

The strategy we recommend instead is *incremental* construction and testing, whereby the program is constructed gradually by adding a module at a time. The testing of each module is facilitated by using modules that have already been tested. This simplifies the problem of creating a test environment for each module, allows design and interface errors to be discovered and corrected as early as possible, and eliminates the distinct integration phase.

When a module `M` is to be tested before the module that eventually will call `M` is available, we need a *driver module* to test `M`. This is a temporary module that simply calls `M`, supplying suitable test inputs, and displays `M`'s outputs.

When a module `M` is to be tested before all its subordinates are available, we need a *surrogate module* (sometimes called a *stub*) in place of each of the missing subordinates. A surrogate is a temporary version of the missing module, presenting the same interface to `M`. In Ada terms, each surrogate module must have a (subprogram or package) declaration identical to that of the module it temporarily replaces. What a surrogate module should actually *do* is a matter of convenience. It might do nothing at all, or it might display its own name (to confirm that it has been called) and its inputs, or it might actually perform the intended function of the module using some quick-and-dirty algorithm.

Example 16.1 *Incremental testing of* `Sort_Names`

The design displayed in Figure 16.3(b) consists of a main-program module, `Sort_Names`, and two package modules, `Name_IO` and `Sort_Service`. In what order should we test these modules? If we were to test the main-program module first, we would need surrogates for all the other modules; and since `Get_Name` produces an output value (a name read from the input text) we would face the problem of making the surrogate `Get_Name` return a sensible output value. In fact, the surrogate `Get_Name` would be no easier to implement than the final version.

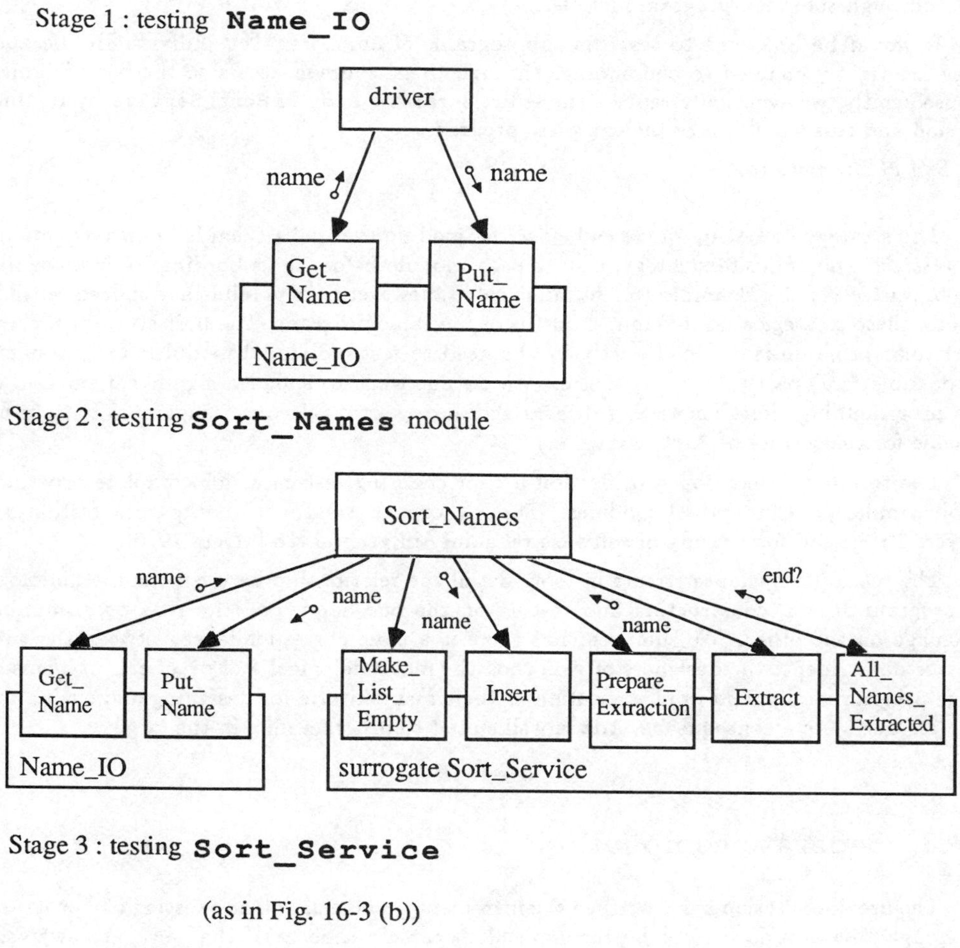

Fig. 16.4 Incremental testing of `Sort_Names` (Case Study II)

Therefore we start by testing `Get_Name` with a driver. Since this driver will have to display each name read by `Get_Name`, we might as well test the whole of the package module `Name_IO`. Its driver should incorporate the declaration and body of `Name_IO`, and it could (for example) call `Get_Name` and `Put_Name` alternately, allowing the output text to be compared with the input text. See Figure 16.4, stage 1.

Next we could test the main-program module, using the already-tested `Name_IO` and a surrogate version of `Sort_Service`. Each subprogram of the latter could display its own name, and `Insert` could also display its input parameter. `Extract` and `All_Extracted` are to produce outputs, always a problem for surrogate modules. We could make them constant outputs, or possibly we could generate random outputs. In any case, we would use the final version of `Sort_Service`'s package declaration together with a surrogate package body. See Figure 16.4, stage 2. This test would allow us to check the flow of control and the flow of data through the main-program module.

It would be awkward to test the subprograms of `Sort_Service` individually, because they are tightly coupled to one another through their common access to the list of names. Consequently, we eventually replace the entire surrogate body of `Sort_Service` by its final version and test what is now the complete program.

□ *End of Example 16.1*

The strategy of testing modules before the module that calls them is known as ***bottom-up testing***. The opposite strategy, testing each module before its subordinates, is known as ***top-down testing***. As Example 16.1 has illustrated, however, it is possible and indeed sensible to mix these strategies for different modules of the same program. The best strategy for any particular program is dictated partly by the need to test individual modules as thoroughly as possible, and partly by convenience. We do not want to spend a significant portion of the programming effort on writing drivers and surrogates! (*Exercise*: suggest a bottom-up scheme for the testing of `Sort_Service`.)

The techniques mentioned in Section 5.2 for choosing test cases for complete programs apply similarly to individual modules. For a thorough treatment of program testing see [Myers 1979], and for a study of software reliability in general see [Myers 1976].

The rest of this chapter treats in more detail the relationship between the methodology of program design, construction and testing on the one hand, and the Ada programming language on the other. We shall see that there is a close correspondence between the two. This is no accident: the designers of Ada took the methodological and practical problems of large program design and implementation as their main criteria for designing and evaluating the language. As a consequence, Ada is well suited to programming in the large.

16.3. Separate compilation

The previous section has described the incremental construction and testing of a program. Although this approach is to be recommended, certain aspects of the work are awkward when the program is a single text. Firstly, each new module has to be edited into the existing (partially completed) program text, perhaps replacing a surrogate module used in earlier testing. Secondly, modules that have already been tested, and are believed to be correct, nevertheless will be repeatedly recompiled, without change, every time the rest of the program is recompiled.

One of the most important features of Ada is the way it allows programs to be put together from a number of source texts that have been compiled separately from one another. The texts compiled on a single occasion are known collectively as a ***compilation***. Each compilation is a sequence of one or more ***compilation units***. A compilation unit is a separately compiled declaration or body of a package or subprogram (treated in Section 16.4), or a subunit (treated in Section 16.6).

When compiled successfully, each compilation unit is added to a ***program library*** nominated by the programmer. Units stored in a program library can be used as components of several programs. A particular object program is obtained by linking together its component units. One of these will be the ***main-program unit***, which will be a subprogram. (Most of the examples in this book are parameterless procedures, but a main-program unit could be a function and/or have parameters.) Of course, a small program might well consist of a main-program unit alone.

Facilities for creating and updating program libraries are not defined as part of the Ada language. They are the concern of the ***Ada Programming Support Environment*** (***APSE***), which is essentially an operating system oriented to the development and maintenance of Ada programs. A description of an APSE is beyond the scope of this book. (Unlike the Ada language itself, there is no standard for the APSE.) Nor does the Ada language specify how a program is invoked; that depends on the run-time system.

What benefits do we get from separate compilation? The traditional answer is that separate compilation reduces the computer time needed to develop and maintain a large program, by reducing the amount of text that must be re-compiled when part of the program is changed. This argument is less convincing in an era of fast computers and efficient compilers. However, not every programmer is blessed with these modern conveniences, and certainly there are truly enormous programs that tax the capabilities of the most powerful programming systems.

A deeper answer is that separate compilation allows a program to be built from a number of relatively small texts, instead of one large text. All the benefits derive from this.

Small source texts are generally easier to handle than large ones. This applies not only to compilation: many software tools such as editors, cross-referencers and syntax checkers will work better, and more reliably, on small texts.

Equally important is the human element. It is a lot easier for the members of a programming team to work on their own separate source texts, than for them all to coordinate their access to a single, shared source text. This alone makes separate compilation almost essential in large projects. On an equally practical level, incremental program construction and testing are greatly simplified by separate compilation.

It might seem paradoxical, but separate compilation encourages the sharing of useful subprograms and packages among programmers (who might not even be working on the same project). As long as your best work lies hidden inside a large program it is tedious to dig it out and make it widely available. But when modules of general utility are written and compiled separately, in conjunction with a program library facility, releasing them to your colleagues is comparatively easy. In this way separate compilation can help to reduce the enormously wasteful duplication of effort that mars the software industry.

Finally, and perhaps most importantly, separate compilation in Ada encourages the designer of a program to give it a highly modular (loosely coupled) structure. Because of the discipline that Ada imposes on separate compilation units, it is harder to introduce an unnecessary coupling between two modules of a program when they are represented by physically separate texts than when they are part of the same compilation unit.

In older languages such as FORTRAN it was possible to compile subprograms independently of each other and of the main program. However, the linking together of the compiled modules into a complete executable program was done by a program (variously called a linkage editor, binder, or loader) that had no knowledge of the interfaces defined in the source program. So it was possible, for example, to call a function defined with an array formal parameter and supply instead a scalar actual parameter. The resulting disasters can be imagined!

No similar danger exists in Ada. The separate compilation facility is part of the language, and is defined in such a way that no consistency checks need be sacrificed. This is achieved through the medium of the program library. An Ada compiler stores in the program library not only the compiled code of a compilation unit, but also declarative information that allows the compiler to check any references that one compilation unit makes to another. The key point is that Ada provides for *separate* compilation, not *independent* compilation.

In order to achieve full consistency checks at reasonable cost Ada imposes a discipline on the use of separate compilation. The rule is simply this: if compilation unit `A` is required to be visible from compilation unit `B`, then `A` must be compiled before `B`. By this means the compiler is assured that the declarative information needed to check `B`'s references to `A` will be available in the program library when `B` is compiled.

16.4. Library units and secondary units

In this section we consider subprograms and packages that can be compiled completely separately from the rest of the program(s) in which they are to be incorporated. Typical examples are subprograms and packages of wide utility, such as standard input-output packages or packages of common mathematical functions.

Such a subprogram or package is added to the program library by supplying its declaration as a compilation unit, and later its body as a compilation unit. A subprogram or package *declaration* supplied as a compilation unit is called a ***library unit***: it serves to define the interface between the subprogram or package and the rest of the program. A subprogram or package *body* supplied as a compilation unit is called a ***secondary unit***: it serves to define the executable code of the corresponding library unit.

Once a library unit has been compiled, it can be made visible to another compilation unit by means of a *with clause*. For example, '`with Text_IO;`' in the context clause of a compilation unit `U` tells the compiler that the previously-compiled library unit `Text_IO` is required by `U`. The declaration of `Text_IO` will be used by the compiler to check all references in `U` to entities exported by `Text_IO`, and the object code of the body of `Text_IO` (a secondary unit) will be linked into the program of which `U` forms a part.

See the syntax diagram 'context_clause' in Appendix A. The context clause precedes the declaration or body in a compilation unit. Its with clause(s) name all the library units that are to be made visible. If any of them is a package, the context clause may optionally include a use clause that makes the package's exported components directly visible.

In a context clause each previously-compiled library unit is referred to by its identifier. Therefore all the library units in a given program library must have distinct identifiers.

The context clause prefixing a compilation unit declares its dependence on other library units. The compiler needs this information, of course, but it is also helpful to a human reader who is trying to form a picture of the coupling between the modules of a program. Only those library units mentioned in the context clause of a compilation unit are visible within the compilation unit. Conversely, only those identifiers declared in the subprogram or package declaration of a library unit are visible to other compilation units. By careful use of these facilities the Ada program designer can exert fine control over the coupling between the compilation units of a program. It follows that separate compilation in Ada is a powerful way of documenting and *enforcing* (by compiler checks) the modular program structure intended by the designer.

In the following examples we adopt the convention that compilation units are submitted in the order given, though not necessarily in a single compilation.

Example 16.2 A separately-compiled subprogram

In Example 12.4 we illustrated a program that assumed the existence of a library function, Sqrt, which it called to calculate the square root of a real number:

```
with Sqrt;
with Text_IO;  use Text_IO;
procedure Demonstrate_Complex is
   ...  Sqrt (...)  ...
end Demonstrate_Complex;
```

The following compilation units supply a (somewhat naive) version of this library function:

```
function Sqrt (X : Float) return Float;

function Sqrt (X : Float) return Float is
   Root : Float := X / 2.0;
begin  -- approximate square root by Newton's method
   while abs (X - Root**2) > 2.0 * X * Float'Epsilon loop
      Root := (Root + X / Root) / 2.0;
   end loop;
   return Root;
end Sqrt;
```

Once the declaration of Sqrt has been compiled it is possible to compile Demonstrate_Complex; the body of Sqrt can be compiled at any time after its declaration.
□ *End of Example 16.2*

As a matter of fact, compiling the body of a subprogram alone is sufficient to declare it. It is not actually necessary to compile both its declaration and its body.

Example 16.3 Separately-compiled packages

A package **Auto_Dialing_Service** is required to provide facilities for calling remote computers, through a modem and auto-dialing hardware. It is to make use of the **Directory_Service** package of Example 13.6 to look up telephone numbers and the **Modem_Data** package of Example 13.1 to operate the modem. The intended structure is shown, in outline, in Figure 16.5. We can see that there is to be an interface between **Auto_Dialing_Service** and the other two packages, but no interface between **Directory_Service** and **Modem_Data**.

The following is a legal, but careless, attempt to realize this structure in Ada.

```
package Auto_Dialing_Service is
    exported subprogram declarations;
    package Directory_Service is
        as before
    end Directory_Service;
    package Modem_Data is
        as before
    end Modem_Data;
end Auto_Dialing_Service;

package body Auto_Dialing_Service is
    internal declarations;
    package body Directory_Service is
        as before
    end Directory_Service;
    subprogram bodies;
```

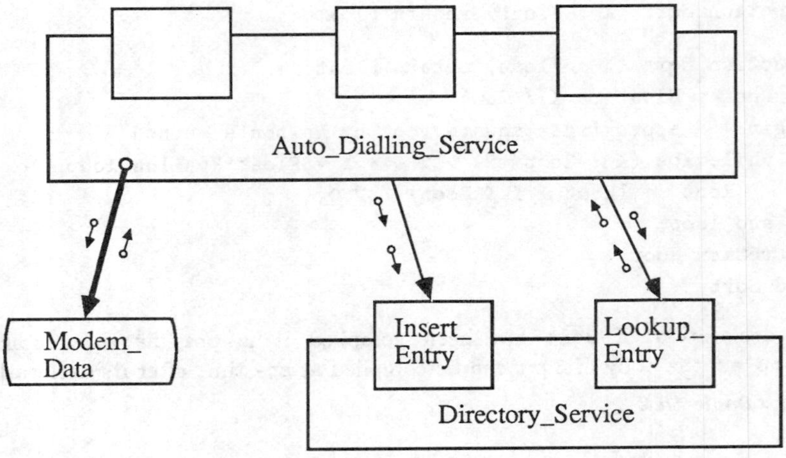

Fig. 16.5 Outline structure diagram for **Auto_Dialing_Service**

```
end Auto_Dialing_Service;
```

Compiled in this way, Modem_Data and Directory_Service are not library units and are therefore available only to programs that incorporate the whole of Auto_Dialing_Service. Moreover, there is the major disadvantage that the intended program structure is not achieved. The operation of Ada's visibility rules sets up the following interfaces (potential couplings) between Auto_Dialing_Service and its components:

- The subprograms exported by Auto_Dialing_Service are visible within Directory_Service and within Modem_Data.
- Directory_Service is visible not only within Auto_Dialing_Service, but also within Modem_Data.
- Modem_Data is visible not only within the body of Auto_Dialing_Service, but also within the body of Directory_Service.
- The internal declarations of the body of Auto_Dialing_Service are visible within the body of Directory_Service.

There are seven interfaces in all, whereas only two are wanted. The five extra interfaces are presumably unused. Nevertheless their presence is undesirable. A program text should, as far as practicable, say exactly what the programmer intends. If you were given the job of maintaining Auto_Dialing_Service you would have to read it through completely, and in detail, to verify that only two of the seven interfaces are in fact used.

A more insidious danger is that you might exploit the extra interfaces (perhaps inadvertently) as an easy way to implement a 'quick fix'. The author of Auto_Dialing_Service has tempted you to undermine the modular design of the package.

By means of separate compilation it is possible to get rid of all the unwanted interfaces and the threat they pose to the maintainability of the package. In the following compilation units the structure depicted in Figure 16.5 is actually achieved:

```
package Modem_Data is
   as before
end Modem_Data;

package Directory_Service is
   as before
end Directory_Service;

package body Directory_Service is
   as before
end Directory_Service;

package Auto_Dialing_Service is
   exported subprogram declarations;
end Auto_Dialing_Service;

with Modem_Data;  use Modem_Data;
with Directory_Service;  use Directory_Service;
package body Auto_Dialing_Service is
   internal declarations;
   subprogram bodies;
end Auto_Dialing_Service;
```

Since `Modem_Data` and `Directory_Service` have empty context clauses, neither has any possible dependency on any other module. The context clause of the body of `Auto_Dialing_Service` makes explicit its dependency on `Modem_Data` and `Directory_Service` (to be more precise, on their declarations).

When a library unit has a context clause, all identifiers made visible by the context clause are visible in the corresponding secondary unit (a body) as well as in the library unit itself (a declaration). Consequently, the context clause in front of the body of `Auto_Dialing_Service` could alternatively have been put in front of its declaration, allowing `Modem_Data` and `Directory_Service` (and their components) to be referenced both within the declaration and within the body of `Auto_Dialing_Service`. Since only the body needs to refer to them, however, the above placement of the context clause is preferable: the declaration of `Auto_Dialing_Service` can be compiled independently of all the other program units. In particular, it is not necessary for the declarations of `Modem_Data` and `Directory_Service` to have been compiled previously. (They must, though, be compiled before the *body* of `Auto_Dialing_Service`.) Once the declaration of `Auto_Dialing_Service` has been compiled, it too can be named in the context clauses of further compilation units and so incorporated in a complete program.

□ *End of Example 16.3*

It has probably occurred to you by now that the writing and testing of library units and the corresponding secondary units, followed by their use in the construction of higher-level modules, is a natural way to put into practice the ideas of bottom-up construction and testing. The following case study illustrates this relationship between language and methodology.

16.5. Case Study III: text formatting

Requirement

A word-processing facility is required as part of the office information system mentioned in Section 14.6. In the first instance, a program is needed to reformat a natural-language text. The formatted text is to be written in paragraphs, and the lines are to be adjusted so as to give straight left and right margins.

The input text is in free format, successive words being separated by one or more spaces or line terminators. Every punctuation mark immediately follows a word, with no intervening spaces or line terminators. To indicate the start of a new paragraph the special word `/PAR/` is used. `/PAR/` need not be the first word of the input text. It is never followed by punctuation. No word of the input text (including any punctuation) is longer than 20 characters.

The formatted text consists of lines within which successive words are separated by one or more spaces. Any punctuation mark must follow the preceding word directly, with no intervening spaces or line terminators. Each line is to be adjusted, if necessary, by distributing additional spaces between the words as evenly as possible. (The output device cannot space more finely than the standard character pitch.) As many words as possible are to be written in each line, but no word may be split between two lines.

Each paragraph must start on a new line, indented from the left margin by four spaces. The last line of a paragraph and the last line of the entire text are not to be right-adjusted.

The formatting program is to be a procedure with a parameter that specifies the width of the output field, i.e., the number of character pitches between the left and right margins, which will not be greater than 80. The program is to ensure that the output field width is sufficient to adjust a line containing two of the longest allowed words.

Analysis

The requirement, as stated, leaves a number of issues unresolved.

- What is to be done if the specified output field width is too small or too large? (We shall make the program propagate the exception `Constraint_Error`.)
- What is to be done if an input word is longer than allowed? (We shall truncate it to the maximum length and discard the excess characters.)
- Where is the input text to be read from? (We shall read from the standard input.)
- Where is the formatted text to be written? (We shall write to the standard output.)

In practice questions like these would be settled by discussion with the customer.

Design

This is one of those problems where a little study of the requirement reveals possibilities for simplification. The requirement is stated in terms of words and punctuation, but in fact any punctuation that follows a word immediately in the input text will also follow the word immediately in the formatted text. Thus it is convenient to treat any such punctuation as part of the word. Let us define a ***token*** as any sequence of consecutive nonblank characters. The input text then is a sequence of tokens separated by spaces and line terminators. A token is either a paragraph marker (if its spelling is `/PAR/`) or a word (possibly with attached punctuation).

These considerations lead to the outline data flow diagram of Figure 16.6(1). The input text is first transformed, by 'get tokens', into a stream of tokens (and the spaces and line terminators that separate them are discarded); the tokens are then input to the transform 'generate reformatted text'.

We can now refine the transform 'get tokens'. A text is a two-dimensional object, but analysis into tokens will be more convenient if we first transform the text into a one-dimensional stream of characters, line terminators being replaced by spaces (which are equivalent in this application). Hence the refinement of 'get tokens' shown in Figure 16.6(2).

The refinement of 'generate reformatted text' is more difficult. It is clear, however, that each word cannot be written out immediately, since a whole line of text will have to be transformed (by distributing extra spaces between words) whenever a new word fails to fit into the line. Therefore we introduce a data store to contain a (partial) line of text. Words and spaces will be added to this line until either a new word cannot be fitted in (in which case the line will be written with adjustment) or the end of the text or paragraph is reached (in which case the line will be written without adjustment); in either case the line will then be emptied. These considerations are reflected in the refinement of 'generate reformatted text' in Figure 16.6(2).

The outline data flow diagram suggests that an appropriate design would be to specify a module responsible for the getting of tokens, say `Token_Handler`, a module responsible for the reformatting of the text, say **Line_Handler**, and a main-program module to coordinate the first two, say **Format_Text**. We should like these three modules to be compiled and tested individually, rather than having the two subordinate modules nested inside the main-program module. However, there are a number of constants that influence the external behavior of the program and are therefore of global effect, for example the maximum word size, the spelling of the paragraph marker, and so on. It will be convenient to group these in a fourth module, a package that will be compiled first:

```
package Format_Definitions is
   Max_Token_Size : constant Positive := 20;
   Space          : constant Character := ' ';
   Para_Mark      : constant String := "/PAR/";
   Para_Indent    : constant String := "    ";  -- 4 spaces
   Min_Field_Width : constant Positive
                  := Para_Indent'Length + 2*Max_Token_Size + 1;
   Max_Field_Width : constant Positive := 80;
end Format_Definitions;
```

Other modules that depend on these global constants will nominate **Format_Definitions** in their context clauses.

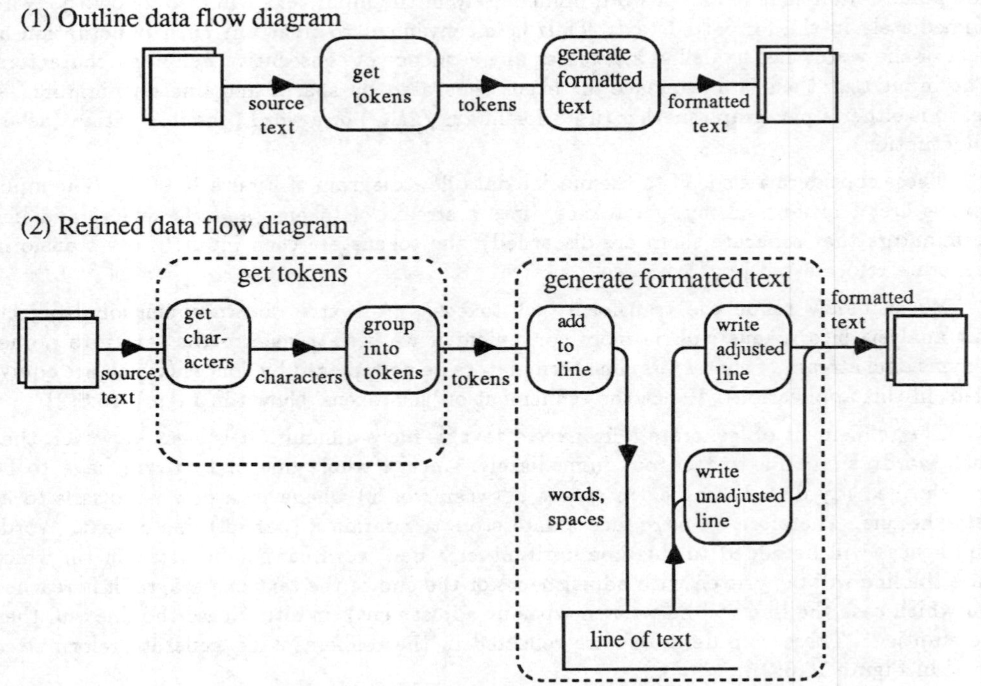

Fig. 16.6 Data flow diagrams for **Format_Text**

We now turn to the design of the main-program module, `Format_Text`. It is to be a procedure with an in parameter that specifies the desired field width. Hence its declaration is:

```
procedure Format_Text (Field_Wanted : in Integer);
```

Without starting the implementation of `Format_Text`, we can deduce what resources it will require from the modules `Token_Handler` and `Line_Handler`, and hence specify these modules.

Consider `Token_Handler` first. It is clear that it must export a subprogram, `Get_Next_Token` say, to get the next token from the input text. We have already identified two different kinds of tokens — word tokens and paragraph tokens. Since the main-program module will have to know when the end of the input text has been reached (so that it can cause the last line of the formatted text to be written), we can make `Token_Handler` present a clean interface to the main-program module by adding a third kind of token, one that corresponds to the end of the input text. Now the problem is to decide how each token should be made available to the calling module for inspection: paragraph tokens and end-of-file tokens are completely described by their kind, but a word token additionally has a size and spelling. One possibility is for `Get_Next_Token` to have an out parameter that is a record consisting of a kind, a size and a spelling, on the understanding that the latter two components are to be ignored unless the token is a word. A slightly cleaner design is to make `Get_Next_Token` parameterless, and to export functions that return, respectively, the kind of the last token read, its size (if it is a word), and its spelling (if it is a word). Adopting this solution, we have the following declaration of `Token_Handler`:

```
with Format_Definitions; use Format_Definitions;

package Token_Handler is

   type Token_Kinds is (Word_Token, Para_Token, EOF_Token);
   subtype Token_Sizes is Natural range 0 .. Max_Token_Size;

   procedure Get_Next_Token;

   function Kind_of_Token return Token_Kinds;
   function Size_of_Word  return Token_Sizes;
      -- assumes that Kind_of_Token = Word_Token
   function Text_of_Word  return String;
      -- assumes that Kind_of_Token = Word_Token

end Token_Handler;
```

Note that we have used comments to state explicitly the preconditions that must hold when `Size_of_Word` and `Text_of_Word` are called.

This design has the advantages that the size and spelling of the word are not returned to the calling module unless they are actually needed; and that the spelling is returned as a variably-sized string, avoiding conventions such as padding out to fill a fixed-sized string. (This is possible because a function or parameter, unlike a variable, may be of an unconstrained array type.)

Now we turn to `Line_Handler`. This is to encapsulate a data structure that contains a (partial) line of text. From the data flow diagram we can see that `Line_Handler` must export a subprogram to add a word or spacing to the line, and subprograms to write the line with and without adjustment. Additionally it must export a subprogram to set the field width and a subprogram to make the line empty. (These are initializations and do not appear in the data flow diagram.) Finally, the logic of the main-program module will require it to know whether a word of a given size will fit into the current line, so a subprogram to answer this question is also to be exported. These considerations lead to the following declaration:

```
package Line_Handler is
    procedure Set_Field_Width (Field_Wanted : in Integer);

    procedure Make_Line_Empty;
    procedure Append_to_Line (Appendage : in String);
       -- assumes that Line_has_Room_for (Appendage'Length)
    function Line_has_Room_for (Size_Wanted : Positive)
             return Boolean;
    procedure Write_Adjusted_Line;
    procedure Write_Unadjusted_Line;

end Line_Handler;
```

Our design is summarized by the structure diagram of Figure 16.7.

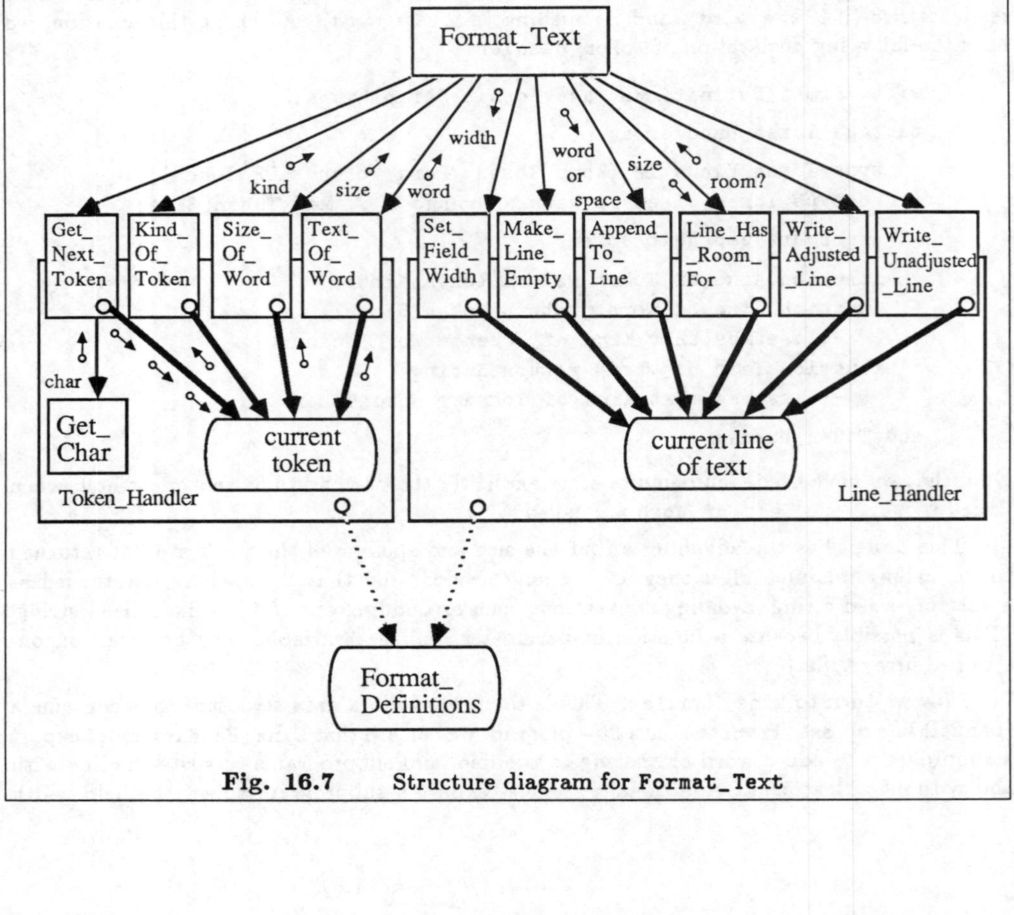

Fig. 16.7 Structure diagram for `Format_Text`

Bottom-up construction and testing

We have a program design, displayed in the structure diagram and also formally specified in Ada terms. We can now compile the library units `Format_Definitions`, `Token_Handler` and `Line_Handler` (and also the declaration of `Format_Text`, if desired).

What remains is to implement the modules `Token_Handler`, `Line_Handler` and `Format_Text`, by writing, compiling and testing their bodies. They can be *compiled* in any order at all, but no module can be *tested* until we have compiled a body for each module on which it depends. In this case the bodies of both `Token_Handler` and `Line_Handler` must be compiled before `Format_Text` can be tested. A suitable strategy is to write, compile and test each of the package modules with a driver, and finally to write, compile and test `Format_Text`.

Let us start with `Token_Handler`. Since `Kind_of_Token`, `Size_of_Word` and `Text_of_Word` are to return data about the latest token read by `Get_Next_Token`, the package must encapsulate a representation of the token. The only problem here is the variable length of the token's spelling. Fortunately the requirement allows us to assume an upper limit on the size of a word, given by the constant `Max_Token_Size` of the library package `Format_Definitions`. Thus we can use a string variable with that number of characters. However, `Text_of_Word` should return only the significant substring of this variable.

In line with the refinement of 'get tokens' in Figure 16.6(2), `Token_Handler` should contain a local subprogram, `Get_Source_Char`, that reads and returns a single character, or skips a line terminator and returns a space, as the case may be. This simplifies the logic of `Get_Next_Token`.

The programming of `Token_Handler` can now be completed straightforwardly, by stepwise refinement. Only the complete solution is given here, for the sake of brevity.

```
with Text_IO;  use Text_IO;
package body Token_Handler is
   Token_Kind : Token_Kinds;
   Token_Size : Token_Sizes;
   Token_Text : String (1 .. Max_Token_Size);
   procedure Get_Source_Char (Char : out Character) is
   begin
      if End_of_Line then
         Skip_Line;
         Char := Space;
      else
         Get (Char);
      end if;
   end Get_Source_Char;
   procedure Get_Next_Token is
      Char : Character;
   begin
      -- skip spaces preceding the next token --
      loop
         if End_of_File then
            Token_Kind := EOF_Token;
            return;
```

```
            end if;
            Get_Source_Char (Char);
            exit when Char /= Space;
         end loop;
         -- read the token text --
         Token_Size := 0;
         loop
            if Token_Size < Max_Token_Size then
               Token_Size := Token_Size + 1;
               Token_Text(Token_Size) := Char;
            end if;
            Get_Source_Char (Char);
            exit when Char = Space;
         end loop;
         if Token_Text(1..Token_Size) = Para_Mark then
            Token_Kind := Para_Token;
         else
            Token_Kind := Word_Token;
         end if;
      end Get_Next_Token;
      function Kind_of_Token return Token_Kinds is
      begin
         return Token_Kind;
      end Kind_of_Token;

      function Size_of_Word  return Token_Sizes is
      begin
         return Token_Size;
      end Size_of_Word;

      function Text_of_Word  return String is
      begin
         return Token_Text(1..Token_Size);
      end Text_of_Word;

   end Token_Handler;
```

It is easy to write a driver module to test **Token_Handler**. The driver can call **Get_Next_Token** repeatedly. For each token read, it writes the token kind and (if a word) its size and spelling.

Let us now turn to the module **Line_Handler**. This encapsulates a data structure that represents a line of text. Since we know that no line can be longer than **Max_Field_Width** characters, a string variable with that number of components will suffice, together with a count of the actual size of the current partial line. All the subprograms of **Line_Handler** are straightforward to write, with the exception of **Write_Adjusted_Line**.

We need to devise an algorithm that will distribute extra spaces between the words in the current line so as to increase the line size up to the field width. Let us call this number of spaces **Extra**, and the number of inter-word gaps **Gap_Count**; both are easy to compute. Now the necessary widening of each gap is approximately **Extra/Gap_Count**; the difficulty is that we are working with integers, and we cannot in general widen every gap by the same amount. However, we can use this expression to compute the widening of each gap, *provided* that we reduce Extra by the amount of the widening, and reduce Gap_Count by one, before going on to the next gap. For example, if there are 10 extra spaces to be distributed among 4 gaps, the widening of successive gaps will be:

1. 10/4 = 2 spaces;
2. (10-2)/(4-1) = 8/3 = 2 spaces;
3. (8-2)/(3-1) = 6/2 = 3 spaces;
4. (6-3)/(2-1) = 3/1 = 3 spaces.

The refinement is as follows:

```
procedure Write_Adjusted_Line is
   declarations of Left, Right, Extra, Gap_Count, Widening;
begin
   make Left and Right the positions of the
      leftmost and rightmost nonspaces in the line;
   make Gap_Count the number of gaps in the line;
   Extra := actual field width - Right;
   for each position Pos in the line (up to Right) loop
      if there is an gap at Pos then
         Widening := Extra / Gap_Count;
         write Widening+1 spaces;
         reduce Extra by Widening;
         reduce Gap_Count by 1;
      else
         write the character at Pos;
      end if;
   end loop;
   New_Line;
end Write_Adjusted_Line;
```

To see that this algorithm does indeed distribute exactly the correct number of spaces among the gaps, note that at the last gap Extra will have been reduced to the number of extra spaces not yet distributed and Gap_Count will have been reduced to 1. Then Extra/Gap_Count will be equal to Extra, thus accounting for all the remaining extra spaces.

The remaining refinement of Write_Adjusted_Line is straightforward, so we can now complete the implementation of Line_Handler.

```
with Format_Definitions;  use Format_Definitions;
with Text_IO;  use Text_IO;

package body Line_Handler is
   subtype Field_Widths is
         Positive range Min_Field_Width .. Max_Field_Width;
   subtype Line_Sizes is
         Natural range 0 .. Max_Field_Width;
   subtype Line_Positions is
         Positive range 1 .. Max_Field_Width;

   Actual_Field_Width : Field_Widths;
   Line_Size : Line_Sizes;
```

```
Line_Text : String (Line_Positions);
procedure Set_Field_Width (Field_Wanted : in Integer) is
begin
   Actual_Field_Width := Field_Wanted;
end Set_Field_Width;
procedure Make_Line_Empty is
begin
   Line_Size := 0;
end Make_Line_Empty;
procedure Append_to_Line (Appendage : in String) is
   New_Line_Size : constant Line_Sizes
            := Line_Size + Appendage'Length;
begin
   Line_Text(Line_Size+1..New_Line_Size) := Appendage;
   Line_Size := New_Line_Size;
end Append_to_Line;
function Line_has_Room_for (Size_Wanted : Positive)
      return Boolean is
begin
   return (Line_Size + Size_Wanted <= Actual_Field_Width);
end Line_has_Room_for;
procedure Write_Unadjusted_Line is
begin
   Put_Line (Line_Text(1..Line_Size));
end Write_Unadjusted_Line;
procedure Write_Adjusted_Line is
   Extra, Gap_Count, Widening : Line_Sizes;
   Left : Line_Positions := 1;
   Right : Line_Positions := Line_Size;
begin
   -- make Left and Right the positions of the
   --  leftmost and rightmost nonspaces in the line --
   while Line_Text(Left) = Space loop
      Left := Left + 1;
   end loop;
   while Line_Text(Right) = Space loop
      Right := Right - 1;
   end loop;
   -- make Gap_Count the number of gaps in the line --
   Gap_Count := 0;
   for Pos in Left .. Right loop
      if Line_Text(Pos) = Space then
         Gap_Count := Gap_Count + 1;
      end if;
   end loop;
   Extra := Actual_Field_Width - Right;
   for Pos in 1 .. Right loop
```

```
          if Pos > Left and then
              Line_Text(Pos) = Space then
              -- there is an gap at Pos
              Widening := Extra / Gap_Count;
              for J in 1 .. Widening + 1 loop
                  Put (Space);
              end loop;
              Extra := Extra - Widening;
              Gap_Count := Gap_Count - 1;
          else
              Put (Line_Text(Pos));
          end if;
      end loop;
      New_Line;
  end Write_Adjusted_Line;

end Line_Handler;
```

Line_Handler is concerned with output. Output modules are often most conveniently tested top-down, but this particular one can easily be tested bottom-up. What is needed is a driver program that is capable of calling the subprograms of Line_Handler in a variety of sequences. The driver could be written to allow the programmer to choose interactively which subprogram to call next, and to supply its parameters. This technique has the advantage of allowing the module's robustness to be tested, if desired, with sequences of calls that should never arise from Format_Text itself. For example, Append_to_Line could be tested with a parameter string that is too long to fit into the current line.

The following hypothetical dialog should clarify this idea. The programmer's responses are distinguished; ◇ represents a space.

```
Type    S for Set_Field_Width          E for Make_Line_Empty
A for Append_to_Line              R for Line_has_Room_for
J for Write_Adjusted_Line     U for Write_Unadjusted_Line

Operation? S    Width_Wanted? 32
Operation? E
Operation? A    Appendage? Familiarity
Current line is:  "Familiarity"
Operation? A    Appendage? ◇
Current line is:  "Familiarity "
Operation? A    Appendage? breeds
Current line is:  "Familiarity breeds"
Operation? A    Appendage? ◇
Current line is:  "Familiarity breeds "
Operation? A    Appendage? contempt.
Current line is:  "Familiarity breeds contempt."
Operation? U
Familiarity breeds contempt.
Operation? J
Familiarity   breeds   contempt.
```

```
Operation? A      Appendage? Proverb.
Exception CONSTRAINT_ERROR raised in APPEND_TO_LINE
```

(*Exercise*: write a driver module that conducts such a dialog, and test Line_Handler.)

Having tested all the subordinate modules, the last step is to write, compile and test the main-program module Format_Text. Essentially it is a loop that repeatedly fetches a token and acts on it. In the case of a word token, it is essential to check whether the word will fit into the current line before actually appending it; if not, the current line must be written with adjustment and a fresh line started before appending the word. After that, a single space is appended to provide the minimum separation between this word and the next one (if any). In the case of a paragraph token, the current line is written without adjustment, and four spaces are appended to a fresh line. In the case of an end-of-file token, the current line is written without adjustment, and the program terminates.

```
with Format_Definitions;  use Format_Definitions;
with Line_Handler;  use Line_Handler;
with Token_Handler;  use Token_Handler;

procedure Format_Text (Field_Wanted : in Integer) is
begin
   Set_Field_Width (Field_Wanted);
   Make_Line_Empty;
   loop
      Get_Next_Token;
      case Kind_of_Token is
         when Word_Token =>
            if not Line_has_Room_for (Size_of_Word) then
               Write_Adjusted_Line;
               Make_Line_Empty;
            end if;
            Append_to_Line (Text_of_Word);
            if Line_has_Room_for (1) then
               Append_to_Line (" ");
            end if;
         when Para_Token =>
            Write_Unadjusted_Line;
            Make_Line_Empty;
            Append_to_Line (Para_Indent);
         when EOF_Token =>
            Write_Unadjusted_Line;
            return;
      end case;
   end loop;
end Format_Text;
```

This can be compiled and then tested with the previously-tested Token_Handler and Line_Handler. The program is then complete.

16.6. Subunits

The advantages of separately compiling a package or subprogram have already been emphasized. For a module S to be compilable as a library unit, however, it is necessary that S does not refer to any higher-level module P in the structure diagram. Any such coupling would make it impossible to compile S before the higher-level module, as Ada requires. If such a coupling exists, the declaration of S must be nested within the higher-level module. This nested position allows S to import identifiers declared within P without formality.

It is possible, however, to arrange for the *body* of a nested program unit S to be compiled separately. Such a separately-compiled body is known as a *subunit* and the unit within which it is nested is known as its *parent unit*. In the parent unit only the declaration of S and a *body stub* are present. The body stub replaces the body in the parent unit and informs the compiler that the body is to be compiled separately.

Here is an example of a package body stub:

```
package body Comms_Control is separate;
```

This would follow the package declaration of `Comms_Control` and would inform the compiler (and the reader) that the body of this package is to be compiled separately and later.

Here is an example of a subprogram body stub:

```
procedure Transmit_Reply (Reply : String) is separate;
```

This indicates that the body of the procedure `Transmit_Reply` (which might or might not have been previously declared) is to be compiled separately. See the syntax diagram 'body_stub' in Appendix A.

The identifiers visible within a subunit are just those that would be visible to a nested body inserted in the parent unit at the place of the body stub. Therefore the use of subunits makes no difference to the *logical* structure of a program.

Every body compiled as a subunit must be preceded by a clause of the form:

separate (*parent_unit_*name)

This tells the compiler which compilation unit is the parent of the subunit, so that the compiler can retrieve from the program library details of identifiers declared inside the parent unit and visible at the body stub. The subunit must be declared at the highest level of its parent unit, and not within any nested program unit it might contain.

The parent unit may itself be a subunit. Therefore the *parent_unit_*name is given in general by a fully qualified name starting at the name of a library unit. The parent unit of each subunit must be compiled before the subunit itself. This rule, together with information obtained from `separate` clauses and the program library, makes it possible to deduce the logical structure of the program unambiguously, so that subunits can be subjected to the same rigorous compile-time checks as nested units.

Example 16.4 *Package subunits*

The following is a reworking of Case Study II, using subunits to split up the text for compilation. Note how much clearer the `Sort_Names` procedure is, now that the details of the package bodies are given elsewhere.

```
with Text_IO; use Text_IO;
```

```
procedure Sort_Names is
   subtype Names is String (1 .. 20);
   package Sort_Service is
      procedure Make_List_Empty;
      procedure Insert (New_Name : in Names);
      procedure Prepare_Extraction;
      procedure Extract (Old_Name : out Names);
      function All_Extracted return Boolean;
   end Sort_Service;

   package Name_IO is
      procedure Get_Name (Name : out Names);
      procedure Put_Name (Name : in Names);
   end Name_IO;

   use Sort_Service, Name_IO;
   Current_Name : Names;
   package body Sort_Service is separate;
   package body Name_IO is separate;
begin
   Make_List_Empty;
   while not End_Of_File loop
      Get_Name (Current_Name);  Skip_Line;
      Insert (Current_Name);
   end loop;
   Prepare_Extraction;
   while not All_Extracted loop
      Extract (Current_Name);
      Put_Name (Current_Name);  New_Line;
   end loop;
end Sort_Names;

separate (Sort_Names)
package body Sort_Service is
   as before
end Sort_Service;

separate (Sort_Names)
package body Name_IO is
   as before
end Name_IO;
```

□ *End of Example 16.4*

Subunits allow for the separate compilation of program units that are too specialized to be suitable as library units. Such units can arise when subdividing modules that are strongly cohesive but are too large for convenience. For example, a large package body can be divided among several programmers by means of subunits. They are also convenient when we want to postpone working out the low-level details of an algorithm, but still want to be able to construct a complete compilation unit.

Example 16.5 *Subprogram subunits*

In Section 13.5 it was suggested that the Sort_Names program could be made to cope with a changed input format by suitable amendments to the procedures Get_Name and Put_Name of the Name_IO package. Let us recast the body of Name_IO so as to anticipate this change and make it easy to put into effect.

```
separate (Sort_Names)
package body Name_IO is
   function Transformed_Name (Name : Names) return Names
            is separate;
   function Reformed_Name (Name : Names) return Names
            is separate;
   procedure Get_Name (Name : out Names) is
      Original_Name : Names;
   begin
      read Original_Name from a single line of input;
      Name := Transformed_Name (Original_Name);
   end Get_Name;
   procedure Put_Name (Name : in Names) is
   begin
      Put (Reformed_Name (Name));
   end Put_Name;
end Name_IO;
```

The initial versions of Transformed_Name and Reformed_Name just return the given name without alteration:

```
separate (Sort_Names.Name_IO)
function Transformed_Name (Name : Names) return Names is
begin
   return Name;
end Transformed_Name;

separate (Sort_Names.Name_IO)
function Reformed_Name (Name : Names) return Names is
begin
   return Name;
end Reformed_Name;
```

Now, when we want to enhance Sort_Names, we need only write and compile the new versions of Transformed_Name and Reformed_Name, replacing the old versions in the program library. The rest of Sort_Names need not be changed in any way.

Note that we have had to declare these functions in a wider scope than is methodologically desirable, because of the rule that subunits must be declared at the highest level of their parent unit.

□ *End of Example 16.5*

We saw in Section 16.4 that building a program from library units corresponds closely to the discipline of bottom-up construction and testing. Now we have a similar correspondence to explore between the use of subunits and the top-down discipline. That is an important theme of the following case study.

16.7. Case Study IV: alternative vote elections

Requirement

In an election held under the alternative vote system, the successful candidate must gain an absolute majority of the votes cast, even when there are more than two candidates. Each voter must complete a ballot by ranking *all* the candidates in order of preference. When the votes are first counted, only the first choice of each voter is taken into account. If there is no overall majority for any candidate, the candidate who has gained the fewest votes is eliminated from the contest. A recount then takes place in which each vote cast for the eliminated candidate is re-assigned to the benefit of the next-choice candidate. Eliminations and recounts continue in this fashion until one candidate accumulates an overall majority (or until all the candidates remaining have exactly equal votes, in which case the election has been tied).

For example, suppose the votes cast in a three-candidate election are as follows:

Voter A	3	1	2
Voter B	2	3	1
Voter C	2	1	3
Voter D	1	3	2
Voter E	2	1	3
Voter F	3	2	1
Voter G	1	3	2
Voter H	3	1	2
Voter I	2	3	1

where the candidates have been numbered 1, 2 and 3 for identification, and where voter must specify a first, second and third choice (in that order). On the first count, candidates 1, 2 and 3 receive (respectively) 2, 4 and 3 votes. As there is no overall majority, candidate 1 is eliminated. On the recount the second choices of voters D and G are taken into consideration. The recount results in candidates 2 and 3 receiving (respectively) 4 and 5 votes. Candidate 3 is therefore the winner.

A program is required that will process an alternative vote election. The program is to report the winner of the election, or a list of the remaining candidates in the event of a tie. The program is to be a procedure with a parameter that is the number of candidates. In the first instance, the candidates are identified by the numbers 1, 2, ..., and each ballot will be presented as a single line of input, on which the candidates are listed in order of preference, as in the example above. However, changes in the form of the ballot are to be anticipated. (For example, each candidate might be identified by name instead of by number, or the ballot itself might be given as the rank assigned to each candidate.)

The program must ignore invalid ballots. A ballot is valid if every candidate has been placed in exactly one position in the ranking. (For example, with three candidates, '2 1 2' and '3 1 4' are invalid ballots).

Analysis

The requirement leaves several things unstated or unclear:

- What is the source of the input ballots? (We shall assume the standard input file.)
- Where is the report to be written? (We shall assume the standard output file.)
- What is to be done if, after any count, there is no winner and several candidates tie for last place? (Consulting the rules for this kind of election, we find that any one of the last-placed candidates may be eliminated.)
- How exactly is each ballot to be interpreted after several candidates have been eliminated? (Consulting the rules again, we find that the most-preferred candidate on the ballot who has not already been eliminated is to receive a vote from that ballot. For example, if the ballot contains '3 1 2 4' and candidates 1 and 3 have already been eliminated, then candidate 2 receives the vote.)

Design

It is clear from the requirement that the ballots are liable to be scanned repeatedly, once on each count or recount, so it will be necessary to store the ballots. While doing this we might as well throw away all the invalid ballots so that only valid ones reach the counting stage. Thus the input ballots will pass through a transform 'store valid ballots' into a 'ballot store'.

It is easy to identify another transform, 'count votes', that inspects the stored ballots and counts the votes for each candidate still in contention. The set of candidates still in contention will therefore be a second input to this transform. There is no need for this transform to output the actual vote counts. Instead, it should output the outcome of the count, (i.e., whether there is a clear winner, a tie, or neither); and either the identity of the winner(s) or the identity of the last-placed candidate (as the case may be). In the event of a clear winner or tie, the identity of the winner(s) must be sent to a transform, 'announce result', that produces the final report. Otherwise, the identity of the loser must be sent to a transform, 'eliminate loser', that removes the unfortunate candidate from the set of candidates still in contention.

This suggests a data-flow diagram like that in Figure 16.8. The data store 'ballot store' allows the valid ballots to be retrieved as often as required. The data store 'state of the poll' gathers together data about the poll, namely the set of candidates still in contention, the outcome of the latest count, and the identity of the winner or loser on the latest count.

Top-level design

The data flow diagram of Figure 16.8 maps almost directly on to a top-level structure diagram for this program: see Figure 16.9(1). Each of the four transforms becomes a subprogram. The subprograms are coordinated by the main-program module, `Find_Election_Result`, which will be a procedure with an in parameter, the number of candidates. The subprograms `Store_Valid_Ballots` and `Count_Votes` will refer to the 'ballot store', and the subprograms `Count_Votes`, `Eliminate_Loser` and `Announce_Result` will all refer to the 'state of the poll'. We can avoid allowing the main-program module to refer directly to the 'state of the poll', provided that `Count_Votes` returns an indication of whether a result has been obtained or not; details of the result itself can be kept in the data store. This avoids complicating the main-program module with the details of the result, which depend very much on the kind of result (clear win or tie). The four subprograms are collected in a package `Count_Handler` in order to encapsulate the data stores, thus reducing the potential coupling in the program.

Top-down construction and testing

The algorithm of the main-program module must be as follows. First, store the valid ballots. Then repeatedly count the votes and eliminate the losing candidate, until a count produces a result.

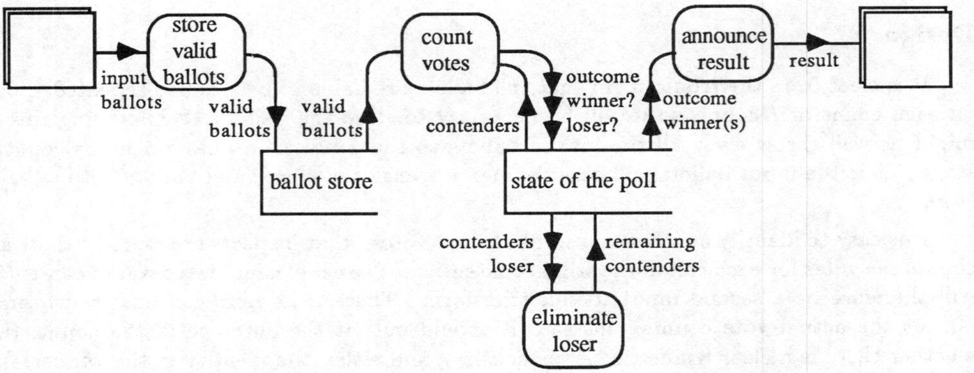

Fig. 16.8 **Data flow diagram for `Find_Election_Result`**

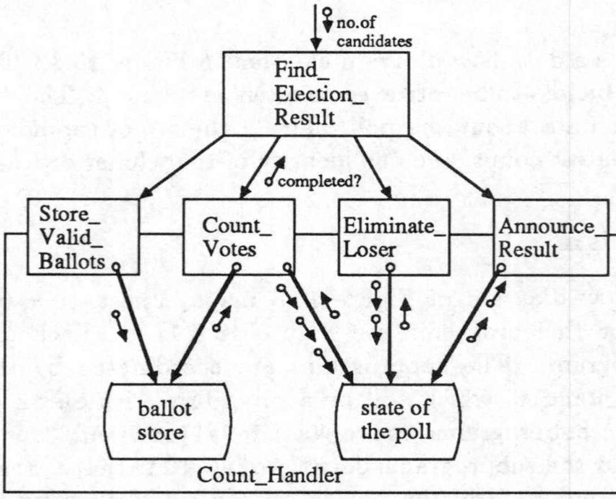

Fig. 16.9 **(1) Structure diagram for `Find_Election_Result`**

The package Count_Handler will have to be (logically) nested within the main-program unit, since its internal logic must depend on the number of candidates, which is a parameter to the main program. In order to keep the main-program unit concise, however, let us choose to compile the package body separately. Therefore the main-program unit will be:

```
with Text_IO;  use Text_IO;
procedure Find_Election_Result (Nr_Candidates : in Positive) is
   Election_Completed : Boolean;
   package Count_Handler is
      procedure Store_Valid_Ballots;
      procedure Count_Votes (Result_Obtained : out Boolean);
      procedure Eliminate_Loser;
      procedure Announce_Result;
   end Count_Handler;
   use Count_Handler;
   package body Count_Handler is separate;
begin
   Store_Valid_Ballots;
   loop
      Count_Votes (Election_Completed);
      exit when Election_Completed;
      Eliminate_Loser;
   end loop;
   Announce_Result;
end Find_Election_Result;
```

This unit can be compiled as it stands, and tested if we also supply a surrogate body for Count_Handler.

The next step is to implement the body of Count_Handler. This module is centered on two data stores.

The 'state of the poll' is to contain the following data:

- The set of candidates still in contention, Still_Contending. A natural representation for this variable is a Boolean array indexed by the candidate numbers.
- The outcome of the latest count, Latest_Outcome. This has three possible values, so an enumeration type is indicated.
- The winner of the election (when known), Winner.
- The loser in the latest count, Loser.

The latter two variables are candidate numbers.

We see that an important type will be that of the candidate numbers. It is better to talk in terms of *candidate identities*, since we are required to anticipate future changes in the way candidates are identified. Let us name this type Candidate_Ids, and encapsulate it in a lower-level package, Candidate_Id_Handler. This package must export operations on candidate identities, namely subprograms for input and output. Since we are also interested in sets of candidates, the package might as well handle such sets too:

```
package Candidate_Id_Handler is
```

```
      subtype Candidate_Ids is ...;
      type Set_of_Candidates is array (Candidate_Ids) of Boolean;
      ...
      procedure Get_Id (Id : out Candidate_Ids);
      procedure Put_Id (Id : in Candidate_Ids);
   end Candidate_Id_Handler;
```

The actual declaration of Candidate_Ids will depend on how candidates are identified. It would be preferable, ideally, for Candidate_Ids to be a private type. However, it will be used to index certain arrays (such as the vote counts), so it must be visibly a discrete type. Other modules might be coupled to Candidate_Id_Handler by using knowledge of the type class of Candidate_Ids; we shall just have to rely on discipline to minimize this coupling. (For example, no module should exploit the fact that Candidate_Ids is a subtype of Integer.)

Another important type in the context of this program will be that of the *ballots*. Store_Valid_Ballots will have to read, check and store ballots, and Count_Votes will have to retrieve them and use them to count the votes. It should be clear that only two operations actually depend on the representation of the ballots: reading and checking a ballot, and determining the preferred candidate in a ballot. Therefore we encapsulate the new type, Ballots, in a package Ballot_Handler, together with these operations:

```
   package Ballot_Handler is
      type Ballots is private;
      procedure Read_and_Check
                  (Ballot : out Ballots;
                   Valid  : out Boolean);
      function All_Read  return Boolean;
      function Preferred_Candidate
                  (Ballot : Ballots;
                   Still_Contending : Set_of_Candidates)
            return Candidate_Ids;
   private
      ...
   end Ballot_Handler;
```

The function All_Read is provided in order to indicate when all ballots have been read.

The next design problem is how to organize the ballot storage. The subprograms Store_Valid_Ballots and Count_Votes require to store and retrieve ballots in the ballot store. If we allow these subprograms to refer *directly* to the ballot store, however, they will be common-environment coupled to each other. This can be avoided if we encapsulate the ballot store in a package, Ballot_Storage, that exports subprograms for storing and retrieving ballots. This package will need to refer to the type Ballots but needs no knowledge of how ballots are represented.

```
   package Ballot_Storage is
      procedure Prepare_Storage;
      procedure Store (Ballot : in Ballots);
      procedure Prepare_Retrieval;
      procedure Retrieve (Ballot : out Ballots);
      function All_Retrieved  return Boolean;
   end Ballot_Storage;
```

As usual, we include subprograms for initialization and finalization.

These considerations lead to the refined structure diagram of Figure 16.9(2). Note that we use boxes with curved ends to represent exported types as well as data objects. A broken arrow pointing to the edge of a type box represents a reference to the type *name* alone; this is (necessarily) the case with the private type `Ballots`. A broken arrow pointing inside a type box represents a reference to the declared representation of the type; this is the case with `Candidate_Ids` and `Set_of_Candidates`.

Because of their dependencies on `Nr_Candidates` (not shown in Figure 16.9) and on one another, the packages `Candidate_Id_Handler`, `Ballot_Handler` and `Ballot_Storage` must be logically nested within the program. To keep the body of `Count_Handler` reasonably short, we shall make all three packages subunits. The subprograms of `Count_Handler` are mostly straightforward to write. `Count_Votes` is relatively complicated and should be tackled by stepwise refinement. We omit this for the sake of brevity. (You might like to carry out

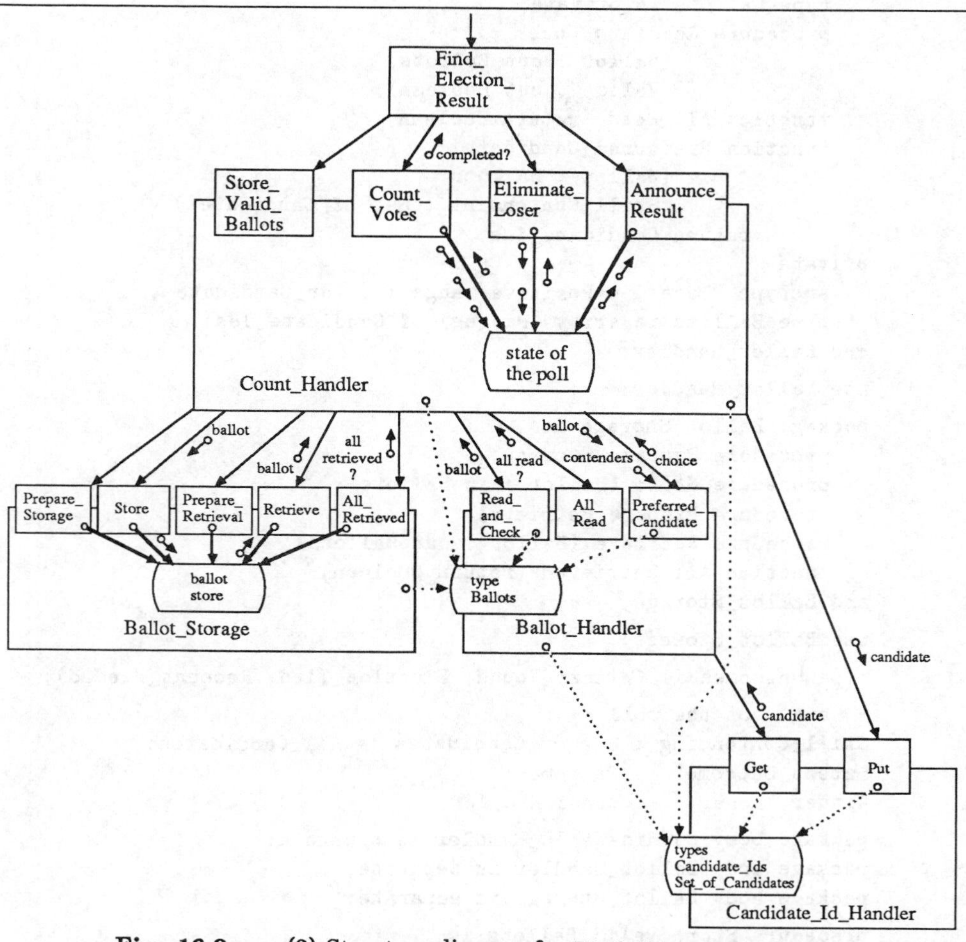

Fig. 16.9 (2) Structure diagram for `Find_Election_Result`

the refinement yourself, as an exercise.) Here is the completed body of Count_Handler:

```
separate (Find_Election_Result)
package body Count_Handler is
   package Candidate_Id_Handler is
      subtype Candidate_Ids is Positive range 1 .. Nr_Candidates;
      type Set_of_Candidates is array (Candidate_Ids) of Boolean;
      All_Candidates : constant Set_of_Candidates
                     := (Candidate_Ids => True);
      procedure Get_Id (Id : out Candidate_Ids);
      procedure Put_Id (Id : in Candidate_Ids);
   end Candidate_Id_Handler;
   use Candidate_Id_Handler;
   package Ballot_Handler is
      type Ballots is private;
      procedure Read_and_Check
                (Ballot : out Ballots;
                 Valid  : out Boolean);
      function All_Read  return Boolean;
      function Preferred_Candidate
                (Ballot : Ballots;
                 Still_Contending : Set_of_Candidates)
            return Candidate_Ids;
   private
      subtype Places is Positive range 1 .. Nr_Candidates;
      type Ballots is array (Places) of Candidate_Ids;
   end Ballot_Handler;
   use Ballot_Handler;
   package Ballot_Storage is
      procedure Prepare_Storage;
      procedure Store (Ballot : in Ballots);
      procedure Prepare_Retrieval;
      procedure Retrieve (Ballot : out Ballots);
      function All_Retrieved  return Boolean;
   end Ballot_Storage;
   use Ballot_Storage;
   type Outcomes is (Winner_Found, Election_Tied, Recount_Needed);
   -- state of the poll --
   Still_Contending : Set_of_Candidates := All_Candidates;
   Latest_Outcome   : Outcomes;
   Winner, Loser    : Candidate_Ids;
   package body Candidate_Id_Handler is separate;
   package body Ballot_Handler is separate;
   package body Ballot_Storage is separate;
   procedure Store_Valid_Ballots is
      One_Ballot : Ballots;
```

```
      Ballot_is_Valid : Boolean;
   begin
      Prepare_Storage;
      while not All_Read loop
         Read_and_Check (One_Ballot, Ballot_is_Valid);
         if Ballot_is_Valid then
            Store (One_Ballot);
         end if;
      end loop;
   end Store_Valid_Ballots;
   procedure Count_Votes (Result_Obtained : out Boolean) is
      Votes_For : array (Candidate_Ids) of Natural
                    := (Candidate_Ids => 0);
      Best, Worst, Choice : Candidate_Ids;
      Ballot_Count : Natural := 0;
      Best_Count, Worst_Count : Natural;
      One_Ballot : Ballots;
   begin
      -- count the votes --
      Prepare_Retrieval;
      while not All_Retrieved loop
         Retrieve (One_Ballot);
         Ballot_Count := Ballot_Count + 1;
         Choice := Preferred_Candidate (One_Ballot, Still_Contending);
         Votes_For(Choice) := Votes_For(Choice) + 1;
      end loop;
      -- determine outcome of count --
      Best_Count := 0;  Worst_Count := Ballot_Count;
      for Candidate in Candidate_Ids loop
         if Still_Contending(Candidate) then
            if Votes_For(Candidate) > Best_Count then
               Best := Candidate;
               Best_Count := Votes_For(Best);
            end if;
            if Votes_For(Candidate) < Worst_Count then
               Worst := Candidate;
               Worst_Count := Votes_For(Worst);
            end if;
         end if;
      end loop;
      if Best_Count > Ballot_Count/2 then
         Latest_Outcome := Winner_Found;  Winner := Best;
      elsif Best_Count = Worst_Count then
         Latest_Outcome := Election_Tied;
      else
         Latest_Outcome := Recount_Needed;  Loser := Worst;
      end if;
      Result_Obtained := Latest_Outcome /= Recount_Needed;
```

```
      end Count_Votes;

      procedure Eliminate_Loser is
      begin
         Still_Contending(Loser) := False;
      end Eliminate_Loser;

      procedure Announce_Result is
      begin
         New_Line;
         case Latest_Outcome is
            when Winner_Found =>
               Put ("The winning candidate is ");
               Put_Id (Winner);
            when Election_Tied =>
               Put ("The following candidates have tied:");
               for Candidate in Candidate_Ids loop
                  if Still_Contending(Candidate) then
                     Put ("  ");  Put_Id (Candidate);
                  end if;
               end loop;
            when Recount_Needed =>
               raise Constraint_Error;
         end case;
         New_Line;
      end Announce_Result;

   end Count_Handler;
```

The implementation of Candidate_Id_Handler is straightforward:

```
   separate (Find_Election_Result.Count_Handler)
   package body Candidate_Id_Handler is
      package Candidate_IO is new Integer_IO (Candidate_Ids);
      procedure Get_Id (Id : out Candidate_Ids)
            renames Candidate_IO.Get;
      procedure Put_Id (Id : in Candidate_Ids)
            renames Candidate_IO.Put;
   end Candidate_Id_Handler;
```

In the implementation of Ballot_Handler, care must be taken in Read_and_Check to anticipate and catch as many errors as possible. Each input ballot is supposed to rank all the candidates in order of preference. Get_Id will be used to read each candidate identity. That will raise Data_Error if the datum is not an integer or is not in the range 1 through Nr_Candidates. Read_and_Check must itself check for duplicates in the ballot. (If a ballot has the correct number of entries and there are no duplicates, there can be no missing candidates either.)

Since some of the possible errors are propagated from Get_Id to Read_and_Check as exceptions, it is necessary for this procedure to contain an exception handler that sets the out parameter Valid to False and avoids propagating the exception any further. Given this handler, the procedure might as well react to errors it detects itself by raising an exception.

The implementation of Ballot_Handler follows:

```
separate (Find_Election_Result.Count_Handler)
package body Ballot_Handler is
   procedure Read_and_Check
               (Ballot : out Ballots;
                Valid  : out Boolean) is
      Not_Yet_Chosen : Set_of_Candidates := All_Candidates;
      Choice : Candidate_Ids;
   begin
      for Place in Places loop
         Get_Id (Choice);
         if Not_Yet_Chosen(Choice) then
            Ballot(Place) := Choice;
            Not_Yet_Chosen(Choice) := False;
         else
            raise Constraint_Error;
         end if;
      end loop;
      Valid := True;
      Skip_Line;
   exception
      when End_Error | Data_Error | Constraint_Error =>
         Valid := False;
         Skip_Line;
   end Read_and_Check;
   function All_Read  return Boolean
         renames End_of_File;
   function Preferred_Candidate
               (Ballot : Ballots;
                Still_Contending : Set_of_Candidates)
         return Candidate_Ids is
   begin
      for Place in Places loop
         if Still_Contending(Ballot(Place)) then
            return Ballot(Place);
         end if;
      end loop;
   end Preferred_Candidate;
end Ballot_Handler;
```

The error-checking in Read_and_Check is not exhaustive. For example, it does not detect a wrong number of entries on a ballot.

Last of all we must implement Ballot_Storage. We observe that successive calls of Store are to place the given ballots in the ballot store, and that successive calls of Retrieve are to fetch the ballots from the ballot store, but *no retrieval order is prescribed.* The only requirement is that every ballot should be retrieved exactly once in each scan (i.e., until `Prepare_Retrieval` is called again). We could, for example, store the ballots in an array. Instead, recognizing that the number of ballots could be large, we propose to use a (temporary) serial file as the ballot store. This decision makes the implementation of `Ballot_Storage` straightforward:

```
with Sequential_IO;

separate (Find_Election_Result.Count_Handler)
package body Ballot_Storage is

   package Ballot_IO is new Sequential_IO (Ballots);
   use Ballot_IO;

   Ballot_File : File_Type;

   procedure Prepare_Storage is
   begin
      Create (Ballot_File, Mode=>Out_File);
   end Prepare_Storage;

   procedure Store (Ballot : in Ballots) is
   begin
      Write (Ballot_File, Ballot);
   end Store;

   procedure Prepare_Retrieval is
   begin
      Reset (Ballot_File, Mode=>In_File);
   end Prepare_Retrieval;

   procedure Retrieve (Ballot : out Ballots) is
   begin
      Read (Ballot_File, Ballot);
   end Retrieve;

   function All_Retrieved  return Boolean is
   begin
      return End_of_File (Ballot_File);
   end All_Retrieved;

end Ballot_Storage;
```

16.8. Compilation strategy

We now summarize some of the practical considerations involved in choosing a program development strategy and putting it into practice with Ada.

Order of compilation and recompilation

An important issue in managing a large program composed of many compilation units is the order in which these compilation units may be compiled and recompiled. The fundamental rule is that a compilation unit must be compiled before all other compilation units that depend on it. Specifically:

- A library unit (a subprogram or package declaration) must be compiled before the corresponding secondary unit (its body).
- A library unit must be compiled before any compilation unit that names the library unit in a with clause.
- A compilation unit containing a body stub must be compiled before the corresponding subunit.

(In connection with the first point, however, a subprogram body may act as both a library unit and a secondary unit.)

These rules are illustrated by the dependency diagrams of Figure 16.10 and Figure 16.11. In Case Study III, for example, the `Token_Handler` declaration must be compiled before the `Token_Handler` body, before the `Format_Text` body, after the `Format_Definitions` declaration, but either before or after the `Line_Handler` declaration and body. In Case Study IV, the `Find_Election_Result` body must be compiled first, followed by the `Count_Handler` subunit; the remaining three subunits may be compiled thereafter in any order.

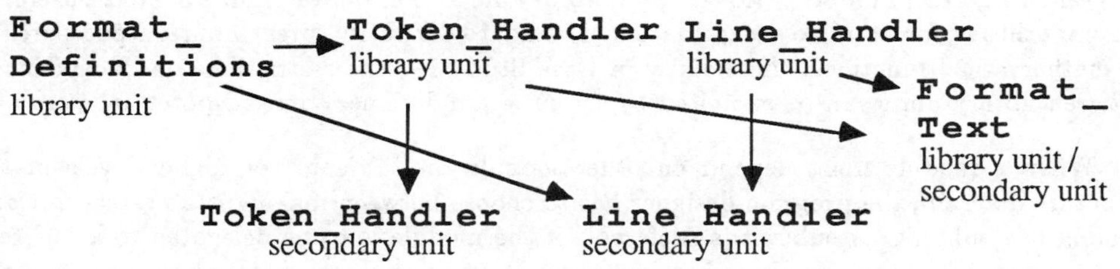

Fig. 16.10 Dependency diagram for `Format_Text`

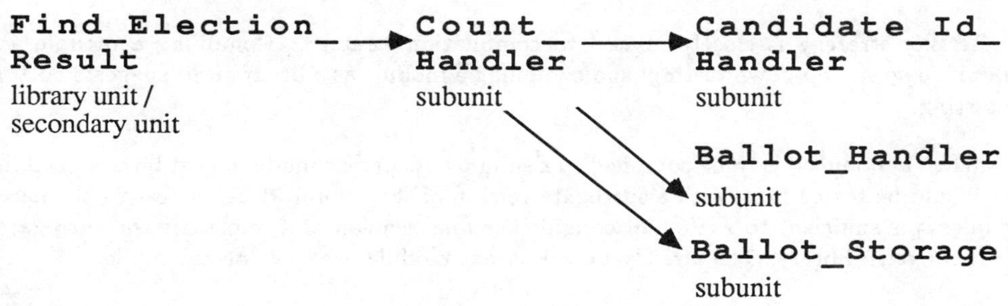

Fig. 16.11 Dependency diagram for `Find_Election_Result`

The same considerations determine the order of recompilation. If a compilation unit has to be recompiled (to correct an error, or perhaps to replace a surrogate version by the final version), then any other compilation units dependent on it must also be recompiled, but no others. In particular, recompiling the body of a library unit never forces recompilation of any other compilation unit (unless it contains body stubs). In Case Study III, for example, if any body is recompiled, nothing else has to be recompiled; if the `Line_Handler` declaration is recompiled, only the `Line_Handler` and `Format_Text` bodies also have to be recompiled; but if the `Format_Definitions` declaration is recompiled, everything else must be recompiled except the `Line_Handler` declaration. In Case Study IV, if any of the `Candidate_Id_Handler`, `Ballot_Handler` or `Ballot_Storage` subunits is recompiled, nothing else need be recompiled; if the `Count_Handler` subunit is recompiled, all the above three subunits must be recompiled; and if the main-program unit is recompiled, everything else must be recompiled.

Choice of nested units, library units or subunits

For any given program unit, the program designer has a choice of compiling it as part of its parent unit, compiling it as a subunit, or compiling it as a library unit. The best choice is determined by management considerations.

A library unit has the advantage of being reusable, capable of being shared by a number of programs. A library unit has the limitation, however, that it cannot depend on any other program unit, except for other (lower-level) library units. Thus library units are most useful as general utilities, for example encapsulation of standard data structures, input-output, sorting, or mathematical functions. As we saw in Case Study III, the restrictions on dependencies between library units can be exploited by the program designer to avoid potential coupling.

When a module must depend on other modules at the same or higher levels in the structure diagram, the program designer has to choose between making it a nested unit and making it a subunit. A subunit is preferable if the module is to be delegated to a different programmer, who then has his or her own source text to work on. It also has the advantage in terms of readability of the parent unit.

Compilation strategy and testing strategy

Testing strategy is closely related to compilation strategy. Compiling a module as a subunit suggests top-down testing; and compiling a module as a library unit suggests bottom-up testing.

When a module `M` is to be compiled as a subunit, its parent module must be compiled first and should be tested first, with a surrogate version of the subunit `M`. After testing the parent module, it is sufficient to write and compile the final version of `M`, replacing the surrogate `M` in the program library. The already-tested parent module need not be recompiled.

When a module M is to be compiled as a library unit, it can be compiled and tested with a driver. Thereafter the parent module can be compiled and tested. The already-tested library module M need not be recompiled.

16.9. Visibility rules and separate compilation

A consequence of separate compilation is that the visibility rules given in Section 12.7 and in Section 13.6 have to be generalized to extend from one compilation unit to another.

A with clause in the context clause of a compilation unit may name any library units that have already been compiled and placed in the program library. The names of these library units are then visible throughout the compilation unit.

A context clause may contain use clauses as well as with clauses. These use clauses may name only library packages named in preceding with clauses. The names of entities exported by these library packages then become directly visible in the compilation unit, in accordance with the usual rules for use clauses discussed in Section 13.6. A familiar example of this is the appearance of the context clause:

```
with Text_IO;  use Text_IO;
```

which not only makes the package `Text_IO` visible but also makes exported subprograms such as `New_Line` directly visible.

In the case of a subunit, the visibility rules can be deduced by imagining the subunit physically substituted into its parent unit in place of the corresponding body stub. Thus all identifiers visible at the position of the body stub are also visible within the subunit. If the subunit has a context clause, the effect (within the subunit) is as if that context clause were appended at the end of the parent unit's context clause. For example, in Case Study IV, the subunit `Ballot_Storage` was able to refer to the library unit `Sequential_IO` and to the type `Ballots`, exported from `Ballot_Handler` and directly visible at the body stub.

The package Standard

You might have noticed that the effect of a with clause is to make named library units visible in much the same way as the names of standard types and other entities, such as `Integer`, `Boolean` and so on. In fact all the standard entities behave as if they are declared in a global package, `Standard`, that is automatically available to every Ada program. Thus their fully qualified names are in fact `Standard.Integer`, `Standard.Boolean`, and so on. (These fully qualified names may always be used if, for any reason, the names `Integer`, `Boolean` and so on have been hidden.) A listing of `Standard` may be found in Appendix D.

In a sense, compiling a library unit has the effect of adding the unit to `Standard` (and recompiling the library unit has the effect of replacing the unit in `Standard`). Thus the fully-qualified name of a library unit `U` is, in fact, `Standard.U`. Despite this, no reference to `U` is allowed in a compilation unit that does not name `U` in its context clause.

Exercises 16

16.1. Draw a data flow diagram for a programming system (editors, compilers, linkers, and so on) with which you are familiar.

16.2. Find a moderately large program you are familiar with, written in any language. Carefully document its structure with a data flow diagram and a structure diagram. (You may omit the lower levels of detail if the program is very large.) How loosely or tightly are the modules coupled? How cohesive is each module? Could you improve the design of the program? Document your improved design with a data flow diagram, a structure diagram, and Ada declarations of all modules.

16.3. (a) Does the requirement for the text-formatting program (Case Study III) specify clearly what is to happen if the source text starts with `/PAR/`?

(b) What does the given solution actually do in this case?

(c) Suppose the requirement stated clearly that any blank lines at the start of the formatted text are to be suppressed. What modifications, if any, would be needed to the solution? Which of the compilation units would have to be recompiled?

16.4. In Case Study III the procedure `Write_Adjusted_Line` assumes that only *one* space ever separates words. Is this a reasonable assumption? How could it be relaxed, and would the structure of the program thereby be improved?

16.5. An alternative strategy in Case Study III would have been to test the main-program module `Format_Text` *before* `Line_Handler`. Describe how this could be done.

16.6. Consider what modifications to program `Find_Election_Result` would be necessary to change the identification of candidates as follows:

(a) Candidates are identified by the letters A, B, C, ...

(b) Candidates are identified by their surnames. Each surname consists of at most 20 letters. Each input ballot is a single line of text in which the candidates' surnames are separated by commas (only). A second input file is provided, containing a list of the candidates' surnames, for the purpose of checking the ballots.

16.7. In Case Study IV the procedure `Announce_Result` contains the statement:

```
raise Constraint_Error;
```

In what circumstances can this statement be obeyed? Is raising an exception a reasonable thing to do in these circumstances? What are the alternatives and how do they compare with using an exception?

PART III

Advanced Data Types

17

Access Types and Dynamic Data Structures

17.1. Dynamic data structures

Arrays and records are data structures of fixed shape. This is obviously true for records, since each record has a number of components fixed by its type definition. The number of components of an array is also fixed, although in the case of a dynamic array the number is not known until the array declaration is elaborated at run-time.

Many programs require data structures where the number of nodes (or entries) varies dynamically. A common example of such a data structure is a *list*, which will expand as entries are inserted into the list and contract as entries are removed from it. We used such a data structure in Case Studies II and III: this was a list of names used in an insertion sort.

As illustrated by these case studies, a list can be represented by an array. This representation is not entirely satisfactory, however, for the following reasons:

- The size of the array must be fixed on declaration (i.e. before insertion of list entries commences). Therefore the index bounds of the array impose a limit on the number of entries in the list. This limit might well be completely arbitrary, such as the limit of 100 in Case Studies II and III.
- In general, only some of the array components will contain actual list entries, so the storage occupied by the remaining array components is wasted. This is a direct consequence of the fact that the lifetime of the array (and each of its components) is the entire activation of the program unit in which the array is declared, whereas the lifetime of each list entry will be shorter.
- Inserting (or deleting) an entry in the array requires all following entries to be shifted. This is very time-consuming when the list contains many entries.

Thus, although arrays *can* be used to represent lists and other dynamic data structures (and in some programming languages they are the only possible representation), they are really too inflexible for the representation to be efficient.

A data structure is much more flexible if its nodes can be created whenever necessary and if the nodes are allowed to contain explicit interconnections — *pointers* from one node to one another. Expansion and contraction of the data structure can then be achieved efficiently by simple manipulation of the pointers, as we shall see.

Figure 17.1(a) shows a list of integers in which each node contains not only an integer but also a pointer to the next node in the list. The advantage of using pointers becomes apparent when we update the list by inserting a new entry. For example, inserting 21 between 13 and 25 in the list of Figure 17.1(a) is achieved simply by: (1) creating a new node containing the integer 21 and a pointer to the 25 node (which will be the new node's follower); and (2) redirecting the pointer in the 13 node (the new node's predecessor) to point to the new node. The other nodes in the list are not disturbed at all. The result is shown in Figure 17.1(b).

Removal of an entry from such a list is equally easy and efficient. To delete 73 from the list of Figure 17.1(b), for example, all that needs to be done is to redirect the pointer in the 37 node (the 73 node's predecessor) to point to the 74 node (the 73 node's follower), with the result shown in Figure 17.1(c). (The 73 node still exists, but it is no longer linked into the list.)

A list of nodes linked by pointers is known as a *linked list*. This is the simplest and most common form of dynamic data structure. More complicated forms will be described in Section 17.4.

17.2. Access types

Suppose that we wish to declare in Ada a linked list containing items of some type `Items`. (These items could be integers, or strings, or of some other type; that does not concern us here.) We need a type, say `Item_Node`, for the nodes of the list. Since each node must contain both an item and a pointer to the next node, we must declare `Item_Node` to be a record type with these two components. We also need a type for the pointers themselves; let us call that type `Item_Ptr`. Here are the type declarations:

```
type Item_Node;
type Item_Ptr is access Item_Node;
type Item_Node is
```

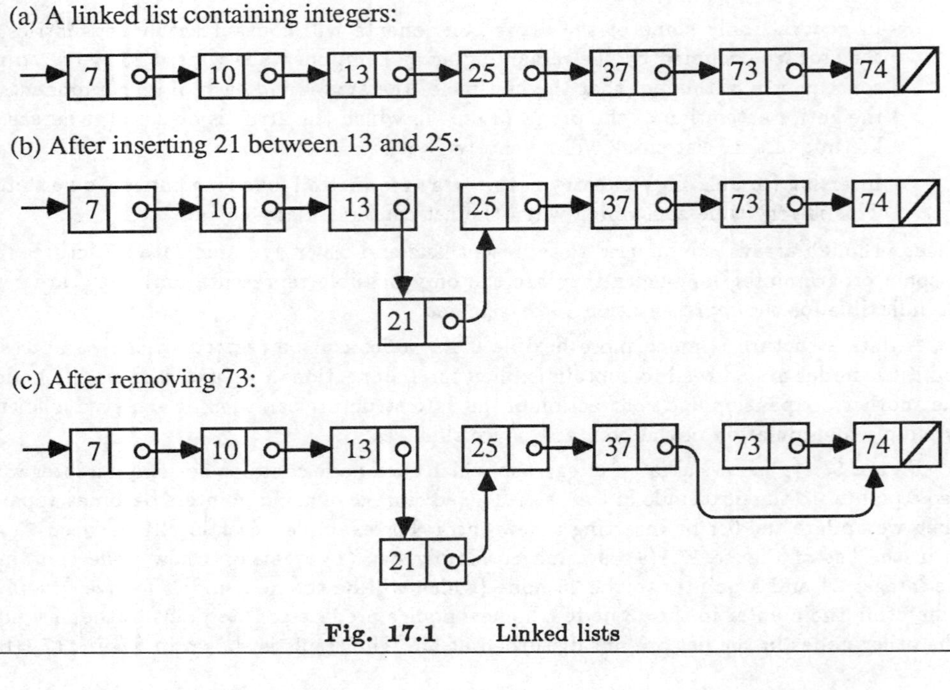

Fig. 17.1 Linked lists

```
        record
           Item : Items;
           Next : Item_Ptr;
        end record;
```

Item_Ptr is declared to be the *access type* 'access Item_Node'. This means that each value of type Item_Ptr will be a pointer to an object of type Item_Node. See the syntax diagram 'access_type_definition' in Appendix A.

Note that the type declarations of Item_Ptr and Item_Node are mutually recursive. (This is a feature of all dynamic data structures.) Since Ada requires every identifier to be declared before it is used, the very first type declaration above is an *incomplete type declaration*, which merely declares that Item_Node is to be a type name, with further details to be provided later (in the same declarative part). The order illustrated above is mandatory: (1) an incomplete type declaration for the node type, followed by (2) a type declaration for the access type, in terms of the node type, followed by (3) a complete type declaration for the node type.

The component Item of each node will contain one of the items in the list, and the component Next will point to the next node in the list. Thus each node can be accessed from the preceding node. We also need an object such as:

```
Item_List_Head : Item_Ptr;
```

to contain a pointer to the *first* node of the list. Finally, to indicate that the last node in the list has *no* follower, we store in its Next component the special access value null, which points to nothing at all. An empty list can be represented by storing null in Item_List_Head itself.

All access objects are, by default, initialized to null. We do not recommend exploiting this anomalous feature, however, preferring that initializations should be explicit:

```
Item_List_Head : Item_Ptr := null;
```

In the following, we assume that P and Q are variables of type Item_Ptr.

Nodes are created dynamically by means of *allocators*. For example, consider the statement:

```
P := new Item_Node;
```

The allocator 'new Item_Node' creates a new object of type Item_Node, and the value of the allocator is a pointer to the new object. The value of the new object itself is undefined. In this particular statement, the value of the allocator is assigned to the access variable P. Thus P may subsequently be used to access the new object.

It is often possible to initialize the new object at the time of creation. This may be specified by an allocator containing a *qualified expression*, which is evaluated to determine the initial value of the new object. A qualified expression contains principally a (sub)type name and a parenthesized expression or aggregate of the appropriate type. The above statement could be modified to:

```
P := new Item_Node' (I, null);
```

Here (I,null) is a record aggregate of type Item_Node. This statement would have the additional effect of initializing the components Item and Next of the new object to I and null respectively.

See the syntax diagrams 'allocator' and 'qualified_expression' in Appendix A.

Access values may be assigned to access variables, as illustrated above, or used to initialize access objects. They may also be compared using the relational operators `=` and `/=`; two access values are equal if they point to the same object or if they are both `null`. Finally, access values may be passed as parameters or returned as function results. In none of these operations may different access types be mixed. (This is a consequence of Ada's strong type rules.)

The notation `P.all` names the entire object that `P` currently points to. Thus the declaration:

```
N : Item_Node := P.all;
```

initializes `N` to a copy of this object.

Contrast the two statements:

```
P := Q;          P.all := Q.all;
```

The difference between them is illustrated by Figure 17.2. The first statement copies the value of `Q` (a pointer); thus it makes `P` point to the same object as `Q`, but it does not affect the value of the object that `P` formerly pointed to. The second statement assigns the entire object pointed to by `Q` to the object pointed to by `P`; however, `P` still points to the same node as before.

In our example `P` points to a record of type `Item_Node`. The components of that record may be named using the same selected component notation as that used for ordinary records. Thus `P.Item` names the component `Item` of the object pointed to by `P`, and `P.Next` names the component `Next` of the same object.

The type rules ensure that `P` can never point to an object of any type other than `Item_Node`, but it is possible for `P` to be `null`. If its value is `null` when an attempt is made to refer to `P.all`, `P.Item` or `P.Next`, the exception `Constraint_Error` is raised.

The necessary run-time checks on access values can, however, be suppressed by:

```
pragma Suppress (Access_Check);
```

Objects allocated by **new** are created in a region of storage known as the *heap*, logically separate from the region used for objects created by object declarations. We shall henceforth call the latter objects *local objects*, to distinguish them from *heap objects*. All local objects are named, and no access value can ever point to a local object. All heap objects are anonymous, and can be accessed *only* through access values that point to them.

A further important distinction is that local objects exist (i.e. occupy storage) from elaboration of their declaration until termination of the program unit that is their scope; whereas heap objects exist from their allocation by **new** until they become inaccessible.

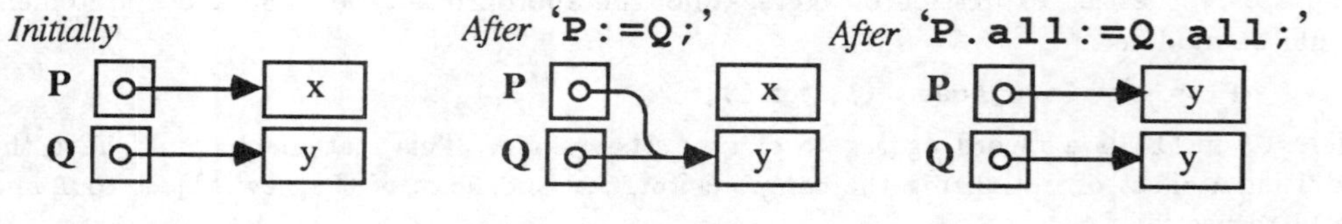

Fig. 17.2 Assignment of access values and of heap objects

Assignment makes it possible for more than one access value to point to the same heap object. This is another form of *aliasing*. It is illustrated by the effect of 'P := Q;' in Figure 17.2.

17.3. Linked list processing

In this section we illustrate the use of pointers by examples of linked list manipulation.

Example 17.1 *Linked list traversal*

Assume the declarations of the types Item_Node and Item_Ptr from the previous section. Let us write a function with the following declaration:

```
function List_Length (List_Head : Item_Ptr) return Natural;
```

List_Length is to take List_Head as pointing to the first node of a linked list, and is to return the number of nodes in that list.

This problem can easily be solved by a loop that makes Ptr (a local access variable) point to each node of the list in turn. The loop is terminated when Ptr is null. Ptr is initialized to point to the first node of the list. A while loop allows for an empty list.

```
function List_Length (List_Head : Item_Ptr) return Natural  is
   Ptr    : Item_Ptr := List_Head;
   Length : Natural := 0;
begin
   while Ptr /= null loop
      Length := Length + 1;
      Ptr := Ptr.Next;
   end loop;
   return Length;
end List_Length;
```

Within the body of the loop, we can be sure that Ptr is not null, so it must point to a record of type Item_Node. Therefore Ptr.Next names the component Next of that record, and the statement 'Ptr := Ptr.Next;' advances Ptr from one node to the next.

□ *End of Example 17.1*

The function List_Length illustrates an important point about access values. Since List_Head is an in parameter, it acts as a local *constant*, so the compiler will prevent any attempt to change its value. Thus the function cannot make List_Head point to a different node. The object List_Head.all is a *variable*, however, so this object or any component of it may be assigned to by the function. Thus an access value passed as an in parameter is itself protected, but not the object it points to. This observation applies to all access-valued constants as well as to in parameters.

Example 17.2 *Linked list linear search*

Assume once again the declarations of the types Item_Node and Item_Ptr from the previous section. Let us write a procedure with the following declaration:

```
procedure Search_List
        (List_Head  : in Item_Ptr;
         Target     : in Items;
         Target_Ptr : out Item_Ptr);
```

`Search_List` is to take `List_Head` as pointing to the first node of a linked list of items, and is to make `Target_Ptr` point to the first node containing an item that equals `Target`, or set `Target_Ptr` to `null` if the list contains no such node. We do not assume that the items in the list are in any particular order.

This problem illustrates linear search in a linked list. (Compare Example 10.2.) The technique is similar to the previous example, except that the loop should terminate as soon as a match is found.

```
procedure Search_List
        (List_Head  : in Item_Ptr;
         Target     : in Items;
         Target_Ptr : out Item_Ptr)  is
   Ptr : Item_Ptr := List_Head;
begin
   while Ptr /= null and then Ptr.Item /= Target loop
      Ptr := Ptr.Next;
   end loop;
   Target_Ptr := Ptr;  -- possibly null
end Search_List;
```

The loop terminates when either `Ptr` is `null` or `Target` matches the `Item` component of the record `Ptr` points to. Note the use of '`and then`' to avoid raising `Constraint_Error` if `Ptr` is `null`.

(*Exercise*: recast this procedure as an access-valued function.)

□ *End of Example 17.2*

Example 17.3 *Linked list insertion*

The program of Case Study II sorted a list of names by insertion sort, in which each name was read and inserted immediately into its correct position in an ordered list of names. The list of names was represented by an array. Let us modify the program to use a linked list instead. This will improve the program substantially in several respects, as discussed in Section 17.1.

Showing good foresight, we decided to encapsulate the list of names by the package `Sort_Service`. Therefore only the body of `Sort_Service` depends on the list representation and needs to be modified now. Here is the package declaration again:

```
package Sort_Service is
   procedure Make_List_Empty;
   procedure Insert (New_Name : in Names);
   procedure Prepare_Extraction;
   procedure Extract (Old_Name : out Names);
   function All_Extracted return Boolean;
end Sort_Service;
```

The package body must contain the type and object declarations for the linked list. Other than that, it is necessary to rewrite the five subprogram bodies to work on the new data structure.

The only subprogram that is tricky is Insert. Its original refinement (Section 12.8) is now largely inappropriate, so we revise it as follows:

```
procedure Insert (New_Name : in Names)  is
   local declarations;
begin
   find the insertion position for New_Name;
   create a new node containing New_Name;
   link the new node into the list;
end Insert;
```

(There is no longer any need to test whether the list is already full.) The refinement of '*find the insertion position for* Name' must find both the node that will follow the new node and the node that will precede it, so we introduce two access variables, Ptr and Prev_Ptr, to point to these nodes. The refinement of '*create a new node containing* Name' must allocate a new node and initialize it to contain Name and a copy of the pointer Ptr. The refinement of '*link the new node into the list*' must redirect the pointer in the node to which Prev_Ptr points, except in the case that Ptr points to the *first* node of the list, in which case it is the list head pointer that must be redirected.

```
package body Sort_Service is

   type Name_Node;
   type Name_Ptr is access Name_Node;
   type Name_Node is
         record
            Name : Names;
            Next : Name_Ptr;
         end record;

   Head, Extract_Ptr : Name_Ptr;

   procedure Make_List_Empty is
   begin
      Head := null;
   end Make_List_Empty;

   procedure Insert (New_Name : in Names)  is
      Ptr : Name_Ptr := Head;
      Prev_Ptr, New_Ptr : Name_Ptr;
   begin
      -- find the insertion position for New_Name --
      while Ptr /= null and then New_Name > Ptr.Name loop
         Prev_Ptr := Ptr;  Ptr := Ptr.Next;
      end loop;
      -- create a new node containing New_Name --
      New_Ptr := new Name_Node' (New_Name, Ptr);
      -- link the new node into the list --
      if Ptr = Head then
         Head := New_Ptr;
```

```
         else
            Prev_Ptr.Next := New_Ptr;
         end if;
      end Insert;
      procedure Prepare_Extraction is
      begin
         Extract_Ptr := Head;
      end Prepare_Extraction;
      procedure Extract (Old_Name : out Names) is
      begin
         Old_Name := Extract_Ptr.Name;
         Extract_Ptr := Extract_Ptr.Next;
      end Extract;
      function All_Extracted return Boolean  is
      begin
         return (Extract_Ptr = null);
      end All_Extracted;
   end Sort_Service;
```

Note that each node created by the allocator in `Insert` outlives `Insert` itself.

□ *End of Example 17.3*

This example has illustrated the possibility of changing the implementation of an encapsulated data structure without any change to the package declaration or to the rest of the program. It is precisely this possibility that makes packages such a powerful aid to modularity in Ada programs.

17.4. Binary trees and hash tables

In this section we shall briefly describe some more complicated dynamic data structures and see how they may be defined in Ada. We shall see that many applications allow a choice of different kinds of data structure, the best choice being dictated by efficiency considerations.

Recall the `Directory_Service` package of Example 13.6. Its declaration was as follows:

```
package Directory_Service is
   subtype Names   is String (1 .. 20);
   subtype Numbers is String (1 .. 12);
   procedure Insert_Entry
               (New_Name   : in Names;
                New_Number : in Numbers);
   procedure Lookup_Entry
               (Given_Name  : in Names;
                Name_Found  : out Boolean;
                Corr_Number : out Numbers);
end Directory_Service;
```

This package encapsulates a telephone directory. `Insert_Entry` is to add a new entry to the directory, and `Lookup_Entry` is to find the telephone number (if any) corresponding to a given name.

The `Directory_Service` package body in Example 13.6 declared the directory as an array of entries, together with a count of the current number of entries. A simplistic implementation of `Insert_Entry` would simply add the new entry at the end of the directory, and then `Lookup_Entry` would have to work by linear search. The search time is proportional to the current number of entries. For large directories this would be unacceptably slow.

An alternative is to maintain the directory entries in lexicographic order of names. Then `Lookup_Entry` can work by binary search. The search time is proportional to the *logarithm* of the current number of entries, a substantial improvement. `Insert_Entry` is slower, on the other hand, because it must insert each new entry in its correct lexicographic position (which implies shifting entries in the array, as in insertion sort).

Whether linear search or binary search is used, the array representation has the disadvantages discussed in Section 17.1 — an arbitrary limit on the size of the directory, combined with waste of storage when the directory is not full.

What we want is a dynamic data structure that allows both insertion and search to be implemented efficiently. A linked list would not be satisfactory because it would entail slow linear search. We shall describe two kinds of data structure that are suitable for applications like this: ***binary trees*** and ***hash tables***. We shall illustrate their use by demonstrating alternative implementations of `Directory_Service`.

Binary trees

In a ***binary tree***, each node contains *two* pointers to other nodes, and no two pointers may point to the same node. These interconnections lead to the structure illustrated by Figure 17.3. Each binary tree has a unique node to which no other node points; this node is called the ***root*** of the binary tree. (Perversely, in view of all this arboreal terminology, it is customary to picture a binary tree with its root at the top!) The two pointers in each node P are called its ***left branch*** and ***right branch*** respectively. If you consider the set of nodes that can be reached by following the left branch of P, you will see that they themselves form a binary tree, which we call the ***left subtree*** of P. Likewise we define the ***right subtree*** of P. For the example, the right subtree of the 25 node in Figure 17.3(a) consists of the 37, 73 and 74 nodes; the left subtree of the 73 node consists of the 37 node alone; and both the left and right subtrees of the 37 node are empty.

A binary tree is said to be ***sorted*** if, for every node P of the binary tree, the value contained in P is not less than any value contained in the left subtree of P and not greater than any value contained in the right subtree of P. The binary trees of Figure 17.3 are all sorted.

Given any sorted binary tree, it is always possible to insert a new node in such a way as to keep the binary tree sorted and without changing the existing interconnections among the nodes of the tree. Figure 17.3(b) shows an example: 21 is to be inserted in the sorted binary tree of Figure 17.3(a). The root node contains 25, and 21 is *less* than 25, so we can deduce that 25 must go in the root node's *left* subtree. That subtree's root contains 13, and 21 is *greater* than 13, so we can deduce that 21 must go in the 13 node's *right* subtree. But the latter subtree is empty, so we add a single node containing 21 as the right subtree of the 13

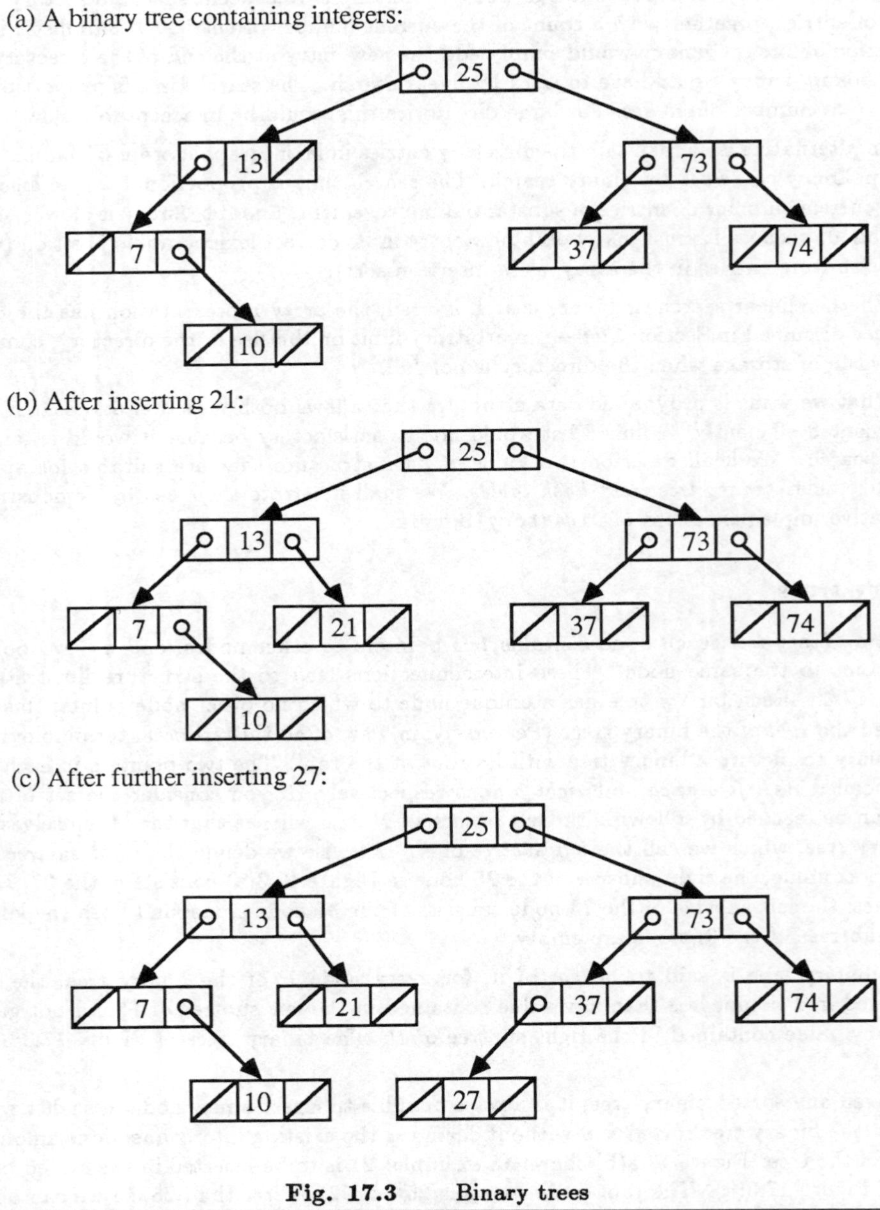

Fig. 17.3 Binary trees

node. Figure 17.3(c) shows another example of insertion. Sorted binary tree insertion always works by replacing an empty subtree by the new node.

To *search* an ordered binary tree for a node matching a given target value, we start at the root node and track left or right in a similar fashion. The search terminates when we find either a matching node or an empty subtree. In Figure 17.3(c), for example, we search for a node containing 21 as follows. The root node contains 25, and 21 is *less* than 25, so we must seek 21 in the root node's *left* subtree. That subtree's root node contains 13, and 21 is *greater* than 13, so we must seek 21 in the 13 node's *right* subtree. There we are successful, for that subtree's root node contains 21. If the target had been 22 instead, we would have followed the same track, but we would now find the target to be *greater* than 21, so we must continue the search in the 21 node's *right* subtree; since that subtree is empty, the search would have proved unsuccessful.

Note that the amount of time required for both insertion and search depends on the (local) depth of the binary tree, rather than on the total number of nodes. This is a substantial improvement over a linked list when the number of nodes is large, provided that the binary tree is reasonably balanced (i.e. its depth does not vary greatly from place to place).

Example 17.4 *A binary tree package*

Here is a revised implementation of `Directory_Service`. The directory is represented by a binary tree, sorted on the names. Each node is a record containing a name and telephone number, plus two access values pointing to two subtrees. An encapsulated variable, `Directory_Root`, points to the root node of the tree. An empty tree or subtree is represented by `null`.

```
package body Directory_Service is
   type Directory_Node;
   type Directory_Ptr is access Directory_Node;
   type Directory_Node is
         record
            Name   : Names;
            Number : Numbers;
            Left, Right : Directory_Ptr;
         end record;
   Directory_Root : Directory_Ptr := null;
         -- directory is initially empty
   procedure Insert_Entry
             (New_Name   : in Names;
              New_Number : in Numbers) is
      procedure Insert_in_Subtree
                 (Subtree_Root : in out Directory_Ptr)  is
      begin
         if Subtree_Root = null then
            Subtree_Root :=
                  new Directory_Node'
                     (New_Name, New_Number, null, null);
         elsif New_Name < Subtree_Root.Name then
```

```
                Insert_in_Subtree (Subtree_Root.Left);
             else
                Insert_in_Subtree (Subtree_Root.Right);
             end if;
          end Insert_in_Subtree;
       begin
          Insert_in_Subtree (Directory_Root);
       end Insert_Entry;
       procedure Lookup_Entry
                  (Given_Name  : in Names;
                   Name_Found  : out Boolean;
                   Corr_Number : out Numbers) is
          Ptr : Directory_Ptr := Directory_Root;
       begin
          loop
             if Ptr = null then
                Name_Found := False;
                exit;
             elsif Given_Name = Ptr.Name then
                Name_Found := True;
                Corr_Number := Ptr.Number;
                exit;
             elsif Given_Name < Ptr.Name then
                Ptr := Ptr.Left;
             else
                Ptr := Ptr.Right;
             end if;
          end loop;
       end Lookup_Entry;

    end Directory_Service;
```

□ *End of Example 17.4*

Hash tables

A hash table is based on the idea of partitioning the data structure into a number of small substructures called ***buckets***. The bucket to which a given node belongs is determined only by the node's content. Insertion or search is performed by (1) deciding which bucket the new or target node belongs to, and (2) inserting or searching in that bucket.

To take a very simple example, a hash table containing integers might consist of 10 buckets, where each integer's least significant decimal digit decides which bucket it belongs to. This simple hash table is illustrated in Figure 17.4, where each bucket is a linked list and an array of 10 pointers provides access to these lists. Provided that each bucket contains only a small number of nodes, linear search within each bucket would be acceptable.

The computation that decides which bucket a node belongs to is called a ***hash function***. In Figure 17.4 the hash function is computed by taking the integer modulo 10. Provided that the same hash function is used for both insertion and search, any hash function is formally correct. The key to efficiency, however, is to choose a hash function that is simple and fast, but will also distribute the nodes as evenly as possible among the buckets. (In the worst case, a hash function that allocated every node to the same bucket would make the hash table no better than a single linked list!)

Example 17.5 *A hash table package*

Let us now rework the `Directory_Service` package using a hash table. We shall use a structure similar to that of Figure 17.4, namely an array of linked lists, but we must decide on a hash function suitable for names rather than integers.

A simple but naive solution would be to have 26 buckets and allocate each name to a bucket according to its initial letter. Unfortunately, the letters of the alphabet vary widely in frequency, so some buckets would contain many more entries than others. Since most searches would be for names in the most crowded buckets, the average search time would be much worse than we would expect from a hash table with evenly distributed nodes.

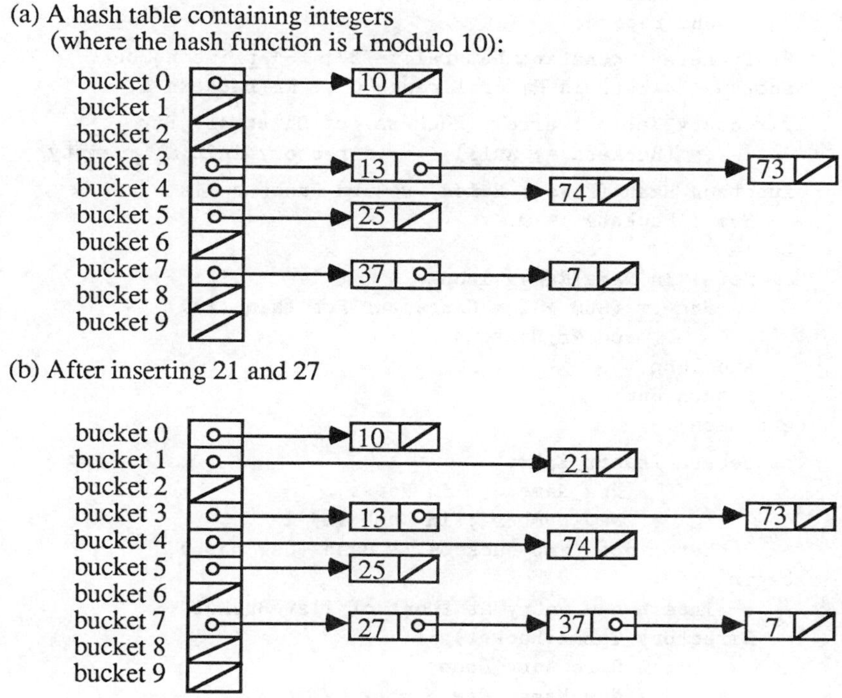

Fig. 17.4 Hash tables

A body of theory has been developed for the design of hash functions [Knuth 1973]. The solution adopted here is simple but adequate; compute a weighted sum of the position numbers of the characters of the name, *modulo* the number of buckets. The function **Hash** is for use inside the package body only, so its declaration is also inside the package body.

To insert a new entry, we use **Hash** to decide which bucket should contain the new entry, then insert it in that bucket's linked list. For simplicity, we can insert the new entry at the front of this list. To look up a name, we use **Hash** to decide which bucket should contain that name, then linearly search the corresponding linked list.

The package body contains an encapsulated variable, Directory_Table, which is an array of pointers to the linked lists, one for each bucket. This array will be indexed by the result of **Hash**, so its index subtype must match the function's result subtype.

```
package body Directory_Service is
   type Directory_Node;
   type Directory_Ptr is access Directory_Node;
   type Directory_Node is
         record
            Name   : Names;
            Number : Numbers;
            Next : Directory_Ptr;
         end record;
   Nr_Buckets : constant Natural := 37;  -- prime number
   subtype Buckets is Natural range 0 .. Nr_Buckets-1;
   Directory_Table : array (Buckets) of Directory_Ptr
         := (Buckets => null);  -- directory initially empty
   function Hash (Name : Names) return Buckets  is
      Sum : Buckets := 0;
   begin
      for I in Name'Range loop
         Sum := (Sum + I * Character'Pos (Name(I)))
               mod Nr_Buckets;
      end loop;
      return Sum;
   end Hash;
   procedure Insert_Entry
               (New_Name   : in Names;
                New_Number : in Numbers) is
      Bucket : constant Buckets := Hash (New_Name);
   begin
      -- insert new entry at front of list Bucket --
      Directory_Table(Bucket) :=
            new Directory_Node'
               (New_Name, New_Number,
                Directory_Table(Bucket));
   end Insert_Entry;
   procedure Lookup_Entry
               (Given_Name  : in Names;
```

```
                        Name_Found   : out Boolean;
                        Corr_Number : out Numbers) is
            Bucket : constant Buckets := Hash (Given_Name);
            Ptr : Directory_Ptr := Directory_Table(Bucket);
        begin
            loop
                if Ptr = null then
                    Name_Found := False;
                    exit;
                elsif Given_Name = Ptr.Name then
                    Name_Found := True;
                    Corr_Number := Ptr.Number;
                    exit;
                else
                    Ptr := Ptr.Next;
                end if;
            end loop;
        end Lookup_Entry;

    end Directory_Service;
```

□ *End of Example 17.5*

In this book we can only scratch the surface of the important subject of data structures. A fuller treatment may be found in any textbook on the subject, for example [Knuth 1973]. Having studied the examples, however, you should have no trouble in using Ada to declare and manipulate other kinds of data structures.

17.5. Programming methodology and data structures

We have now presented three versions of the `Directory_Service` package body. Which is the best? It is clear that the original version, using an array and relying on linear search, is the *worst*: search time is proportional to the number of directory entries. As between the two versions presented in Section 17.4, the answer is less clear-cut. In the binary tree version, search time is proportional to the (local) depth of the tree, which in a well-balanced tree is proportional to the logarithm of the number of entries. In the hash table version, search time is potentially almost independent of the number of entries, provided that no bucket contains more than one or two entries; but if the hash function is badly chosen or the hash table is allowed to become overcrowded, search time deteriorates to that required for linear search.

The point of this discussion is not to claim that one data structure is always better than others. Lists, binary trees, hash tables and other data structures are all suitable choices in different applications. The next example illustrates the importance of the particular application.

Example 17.6 *Binary tree traversal*

Suppose that the `Directory_Service` package were required to export the following additional procedure:

```
procedure List_All_Entries;
```

which is to write a lexicographically ordered listing of the directory entries.

This modification of the package declaration makes the hash table implementation (Example 17.5) unattractive, since the hash table structure is unrelated to lexicographic ordering. In the sorted binary tree implementation (Example 17.4), however, the required listing can be achieved easily by a left-root-right traverse of the tree: for each node P, list all the entries in P's left subtree, then list the entry in P itself, then list all the entries in P's right subtree. If this is wrapped up as a procedure with `P` as parameter, the first and third steps can be achieved by recursive calls on this procedure. The necessary degenerate case for the recursive procedure is when the subtree to be listed is empty.

```
procedure List_All_Entries is
   procedure List_Subtree (Subtree_Root : Directory_Ptr)  is
   begin
      if Subtree_Root /= null then
         List_Subtree (Subtree_Root.Left);
         write entry Subtree_Root.Name, Subtree_Root.Number;
         List_Subtree (Subtree_Root.Right);
      end if;
   end List_Subtree;
begin
   List_Subtree (Directory_Root);
end List_All_Entries;
```

□ *End of Example 17.6*

We suggest the following methodology for programs using nontrivial data structures. When the need for a data structure becomes apparent, declare a package that will encapsulate the data structure and will export *only* the required operations (such as insertion, deletion, search, traversal). Continue with the development of the rest of the program. This might show up necessary modifications to the package declaration. Therefore it is essential to delay implementation of the package body until the package declaration is finalized. Only then can the most suitable implementation be chosen.

The kind of data structure chosen must, first of all, be *capable* of supporting the required operations. Among those that satisfy that fundamental requirement, the choice should be based on efficiency considerations. Some programmers tend to misplace their efforts in the quest for efficiency. Coding tricks of the bit-picking variety might improve efficiency by a few percent. Programming in a low-level language might give double or triple the efficiency of a high-level language program. But choosing the most effective data structures and algorithms can often make a *order-of-magnitude* difference to the efficiency of a program. It follows that programmers' efforts are usually most productively invested in the selection of appropriate data structures and algorithms.

It might sometimes be desirable to provide an early implementation of the package encapsulating a data structure, for example to allow some other module to be tested, or to complete a demonstration version of the program. Then there is much to be said for providing a ***prototype*** implementation using some simple data structure (such as the linear search version of the Directory_Service package). This implementation can later be replaced by a more elaborate but more efficient implementation, simply by replacing the package body.

An advantage of this approach is that the prototype version of the package can be made to collect statistics about its own usage. These statistics can be used in a quantitative analysis to determine the best data structure, in an application where the best choice depends on the relative frequency of the various operations provided by the package. For example, if an array ***had*** to be used in Directory_Service, the choice between linear search and binary search should be based on the relative frequencies of the Insert_Entry and Lookup_Entry operations. Of course, such statistics gathering would be hidden inside the package body and would not affect the rest of the program.

Data structures such as the ones described in this chapter are quite standard, so packages encapsulating them can be written, tested, put in a program library, and subsequently selected 'off the shelf' for use whenever needed. This possibility is made all the more practicable by declaring them as ***generic packages***, which will be described in Chapter 22.

Each of the examples in this chapter has illustrated a single, encapsulated, instance of a data structure. Instead, a package can export the data structure type as an abstract data type. This is the style we prefer. A program written to use an encapsulated variable may need major alterations if more variables of the same type need to be introduced. However, a program using an abstract data type can trivially declare as many variables of the type as become necessary.

Example 17.7 A package for sorting several lists of names

Here is a modified package declaration for Sort_Service that exports a limited private type, Name_Lists, to allow declarations of several linked lists of names:

```
package Sort_Service is
    type Name_Lists is limited private;
    procedure Make_List_Empty
                (List : out Name_Lists);
    procedure Insert
                (New_Name : in Names;
                 List : in out Name_Lists);
    procedure Prepare_Extraction
                (List : in out Name_Lists);
    procedure Extract
                (Old_Name : out Names;
                 List : in out Name_Lists);
    function All_Extracted
                (List : Name_Lists) return Boolean;
private
    type Name_Node;
    type Name_Ptr is access Name_Node;
    type Name_Node is
          record
```

```
            Name : Names;
            Next : Name_Ptr;
        end record;
    type Name_Lists is
        record
            Head, Extract_Ptr : Name_Ptr;
        end record;
end Sort_Service;
```

Each list of names must contain its own list head and extraction position. Hence the type `Name_Lists` is declared in the private part to be a record type with these two components.

Note that `Name_Lists` is a *limited private* type. Suppose that `Name_Lists` were made simply *private*, and suppose that `ListA` and `ListB` are variables of this type. Then the assignment '`ListA := ListB;`' would simply make `ListA` point to the same list as `ListB`, rather than copying the whole of `ListB`. Thus a subsequent modification to `ListB` would affect `ListA` as well as `ListB`. The relation '`ListA = ListB`' would also be misleading. Its value would be `True` if and only if `ListA` and `ListB` point to the same list, rather than if the two lists had similar contents. It was to prevent such counterintuitive effects that `Name_Lists` was made limited private.

□ *End of Example 17.7*

Style

Pointers are rather a low-level feature in a high-level language. They are really *too* powerful, allowing data structures to be formed and reformed with few restrictions. Experience has shown that manipulation of pointers is exceedingly tricky and error-prone, even for experienced programmers, because they point to anonymous objects and because of the possibility of aliasing.

Pointers should be exploited for defining abstract data types, such as lists and directories, rather than treated as useful data objects in themselves. When a package defines an abstract data type in terms of an access type, the abstract data type should be specified as limited private in order to limit the manipulation of pointers to the package body.

17.6. Other applications of access types

This chapter might have given you the impression that access values always point to records. That is the most common case, but not the only one. In fact, Ada places no restriction on the type specified after `access` in an access type definition.

It is sometimes useful to be able to allocate and deallocate a large object, such as an array, whose lifetime does not correspond to the entire activation of some program unit. This can be done by allocating the array on the heap and accessing it through a pointer. This even allows the size of the array to be varied dynamically. This possibility is illustrated by the following example.

Example 17.8 *An editing package*

Suppose that we are required to write a simple text file editing package with the following declaration:

```
package Editing_Service is
   Max_Line_Number : constant Integer := 2000;
   subtype Line_Numbers is
         Integer range 0 .. Max_Line_Number;
   procedure Read_File
            (Filename : in String);
   procedure Replace_Line
            (Place : in Line_Numbers;
             Line  : in String);
   procedure Add_Line
            (Place : in Line_Numbers;
             Line  : in String);
   procedure Delete_Line
            (Place : in Line_Numbers);
   procedure Write_File;
   Bad_Operation : exception;
end Editing_Service;
```

`Read_File` is to copy the named external file into a 'buffer', where the actual editing operations are to take place. `Write_File` must be called later to copy the edited contents of the buffer back to the external file. The other exported operations provide for replacement, insertion and deletion of single lines at specified places in the buffer. The user is free to edit lines in any order. All line numbers refer to the *current* buffer contents, not to the original contents.

The specification strongly suggests that the buffer should be structured to allow immediate access to any specified line. For the sake of simplicity we shall use an array indexed by line number. (More elaborate data structures that impose no arbitrary limit on the number of lines are, of course, possible.) An array of strings (one string per line) would, however, be grossly wasteful of storage when there are many fewer than 2000 lines, or when the lines are much shorter than the fixed length that would have to be chosen for the strings. Much better would be an array of *pointers* to strings, since a single pointer occupies much less space than (say) a 256-character string. The editing operations then can allocate space for just as many strings as the number of lines in the buffer, and just enough space for each of these strings.

Here is a (partial) solution:

```
with Text_IO;  use Text_IO;
package body Editing_Service is
   type String_Ptr is access String;
   Size   : Line_Numbers;
   Buffer : array (1 .. Max_Line_Number) of String_Ptr;
   Edit_Filename : String_Ptr;
   procedure Read_File
               (Filename : in String) is
      Edit_File   : File_Type;
```

```
      Line_Text   : String (1 .. 256);
      Line_Length : Natural;
   begin
      Edit_Filename := new String' (Filename);
      Size := 0;
      Open (Edit_File, In_File, Filename);
      while not End_of_File (Edit_File) loop
         Get_Line (Edit_File, Line_Text, Line_Length);
         Size := Size + 1;
         Buffer(Size) :=
               new String' (Line_Text(1..Line_Length));
      end loop;
      Close (Edit_File);
         -- to allow other processes to use it meanwhile
   exception
      when others => raise Bad_Operation;
   end Read_File;

   procedure Replace_Line
               (Place : in Line_Numbers;
                Line  : in String)  is
   begin
      if Place not in 1 .. Size then
         raise Bad_Operation;
      end if;
      Buffer(Place) := new String' (Line);
   end Replace_Line;

   ...

end Editing_Service;
```

A number of observations are appropriate here. The type declaration of String_Ptr makes it an access type whose values point to objects of type String. Since the latter is an unconstrained array type, different values of type String_Ptr can point to strings of different lengths.

The allocator 'new String' (Filename)' in Read_File contains an expression that initializes the allocated string. The bounds of the allocated string are the bounds of Filename. Note that by making Edit_Filename contain a *pointer* to a string rather than the string itself, we avoid having to choose an arbitrary length for the filename stored by the package. (It will be needed by Write_File.)

The allocator 'new String' (Line_Text(1..Line_Length))' in the same procedure likewise contains an expression that initializes the allocated string. This time its bounds are the bounds of the slice, which will depend on the length of the line read from Edit_File. Since successive evaluations of this allocator might allocate strings of different lengths, we obtain a 'ragged array' effect as illustrated in Figure 17.5. Moreover, the string pointed to by a particular component of Buffer can be changed at any time. For example, the last statement of Replace_Line allocates a completely new string and makes Buffer(Place) point to that new string.

(*Exercise*: complete the package body. `Add_Line` is to insert `Line` *after* the line numbered `Place`, so `Place` may be zero. Both `Add_Line` and `Delete_Line` will require shifting of some components of `Buffer`.)

□ *End of Example 17.8*

Whenever an unconstrained array type name is given in an allocator, either an initializing expression or an index constraint must also be given. Thus the allocator '`new String`' would be illegal, since it does not give the bounds of the allocated object. But '`new String' (1 .. 80)`' would be permissible; it would allocate a 80-character string object on the heap without initializing it.

17.7. Heap space management

(This section may be omitted on a first reading.)

As mentioned in Section 17.2, allocators create new objects in a separate region of storage called the *heap*. We shall not concern ourselves here with details of how the capacity of the heap is set. It is sufficient to note that a program might eventually use up all available heap space, by evaluating too many allocators. If this happens, the exception `Storage_Error` is raised.

Example 17.9 *Exporting exceptions from the sorting package*

Let us modify the `Sort_Service` package of Example 17.3 to export exceptions `List_Full` and `List_Empty`, as was done in Example 14.2 and 3. The package declaration is:

```
package Sort_Service is
   procedure Make_List_Empty;
```

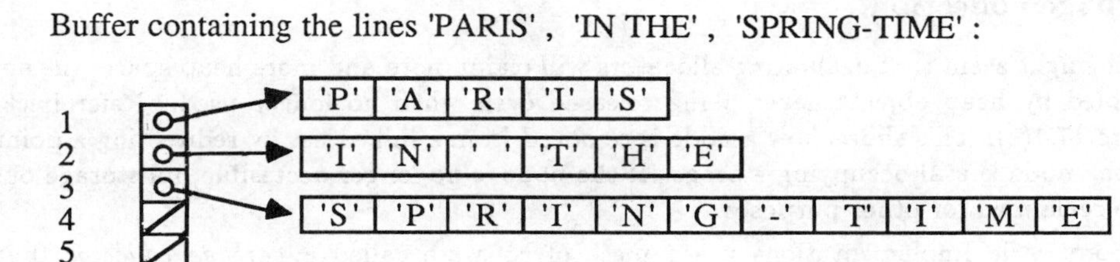

Fig. 17.5 The file buffer of `Editing_Service`

```
      procedure Insert (New_Name : in Names);
      procedure Prepare_Extraction;
      procedure Extract (Old_Name : out Names);
      function All_Extracted return Boolean;
      List_Full, List_Empty : exception;
   end Sort_Service;
```

The exception List_Empty must be raised by Extract, if Extract_Ptr is found to be null:

```
      procedure Extract (Old_Name : out Names)  is
      begin
         if Extract_Ptr = null then
            raise List_Empty;
         end if;
         Old_Name := Extract_Ptr.Name;
         Extract_Ptr := Extract_Ptr.Next;
      end Extract;
```

The exception List_Full must be raised by Insert, but only if all heap space is used up. In this event the allocator in Insert will raise the exception Storage_Error. Therefore we must provide Insert with a handler for Storage_Error that simply raises List_Full:

```
      procedure Insert (New_Name : in Names)  is
         ...
      begin
         ...
         New_Ptr := new Name_Node' (New_Name, Ptr);
         ...
      exception
         when Storage_Error => raise List_Full;
      end Insert;
```

□ *End of Example 17.9*

Garbage collection

It might seem that evaluating allocators will claim more and more heap space, the space occupied by heap objects never being released even when no longer used. Refer back to Figure 17.1(c). This shows how a node is removed from a linked list by redirecting a pointer, but the node is still occupying storage. If the node is no longer accessible, its storage ought to be reclaimed for other purposes.

Some Ada implementations use a piece of software called a *garbage collector* that is responsible for automatically deallocating inaccessible heap objects (i.e. reclaiming the storage they occupied). In the case of the linked list example of Figure 17.1, any node that is removed from the list in the manner shown in Figure 17.1(c) would indeed become inaccessible and therefore could be deallocated.

The key word here is 'accessible'. A heap object is *accessible* only if it can be reached by following pointers from *local* objects (i.e. objects declared in blocks, subprograms and packages). In Example 17.3, Head and Extract_Ptr are local objects, and both point into a linked list of nodes. Consider what happens if Make_List_Empty is called a second time, resetting Head to null. If Extract_Ptr is also null, then all the nodes in the list become inaccessible and therefore may be deallocated. On the other hand, if Extract_Ptr is pointing to a node in the list (because Extract has not yet been called often enough to extract every name in the list), then all the nodes pointed to (directly or indirectly) by Extract_Ptr are still accessible and cannot be deallocated until Prepare_Extraction is called.

Garbage collection is desirable to reclaim unused storage automatically, but it is also very time-consuming. The garbage collector must, whenever activated, trace every path from every existing local access object, in order to ensure that no accessible heap object is incorrectly deallocated. Furthermore, the timing is unpredictable. This is a severe problem in real-time applications, where unpredictable variations in speed of execution are unacceptable.

One time when automatic deallocation is both easy and fast is on termination of a program unit that is the scope of an access type T, for at that point all local objects of type T must cease to exist, and therefore all heap objects created by allocators of type T must become inaccessible. The following pragma:

```
pragma Controlled (T);
```

may be used to request that deallocation of these heap objects take place only on leaving the scope of T. (This pragma must be placed after the type declaration of T, in the same declarative part.)

In some applications time and space resources are so scarce that neither the overheads of automatic garbage collection nor any waste of storage by inaccessible objects can be tolerated. In such circumstances the programmer needs a mechanism for explicitly deallocating individual heap objects. This mechanism is provided in Ada by a library unit called Unchecked_Deallocation. Use of this mechanism is notoriously error-prone, and in any case will not be described until Chapter 24.

Exercises 17

17.1. The length of a list L can be defined recursively: (a) if L is empty, its length is zero; (b) if L is non-empty, its length is one more than the length of the tail of L. (The tail of L is the list containing all but the first node of L.) Rewrite the function body of List_Length, Example 17.1, by transcribing this recursive definition.

17.2. (a) Write a procedure with the following declaration:

```
procedure Delete_Node
            (Del_Ptr : in Item_Ptr;
             List_Head : in out Item_Ptr);
```

List_Head points to the head of a linked list of items (see Section 17.2), and Del_Ptr points to a node that is to be removed from this list. Why is this operation awkward?

(b) Suppose now that the linked list is redesigned so that each node points to both its predecessor and its follower in the list. (The first node in the list will have null as its predecessor.) Modify the type declarations defining the linked list of items accordingly. Rewrite Delete_Node to take advantage of the predecessor links.

17.3. Write a non-recursive version of the procedure Insert_Entry of Example 17.4.

17.4. Provide a package body for `Sort_Service` in Example 17.7.

17.5. (a) Provide a body for the `Multi_Directory_Service` package of Example 13.8, using a binary tree representation for the limited private type `Directories`.

(b) Add to the package a subprogram `Copy_Directory` that makes a *complete* copy of a directory.

17.6. Write a program that simulates a queue of customers at an office counter or supermarket checkout. A customer on arrival joins the end of the queue. The customer at the front of the queue is served first and then departs. The times of customers' arrivals and departures are supplied as input data to the simulation program. An arrival is indicated by a line of input data containing the letter 'A' and the time of day (hours, minutes, seconds); a departure is similarly indicated by a line of input data containing the letter 'D' and the time of day. Assume that the input data is ordered by the time of day. The program is to output a histogram showing the number of customers in the queue at intervals of one minute. It is also to compute the mean and standard deviation of the time spent by customers in the queue. (See Exercises 10 for a definition of 'standard deviation'.)

18

Types with Discriminants

18.1. Records and discriminants

The data objects in a program model the entities of some physical or conceptual system in the real world. Consider a payroll program, for example. The master file models the work force, and each employee is modeled by one of the master file records. We cannot depict the real world exactly, in all its richness of detail. We are forced to *abstract* — a record in a payroll master file does not contain everything there is to know about an employee, only *relevant* information. But abstraction is not the same thing as impreciseness. We want the features that are included in the model to be represented as faithfully as possible.

In practical terms, this means choosing data types with great care. Most often we want to model entities as aggregations of values, each of which in turn models some attribute of the entity. In the payroll system, for example, each employee record is an aggregation of components such as name, social security number and salary. Such aggregations of data are represented in Ada by arrays or records. Array types and record types are therefore fundamental to the accurate modeling of many applications.

Using the Ada features described so far, the structure of an array or record object cannot be made to vary during its lifetime. By use of an unconstrained array type we can delay fixing the index range of an array object until it is created, and different array objects of the same type can have different index ranges. Once created, however, an array object belongs to a specific subtype and its structure is fixed. Records, as described in Chapter 11, have no flexibility of structure at all.

What should we do when the best model for an entity is a record with a flexible structure? We get a clue as to how this difficulty is resolved by considering array types and their subtypes. There is a facility that allows us to declare *record* types having several subtypes, where the subtypes may have different internal structures, just as array subtypes may have different sizes. Moreover, a record variable of such a type can vary its structure dynamically. This new facility is the *discriminant.*

Example 18.1 *Payroll records*

In a payroll system, employees might be modeled by the following record type:

```
type Grade is (Monthly_Paid, Weekly_Paid);
type Employee is
      record
         Status    : Grade;
         Name      : String (1 .. 20);
         Birthdate : Date;
         Salary    : Money;
```

```
            Self, Supervisor : Employee_Id;
        end record;
```

One payroll program handles monthly paid staff, a second handles weekly paid staff. It would be appropriate to define subtypes Monthly_Paid_Employee and Weekly_Paid_Employee in order to specify these subsystems. But a plain record type such as Employee has no subtypes (apart from itself). By making Status a discriminant of the type, however, it becomes possible to define the subtypes we want:

```
type Employee (Status : Grade) is
    record
        Name      : String (1 .. 20);
        Birthdate : Date;
        Salary    : Money;
        Self, Supervisor : Employee_Id;
    end record;
```

The type Employee now has two distinct subtypes, Employee(Monthly_Paid) and Employee(Weekly_Paid). We can declare variables of these subtypes:

```
Programmer : Employee (Monthly_Paid);
Caretaker  : Employee (Weekly_Paid);
```

□ *End of Example 18.1*

We use the selected component notation for the discriminant, Programmer.Status, just as for the ordinary record components like Programmer.Name.

Both Programmer and Caretaker are said to be *constrained* to take only values of their subtype. In other words, Programmer.Status is fixed to be Monthly_Paid, and Caretaker.Status is fixed to be Weekly_Paid. Any statement that attempts to change these discriminants will raise Constraint_Error.

A declaration such as 'Recruit : Employee;' is not permitted, because Recruit.Status would be initially undefined and therefore the subtype of Recruit would be undefined.

We can write subtype declarations for record subtypes in the usual way:

```
subtype Monthly_Paid_Employee is Employee (Monthly_Paid);
subtype Weekly_Paid_Employee  is Employee (Weekly_Paid);

Programmer : Monthly_Paid_Employee;
Caretaker  : Weekly_Paid_Employee;
```

A discriminant can be given a default value. For example, if most employees are monthly paid, we could make that the default by writing:

```
type Employee (Status : Grade := Monthly_Paid) is
  record
    as above
  end record;
```

The most important point is that now the declaration:

```
Recruit : Employee;
```

is permitted, and Recruit.Status is initially Monthly_Paid; but Recruit is *unconstrained*, and can have its subtype changed at any time. However, we are not allowed to change the discriminant by itself, for example by 'Recruit.Status := Monthly_Paid;' — it can be given a new value only as the result of an assignment to the entire record variable, for example:

```
Recruit := Programmer;
```

The type of a discriminant must always be discrete. In the subtype indication `Employee(Weekly_Paid)`, the phrase in parentheses is an example of a *discriminant constraint.* Its effect is to fix the value of the discriminant for all values of the subtype. (See the syntax diagrams 'subtype_indication' and 'discriminant_constraint' in Appendix A.)

The attribute `Constrained` indicates whether an object is constrained or not. In Example 18.1, `Programmer'Constrained` is `True`, while `Recruit'Constrained` is `False`.

A type may have several discriminants. (See the syntax diagrams 'type_declaration' and 'discriminant_part' in Appendix A.) If any of the discriminants has a default value, they all must have default values. Only a record type (or a private type implemented as a record type) can have a discriminant. This is not a serious restriction, because a record can have components of any type.

The discriminant is in most respects an ordinary component of the record, but it does have some special properties:

- The discriminant acts as a parameter of the type, and each value of the discriminant defines a distinct subtype.
- The discriminant always has a value (unlike ordinary record components, which might initially be undefined). The discriminant of a constrained object has its value determined at its declaration and is fixed thereafter. The discriminant of an unconstrained object has its value initialized to the default value, although it may be changed later by assignment to the whole record.

Declaring objects with appropriate constraints helps us to model real-world entities more precisely. This makes the program more expressive of our intentions, and so is an aid both to the maintenance programmer and to the Ada compiler. In particular the compiler is helped in checking the source program, and in mapping its data types on to computer storage. Efficient programs are the happy byproduct. This is as true for discriminant constraints as for range constraints. When declaring an unconstrained type or object, always consider whether it should be constrained.

18.2. Variant records

Example 18.1 illustrated a record type whose subtypes are structurally identical. We also sometimes need record types with subtypes that contain different components. These are called *variant records.* A variant record has some components that are common to all subtypes, but also some components that are peculiar to particular subtypes.

The variant record is to data as the case statement is to control flow. For that reason Ada uses a syntax for variant records that is reminiscent of the syntax of case statements. (See the syntax diagrams 'record_type_definition' and 'variant_part' in Appendix A.)

Example 18.2 *An inventory control system*

Consider an inventory control system that is concerned with three classes of warehouse

— large, medium and small. Some data are common to all warehouses; others are peculiar to one class of warehouse. Correspondingly, some modules of the system will operate on warehouses in general, while others will be specialized to large, medium or small warehouses.

We introduce a type to represent the three warehouse classes:

```
type Warehouse_Class is (Small, Medium, Large);
```

Now we need a type, `Warehouse`, representing warehouses in general. This will be a record type, to contain several components of different types. The general modules can then be specified in terms of `Warehouse`. But the specialized modules for small warehouses (for example) should not be specified in terms of this type, because they work only on data peculiar to small warehouses. In fact we want three subtypes of `Warehouse`, each containing only the components peculiar to one class of warehouse. The declaration of `Warehouse` is, in outline:

```
type Warehouse (Class : Warehouse_Class := Small) is
   record
      other fields
   end record;
```

where we have (somewhat arbitrarily) made `Small` the default value for the discriminant `Class`. The advantage of this is that we shall be able to declare unconstrained objects of type `Warehouse`.

Suppose that we must hold the floor space for warehouses of all classes. Suppose also that the person in charge of a warehouse has a rank that depends on the warehouse class (a manager for a large warehouse, a storeman for a medium warehouse, a clerk for a small warehouse). Furthermore, for medium and small warehouses we wish to store the identity and distance of the nearest large warehouse (for restocking purposes). The type declaration then becomes (*version 1*):

```
type Warehouse (Class : Warehouse_Class := Small) is
   record
      Space : Area;      -- square meters
      case Class is
         when Large =>
            Manager     : Employee;
         when Medium =>
            Storeman    : Employee;
            Supplier_M  : Large_Warehouse_Id;
            Distance_M  : Distance;     -- kilometers
         when Small =>
            Clerk       : Employee;
            Supplier_S  : Large_Warehouse_Id;
            Distance_S  : Distance;  -- kilometers
      end case;
   end record;
```

Note that all components must have different identifiers, so we have had to distinguish between `Supplier_M` and `Supplier_S`, and between `Distance_M` and `Distance_S`. This could be avoided by using nested variants (*version 2*):

```
type Warehouse (Class : Warehouse_Class := Small) is
   record
```

```
            Space : Area;     -- square meters
            case Class is
               when Large =>
                  Manager  : Employee;
               when others =>
                  Supplier : Large_Warehouse_Id;
                  Distance_to_Supplier : Distance;
                  case Class is
                     when Medium =>
                        Storeman : Employee;
                     when Small =>
                        Clerk    : Employee;
                     when others =>
                        null;
                  end case;
            end case;
         end record;
```

The **others** in the nested variant part ensures that all possible values of Class are listed. This is required by Ada for all variant parts, although it is logically unnecessary in this particular example. The explicit **null** indicates an empty list of components.

Assume the declaration 'W : Warehouse;'. The components of W actually existing at a given time depend on the current value of the discriminant W.Class. For example:

- W.Space exists at all times.
- W.Manager exists only when the discriminant is Large.
- W.Supplier (in version 2) exists only when the discriminant is Medium or Small.
- W.Clerk exists only when the discriminant is Small.

The analogy between the variant record and the case statement is best seen when we write statements to inspect the contents of a variant record. Here is a procedure to display the details of a given warehouse (assuming version 1 of the type declaration):

```
procedure Put_Warehouse_Details (W : in Warehouse) is
begin
   Put ("Class: ");  Put (W.Class);  New_Line;
   Put ("Space: ");  Put (W.Space);  Put ("sq.m.");  New_Line;
   case W.Class is
      when Large =>
         Put ("Manager: ");  Put (W.Manager);  New_Line;
      when Medium =>
         Put ("Storeman: ");  Put (W.Storeman);  New_Line;
         Put ("Supplied from ");  Put (W.Supplier_M);
         Put (" at distance ");  Put (W.Distance_M);
         Put ("km.");  New_Line;
      when Small =>
         Put ("Clerk: ");  Put (W.Clerk);  New_Line;
         Put ("Supplied from ");  Put (W.Supplier_S);
         Put (" at distance ");  Put (W.Distance_S);
         Put ("km.");  New_Line;
```

```
    end case;
  end Put_Warehouse_Details;
```

This case statement ensures that each component of `W` is referred to only when the discriminant `W.Class` has the appropriate value.

□ *End of Example 18.2*

A component in the variant part of a record exists only if the record has a discriminant value appropriate to that component. On each reference to such a component, the Ada compiler inserts a check that the current value of the discriminant is appropriate, and if this check fails, the `Constraint_Error` exception is raised. This would happen, for example, if we attempted to refer to `W.Manager` when `W.Class` is not `Large`. This is a programming error that must be guarded against, in the same way as an array index outside the index range. The compiler will usually generate code to check the variant at run time. However, if we declare:

```
  Central_Warehouse : Warehouse (Large);
```

no such check is required on a reference to `Central_Warehouse.Manager`, because `Central_Warehouse` is constrained and `Central_Warehouse.Class` is always `Large`.

The amount of storage space needed for a variant record depends on the discriminant value. If the object is unconstrained, the discriminant value could change during the object's lifetime, so the compiler will allow space for the largest variant. If the object is constrained, on the other hand, the compiler can allow just enough space for the appropriate variant. This point is illustrated by Figure 18.1; part of the space occupied by an unconstrained variant record is sometimes unused.

18.3. Arrays and discriminants

Each index range of an array object is normally fixed throughout the object's lifetime. The one exception to this rule is an array component of a record with discriminants. Ada allows such an array to have an index bound determined by the *current* value of a discriminant. Changing the discriminant is, as always, possible only by assignment to the entire record. Therefore it is impossible to change the index bounds of the array without simultaneously providing new values for the array's own components.

Example 18.3 *OIS: database subsystem*

We return to the Office Information System introduced in Section 14.6. One part of this is to be a database subsystem. This is to support a collection of named files, with a variety of data formats, and a set of operations on these files. Some of these operations must be capable of working on all files (e.g. *create*, *delete*, *join*); others are to work only on files with a specific data format or a narrow range of formats.

In a conventional file system, the structure of each file (i.e. the type of the file elements) is rigidly fixed by the numerous programs that process it. For example, one file might contain payroll records, with its elements being of type `Employee` (Example 18.1); a second file might contain a mailing list, with its elements being of some other type `Name_and_Address`. We cannot write in Ada a sufficiently general system to handle files of all such types. For example, a subprogram whose parameter is a file containing elements of type `Employee` cannot accept a file whose elements are of type `Name_and_Address`, nor *vice versa*.

The database subsystem must, on the other hand, handle files with a variety of data formats. In order to implement this, we must design a single type for all data formats permitted in the subsystem.

The operator is provided with a command to create a file and specify that file's data format. Each file consists of a sequence of *tuples*, and each tuple consists of a fixed number of *fields*; for each field the operator specifies a *name* and a *kind* — either *alphanumeric* or *numeric*. An alphanumeric field consists of a sequence of characters, whose length is also specified by the operator (and thereafter is fixed). A numeric field contains a single number. We shall not concern ourselves here with the type of the numbers; let us assume that they are of a globally declared type `Number`.

In each file all tuples have the same format. However, different files may differ in the number, names and kinds of the fields, and in the lengths of the alphanumeric fields. The database subsystem must maintain a central *catalog* containing, for each file, its file name and a description of its tuples. Figure 18.2 illustrates the logical structure of some typical files.

We need to design types to describe and represent all possible tuples. It will be conve-

Assume version 1 of the declaration of **`Warehouse.`**

(a) **`W : Warehouse;`**

Size=Large	Space	Manager	(not used)	

or

Size=Medium	Space	Storeman	Supplier_M	Distance_M

or

Size=Small	Space	Clerk	Supplier_S	Distance_S

(b) **`Central_Warehouse : Warehouse (Large);`**

Size=Large	Space	Manager

(c) **`District_Warehouse : Warehouse (Medium);`**

Size=Medium	Space	Storeman	Supplier_M	Distance_M

(d) **`Local_Warehouse : Warehouse (Small);`**

Size=Small	Space	Clerk	Supplier_S	Distance_S

Fig. 18.1 Storage layout for variant records

nient to collect all the alphanumeric fields of each tuple together in a single string (formed by concatenating the alphanumeric fields), so the tuple representation will be parametrized only by the total length of the alphanumeric fields (and not separately by all their individual lengths). The numeric fields can be represented by an array of numbers, so the tuple representation must also be parametrized by the number of numeric fields. Each alphanumeric field is then specified by its lower and upper bounds in the string, and each numeric field is specified by an index into the array. Figure 6.3 illustrates the representation of the files of Figure 6.2. Thus we arrive at our type for the tuple representation. It will be a record type with a discriminant for the total length of the alphanumeric fields and a second discriminant for the number of numeric fields:

```
type Number_Sequence is array (Positive range <>) of Number;
type Tuple_Contents
      (Total_Alph_Length, Nr_Numeric_Fields : Natural) is
   record
      A : String (1 .. Total_Alph_Length);
      N : Number_Sequence (1 .. Nr_Numeric_Fields);
   end record;
```

Thus we have two array components, A and N, whose index bounds are fixed by the discriminant values.

File 'STAFF'

'STAFF#' numeric	'NAME' 12 chars.	'DEPARTMENT' 10 chars.
9134	Jane Doe	Research
170	Joe Foot	Sales
5311	Al Penpusher	Admin
13	Benito Duce	Admin

File 'COMMITTEES'

'COMM#' numeric	'NAME' 10 chars.	'CONVENER' numeric	'FREQ' numeric
801	Planning	13	13
841	Personnel	199	8
842	Sales	170	1

File 'JOBS'

'STAFF#' numeric	'COMM#' numeric
9134	801
9134	841
170	842
13	801
13	841

Fig. 18.2 Logical structure of files in the database subsystem

An individual tuple field is described by its kind, name, and position within `A` or `N`:

```
type Field_Kind is (Alphanumeric, Numeric);
type Field_Description (Kind : Field_Kind) is
    record
        Name : String (1 .. 16);
        case Kind is
            when Alphanumeric =>
                Lower, Upper : Positive;  -- field is A(Lower..Upper)
            when Numeric =>
                Index : Positive;         -- field is N(Index)
        end case;
    end record;
```

The tuple description will be parametrized by the number of fields:

```
type Field_Sequence is
    array (Positive range <>) of Field_Description;
type Tuple_Description (Nr_Fields : Natural) is
    record
        Field_Descr : Field_Sequence (1 .. Nr_Fields);
    end record;
```

Note that no defaults are provided for the discriminants of the types we have designed. Whenever a file is created, values must therefore be provided for all discriminants, and the resulting objects are constrained. In other words, the structure of a given file will be frozen on creation. Different files, however, may have different values for the discriminants.

File 'STAFF'

A	N(1)
´Jane Doe Research `	9134
´Joe Foot Sales `	170
´Al PenpusherAdmin `	5311
´Benito Duce Admin `	13

File 'COMMITTEES'

A	N(1)	N(2)	N(3)
´Planning `	801	13	13
´Personnel `	141	199	8
´Sales `	842	170	1

File 'JOBS'

A	N(1)	N(2)
´ `	9134	801
´ `	9134	841
´ `	170	842
´ `	13	801
´ `	13	841

Fig. 18.3 Representation of files in the database subsystem

Nevertheless they all have the same element type, `Tuple_Contents`, and can be handled by the same modules.

□ *End of Example 18.3*

As illustrated above, an array that is a record component can have a discriminant of the record as an index bound. Only the discriminant value itself may be used as an index bound, however, not a more general expression containing the discriminant.

18.4. Access types and discriminants

We have seen that discriminants are used to define data structures that possess some flexibility of structure. We have also seen, in Chapter 17, how dynamic data structures can be defined using access types. Discriminants and access types are quite distinct features of Ada, but they can profitably be used in conjunction.

An access type definition can specify a constraint on the values pointed to. One possibility is a discriminant constraint, for example:

```
type Large_Warehouse_Id is access Warehouse (Large);
```

This type declaration guarantees that every value of type `Large_Warehouse_Id` points to a record describing a large warehouse. On the other hand:

```
type Warehouse_Id is access Warehouse;
```

allows values of type `Warehouse_Id` to point to records describing any warehouses.

Example 18.4 *OIS: reminder subsystem*

Some calculators have a clock with an alarm that can be a useful reminder for appointments. Our Office Information System is to have a similar, but more sophisticated, facility. Each reminder has a message associated with it, and can be repeated just once, weekly, monthly or annually.

A suitable data structure would be a linked list of records, each record containing one message, and stored in time order so that the next reminder can easily be found. Rather than allowing space for the longest possible message, we wish to minimize the size of each record by storing only the characters of the message. Hence the record has the message length as a discriminant. This gives:

```
type Frequency is (Once, Weekly, Monthly, Annually);

type Reminder_Node (Message_Length : Natural);
type Reminder_Ptr is access Reminder_Node;
type Reminder_Node (Message_Length : Natural) is
      record
         Alarm_Time : Time;
         Freq       : Frequency;
         Message    : String (1 .. Message_Length);
         Next       : Reminder_Ptr;
      end record;
```

The first reminder in the list will be interrogated at regular intervals. When Alarm_Time has come, the message will be sent and the reminder node will be either deleted (if Freq is Once) or moved to a new position in the list with Alarm_Time altered.

□ *End of Example 18.4*

18.5. Private types and discriminants

In Example 18.2, the type Warehouse had two levels of detail, the discriminant and the other components, and both levels are visible to the user of the type. A private type that is implemented as a record has components that are completely hidden from the user of the private type. Such a private type can also have discriminants, but these are *visible* to the user. This means that the two levels of detail are distinguished by the language rules — the upper level is visible, and the lower level invisible, outside the defining package. This possibility suggests that we can use discriminants for reasons of modularity, as well as for flexibility. The use of discriminants to define levels of visibility for private types is, however, severely restricted in practice by the rule that discriminants must have discrete types.

Example 18.5 A varying length string package

A string handling package is to be provided, following the semantics of PL/I varying length strings. Each string variable S is declared with a given maximum length. Thereafter a string of any number of characters (up to the maximum) may be assigned to S, *without padding*. For example, if S has maximum length 10, then S may at different times contain values such as "" (the empty string), "apple", "paw paw" and "grapefruit"; but never "passion fruit", which is too long. (By contrast, the Ada declaration 'S : String(1..10);' allows S to contain only strings of *exactly* 10 characters.)

Our package declaration is to export subprograms that return the length of a varying length string, append one string to another, place a value of type Character or String in a varying length string, extract the String value corresponding to a varying length string, and perform simple pattern matching. It should also permit assignment and equality tests for varying length strings. We are allowed to assume an upper limit of 100 for the length of any string.

```
package Flex_String_Handler is
   String_Limit : constant Positive := 100;
   subtype String_Index is Natural range 0 .. String_Limit;
   type Flex_String (Max_Length : String_Index := String_Limit) is
         private;
   function Length  (X : Flex_String) return String_Index;
   function Flex1   (C : in Character) return Flex_String;
   function Flex    (S : in String)    return Flex_String;
   function Extract (X : Flex_String) return String;
   procedure Append (X : in out Flex_String;
                     Y : in Flex_String);
   function Find (Pattern, Text : Flex_String) return String_Index;
```

```
private
   implementation details
end Flex_String_Handler;
```

Since assignment and equality tests are defined for `Flex_String`, we have made it a non-limited private type. We must be careful to ensure that the representation of the type gives the required semantics for these operations. A suitable representation is an array of `Max_Length` characters, within which the characters of the varying length string are stored left justified. To ensure that the operators `=` and `/=` work correctly, we pad on the right with spaces. (These padding spaces are present only in the *representation*; the user of the package should never be aware of their presence.)

```
type Flex_String (Max_Length : String_Index := String_Limit) is
   record
      Length : String_Index := 0;
      Ch     : String (1 .. Max_Length)
                 := (1 .. Max_Length => ' ');
   end record;
```

Here we have chosen to make the empty string the default initial value for `Flex_String` objects.

The package body is fairly straightforward to program. For instance:

```
function Flex1 (C : in Character)
      return Flex_String is
begin
   return (1, (1 => C, others => ' '));
end Flex1;
```

(*Exercise*: program the complete package body.)

□ *End of Example 18.5*

Exercises 18

18.1. Declare a variant record to represent one of the 'tokens' of Case Study III.

18.2. Design types for representing a family tree. Make the simplifying assumption that nobody marries more than once. Produce a package declaration exporting operations for construction and interrogation of such a family tree.

18.3. Specify and implement a package that handles polynomials in x, of any order, e.g. $2x^4 - 9.5x^2 + 3.5$ (of order 4) or $5x$ (of order 1). The package must export an abstract data type, `Polynomial`, and subprograms to create, add, subtract, multiply and copy polynomials, to return the order of a polynomial, to return the coefficient of a given power, and to change a coefficient.

18.4. (a) Complete the type declaration:

```
type Matrix (Nr_Rows, Nr_Cols : Natural) is ...;
```

so that an object of subtype `Matrix(M,N)` represents an `M` × `N` matrix (both lower bounds being 1).

(b) Using this type, or otherwise, complete the type declaration:

```
type Square_Matrix (Side : Natural) is ...;
```

which is to represent square matrices.

(c) Write a subprogram that computes the product of two square matrices.

19

Numeric Types

19.1. Introduction

There are two distinct kinds of computer arithmetic: integer arithmetic for exact computation, and real arithmetic for approximate computation. Ada provides two corresponding classes of numeric types: integer types, exemplified by the predefined type `Integer`, and real types, exemplified by the predefined type `Float`. Preview Figure 20.1.

The design of the numeric types in Ada addresses an important problem. We shall illustrate this in the case of integer arithmetic, but the case of real arithmetic is similar.

Each machine can easily handle integer numbers up to a certain maximum size. For example, on most 16-bit machines 32-bit arithmetic is expensive. Consequently it is important that Ada does not require 32-bit arithmetic to be used in all programs. Since different machines have different properties, no rigid rules on the capacity of integer computations are included in the language. Instead the *programmer* is enabled to define each numeric type with a range of values determined by the requirements of the problem. This allows the compiler to choose a representation for the type that is as economical as possible on the target machine. Moreover, specifying a range of values for each integer type helps to document the program and focuses attention on the algorithm instead of the machine.

Analogous arguments hold for the *precision* of a real type. As we shall see, Ada allows the programmer to specify this too.

19.2. Integer types

Predefined integer types

`Integer` is an example of an *integer type*. For a specific implementation, it corresponds to the most easily handled range of integer values, typically occupying one machine word. See Figure 2.1.

Apart from `Integer` (which must be provided), an implementation is free to provide further predefined types `Short_Integer` (with a smaller range than `Integer`) and/or `Long_Integer` (with a larger range than `Integer`). The operations available on these types are exactly the same as the `Integer` operations. For example, if `I` is of type `Integer`, and `L1` and `L2` are of type `Long_Integer`, then the expressions `L1+L2` and `L1+3` are legal (and of type `Long_Integer`), but the expression `L1+I` is ill-typed. The general rule with the predefined integer operations is that the operands must be of the same type, and the result is of that same integer type (or of type `Boolean`). See the package `Standard` (Appendix D).

Casual use of the type Integer is safe only if you can be sure that the range Integer'First through Integer'Last is adequate for your needs. (It is reasonably safe to assume that 16-bit capacity at least is available.) Short_Integer and Long_Integer are not guaranteed to be provided at all, so explicit use of these types in a program is inadvisable.

Example 19.1 *Integer computation*

A pair of distinct nonnegative integers M and N are an ***amicable pair*** if the sum of the divisors of M equals N, and ***vice versa***. A function to test for an amicable pair is simply expressed in terms of this definition:

```
function Is_Amicable_Pair (N, M : Natural) return Boolean is
begin
   return (N /= M
          and then Sum_Divisors (N) = M
          and then Sum_Divisors (M) = N);
end Is_Amicable_Pair;
```

The function Sum_Divisors can now be written to complete the implementation:

```
function Sum_Divisors (N : Natural) return Natural is
   Sum : Natural := 1;
begin
   for D in 2 .. N/2 loop
      if N mod D = 0 then
         Sum := Sum + D;
      end if;
   end loop;
   return Sum;
end Sum_Divisors;
```

This solution is formally correct, but unfortunately it contains a gross design error. The problem is that the range of values on which Sum_Divisors will operate, namely 0 .. Integer'Last, is inadequate. On a 16-bit machine, for example, this range would contain only 8 amicable pairs, which could be stored in a table! Nor would it be appropriate to use (a subtype of) Long_Integer instead, because an implementation might not provide this type, or it might be needlessly expensive. The best solution is to declare a suitable new integer type that has just the desired range of values. That will be discussed a little later.

□ *End of Example 19.1*

Using type Integer is so much a matter of habit for most programmers, trained in other languages, that you should make a deliberate effort to avoid it. A fairly safe guideline is to use Integer only in contexts where 30,000 is very large (e.g. as a column number, or as a number of terminals).

Declaring new integer types

The type definition for a new integer type simply gives the range of values needed. See the syntax diagram 'integer_type_definition' in Appendix A. For instance, suppose that the function `Is_Amicable_Pair` of Example 19.1 is intended to work on integers up to 100,000. Instead of using (a subtype of) `Integer`, the following type should be declared:

```
type Pair_Integer is range 0 .. 100_000;
```

and each occurrence of `Natural` should be replaced by `Pair_Integer`.

All integer types are distinct from one another, so values of one integer type cannot be mixed arbitrarily with values of another. This type checking barrier can be used to protect logically distinct data values against misuse (e.g. mixing sums of money with populations or social security numbers). The operations appropriate to one type can be provided by subprograms that accept parameters of the intended type only. For example, the function `Is_Amicable_Pair` with `Pair_Integer` parameters is *not* available for `Integer` actual parameters.

You should declare your own integer type whenever a logically distinct set of integer values arises. For example:

```
type Bank_Balance is range -9999 .. +9999;

type Card_Count is range 0 .. 52;

type Disk_Address is range 0 .. 2**30 - 1;
```

Suppose that `Balance`, `Count` and `Addr` are variables of these three types (respectively). Then expressions like '`Balance + Addr`' and assignments like '`Addr := Count;`' are illegal as well as meaningless, because distinct types may not be mixed in these ways. On the other hand, '`Balance + 1000`' and '`Count := 13;`' are legal. In this way the type rules can be a useful protection against logical errors that might otherwise go undetected.

An important aspect of program design is to decide when new types should be introduced, the basis for the decision being that values of the different types will be kept quite separate. Later we shall see how values *can* be converted from one integer type to another, but initially you should choose new types on the assumption that no such conversions should be needed.

The lower and upper bounds in an integer type definition must be static integer expressions. These values are computed at compile time and are used to choose a suitable representation for values of the new type.

The integer operations are applicable to *all* integer types. See the package `Standard` (Appendix D). Note that in a particular application some of these operations might be meaningless. For example, if `B1` and `B2` are of type `Bank_Balance`, then the expressions `B1+B2`, `B1-B2`, `B1*B2` (and so on) are all legal, although only the first two are sensible.

Integer subtypes

Any object of an integer type can be declared with a range constraint. It is often better to use an appropriate subtype identifier. This can be a valuable localization when several objects share the same constraint. The limits of a subtype range constraint can be any expressions of the base type — they are not restricted to static expressions as in the constraint of an integer type definition. (The reason is that the bounds of an integer type definition must be known to the compiler, so that a suitable representation can be chosen; whereas the bounds of a subtype need not be known until run time.) For example, if we declare:

```
subtype Credit_Balance is
        Bank_Balance range 0 .. Bank_Balance'Last;
```

we can now declare variables of subtype `Credit_Balance` without having to repeat the base type name and the range constraint. Given the object declaration '`CB : Credit_Balance;`', the operations that are applicable to `CB` are just those applicable to type `Bank_Balance`, except that any assignment to `CB` is checked for compliance with the range constraint.

Integer type conversions

Type conversions are allowed between any two integer types. The target type name is used as a function name for such a conversion, for example:

```
Addr := Disk_Address (I);
```

Here the `Integer` value of `I` is converted to the integer type `Disk_Address`. The type conversion would raise `Constraint_Error` if the value of `I` did not lie within the range of `Disk_Address`.

Type conversions typically require no code to be executed at run time (except possibly for a range check). They are essential for type security, however, and they make any circumvention of the normal type rules absolutely explicit. Nevertheless, a well-designed program should make minimal use of type conversions, because a compiler cannot check that the conversion makes sense.

Example 19.2 Temperature scales

An automatic weather monitoring station handles temperature data in both the Celsius and Fahrenheit scales. Mixing the values on the two scales should not be permitted, so they should be represented by two distinct types. For the purposes of this example we shall use integer types. Fractions of a degree, on either scale, are ignored. The two types might be declared as follows:

```
type Celsius    is range -40 .. +100;
type Fahrenheit is range -40 .. +212;
```

The small range of values required means that the compiler can choose a compact representation.

We need a pair of functions to convert temperatures from one scale to the other. The results must be correct to the nearest degree. If `F` is of type `Fahrenheit`, `Celsius(F)` does not perform the necessary conversion, because only the type and not the numerical value is changed. (This illustrates why type conversions must be used with caution.) The following solution is a little complicated because the integer division operator `/` truncates the quotient, whereas we want the results rounded:

```
function F_to_C (F : Fahrenheit) return Celsius is
begin
   if F > 32 then
      return Celsius ((5*(F-32) + 4) / 9);
   else
      return Celsius ((5*(F-32) - 4) / 9);
   end if;
end F_to_C;

function C_to_F (C : Celsius) return Fahrenheit is
begin
```

```
      if C > 0 then
         return Fahrenheit ((C*9 + 2) / 5 + 32);
      else
         return Fahrenheit ((C*9 - 2) / 5 + 32);
      end if;
   end C_to_F;
```

□ *End of Example 19.2*

Relationship between declared and predefined integer types

(This subsection may be omitted on a first reading.)

Each new integer type is based on one of the predefined integer types. For example, the predefined type used to implement **Pair_Integer** must include the whole of **Pair_Integer'Range**, but otherwise the compiler is free to choose any predefined integer type. Suppose that a particular compiler chooses the type **Integer**, on the grounds that in the target machine **Integer'Range** includes the whole of the range 0 through 100,000. Then the type **Pair_Integer** is said to be *derived* from **Integer**, and **Integer** is called the *parent type* of **Pair_Integer**. All declared integer types are derived types. The derivation can be made explicit by using a *derived type definition*. The declaration of **Pair_Integer** is equivalent (as we suppose) to:

```
   type Pair_Integer is new Integer range 0 .. 100_000;
```

This means that **Pair_Integer** is a copy of the type **Integer**, but with the constraint that all **Pair_Integer** values are within the range 0 through 100,000.

It is the *compiler* that determines the parent type from an integer type definition. **Integer** could be chosen as the parent type of **Pair_Integer** only if **Integer'Range** includes the whole of **Pair_Integer'Range**. On a 16-bit machine this would not be the case, and the parent type might then be **Long_Integer** instead (if this type is available).

From the programmer's point of view, what is really important is that the logic of the program is not affected by the compiler's choice of parent type. **Pair_Integer** is a new integer type, with a range of values chosen by the programmer. It is distinct from all other types, even its own parent type, so **Pair_Integer** may not be mixed with any other integer types in expressions or assignments.

Example 19.2 illustrates an important point about arithmetic in a declared integer type. Let us suppose that **Short_Integer** has a 16-bit representation, and that this is chosen as the parent type of **Celsius** and **Fahrenheit**. The expression **(C*9+2)/5+32** is of type **Celsius**, but its value could easily be outside the range of values of **Celsius**, for example if **C** is +100. Fortunately, however, the value of the expression (and each of its subexpressions) will remain within the range of the parent type **Short_Integer**. Such expressions *can* be evaluated, within what is called the *extended range* of the type **Celsius**. The reason for permitting this extended range is that the arithmetic operations of **Celsius** are based on the arithmetic operations of **Short_Integer**, rather than being new operations special to the new type. This has the advantage that range checking is not performed after every individual operation, but only when the value is assigned, used in a type conversion (as in Example 19.2), or whatever. You must be careful not to assume too large an extended range, because the actual range provided depends upon the parent predefined type, which is implementation-dependent. If the machine has an 8-bit representation for `Short_Integer`, the parent type of `Celsius` (but not of `Fahrenheit`) might still be `Short_Integer`, but the extended range would then be inadequate.

19.3. *Universal integer* and number declarations

One problem arising from the multiplicity of integer types has so far been glossed over: what is the type of an integer literal? An integer literal can appear in an expression of any integer type. Logically, we should have to convert each literal to the appropriate type by an explicit type conversion. That would be tedious, however, so literals are automatically converted to the type required by the context.

Integer literals are regarded as being of the hypothetical type ***universal integer***. All the predefined integer operations are available for the type ***universal integer***, giving a ***universal integer*** (or `Boolean`) result.

To illustrate the implicit conversions, consider the expression `(C*9-2)/5+32` from Example 19.2. The literal `9` is converted to type `Celsius` to permit the `*` operator to be applied, yielding a result of type `Celsius`. Similarly the literal `2` is converted to type `Celsius` so that the `-` operator can be applied. The same reasoning applies to the remaining operators and literals. If we inserted the conversions explicitly, we would have:

```
(C * Celsius(9) - Celsius(2)) / Celsius(5) + Celsius(32)
```

The implicit conversion of an integer literal is applied whenever it avoids operations of type ***universal integer***. If the expression `5*(F-32)` had been written as `5*F-5*32`, then the second multiplication would have been of type `Fahrenheit` rather than ***universal integer***. This distinction is important because an operation on values of type `Fahrenheit` might raise an exception, whereas a ***universal integer*** operation cannot.

The type ***universal integer*** does not have an Ada name, so the programmer cannot declare variables of this type. ***Number declarations*** do, however, allow constants of this type to be declared. This is very useful when the use of an explicit integer type is inappropriate. The example given in Section 19.2 is better expressed as:

```
Disk_Limit : constant := 2**30 - 1;
type Disk_Address is range 0 .. Disk_Limit;
```

In this version, although `Disk_Limit` and `Disk_Address'Last` have the same numerical value, they have different types. The declaration of `Disk_Limit` may be considered to have the effect of:

```
Disk_Limit : constant universal integer := 2**30 - 1;
```

The type of `Disk_Address'Last`, on the other hand, is just `Disk_Address`. It would be a mistake to declare `Disk_Limit` as an `Integer` constant, because the value $2^{30} - 1$ might be outside the range of `Integer`.

Expressions of type ***universal integer*** are useful in contexts where no type yet exists. Recall the two type declarations of Example 19.2:

```
type Celsius    is range -40 .. +100;
type Fahrenheit is range -40 .. +212;
```

Here the expressions -40, +100 and +212 are all of type *universal integer*. The two type declarations cover the same physical temperature range, but that is not evident from the literals used. To make this clearer, we could revise the declaration for Fahrenheit to use the bounds of Celsius:

```
type Fahrenheit is range ((-40)*9-2)/5+32 .. (100*9+2)/5+32;
```

The expressions here are also of type *universal integer*. Better still, we could replace -40 by Celsius'First and 100 by Celsius'Last, making the type of the expressions Celsius. (But this would not matter: the bounds in an integer type definition may be of *any* integer type.) This formulation is to be preferred, because the relationship between the two type declarations is more explicit. We can avoid the requirement to put the Celsius declaration first by using number declarations:

```
C_Min : constant := -40;
C_Max : constant := +100;
type Celsius    is range C_Min .. C_Max;
type Fahrenheit is range (C_Min*9-2)/5+32 .. (C_Max*9+2)/5+32;
```

(The latter declaration assumes that C_Min is negative and C_Max is positive.)

Example 19.3 OIS: System constants

The office information system (OIS) introduced in Chapter 14 consists of a basic system and a number of subsystems. Several constants of system-wide importance are to be declared in a common package. Some of these constants are integers and will be used to define integer types in various subsystems. These constants are not typed, so they should be declared by means of number declarations:

```
package System_Constants is
   Characters_per_Line : constant := 127;
   Characters_in_File  : constant := 2**32 - 1;
   ...
end System_Constants;
```

□ *End of Example 19.3*

Finally, certain attributes are considered to be of type *universal integer*. Two examples we have met already are A'Length, which yields the number of components of an array type or object A, and T'Pos, which is a function that converts a value of the discrete type T into its position number, the latter being of type *universal integer*. Therefore A'Length or a call of T'Pos may occur in an expression of any integer type.

Based literals

(This subsection may be omitted on a first reading.)

It is sometimes convenient to express integer literals in a radix (base) other than 10. For example, it is common to use radixes of 2, 8 and 16 to express values related to some aspect of the hardware in low-level programming.

In Ada any radix from 2 through 16 may be used. A based literal consists of the digits of the number enclosed between two # characters, preceded by the radix (which is itself in decimal). The decimal literal 16 could be written, for example, as 2#10000#, 8#20#, 12#14# or 16#10#. The digits with values ten through fifteen are represented by the letters A through F (in upper or lower case). The decimal literal 255 could therefore be written as 16#FF#. As in ordinary decimal literals, medial underscores can be inserted among the digits, for example 16#7E00_0000#.

A nonnegative exponent can also be given, in both decimal and based integer literals. The exponent applies to the radix being used. Hence 55e6 represents 55 million, and sixteen could also be written as 2#1#e4.

19.4. Real types

The real types of Ada allow us to model continuously varying quantities such as we obtain from physical measurement and mathematical analysis. These quantities cannot all be represented in a computer with complete accuracy. Fortunately it is sufficient to represent such numbers approximately, especially when modeling physical measurements having inherent observational errors.

Two quite distinct methods are available for performing approximate computations, and both are available in Ada.

The most common method used for scientific computation is *floating-point* arithmetic. In this form each real number is represented by an exponent and a mantissa. Over a very wide range, numbers can be represented with small relative error. The absolute error, however, is roughly proportional to the magnitude of the number and may be large. For a conceptual view of floating point, think in terms of a machine that (for example) has two decimal digits for the exponent and three for the mantissa: this can handle positive numbers in the range $.100 \times 10^{-99}$ through $.999 \times 10^{+99}$ (assuming a 'normalized' mantissa). The number 1/3 would be represented as $.333 \times 10^0$, that is with an error of about one part in a thousand. This floating-point representation can be thought of as having the format $\pm .ddd \times 10^{\pm dd}$, where each d stands for a decimal digit.

The second method of handling approximate values is called *fixed-point* arithmetic, because there is no exponent and the position of the decimal point is fixed. A variety of fixed-point formats are possible: $\pm d.dd$, $\pm ddd0.0$ and $\pm 0.00ddd$ are just some of the possible three-digit formats. In these formats the number 1/3 would be (respectively) 0.33, 0.0, and out-of-range. The absolute error is independent of the magnitude of the number. The relative error, however, may be large if the number is small. These properties are in contrast to the properties of floating point.

Within each format, only a narrow range of values can be accommodated. For this reason different scales may be needed to represent large and small numbers adequately. It was just such difficulties that led to the introduction of floating-point arithmetic together with quite complex hardware to support it. Fixed-point arithmetic still has advantages, however. The representation is more economical of storage, because no exponent is stored. (The position of the decimal point is remembered by the compiler.) In any case, some minicomputers and many microprocessors have no floating-point hardware. Floating-point arithmetic can be implemented by software, but that might be 100 times slower than fixed-point arithmetic. For these reasons, Ada allows the programmer to specify approximate computation in fixed point.

Ada real types are formally defined in terms analogous to the format notation used above. Real types are subdivided into ***floating-point types***, whose values are numbers held in formats such as $\pm.ddd\times 10^{\pm dd}$, and ***fixed-point types***, whose values are numbers held in formats such as $\pm d.dd$, $\pm ddd0.0$ or $\pm 0.00ddd$. The important point about the formats is that they determine both the range of values that can be represented and the accuracy of the representation. These essential characteristics are specified explicitly by a ***real type definition***.

A floating-point type is defined entirely by the number of digits held, whereas a fixed-point type definition requires the resolution to be specified also. For this reason programming with fixed point is likely to be more difficult than with floating point. We suggest that you read only Section 19.5 first. Once you have gained practical experience with floating point, you can go on to study the details of fixed point, the model used to define the accuracy of computation, and how to avoid machine dependencies in numerical programming.

19.5. Floating-point types

Predefined floating-point types

Each implementation must provide one or more predefined floating-point types. By convention, these are named `Short_Float`, `Float` and `Long_Float`, in order of increasing precision. Of these, `Float` is the only one that *must* be provided by every implementation, so no program should rely on the existence of the others.

Declaring new floating-point types

Consider a program that deals with distances measured and recorded (in meters) with an accuracy of at most 5 significant digits. We can declare a type for these values as follows:

```
type Distance is digits 5;  -- in meters
```

The new type `Distance` is a floating-point type with 5 decimal digits of precision. We can declare and use objects of this type, for example:

```
My_Height  : Distance := 1.7907;
Angstrom   : constant Distance := 1.0e-10;
Light_Year : constant Distance
               := Physical_Constants.c * 3600.0 * 24.0 * 365.24;
```

All computations on `Distance` values will be performed with about 5 digits of precision. For example, the value used to initialize `Light_Year` will be approximately 9.4605×10^{15}, correct to 5 significant digits, notwithstanding the fact that `Physical_Constants.c` might be defined with much greater precision (see Example 19.8). The type `Distance` is distinct from `Float` or any other floating-point type, so the compiler would detect the error in:

```
type Time is digits 5;
T : Time := Light_Year;  -- illegal
```

The phrase '`digits 5`' is an example of a ***floating-point constraint***. The expression after `digits` is a static integer expression (often just a literal), giving the minimum number of decimal digits of precision that the type must have. The implemented precision might be greater, because only a few different precisions are available in each machine.

A range constraint can also be given as part of the floating-point constraint. For example:

```
type Weight is digits 8 range 0.0 .. 1.0e6;
```

Each assignment to a variable of type `Weight` will then invoke a range check to ensure that the assigned value lies in the specified range.

The operations available for each floating-point type are exactly those available for `Float`. (Refer to Appendix D.) For example, `My_Height+Angstrom` is valid and yields a `Distance` result; `Angstrom+T` is invalid because `+` is not defined between two different floating-point types. Note that `My_Height*Angstrom` is also valid, but yields a result of type `Distance` (*not* `Area`!), so do not be misled into thinking that Ada automatically supports any kind of dimensional analysis.

Care must be taken in using the relational operators, because the approximate nature of floating point can give a result different from the mathematical result. The properties that *can* be relied upon are described in Section 19.8.

Floating-point subtypes

Subtypes of a floating-point type may be declared. A possible constraint is a range constraint, such as we have already seen with discrete types. If such a constraint is violated, the `Constraint_Error` exception is raised as usual. A floating-point subtype can also have a floating-point constraint specifying a reduced precision, for example:

```
subtype Astronomical_Distance is Distance digits 2;
Universe_Diameter : Astronomical_Distance;
```

There is no exception corresponding to such a floating-point constraint: when a more precise value is assigned to a variable of a less precise subtype:

```
Universe_Diameter := 3.2e10 * Light_Year;
```

the excess precision (about 3 digits in this case) is lost.

Floating-point constraints can be used when declaring individual objects as well as named subtypes. For example, the above object declaration is equivalent to:

```
Universe_Diameter : Distance digits 2;
```

Floating-point attributes

There are more attributes for floating-point types than for discrete types. The attributes `First` and `Last` have the same meanings as usual, being the smallest and largest values of the type or subtype. The other attributes characterize the approximate nature of the floating-point type and the range of numbers over which the approximation holds. For any floating-point type or subtype `F`:

- `F'Digits` is the precision in decimal digits;
- `F'Mantissa` is the corresponding length of the binary mantissa (see Section 19.8);
- `F'Epsilon` is the relative precision of numbers around 1.0;
- `F'Safe_Emax` is the maximum value of the binary exponent (see Section 19.8);
- `F'Safe_Small` and `F'Safe_Large` are the smallest and largest positive numbers that can be relied upon to be handled accurately.

Floating-point type conversions

Conversion of values between floating-point types is similar to conversion between integer types. The target type name is used as a function.

Example 19.4 *Double-precision square root function*

Let us write a Long_Float square root function, given a Float square root function Sqrt. The latter can be used to yield a first approximation to the Long_Float result, then one application of Newton's formula can be used to improve the accuracy of the result:

```
function Long_Sqrt (X : Long_Float) return Long_Float is
   Estimate : Long_Float := Long_Float (Sqrt (Float (X)));
begin
   return 0.5 * (Estimate + X/Estimate);
end Long_Sqrt;
```

Although Estimate is of type Long_Float, its value is accurate to Float'Digits digits only. One application of Newton's formula gives sufficient additional accuracy, provided that Float'Digits is at least half Long_Float'Digits.
□ *End of Example 19.4*

Example 19.5 *Inner product of vectors*

It is required to write a function that computes the inner (scalar) product of two values of type Vector. Assume the declarations:

```
type Real is digits ...;
type Vector is array (Integer range <>) of Real;
```

It is well known that this function can be most accurately computed by working in double precision. If the vector elements were of type Float, we would use Long_Float arithmetic. But here we are working with the declared type Real, and we do not wish to make any assumption about its precision. This is no problem in Ada — we can easily declare a floating-point type with twice the precision of Real. The solution is:

```
function Inner_Product (V1, V2 : Vector) return Real is
   type Long_Real is digits 2*Real'Digits;
   Sum : Long_Real := 0.0;
begin  -- assume that V1'Range = V2'Range
   for I in V1'Range loop
      Sum := Sum + Long_Real (V1(I)) * Long_Real (V2(I));
   end loop;
   return Real (Sum);
end Inner_Product;
```

The type declaration of Long_Real is legal because the expression 2*Real'Digits is static.

□ *End of Example 19.5*

Example 19.6 Probabilities

As part of a package designed to handle statistical events, a function is needed to calculate the probability of an event using the binomial distribution:

$$binomial(n,r,P) = \binom{n}{r} P^r(1-P)^{n-r} \qquad (n > 0, r > 0, 0.0 \leq P \leq 1.0)$$

The values given by this function, being probabilities, lie in the range 0.0 through 1.0. Should we declare a type with this range? Almost certainly not, because computations using probabilities often involve values outside that range. We choose instead to make `Probability` a subtype of `Float`:

```
package Chance is
   subtype Probability is Float range 0.0 .. 1.0;
   function Binomial
               (N, R : Positive;
                P : Probability)
         return Probability;
   function Poisson
               (Mean : Float;
                X : Positive)
         return Probability;
end Chance;
```

The body of the package could be:

```
with Math_Lib;
package body Chance is
   function Binomial
               (N, R : Positive;
                P : Probability)
         return Probability is
      NCR : Float := (1.0-P)**N;
   begin
      for I in 1 .. R loop
         NCR := NCR * P * Float (N+1-I) / ((1.0-P) * Float (I));
      end loop;
      return NCR;
   end Binomial;

   function Factorial (N : Positive) return Float is
      F : Float := 1.0;
   begin
      for I in 2 .. N loop
         F := F * Float (I);
      end loop;
      return F;
   end Factorial;

   function Poisson
               (Mean : Float;
```

```
                X : Positive)
            return Probability is
      begin
         return Math_Lib.Exp (-Mean) * Mean**X / Factorial (X);
      end Poisson;
   end Chance;
```

The reason for making Probability a subtype should now be clear. The terms in the expression for Poisson yield values of type Float, and are not restricted to the range 0.0 through 1.0.

□ *End of Example 19.6*

Relationship between declared and predefined floating-point types

(This subsection may be omitted on a first reading.)

Each declared floating-point type is implicitly derived from one of the predefined floating-point types. For example, consider the declaration:

```
type Weight is digits 8 range 0.0 .. 1.0e6;
```

If Float provides at least 8 digits of precision, the type might be equivalent to:

```
type Weight is new Float digits 8;
```

Otherwise Weight might be derived from Long_Float instead. If *none* of the predefined types has the required precision, the Ada compiler is free to reject the declaration of Weight altogether.

Note that the provision of floating-point types is closely analogous to the provision of integer types, the main difference being that the choice of predefined floating-point type is determined by the precision required, rather than by the range of values.

What is important is that the programmer has little need to be concerned with how each floating-point type is derived: the *compiler* chooses the representation for each declared floating-point type. If the programmer specifies a degree of precision that cannot be provided, the compiler makes this clear. This is a great improvement on older languages. (In FORTRAN the programmer just chooses between REAL and DOUBLE PRECISION and might be completely unaware whether the corresponding arithmetic is sufficiently precise or not.)

19.6. Fixed-point types

(This section may be omitted on a first reading.)

The previous section showed a declaration of Time as a floating-point type. That would be appropriate in an application involving times with a wide range of magnitudes, and observational errors proportionate to the magnitudes of the measured times. In sports timing, on the other hand, we are interested in times within quite a narrow range (up to three hours, say), measured and recorded with a fixed accuracy of 0.1 seconds. It is appropriate to declare Race_Time as a fixed-point type:

```
Minute : constant := 60.0; -- seconds
```

```
type Race_Time is delta 0.1 range 0.0 .. 180.0 * Minute;
```

The phrase starting with the reserved word `delta` is called a *fixed-point constraint*. (See the syntax diagram 'fixed_point constraint' in Appendix A.) The expressions in the fixed-point constraint must all be static real expressions. They are evaluated by the compiler to determine the range and precision of the values of the declared fixed-point type:

- The expression following `delta` gives the *delta* or resolution of the fixed-point type, which is the (maximum) interval between successive values of the type. The delta is available to the programmer through the attribute `Delta`.
- The range, if present, gives the lower and upper bounds on values of the fixed-point type. They are provided, as usual, by the attributes `First` and `Last` (respectively).

For example, `Race_Time'Delta` is approximately 0.1, `Race_Time'First` is 0.0, and `Race_Time'Last` is 10800.0, all these attributes being of type `Race_Time`.

Unlike integer and floating-point types, no fixed-point types are provided by `Standard`. (However, the standard package `Calendar` exports a fixed-point type `Duration`, intended specifically for machine timing; see Appendix D.) Fixed-point types are more varied than other numeric types because both the range and the resolution must be specified. For this reason, fixed-point types do not inherit their properties from a few predefined types by means of the derived type mechanism. The compiler will choose a representation such that the difference between two successive values of the type is no more than the specified delta, and such that the whole of the specified range of values can be represented. This determines the storage needed for values of the type — typically one or two machine words. (The values of the attributes `First` and `Last` could differ by a small amount from the range bounds, because of the errors involved in converting the range bounds to the declared type.)

The operations on fixed-point types fall into two categories: operations *without* rescaling (i.e. keeping the same range and delta), and operations *with* rescaling. If rescaling is not done, then the result of the operation can be of the same fixed-point type as the operands. Here is a list of the predefined fixed-point operations without rescaling:

Operation	*Result type*	*Meaning*
`+ X`	type of `X`	identity operation
`- X`	type of `X`	negation
`abs X`	type of `X`	absolute value
`X + Y`	type of `X` and `Y`	addition
`X - Y`	type of `X` and `Y`	subtraction
`I * X`	type of `X`	equivalent to repeated addition
`X * I`	type of `X`	equivalent to repeated addition
`X / I`	type of `X`	division without rescaling
`X = Y`	`Boolean`	equality
`X /= Y`	`Boolean`	inequality
`X < Y`	`Boolean`	less than
`X <= Y`	`Boolean`	less than or equal
`X > Y`	`Boolean`	greater than
`X >= Y`	`Boolean`	greater than or equal
`X in Y .. Z`	`Boolean`	range membership
`X not in Y .. Z`	`Boolean`	converse of range membership

(Here `X`, `Y` and `Z` are of the same fixed-point type, and `I` is of type `Integer`.) If the result exceeds the capacity of the machine, `Numeric_Error` will be raised. The operation of multiplication by an integer is merely a shorthand for repeated addition. No scaling is performed, so overflow is likely if the integer operand is large.

Consider now the operations that do require rescaling. This means that more than one fixed-point type is involved. To see the nature of the problem, consider the following types and variables:

```
type Small  is delta 0.0001 range -0.1 .. +0.1;
type Medium is delta 0.1    range -100.0 .. +100.0;
type Large  is delta 100.0  range -100_000.0 .. +100_000.0;
S : Small;  M : Medium;  L : Large;
```

If we wish to add ten times S to M, then we can write:

```
M := M + Medium (10 * S);
```

This is satisfactory unless 10*S (of type Small) is likely to overflow, in which case we could write instead:

```
M := M + 10 * Medium (S);
```

The disadvantage of this version is that S may be less than Medium'Delta, in which case Medium(S) may be zero! There is no adequate solution without rescaling. As usual with fixed point, the choice of coding will depend upon the values concerned and an analysis of the likely rounding errors.

With the operations +, - and abs, the choices are simple. With * and /, the operations given above are clearly inadequate. We might wish to square M and assign the result to L. The square of M is potentially outside the range of Medium. In general, the range of values for the result of multiplication or division is not the range of values of either operand. The rule in Ada is that the multiplication or division of two fixed-point values results in a value of the hypothetical type *universal fixed*. This type does not match any other type and has no operations defined upon it, so the result must always be explicitly converted to a declared fixed-point type. This forces the programmer to decide the type of the result. The expressions M*M, L*S and M/S are all valid and of type *universal fixed*. So we can write:

```
L := Large (M * M);
M := Medium (L * S);
L := L + Large (M / S);
```

If a real literal is used as one operand of a fixed-point multiplication or division, it must be converted to a fixed-point type:

```
L := Large (Medium (99.0) * M);
S := Small (Large (1.0e4) / L);
M := M + Medium (Medium (10.0) * S);
```

The important issue with fixed-point expressions is to ensure that the type of each intermediate result is clearly determined; this in turn determines the precision of the result (bounded by an interval whose width is the delta).

Example 19.7   Fixed-point arithmetic

A function is to be written to calculate the mean value of a list of race times, values of the type Race_Time declared above:

```
type List_of_Times is array (Positive range <>) of Race_Time;
```

```
function Mean_Time (List : List_of_Times) return Race_Time;
```

It would appear to be a simple matter to implement this function:

```
function Mean_Time (List : List_of_Times) return Race_Time is
   Sum : Race_Time := 0.0;
begin
   for I in List'Range loop
      Sum := Sum + List(I);
   end loop;
   return Sum / List'Length;
end Mean_Time;
```

(Recall that division by an integer does not require an explicit type conversion.) The problem with this implementation is that the value of Sum is likely to overflow if the list is long, although the final result cannot possibly be out of range.

The obvious alternative is to perform the division on each time value:

```
   for I in List'Range loop
      Sum := Sum + List(I) / List'Length;
   end loop;
   return Sum;
```

This implementation also has a flaw: if the list is long, the division by `List'Length` will lose a lot of the precision, perhaps even rounding to zero.

The best choice depends upon the circumstances. Such difficulties are precisely the reason why floating point is widely preferred — its automatic scaling prevents overflow and loss of precision in most cases.

□ *End of Example 19.7*

19.7. *Universal real*

(This section may be omitted on a first reading.)

The hypothetical type ***universal real*** is used in Ada as the type of all real literals. It is analogous to the type ***universal integer*** for integer literals. ***Universal real*** operands can occur in both fixed-point and floating-point expressions.

The mixed integer and real operands in ***universal real*** expressions like `2*3.0`, `4.0*10` and `10.0/2` would normally be permitted only when the real operand is fixed-point. On the other hand, `**` is not permitted for a fixed-point operand, so the operation in `3.0**3` is a floating-point operation. Hence ***universal real*** encompasses the operations of both fixed-point and floating-point types. The six relational operators and the two membership operators can also be used with ***universal real*** operands giving the usual `Boolean` result. All ***universal real*** expressions are evaluated exactly, in principle, although the compiler will probably place some limit on the precision.

Literal expressions should be used to show relationships between literals that would not otherwise be clear. For example:

```
Pi              : constant := 3.14159_26535_89793_23846;
```

```
Half_Pi        : constant := Pi / 2;
Reciprocal_Pi  : constant := 1.0 / Pi;
```

These three constants are of type *universal real*. They be used in expressions of any (real) type, and the compiler will ensure conversion to the precision required.

Example 19.8 A physical constants package

For physical calculations, a package is to be provided containing the values of commonly used constants. Such an encapsulation helps to ensure consistency among different program modules using these constants.

The constants might be used in expressions of a variety of real types, so it would be premature to specify their types here. Therefore we use number declarations:

```
package Physical_Constants is
   c : constant := 2.997_924_580e8;   -- speed of light, m/s
   h : constant := 6.626_176e-34;     -- Planck constant, J/Hz
   G : constant := 6.672_0e-11;       -- gravitational constant
   k : constant := 1.386_62e-23;      -- Boltzmann constant, J/K
end Physical_Constants;
```

□ *End of Example 19.8*

Based literals

The facility for writing integer literals in a radix other than ten extends to real literals also. The advantage of this is that we can ensure that a particular bit pattern is used. (This is important in certain rare situations.) Also, many fractional values cannot be expressed exactly in decimal; an example is one-third, which can conveniently be expressed as the based literal `3#0.1#`. See the syntax diagram 'numeric_literal' in Appendix A.

19.8. The Ada model for real arithmetic

(This section may be omitted on a first reading.)

Each real type definition establishes a set of ***model numbers*** for that type. These model numbers are values of the type and are represented exactly. For example, 1.0 is a model number of every floating-point type. On the other hand, 0.1 is not a model number of any floating-point type, reflecting the reality that this value cannot be represented exactly in a binary machine. In fact, Ada assumes that floating-point arithmetic is implemented with a radix that is a power of two. (2, 8 and 16 are used in current machines).

The floating-point model

The model numbers of a floating-point type `F` are *zero* and all values of the form:

$$\pm mantissa \times 2^{exponent}$$

where:

- $0.5 \le mantissa < 1.0$;
- *mantissa* consists of exactly `F'Mantissa` binary digits;
- `F'Mantissa` $= \lceil$`F'Digits` $\times \log_2 10 + 1\rceil$;
- $-4 \times$ `F'Mantissa` $\le exponent \le +4 \times$ `F'Mantissa`.

Note that the maximum exponent is four times the mantissa length. This maximum exponent is given by the attribute `F'Emax`.

Consider, for example, the floating-point type declared by:

```
type F is digits 5;
```

Its attributes are determined as follows:

`F'Mantissa` (mantissa length of `F`)	$=$	$\lceil 5 \times \log_2 10 + 1\rceil$
	$=$	$\lceil 17.6\rceil$
	$=$	18
`F'Emax` (maximum exponent of `F`)	$=$	4×`F'Mantissa`
	$=$	72
`F'Small` (smallest positive model number of `F`)	$=$	$0.1_2 \times 2^{-72}$
	$\approx$	1.05×10^{-22}
`F'Large` (largest model number of `F`)	$=$	$0.111111111111111111_2 \times 2^{72}$
	$\approx$	4.72×10^{21}
Smallest model number of `F` greater than 1.0	$=$	$0.100000000000000001_2 \times 2^1$
	$=$	1.0+`F'Epsilon`

For a floating-point type a further set of values is defined. This is the set of *safe numbers.* Safe numbers have all the properties of model numbers but are dependent upon the implementation and not just upon the real type definition. Safe numbers are defined in the same way as model numbers but have a possibly larger exponent range. (Therefore the model numbers of a given type are a subset of its safe numbers.) The attribute `F'Safe_Emax` is defined to be the maximum exponent for safe numbers of the type `F`.

For the type `F` above, the compiler might choose a representation with one byte for the exponent, giving an exponent range of -127 through $+127$. Hence:

`F'Safe_Emax` (maximum exponent of F's safe numbers)	$=$	127
`F'Safe_Small` (smallest positive safe number of `F`)	$=$	$0.1_2 \times 2^{-127}$
	$\approx$	2.94×10^{-39}
`F'Safe_Large` (largest safe number of `F`)	$=$	$0.111111111111111111_2 \times 2^{127}$
	$\approx$	1.70×10^{38}

The importance of model (and safe) numbers lies not in the fact that they are handled exactly, but in their use for determining the accuracy of *any* real operation. This is defined in terms of *model intervals.* A model interval is a range of real numbers bounded by a pair of model numbers. An important special case is a model interval containing a single model number.

To determine the error bound on a real arithmetic operation, say `X+Y`, we proceed as follows:

1. Calculate the smallest model intervals enclosing the values of `X` and `Y` respectively.

2. Calculate the set of values $x + y$ for all x and y within the respective model intervals (this '+' being the exact mathematical operation).
3. Find the smallest model interval enclosing this set of values.

The resulting model interval bounds the result of `X+Y`. Model intervals for other real arithmetic operations are determined similarly.

An interesting special case is when the operands and the (mathematical) result all happen to be model numbers; in that case the operation is guaranteed to be exact. In floating point, all sufficiently small integer numbers are model numbers, and therefore addition, subtraction and multiplication of such numbers is exact.

A model interval overflows if a bounding value is outside the range `-F'Safe_Large` through `+F'Safe_Large`. When this happens, the exception `Numeric_Error` might be raised. However, an implementation is at liberty to provide values outside the range of safe numbers, or even to yield an 'infinite' value, instead of raising `Numeric_Error`.

Similar considerations apply to the relational and membership operators with real operands. The possible results are found by comparing the model intervals of the operands. If the intervals overlap, the result is implementation-dependent. Consider, for example, the evaluation of `X=Y`. If the model intervals of `X` and `Y` are disjoint, the result is guaranteed to be `False`; if they overlap, the result is implementation-dependent; and only if both model intervals happen to contain one and the same number is the result guaranteed to be `True`. This clearly demonstrates the danger of using `=` and `/=` with real numbers. The other relational operators also can give fuzzy results.

It is not expected that you should calculate model intervals for each real operation in a program. What *is* important about the model is that it allows classical error analysis to be applied.

Example 19.9 Quadratic equations

A procedure to calculate the real roots of a quadratic equation might be written as:

```
procedure Solve_Quadratic_Equation
               (A, B, C        : in Float;
                Roots_are_Real : out Boolean;
                Root1, Root2   : out Float) is
   D : Float := B**2 - 4.0*A*C;
begin
   if D < 0.0 then
      Roots_are_Real := False;
   else
      D := Sqrt (D);
      Root1 := (-B + D) / (2.0*A);
      Root2 := (-B - D) / (2.0*A);
      Roots_are_Real := True;
   end if;
end Solve_Quadratic_Equation;
```

This procedure could fail, or even give incorrect results, for a number of reasons. A multiplication might overflow, for example in the initialization of `D`, even though the final value for `D` cannot be out of range. This particular problem can be avoided by normalizing `A`, `B` and C so that the largest absolute value is 1.0. A multiplication can also *underflow*, yielding zero although neither operand is zero. This can happen if the mathematical result is less than Float'Small. Overflow cannot lead to incorrect results, provided that Numeric_Error is raised by overflow. Underflow *can* lead to incorrect results, however, because no exception is raised.

In practice, the major cause of inaccuracy with floating point is not underflow but *cancellation*. For instance, if the value of B**2 is nearly equal to that of 4.0*A*C, then the value assigned to D will be much less accurate than the values of A, B and C. This could even result in D having the wrong sign, leading to a false conclusion as to the nature of the roots.

□ *End of Example 19.9*

The fixed-point model

Let us now consider the Ada model for fixed-point arithmetic. The logic of model intervals is similar to the above, so we need only define the model numbers. The model numbers of a fixed-point type F are integer multiples of a certain real number. They are of the form:

$$\pm mantissa \times \texttt{F'Small}$$

where:

- F'Small is normally the largest power of two not greater than F'Delta;
- *mantissa* is a nonnegative integer that can be represented in exactly F'Mantissa binary digits;
- the value of F'Mantissa is the smallest integer such that F'First and F'Last (or rather the closest numbers of the above form) lie within the range of model numbers.

From this we can see that fixed-point arithmetic is essentially an approximate form of computation implemented with integers.

Example 19.10 Smoothing data

At regular intervals a reading is taken from a sensor. The values of these readings are of the following fixed-point type:

```
type Reading is delta 1.0/128 range -1.0 .. 1.0;
```

Because of natural variations in the readings it is necessary to smooth this data. The method adopted is to take 10% of the current reading (R) together with 90% of the previous smoothed reading (S). The obvious way to implement this is as follows:

```
W1 : constant Reading := 0.1;
W2 : constant Reading := 1.0 - W1;
R, S : Reading;
...
loop
   ...
   store the current sensor reading in R;
   S := Reading (W2*S) + Reading (W1*R);  -- smoothing
   ...
```

```
end loop;
```

We can now examine the accuracy of this computation using model interval arithmetic. `Reading'Small` will be 1/128 exactly, and the model numbers of `Reading` will be integer multiples of this number. To be concrete, suppose that `S` is 125/128 and that the reading assigned to `R` is also 125/128.

- Analyzing the sub-expression `Reading(W2*S)`, we find that: the model interval of `W2` is [115/128, 116/128]; the model interval of `S` is [125/128, 125/128]; therefore the model interval of `Reading(W2*S)` is [112/128, 114/128] — because 112/128 is the largest model number not greater than (115/128)×(125/128), and 114/128 is the largest model number not less than (116/128)×(125/128).
- Similarly analyzing the sub-expression `Reading(W1*R)`, we find that: the model interval of `W1` is [12/128, 13/128]; the model interval of `R` is [125/128, 125/128]; therefore the model interval of `Reading(W1*R)` is [11/128, 13/128].
- Adding together the model intervals [112/128, 114/128] and [11/128, 13/128], we find that the new model interval of `S` is [123/128, 127/128].

Suppose now that the next reading for `R` is also 125/128. Repeating our interval arithmetic with the new model interval of `S`, we find that after the second iteration of the loop the model interval of `S` has expanded to [121/128, 129/128]. Indeed, with consistent readings of 125/128 for `R`, further iterations make the model interval of `S` expand eventually to [108/128, 139/128]. Thus `S` could eventually be as low as 108/128 or, worse still, it could overflow.

A better solution is to rewrite the smoothing assignment as:

```
S := S + Reading (W1 * (R - S));
```

This involves only one multiplication and is likely to be faster, as well as avoiding the rounding error in the constant 0.9. If `S` and the reading for `R` are equal, then `S` will remain unchanged because the subtraction will give 0.0 exactly (both operands are model numbers). In general, `R-S` has an error bound of at most 2*`Reading'Small`. Hence when `R-S` is multiplied by 0.1, the error bound is less than `Reading'Small`. However, on conversion to type `Reading`, the error bound might still be 2 × `Reading'Small` if the resulting interval straddles more than one model interval.

□ *End of Example 19.10*

The conclusion to be drawn from this example is that limiting errors in fixed-point arithmetic requires great care, but the Ada definition provides guaranteed error bounds. These can be calculated in order to ensure that the proposed algorithm is stable.

19.9. Avoiding machine dependencies

(This section may be omitted on a first reading.)

The numeric facilities of current computers vary widely. Ada does not disguise these differences, but makes it possible for the programmer to choose between portability and efficiency (at the expense of machine dependence). In this section we consider that trade-off.

For both fixed-point and floating-point types, the precision actually provided might exceed the requested precision. A program might work because of this fortuitous additional precision, but give incorrect results on another implementation that provides just the precision requested. The only certain defense against this is to make a detailed analysis of the rounding errors inherent in the algorithm. Failing that, you should write the program so that all convergence criteria are expressed in terms of the attributes of the types involved. Then, simply by changing the type declarations from `Float` to `Long_Float` (or single-word to double-word fixed point), you can check that a corresponding increase in precision is obtained.

Ada does provide a set of machine-dependent attributes for numeric types. They allow a program to configure itself to properties of the machine.

- The integer attribute `F'Machine_Radix` gives the radix of the floating-point type `F`. The value can be important when very close analysis of rounding errors is needed.
- For any real type `F`, the `Boolean` attribute `F'Machine_Rounds` is `True` if all operations on `F` are rounded (rather than truncated). This can influence the results of a computation, because rounding gives about one bit of precision more than truncation.
- The attribute `F'Machine_Overflows` is `True` if `Numeric_Error` is always raised by overflow. Most floating-point implementations do detect overflow. Unfortunately, some computers generate an 'infinite' value and continue without raising an exception, and some even continue without any indication at all.

For a complete list see Appendix B.

Attributes like `Integer'Last` can be used to anticipate overflow problems, but the following example illustrates that care is essential.

Example 19.11 *A random number generator*

Many random number generators work by arithmetic on large integers. Such generators are unsatisfactory on small machines in which 32-bit arithmetic is slow, and useless if 32-bit arithmetic is unavailable. Hence a portable generator should not rely upon such a wide range of integers.

The random numbers package given here has two alternative implementations — one that will work when the range of `Integer` is small, and a second that will exploit a larger `Integer` range to run more efficiently. The package declaration hides this implementation detail from the users of the package.

Every random number generator uses a *seed* that determines the next random number to be generated. Here we shall use a group of three small integers as the seed. We use the type `Integer` for each of the three integers, because this will provide the most efficient implementation. In order to allow repetition of a sequence of random numbers, subprograms to inspect and (re)set the current seed are exported by the package:

```
package Random_Numbers is

   type Seed is
         record
            X, Y, Z : Integer;
         end record;

   function Random return Float;
      -- Returns a random number in range 0.0 .. 1.0.

   function Current_Seed return Seed;
      -- Returns the current value of the seed.
```

```
    procedure Restart (Restart_Seed : in Seed);
        -- Restarts from the given seed value.

end Random_Numbers;
```

First we must decide whether the package should always generate the same sequence of random numbers. This is unsatisfactory in practice, so let us initialize the seed using the current time. (The current time is returned by the function `Clock` in the standard package `Calendar`, see Appendix D). Repeatability can still be obtained, if required, by use of the `Restart` procedure.

The second issue is more difficult, and that is how to supply the alternative implementations. One possibility is to have two distinct package bodies, leaving the programmer to select the one appropriate to the particular machine. It would be easy to make the wrong choice, however, and moreover two package bodies would have to be maintained separately. What we propose is a single package body in which the implementation is selected by use of machine attributes. There are three cases:

- if `Integer'Last` is less than 30323, then the algorithm will not work at all;
- if `Integer'Last` is less than 5212632, then the small-range implementation must be used;
- otherwise the large-range implementation can be selected.

The problem now is that if we write:

```
if Integer'Last < 5212632 then
    deal with small range;
else
    deal with large range;
end if;
```

the test will raise `Constraint_Error` if its value is mathematically true. The method adopted below is to use `Integer'Size` to select the implementation. (The attribute `Size` gives the number of bits used to represent values of the type, see Chapter 24.) We include tests to make the package initialization raise `Constraint_Error` in case this does not succeed in selecting the correct implementation.

A good Ada compiler will avoid generating code for the case that is not executed. So the effect of the body given below should be to select the correct implementation at compile time.

```
with Calendar;

package body Random_Numbers is

    Large_Range : constant Boolean := Integer'Size >= 24;
        -- Large_Range is true if the Integer range
        -- allows the simple algorithm to be selected.
        -- The selection should be done by the compiler.

    S : Seed;    -- the current seed

    function Random return Float is
        W : Float;
    begin
        if Large_Range then
            S := ((171 * S.X) mod 30269,
```

```
                     (172 * S.Y) mod 30307,
                     (170 * S.Z) mod 30323);
         else -- not Large_Range
            S := (171 * (S.X mod 177) - 2 * (S.X / 177),
                     172 * (S.Y mod 176) - 35 * (S.Y / 176),
                     170 * (S.Z mod 178) - 63 * (S.Z / 178));
            if S.X < 0 then
               S.X := S.X + 30269;
            end if;
            if S.Y < 0 then
               S.Y := S.Y + 30307;
            end if;
            if S.Z < 0 then
               S.Z := S.Z + 30323;
            end if;
         end if;
         W := Float (S.X) / 30269.0 +
               Float (S.Y) / 30307.0 +
               Float (S.Z) / 30323.0;
         return W - Float (Integer (W - 0.5));
      end Random;
      function Current_Seed return Seed is
      begin
         return S;
      end Current_Seed;
      procedure Restart (Restart_Seed : in Seed) is
      begin
         if (Restart_Seed.X not in 1..30268) or
               (Restart_Seed.Y not in 1..30306) or
               (Restart_Seed.Z not in 1..30322) then
            raise Constraint_Error;
         end if;
         S := Restart_Seed;
      end Restart;
   begin
      -- Check that Integer has sufficient range
      -- for the generator to work at all --
      if Integer'Last < 30323 then
         raise Constraint_Error;
      end if;
      -- Check that Large_Range gives correct selection --
      if Large_Range and then Integer'Last < 5212632 then
         raise Constraint_Error;  -- (unlikely)
      end if;
      -- Initialize the seed --
      declare
         use Calendar;
```

```
      T : Time := Clock;
   begin
      S := (Month (T), Day (T),
            Integer (Seconds (T) / 3) + 1);
         -- gives S.Z in range 1..28801
   end;
end Random_Numbers;
```

□ *End of Example 19.11*

This example illustrates a number of points. Firstly, the external specification of a package should be machine-independent. Secondly, careful use of machine attributes can obtain an implementation that is both portable and efficient over a wide range of machines. Lastly, alternative implementations of a package can often be provided within one package body.

Exercises 19

19.1. Consider again the problem of an automatic weather station working in Celsius and Fahrenheit (Example 19.2). Declare different ***floating-point*** types for each temperature scale, and write appropriate conversion functions. What are the advantages and disadvantages of floating point against the use of integers in this particular example?

19.2. Repeat the automatic weather station example again, this time with ***fixed-point*** types for Celsius and Fahrenheit temperatures. Code the two conversion functions. What are the advantages and disadvantages of fixed point against the use of integers and floating point in this application?

19.3. Analyze the floating-point and fixed-point temperature scale conversion functions for rounding errors. Do repeated conversions accumulate rounding errors?

19.4. Write type declarations for masses (expressed in kilograms), volumes (in cubic meters) and densities (in kilograms/cubic meter). Assume that all these quantities are to be held accurate to six significant digits. Which of the predefined floating-point operations are appropriate to each of these types? Write a subprogram that returns the density of a substance, given the mass and volume of a quantity of the substance.

19.5. Repeat the previous exercise using fixed point, where each mass is to be held accurate to the nearest gram and each volume accurate to the nearest cubic centimeter.

19.6. Refer to Example 19.7. Calculate the results of both versions of `Mean_Time`, given a list of times that contains 50 occurrences of 20.0 and 50 occurrences of 20.2.

19.7. Refer to Example 19.10.

(a) Using the first version of the smoothing assignment, perform a few more calculations of the model interval of `S` on successive iterations of the loop, assuming that every reading assigned to `R` is 125/128.

(b) Using the improved version of the smoothing assignment, calculate the model interval of `S` for the first two iterations of the loop.

20

Data Types in General

20.1. Types and program design

In an important sense, any program can be considered as a working model of some universe of discourse. Each object in the program models some entity in that universe, and should have properties modeling as closely as possible the properties of that entity.

In Ada the properties of an object are determined by its type. The type of an object specifies the set of possible values that the object can take, and the set of possible operations on those values. Consequently the choice of a particular type for an object is a crucial design decision in an Ada program, affecting the closeness of fit between the program and the universe that it models. That in turn has important implications for the structure of the program. We have now introduced most of the type classes provided by Ada, and the time has come to consolidate this knowledge with our approach to program design. The aim is to exploit the type system of Ada with benefit to the security, efficiency and maintainability of our programs.

A bad choice of types can seriously impair the modularity of a program, by introducing unnecessary coupling between modules that should be relatively independent. This happens when we use types that poorly model abstractions from the universe of discourse. It follows that great care should be taken when inventing data types and giving types to objects. Often the best choice is an abstract data type, exported by a package, but this chapter concentrates on doing as well as we can with the types provided by the language.

There are six major classes of type in Ada:

- *Scalar types.* These are subdivided into ***discrete types*** and ***real types***. Discrete types are used for counting (integer types) and enumeration (enumeration types). Real types are for approximate computation and for modeling continuous quantities, such as lengths and probabilities. (See Chapters 2, 3, 6, 7, 9, 19).
- *Composite types.* An object of a composite type contains simpler objects as components. The two classes of composite types are array types and record types. Record types can have discriminants. (See Chapters 10, 11, 18).
- *Access types.* Access values are essentially pointers to objects of other types, and are used to build up data structures of a more dynamic nature than arrays and records. (See Chapter 17).
- *Private types.* These come in two forms: private types and limited private types. They allow the programmer to exercise precise control over the operations that are applicable to the type. Private types form the basis on which abstract data types can be implemented in Ada. (See Chapter 13).
- *Task types.* These are described in Chapter 23.

- *Derived types.* The derivation mechanism allows us to construct a new type from any existing type or subtype.

The relationships among these type classes are shown in detail in Figure 20.1. Actually, some relationships have been omitted for simplicity. For instance, the components of arrays and records are themselves typed, and components of arrays are selected by an index that is itself of a discrete type. Integer and real types are classified as *numeric types.* Limited private types and task types are classified as *limited types.*

Each time you choose a type for some data objects, keep the following criteria in mind:

- The proposed type should have all the properties needed in the application.
- The proposed type should have no other properties.

A predefined type is unlikely to pass both tests, except in the simplest of situations. Thus we often need to declare a new type with properties closer to the desired properties. Although Ada provides a variety of type structures for this purpose, we will be lucky indeed to find a type that provides *exactly* the desired properties. Nevertheless, it is important to try.

For example, consider choosing Ada types to describe a pack of playing cards. We will require an ordered type to represent the rank of a card. A first attempt might be:

```
type Rank is range 2 .. 14;   -- Ace is high
```

However, this fails the second criterion above, because there is nothing to prevent a program from performing addition and other arithmetic operations on objects of type Rank. These inappropriate operations are made possible by the choice of a type with richer semantics than we need. It is better to define a type with no unneeded operations, such as:

```
type Rank is (Two, Three, Four, Five, Six, Seven,
              Eight, Nine, Ten, Jack, Queen, King, Ace);
```

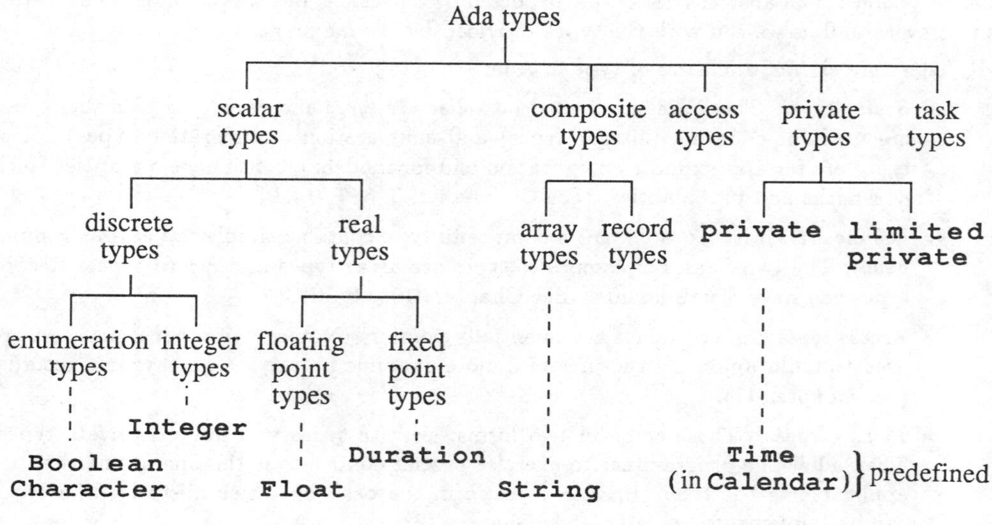

Fig. 20.1 Classification of types in Ada

This avoids the gratuitous arithmetic operations, and also gives meaningful names to the face cards. The enumeration type does have properties that go beyond those normally associated with the ranks of playing cards, for example the operations `Rank'Succ` and `Rank'Pred`. However, we shall quite possibly want to be able to range over all the ranks in a suit, so these properties are likely to be useful in practice. Even if they were not, introducing a package in order to make `Rank` an abstract data type would probably be excessive.

Example 20.1 *Sparse matrices*

A sparse matrix is a two-dimensional array of numbers in which most of the components are zero. Many computing problems involve very large sparse matrices. It is desirable to exploit their sparseness to economize on storage, by storing only the nonzero components. Let us declare a package to handle sparse matrices, hiding their implementation and exporting only the conventional abstract operations on arrays.

The two most basic operations are fetching and storing component values. The `Store` operation updates a component of an array, given the array itself, a row index, a column index, and the new component value. The `Fetch` returns the value of an array component, given the array itself and a pair of indices.

In order to preserve the integrity of the data structure we make `Sparse_Matrix` a limited private type. If copying and comparison operations on complete sparse matrices were needed, they could be added as exported subprograms.

```
package Sparse_Matrix_Handler is
   type Sparse_Matrix is limited private;
   function Fetch
              (A : Sparse_Matrix;
               Row, Col : Positive)
         return Real;
   procedure Store
              (A : in out Sparse_Matrix;
               Row, Col : in Positive;
               Component : in Real);
   ...
private
   implementation details
end Sparse_Matrix_Handler;
```

We assume here that the array components are of some type `Real`, already declared. This makes the package somewhat inflexible, but we shall pass over that point for now.

We must also provide an operation that creates an all-zero sparse matrix. Its parameters are the array itself and the upper bounds for the two indices. Its declaration is:

```
   procedure Zero
              (A : out Sparse_Matrix;
               Last_Row, Last_Col : in Natural);
```

Finally, we need to provide functions analogous to the attribute `Last` for ordinary arrays. These are specified as follows:

```
   function Last_Row (A : Sparse_Matrix) return Natural;
   function Last_Col (A : Sparse_Matrix) return Natural;
```

At this stage we must check that the abstract type Sparse_Matrix has all the essential properties and (as far as possible) no unneeded ones.

Having completed the package declaration, we must decide upon an implementation that conserves storage in the intended manner. The most frequently executed operations will be Fetch and Store. These must be as fast as possible, if necessary at the expense of the other operations. One suitable method is to hash the pair of index values and thus select a linked list of components with the same hash value. (For another treatment of sparse matrices, see [Knuth 1968]). A representation of Sparse_Matrix can now be defined:

```
private
   type Component_Node;
   type Component_Ptr is access Component_Node;
   type Component_Node is
         record
            Row, Col : Positive;
            Value    : Real;
            Next     : Component_Ptr;
         end record;
   Hash_Size : constant := 137;  -- should be prime
   type Hash_Range is range 0 .. Hash_Size-1;
   type Hash_Array is array (Hash_Range) of Component_Ptr;
   type Sparse_Matrix is
         record
            Last_Row, Last_Col : Natural := 0;
            Head : Hash_Array;
         end record;
```

The Hash_Size value is chosen as a compromise between minimizing storage for the array Head and minimizing the access time for Store and Fetch. Note that the component initializations in the Sparse_Matrix type correspond to an array with bounds of 0; an object declaration like:

```
X : Sparse_Matrix;
```

will therefore automatically initialize X to be a null array. (*Exercise*: complete the package body.)

□ *End of Example 20.1*

20.2. Subtypes and constraints

An Ada type determines both a set of values and a set of operations on those values. A subtype of a type is defined by imposing some constraint on the set of values of that type. Different kinds of constraint are applicable to different type classes:

- ***Range constraints.*** These apply to discrete types. A range constraint specifies a range of consecutive values.
- ***Index constraints.*** These apply to the index types of arrays. Since all index types must be discrete types, this form of constraint is closely related to the range constraint.

- *Floating-point constraints.* These apply to floating-point types, and specify the precision of the values. A floating-point constraint may also include a range, similar to a range constraint for a discrete type.
- *Fixed-point constraints.* These apply to fixed-point types, and specify the precision and range of the values.
- *Discriminant constraints.* These apply to record types (and to private types implemented as record types). Discriminants provide a degree of flexibility in the structure of these types.

The violation of any constraint raises the exception `Constraint_Error`.

Example 20.2 *Contract Bridge*

A library package `Contract_Bridge` is to be provided, containing global declarations for a program to play the card game Contract Bridge. The basic notions here are cards, ranks, suits, packs and hands.

The lower-ranked cards are numbered from 2 to 10, but above them are ranked the Jack, Queen, King and Ace. It is appropriate to define the set of ranks by an enumeration type `Rank`; this has already been illustrated in Section 20.1.

In assessing the strength of a hand (for bidding purposes) it is conventional to weight the Jack, Queen, King and Ace at 1, 2, 3 and 4 points respectively. (Other ranks are weighted 0.) To obtain the points value of a card from its rank, we could provide a simple function, but a constant array is even better:

```
type Rank is (Two, Three, Four, Five, Six, Seven,
              Eight, Nine, Ten, Jack, Queen, King, Ace);
Points : constant array (Rank) of Natural range 0 .. 4
         := (Jack => 1, Queen => 2, King => 3, Ace => 4, others => 0);
```

The concept of a suit is well modeled by an enumeration type, including subtypes for the major and minor suits. The order of the `Suit` values is important, because a bid in Spades is stronger than an equivalent bid in Hearts, Hearts is stronger than Diamonds, and Diamonds is stronger than Clubs:

```
type Suit is (Clubs, Diamonds, Hearts, Spades);
subtype Minor_Suit is Suit range Clubs .. Diamonds;
subtype Major_Suit is Suit range Hearts .. Spades;
```

A card is characterized by a suit and a rank:

```
type Card is
      record
         R : Rank;
         S : Suit;
      end record;
```

For counting cards within a pack we need:

```
type Card_Count is range 0 .. 52;
```

We can represent a set of cards by an array:

```
type Card_Set is array (Card_Count range <>) of Card;
```

This implementation of `Card_Set` is not ideal: it actually gives a *sequence* of cards rather than a set, and it does not enforce the rule that all the cards in a set must be distinct.

Certain sets of cards have special significance, namely a trick (4 cards), a hand (13 cards) and the whole pack (52 cards). These can be subtypes of `Card_Set`:

```
subtype Trick is Card_Set (Card_Count range 1 .. 4);
subtype Hand  is Card_Set (Card_Count range 1 .. 13);
subtype Pack  is Card_Set (Card_Count range 1 .. 52);
```

It remains to deal with bidding. Here we come to a problem. In Contract Bridge, it is possible to make a bid *either* in one of the suits *or* in 'no-trumps'. No-trumps has many, but not all, of the properties of a suit. Therefore we cannot accurately model the bidding system simply by extending the enumeration type `Suit` to include a fifth value, `No_Trumps`. Each bid consists of an integer between 1 and 7 for the number of tricks, and either a suit or no-trumps. A record is needed to hold this information. It should also include 'no-bid' for the sake of completeness. This leads to:

```
subtype Trick_Count is Card_Count range 1 .. 7;
type Bid_Class is (Trump_Bid, No_Trump_Bid, No_Bid);
type Bid (Class : Bid_Class) is
      record
         case Class is
            when Trump_Bid =>
               Trump_Suit   : Suit;
               Trump_Tricks : Trick_Count;
            when No_Trump_Bid =>
               No_Trump_Tricks : Trick_Count;
            when No_Bid =>
               null;
         end case;
      end record;
```

Although the component giving the number of tricks is common to two of the variants, it must be duplicated and given different identifiers. The variant without a bid has no components, because the discriminant itself contains all the necessary data.

The last type is that of the players' positions on the table:

```
type Position is (North, East, South, West);
```

This reflects the ordering round the table: North precedes East, who precedes South, who precedes West. However, West precedes North, and enumeration types such as `Position` do not possess this cyclic property. Therefore we must add a function to provide the cyclic successor of a `Position` value:

```
function Next (P : Position) return Position is
begin
   if P = Position'Last then
      return Position'First;
   else
      return Position'Succ (P);
   end if;
end Next;
```

□ *End of Example 20.2*

The attribute Base is applicable to any subtype name. It denotes the subtype's base type, that is, the type obtained by stripping away all constraints. In Example 20.2, `Trick'Base`, `Hand'Base` and `Pack'Base` all denote the type `Card_Set`; and `Trick_Count'Base` denotes the type `Card_Count`. `Base` may be used only for constructing other attributes, for example `Hand'Base'Length` or `Trick_Count'Base'Last`.

20.3. Derived types

In Chapter 19 we saw how newly declared numeric types are derived from the predefined numeric types. The purpose of this mechanism is to provide a new type from an existing type. In the case of integer and floating-point types, you can either choose the existing type yourself or leave the choice to the compiler.

Deriving a new type from an existing type produces a new set of operations, as well as a new set of values. The derived type is said to *inherit* the original operations of the old type, its *parent* type. This is achieved by systematically replacing the parent type name by the derived type name throughout the declarations of these operations. Thereafter it is always possible to define additional operations for the derived type. Any such additional operations apply only to the derived type, and not to its parent type.

Consider, for example, the following declaration of a new integer type:

```
type Money is range 0 .. 999_999;
```

and assume that the compiler chooses to derive `Money` from the type `Integer`. Then `Money` inherits the original operations of `Integer`. Take `+`, for example: this accepts two `Integer` operands and yields an `Integer` result. Now it also accepts two `Money` operands and yields a `Money` result.

More generally, when we derive a type:

```
type NT is new PT ...;
```

the new type `NT` inherits only certain operations from its parent type `PT`. These operations are:

- assignment, `=` and `/=`;
- all attributes of PT;
- operations like array indexing and record component selection;
- if `PT` is exported by a package, any subprograms with parameters or result of type `PT` that the package also exports.

Parameter passing and returning a function value are available to all types in Ada, including derived types, as a matter of course. Note also that the operations inherited from a parent type that is predefined, like `Integer`, can be deduced by recalling that these types and their basic operations are all considered to be exported by the package `Standard`. If the parent type is a (limited) private type, the derived type is also (limited) private.

The derived type can be restricted to a subset of the values of its parent type, by giving a subtype indication (instead of just a type name) after the reserved word `new` in the derived type definition.

In Example 20.2, we had a problem in representing no-trumps because it has some, but not all, of the properties of a suit. One possibility is to use the derived type mechanism as follows:

```
type Trumps is (Clubs, Diamonds, Hearts, Spades, No_Trumps);
type Suit   is new Trumps range Clubs .. Spades;
```

The type Suit now has the same properties as before, but Trumps has the additional value No_Trumps, as required. Any subprograms subsequently declared for type Suit will be inapplicable to type Trumps, as a consequence of the ordinary type rules. However, any subprogram applicable to type Trumps, and declared in package Contract_Bridge *before* the declaration of Suit, will be applicable to Suit as well. This approach would improve the description of the bidding system. For instance, the declaration of type Bid in Example 20.2 could be simplified as follows:

```
type Bid (Bid_Made : Boolean) is
      record
         case Bid_Made is
            when True =>
               Trump  : Trumps;
               Tricks : Trick_Count;
            when False =>
               null;
         end case;
      end record;
```

The even simpler definition:

```
type Bid is
   record
      Bid_Made : Boolean;
      Trump    : Trumps;
      Tricks   : Trick_Count;
   end record;
```

is not satisfactory, because it fails to model the fact that Trump and Tricks are undefined when Bid_Made is equal to False.

Example 20.3 *Personnel records*

Consider a filing system for personnel records of the type:

```
type Person (Married : Boolean := False) is
      record
         Own_Id     : Person_Id;
         Name       : String (1 .. 20);
         Birth_Date : Date;
         case Married is
            when True =>
               Spouse_Id : Person_Id;
            when False =>
               null;
         end case;
```

```
        end record;
```

Suppose we need to analyze a sequential file that is known to contain records of married persons only. We could approach this by declaring a subtype:

```
subtype Married_Person is Person (Married => True);
```

and instantiating an input-output package:

```
package Person_IO is new Sequential_IO (Person);
use Person_IO;
subtype Marriage_File is Person_IO.File_Type;
```

To print details from a file containing elements of the subtype Married_Person only, we might write the following procedure:

```
procedure Print_Couples (F : in out Marriage_File) is
   P : Married_Person;
begin
   Reset (F, In_File);
   while not End_of_File (F) loop
      Read (F, P);
      Put (P.Own_Id);  Put (P.Spouse_Id);  New_Line;
   end loop;
end Print_Couples;
```

The references to P.Own_Id and P.Spouse_Id do not require any discriminant checks, because we have declared P with the subtype Married_Person. On the other hand, the statement 'Read(F,P);' does require such a check, because the declaration of F as a file with elements of type Person does not state that every element will have the discriminant Married equal to True. We know that only records of married persons should be stored in the file, so this check is unnecessary. We can avoid it by introducing a *type* whose values are necessarily records of married persons only:

```
type Married_Person is new Person (Married => True);
```

Since Person and Married_Person are distinct types, values can be converted from one to the other only by explicit type conversion:

```
A : Person;  -- could be either married or not
B : Married_Person;
...
A := Person (B);               -- always OK
B := Married_Person (A);       -- might raise Constraint_Error
```

The type conversion uses the name of the target type as a function. Note that only explicit type conversions from Person to Married_Person need check for values with Married being False, so that processing objects of type Married_Person will not require any check on the discriminant.

If we now declare:

```
package Married_Person_IO is new Sequential_IO (Married_Person);
use Married_Person_IO;
subtype Marriage_File is Married_Person_IO.File_Type;
```

the procedure Print_Couples can be written as above, and the discriminant check will disappear.

□ *End of Example 20.3*

Apart from reducing checking overhead, a derived type has the advantage of isolating the new type from the old type. If it later becomes necessary to represent married persons differently, the job will be made much easier by the fact that all conversions between `Person` and `Married_Person` are explicit.

A derived type can often be represented in the computer in a different manner from the parent type, and this can even be controlled by the programmer (see Chapter 24). For example, values of type `Married_Person` could, in principle, be represented without storing the discriminant.

See the syntax diagram 'derived_type_definition' in Appendix A.

20.4. Type conversions

We have seen how types allow data objects to be separated into a number of classes, affording a degree of security that is not available in languages without a rich type system. A type conversion takes a value of one type and converts it to a value of another (related) type. Type conversions are permitted in Ada, but they must be explicit. This should make the programmer's intention clear and prevent many careless errors.

As we have seen already (Chapter 7), conversions between values of enumeration types and integers are made possible by the attributes `Pos` and `Val`. In Example 7.3, the enumeration type `Months` was defined in the obvious way. To calculate ages in months, it was necessary to subtract two values of type `Months` — not a permitted operation. The solution was to use the attribute `Pos` to convert `Months` values into integers in the range 0 through 11, so that the age in months can be calculated by:

```
Age := 12 * (Census_Year - Birth_Year)
         + Months'Pos (Census_Month) - Months'Pos (Birth_Month);
```

The result type of `Pos` is ***universal integer***, which, uniquely, can be converted implicitly into any integer type required by the context. In this case the required type is the type of `Age`, `Census_Year` and `Birth_Year`.

Type conversions, although they are explicit, should be thought of as providing a means of escape from the type system, to be invoked as a last resort. Every type conversion blurs the distinction between the types involved, and so reduces the protection they afford. Furthermore, any conversion between types `T1` and `T2` sets up a coupling between the declarations of these types. Thus type conversions are inimical to modularity. There is usually a better alternative. In the above example, we should really define a subtraction operation that takes two dates and returns their difference in days. (Such an operation is provided by the package `Calendar`, see Appendix D.)

A form of type conversion that has already been introduced is numeric conversion. A value may be converted from any numeric type to any other numeric type. Unlike nonnumeric conversions, which merely change the type of a value, numeric conversions can affect the value itself by rounding. Numeric conversions should be used with caution, because they are not always meaningful. For instance, in Example 19.2 a plain type conversion between `Fahrenheit` and `Celsius` would merely copy the numerical value:

```
F : Fahrenheit;  C : Celsius;
...
```

```
F := 32;  C := Celsius (F);
```

would result in C having the value 32, not 0. If the intention was to model freezing point, a mistake has been made and the compiler cannot detect it.

A form of conversion between derived types was introduced in Example 20.3. Here we have two types, Person and Married_Person, directly related because one is derived from the other. Since the very purpose of introducing the type Married_Person was to make a clear distinction between its values and values of type Person, conversions between the two types should be used sparingly.

Conversion is also possible between two array types, provided that the index and component types are either the same as or derived from each other. For example:

```
type Vector is array (Integer range <>) of Float;
Y : Vector (1 .. 10);
X : array (1 .. 10) of Float;
...
Y := Vector (X);
```

The type conversion is valid, because the index types of X and Y are both Integer, and because the component types of X and Y are both Float. However, a type conversion from Y to X would not be possible because X does not have a named type. In this example, X would better have been declared to be of type Vector, which would have avoided the need for any type conversion. However, there are circumstances in which such type conversions cannot be avoided. Suppose that we have two independently produced packages, already available in a library:

```
package Sort_Service is
   type Sequence is array (Integer range <>) of Float;
   procedure Sort (X : in out Sequence);
end Sort_Service;

package Disk_Service is
   type Vector is array (Integer range <>) of Float;
   procedure Read_from_Disk (X : out Vector);
   procedure Write_to_Disk (X : in Vector);
end Disk_Service;
```

The types Sort_Service.Sequence and Disk_Service.Vector are distinct, because they are declared in different places. A program using both packages cannot declare a variable with a type that matches the parameters of all the subprograms in these packages. Explicit conversion to the required parameter type can be used to overcome this problem:

```
with Sort_Service;  use Sort_Service;
with Disk_Service;  use Disk_Service;
procedure P is
   A : array (1 .. 10) of Float;
begin
   ...
   Read_from_Disk (Vector (A));
   Sort (Sequence (A));
   Write_to_Disk (Vector (A));
   ...
```

```
    end;
```

The declaration of A could have been somewhat different:

```
    type Height is digits 4 range 0.0 .. 2.0;
    A : array (1 .. 10) of Height;
```

but the type conversions involving A would still be legal, *provided* only that the compiler chooses to derive Height from Float.

20.5. Qualified expressions

The type of an expression is not usually stated explicitly, but must be deduced from the context by the reader. The programmer can usually make this easy by, for example, good choice of identifiers. The subtype of a expression, however, often depends upon the dynamic behavior of the program and might be far from obvious.

Suppose that we have an Integer variable I, and suppose that one particular statement is expected to assign a nonnegative value to I. To assist the reader we might use a comment:

```
    I := expression;        -- I >= 0
```

However, the comment is ignored by the compiler, and the assertion might be incorrect. An improvement is to state explicitly that the value of *expression* is expected to be in the range of Natural. This can be done by means of a *qualified expression*:

```
    I := Natural' (expression);
```

Now if the value of *expression* turns out to be negative, the Constraint_Error exception is raised.

Qualified expressions are also used in initialized allocators (Section 17.2) where it is essential to state precisely the subtype of the allocated object.

Exercises 20

20.1. Suppose that it is decided to implement a prototype version of the sparse matrix package of Example 20.1, using ordinary 2-dimensional arrays to represent sparse matrices. Revise the private part of the package declaration, and write the package body, accordingly. How do the properties defined for sparse matrices in the package differ from the properties of ordinary 2-dimensional arrays?

20.2. Complete the declaration and body of the Contract_Bridge package of Example 20.2. Include in the package: (a) a type that describes a 'deal' (4 hands of 13 cards each); (b) a subprogram that computes the total points value of a given hand; (c) a subprogram that sorts a given hand, primarily by suit and secondarily by rank; (d) a subprogram that displays a given deal, in something like the conventional format; (e) a subprogram that generates a random deal (using the package Random_Numbers of Example 19.10).

PART IV

Advanced Program Structures

21

Operator Declarations and Overloading

21.1. Operators and functions

A widely accepted and convenient notation is the *infix operator* used in mathematical formulae. Nearly all high-level languages adopt the same notation in expressions, for predefined operations such as addition, subtraction and relations.

Ada allows the programmer to declare operators. An operator takes either one or two operands and delivers a single result. This is analogous to a function with one or two parameters. For example, the addition operation has the name `"+"`, and the expression `I+J` is exactly equivalent to the function call `"+"(I,J)` . Naturally, the infix notation is to be preferred for the standard mathematical operations.

The operator `"+"` is used in Ada for addition. However, the meaning of addition depends on the types of the operands. The addition of two integers is exact, whereas the addition of two floating-point values is approximate. For most machines the Ada compiler must generate different instructions in the two cases. The fact that `"+"` can have more than one meaning, depending upon the types involved, is called *overloading*. All but the simplest high-level languages have some form of overloading. In Ada, operators, subprograms and enumeration literals can be overloaded.

We often declare new data types, with benefit to the reliability and readability of our programs. For some data types (such as `Complex`), it is desirable to define and use operators such as `"+"` and `"*"`. With such operators defined, these new data types have similar status to the predefined types.

Example 21.1 *Operators for* `Time` *and* `Duration`

As an example of operator declarations, consider the modeling of times in the standard package `Calendar` (see Appendix D). This package defines a type `Time` and various operations associated with it.

Time intervals are represented by values of the predefined fixed-point type `Duration` (whose units are seconds). There are natural relationships between the types `Time` and `Duration`. For example, it makes sense to subtract two `Time` values to yield a `Duration` value. Operations like this are defined in `Calendar`. This package illustrates how to declare operators applicable to a new type. The usual syntax for function declarations (and bodies) is used, but with the function identifier replaced by an operator symbol between quotes. For example:

```
function "-" (Left, Right : Time) return Duration;
function "<" (Left, Right : Time) return Boolean;
```

`Duration` is predefined as a fixed-point type (see Appendix D), so operations like addition and subtraction of `Duration` values are already defined, giving results of the same type.

Given the declarations:

```
use Calendar;
T : Time := Clock;
Off_Interval, On_Interval : Duration;
```

the following statements are legal:

```
Off_Interval := Clock - T;
On_Interval  := Off_Interval * 5 / 2;
```

but the following are *illegal*:

```
T := 2 * T;      -- no "*" defined for Time.
T := T ** 2;     -- no "**" defined for Time.
T := T - T;      -- RHS is of type Duration (not Time).
T := + T;        -- no unary "+" defined for Time.
```

□ *End of Example 21.1*

In `Calendar` only binary operators are declared: these are analogous to functions with exactly two parameters. A unary operator is declared like a function with exactly one parameter: see Example 21.2.

21.2. Overloading of operators

There is a fixed set of operator symbols in Ada. This set corresponds roughly to the common mathematical operations. Therefore if a new operation is to be defined, but none of the existing operator symbols is suitable, the new operation should be given an identifier as usual.

Each operator has a fixed precedence. This ensures that the structure of each expression can be determined independently of the types of its operands and independently of the declarations of its operators. One consequence of this is that `"not"` and `"abs"` can only be overloaded as unary operators, whereas `"+"` and `"-"` can be either unary or binary. The overloadable binary operators are `"+"`, `"-"`, `"*"`, `"/"`, `"mod"`, `"rem"`, `"**"`, `"<"`, `">"`, `"<="`, `">="`, `"and"`, `"or"`, `"xor"`, `"&"` and (exceptionally) `"="`.

The `"="` operation may be explicitly defined only for a type that does not have it already defined, in other words a limited private type. (See Section 13.4.) The defined `"="` operation must have `Boolean` as its result type, and it implicitly defines the complementary `"/="` operation. No explicit declaration of `"/="` is ever permitted.

Example 21.2 Operations on rational numbers

As a further example of operator declarations and overloading, consider a rational arithmetic package. The package is to export a type named `Rational`, together with a set of arithmetic operations permitted on this type. For these operations it is natural to use the operator symbols `"+"`, `"-"`, and so on.

```
package Rational_Arithmetic is
   type Rational is
```

```
            record
               Num, Den : Integer;
            end record;
      function "-" (R : Rational) return Rational;
      function "+" (L, R : Rational) return Rational;
      function "-" (L, R : Rational) return Rational;
      function "*" (L, R : Rational) return Rational;
      function "/" (L, R : Rational) return Rational;
   end Rational_Arithmetic;
```

As usual, the package body must provide the bodies of the declared functions (in this case operators):

```
   package body Rational_Arithmetic is
      function "-" (R : Rational) return Rational is
      begin
         return (-R.Num, R.Den);
      end "-";

      function "+" (L, R : Rational) return Rational is
      begin
         return (L.Num*R.Den+R.Num*L.Den, L.Den*R.Den);
      end "+";

      function "-" (L, R : Rational) return Rational is
      begin
         return L + (- R);
      end "-";

      function "*" (L, R : Rational) return Rational is
      begin
         return (L.Num*R.Num, L.Den*R.Den);
      end "*";

      function "/" (L, R : Rational) return Rational is
      begin
         return (L.Num*R.Den, L.Den*R.Num);
      end "/";

   end Rational_Arithmetic;
```

The definition of the unary "-" for Rational uses the predefined unary "-" for Integer (in the expression -L.Num). Similarly the binary "+" for Rational is defined in terms of "+" and "*" for Integer. On the other hand, the binary "-" for Rational is defined in terms of "+" and unary "-" for Rational. However, if the expression were written as L-R, then it would call the operator "-" for Rational (which would be infinite recursion!).

Note that "=" and "/=" are automatically defined for the type Rational. Unfortunately (in this case), these definitions are in terms of equality of the components. This implies that the expression (1,2)=(2,4) has the value False, although the two rational numbers are equal in the mathematical sense. It would therefore be preferable to declare Rational as a limited private type so that "=" could be declared explicitly in the package:

```
   package Rational_Arithmetic is
      type Rational is limited private;
```

```
        function "-" (R : Rational) return Rational;
        function "+" (L, R : Rational) return Rational;
        function "-" (L, R : Rational) return Rational;
        function "*" (L, R : Rational) return Rational;
        function "/" (L, R : Rational) return Rational;
        function "/" (L, R : Integer) return Rational;
        function "=" (L, R : Rational) return Rational;
    private
        type Rational is
              record
                 Num, Den : Integer;
              end record;
    end Rational_Arithmetic;
```

The "=" operator would be implemented as follows:

```
        function "=" (L, R : Rational) return Boolean is
        begin
           return (L.Num*R.Den = L.Den*R.Num);
        end "=";
```

Note that we have also added an operator "/" to construct a Rational value from two Integer values. This is necessary since the record aggregate notation (1,2) is no longer available; we write 1/2 instead. This operator would be implemented as follows:

```
        function "/" (L, R : Integer) return Rational is
        begin
           return (L, R);
        end "/";
```

□ *End of Example 21.2*

21.3. Overloading of subprograms

We have already encountered examples of overloading of subprograms. For example, Put has been used to output values of type Character, String, Integer, and so on. In fact, the Text_IO package defines a number of distinct procedures named Put. They differ principally in the types of their parameters. The compiler selects the appropriate procedure according to the type of the actual parameter in the procedure call. If more than one procedure can be selected, the procedure call is ambiguous and therefore invalid. For instance, since Put is defined for more than one integer type, the call 'Put(2);' is illegal.

The example of Put illustrates the typical use of overloading. All the Put procedures perform the same abstract operation, so it is reasonable to give them all the same name. The use of the single name Put is an aid to readability in this case; having to invent a variety of names such as Put_Character, Put_String and Put_Integer would be less attractive. On the other hand, the use of the same name for procedures not performing the same abstract operation should be avoided.

Example 21.3 Overloading of a procedure

New procedures also called `Put` could be added to the packages `Complex_Arithmetic` (Example 13.7) and `Rational_Arithmetic` (Example 21.2) without difficulty. The declaration of `Rational_Arithmetic` should be augmented by:

```
procedure Put (Item : in Rational);
```

and its body by something like:

```
procedure Put (Item : in Rational) is
begin
   Put (Item.Num);  Put (" / ");  Put (Item.Den);
end Put;
```

This itself calls two different overloadings of `Put`: the first and last calls have parameters of type `Integer`, and the middle one a parameter of type `String`. Of course, the package body of `Rational_Arithmetic` must have access to `Text_IO` for these calls to be valid.

Similarly, the body of `Put` in `Complex_Arithmetic` might be:

```
procedure Put (Item : in Complex) is
begin
   Put (Item.Re);  Put (" + ");  Put (Item.Im);  Put ("i");
end Put;
```

Suppose now that the name of the `Sum` function in `Complex_Arithmetic` has been changed to `"+"`. Consider an application that uses both these packages:

```
use Rational_Arithmetic, Complex_Arithmetic;
C, D : Rational;
R, S : Complex;
...
Put (C + D);
Put (R + S);
```

Here both `Put` and `"+"` are overloaded, but each procedure call has a unique interpretation and is therefore legal. If we omit the use clause, we avoid the overloading of `Put` and `"+"`, but the coding is much less concise:

```
C, D : Complex_Arithmetic.Complex;
R, S : Rational_Arithmetic.Rational;
...
Rational_Arithmetic.Put (Rational_Arithmetic."+" (R, S));
Complex_Arithmetic.Put (Complex_Arithmetic."+" (C, D));
```

□ *End of Example 21.3*

Example 21.4 Overloading of a function

The following overloaded functions compute the maximum of two or three integers:

```
function Max (X, Y : Integer) return Integer is
begin
   if X > Y then
      return X;
```

```
      else
         return Y;
      end if;
   end Max;

   function Max (X, Y, Z : Integer) return Integer is
   begin
      return Max (Max (X, Y), Z);
   end Max;
```

Here the two functions are distinguished by the number of parameters rather than by the types of the parameters. A function call with three parameters, such as `Max(0,2*N,M)`, clearly calls the ternary `Max` function, whereas a call with two parameters clearly calls the binary `Max` function. Thus both function calls inside the body of the ternary `Max` are calling the binary `Max` and are not recursive.

□ *End of Example 21.4*

21.4. Overloading of enumeration literals

Apart from subprograms and operators, Ada also permits the overloading of enumeration literals. Consider enumeration types to model colors of the rainbow and states of a traffic signal:

```
type Color  is (Red, Orange, Yellow, Green, Blue, Indigo, Violet);
type Signal is (Red, Amber, Green);
```

If both of these declarations occurred in the same scope, then the names `Red` and `Green` would both be ambiguous. This overloading is permitted in Ada, however, in a fashion similar to the overloading of subprograms. If the types `Color` and `Signal` were declared in separate packages, then the selected-component notation could be used to select the appropriate `Red` and `Green`. This notation tends to be verbose, however, and in many cases it is preferable to allow overloading:

```
State : Signal;  Paint : Color;
...
State := Red;  Paint := Red;
```

Neither of these assignment statements is ambiguous.

Character types

The predefined type `Character` is an ordinary enumeration type. We simplified the introduction to enumeration types in Section 7.1 by omitting to mention that character literals as well as identifiers may be used as enumeration literals. (See the syntax diagram 'enumeration_literal' in Appendix A.) The declaration of `Character` looks like this, in outline:

```
type Character is (..., ' ', ..., 'A','B','C', ...);
```

Nearly all the properties of the type may be deduced from its declaration, which is given in full in Appendix D.

Since the character literal is just one form of enumeration literal, character literals may be overloaded in exactly the same way as the identifiers `Red` and `Green` above. An enumeration type that is defined using character literals is called a *character type*. Character types are an important special case of overloading.

Example 21.5 *Roman numerals*

The following is a convenient way of modeling Roman numerals:

```
type Roman is ('I', 'V', 'X', 'L', 'C', 'D', 'M');
type Roman_Numeral is array (Positive range <>) of Roman;
```

Now the values of type `Roman` are denoted by the character literals `'I'`, `'V'` and so on, and these overload some of the `Character` literals. The value denoted by `'I'` in `Roman` is quite distinct from the value denoted by `'I'` in `Character` (they belong to distinct types). There is no ambiguity in the following statements:

```
C : Character;  R : Roman;
...
C := 'I';  R := 'I';
```

but an expression like `'I'<'C'` would be ambiguous in every sense. (We shall see in the next section how to avoid such ambiguities.)

The string literal `"XIV"` is *defined* in Ada to be equivalent to the array aggregate `('X','I','V')`, and therefore its type could be either `String` or `Roman_Numeral`. On the other hand, the string literal `"IXY"` can only be of type `String`, since the character literal `'Y'` cannot be of type `Roman`.

The following function will convert a given Roman numeral to the corresponding integer value:

```
function Value (Numeral : Roman_Numeral) return Positive is
   Digit_Value : constant array (Roman) of Positive
                 := (1, 5, 10, 50, 100, 500, 1000);
   Sum : Positive := 0;
   Previous : Roman := 'I';
begin
   for Pos in reverse Numeral'Range loop
      if Numeral(Pos) < Previous then
         Sum := Sum - Digit_Value (Numeral(Pos));
      else
         Sum := Sum + Digit_Value (Numeral(Pos));
      end if;
      Previous := Numeral(Pos);
   end loop;
   return Sum;
end Value;
```

The function call `Value("MCMLXXXVIII")` is legal since the string literal can be of type `Roman_Numeral`, and its value will be 1988. On the other hand, the function call `Value("IXY")` will not compile because, as explained above, this string literal is not of type `Roman_Numeral`. For a similar reason, '`R(1):='Y';`', where `R` is of type `Roman_Numeral`, also will not compile. Hence the function above does not need to check that the parameter contains only permitted characters: that is guaranteed by the type rules. (The function does permit sequences not usually allowed for Roman numbers, such as "IC", giving 99. However, that is a separate matter.)

□ *End of Example 21.5*

21.5. Overloading and ambiguity

Overloading is a potential source of ambiguity. The rule in Ada is that if an expression or subprogram call is ambiguous (in its context), then it is illegal. Hence programmers are assured that the compiler will reject ambiguous constructs rather than guess the 'correct' interpretation.

The detection of ambiguities involves ***overload resolution*** by the compiler. To see how this works, consider the following example:

```
use Rational_Arithmetic;
package Int_IO is new Integer_IO (Integer);  use Int_IO;
I, J, K : Integer;  R : Rational;
...
I := J / K;
R := J / K;
Put (J / K);
```

The expression J/K calls a function named "/" with two actual parameters of type Integer. This could be *either* (a) the predefined operator "/" with two Integer operands and an Integer result, *or* (b) the operator "/" with two Integer operands and a Rational result (exported by Rational_Arithmetic). In the statement 'I:=J/K;' only interpretation (a) is possible, since the left and right sides of an assignment statement must be of the same type. In the statement 'R:=J/K;' only interpretation (b) is possible. In the statement 'Put(J/K);' only interpretation (a) is possible — ***unless*** the procedure Put of Example 21.3 is also visible, in which case both interpretations would be possible, and the statement would be illegal.

We can avoid ambiguity by means of a qualified expression that explicitly specifies the type of the expression. For example, the type declaration of Roman in Example 21.5 makes the expression 'I'<'C' ambiguous, but it could be written unambiguously as either Character'('I')<Character'('C') or Roman'('I')<Roman'('C'). Similarly, our ambiguous statement 'Put(J/K);' could be made unambiguous by suitable qualification:

```
Put (Integer' (J / K));
Put (Rational' (J / K));
```

A more common form of ambiguity arises from aggregates. We have already seen this in the case of a string literal, which is a special form of array aggregate. Record aggregates can also be ambiguous. Suppose, for example, that the following declarations occur in the same scope as Rational_Arithmetic:

```
type Coordinate is
      record
         X, Y : Integer;
      end record;
```

```
procedure Put (Item : in Coordinate);
```

If Rational is not private, then 'Put((1,2));' would be ambiguous, but could be rewritten in either of the forms:

```
Put (Rational' (1, 2));
Put (Coordinate' (1, 2));
```

(*Exercise*: what if Rational *is* private?)

Style

Overloading is common in natural language. There we have no formal notation for expressing the context, so ambiguity is a serious problem. Precise expression is essential in programming, on the other hand, and yet the notation should be as natural as possible. Hence any use of overloading should satisfy the following two criteria:

- The proposed use of overloading should be natural. For example, the use of "+" for addition of complex numbers is natural, but its use for comparing two strings would not be.
- There should be no possibility of confusion with other widely accepted notations.

Obviously it is easy to abuse overloading. This is not a new possibility, however. Overloading extends the naming freedom that is common to all programming languages, and that freedom can always be abused, for example by defining a subprogram for subtracting matrices and naming it ADD.

21.6. Visibility rules and overloading

In previous discussions of the visibility rules (Section 12.7, Section 13.6 and Section 16.9), we have simplified the rules by pretending that each identifier stands for (at most) one entity at each point of the program text. This simplification implies that no identifier may be declared twice in the same declarative region, and a declaration of an identifier in an inner declarative region hides any declaration of the same identifier in an enclosing declarative region.

Actually, these rules are accurate for all entities except subprograms, operators and enumeration literals, which are known collectively as ***overloadable entities***. An identifier (or operator symbol or character literal) may stand for several overloadable entities at the same point of the program text, provided that these entities are distinguishable from one another. For example, the operator symbol "+" stands for several predefined functions including:

```
function "+" (Right : Integer) return Integer;
function "+" (Right : Float)   return Float;
function "+" (Left, Right : Integer) return Integer;
function "+" (Left, Right : Float)   return Float;
```

These functions are distinguishable from one another by their parameter and result types, so that in an expression containing "+" the appropriate function can be selected by overload resolution, described above.

To state the visibility rules more precisely, it is convenient to define a property called the ***signature*** of each subprogram, operator and enumeration literal. The signature consists of the sequence of parameter types (if any), together with the result type (if any). For example, the four "+" functions declared above, the two Put procedures in Example 21.3 and the two enumeration literals Red declared at the beginning of Section 21.4 have the following signatures:

Entity	*Signature* *parameter types* → *result type*
`function "+" (Right : Integer) return Integer`	`Integer` → `Integer`
`function "+" (Right : Float) return Float`	`Float` → `Float`
`function "+" (Left, Right : Integer) return Integer`	`Integer, Integer` → `Integer`
`function "+" (Left, Right : Float) return Float`	`Float, Float` → `Float`
`procedure Put (Item : in Rational)`	`Rational` → *(no result)*
`procedure Put (Item : in Complex)`	`Complex` → *(no result)*
Enumeration literal `Red` of type `Color`	*(no parameters)* → `Color`
Enumeration literal `Red` of type `Signal`	*(no parameters)* → `Signal`

Note that it is the *types*, not the subtypes, of the parameters and results that matter. Also, the parameter modes (in, out and in out) of a subprogram are not taken into account. The reason is that subtypes and modes are not apparent in a subprogram call, only the types of the actual parameters. For the purpose of defining its signature, an enumeration literal is treated like a parameterless function.

Armed with the concept of a signature, the interaction between overloading and the visibility rules can now be stated quite simply:

- An identifier (or operator symbol or character literal) *may* be declared more than once in the same declarative region, provided that all these declarations introduce overloadable entities with different signatures.
- A declaration of an overloadable entity hides an outer declaration of an overloadable entity with the same identifier (or operator symbol or character literal) only if the two declarations have the same signature.

Exercises 21

21.1. The package body of `Rational_Arithmetic` in Example 21.2 has the defect that some of the functions could raise `Numeric_Error` even when the result is in range. Revise the body of `"+"` to avoid this, using an exception handler for `Numeric_Error`. Would it be better to use cautious coding always and not rely upon `Numeric_Error`?

21.2. Add an operator `"<"` to the declaration of `Rational_Arithmetic`. Implement it: (a) using subtraction; and (b) without using subtraction and avoiding unnecessary overflow.

21.3. Add:

```
function "abs" (X : Rational) return Rational;
```

to the package `Rational_Arithmetic`.

21.4. Write a package `Days_of_Week` that exports a private type `Day`, with constants `Monday`, `Tuesday`, and so on. It must also export operators `"+"` and `"-"`, each with a `Day` first parameter, an `Integer` second parameter, and a `Day` result. For example, `Friday+12` should yield `Wednesday`.

21.5. Write a subprogram `Put` to output a value of type `Time` in ISO format:

year:month:day:hour:minute:second

(An example would be `1987:6:21:5:30:15`.) Also write a statement that outputs the *current* time (returned by `Clock`).

21.6. Consider the following declarations:

```
function "+" (X : Integer;  Y : Integer)  return Integer;
function "+" (X : Real;     Y : Real)     return Real;
function "/" (X : Integer;  Y : Integer)  return Integer;
function "/" (X : Real;     Y : Real)     return Real;
function "/" (X : Integer;  Y : Integer)  return Real;
I : Integer;  R : Real;
```

Which of the following statements are legal? For those that are legal, identify which declaration corresponds to each operator.

```
I := 7/3;
R := 7/3;
I := 2 + 1/3;
R := (1/2) / (3/4);
```

How would your answers be affected if the second declaration of `"/"` were removed? or its first declaration?

22

Generic Program Units

22.1. Introduction

In large software systems it is sometimes found necessary to incorporate two or more modules that are distinct but very similar (or even textually identical). For example, we might need several sorting procedures that use identical algorithms but differ in the types of the objects to be sorted; the Ada type rules make it impossible to use a single procedure in such a case. As another example, we might need a package that encapsulates a bounded queue, and a second package that encapsulates a second bounded queue, perhaps of a different size.

Generic program units (or simply *generics*) provide a mechanism whereby the text of a subprogram or package can be generalized to a *template*, which can then be used to produce several distinct instances for actual use. This is called *instantiating* the generic. Such an instantiation then provides a subprogram or package that can be used directly in the usual manner. The generic mechanism thus has three aspects:

- A *generic declaration* is a subprogram declaration or package declaration specifying that the corresponding subprogram or package is a template.
- *Generic instantiation* creates a specific instance from the template.
- The instantiated subprogram or package is used in the ordinary way.

See the syntax diagrams 'generic_declaration' and 'generic_instantiation' in Appendix A. The generic mechanism in Ada has no direct analogy in other widely used languages.

22.2. Parameterless generics

A package containing only object declarations is somewhat similar to a single record object. However, packages are much more general than records in that they may contain declarations of types, subprograms, etc., in addition to objects. On the other hand, we can easily create several instances of a record, by declaring several objects of the same record type. It would appear that Ada does not allow multiple instances of a package. This is true for an ordinary package, but multiple copies can easily be formed by making the package generic.

A package is made generic simply by prefixing the reserved word `generic` to the package declaration. No change at all is made to the package body. Then multiple copies can be formed by instantiations of the generic package.

Example 22.1 *OIS: Multiple device drivers*

Consider again the office information system (OIS) introduced in Example 14.6. Suppose that the OIS hardware includes a single VDU. This device is to be driven by a package named VDU. The package encapsulates a display table that is a copy of the characters currently displayed on the VDU screen. The package also keeps track of the current cursor position, which is marked in a distinctive manner on the screen.

```
package VDU is
   subtype Y_Range is Integer range 1 .. 24;
   subtype X_Range is Integer range 1 .. 80;
   procedure Write (S : String);
      -- writes S to the display at the cursor position.
   procedure Move (Y : in Y_Range;  X : in X_Range);
      -- changes the cursor position to line Y and column X.
   ...
end VDU;

package body VDU is
   Display : array (Y_Range, X_Range) of Character;
   Cursor_Y : Y_Range;  Cursor_X : X_Range;
   ...
end VDU;
```

Now suppose that the OIS is enhanced to include two similar VDUs. This would appear to require either a duplication of the package or substantial modifications to the software (giving each procedure a parameter to indicate the actual VDU involved).

A much better solution is to make the package generic. The package then becomes a template, which can be used to instantiate a distinct package for each VDU. The declaration of the generic package is:

```
generic
package VDU is
   subtype Y_Range is Integer range 1 .. 24;
   subtype X_Range is Integer range 1 .. 80;
   procedure Write (S : String);
   procedure Move (Y : in Y_Range;  X : in X_Range);
   ...
end VDU;
```

The only change is inserting the word **generic** at the beginning of the package declaration. The generic package body is identical to the package body above. The two drivers are now created by instantiations of this generic package:

```
package VDU1 is new VDU;
package VDU2 is new VDU;
```

The first of these instantiations creates a new package that is identical to the generic package VDU, except that **generic** is stripped off and the package is renamed VDU1. Similarly, the second instantiation creates an identical package called VDU2. These two new packages can now be used just like any ordinary package, for example:

```
VDU1.Write ("VDU 1");  VDU2.Write ("VDU 2");
```

We can see from this simple example how powerful the generic mechanism is. Merely adding the single symbol **generic** in front of a package declaration gives us the ability to make copies of it. In this example, the procedures `Write` and `Move` are identical except for the data on which they operate: `VDU1.Write` operates on `VDU1.Display`, whereas `VDU2.Write` operates on `VDU2.Display`.

The two instantiated packages have distinct identifiers, `VDU1` and `VDU2`. This is appropriate if they are to be used in distinct ways, say one for control and the other for input. However, if we had 20 VDUs and wished to broadcast messages to all of them, having 20 distinct packages would not be convenient! A different approach would then be needed.

□ *End of Example 22.1*

In Example 22.1 there was no distinction between the two instantiated packages (apart from their names). For this reason, the generic package was parameterless. Instances that are not identical to one another can be created from a generic with parameters. Objects, types and subprograms can all be used to parametrize a generic program unit. These ***generic parameters*** are introduced in the following sections.

22.3. Generic object parameters

Generic in parameters

Sometimes a generic must be parametrized by a value that is fixed at the time of instantiation. Such cases can be handled by means of ***generic in parameters.***

Example 22.2 OIS: Multiple device types

Example 22.1 assumed that all the VDUs were identical. In reality, it is common to attach a mix of VDUs to the same computer, where certain characteristics (such as the control characters used for cursor movement) tend to vary from one kind of VDU to another. Let us modify the package to accommodate this variation.

Firstly, the various kinds of VDU must be specified:

```
type VDU_Kind is (Basic_Kind, Kind_A, Kind_B, ...);
```

Secondly, the kind of a particular VDU must be provided as a generic parameter, so that it can be fixed at instantiation of the package for that particular VDU. Since the kind of the VDU is a ***value*** used by the package, it is specified as a generic in parameter:

```
generic
   Kind : in VDU_Kind;
package VDU is
   as before
end VDU;
```

The body of the package can now use `Kind` as a constant. For instance, the initialization of the package could output the kind of the VDU:

```
package body VDU is
   Display : array (Y_Range, X_Range) of Character;
```

```
      Cursor_Y : Y_Range;   Cursor_X : X_Range;
      ...
   begin
      Move (1, 1);
      Write (VDU_Kind'Image (Kind));
   end VDU;
```

Each instantiation of the package must provide a value for Kind as a *generic actual parameter*, for example:

```
   package Control is new VDU (Basic_Kind);
   package Monitor is new VDU (Kind_A);
```

The instantiation of Control will write 'BASIC_KIND', and the instantiation of Monitor will write 'KIND_A', on the top lines of the respective VDU screens.
□ *End of Example 22.2*

The actual parameter that corresponds to a generic in parameter must be an expression of the same type. This expression is evaluated at the time of instantiation, and it is the *value* of the expression that is used in the instantiated subprogram or package.

A generic in parameter can have a default value (similarly to a subprogram in parameter). We could have specified Kind as follows:

```
   generic
      Kind : in VDU_Kind := Basic_Kind;
   package VDU is
      as before
   end VDU;
```

and then the instantiation of Control could be simplified to:

```
   package Control is new VDU;
```

Example 22.3 Range tests on strings

Suppose that a string handling package is being developed. As part of this, it is necessary to test strings to see if each character within them is contained in a specified range of character values. A generic function could be used to avoid implementing several logically equivalent functions:

```
   generic
      Lower, Upper : in Character;
   function In_Range (S : String) return Boolean;

   function In_Range (S : String) return Boolean is
   begin
      for I in S'Range loop
         if S(I) not in Lower .. Upper then
            return False;
         end if;
      end loop;
      return True;
   end In_Range;
```

```
function Is_All_Upper_Case is new In_Range ('A', 'Z');
function Is_All_Lower_Case is new In_Range ('a', 'z');
function Is_All_Decimal    is new In_Range ('0', '9');
```

The generic function `In_Range` illustrates two levels of abstraction, embodied by the generic parameters and the function's own parameter, respectively. The generic function is instantiated, with generic actual parameters `'A'` and `'Z'`, to create an ordinary function `Is_All_Upper_Case`. This function has a `String` formal parameter `S` and a `Boolean` result, and it uses the values `'A'` and `'Z'` as internal constants (in place of `Lower` and `Upper`). The alternative of providing one function with three parameters is less attractive because the three different uses could not be distinguished by name: `In_Range(S,'A','Z')` is not so clear as `Is_All_Upper_Case(S)`. A modest investment of effort in making the function generic allows us to generate a family of functions, each of which would otherwise require nine lines to express. The generic function `In_Range` expresses a more general test than each function instantiated from it. Generics provide the key to this higher level of abstraction.

□ *End of Example 22.3*

Generic in out parameters

Generic **in** parameters allow a generic to be parametrized with respect to a *value* computed at the time of instantiation. It is also possible to parametrize a generic with respect to a *variable* that is external to the generic itself: that is achieved by means of a *generic in out parameter*.

Example 22.4 Device control blocks

Consider again the problem of multiple device drivers, but this time in a more realistic context. At a high level we have subprograms to transfer data to and from the device. In the case of the VDUs we needed a display table to implement this level. At a lower level, actual device control is needed. This can be both complicated and machine-dependent. The details of the data upon which this package works should therefore be hidden within the package. However, the *existence* of this data must be controlled at a high level, in order to ensure its correct allocation. Many operating systems that have this problem simply allocate the data for device drivers statically, i.e. when the system is set up. Here we assume that the data is defined by a private type called `Device_Data`. Our generic device-driver package has an object of type `Device_Data` as an **in out** parameter. The package now looks like this:

```
generic
   Control_Block : in out Device_Data;
   Kind : in VDU_Kind := Basic_Kind;
package VDU is
   as before
end VDU;
```

The package body can now use `Control_Block` as a variable. The instantiation determines the actual variable denoted by `Control_Block`. It could, for example, be a component of an array of control blocks:

```
Device_Table : array (1 .. N) of Device_Data;
```

```
package Control is new VDU (Device_Table(1), Kind_A);
```

Now all references to `Control_Block` within the body of the instantiated package `Control` represent references to `Device_Table(1)`.

The importance of this solution is that now we have isolated the allocation of space for the `Device_Data` objects from the instantiation of the package itself. In consequence, much more freedom is available in the way in which the package is used.

□ *End of Example 22.4*

22.4. Generic type parameters

A designer of general-purpose library software, such as mathematical functions or sorting procedures, faces a dilemma. Such software cannot be written in terms of types declared in individual programs. But if it is written in terms of predefined types only, then it is almost unusable with types declared in individual programs. For example, a library unit like:

```
function Sqrt (X : Float) return Float;
```

could not be used to obtain a `Long_Float` square root accurately. This is unfortunate, since there is no reason for the algorithm used in the subprogram to depend on the particular floating-point type. Nor would replacing each occurrence of `Float` by (say) `Real` help much, since the library unit could only depend on a specific declaration of `Real` in another library unit.

What we need is to be able to parametrize software by the types of the data involved. In other words, we need to allow ***generic type parameters*** so that different instantiations of a generic can provide the same algorithm for different types of data.

The critical aspect of a generic type parameter is what knowledge the generic may assume about the properties of the type. The less the generic assumes about the properties of its type parameter, the wider the class of types acceptable as actual parameters.

Example 22.5 *Value interchange*

Consider a procedure `Swap` that interchanges two values of some *specific* type `Items`:

```
procedure Swap (X, Y : in out Items) is
   Old_X : Items := X;
begin
   X := Y;  Y := Old_X;
end Swap;
```

This procedure assumes only assignment for the type `Items`. It will therefore work for any type `Items` other than a limited type. However, it cannot be used to interchange values of any type other than `Items`. We can generalize `Swap`, so that it can be instantiated for a variety of types, by making `Items` into a generic type parameter:

```
generic
   type Items is private;
procedure Swap (X, Y : in out Items);
```

```
procedure Swap (X, Y : in out Items) is
   Old_X : Items := X;
begin
   X := Y;  Y := Old_X;
end Swap;
```

This generic can now be instantiated for any type other than a limited type:

```
procedure Swap_Int  is new Swap (Integer);
procedure Swap_Char is new Swap (Items => Character);
```

The instantiated procedures can now be called directly, just as if separate procedures had been written for each type:

```
Swap_Int  (I1, I2);  -- swap I1 and I2 of type Integer
Swap_Char (C1, C2);  -- swap C1 and C2 of type Character
```

The generic actual parameter corresponding to `Items` must be a type name. Moreover, this type must not be limited. This restriction guarantees that assignment, used in the body of `Swap`, is indeed available for the actual parameter type.

□ *End of Example 22.5*

The Ada compiler checks the generic declaration and body for internal consistency. (In `Swap`, for example, the compiler checks that no operations are assumed for the private type parameter `Items` other than assignment, `"="` and `"/="`.) The compiler also checks each generic instantiation for internal consistency. (In each instantiation of `Swap`, for example, the compiler checks that the generic actual parameter corresponding to `Items` is not a limited type.) In nearly every case these checks are sufficient to guarantee that the instantiated program unit is error-free.

It is, however, possible for an instantiation to be illegal for reasons that are not immediately obvious. For instance,

```
procedure Swap_String is new Swap (String);
```

is *illegal* because the instantiation, obtained by substituting `String` for each occurrence of the generic formal parameter `Items`, would contain a declaration of an unconstrained array variable, `Old_X`. (*Exercise*: Find a simple improvement to the body of `Swap` that would avoid this problem.)

The generic procedure `Swap` was introduced as a generalization of the ordinary non-generic procedure. The generic procedure corresponds to the abstract concept of performing an interchange for *any* type.

Generic type parameters of specific classes

In Example 22.5, the generic type parameter was specified by:

```
type Items is private;
```

This says that, within the generic body, no properties may be assumed for `Items` other than those possessed by a private type, namely assignment and (in)equality tests. In that particular example, no other properties were needed.

The generic mechanism would be very restrictive if generic types always had only assignment and (in)equality tests. So the generic type parameter can be characterized in various ways, to let the generic body know exactly what properties of the generic type may be exploited. The classes of generic type parameters are as follows:

Generic formal parameter	*Actual parameter*
`type T is limited private;`	any type
`type T is private;`	any non-limited type
`type T is ( <> );`	any discrete type
`type T is range <>;`	any integer type
`type T is digits <>;`	any floating-point type
`type T is delta <>;`	any fixed-point type

These generic type classes form a hierarchy as shown in Figure 22.1. As we ascend the hierarchy, fewer and fewer properties of the generic type can be exploited by the generic body, but conversely more and more types can legally be supplied at instantiation. Therefore for a generic type parameter you should choose the most general class that still provides the operations needed in the generic body.

Example 22.6 *Generic square root*

Consider the square-root example discussed at the start of this section. We wish to write a generic function `Square_Root`, with a generic type parameter `Real` that represents the actual type of the square-root function's argument and result. The implementation of the function must use various operations that are unique to floating-point types, so `Real` must be specified as a floating-point type in the generic function declaration:

```
generic
   type Real is digits <>;
function Square_Root (X : Real) return Real;
```

The phrase '`digits <>`' is interpreted as specifying a floating-point type, but not its precision.

The generic function body can now assume that floating-point operations such as `"*"`, `"-"`, `abs` and the attribute `Epsilon` are available for `Real`:

```
function Square_Root (X : Real) return Real is
   Root : Real := X / 2.0;
```

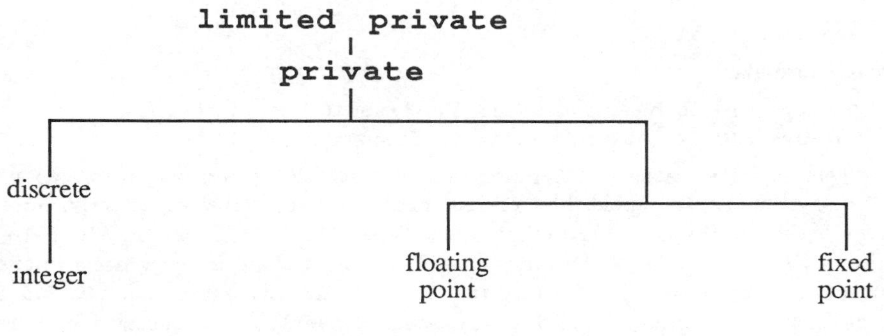

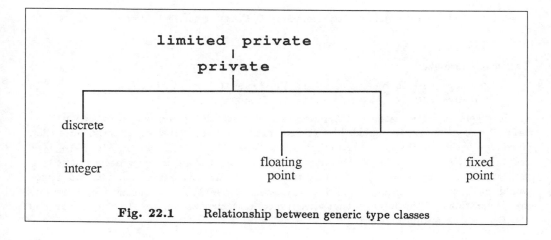

Fig. 22.1 Relationship between generic type classes

```
begin
   while abs (X - Root**2) > 2.0 * X * Real'Epsilon loop
      Root := (Root + X / Root) / 2.0;
   end loop;
   return Root;
end Square_Root;
```

This generic function can be instantiated for any floating-point type, for example:

```
function Sqrt is new Square_Root (Float);
function Sqrt is new Square_Root (Long_Float);
```

These instantiations illustrate a typical use of overloading. Which of the two instantiated functions is called by `Sqrt(R)` depends on whether `R` is declared as `Float` or `Long_Float`. The function call `Sqrt(2.0)` would be ambiguous and therefore illegal.

□ *End of Example 22.6*

The input-output packages revisited

Some excellent illustrations of generic type parameters are provided by the standard input-output packages. We are now in a position to show exactly what they look like, and to explain the 'magic formulae' we have been using up to now.

`Sequential_IO` (described in Section 15.3) is a generic package, with a generic type parameter `Element_Type` that corresponds to the type of the file elements. The package does nothing to these elements other than copy them to or from the file, so `Element_Type` is specified as `private` in the generic package declaration:

```
generic
   type Element_Type is private;
package Sequential_IO is
   type File_Type is limited private;
   ...
   procedure Read (File : in File_Type;
                   Item : out Element_Type);
   ...
   End_Error : exception renames IO_Exceptions.End_Error;
   ...
end Sequential_IO;
```

The 'magic formulae':

```
package TIO is new Sequential_IO (Transactions);
package AIO is new Sequential_IO (Accounts);
```

are just generic instantiations of `Sequential_IO`, with the generic type parameter `Element_Type` systematically replaced by `Transactions` and `Accounts` respectively. Note that, since two distinct packages are instantiated, the types `TIO.File_Type` and `AIO.File_Type` are quite distinct. Likewise, if the input-output exceptions had ordinary declarations (e.g. '`End_Error : exception;`') in `Sequential_IO`, then `TIO.End_Error` and `AIO.End_Error` would be distinct exceptions. In fact, however, `Sequential_IO` contains only renaming declarations of the input-output exceptions, as shown above, so `TIO.End_Error` and `AIO.End_Error` are just aliases.

Direct_IO (described in Section 15.4) is also a generic package, analogous to Sequential_IO.

Text_IO is an ordinary package, but within it Enumeration_IO, Integer_IO, Float_IO and Fixed_IO are declared as generic packages. Each of them has a single generic type parameter of the appropriate class:

```
package Text_IO is
   ...
   type File_Type is limited private;
   ...

   generic
      type ENUM is ( <> );
   package Enumeration_IO is
      procedure Get  (File : in File_Type;
                      Item : out ENUM);
      ...
   end Enumeration_IO;

   generic
      type NUM is range <>;
   package Integer_IO is
      procedure Get  (File  : in File_Type;
                      Item  : in NUM;
                      Width : in Field := 0);
      ...
   end Integer_IO;

   generic
      type NUM is digits <>;
   package Float_IO is
      ...
   end Float_IO;

   generic
      type NUM is delta <>;
   package Fixed_IO is
      ...
   end Fixed_IO;

   ...
end Text_IO;
```

The fact that the generic type parameter NUM is specified as 'range <>' allows the body of Integer_IO to exploit the integer operations for NUM. (For example, Put can convert the integer value of Item into decimal digits by means of integer division.) The 'magic formula':

```
package Int_IO is new Text_IO.Integer_IO (Integer);
```

instantiates a copy of the package Text_IO.Integer_IO with each occurrence of NUM replaced by Integer.

22.5. Generic subprogram parameters

In some programming languages a subprogram is a kind of value. In FORTRAN and Pascal such use of a subprogram is restricted to passing it as a parameter to another subprogram. Ada does not permit even this, but a subprogram can be a generic parameter.

Example 22.7 *Numerical integration*

It is straightforward to write down an algorithm that uses Simpson's rule (for example) to compute the direct integral of a given (continuous) function $F(x)$ between limits $x = A$ and $x = B$. We would like to formulate this algorithm as a subprogram. In Ada a function may not be passed as a parameter to another subprogram. What we can do, however, is to formulate the integration algorithm as a *generic* subprogram, with the function to be integrated, `F`, as a generic function parameter:

```
generic
   with function F (X : Float) return Float;
function Integral (A, B : Float) return Float;
```

We can now express the body in terms of the generic parameter `F` and the subprogram's parameters `A` and `B`:

```
function Integral (A, B : Float) return Float is
   N : constant := 100;   -- no. of intervals (must be even)
   H : constant Float := (B - A) / Float(N);    -- interval width
   Sum, X : Float;
begin
   Sum := F (A) + F (B);
   for I in 1 .. N - 1 loop
      X := A + Float (I) * H;
      if I mod 2 = 0 then
         Sum := Sum + 2.0 * F (X);
      else
         Sum := Sum + 4.0 * F (X);
      end if;
   end loop;
   return Sum * H / 3.0;
end Integral;
```

Here is an instantiation of `Integral` that can be used to integrate the specific function `Sqrt`:

```
function Integral_of_Sqrt is new Integral (Sqrt);
```

Now the function call `Integral_of_Sqrt(1.0,2.0)` will evaluate the definite integral of `Sqrt` from 1.0 to 2.0.

The two levels of abstraction in the definition of the integration subprogram require two levels of concretization. Firstly, the instantiation of the generic specifies the particular function to be integrated. The latter function (`Sqrt` above) must be compatible with the generic function parameter `F` in its result type, parameter types and parameter modes. Secondly, to perform a particular integration, ordinary parameters must be passed to the instantiated function (`Integral_of_Sqrt` above).

Another possibility would be to make A and B generic parameters too, but that would mean that each instantiation of Integral could only integrate a specific function between specific limits. The version given is above is more general and far more useful.

□ *End of Example 22.7*

Example 22.8 *A generalized sorting package*

Recall the package Sort_Service developed in Case Study II and extended with exceptions in Example 14.2:

```
package Sort_Service is
   procedure Make_List_Empty;
   procedure Insert (New_Name : in Names);
   procedure Prepare_Extraction;
   procedure Extract (Old_Name : out Names);
   function All_Extracted  return Boolean;
   List_Full, List_Empty : exception;
end Sort_Service;
```

This assumes that Names has previously been declared as a type. The package body of Sort_Service assumes nothing about the type Names other than the availability of assignment and the operator ">".

This package clearly ought to be generic with respect to the type, and ought to be formulated for any type for which an ordering operation such as ">" is available. This is achieved by declaring it as:

```
generic
   type Names is private;
   with function ">" (L, R : Names) return Boolean is <>;
package Sort_Service is
   as before
end Sort_Service;
```

The generic type parameter Names is specified as private, with only the implicit operations of assignment and (in)equality tests, in order to allow the package to be instantiated for as many actual types as possible. Therefore ">" must also be a generic parameter. (Recall that an operator is analogous to a function with one or two parameters.) The phrase 'is <>' in the specification of ">" will be explained shortly.

The generic package can be instantiated for sorting Integer values as follows:

```
package Integer_Sort is new Sort_Service (Integer, ">");
```

The second generic actual parameter is the predefined operation ">" for type Integer. (">" is overloaded, but the version just mentioned is the only one that is compatible with the generic formal parameter after substitution of Integer for Names.) It is just as easy to sort integers in reverse order:

```
package Integer_Rev_Sort is new Sort_Service (Integer, "<");
```

Suppose that the following type describes entries in a directory:

```
type Directory_Entries is
   record
```

```
            Name   : String (1 .. 20);
            Number : String (1 .. 12);
        end record;
```

The following function defines a lexicographic ordering on such directory entries:

```
function Ordered (Entry1, Entry2 : Directory_Entries)
     return Boolean  is
begin
   return Entry1.Name > Entry2.Name;
end Ordered;
```

Then `Sort_Service` could be instantiated to sort such directory entries:

```
package Directory_Sort is
     new Sort_Service (Directory_Entries, Ordered);
```

The phrase '`is <>`' in the specification of the generic function parameter `">"` allows the corresponding generic actual parameter to be defaulted to a function of the same name. Thus the instantiation of `Integer_Sort` could be abbreviated to:

```
package Integer_Sort is new Sort_Service (Integer);
```

This example shows an important and unique property of generic parameters. The generic type parameter `Names` was used in the specification of the generic function parameter `">"`. This establishes a relationship between the two generic parameters. (No such relationship can exist between the parameters of a subprogram.) This relationship must be preserved by the generic actual parameters. Thus it would be illegal to supply `Ordered` in the instantiation of `Integer_Sort`.

The generic version of `Sort_Service` captures all the essential characteristics of sorting. In consequence, one single generic package can provide all that should be needed for internal sorting. The same declaration could be used for an external sorting package; merely the implementation has to change. The generic embodies the abstract properties of all types that can be sorted. Hence the generic mechanism provides a powerful means of exploiting abstract data types. It would have been better style to reflect this by choosing a less specific name for the generic type parameter, for example `Items` rather than `Names`.

As mentioned in Section 22.4, each instantiation creates a new and distinct package. Therefore `List_Full` and `List_Empty` will be distinct exceptions in each instantiation of `Sort_Service`. This means that handlers must treat them as distinct, for example:

```
exception
   when Integer_Sort.List_Full |
        Integer_Rev_Sort.List_Full =>
        ...
```

□ *End of Example 22.8*

22.6. Generic abstract data types

A package can be used in Ada to define an abstract data type, by grouping the type declaration with the operations on that type. Generics carry this process one step further by permitting us to define a whole *class* of abstract data types. For example, the abstract data types 'list of integers', 'list of characters' and so on all belong to the class of abstract data types 'list'. The key to this higher level of abstraction is the use of generic type parameters together with any associated operations.

Example 22.9 Generalized stack handling

A commonly used data structure is a *stack*. We wish to encapsulate a type Stacks whose values will be stacks of elements of some type Items. A possible set of operations on a given stack might be: empty the stack; push a new element on to the top of the stack; pop the top element from the stack; test the stack for emptiness; traverse the stack to apply a given procedure Operate to each element in the stack.

In order to allow the same package to be used for stacks of integers, stacks of characters and so on, we make the package generic in Items:

```
generic
   type Items is private;
package Stack_Service is
   type Stacks is limited private;
   procedure Clear (S : out Stacks);
   procedure Push  (Elem : in Items;  S : in out Stacks);
   procedure Pop   (Elem : out Items;  S : in out Stacks);
   function Empty  (S : Stacks) return Boolean;
   generic
      with procedure Operate (Elem : in out Items);
   procedure Traverse (S : in out Stacks);
private
   implementation details
end Stack_Service;
```

As an example of the use of such a package, consider the manipulation of a stack of integers. To achieve this we instantiate the package:

```
package Integer_Stack_Service is new Stack_Service (Integer);
```

The use of the instantiated package is now straightforward:

```
use Integer_Stack_Service;
Result_Stack : Stacks;
Left, Right  : Integer;
...
Clear (Result_Stack);
...
Pop (Right, Result_Stack);  Pop (Left, Result_Stack);
Push (Left - Right, Result_Stack);
```

Note that Traverse is itself generic, with Operate as its generic subprogram parameter. In order to display the contents of a stack, we must first provide a procedure to display a single integer, for example:

```
procedure Display (I : in out Integer) is
begin
   Put (I, Width => 1);  Put ("  ");
```

```
      end Display;
```

Now we can instantiate the generic procedure `Traverse`:

```
      procedure Display_All is new Traverse (Display);
```

and lastly call the instantiated procedure:

```
      Display_All (Result_Stack);
```

Note that the formal parameter of `Display` has to be an `in out` parameter in order that this procedure may be compatible with the formal subprogram parameter `Operate`.

□ *End of Example 22.9*

22.7. More on generic parameter matching

We have now considered each class of generic parameters in isolation. However, it can happen that there are several generic parameters that *interact*. Indeed, we already have met one example of this, in Example 22.8, where the generic type parameter `Names` was also the type of the parameters of the generic function parameter `">"`. Such interactions are common.

Generic formal parameters are processed sequentially, like other declarations. In Example 22.8, therefore, the type `Names` had to be specified before the function `">"` whose declaration uses `Names`. An interaction such as this is a restriction on the permitted generic actual parameters in the instantiation. This restriction is essential for the correct functioning of the generic body. The body of the sorting package uses the fact that two `Names` values can be compared using `">"` to give a `Boolean` result. (Even if the body did not use this fact, the generic declaration would still enforce the same restriction on the generic actual parameters.)

Another situation where generic parameters might interact is when a generic parameter is to be an array type, where the index type(s) and/or the component type are also to be generic parameters.

Example 22.10 *A vector operation*

Given two vectors X and Y, and a vector element A, we want to perform the vector-algebra operation of adding AX to Y. One possibility would be to define individual subprograms for vector addition and multiplication. In this example, however, we wish to provide a specialized (and more efficient) procedure.

Now, the type of the vector elements could be any numeric type, or even `Complex`. Hence this element type must be a generic parameter. Similarly the vector type must be a generic parameter also. The relationship between the two types is simply stated:

```
      generic
         type Element is private;
         type Vector is array (Integer range <>) of Element;
```

This relationship must be preserved by the actual types provided on generic instantiation. In fact the following points are checked by the compiler, assuming that `E` and `V` are the actual types corresponding to `Element` and `Vector` respectively:

- that `E` is not limited;

- that V is a one-dimensional array type;
- that the index type of V is Integer;
- that the component type of V is E.

The parameters Element and Vector do not suffice to write the generic procedure, since the generic body will need to use the operators "*" and "+" for operands of type Element. These must be imported by means of generic function parameters. Each of them can be defaulted to the synonymous operation on the actual element type. The whole generic declaration can now be completed:

```
generic
   type Element is private;
   type Vector is array (Integer range <>) of Element;
   with function "+" (L, R : Element) return Element is <>;
   with function "*" (L, R : Element) return Element is <>;
procedure Add_AX_to_Y
         (A : in Element;
          X : in Vector;
          Y : in out Vector);
```

The body of the procedure is simple to write:

```
procedure Add_AX_to_Y
         (A : in Element;
          X : in Vector;
          Y : in out Vector) is
begin
   if X'Length /= Y'Length then
      raise Constraint_Error;
   else
      for I in Y'Range loop
         Y(I) := A * X(I-Y'First+X'First) + Y(I);
      end loop;
   end if;
end Add_AX_to_Y;
```

Typical instantiations would use the default "+" and "*", for example:

```
type Vector is array (Integer range <>) of Float;
procedure Add_Float_AX_to_Y is
      new Add_AX_to_Y (Float, Vector);

use Complex_Arithmetic;  -- exports Complex, Sum, Prod, etc.
type Complex_Vector is array (Integer range <>) of Complex;
procedure Add_Complex_AX_to_Y is
      new Add_AX_to_Y (Complex, Complex_Vector, Sum, Prod);
```

Although the specification of the generic parameters is tedious, compared to the shortness of the procedure body, the effort rapidly justifies itself since only one source text needs to be maintained.

□ *End of Example 22.10*

It is tempting to think of the generic mechanism entirely in terms of textual substitution, in other words to imagine that a generic instantiation causes the generic parameters to be substituted and then the resulting text to be submitted to the compiler. This is not the case. Firstly, the text of each generic body is fully checked by the compiler before any instantiation is processed. This is important for the early detection of errors, and also to ensure (as far as possible) that errors are not left to to be discovered by the programmer instantiating the generic, who might have no knowledge of the generic body. Secondly, any nonlocal entity in a generic body is interpreted in the context of the body and not in the context of the instantiation.

Generics are a powerful tool that provide a level of abstraction over and above that provided by ordinary subprograms and packages. As illustrated by the generic input-output packages, generics can be used by a programmer without detailed knowledge of their implementation.

Exercises 22

22.1. Write a generic procedure that increments a value of any given discrete type. Use it to instantiate a procedure that increments an `Integer` value.

22.2. Write a generic function that returns the maximum value of the elements of *any* one-dimensional array. Then write an instantiation that returns the maximum of a vector (index type `Integer`, element type `Float`). How could we instantiate the generic function to compute the *minimum* value instead?

22.3. Write a body for the generic package `Stack_Service` of Example 22.9.

22.4. (For readers familiar with elementary compiling techniques.)

(a) Use `Stack_Service` to implement a translator from infix real expressions to postfix. (For example, `a+b/c-d` should be translated to `abc/+d-`.)

(b) Use `Stack_Service` to implement an evaluator for postfix real expressions. The evaluator should use

```
Store : array ('a' .. 'z') of Real;
```

to provide values for the variables in the expression.

22.5. Write the declaration and body of a generic bounded-queue package. The type of the queue elements and its maximum size are to be generic parameters. (If you are unfamiliar with bounded queues, see the description in Example 23.8.)

22.6. (a) Add a generic `Traverse` procedure to the declaration of the `Directory_Service` package of Example 13.6. `Traverse` is to traverse the directory in lexicographic order and apply its own procedure parameter `P` to each entry of the directory. (Compare Example 22.9.)

(b) Write a procedure `List_All_Entries`, external to `Directory_Service`, that writes all the entries of the directory in lexicographic order, by calling an instantiation of `Traverse`.

(c) Write the body of `Traverse`, in the context of the binary-tree implementation of `Directory_Service` (Example 17.4).

23

Tasks

23.1. Programs and processes

We have now reached the point in our study of Ada when it becomes important to distinguish between two ideas that previously we were happy to confuse. We must be able to see the difference between a ***program*** and a ***process***. There is an analogy with the theater that can help us in this, for the difference is exactly that between a ***script*** and a ***performance***. A script is a text written in a natural language such as English. It describes the actions to be performed by the cast. A script is a static object. But a performance is dynamic — it unfolds in time. Analogously, a program is a text written in a programming language such as Ada. It describes the actions to be performed by a computer. Like a script, a program is a static object. A process, on the other hand, is the dynamic ***activity*** of obeying a program.

In a simple computer system a new process comes into existence each time we run a program. Conversely, each process active in the system has a separate program to obey. When these conditions hold, as they did in early operating systems and still do in many personal computers, no harm is done by identifying programs with processes.

In more complex systems this one-to-one correspondence no longer holds. For example, the technique known as ***chaining*** allows a single process to transfer control from one program to another, rather as control passes from statement to statement within a program. In this way a single process can obey instructions from several programs in succession. (This is often done when a program is too large to fit into main store and must be divided up.) We can no longer say that the job is done in one program, although it is still done in one process.

Conversely, in multi-access systems it often happens that several users want to run the same program at the same time. This is especially likely to happen with popular programs like text editors and compilers. If each user process had its own copy of such a program, storage would be wasted by replicating the instructions. It is possible to avoid this waste by sharing a single copy of the program among the processes that need it. Now we have several processes to consider, but only one program.

Sequential programs

In the kind of program we have considered so far the instructions are obeyed ***sequentially***; that is, one after another. Each instruction is completed before the next one starts. Executing a program in this manner defines a single ***sequential process***. A ***sequential program*** controls a single sequential process. In terms of our theatrical analogy, a sequential program is more like a dramatic monologue than a play.

No computer system is actually sequential in this strict sense. For example, the input-output statements in a program call upon the operating system's services. The operating system tries to have as many input and output operations as possible going on at once.

To this end elaborate buffering schemes are used and peripheral devices are made able to operate simultaneously with the CPU. By careful use of these techniques the operating system attempts to minimize the time a process spends waiting for input-output operations to complete. This implies that a system is usually controlling several things at once: some computation, some input, and some output. It is reasonable to regard these activities as separate processes. However, they are managed by the operating system so that the illusion of a single sequential process is preserved. The sequential process is therefore an abstraction from the details of an actual system. It allows us to forget the hardware and the operating system, the better to concentrate on the application.

When, despite the best efforts of the operating system, a process must wait for an input-output operation to finish, control can be switched to some other process that is ready to go ahead. The latter uses the CPU time that would otherwise be wasted. This is known as *multiprogramming*. It might substantially increase the throughput of the computer. The decision as to which process should be running at any time is known as *scheduling*. Good scheduling is crucial to efficient use of the hardware.

Concurrent programs

A computer system is *concurrent* if it involves the parallel activity of several processes. A *concurrent program* controls the concurrent execution of several sequential processes. If a sequential program is like a dramatic monologue, a concurrent program is more like a play with several characters.

Operating systems are examples of programs that sustain much concurrency. On the other hand, most application programs are still written as if the computer could do only one thing at a time. This is adequate for many business, administrative and technical applications. Increasingly, though, a computer is being used as a component of some larger system whose concurent activities it must monitor or control. These are known as *embedded computer systems*. Examples of such systems abound in industrial plant control, as well as in the military and aerospace fields. Indeed it was the need for a suitable programming language for embedded computer systems that stimulated the development of Ada.

As the techniques of concurrent programming become more widely understood we can expect to see them being used in less exotic applications. In particular, local area networks provide many opportunities to exploit the benefits of concurrency, whether in terms of improved performance, greater functionality or increased reliability. The next section gives a brief introduction to the elements of concurrent programming. If you wish to pursue the topic further we recommend a study of [Ben-Ari 1982] or [Hansen 1973].

23.2. Concurrent programming

Concurrent programming presents difficulties that do not arise in sequential programming. In particular, concurrent programs can fail for reasons that do not affect sequential programs at all.

Lack of progress

A sequential process has a property so fundamental that we take it for granted: it makes *finite progress* in finite time spans. That is to say, if we observe it long enough we will see it obeying more and more instructions. A concurrent system may not share this desirable property, for either of two reasons.

- A process is said to be *starved* if it makes no progress because the resources it needs are withheld from it by the actions of other processes.
- A set of processes is said to be *deadlocked* if they make no progress because of mutually irreconcilable demands for additional resources.

Starvation results from an *unfair* scheduling rule. For example, consider a system in which free resources are always granted to the process at the head of a queue of waiting processes. The position of a process in the queue is determined by its priority. High-priority processes are inserted near the head of the queue and low-priority processes are inserted near the tail. If high-priority processes are inserted often enough, low-priority processes might never reach the head of the queue. Thus a strict priority rule is unfair and can cause starvation. By contrast, if the queue is organized on a 'first-in first-out' basis every process is inserted at the tail of the queue and eventually makes its way to the head. Starvation is therefore impossible.

Deadlock is another scheduling disaster. A deadlock can occur in a system of processes and resources if and only if the following conditions hold:

- Processes may be granted exclusive access to some resources.
- Once granted, resources cannot be taken away from a process until it voluntarily gives them up.
- Processes continue to hold previously allocated resources when they have to wait for a new demand to be fulfilled.
- It is possible to set up a cycle of processes and resources in which each process holds a resource that is demanded by the next process in the cycle.

For a simple example, suppose that we want to run two processes concurrently, each executing a tape-to-printer utility. Process P has been granted access to all the tape decks, and process Q has been granted the use of the line printer. Process P then demands the line printer and process Q demands a tape deck. Neither request can be met, and neither process can go ahead until it is. Deadlock! The only way out is to abort one of the two processes (or both).

The programmer who exploits concurrency must take steps to avoid both starvation and deadlock.

Speed dependence

A sequential process is defined only by the instructions executed and by the *order* in which they are executed. It makes no difference how much time it takes to execute any of those instructions (so long as that time is finite). Thus the correctness of a sequential process does not depend in any way on the speed with which it is executed. A system of interacting sequential processes no longer has this property, in general. This is an important point, because if a system is speed-dependent its behavior is not reproducible. We say that such a system displays *indeterminacy*. The output obtained depends not only on the inputs, but also on the speed of execution of its constituent processes. Since the exact timing of peripheral transfers, and even of CPU cycles, is subject to (small) random variations, the system can misbehave at random. In turn that makes testing almost impossible — is incorrect output due to a logical error or to a speed fluctuation? An important rule of concurrent programming is therefore: ***Do not write speed-dependent programs.***

Unfortunately, it is not always possible to follow this rule. In ***real-time programming*** we are dealing with external activities whose speed cannot be chosen for the convenience of the computer. It is then necessary to ensure that any process involved executes fast enough to keep up. This adds a further level of difficulty to the already difficult job of concurrent programming.

Structures of concurrent systems

A system of several processes that interact with each other in arbitrarily complicated ways will almost certainly suffer from the problems described above. Moreover, it will be difficult, perhaps economically impossible, to debug and maintain. Such a system can be characterized as having tight inter-process coupling. Tight coupling between processes is an even bigger source of trouble than tight coupling between the modules of a sequential program. It is therefore important in the design of a concurrent program to try to remove as many interactions between processes as possible, and to make the remaining interactions well-disciplined. We would like to approach the ideal of no interactions at all, but of course we never quite get there.

Non-interacting processes

Two processes, P and Q, are ***non-interacting*** if it does not matter whether any action of P precedes or follows any action of Q. In particular *all* of P may precede *all* of Q, or *vice versa*. It follows that a system composed entirely of non-interacting processes is not speed-dependent. Unfortunately, there is no general method of telling whether two arbitrary processes are non-interacting. However, it is a ***sufficient*** condition that neither process can alter a variable whose value is used by the other process. So if the set of variables that can be accessed by one process is disjoint from those that can be accessed by another process, the processes are certainly non-interacting. We have to interpret the term 'variable' quite broadly here. It includes not only variables as defined by the programming language but any computer resource, such as a disk file or a peripheral interface, whose state can be sensed and changed by a process.

Communicating processes

There is (one-way) ***communication*** from the process P to the process Q if some action of P must entirely precede some action of Q. It is possible for *all* of P to precede *all* of Q, but not *vice versa*. In essence, process P is producing data for use by process Q. For example, P might write a number of records into a shared file to be read by Q.

A system of communicating processes is more tightly coupled than a system of non-interacting processes, but in practice the additional complexity is quite manageable. In large measure this is due to the unidirectional nature of the interaction. Two-way communication between processes is a lot more complex.

Competing processes

Two processes, P and Q, *compete* with each other if each contains an action that requires exclusive access to the same resource, R. These actions are called ***critical sections*** with respect to R, and the processes involved must ensure that their critical sections do not overlap in time. One critical section must be completed before the other one starts. In particular, either process could entirely precede the other, although that would not allow for any concurrency between them.

A typical system of this kind is one in which each process has access to a shared database, which it is able to update and interrogate. When two such processes require to update the same record in the database, it is necessary to allow only one update at a time. Otherwise the record could end up scrambled.

Example 23.1 The need for mutual exclusion

Suppose that one process executes the statement:

```
I := I + 1;
```

and another executes the statement:

```
I := I + 2;
```

both referring to the same global variable `I`, whose initial value is zero. Let us call these statements 1 and 2 respectively, let us call their right-hand sides 1R and 2R, and let us call their left-hand sides 1L and 2L. Each of 1R and 2R calculates a value that depends on the value of `I` when it inspects the variable. Both 1L and 2L change the value of `I`. The outcome depends on the way these actions are ordered in time.

- The sequence 1R–2R–2L–1L leaves the value 1 in `I`. The sequence 2R–1R–2L–1L also leaves the value 1.
- The sequence 2R–1R–1L–2L leaves the value 2, as does 1R–2R–1L–2L.
- The sequence 1R–1L–2R–2L leaves the value 3, as does the sequence 2R–2L–1R–1L.

Presumably the result 3 is what the programmer intended. Note that this is obtained only when each assignment statement is obeyed ***indivisibly***, that is, when its component instructions are obeyed with no component of the other statement intervening. To make an action on a shared variable indivisible, we give it exclusive access to the variable until the action is complete.

□ *End of Example 23.1*

We cannot assume that assignments (or any other predefined operations) are indivisible in Ada. For example, many computers assigning an array or record value will require a loop of machine instructions that copy the value word by word. Such a loop will almost certainly not be indivisible. Even simple assignments such as '`I:=1000;`' are not executed indivisibly on some computer architectures. If you require an operation in an Ada program to be indivisible, you must take the necessary steps to make it so. As we shall see in Section 23.4, Ada provides the means by which processes can exchange data without the use of critical sections.

A system of competing processes will be speed-dependent if the effect of some critical section depends on the state of the shared resource when it is acquired, and if some critical section changes the state of the resource. In these circumstances the outcome depends on the order in which critical sections get access to the resource. Such a system exhibits indeterminacy.

Example 23.2 *Indeterminacy*

Suppose that one process executes the statement:

```
I := I + 1;
```

and another executes the statement:

```
I := I * 2;
```

both referring to the same variable I, whose initial value is zero. Assume that they arrange for mutual exclusion so that I is updated indivisibly in both cases. If the addition is done first the final value of I is 2, but if the multiplication is done first the final value is 1.

We can see from this example that mutual exclusion does not of itself prevent indeterminacy.

□ *End of Example 23.2*

To ensure speed-independence competing processes must agree as to which of them will enter its critical section first, and to reach agreement they must communicate with each other.

Sometimes it does not matter which of two competing processes goes first. For example, if two processes compete for a line printer to output a listing, and either may go first at random, the order in which the listings appear will also be random. This might not matter at all. On the other hand it would most certainly not be acceptable for the *lines* of the two listings to be interspersed at random! We can express this by saying that a degree of *bounded indeterminacy* is often acceptable (or even desirable) in a concurrent system.

23.3. Tasking

In Ada terminology a process is known as a ***task***. A ***task unit*** is an Ada program unit whose characteristic feature is that it executes concurrently with the rest of the program. A concurrent Ada program therefore consists of one process representing the execution of the main program, and one or more tasks representing the execution of task units. (For most purposes the main program itself can be considered a task unit.)

Like any other program unit, a task unit has a declaration and a body. Both must be given. Regrettably, a task unit cannot be generic. Moreover, a task unit cannot be a library unit; it can be declared only within a subprogram or package. It is possible to compile a task body separately, as a subunit. This is done in the usual way, a body stub taking the place of the task body in its parent unit.

Subject to the restriction that task units cannot be library units, task declarations can appear in the same places as package declarations, and task bodies in the same places as package bodies. The distinction between task declaration and task body is broadly analogous to that between package declaration and package body. The task declaration declares any identifiers to be exported from the task. The task body contains the local declarations and statements of the task.

A ***single task*** is declared as follows:

```
task Single is
    declarations of exported identifiers
end Single;

task body Single is
    local declarations and statements
end Single;
```

If the task does not export any identifiers then the declaration reduces to:

```
task Single;

task body Single is
    local declarations and statements
end Single;
```

As in conventional multiprogramming, the various tasks of a concurrent Ada program may share the use of a single CPU. The Ada run-time system is then responsible for switching control of the CPU from task to task. It is *not* required by the language definition to do this in any particular way. In a multi-processor system there may be as many tasks simultaneously running as there are CPUs, or as few as none. In a distributed system, different tasks may run on different computers, or even move from one computer to another. None of this is specified by the Ada language, although an APSE should provide means for the programmer to control the allocation of processing resources.

Example 23.3 Independent tasks

A 'housekeeping' program to be run in the early hours of the morning does a CPU confidence test and makes a backup copy of important disk files. These operations can profitably run concurrently, the first being CPU bound and the second input-output bound. The structure of a concurrent Ada program for this job is almost trivial:

```
procedure Keep_House is

    task Test_CPU;
    task Copy_Disk;
    task body Test_CPU is
        ...
    end Test_CPU;

    task body Copy_Disk is
        ...
    end Copy_Disk;
begin
    null;
end Keep_House;
```

□ *End of Example 23.3*

As this example shows, there is no need explicitly to invoke a task to set it going — merely supplying the task body is enough.

Task types

Ada also provides for *task types.* This means that several identical tasks (having the same type) can be declared, that tasks can be components of structured types, and that tasks can be allocated dynamically on the heap. By exploiting task types we can write programs with a concurrent control structure that varies during execution, unlike the purely sequential control structure which is fixed at compilation.

A task type is declared by including the reserved word type in the task declaration. A copy of the corresponding task body is created for every object of the task type that is subsequently declared, or allocated on the heap. This means that each such task object has its own distinct set of local objects — these are *not* shared.

A typical task type goes as follows:

```
task type T is
    declarations of exported identifiers
end T;
...
Task_1, Task_2 : T;
...
task body T is
    local declarations and statements
end T;
```

A task object, such as Task_1 or Task_2 above, is declared as a variable of a task type. However, a task type is *limited.* In other words, it is subject to the same restrictions as limited private types: neither assignment (including constant initialization) nor comparison is a permitted operation. Consequently, despite the way it is declared, a task object is effectively constant. It is given a unique value, when it is declared, and that value cannot be changed.

Terminology

Now that we see clearly the difference between a process (single task or task object) and the program (task unit) that it runs, it is more convenient to ignore the distinction. Unless it is essential to the meaning, we shall say just 'task' and let you determine from the context whether we refer to the program or the process.

23.4. Rendezvous

Independent tasks are sometimes useful, but more often we need to structure a program as a set of interacting tasks. It is possible to do this by making the tasks operate on shared global variables. As we have seen, this approach has severe drawbacks. The Ada tasking mechanism has been designed to support a more modular method, in which tasks work on encapsulated data.

Like a package, a task declaration can export identifiers. Unlike a package, these cannot be the names of types, constants, variables, subprograms, nor any of the constructs we have seen so far. Instead, only *entries* can be exported from a task. An entry looks very much like a procedure. It has an identifier and may have parameters of all three modes: `in`, `out` and `in out`. Indeed, an ***entry call*** looks just like a procedure call. This means that we can use tasks in a similar way to packages; for example, a task can be a module encapsulating a data structure, upon which the exported entries operate. The crucial difference is that the operations invoked by an entry call are performed by the task in which the entry is declared, not by the task in which the call is executed. In this way the called task retains complete control, not only of what operations are done, but also of when they are done.

An entry call, in fact, is just a request from the calling task for the called task to perform some service. For that reason we refer to the called task as a ***server task***. If the server task is not ready to provide the service, the calling task is held up. When the server task accepts an entry call, and completes the requested service, the calling task is resumed (but not necessarily at once — some other task may be given preferential use of the CPU, for example). This interaction between calling and server tasks is known as a ***rendezvous***.

The entry call is one side of the rendezvous mechanism. The other side, executed by the server task, is the ***accept statement***. Its simplest form is as follows (for a parameterless entry):

```
accept entry_name;
```

Should a server task perform an accept statement when no calling task is waiting for service, the server is held up at the accept statement. It resumes after a call on the entry is made (again, not necessarily at once). When a rendezvous is complete, the caller resumes execution at the point directly after the entry call; the server continues at the point directly after the accept statement. Thus the entry call and the accept statement behave symmetrically.

Any number of tasks may call the same entry concurrently. At most one of them can be receiving service at any time, however. The rest wait for service in a 'first-in first-out' queue associated with the entry. Each time the server task accepts an entry call, one waiting task is taken from the front of the queue.

Example 23.4 Rendezvous

A certain task falls naturally into two phases, the first of which can run concurrently with its parent. The second phase can also run concurrently, but only after the parent has completed some preparations. The task therefore waits for a 'go ahead' before entering its second phase.

```
procedure Parent is

   task Two_Phase is
      entry Go_Ahead;
   end Two_Phase;

   task body Two_Phase is
      ...
   begin
      perform first phase;
      accept Go_Ahead;
      perform second phase;
   end Two_Phase;

begin
```

```
      prepare for second phase;
      Two_Phase.Go_Ahead;
      ...
   end Parent;
```

□ *End of Example 23.4*

Note that in an entry call the entry name must be qualified by the task name. An entry name cannot be made directly visible by a use clause, which applies only to packages.

A more complicated form of the accept statement must be used with entries that have parameters. See the syntax diagram 'accept_statement' in Appendix A.

When the full form of the accept statement is executed, firstly any **in** or **in out** formal parameters are given the values of the corresponding actual parameters — just like parameters of a subprogram. Then the statements inside the accept statement are executed. Finally, the values of any **out** or **in out** formal parameters are given to the corresponding actual parameters — again, just like parameters of a subprogram. Now the calling task may be resumed, at the point following the entry call; and the server task may continue, independently, at the point following the accept statement.

The formal parameters of an entry are accessible only within accept statements. The passing of parameters, and the execution of the statements inside the accept statement, constitute an *extended rendezvous*.

It is possible, though not very useful, to omit the body of an accept statement for an entry with parameters. The formal parameter list must always be present. It is also possible, and sometimes useful, to have the full form of accept statement, and an extended rendezvous, even for a parameterless entry.

Example 23.5 Extended rendezvous

In a *sequential* program the following package might be used to implement a buffer, with room for a single data item of the global type Items.

```
package Buffer is
   procedure Insert (Item : in Items);
   procedure Remove (Item : out Items);
end Buffer;

package body Buffer is
   Datum : Items;

   procedure Insert (Item : in Items) is
   begin
      Datum := Item;
   end Insert;

   procedure Remove (Item : out Items) is
   begin
      Item := Datum;
   end Remove;
end Buffer;
```

This formulation is too simple, even for a robust sequential program, because it fails to enforce the strict alternation of insertion and removal implied by the semantics of a buffer. A second drawback makes it useless in a *concurrent* program. Several tasks could call the `Insert` and `Remove` procedures in parallel. But nothing has been done to make the assignments to and from `Datum` indivisible. It follows that a concurrent program using this package will eventually corrupt data on its way into or out of the buffer.

Both problems can be avoided by recasting the module as a task:

```
task Buffer is
   entry Insert (Item : in Items);
   entry Remove (Item : out Items);
end Buffer;

task body Buffer is
   Datum : Items;
begin
   loop
      accept Insert (Item : in Items) do
         Datum := Item;
      end Insert;
      accept Remove (Item : out Items) do
         Item := Datum;
      end Remove;
   end loop;
end Buffer;
```

In this version the operations of insertion and removal are obeyed only when the task performs the corresponding accept statements. Since the task executes these statements in alternation, beginning with an `Insert` operation, the desired sequence of operations on the buffer is enforced. Even if calling tasks call `Remove` out of sequence, a removal cannot take place until after an insertion. Note the loop. Without it the task would terminate after buffering just one item of data. (For the time being you need not worry about the absence of a terminating condition for the loop. This issue will be covered in Section 23.6.)

The concurrency problem is solved as well, because now there is *no* concurrency of access to `Datum`. Only the `Buffer` task itself ever accesses it. Concurrent calls on the `Insert` and `Remove` operations are sequenced by the queuing mechanism, and released one at a time to rendezvous with the accept statements.

Other tasks call on the service provided by `Buffer` as follows:

```
Buffer.Insert (My_Item);
...
Buffer.Remove (My_Item);
```

In practice it would probably be more convenient to have a task type, rather than a single task, in an application such as this. The change is trivial:

```
task type Buffer is
   entry Insert (Item : in Items);
   entry Remove (Item : out Items);
end Buffer;
```

Now we can write, for example:

```
Buffer_Pool : array (1 .. Pool_Size) of Buffer;
...
Buffer_Pool(I-1).Remove (My_Item);
Buffer_Pool(I+1).Insert (My_Item);
```

□ *End of Example 23.5*

Accept statements for the entries of a task can appear only directly within the body of that task, and not within any unit nested inside the task. However, as Example 23.5 shows, they can be nested within any control structure forming the statement part of the task body. Moreover, there may be more than one occurrence of an accept statement for each entry, perhaps with different statement parts at each occurrence. In this way the task exerts complete control over the sequence of entry calls that it accepts, and the actions performed on each acceptance.

Example 23.6 Multiple rendezvous

The two-phase task of Example 23.4 can be extended to several phases by including an accept statement for each 'go ahead'.

```
procedure Parent is

   task Multi_Phase is
      entry Go_Ahead;
   end Multi_Phase;

   task body Multi_Phase is
      ...
   begin
      perform first phase;
      accept Go_Ahead;
      perform second phase;
      accept Go_Ahead;
      perform third phase;
   end Multi_Phase;

begin
   prepare for second phase;
   Multi_Phase.Go_Ahead;
   prepare for third phase;
   Multi_Phase.Go_Ahead;
   ...
end Parent;
```

□ *End of Example 23.6*

23.5. Selective waiting

In Example 23.5 we saw how a task can be used to encapsulate a buffer, permitting only alternating insertion and removal operations. Can we write a task that encapsulates a variable, permitting its value to be read and written in any order? The problem we face is how to introduce bounded indeterminacy to the sequence of entry calls accepted by a server task. In fact this *can* be done, using a new control structure, the *selective wait statement*.

The selective wait acts as a kind of nondeterministic case statement. Several alternatives are given, each a sequence of statements beginning with an accept statement. When the selective wait statement is executed, one of these alternatives is *selected* and the others are rejected. The selected alternative is then executed, and control passes on to the point after the selective wait. See the syntax diagram 'selective_wait' in Appendix A.

If only one of the accept alternatives has a waiting entry call, that is the alternative selected. If two or more accept alternatives have waiting entry calls, the implementation is free to select any one of them. The language does not specify what criteria are used in making the selection. For example, it is allowed to select the entry with the longest queue of calls, or the entry nearest the top of the selective wait statement, or even a random entry. A correct Ada program is independent of the method used.

Example 23.7 An encapsulated variable

A variable of some global type `Items` is to be used as a data store by several cooperating tasks. They need to be able to store a value in the variable, or to fetch its current value, subject only to the restriction that the first operation must be to store a value in it. The following task provides this service:

```
task Encapsulated_Variable is
   entry Store (Item : in Items);
   entry Fetch (Item : out Items);
end Encapsulated_Variable;

task body Encapsulated_Variable is
   Datum : Items;
begin
   accept Store (Item : in Items) do
      Datum := Item;
   end Store;
   loop
      select
         accept Store (Item : in Items) do
            Datum := Item;
         end Store;
      or
         accept Fetch (Item : out Items) do
            Item := Datum;
         end Fetch;
      end select;
   end loop;
end Encapsulated_Variable;
```

□ *End of Example 23.7*

Another variation on the buffering theme of Example 23.5 is to expand the buffer so that it can hold several data items at a time. Sometimes data is produced faster than it can be consumed; sometimes the reverse. A buffer with room for several items allows the producing task to work at full speed even during a period when the consumer cannot keep up with it; and allows the consumer to work at full speed, clearing off a backlog, even during a period when the producer is working slowly. Such a buffer is, in effect, a *queue* of data waiting to be processed by the consumer.

Example 23.8 *A buffer queue*

A good way to implement a buffer queue is by clever management of an array of adequate size. Associated with the array there are two indexes. One gives the index of the array component containing the next item to be removed (i.e. the head of the queue). The other gives the index of the next free array component (i.e. the tail of the queue). These indexes are incremented each time the corresponding operation is called, if necessary 'wrapping around' from the last to the first array component. Attempting to insert too many items causes the insertion index to overtake the removal index. Similarly, trying to extract an item from an empty buffer queue causes the removal index to overtake the insertion index. In either case we raise the exception `Constraint_Error`.

```
task Buffer_Queue is
   entry Insert (Item : in Items);
   entry Remove (Item : out Items);
end Buffer_Queue;

task body Buffer_Queue is
   Q_Size : constant Integer := 100;
   subtype Q_Range is Integer range 1 .. Q_Size;
   Length       : Integer range 0 .. Q_Size := 0;
   Head, Tail : Q_Range := 1;
   Data         : array (Q_Range) of Items;
begin
   loop
      select
         accept Insert (Item : in Items) do
            if Length = Q_Size then
               raise Constraint_Error;
            end if;
            Data(Tail) := Item;
         end Insert;
         Tail := Tail mod Q_Size + 1;
         Length := Length + 1;
      or
         accept Remove (Item : out Items) do
            if Length = 0 then
               raise Constraint_Error;
            end if;
```

```
                Item := Data(Head);
            end Remove;
            Head := Head mod Q_Size + 1;
            Length := Length - 1;
        end select;
    end loop;
end Buffer_Queue;
```

Note that Length, Head and Tail are updated outside the accept statements. These updates could be included in the rendezvous, but that would (slightly) delay the resumption of the caller, for no good reason — the updates are independent of the entry call's parameters. More generally, the only statements included in a rendezvous should be those that refer to entry parameters, or must be executed while the calling task is suspended.

In a sequential program, buffer queue insertion and removal are done by subprograms responding passively to calls. When Insert is called and the queue is full, or Remove is called and the queue is empty, the best they can do is raise an exception. The task above follows this model, with entries in place of procedures. But a concurrent program has more freedom. A task need not accept an entry call that it knows must fail — instead the call can be made to wait until circumstances change. A first attempt to program this strategy might be the following:

```
...
begin
    loop
        if Length < Q_Size then
            accept Insert (Item : in Items) do
                Data(Tail) := Item;
            end Insert;
            Tail := Tail mod Q_Size + 1;
            Length := Length + 1;
        else -- Length = Q_Size
            accept Remove (Item : out Items) do
                Item := Data(Head);
            end Remove;
            Head := Head mod Q_Size + 1;
            Length := Length - 1;
        end if;
    end loop;
end Buffer_Queue;
```

This is not satisfactory. Because of the way the if statement works, the task will accept only insertions when there is any room left in the buffer queue. Reversing the logic does not help, as the task then will accept only removals when the buffer queue is not empty. Either way, the effect is to degrade the queue to a single-slot buffer.

The selective wait statement has a feature that avoids this problem, and is more convenient as well. We can use ***guards*** for alternatives in selective wait statements. A guard is a clause of the form:

when *boolean*_expression =>

and goes directly in front of the alternative it governs. If an alternative has no guard, the clause:

```
when True =>
```

is assumed by default. All the guards in a selective wait statement are evaluated, in an arbitrary order. Each alternative that has a True value for its guard is said to be an *open* alternative. The alternative that is selected by the selective wait is chosen from among those that are open. In this way the selective wait combines conditional acceptance with bounded indeterminacy.

Using guards, Buffer_Queue goes as follows:

```
...
begin
   loop
      select
         when Length < Q_Size =>
            accept Insert (Item : in Items) do
               Data(Tail) := Item;
            end Insert;
            Tail := Tail mod Q_Size + 1;
            Length := Length + 1;
      or
         when Length > 0 =>
            accept Remove (Item : out Items) do
               Item := Data(Head);
            end Remove;
            Head := Head mod Q_Size + 1;
            Length := Length - 1;
      end select;
   end loop;
end Buffer_Queue;
```

When the buffer queue is full the task will not accept a call on the insertion operation. When it is empty no call on the removal operation will be accepted. In all other cases either an insertion or a removal is acceptable.

☐ *End of Example 23.8*

If none of the alternatives in a selective wait is open, no alternative can be selected. This is considered to be an error and raises the predefined exception Program_Error.

Entry families

Example 23.5 showed how a buffer pool (an array of buffers) could be set up by declaring a task type with the behavior of a buffer, and then declaring an array of these tasks. This approach allows the maximum possible concurrency — each buffer task can (in principle) be simultaneously active. On most computers, however, there are not nearly enough CPUs to exploit this concurrency. In fact the normal case is a single CPU, switched between the calling task and the buffer tasks. In these circumstances, implementing a buffer pool as an array of tasks has few advantages to balance the costs:

- Each task object occupies considerable storage space, in excess of that required for the encapsulated buffer. This space is needed to record the state of the task, and includes enough storage for a stack of subprogram activations.

- The declaration of a task requires more CPU time than the declaration of a non-task variable. This is consumed in setting up the data structures needed to support task interactions. An array of tasks requires commensurately more CPU time.

In view of these disadvantages, it is worth considering an implementation of a buffer pool in which the whole array of buffers is represented by one task. In such an implementation we incur the overheads of declaring a task object only once, however many buffers the pool contains. The penalty we pay is that only one buffer operation can be in progress at a time.

To fix ideas, suppose that the type of the data items to be stored in the buffer is `Items`, and that individual buffers are identified by values of:

```
type Buffer_Id is range 1 .. 4;
```

A first attempt at a declaration for the buffer pool might go as follows:

```
task Buffer_Pool is
   entry Insert (Item : in Items;  Place : in Buffer_Id);
   entry Remove (Item : out Items;  Place : in Buffer_Id);
end Buffer_Pool;
```

and we would then write, for example:

```
Buffer_Pool.Remove (My_Item, I);
Buffer_Pool.Insert (My_Item, I+1);
```

The problems start when we try to write the task body. Assume that the task body declares two arrays:

```
Data   : array (Buffer_Id) of Items;
Filled : array (Buffer_Id) of Boolean := (Buffer_Id => False);
```

where `Data(I)` is to contain the I'th buffered item, and `Filled(I)` is to show whether buffer `I` is occupied or not. Now consider the implementation of the `Insert` operation for one of the buffers, say buffer `I`. It must take the form:

```
when not Filled(I) =>
   accept Insert (Item : in Items;  Place : in Buffer_Id) do
      Data(Place) := Item;   -- ??
   end Insert;
   Filled(Place) := True;
```

There is nothing in this to enforce the requirement that the entry call to be accepted must relate to buffer `I`. In other words, there is nothing to ensure that `Place` is equal to `I`. Nor, with the mechanisms we have seen so far, is it possible to ensure this. What we need is a way of including the value of `Place` in the guard for the accept statement. But we do not know the value of `Place` until after an entry call has been accepted!

The resolution of this problem requires a new construction: the *entry family*. This allows several entries to have the same name, being distinguished by the value of an index. A call to an entry of the family must specify its index, and such a call will be accepted only by an accept statement that specifies the same index. In this way the index associated with a family member acts as a criterion for the acceptance of an entry call, and can be used to communicate information about the call to the task.

Example 23.9 A buffer pool

Here is a version of task Buffer_Pool using entry families:

```
task Buffer_Pool is
   entry Insert (Buffer_Id) (Item : in Items);
   entry Remove (Buffer_Id) (Item : out Items);
end Buffer_Pool;

task body Buffer_Pool is
   Data   : array (Buffer_Id) of Items;
   Filled : array (Buffer_Id) of Boolean := (Buffer_Id => False);
begin
   loop
      select
         when not Filled(1) =>
            accept Insert(1) (Item : in Items) do
               Data(1) := Item;
            end Insert;
            Filled(1) := True;
      or
         when Filled(1) =>
            accept Remove(1) (Item : out Items) do
               Item := Data(1);
            end Remove;
            Filled(1) := False;
      or
         ...  -- similarly for buffers 2, 3 and 4
      end select;
   end loop;
end Buffer_Pool;
```

Here there are only four entries in each family. Even so it would be tedious to write out the task body in full. What if we need a buffer pool with 100 components? — it would not be sensible to implement such a pool in terms of 200 accept statements! (*Exercise*: find a solution to this problem.)

□ *End of Example 23.9*

23.6. Activation and termination

Activation

As each task progresses it synchronizes at suitable points with other tasks. These points represent important milestones in the progress of the task. A task that has passed such a milestone is said to be in a corresponding *state*. The first milestone is the elaboration of declarations local to the task body. This is known as the *activation* of the task, and leaves it in the *active* state.

A task is activated when control reaches the begin of the enclosing program unit. All tasks declared in the same declarative part are activated concurrently with each other. It is only when these activations have taken place that the statements of the enclosing unit are executed. Concurrently with that, the active tasks change state to *running* and start to execute the statements in their bodies. (Any tasks that are created by evaluating an allocator are activated immediately. They are all in the active state by the time the allocator delivers the access value.)

This gives the gist of the rules relating to task activation. For the full details see [Ada 1983].

Normal termination

Some tasks have a natural conclusion and terminate by reaching the end of their statements (just like a subprogram). But many tasks, especially server tasks, are characterized by an 'infinite loop' around a selective wait statement. They are perpetually either responding to, or waiting for, an entry call.

This is important because control cannot leave a task's *master* until the task terminates. A master is either a block statement, a subprogram, a task or a library package (but not a nested package). A task *depends* on a master if it is declared within the master, or if it allocated on the heap and the relevant access type is declared within the master.

It would be possible for each task to export an entry used only to indicate that no further entry calls will be made. This is not very attractive, as it increases the coupling between the task and its environment. A better solution is provided in Ada. One of the alternatives in a selective wait statement can be a *terminate alternative.* Provided that certain conditions are satisfied, the terminate alternative is selected and the task then terminates.

A terminate alternative takes effect only if:

- The terminate alternative is open.
- The task depends on some master that is already in the *completed* state. In other words, the master must have run out of statements, and would terminate but for the presence of one or more dependent tasks.
- Every other task depending on the same master has either terminated, or selected a terminate alternative in a selective wait statement.

When all of the tasks involved satisfy these requirements then they all 'bow out' together. (The termination of tasks declared within library packages is not defined by the language.)

Again, this is only the gist of the matter. For full details see [Ada 1983].

Example 23.10 *A terminating buffer task*

The single-slot buffer task of Example 23.5 is not adequate as it stands, having no provision for normal termination. The following version removes this defect:

```
task body Buffer is
   Datum : Items;
begin
   loop
      select
```

```
            accept Insert (Item : in Items) do
               Datum := Item;
            end Insert;
         or
            terminate;
         end select;
         select
            accept Remove (Item : out Items) do
               Item := Datum;
            end Remove;
         or
            terminate;
         end select;
      end loop;
   end Buffer;
```

□ *End of Example 23.10*

(*Exercise*: Add terminate alternatives to all tasks in this chapter that need them.)

Abnormal termination

Normal termination assumes a willingness to terminate on the part of the tasks involved. In fact, they must cooperate in order to terminate properly. We are not always so lucky. A task might contain an infinite loop, or some other fault, that keeps it from a normal conclusion. Or it might be necessary to abandon tasks in response to some emergency, without waiting for any of them to terminate normally. In both cases we need the means to terminate one or more tasks forcibly.

Of course, this is a very serious step to take and you should consider all feasible design options before committing yourself to forcible termination. It is sometimes necessary, however, and Ada provides a special statement for the purpose. This is the *abort statement*. See the syntax diagram 'abort_statement' in Appendix A.

The abort statement causes the named task, and any dependent task, to change to the *abnormal* state, regardless of its present activities. If it was waiting in an accept statement, delay statement, select statement or entry call, an abnormal task is deemed completed, and executes no more statements. This must happen before the completion of execution of the abort statement itself. Otherwise an abnormal task is allowed to continue executing until it reaches a synchronization point, such as the beginning or ending of a rendezvous. Then it becomes completed.

Once a task becomes abnormal, no other task can successfully call any of its entries. Again, the full details are to be found in [Ada 1983].

23.7. Real-time programming

A *real-time program* is one that has, as an important criterion of its correctness, bounds on the amount of physical (real) time it may spend between certain points in its progress, such as consuming inputs or producing outputs. A (tongue-in-cheek) example is a weekly payroll program, which must not take more than a week to run! More serious examples are aircraft navigation, patient monitoring and industrial control systems. Most real-time programs are also concurrent programs, so it is appropriate to discuss the topic here.

The features in Ada that support real-time programming fall into two categories: means to measure the passage of time, and extensions of the tasking mechanism.

A program can discover the current time, and manipulate measurements of time, using the facilities provided by the predefined library package `Calendar` (Appendix D).

The simplest real-time facility in Ada is the ***delay statement***. The statement '`delay` D;' where D is an expression of the predefined fixed-point type `Duration`, holds up execution of the task for ***at least*** D seconds. The actual delay may be longer, because there might be no processing resources available for the task immediately after the interval expires.

You are guaranteed that the range of `Duration` allows for both positive and negative values up to and including one day (86400 seconds) and that intervals as small as 20 milliseconds can be represented. (It is recommended that intervals as small as 50 microseconds should be handled, but this is not guaranteed.)

Example 23.11 Real-time delay

The following task takes in characters and sends them to a slow output device at the rate of one character about every tenth of a second.

```
task Slow_Output is
   entry Open  (Device_Name : in String);
   entry Put   (Char : in Character);
   entry Close;
end Slow_Output;
task body Slow_Output is
   use Calendar;
   Pause : constant Duration := 0.1;
   Next_Time : Time;
   package Slow_IO is new Sequential_IO (Character);
   use Slow_IO;
   Slow_Device : File_Type;
begin
   accept Open (Device_Name : String) do
      Open (Slow_Device, Out_File, Device_Name);
   end Open;
   Next_Time := Clock + Pause;
   loop
      delay (Next_Time - Clock);
      select
         accept Put (Char : in Character) do
            Put (Slow_Device, Char);
         end Put;
      or
         accept Close;
```

```
            Close (Slow_Device);
            exit;
         end select;
         Next_Time := (Next_Time + Pause);
      end loop;
   end Slow_Output;
```

You might wonder why the following, more obvious, version of the loop was not used:

```
loop
   delay Pause;
   select
      accept Put (Char : in Character) do
         Put (Slow_Device, Char);
      end Put;
   or
      accept Close;
      Close (Slow_Device);
      exit;
   end select;
end loop;
```

The reason is that the repetitions are timed less accurately by this version.

- There is an error inherent in representing the value 0.1 as a binary fixed-point number. Rounding could make the actual delay either shorter or longer than 0.1 seconds. (Actually, this applies to both versions.)
- More important is the time taken by the statements following the delay statement. They lengthen the cycle time for the loop as a whole.
- Finally, and most importantly, Ada guarantees only that the delay will be at least as long as specified — it may be much longer.

Provided the statements in the loop take less time than the desired delay, we can (partially) compensate for the drift by calculating an actual delay that is relative to the current time. This is what is done in `Slow_Output`.

□ *End of Example 23.11*

The delay statement can also be used in a different way, as part of a new control structure: the *timed entry call.* This allows a calling task to withdraw an entry call if the server task does not accept the call within a specified deadline. The syntax used is that of a select statement with two alternatives. The first alternative begins with the entry call and continues with the statements (if any) to be obeyed after a successful rendezvous. The second alternative begins with a delay statement specifying the maximum tolerable waiting time and continues with the statements (if any) to be obeyed if this time is exceeded.

Example 23.12 *A rendezvous timeout*

A transaction processing system maintains a file with the names and passwords of all authorized operators. To control concurrent access to the password file from multiple terminals, a task named `Password_Server` encapsulates all operations on it. A command is available to operators that lets them change their passwords, updating the file accordingly. To avoid excessive response times, it is required to abandon the update if access to the file is not gained within five seconds.

```
task Password_Server is
   entry Obtain (User : in String;  Password : out String);
   entry Change (User : in String;  Password : in String);
end Password_Server;
...
Login_Name, New_Pass : String(1 .. 14);
...
Put ("Please type your new password:");
Get (New_Pass);  Skip_Line;
select
   Password_Server.Change (Login_Name, New_Pass);
   Put_Line ("OK");
or
   delay 5.0;
   Put_Line ("The system is busy just now.");
   Put_Line ("Please try again later.");
end select;
```

□ *End of Example 23.12*

Be clear that the maximum wait given in a timed entry call relates only to the time spent waiting for the rendezvous to start. Should the server task accept the entry call promptly, and then take an excessive time to complete the rendezvous, the delay alternative in the entry call is *not* executed. If this is a problem, you must deal with it yourself. One approach is to replace a slow entry with a pair of entries. The first of the pair passes data to the server task. The second passes back a result. Server and calling tasks proceed concurrently between rendezvous at the two entries. When a result is required, the caller uses a timed entry call on the second entry of the pair.

Example 23.13 *Functional timeout*

A data collection task sets up matrices of data taken from measurements and submits them to a computational task for processing. The latter may take too long for the data collection task to wait for the result. If necessary the data collection task must abandon the current set of data to ensure that the next set can be captured in time. A limit of one second is allowed for processing.

```
task Matrix_Multiplier is
   entry Take (A, B : in Matrix);
   entry Give (Product : out Matrix);
end Matrix_Multiplier;
...
Raw_Data, Transform, Cooked_Data : Matrix;
...
loop
   collect Raw_Data from sensors;
```

```
      Matrix_Multiplier.Take (Raw_Data, Transform);
      select
         Matrix_Multiplier.Give (Cooked_Data);
         pass Cooked_Data on to display task;
      or
         delay 1.0;
         Log_Error("Matrix_Multiplier too slow.");
      end select;
   end loop;
```

□ *End of Example 23.13*

There is a special notation, the ***conditional entry call***, for use when it is unacceptable to have any delay whatever in achieving rendezvous. It is semantically equivalent to a timed entry call with a delay of zero. See the syntax diagram 'conditional_entry_call' in Appendix A.

Example 23.14 *Conditional entry call*

In Example 23.12 a delay of up to five seconds was acceptable in gaining access to a password file. If we require immediate access a delay of zero could be specified. Better, because it expresses our intention more clearly, is a conditional entry call:

```
   select
      Password_Server.Change (Login_Name, New_Pass);
      Put_Line ("OK");
   else
      Put_Line ("The system is busy just now.");
      Put_Line ("Please try again later.");
   end select;
```

□ *End of Example 23.14*

The timed and conditional entry calls enable a calling task to cope with delays in achieving rendezvous. A server task equally might need to take special action when rendezvous is delayed by the absence of calls on its entries. Ada provides symmetrical facilities to allow this, in the form of delay and else parts for the selective wait statement.

A selective wait statement must have at least one accept alternative and at most one terminate alternative. If there is no terminate alternative, it is permitted to have a ***delay alternative***, consisting of a delay statement, optionally followed by a sequence of statements. The delay alternative is selected only if no accept alternative can be selected before the time interval given in the delay alternative has elapsed. (In fact, it is permitted to have several delay alternatives. The one with the shortest interval is selected from among those that are open. An implementation is free to choose any one of several that have equal smallest intervals.)

Example 23.15 *Server task timeout*

A library package that makes no provision for mutual exclusion is used by several tasks in order to update a shared database. To ensure mutual exclusion the tasks themselves call on another module, a task that provides a service tailored to their requirements:

```
task Database_Mutex is
   entry Acquire (Lease : in Duration);
   entry Relinquish;
end Database_Mutex;
```

A calling task can acquire exclusive use of the database for a maximum period given by `Lease`. No other claim will be accepted until it relinquishes the database, or the lease expires. This is a (crude) way to prevent deadlock.

```
task body Database_Mutex is
   Timeout : Duration;
begin
   loop
      select
         accept Acquire (Lease : in Duration) do
            Timeout := Lease;
         end Acquire;
         select
            accept Relinquish;
         or
            delay Timeout;
         end select;
      or
         terminate;
      end select;
   end loop;
end Database_Mutex;
```

□ *End of Example 23.15*

Again, it may be that no delay in achieving rendezvous is acceptable to a called task. In this case, a selective wait statement with an else part can be used. The else part is executed if and only if none of the alternatives can be selected immediately. (Consequently, `Program_Error` cannot be raised when there is an else part.) It is not permitted to have an else part if a terminate alternative or a delay alternative is present.

Example 23.16 Events

The following task type implements the abstract data type `Event`, used for low-level interprocess communication.

```
task type Event is
   entry Wait;
   entry Signal;
end Event;
```

When the `Signal` operation is invoked, all tasks that are held up in a call of the `Wait` operation are resumed. If a `Signal` operation is invoked when there are no waiting tasks, then it is ignored (in effect). To achieve this we need to be able to accept exactly as many calls on the `Wait` entry as are outstanding when `Signal` is accepted. Accepting too few means that some callers will miss the `Signal`. Accepting too many means that the next `Signal` will be wrongly held up. Fortunately, Ada provides the attribute `Count`, applicable only to an entry and allowed only inside the task declaring the entry. `Count` gives the number of calls currently waiting in the entry queue.

```
task body Event is
begin
   loop
      select
         accept Signal;
         for I in 1 .. Wait'Count loop
            select
               accept Wait;
            else
               null;
            end select;
         end loop;
      or
         terminate;
      end select;
   end loop;
end Event;
```

A selective wait with an else part has been used to prevent any holdup resulting from a reduction in the number of outstanding calls. This can happen if a calling task invokes `Wait` using a timed entry call, then times out after the for loop has been entered, but before its own call on `Wait` is accepted.

□ *End of Example 23.16*

23.8. Tasks and interrupts

The tasking facilities in Ada facilitate a modular approach to concurrent programming. We are encouraged to view a concurrent system as a set of processes that interact only by the disciplined exchange of data. The task and rendezvous constructs provide linguistic support for this style. It is all the more regrettable, then, that most hardware works on different principles.

Hardware support for concurrency is usually limited to a facility to *interrupt* the execution of a program, forcing control to be transferred to a routine associated with the interrupt. This routine may be fixed by software, or dynamically identified by the interrupting device. In either case, what happens is that an invisible procedure call is inserted at a random point in the program! Worse, interrupt routines have no natural scope and so are forced to interact with the rest of the system by means of their effect on global variables. These properties of interrupt driven code combine to give it a structure that is far removed from the ideals proposed in this book.

An interrupt routine typically runs in the most privileged hardware mode available on the processor. It has complete freedom of access to the machine, unhindered by the constraints (such as memory protection mechanisms) that apply to application programs. An error in an interrupt routine can therefore cause havoc in parts of the system that are unrelated to the interrupt. Not surprisingly, interrupt driven programs are notoriously tricky to design, debug and maintain.

Fortunately for the Ada programmer, most of this error-prone complexity is abstracted away by the run-time support routines. These build the mechanisms to sustain tasks and rendezvous on top of hardware primitives such as the interrupt system. Consequently, interrupts do not figure directly in the semantics of Ada. Nevertheless, there are some situations in which interrupts are superior. Essentially these are calls for immediate action to be taken within the application program, regardless of any less urgent computation that happens to be in progress. Such a call might result from an alarm condition in equipment being controlled by the Ada program. Less dramatically, an Ada module might have to respond to interrupts from a device such as a disk controller.

The design of Ada seeks to reconcile the orderly tasking model of concurrency with the anarchic interrupt model. The activity of an interrupt source is treated as if it were a process. Run-time routines encapsulate interrupts of interest to the application program, passing them to higher levels in the form of well-behaved entry calls. The equivalent of an interrupt routine in Ada is therefore an ordinary task, one or more of whose entries may be invoked by an interrupt. It follows that an interrupt will receive service only when (and if) that task executes an accept statement for the entry connected to the interrupt. The occurrence of the interrupt does *not* cause an involuntary change in the flow of control. Adequate real-time response can be maintained only if the task accepts entry calls from the interrupt source with a minimum of delay. In an attempt to ensure this, the execution of a rendezvous due to an interrupt is given higher priority than the execution of any task invoked by software. (See Section 23.9.)

To link an interrupt to an entry of a task, a ***representation specification*** is used. This is an addendum to the declaration of the entry in the task declaration. It takes the form:

```
for entry_name use at interrupt address;
```

where the interrupt address is given by any expression of the type `System.Address` (typically this will be an integer type).

Example 23.17 *Clock interrupts*

A device is available that generates an interrupt to location 100_8 at the frequency of the power supply. The following task uses this device to provide a simple timing service.

```
task Rough_Timer is
   entry Get_Interval (Interval : out Duration);
   entry Line_Interrupt;
   for Line_Interrupt use at 8#100#;
end Rough_Timer;
task body Rough_Timer is
   Ticks : Natural := 0;
   Power_Frequency : constant := 60;  -- cycles/second
begin
   loop
      select
         accept Line_Interrupt;
         Ticks := Ticks + 1;
```

```
        or
            accept Get_Interval (Interval : out Duration) do
                Interval := Duration (Ticks) / Power_Frequency;
            end Get_Interval;
            Ticks := 0;
        end select;
    end loop;
end Rough_Timer;
```

□ *End of Example 23.17*

If an interrupt carries some kind of status information with it, this can be made available to the Ada program as a parameter of the entry call. The details of this depend on the implementation.

The entry call that results from an interrupt can be either a normal entry call, or a timed entry call, or a conditional entry call. A normal entry call would be appropriate in the case of a peripheral device that can wait for service (such as a printer). A timed entry call allows the interrupt source to withdraw the interrupt request if it is not serviced within some *crisis time*. This might be used by a 'watchdog timer' that requires a response within a fixed interval to prove that the system is still operating satisfactorily. A conditional entry call would be a suitable way to connect a low-priority interrupt, perhaps of an advisory nature, that can be safely ignored. The technique used is, in any case, chosen by the implementation and not by the Ada programmer.

An interrupt entry may be called in the normal way from an Ada task, as well as from an interrupt source. However, this is probably best avoided. If a normal task is waiting for the interrupt entry, when the interrupt takes place, the call from the interrupt will have to wait until the normal call has been served. (High priority does not confer the right to jump the queue.)

23.9. Tasking pragmatics

This section draws attention to secondary aspects of tasking that might be very important in some applications.

Priority

As we have seen, an implementation of Ada is free to schedule computational resources such as CPU time in any way it chooses. No scheduling policy is specified by the language. What the language does specify is that a task may be given a priority. A multiprogrammed implementation of tasking is required to ensure that a task of high priority never waits while CPU time is being given to a task of low priority. (This requirement does not apply to a distributed implementation.)

If two or more tasks of the same priority compete for a CPU, it may be granted to either of them. Tasks with no priority specified are treated as having an undefined priority.

If both participants in a rendezvous have defined priorities, the rendezvous is executed with the higher of their two priorities. If only one of them has a priority, the rendezvous is executed with (at least) that priority. The priority of the rendezvous is not defined if neither participant has a defined priority. These rules ensure that a high priority task is not delayed unnecessarily by rendezvous with a low-priority task.

It is very bad practice indeed to write a concurrent program that operates correctly only under certain assumptions about the relative priorities of its tasks. This is tantamount to making it speed-dependent. Priorities should be used only to improve the performance of a concurrent program, for example by exploiting the fact that a particular task is known to be CPU bound.

The relative priority of a task is specified with the `Priority` pragma. This takes the form:

`pragma Priority (`*task priority*`);`

where the parameter is a static expression of the `Integer` subtype `System.Priority`. A small priority value indicates less urgency and a large priority indicates greater urgency. The actual range of priority values is dependent on the implementation.

This pragma must appear in the declaration of the task (or task type) to which it applies, or in the outermost declarative part of the main program. (For this purpose the main program is considered to be a task.)

Tasking and exceptions

The predefined exception `Tasking_Error` is raised in a calling task if the server task has already completed at the time of the entry call, or if it completes before a queued entry call gets accepted. `Tasking_Error` is also raised in a calling task if the server task becomes abnormal (due to an abort statement) while engaged in a rendezvous. The converse does not apply. If a calling task becomes abnormal the server task is unaffected: an unaccepted entry call is simply abandoned, while an accepted entry call proceeds normally in the server to the end of the rendezvous.

`Tasking_Error` is also raised at the place of activation of a local task (i.e. at the `begin` of the parent unit, or on allocation of an object with a task component) if the task become completed during its activation.

The predefined exception `Program_Error` is raised by a selective wait statement if there are no open alternatives, or if an attempt is made to activate a task whose body has not yet been elaborated.

A rendezvous completes prematurely if an unhandled exception is raised within the accept statement. In this case execution of the accept statement is abandoned and the exception is propagated to both of the tasks involved. In the calling task it is reraised at the point of the entry call. In the server task it is reraised immediately after the accept statement.

Tasking attributes

The following attributes are defined for task objects (or types) `T`, or for entries `E`: `E'Address`, `T'Address`, `T'Callable`, `E'Count`, `T'Storage_Size` and `T'Terminated`. See Appendix B for details.

Shared variables

Despite our warnings, you might feel it necessary to use shared variables. If so, you should familiarize yourself with the subtleties of their semantics. You can best do this by referring to [Ada 1983].

Tasks and packages

Although there is an analogy between tasks and packages, it cannot be pressed too far. In particular, tasks export entries only, and this is inadequate for complete encapsulation of many abstract data structures. A solution is to wrap the task itself within a package that defines all the other entities — types, constants, variables, subprograms or exceptions — that the application requires. Other restrictions on tasks can be dealt with similarly:

- A task cannot be a library unit. But a task can be declared within a library package, and so made available to any compilation unit that includes the package in its context clause. (Remember that the language does not define termination for tasks in library packages; and that library packages, unlike nested packages, count as task masters. See Section 23.6.)

- A task cannot be generic. But a task can be declared within a generic package and access the generic parameters through the normal visibility rules.

It is possible to rename an entry as a procedure. This is particularly useful when the task is contained in a package that exports such a procedure name, but not the name of the entry itself. By this means a package, already a powerful tool for abstraction, can decouple the rest of a program from the fact that a module has been implemented concurrently. This might prove very useful when introducing concurrency, during maintenance, to a program that was originally designed to be wholly sequential.

In much the same way, if a task is declared within a package, the package can export procedures that call the entries of the task in the correct sequence. For example, the `Database_Mutex` task of Example 23.15 can profitably be encapsulated in a package, say `Database_Manager`, that exports subprograms for all valid operations on the database. These would work by invoking both the sequential library package, and `Database_Mutex`, according to the acquire/relinquish protocol. In this way, `Database_Manager` can handle access to the database by several tasks, without coupling them to `Database_Mutex` in any way. (*Exercise*: write an outline for `Database_Manager`.)

Finally, recall that task types are *limited*. This means that a task type used as an actual parameter in a generic instantiation must correspond to a generic formal parameter that is a limited private type. A task object used as an actual parameter must correspond to a generic formal parameter that is a limited private object and has mode `in out`. Mode `in` is not allowed. These restrictions make it impossible for the generic unit to call entries of the task (directly), for the simple reason that it is not known to be a task within the generic unit. (See Chapter 22.)

A task type may be exported from a package either as itself, or as a limited private type, but not as an unlimited private type. Again, if it is exported as a limited private type, entries of the type cannot be called (directly) from outside the package.

Exercises 23

23.1. Characterize the use of (a) shared variables and (b) rendezvous in terms of the kinds of coupling they induce.

23.2. Example 23.8 does not attempt to schedule the acceptance of entry calls when the queue is neither full nor empty. What criteria might be used to decide between an insertion and a removal in these circumstances? Modify the example to include your choice of scheduling criterion.

23.3. A *pipeline* is a sequence of processes, connected by buffers so that data flows (one way) from process to process, being transformed somewhat at each stage. The start of the pipeline is the *source* process and the end is the *sink* process. The processes between are called *filters*. Declare a task type suitable for use as a buffer between tasks in a pipeline. Set up a pipeline that reads text from the standard input, breaks it into characters, switches between upper and lower case, and outputs the result on the standard output, with no more than 80 characters per line. Use a separate task for each transformation. Having done this, consider how Case Study III, Chapter 16, could be converted to a concurrent program.

23.4. The `Database_Mutex` task of Example 23.15 assumes that if a task fails to relinquish the database before its lease expires, it will not relinquish it later. Redesign `Database_Mutex` to eliminate this unsafe assumption.

23.5. Modify the data collection task in Example 23.13 so that it cannot be delayed by any misbehavior on the part of the `Matrix_Multiplier` task.

23.6. Use the `Event` task type of Example 23.16 to implement the multi-phase task of Example 23.6, but without the `Go_Ahead` entry.

23.7. The following task type declaration specifies the abstract data structure `Semaphore`, used for low-level interprocess communication and mutual exclusion.

```
task type Semaphore is
   entry Initialize (V : in Integer);
   entry Wait;
   entry Signal;
end Semaphore;
```

`Initialize` must be the first operation applied to each semaphore variable. Thereafter any sequence of `Wait` and `Signal` operations may be used. These operations respect the *semaphore invariant*:

$$0 \leq waits(S) \leq initial(S) + signals(S)$$

where $initial(S)$ is the initial value of S, $signals(S)$ is the number of completed `Signal` operations on S, and $waits(S)$ is the number of completed `Wait` operations on S. Note that a call of `Wait` may hold up the caller until it is possible to complete the operation without violating the invariant. This is the property that makes semaphores useful. Implement a body for this task type. (*Hint*: The semaphore invariant implies that:

$$initial(S) + signals(S) - waits(S) \geq 0$$

at all times.)

23.8. **Write a program to test the user's reaction time to a stimulus (such as the output of the *BEL* character to the terminal).**

24

Portability and Machine-dependent Programming

24.1. Portability

It is commonly said that a portable program is one that can be run on a variety of computer systems without modification. Small programs written in high-level languages can sometimes be moved without any modification, but this is exceptional for larger programs. A better definition of portability is based on the cost of re-implementing the software on a second computer system, as a fraction of its initial development cost. By this definition no program is 100% portable, because media conversion, installation and testing are always required on the second system. Equally, no program is 0% portable, since at the very least the experience gained on the first system should aid any re-implementation.

Defining portability in economic terms is appropriate because of the large investment in software. Making software as portable as possible is a way of protecting that investment against hardware and operating system changes. Almost all items of software are potentially portable, so it is both economically and technically sensible to strive for portability. Of course, portability works both ways: we must consider not only providing our own software in a portable form, but also re-using existing software to minimize costs. Failure to do this resulted in a comment of Hamming that scientists and engineers stand on their predecessors' shoulders, whereas programmers stand on one another's toes.

The key to portability is a proper understanding of the software. Easily-understood software can be corrected if problems arise during conversion. In this respect portability and maintainability are analogous.

There are many obstacles to portability. One obstacle is the failure of many compilers to adhere to the standard definition of the programming language. Many COBOL and FORTRAN compilers are deficient in this respect. Inconsistencies between different compilers can cause a program that works on one system to work differently, or even fail, on another system. Another obstacle is that many programs make use of peculiarities of the operating system or character set. Ada attempts to minimize these obstacles by defining the language very carefully, so that only a few constructs will work on one system but not on another. (These are the *erroneous* constructs.) If possible, you should insist on using a validated compiler. This should give you a much higher degree of confidence in your software, because of the rigid specification of the language with which a validated compiler must comply.

Ada provides an opportunity to write highly portable software in areas where this has not been done in the past. For example, concurrent programs can be written using tasks, in a portable manner. Similarly, programs can be made robust by using exceptions, where in the past a failure in one module might cause an entire program to crash.

A survey of portability problems before Ada was designed may be found in [Brown 1977]. Guidelines for writing highly portable programs in Ada are given in [Nissen 1983].

Portability by encapsulation

In economic terms, it is the portability of large programs that is important, so we shall concentrate on this area. Since we cannot achieve 100% portability, our design objective must be to minimize the scale of the necessary modifications. Firstly, we must anticipate the need for modifications, even if we cannot predict their nature and why they become necessary. Secondly, potential modifications should be localized, otherwise it will be difficult to be sure that all the necessary modifications have been identified.

The latter point is in any case a consequence of good program design. Just as coupling among the modules of a program should be minimized, so also should coupling between the program and the underlying system (hardware and software). Each module should present a clean machine-independent interface to the rest of the program. This implies, for example, the use of abstract data types, rather than predefined types whose properties are machine-dependent.

Example 24.1 OIS: Speech-handling service

We continue our running example of the office information system. The system is to be equipped with a speech input-output facility, so that spoken comments can be attached to stored information. To reduce storage requirements, the digitized speech is to be stored in a compressed form. Procedures for compressing speech and for expanding compressed speech are to be provided.

The facility is highly machine-dependent. In order to avoid making the rest of the software unportable, and to allow for later enhancements to the speech facility, we should encapsulate the speech facility in a package. The package declaration should be machine-independent, although its body will inevitably be machine-dependent.

```
with IO;  use IO;  -- exports File_Type

package Speech_Service is
    type Speech is limited private;
    type Compressed_Speech is limited private;

    procedure Record_Speech (S  : out Speech);
    procedure Playback      (S  : in Speech);

    procedure Compress      (S  : in Speech;
                             CS : out Compressed_Speech);
    procedure Expand        (S  : out Speech;
                             CS : in Compressed_Speech);

    procedure Get (File : in File_Type;
                   S    : out Speech);
    procedure Get (File : in File_Type;
                   CS   : out Compressed_Speech);
    procedure Put (File : in File_Type;
                   S    : in Speech);
    procedure Put (File : in File_Type;
                   CS   : in Compressed_Speech);
private
    implementation details
```

```
    end Speech_Service;
```

The procedures for recording and playback of uncompressed speech are augmented by procedures for compression and expansion of the speech and for storing both forms in files. The software that manipulates compressed and uncompressed speech data can now be programmed independently of the internal representation of the speech data.

□ *End of Example 24.1*

Guidelines and pitfalls

The usual concern with portability is to move an (apparently) working program from one computer system to another. There are two aspects to this. Firstly, how should we write our programs to maximize portability? Secondly, what aspects of Ada could cause portability problems?

Many of the portability issues are not peculiar to Ada. We have mentioned the range of `Integer`. It is safe to rely upon the range provided by a 16-bit representation. For a wider range, declare a new integer type in terms of the desired range. Do not use `Long_Integer`, because there is no guarantee that such a type is predefined. Similarly, it is safe to assume that `Float` has at least 5 digits of accuracy, but for greater precision you should declare a new floating-point type. As far as possible, use attributes rather than constants (or, even worse, literals) that have some subtle relationship to the numeric type involved.

For performance reasons, if no other, the allocation of objects via **new** needs care. This is because the allocation of objects on the heap might lead to excessive storage requirements, and conversely their deallocation might either be ineffective or consume too much time. It is wise to isolate the space allocation so that a system can be tuned if necessary — see Example 24.6 below.

A major pitfall to portability is the possibility of a program appearing to work correctly on a particular system, though it is formally incorrect. For example, a program might use an uninitialized variable. If the system on which the program was developed does not detect this error (and recall that detection is not guaranteed), then the programmer might well be completely unaware of its existence. When the program is subsequently moved to a new system, the results are unpredictable. The error might be detected (perhaps even at compile-time), but more typically the program will execute and give incorrect results. A program that uses an uninitialized variable is an example of an *erroneous* program.

Ada does not define how parameter passing is implemented. A program is erroneous if it depends upon a specific implementation method. The two obvious implementations are by copy and by reference. With an implementation that copies parameters, an **out** or **in out** actual parameter will not be updated until (normal) return from the subprogram. Therefore if the subprogram propagates an exception, the actual parameter will be unchanged. This is clearly not the case when a reference implementation is used. The difficulty with this vagueness in the definition of Ada is that it is quite awkward to be sure that a program is independent of the implementation method. (You might wonder why the language does not define the implementation method. The reason is that the copy mechanism is very inefficient with large parameters, whereas the reference mechanism is prohibitively expensive on distributed systems.)

Another class of erroneous programs that might cause portability problems are those with ***incorrect order dependence***. For example, the order in which library units are elaborated depends only on the order imposed by their dependencies (as reflected in their with clauses). In consequence, a program that depends upon any particular elaboration order is erroneous. Similarly, the order of evaluation of the actual parameters in a subprogram call is not defined.

An important practical problem with an Ada program is to avoid environmental dependencies. A module might appear to contain no such dependencies because none are obvious in its declaration. Nevertheless, the body of the module might, for example, open a file using a system-dependent filename. Therefore, checking for portability necessarily requires both the declaration and body of each module to be examined.

There are specific pitfalls concerned with ensuring that numerical computation is portable. All these arise because an implementation is free to provide a greater range of values, or greater precision, than the program actually requests, and the programmer might unconsciously take advantage of this. This topic has been covered in Chapter 19.

24.2. Machine-dependent programming

The definition of Ada is machine-independent. However, some programs *must* achieve an effect that is machine-dependent. An obvious case is the control of exotic peripheral devices whose properties do not fit the standard input-output packages. Another case is when the programmer requires control over some aspect of the object code generated by the compiler, in some part of the program where efficiency is critical. In all cases such as these, we should still aim to design machine-independent interfaces between modules, while admitting that the bodies of some modules will in part be machine-dependent.

Pragmas

Efficiency is sometimes of critical importance. We cannot expect a compiler to produce optimal object code in all circumstances, because the precise nature of the optimum cannot usually be determined from the source text alone. For example, speed and storage space can often be traded off against each other. If the balance matters, instrument your program to determine which parts of it are time or space critical. Make sure that the optimal algorithms are being used. The pragma `Optimize` can then be used to indicate the 'optimization' needed:

```
pragma Optimize (Space);
pragma Optimize (Time);
```

The pragma must appear in the declarative part of a program unit, and the optimization requested is applied to the whole of that unit. The use of this pragma is not actually machine-dependent. It is advisory (like all pragmas) and does not affect the meaning of an Ada program. Of course, the generated object code might well be inadequately efficient if the pragma is in fact ignored.

The following pragma:

```
pragma Inline ( subprogram_names );
```

indicates that the named subprograms should be compiled in-line. (See also Section 12.6.) Use of this pragma in a separately-compiled package implies that a modification to one of the subprogram bodies could force the recompilation of all units dependent on the package. This could be very expensive in a large program.

The last pragma in this class concerns data representations. It takes the form:

```
pragma Pack ( composite_type_name );
```

This pragma must appear in the same declarative part as the declaration of the named type, say `T`. The pragma indicates that a compact data representation should be chosen for all objects of type `T`. It has no influence upon the representation of the component type(s) of `T`. This pragma, if heeded, is likely to result in bulkier and slower object code for fetching and updating components of objects of type `T`. (On the other hand, object code for comparison and assignment of objects of type `T` might well be faster.) The predefined type `String` has the pragma `Pack` applied to its representation (see Appendix D). It is therefore likely that an individual character in a `String` object will occupy a single byte and not a whole word.

Representation clauses

An Ada compiler has considerable freedom in choosing a representation for data of a particular type. The only restriction is the need to preserve the language's semantics. In only a few cases, such as `Integer` and `Float`, is the choice effectively limited to a hardware-supported representation.

Why should the programmer ever be concerned about data representations? There are two situations where this does matter. Firstly, an efficient representation might be critical, as we have noted in explaining the pragma `Pack`. Secondly, the Ada program might have to interface with other parts of a system in which the data representation is already fixed. This latter requirement can be illustrated by an example.

Example 24.2 *OIS: Speech input-output data*

A hardware unit associated with our OIS has the ability to input and output audio signals. Both input and output are in 1024-byte blocks. Each byte represents the audio signal as a signed fraction of the maximum signal. To represent this in Ada, we must control the representation of two types — `Signal` for the audio signal and `Data_Block` for the 1024-byte blocks.

`Signal` is a fixed-point type declared by:

```
type Signal is delta 1.0/128 range -1.0 .. +1.0;
```

(The value +1.0 will not actually be attained if a 2's complement representation is used.) Ordinarily, a compiler would allocate a whole word (of 16 bits or more) to variables of type `Signal`, since that makes access faster and simpler. This representation is unsuitable, however, because the hardware unit uses its own representation which is a byte. So we must add a *length clause* to enforce the predetermined representation:

```
for Signal'Size use 8;
```

This specifies that each object of type `Signal` is to occupy exactly 8 bits. Thus the representation used for type `Signal` is now constrained to be integer multiples of `Signal'Small`, which must be 1.0/128.

However, if the length clause were not itself adequate to constrain the representation, an alternative would be to specify the value of `Small` explicitly by another form of length clause, as follows:

```
for Signal'Small use 1.0/128;
```

The type **Data_Block** is similarly defined with a corresponding length clause:

```
type Data_Block is array (1 .. 1024) of Signal;
for Data_Block'Size use Signal'Size * Data_Block'Length;
```

Note that it would not be sufficient to write:

```
pragma Pack (Data_Block);
```

since the packing would not necessarily be done at the byte level.

□ *End of Example 24.2*

A length clause can also be used to specify the size of the *collection* of heap objects associated with an access type. We illustrate this by a further example.

Example 24.3 *OIS: Speech data buffers*

In Example 24.1 we gave a machine-independent declaration of a speech package, while in Example 24.2 we defined the lower-level, hardware-implemented, data blocks. In this example, we provide the link between the two. In fact, both the types **Speech** and **Compressed_Speech** are implemented as linked lists of data blocks. In order to ensure that the system does not get congested with data blocks, we shall specify a fixed allocation of 20 blocks. This allows us to complete the private part of the **Speech_Service** package declaration:

```
private
    type Signal is delta 1.0/128 range -1.0 .. 1.0;
    for Signal'Size use 8;
    type Data_Block is array (1 .. 1024) of Signal;
    for Data_Block'Size use
          Signal'Size * Data_Block'Length;
    type Block_Node;
    type Block_Ptr is access Block_Node;
    type Block_Node is
          record
             Data : Data_Block;
             Next : Block_Ptr;
          end record;
    type Speech is new Block_Ptr;
    type Compressed_Speech is new Block_Ptr;
    for Block_Ptr'Storage_Size use
          20 * Block_Node'Size / System.Storage_Unit;
end Speech_Service;
```

The attribute **Block_Ptr'Storage_Size** is the number of *storage units* (e.g., bytes or words) of heap space associated with access types **Block_Ptr**, **Speech** and **Compressed_Speech**. The value of the attribute **Block_Node'Size** is expressed in *bits*, however, so we have divided it by the constant **System.Storage_Unit**, which is the number of bits per storage unit. (The latter is exported by the predefined package **System**.)

□ *End of Example 24.3*

A common interfacing requirement is to be able to specify a data structure associated with the control of peripheral equipment. This is likely to be a record with several components. The exact layout of the components of a record may be specified in Ada by a ***record representation clause***. We illustrate this with a further example.

Example 24.4 *Disk control logic*

A package `Disk_Control` is to be written to control a disk at the lowest level. The hardware disk control unit interprets a *disk control block*, located at memory address 77430_8, with the layout illustrated in Figure 24.1.

The disk control block must be specified in terms of an Ada data type. We first write this specification at a logical level by means of a record type definition, as follows:

```
type Disk_Function is (Read, Write, Write_with_Check, Seek);
type Disk_Control_Record is
    record
        Function_Code        : Disk_Function;
        Disk_Address         : Integer;
        Store_Address        : System.Address;
        Words_Transferred    : Positive;
        Write_not_Permitted  : Boolean;
        Disk_Busy            : Boolean;
        Disk_Off_Line        : Boolean;
    end record;
```

The body of `Disk_Control` can now be programmed entirely in terms of this logical specification. However, to interface the package correctly to the hardware disk control unit,

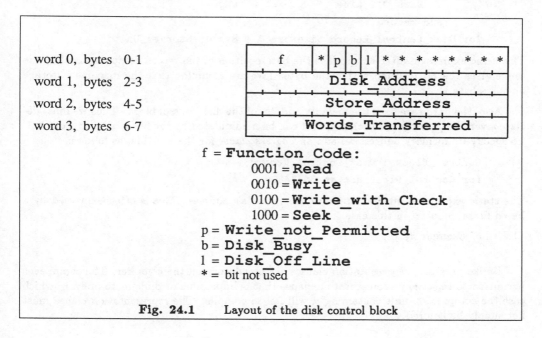

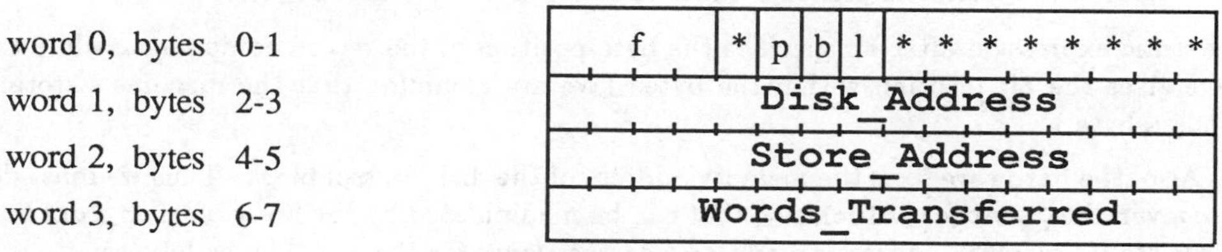

f = **Function_Code:**
0001 = **Read**
0010 = **Write**
0100 = **Write_with_Check**
1000 = **Seek**
p = **Write_not_Permitted**
b = **Disk_Busy**
l = **Disk_Off_Line**
* = bit not used

Fig. 24.1 Layout of the disk control block

we must ensure that the disk control block is laid out exactly in the manner expected by the hardware. This is done by providing representation clauses for both of the above types.

From Figure 24.1 we see that each `Disk_Function` value must be represented by a 4-bit code in which exactly one of the bits is 1. Therefore we need representation clauses to specify both the size and the value representations for `Disk_Function`:

```
for Disk_Function use
    (Read => 1, Write => 2, Write_with_Check => 4, Seek => 8);
for Disk_Function'Size use 4;
```

The first of these is an example of an *enumeration representation clause*. The (integer) representation of each enumeration literal is specified explicitly. The only restriction is that the integer representations must be distinct and increasing. (Otherwise the relational operators "=", "/=", "<", etc., would yield anomalous results.)

Now the layout of a `Disk_Control_Record` can be specified precisely, as required by Figure 24.1, using a record representation clause:

```
for Disk_Control_Record use
    record
        Function_Code          at 0 range 0 .. 3;
        Disk_Address           at 2;
        Store_Address          at 4;
        Words_Transferred      at 6;
        Write_not_Permitted    at 0 range 5 .. 5;
        Disk_Busy              at 0 range 6 .. 6;
        Disk_Off_Line          at 0 range 7 .. 7;
    end record;
for Disk_Control_Record'Size use 8 * System.Storage_Unit;
```

The static expression after **at** specifies the byte position of the record component, while the **range** gives the bit position within the byte. (We are assuming that the machine's storage unit is a byte.)

Also, the hardware fixes the memory address of the disk control block. Thus we must declare a variable, `Control_Block` say, that can be manipulated by the body of `Disk_Control`. To specify its memory address we add an *address clause* for the variable, as follows:

```
Control_Block : Disk_Control_Record;
for Control_Block use at 8#77430#;
```

The static expression after **at** specifies the variable's address. This is often expressed by a based literal — octal in this case.

□ *End of Example 24.4*

Unlike pragmas, representation clauses are mandatory on the compiler. The compiler is permitted to reject any representation clause that is impossible or difficult to obey, in which case the compilation unit containing it will fail to compile. The representation clause must not simply be ignored.

Machine-code insertions

Ada was designed with the intention that complete systems could be programmed entirely in the language. This is particularly important when programming a machine for which no other compiler (or even assembler) is available. Occasionally, however, low-level software is required to achieve effects that cannot be expressed directly in Ada. An example is driving a peripheral by means of a specific machine instruction. It is then necessary to resort to embedding machine-code instructions in the Ada text.

A machine-code insertion is achieved by writing a procedure whose body consists entirely of *code statements*. A code statement corresponds to a single machine instruction and is written as a qualified record aggregate. (See the syntax diagram 'code_statement' in Appendix A.) The machine-code instructions are considered to be records in which each component represents an instruction field. An Ada implementation that provides this facility must provide a library package named Machine_Code that declares the type of these records.

For example, take a (very simple) machine with 16-bit instructions, each composed of a 4-bit operation field F and a 12-bit operand field A:

```
package Machine_Code is
   type Operation is (LOAD, STORE, ADD, ..., STARTIO);
   type Operand   is range 0 .. 4095;
   for Operation'Size use 4;
   for Operand'Size   use 12;
   type Instruction is
         record
            F : Operation;
            A : Operand;
         end record;
   for Instruction use
         record
            F at 0 range 0 .. 3;
            A at 0 range 4 .. 15;
         end record;
   for Instruction'Size use 16;
end Machine_Code;
```

Here is an example of a code statement that generates an ADD instruction:

```
Machine_Code.Instruction' (ADD, 1000);
```

Example 24.5 *Initiating a disk transfer*

Suppose that the package Disk_Control of Example 24.4 must use the machine instruction STARTIO to initiate a disk input-output operation. The instruction's operand is the number of the disk unit, 15. The particular operation to be performed (read, write, etc.), and parameters for that operation, are taken from a disk control block at memory address 77430_8, as described in Example 24.4.

One solution is for the STARTIO instruction to be written in Ada in the form of a machine-code insertion:

```
with Machine_Code;
```

```
package body Disk_Control is
   Disk_Number : constant := 15;
   ...
   procedure Start_Disk is
   begin
      Machine_Code.Instruction' (STARTIO, Disk_Number);
   end;
   pragma Inline (Start_Disk);
   ...
end Disk_Control;
```

If it proves necessary to change the disk unit number, one recompilation of the package body will suffice.

An alternative solution is for `Start_Disk` to be an assembler subroutine containing the `STARTIO` instruction. In the package we simply include a procedure declaration followed by an `Interface` pragma:

```
package body Disk_Control is
   ...
   procedure Start_Disk;
   pragma Interface (Assembler, Start_Disk);
   ...
end Disk_Control;
```

The assembler subroutine must be written in such a way as to interface correctly to the Ada program. (In this simple case the subroutine has no parameters to complicate the interface.) Changing the disk unit number now forces access to some non-Ada text and to the assembler. Also, some special facility will be needed to add the assembler subroutine to the Ada program library. The subroutine is *not* itself a library unit or subunit, but linking clearly requires access to the object code generated by the assembler.

The first solution generates just the single instruction required. The second solution, however, could force all registers to be saved and restored at the subroutine call, resulting in a large overhead to execute a single machine instruction. With both methods, care is needed to avoid corrupting registers and other volatile data.

□ *End of Example 24.5*

The general form of the `Interface` pragma is:

`pragma Interface (` *language*`_name,` *subprogram*`_name );`

The first argument is the name of any language known to the Ada compiler. If it is another high-level language, the programmer must ensure that the Ada compiler and the other compiler use mutually compatible parameter-passing mechanisms.

24.3. Unchecked programming

It is occasionally necessary to cheat; that is, to break the Ada language rules in order to achieve an effect that is otherwise impossible or very inefficient. The Ada rules are not needlessly restrictive, so breaking them is dangerous and not generally recommended.

Ada provides two means of breaking its normal rules, in the form of the generic library units `Unchecked_Conversion` and `Unchecked_Deallocation`. Their names are a reminder of the danger inherent in their use. Also, the need to name them explicitly in a context clause makes it unlikely that they will be used surreptitiously or inadvertently.

The generic function `Unchecked_Conversion`

`Unchecked_Conversion` is provided to convert a value of one type into a value of another type. The types need not be (logically) related to one another, and it is assumed that the conversion is simply a change in the type of the same bit pattern. The conversion is by a *function*, so the converted value must be assigned to an object of the new type, or otherwise processed as such. (This is quite different from FORTRAN's `EQUIVALENCE` 'facility', where one storage area can be regarded as being of more than one type.)

The generic function has the declaration:

```
generic
   type Source is limited private;
   type Target is limited private;
function Unchecked_Conversion (S : Source) return Target;
```

Both generic type parameters are limited private, so the generic function can be instantiated with any types as generic actual parameters. Most implementations will restrict the pair of types, however, requiring them for example to have the same size.

Example 24.6 Unchecked type conversion

Imagine a communications link along which data can be transmitted one byte at a time. The following declarations have been provided:

```
type Byte is range 0 .. 255;
for Byte'Size use 8;
procedure Transmit (Item : in Byte);
```

In terms of these it is desired to implement the following procedure, which is to transmit a complete object of some type `Object`:

```
procedure Transmit (Item : in Object);
```

This can be done by treating the object as an array of bytes. We declare an array-of-bytes type to which the object can be mapped by unchecked type conversion, taking care that the array type has the same size as the object. Then the individual bytes can be transmitted:

```
procedure Transmit (Item : in Object) is
   Object_Size : constant Positive
               := Object'Size / System.Storage_Unit;
   type Mapped_Object is array (1 .. Object_Size) of Byte;
   for Mapped_Object'Size use Object'Size;
   function Mapped is new Unchecked_Conversion (Object, Mapped_Object);
   Mapped_Item : constant Mapped_Object := Mapped (Item);
begin
   for I in Mapped_Item'Range loop
      Transmit (Mapped_Item(I));
   end loop;
```

```
   end Transmit;
```

☐ *End of Example 24.6*

The generic procedure Unchecked_Deallocation

In Section 17.7 the treatment of space allocation for dynamic data structures was left incomplete. The space required for such structures is allocated from a *heap*, and it is the responsibility of the Ada run-time system to manage this. In some implementations the run-time system will perform this job adequately without help from the programmer, by means of a *garbage collector* that periodically searches for inaccessible heap objects and makes the space they occupy available for reallocation. This implies time overheads at unpredictable points during the execution of the program. These time overheads can be minimized by use of the pragma Controlled, as noted in Section 17.7. This might be essential in a real-time program, since unpredictable delays cannot be tolerated in a program that is required always to respond within a limited time. However, this pragma allows the programmer only very loose control over the deallocation of heap objects. It allows heap objects to continue to occupy storage even after they become inaccessible. In some applications, neither waste of memory nor the time overheads of automatic garbage collection can be tolerated. In such applications the programmer needs much tighter control — a mechanism for explicitly deallocating individual heap objects.

The generic library procedure Unchecked_Deallocation provides this mechanism in Ada. This generic procedure must be instantiated for each type of heap object that is to be explicitly deallocated. Its declaration is:

```
generic
   type Object is limited private;
   type Name   is access Object;
procedure Unchecked_Deallocation (X : in out Name);
```

Example 24.7 Deleting entries in a directory

Consider the Directory_Service package of Example 17.5, augmented by a procedure to remove an entry from the directory:

```
package Directory_Service is
   subtype Names   is String (1 .. 20);
   subtype Numbers is String (1 .. 12);

   procedure Insert_Entry ( ... );
   procedure Lookup_Entry ( ... );
   procedure Delete_Entry (Given_Name : in Names);
end Directory_Service;
```

In Example 17.5 a hash table was used to represent the directory. Let us augment this solution to implement Delete_Entry, using explicit deallocation for the sake of efficiency. We must instantiate Unchecked_Deallocation for use within the body of Directory_Service:

```
   procedure Deallocate_Directory_Node is
         new Unchecked_Deallocation (Directory_Node, Directory_Ptr);
```

The body of Delete_Entry must find the entry to be deleted, then unlink this entry from the linked list containing it, and finally deallocate this entry:

```
procedure Delete_Entry (Given_Name : in Names) is
   Bucket  : constant Buckets := Hash (Given_Name);
   Ptr     : Directory_Ptr    := Directory_Table(Bucket);
   Old_Ptr : Directory_Ptr    := null;
begin
   loop
      if Ptr = null then
         exit;     -- specified entry is not present
      elsif Given_Name = Ptr.Name then
         if Old_Ptr = null then
            Directory_Table(Bucket) := null;
         else
            Old_Ptr.Next := Ptr.Next;
         end if;
         Deallocate_Directory_Node (Ptr);
         exit;
      else
         Old_Ptr := Ptr;
         Ptr := Ptr.Next;
      end if;
   end loop;
end Delete_Entry;
```

It must be emphasized that explicit deallocation is notoriously error-prone. Deallocating a heap object that still has other pointers pointing to it leaves the latter pointing to a gap in the heap. This gap might later be used for an object of a different type. Any later attempt to use one of these 'dangling' pointers would have unpredictable consequences! However, by declaring Deallocate_Directory_Node inside the package body, we have restricted use of this inherently insecure facility to the package body itself.

□ *End of Example 24.7*

Exercises 24

24.1. Design a package declaration for the device control of an automatic washing machine. The machine's functions are hot water, cold water, waste, heater, spin (two speeds), door lock and program control.

24.2. The package in Example 19.12 exports a function Random. What portability dangers are there in the use of such a function?

24.3. Study the low-level device control provided by a minicomputer or microprocessor. Write an Ada package declaration for interfacing the device control to an Ada program.

24.4. Write a declaration of the Machine_Code package for your favorite computer.

25

Case Study of a Large System

25.1. An Office Information System

Since Ada is intended to be used for the design and implementation of large systems, it is appropriate that we conclude this book with a case study of a large, realistic, computer system. Space precludes us from studying a large system in full detail, so we shall compromise by reviewing an outline design and then looking more closely at selected parts of the system. Even the requirement must be given only in outline, but you should be able to fill in any details that you feel appropriate.

Our case study is an *Office Information System* (*OIS*). Several parts of this system have already been used as examples in previous chapters. The OIS is to be a component of an 'electronic office', whose hardware includes a keyboard, visual display and printer. A *basic* version of the OIS has software for word processing (WP) and data processing (DP), and includes a filing subsystem. Several other subsystems are to be made available as options:

- a diary subsystem;
- context searching of files;
- telecommunications;
- speech input, output and storage.

The telecommunications and speech subsystems require special-purpose hardware as well as software. These add-on subsystems are designed to allow the system to be marketed with a large range of capabilities (and prices). The customer can specify any combination of add-on subsystems. Figure 25.1 shows a data flow diagram of the OIS.

The OIS is controlled by an operator, using the keyboard and visual display. She (or he) works by typing *commands* on the keyboard. Each subsystem provides an appropriate set of commands.

The OIS is interactive, and many commands such as the editor involve a dialog with the operator. On the other hand, some commands such as printing and telecommunications run for a long time without further interaction. It would be inefficient for the operator to be forced to wait for such a command to complete, before going on to the next command. So the operator is to be enabled (by means of a special key on the keyboard) to start a new command, while the old one is still running in the 'background'. In general, several commands can be running concurrently. Only one of these commands can accept input from the keyboard (the 'foreground' command). By dividing up the visual display into a number of 'windows', it is possible for the output from several commands to be displayed on the one screen.

A typical session might start as follows. At first there is nothing running in the background. The operator types a command to print a file, for example. In order to continue while the printing is done, she moves the printing into the background, and then types a command to send a message using the telecommunications subsystem. She moves that also into the background. Then, after completing a few brief commands, she starts editing a file. The window display at that point might be as shown in Figure 25.2.

This requirement is very informal and incomplete. Before detailed design could be undertaken, in practice, the systems analyst would have to prepare a detailed specification of the hardware, of the commands provided by each subsystem, of the command language used by the operator, and of other control functions available to the operator. For the purposes of this chapter, however, we shall have to be content with an impression of the system requirement.

25.2. The control structure

It is clear that the OIS needs to be a concurrent program. At any time, a foreground process and several background processes could be running concurrently. We do not wish arbitrarily to restrict the concurrency that the system can handle. Therefore we shall define a ***main task*** containing a command interpreter that accepts and executes all commands. We make `Main_Task` a task ***type*** in order to allow several instances of the main task to execute

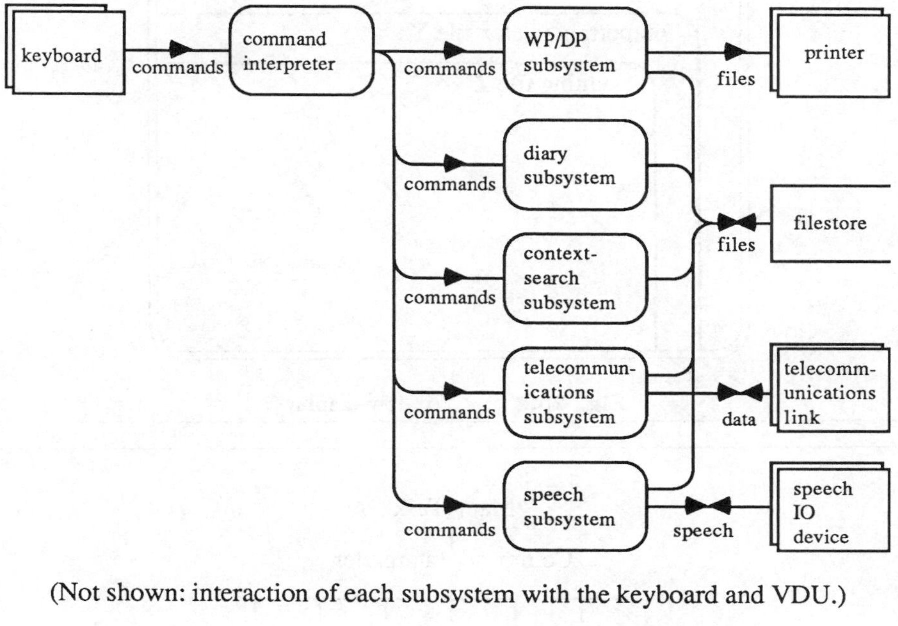

Fig. 25.1 Data flow diagram of the OIS

concurrently. Each foreground and background process will be an instance of the main task. Since all commands can be called from the main task, each process is in effect a copy of the complete system. The top-level control structure of the main task is shown in Figure 25.3.

Seen in this light, we need facilities for initiating a new copy of the main task, for connecting the keyboard to a different task, for terminating a task, and perhaps for changing the display window assigned to a task.

25.3. The package structure

Since the OIS contains four optional subsystems and a customer may select any combination of these, there must be sixteen different versions of the OIS. Clearly it would be absurd to construct sixteen distinct complete source programs. Instead, each of the optional subsystems should be constructed as a separately-compiled package, and then any version of the OIS can be constructed by compiling only the selected subsystems with the rest of the software. It is not quite that simple, however. If the top-level software (specifically, the command interpreter) contains references to all the optional subsystems as well as to the WP/DP subsystem, then the system could not be compiled without *all* the subsystems.

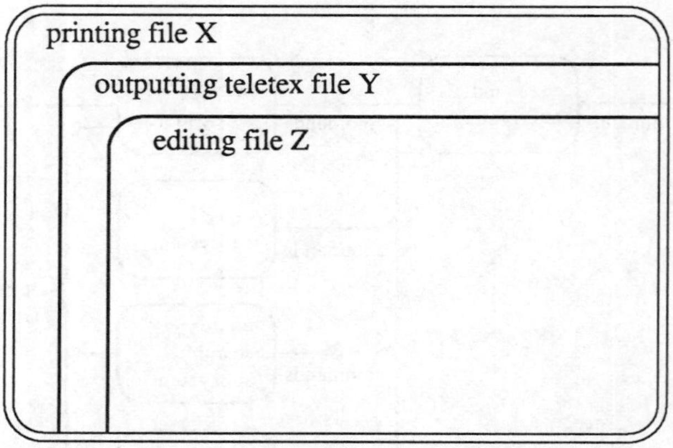

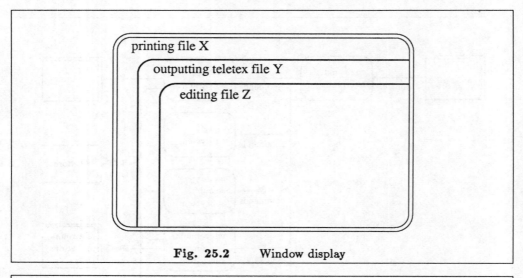

Fig. 25.2 Window display

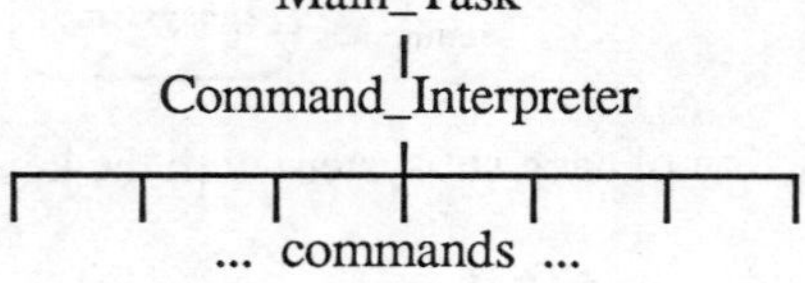

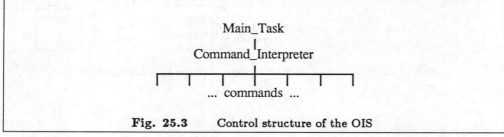

Fig. 25.3 Control structure of the OIS

Therefore it is necessary to construct a distinct version of the command interpreter for each combination of the optional subsystems.

An important design problem is the structure of the program library from which each version of the software is built. This library will contain individual OIS compilation units, test programs for these, and possibly some of the more popular combinations ready-linked. In practice, such a library should have facilities for the management of different versions of the software, but we do not pursue that point here. (Such facilities are a major part of an APSE.)

The OIS commands will be provided by five central packages:

- `WP_and_DP_Subsystem`;
- `Diary_Subsystem`;
- `Context_Search_Subsystem`;
- `Telecom_Subsystem`;
- `Speech_Subsystem`.

Of these, `WP_and_DP_Subsystem` is the basic system, and the others provide the software of the optional subsystems.

The basic system contains a core of lower-level facilities that are also required by the optional subsystems, such as the filing subsystem. Therefore we shall separate out these facilities into a low-level package, `Kernel`, that is used by all the central packages. It is essential that *only* `Kernel` is used by the optional subsystems, otherwise they would not be mutually independent. These design decisions lead to the system structure shown in Figure 25.4. This illustrates a specific version of the system in which `Telecom_Subsystem` and `Speech_Subsystem` are *not* included, and hence no code or data required exclusively for these subsystems will appear in the linked system. As an example, `Telecom_Subsystem` will include a resident task for handling the communications hardware, and procedures to execute the associated operator commands; but none of this will be present in the system version illustrated in Figure 25.4.

Note that this structure implies that the four optional packages can be overlaid in store, since no optional package can call another optional package.

We assume that the standard package `Text_IO` will not be used, for various reasons. Firstly, `Text_IO` is unnecessarily general for this application, and its code is likely to be very bulky. Secondly, the input-output requirements of this application are somewhat exotic, and must be handled by appropriate device drivers. (The need for application-specific input-output software is quite common in real-time systems.)

25.4. The task structure

The system is designed for a single operator, but it is possible for the operator to make several commands execute concurrently. Furthermore, each peripheral device should be driven to provide maximum overlap with the other operations. This implies having a task for each device, called a *device driver*. The device drivers will run continuously. They are:

- `Keyboard_Driver`;
- `VDU_Driver` (see also Examples 22.1, 22.2, 22.4);

- `Printer_Driver`;
- `Disk_Driver` (see also Examples 24.4, 24.5);
- `Telecom_Driver`;
- `Speech_Driver` (see also Examples 24.1, 24.2, 24.3).

The last two are parts of the optional telecommunications and speech subsystems.

The overall control of the system is vested in the tasks of type `Main_Task` as described in Section 25.3. `Main_Task` will look like this:

```
task type Main_Task;
task body Main_Task is
   ...
begin
   claim a display window;
   claim the keyboard;
   Interpret_Commands;
   release the keyboard;
   release the display window;
end Main_Task;
```

where the '*claim*' and '*release*' actions will be implemented by entry calls to `Keyboard_Driver` and `VDU_Driver`.

A specific version consisting of:

WP/DP subsystem
diary subsystem
context-search subsystem

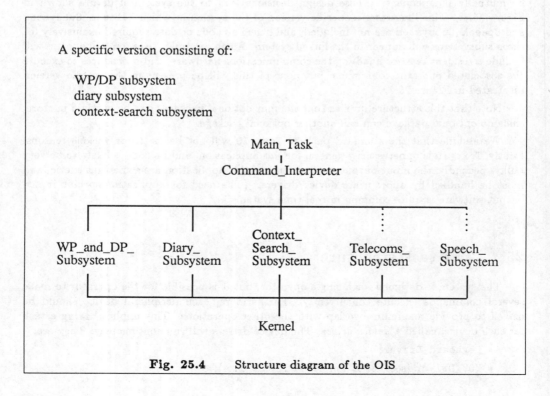

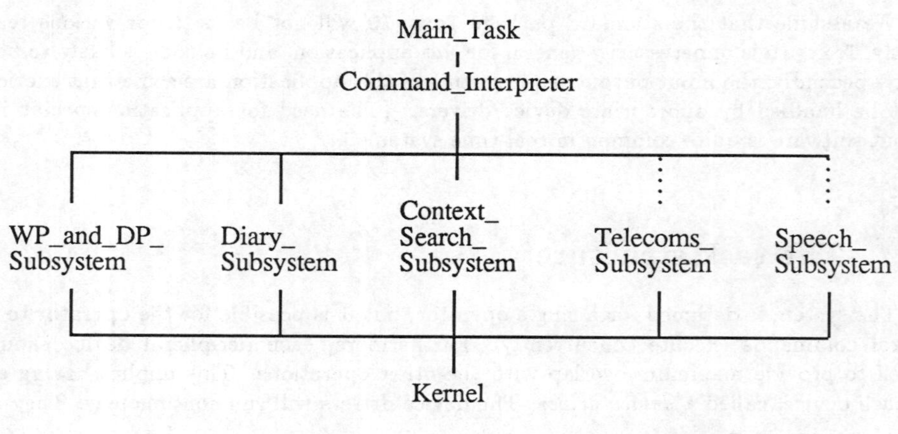

Fig. 25.4 Structure diagram of the OIS

25.5. The command structure

The operator types a command line, consisting of a command name plus appropriate arguments. This sequence of characters is read by the command interpreter. The command name is checked for validity, and the arguments are processed according to the nature of the command. Finally, a procedure is called to execute the command. The command interpreter must handle omitted arguments by inserting default values, unless the default is given by the corresponding procedure.

Each argument is one of the following:

- an input file name;
- an output file name;
- an integer; or
- a string.

It is essential to check all arguments before calling the command procedure, to ensure that the latter is called with valid parameters, and to give the operator an opportunity to retype the command (or perhaps to substitute a valid argument for an invalid one).

This design cleanly separates three distinct activities:

- the input of the command line;
- the processing of the arguments; and
- the actual execution of the command by a command procedure.

By this means, the command procedures are decoupled from the command language, and can (if desired) be called from other parts of the system.

The input of command lines can be encapsulated in the following package:

```
package Command_Input is
   type Command_Type is
         (Edit_Com, Format_Com, Print_Com, ..., Quit_Com);
   type Command is limited private;
   procedure Get_Command (Com : out Command);
      -- reads a command, places the command type and arguments in Com.
   function Arg_Count (Com : Command) return Natural;
      -- yields the number of arguments of Com.
   function Arg (I : Positive; Com : Command) return String;
      -- yields the I'th argument of Com.
   function Type_of (Com : Command) return Command_Type;
private
   implementation details
end Command_Input;
```

We can also encapsulate the processing of arguments in a package. This exports subprograms to process the different kinds of arguments, and an exception that is raised when an argument is found to be invalid:

```
package Argument_Processing is
   procedure Process_Input_Arg   (S : in String; F : out File_Type);
      -- attempts to open file S for input.
   procedure Process_Output_Arg  (S : in String; F : out File_Type);
```

```
      -- attempts to open file S for output.
   procedure Process_Integer_Arg (S : in String; I : out Integer);
      -- attempts to convert S into an integer I.
   Bad_Arg : exception;
      -- raised by above procedures if argument is invalid.
end Argument_Processing;
```

We can now sketch the command interpreter:

```
with Command_Input;          use Command_Input;
with Argument_Processing;    use Argument_Processing;
procedure Interpret_Commands is
   ...
   Current_Com : Command;
begin
   ...
   loop
      Get_Command (Current_Com);
      case Type_of (Current_Com) is
         when Edit_Com =>
            process edit command;
         when Format_Com =>
            process format command;
         when Print_Com =>
            process print command;
         ...
         when Quit_Com =>
            process quit command;
            exit;
      end case;
   end loop;
   ...
end Interpret_Commands;
```

Example 25.1 The edit command

As an example of command interpretation, consider the *edit* command. To edit a file *E* to produce a new file *F*, the operator types:

edit E F

Both files must be existing text files, and *F* must be writable.

Assume that the command procedure corresponding to *edit* is the following:

```
procedure Edit (Old_File, New_File : in File_Type);
```

To process an editing command, the number of command arguments must be checked, the filenames must be checked, the files opened (*E* for input, *F* for output), and then the Edit procedure called. Finally the files must be closed.

The portion of the command interpreter concerned with the *edit* command can now be completed straightforwardly:

```
        when Edit_Com =>
           if Arg_Count (Current_Com) /= 2 then
              Fail ("incorrect number of arguments");
           else
              declare
                 E, F : File_Type;
              begin
                 Process_Input_Arg  (Arg (1, Current_Com), E);
                 Process_Output_Arg (Arg (2, Current_Com), F);
                 Edit (E, F);
                 Close (E);  Close (F);
              end;
           end if;
```

□ *End of Example 25.1*

The operator can terminate an executing command by pressing a special 'break-in' key on the keyboard. As noted in Example 14.7, this event can be signaled by raising a suitably declared exception, Break_in.

The termination of a command cannot always be implemented by a simple transfer of control to the processing of the next command. It is vital that the system be returned to a consistent state so that subsequent commands can be processed correctly. To ensure this, Keyboard_Driver raises the exception Break_in only when data is, or could be, read from the keyboard. In each program unit Break_in may be propagated only if there is no danger of inconsistency resulting; otherwise the program unit must contain an exception handler to restore the system to a consistent state.

Example 25.2 Exception handling in the edit command

Consider the case of the *edit* command above. This could be terminated at any time, possibly leaving one or both files open. That would be inconsistent with normal termination of the *edit* command, since both files are closed before normal termination. Inconsistency could also arise if the second argument is found to be invalid (and Bad_Arg is raised) after processing the first argument: a possibility we neglected above. Here is a more robust implementation of the *edit* command:

```
        when Edit_Com =>
           begin
              if Arg_Count (Current_Com) /= 2 then
                 Fail ("incorrect number of arguments");
                 raise Bad_Arg;
              end if;
              declare
                 E, F : File_Type;
              begin
                 Process_Input_Arg  (Arg (1, Current_Com), E);
                 Process_Output_Arg (Arg (2, Current_Com), F);
                 Edit (E, F);
                 Close (E);  Close (F);
```

```
      end;
   exception
      when Bad_Arg | Break_in =>
         if Is_Open (F) then Close (F); end if;
         if Is_Open (E) then Close (E); end if;
   end;
```

□ *End of Example 25.2*

The strategy for handling Break_in and other exceptions is illustrated in Figure 25.5.

25.6. The database subsystem

Part of Kernel is to be a database subsystem. This subsystem has already been outlined and motivated in Example 18.5, which you should now reread.

In Example 18.5 types were designed to describe and represent the data held in the files of the database. The high-level operations and application programs processing these

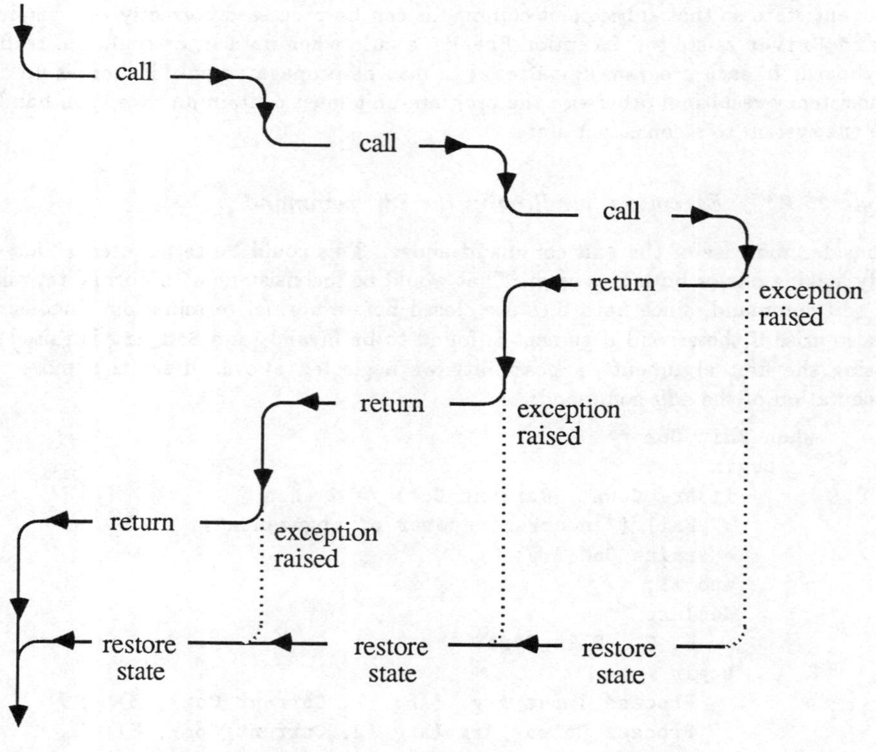

Fig. 25.5 The Break_in exception logic

files do not need to know these details, however, so we design a package providing a more abstract application-level interface. This package exports the basic file operations of creation, deletion, opening, closing, reading and writing. In addition it exports operations for accessing individual fields of a given tuple, given the field descriptions.

```
package Database_IO is
   type File_Type is limited private;
   type File_Mode is (In_File, Out_File);

   type Number is ...;
   type File_Name  is new String (1 .. 20);
   type Field_Name is new String (1 .. 20);
   type Field_Kind is (Alphanumeric, Numeric);
   type Field_Description (Kind : Field_Kind)   is private;
   type Tuple_Description (Nr_Fields : Natural) is private;
   type Tuple_Contents (Total_Alph_Length, Nr_Num_Fields : Natural)
         is private;

   -- File management --
   procedure Get      (Desc : out Tuple_Description);
      -- reads a tuple description from the keyboard,
      -- to be used in creating a file.
   procedure Create   (File : in out File_Type;
                       Name : in File_Name;
                       Desc : in Tuple_Description);
      -- creates a file whose tuples conform to Desc.
   procedure Open     (File : in out File_Type;
                       Mode : in File_Mode;
                       Name : in File_Name);
   procedure Close    (File : in out File_Type);
   procedure Delete   (File : in out File_Type);
   procedure Reset    (File : in out File_Type;
                       Mode : in File_Mode);
   function Valid     (File : in File_Type)
            return Boolean;
      -- true iff File is a database subsystem file.

   -- Input and output operations --
   procedure Read         (File : in File_Type;
                           Item : out Tuple_Contents);
   procedure Write        (File : in File_Type;
                           Item : in Tuple_Contents);
   function End_of_File (File : File_Type)
            return Boolean;

   -- Operations on fields --
  function Description      (File : File_Type;
                             Name : Field_Name;
            return Field_Description;
  function Kind             (Desc : Field_Description)
            return Field_Kind;
  function Field_Value      (Item : Tuple_Contents;
```

```
                                Desc : Field_Description)
                return String;
    function Field_Value      (Item : Tuple_Contents;
                               Desc : Field_Description)
                return Number;
    function Field_Length     (Item : Tuple_Contents;
                               Desc : Field_Description)
                return Natural;
    procedure Update_Field    (Item : in out Tuple_Contents;
                               Desc : in Field_Description;
                               Alph : in String);
    procedure Update_Field    (Item : in out Tuple_Contents;
                               Desc : in Field_Description;
                               Num  : in Number);

     Bad_Field : exception;
        -- raised by Description, Field_Value, Field_Length
        -- or Update_Field if the field is non-existent
        -- or of the wrong kind.
  private
     implementation details (see Example 18.5)
  end Database_IO;
```

In terms of the low-level operations provided by `Database_IO` we can now construct high-level database operations such as:

```
  procedure Join (Name1, Name2, Result_Name : in File_Name);
```

and utilities such as the one outlined in the following example.

Example 25.3 *A histogram utility*

We sketch a command to produce a histogram from numbers in a file supported by the database subsystem. The command has two arguments:

histogram F N

This command requests a histogram to be plotted using the contents of the (numeric) field N in the file F. For this purpose the numerical values are to be partitioned into (say) 20 equal intervals. The number of values within each interval will be represented by a column of proportionate height.

The arguments F and N will be processed along the lines indicated in Section 25.6 and Example 25.1, and then a command procedure, `Make_Histogram`, will be called with these as parameters.

The problem with drawing a histogram is that the scales for the axes cannot be determined without accessing the data. On the other hand, to read all the data before plotting anything would lead to poor response times. It would be nicer to plot the histogram incrementally, as the file is scanned. We can achieve this by estimating the maximum field value and the maximum frequency count in any interval. Then we can start plotting. If the estimated maximum count proves to be exceeded, it will be necessary only to replot the histogram (using the available table of counts) before continuing. If the estimated maximum field value proves to be too small, on the other hand, it will be necessary to increase the estimate and start all over again, since the distribution of the values among the intervals will now be different. We assume that the latter eventuality will occur infrequently.

We can now sketch a solution:

```
with Database_IO;  use Database_IO;
procedure Make_Histogram
            (File : in File_Type;  Fieldname : in String) is
   Desc : constant Field_Description
            := Description (File, Fieldname);
   Nr_Intervals : constant := 20;  -- say
   type Interval is range 1 .. Nr_Intervals;
   Count        : array (Interval) of Natural;
   Tuple        : Tuple_Contents;
   Num, Max_Num : Number;
   Max_Count    : Natural;
   Int          : Interval;
   Replotting   : Boolean;
begin
   if Kind (Desc) /= Numeric then
      raise Break_in;
   end if;
   estimate Max_Num by reading a few tuples from File;
   estimate Max_Count as (say)
      3 * (no. of tuples in File) / Nr_Intervals;
   loop
      Replotting := False;
      Count := (1 .. Nr_Intervals => 0);
      plot axes for the histogram, using
         Max_Num and Max_Count to scale them;
      Reset (File, In_File);
      while not End_of_File (File) loop
         Read (File, Tuple);
         Num := Field_Value (Tuple, Desc);
         if Num > Max_Num then
            Max_Num := Num;
            Replotting := True;
            exit;  -- abandon current scan of File
         end if;
         Int := 1 + Interval (Num) * Nr_Intervals /
                        Interval (Max_Num);
         if Count(Int) >= Max_Count then
            Max_Count := some larger value;
            plot a fresh histogram, using Max_Num and Max_Count
                to scale the axes, and using Count to determine
                the height of the histogram in each interval;
         end if;
         adjust the height of the plotted histogram in
```

```
                    interval Int to correspond to Count(Int);
            end loop;
            exit when not Replotting;
        end loop;
    exception
        ...
    end Make_Histogram;
```

From this sketch, the operations required to perform the plotting of the histogram are clear. The initial plotting of the axes would include annotation and would be based upon the estimated maximum field value and the estimated maximum frequency count. The replotting would adjust the vertical scale to allow for larger frequency counts. Rescaling the horizontal axis requires that the field values be reread and recounted, since the boundaries between the histogram intervals are different.

We could now specify in detail a small package encapsulating the histogram plotting operations. These operations in turn would call upon basic plotting operations. The basic plotting operations might well be dependent upon the hardware in use. It is therefore important to have well-defined and simple interfaces at a higher level, so that any change in the basic plotting operations can be accommodated easily.

(*Exercise*: Complete the histogram utility.)

□ *End of Example 25.3*

25.7. The diary subsystem

The operator of the OIS is to maintain the diaries of a number of executives. The executives themselves also have the means to enquire about the status of their diaries via a communications link.

In Section 25.7 we arrived at a design for the database subsystem from the bottom up, that is, by considering the underlying data structures. Here we invert the process by specifying the functionality of the diary subsystem, devoid of any implementation considerations.

The *diary* is clearly an abstract data structure. Each diary entry is identified by a *person* and a *day*. The content of each diary entry is a *message*. We can now define the data flow of the diary subsystem; see Figure 25.6.

The *enquire* command obtains the message in a person's diary on a given day. The *append* command adds a message to the given diary entry. The *make_meeting* command adds a special form of message; a meeting is arranged by an *organizer*, who specifies the persons who are to be present, the time of the meeting, and an *agenda*. The agenda can be changed by the *change_agenda* command, but we provide no means to delete a meeting altogether (other than changing the agenda to *"CANCELED"*).

Since the diary subsystem is already handling short messages, it is convenient to include a *send_message* command here, the recipient being either a single person or a set of persons.

We can now sketch a package declaration for the diary subsystem:

```
    with Calendar;  use Calendar;
```

```
package Diary_Subsystem is
   type Person         is ...;
   type Set_of_Persons is ...;
   type Day            is ...;
   type Message        is ...;

   procedure Enquire        (Executive      : in Person;
                              Date           : in Day;
                              Stored_Message : out Message);
   procedure Append          (Executive   : in Person;
                              Date        : in Day;
                              New_Message : in Message);
   procedure Make_Meeting    (Organizer : in Person;
                              Invitees  : in Set_of_Persons;
                              At        : in Time;
                              Agenda    : in Message);
   procedure Change_Agenda   (Organizer  : in Person;
                              Invitees   : in Set_of_Persons;
                              At         : in Time;
                              New_Agenda : in Message);

   procedure Send_Message    (Recipient    : in Person;
                              Sent_Message : in Message);
   procedure Send_Message    (Recipients   : in Set_of_Persons;
```

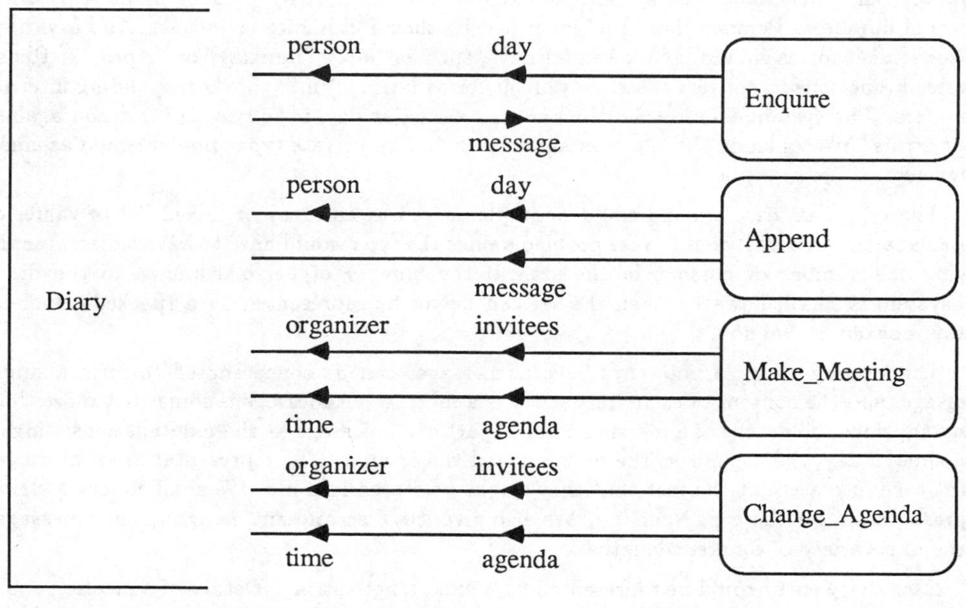

Fig. 25.6 Data flow in the diary subsystem

```
                                    Sent_Message : in Message);
    end Diary_Subsystem;
```

Although the package is not yet complete enough even to compile the declaration, it does capture the essence of Figure 25.6 and we can use it to check our design for consistency and completeness.

On checking the procedure `Make_Meeting`, we should realize that there is no safeguard against 'double-booking'. To allow checks for double-booking, `Make_Meeting` would need an additional parameter that indicates the length of the meeting. We shall assume, however, that the interactive nature of the system makes it unnecessary to complicate the package declaration in this way.

Specifying the procedure `Change_Agenda` raises the question of how the original meeting is to be identified. We assume here that the `Organizer` and `At` parameters are sufficient to identify the meeting. But in that case it seems unnecessary to demand that the invitees be specified again, so let us simplify by removing the parameter `Invitees` of `Change_Agenda`. On the other hand, we need to be able to identify the persons involved in a given meeting, so we add a procedure, `Give_Invitees`, to provide this data.

Checking a specification for consistency and completeness, as we have illustrated, is an important part of design since changes rapidly become more expensive once implementation is under way.

The next stage in the design is to characterize the abstract properties and representation of the main data types. In doing this, we must keep in mind the likely performance requirements. If both `Person` and `Day` were declared as small ranges of integer values, then the diary could be represented efficiently by a direct file or two-dimensional array. Clearly, however, the operator of the system should not have to identify persons or days by their internal numbers. Persons should be identified by their full names or initials. And a variety of convenient forms should be allowed for days, such as *"next Thursday"* or *"April 1"*. Hence we need functions to convert these convenient forms (strings) into the corresponding internal numbers. The system should echo the person's name, or day, in full as a precaution against user errors. We conclude that `Person` and `Day` should be private types implemented as small integers.

The type `Set_of_Persons` could be implemented as an array or linked list of values of type `Person`. An array would cause problems since the type would have to have a discriminant giving the number of persons in the set. If the number of persons known to the diary subsystem is small, however, then the set can better be represented by a (packed) Boolean array indexed by `Person`.

The `Message` type is not easy. Several messages can be concatenated to form a single message, and the content of each diary entry is a message. A message is somewhat more than a string, since the details of a meeting can be (part of) a message — these details consisting of the time of day, the organizer, the invitees, and the agenda. The representation of messages must take into account the fact that they might be stored in a file. We shall choose a string representation for the type `Message`. We also give it a discriminant, `Length`, since messages come in a variety of different lengths.

Each diary entry could be represented by a fixed-length string. Details of a meeting could then be represented by substrings delimited by control characters. The diary entries could be initialized with spaces, or better control characters (such as *NUL*). All these implementation decisions will be encapsulated by the package, so they can easily be changed in the light of experience.

The package declaration can now be revised so that it is complete enough to be compiled:

```
package Diary_Subsystem is
   type Person         is private;
   type Set_of_Persons is private;
   type Day            is private;
   type Message (Length : Natural := 0) is private;
   procedure Enquire        ( ... );
   procedure Append         ( ... );
   procedure Make_Meeting   ( ... );
   procedure Change_Agenda (Organizer  : in Person;
                            At         : in Time;
                            New_Agenda : in Message);
   procedure Give_Invitees (Organizer  : in Person;
                            At         : in Time;
                            Invitees   : out Set_of_Persons);
   procedure Send_Message  ( ... );
   procedure Send_Message  ( ... );
   procedure Put (Item : in Message);
   function Person_Identified_by (Name : String)
         return Person;
   function Day_Identified_by    (Phrase : String)
         return Day;
   function Is_Member (S : Set_of_Persons; P : Person)
         return Boolean;
   function Give_Time (Date : Day; Hours, Mins : Integer)
         return Time;
private
   type Person is Integer range 1 .. 20;   -- say
   type Set_of_Persons is array (Person) of Boolean;
   type Day is range 1 .. 366;
   type Message (Length : Natural := 0) is
         record
            Text : String (1 .. Length);
         end record;
end Diary_Subsystem;
```

Having completed the package declaration, we can now look ahead to implementation of the package body. Note that the format of the diary itself is not yet specified. This is because there is only one diary, which is hidden in the package body. If we define diary entries as follows:

```
type Diary_Entry is Message (60);
```

then the diary could be represented by an array or direct file, indexed by `Person` and `Day`, with elements of type `Diary_Entry`.

Each individual message could be terminated by a control character, say *ETX*, to aid output formatting. The details of a meeting could be represented by a sequence of characters of the form:

SOH time *STX* organizer *ETX* agenda *ETX*

except that in the organizer's own diary entry the second substring should be a list of invitees.

The package body needs access to some additional data such as the range of dates currently being handled, the names and initials of persons known to the diary subsystem, and so on.

The diary will be accessed by the operator and also by executives via the communications link. Therefore access to the diary contents must be controlled by a task to ensure mutual exclusion. Each of the procedures `Enquire` through `Give_Invitees` will invoke an entry of this task. This protects the integrity of the diary against simultaneous updates.

Example 25.4 *Displaying a week of the diary*

To illustrate the use of the diary subsystem, we sketch a command to display a complete week's diary entries for a given person *P*:

diary_week P D

where *D* is any day in the chosen week. This command would be processed as illustrated in Example 25.1. The corresponding command procedure would be:

```
with Diary_Subsystem;  use Diary_Subsystem;

procedure Diary_Week (Executive : in Person; Date : in Day) is
   Day_Message : Message;
begin
   display heading, including name of Executive;
   for Week_Day in the week containing Date loop
      display date of Week_Day;
      Enquire (Executive, Week_Day, Day_Message);
      Put (Day_Message);
   end loop;
end Diary_Week;
```

(*Exercise*: Complete this procedure.)

□ *End of Example 25.4*

To allow executives to use the diary subsystem a simplified user interface would probably be provided, based on menu selection. Whatever the interface, however, the same procedures would be called.

25.8. The context-search subsystem

A large proportion of the information stored in the OIS will be text files processed by the WP subsystem. The operator could be required to maintain an informal catalog of this information in a separate file. It is much more useful, however, to provide a command to search a set of text files for mentions of particular topics. A scan-expression testing for the presence or absence of specified words and prefixes would determine the success or failure of such a search. For example, to find which text files contain references to ICL or IBM in the field of microprogramming, the operator might type the command:

scan S ("ICL" or "IBM") and "micro-"

We can define the syntax of scan-expressions by means of syntax diagrams, similar to those we have used to define the syntax of Ada itself. See Figure 25.7. The semantics of each scan-expression must also be defined. The scan-expression is applied to a text file. A word in a text file is defined to be a sequence of letters, preceded and followed by non-alphabetic characters. The scan-term *"xyz"* is true if and only if the word 'xyz' appears in the file. The scan-term *"xyz-"* is true if and only if a word with prefix 'xyz' appears in the file. Differences of case are ignored in matching. The value of the complete scan-expression is obtained by interpreting *or*, *and* and *not* in the usual way. Thus the scan-expression above will evaluate to true if and only if the text file contains the word 'ICL' or the word 'IBM', *and* contains a word whose prefix is 'micro-'.

The *scan* command applies the scan-expression to all text files in the set indicated by its argument *S*, and displays the names of those files for which the scan-expression is true.

The top level of the *scan* command can now be outlined:

```
check the scan-expression and convert it into a suitable internal representation;
for each text file in S loop
    open the file;
    scan the file, evaluating relevant scan-terms;
    close the file;
    if the value of the scan-expression is true then
        display the name of the file;
    end if;
```

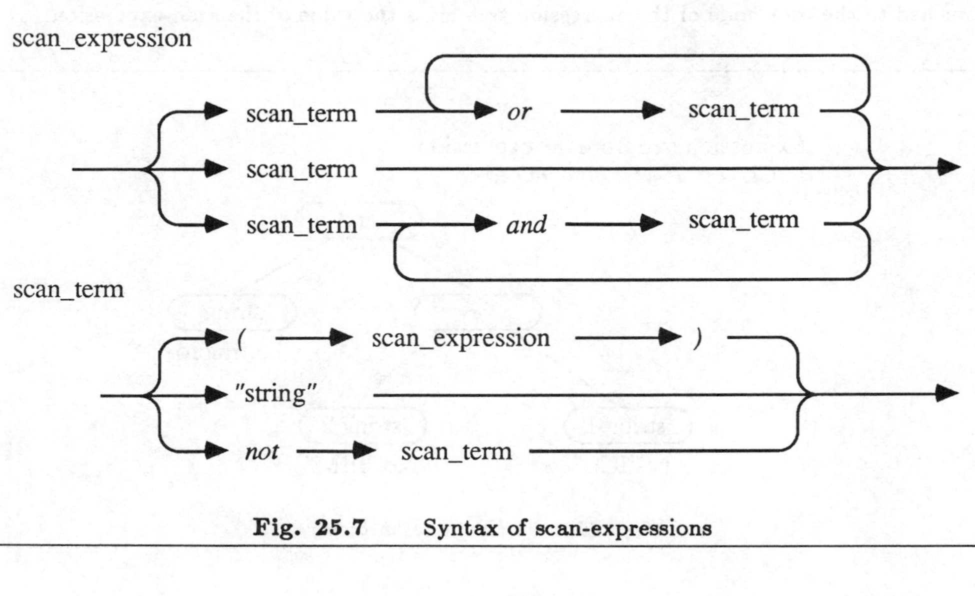

Fig. 25.7 Syntax of scan-expressions

```
    end loop;
```

Presumably the file subsystem in `Kernel` contains some facility for defining sets of text files, but we shall pass over that point here.

The critical issues in this example are the choice of internal representation for a scan-expression, and its use in the scanning of a text file. The details of this internal representation can be encapsulated in a package:

```
    package Context_Search_Subsystem is
        type Expression is limited private;
        procedure Get_Expression (Expr : out Expression);
        procedure Scan_File      (Filename : in String;
                                  Expr     : in Expression;
                                  Result   : out Boolean);
    private
        implementation details
    end Context_Search_Subsystem;
```

The internal representation of a scan-expression must reflect its syntactic structure and must be convenient for evaluation. For this purpose, a tree is the best representation. Each terminal node (leaf) of the expression tree corresponds to a word or prefix to be matched; and each nonterminal node corresponds to one of the operators: *or*, *and*, *not*. Figure 25.8 shows an example of an expression tree.

To evaluate the scan-expression, we can attach a value to each node of the tree. In the tree of Figure 25.8, for example, as soon as we match the word 'ICL' we can attach the value `True` to the *"ICL"* node. Then we can immediately attach the value `True` to the *or* node, regardless of the value attached to the *"IBM"* node. On the other hand, we cannot attach a value to the *and* node until we know the value attached to the *"micro-"* node. If we reach the end of the file without finding a word prefixed by 'micro-', we can attach `False` to the *"micro-"* node, and then deduce the value `False` to attach to the *and* node. The value finally attached to the root node of the expression tree gives the value of the scan-expression.

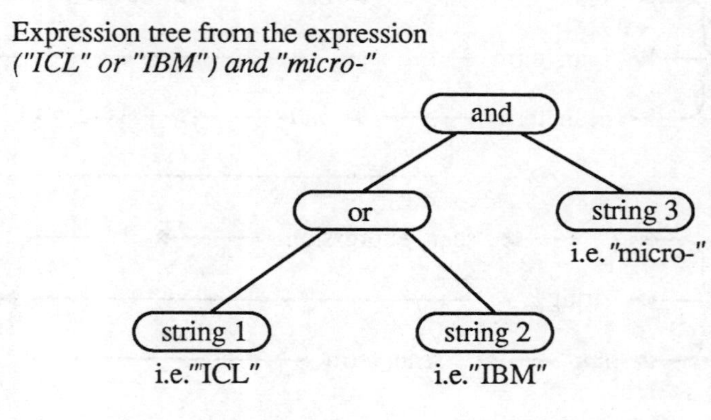

Fig. 25.8 Expression trees

This example illustrates that the value attached to each node can be False, True or unknown, all node values initially being unknown. To represent these possible values, we declare:

```
type Logical is (False, True, Unknown);
```

Note that the literals False and True are now overloaded with the corresponding Boolean literals. By ensuring that every node has one of these three values, we can avoid scanning more of the file than necessary (since False *and* Unknown is False, and True *or* Unknown is True).

To distinguish the four kinds of nodes, we declare:

```
type Node_Kind is (And_Node, Or_Node, Not_Node, String_Node);
```

All nodes contain a value of type Logical, but otherwise different kinds of nodes contain different data. Each *or* node and *and* node has two subtrees, representing the two operands. Each *not* node has one subtree, representing its single operand. Each string node contains only the string itself. Thus the nodes must be represented by variant records. The type Expression will be a pointer to such a record:

```
type Expr_Node (Kind : Node_Kind);
type Expression is access Expr_Node;
type Expr_Node (Kind : Node_Kind) is
      record
         Value : Logical;
         case Kind is
            when Or_Node | And_Node =>
               Left, Right : Expression;
            when Not_Node =>
               Operand : Expression;
            when String_Node =>
               Index : String_Index;
         end case;
      end record;
```

Here we assume that the strings to be matched are stored in some table elsewhere, and are identified by an index into that table. All the above type declarations are placed in the private part of Context_Search_Subsystem, thus completing the package declaration.

In the body of Context_Search_Subsystem, we must provide the bodies of the two subprograms. The procedure Get_Expression can easily grow the expression tree by recursive-descent analysis of the input scan-expression. In other words, we introduce a pair of procedures, Analyze_Term and Analyze_Expr, where the former will analyze (and convert to a tree) a portion of the input that conforms to the syntax of a scan-term, and the latter will likewise analyze a scan-expression. Since a scan-expression can contain a scan-term, and *vice versa*, these procedures will be mutually recursive.

The input scan-expression is read by means of the procedure Get_Symbol, which reads the next symbol and assigns it to a nonlocal variable Current_Symbol. For simplicity we represent each symbol by a single character: '(', ')', '&' (for *and*), '|' (for *or*), '!' (for *not*), or '"'.

We must also introduce a procedure, Analyze_String, to analyze strings in the scan-expression. This must read the string, place it in the string table, and pass out the string's index in the table.

We can now outline the body of Get_Expression:

```
procedure Get_Expression (Expr : out Expression) is
   subtype Symbol is Character;
   Current_Symbol : Symbol;
   procedure Get_Symbol is ...;
     -- reads next symbol and assigns it to Current_Symbol,
     -- or ETX if all symbols have already been read.
   procedure Analyze_String (Index : out String_Index) is ...;
     -- reads and analyzes a string, and sets Index
     -- to its index in the string table.
   procedure Analyze_Term (E : out Expression);
     -- reads and analyzes a scan-term,
     -- and sets E to its tree representation.
   procedure Analyze_Expr (E : out Expression) is
     -- reads and analyzes a scan-expression,
     -- and sets E to its tree representation.
     E1, E2 : Expression;
   begin
     Analyze_Term (E1);
     if Current_Symbol = '|' then
       while Current_Symbol = '|' loop
         Get_Symbol;
         Analyze_Term (E2);
         E1 := new Expr_Node' (Or_Node, Unknown, E1, E2);
       end loop;
     elsif Current_Symbol = '&' then
       while Current_Symbol = '&' loop
         Get_Symbol;
         Analyze_Term (E2);
         E1 := new Expr_Node' (And_Node, Unknown, E1, E2);
       end loop;
     end if;
     E := E1;
   end Analyze_Expr;
   procedure Analyze_Term (E : out Expression) is
     E2 : Expression;
     Index : String_Index;
   begin
     if Current_Symbol = '(' then
       Get_Symbol;
       Analyze_Expr (E);
       if Current_Symbol /= ')' then
         Fail ("bracket mismatch");
         raise Break_in;
       else
         Get_Symbol;
       end if;
```

```
            elsif Current_Symbol = '"' then
               Analyze_String (Index);
               E := new Expr_Node' (String_Node, Unknown, Index);
            elsif Current_Symbol = '!' then
               Get_Symbol;
               Analyze_Term (E2);
               E := new Expr_Node' (Not_Node, Unknown, E2);
            else
               Fail ("unexpected symbol");
               raise Break_in;
            end if;
         end Analyze_Term;
      begin -- Get_Expression
         Get_Symbol;  -- first symbol of the scan-expression
         Analyze_Expr (Expr);
         if Current_Symbol /= ASCII.ETX then
            Fail ("unexpected symbol");
            raise Break_in;
         end if;
      end Get_Expression;
```

Raising an exception on detecting a syntax error would not be appropriate in a compiler. But in this interactive context it is a simple method of signaling the error, and a suitable handler will then allow re-input of the scan-expression.

We omit the details of `Get_Symbol` here. (*Exercise*: Complete this procedure.) So we are left to program `Analyze_String`. Strings must be represented in such as way as to permit efficient matching with the text file. Most words in the text file could be rejected as matches after looking at only one or two characters. In our example, all words not beginning with 'I' or 'm' could immediately be rejected. Therefore whole-word comparisons would be needlessly slow.

The string matching facilities need to be visible inside the bodies of both `Scan_File` and `Analyze_String`, but need not be visible to the rest of `Get_Expression`. We achieve this by defining a package within the body of `Context_Search_Subsystem`, called `String_Matching`, and putting use clauses referring to this only inside `Analyze_String` and `Scan_File`.

`String_Matching` must contain a representation of a set of strings, organized in such a way as to permit efficient matching. An excellent way to do this is by a tree, as illustrated in Figure 25.9 for the strings *"ICL"*, *"IBM"* and *"micro-"*. Some readers might recognize this as a special form of ***finite-state acceptor***. Each branch is labeled by a character, and the nodes are called ***states***. Matching of a word from the text file will start at the initial (root) state. From there the alternatives are 'I' and 'm'. If the first letter of the word does not match either 'I' or 'm' (neglecting case), then scanning can skip immediately to the next word. Suppose, however, that the first character is 'I'. Then we advance along the branch labeled 'I' in the tree, reaching a state where the alternatives are 'C' and 'B'. If the next character of the word matches one of these, then we advance along the corresponding branch to a new state, and so on, otherwise the word can be skipped as a mismatch.

Some of the states are marked as indicating the match of a complete word. Likewise, some states indicate the matching of a prefix. (These sets of states are not necessarily disjoint.)

Filling in the details, we arrive at the declaration of package String_Matching:

```
package String_Matching is
   subtype String_Index is Positive;
   type String_Kind is (Word, Prefix);
   type State is limited private;
   procedure Initial
               (S : out State);
      -- sets S to the initial (root) state.
   procedure Next
               (C : in Character;
                S : in out State;
                Failed : out Boolean);
      -- changes S to the state reached from S by the
      -- branch labeled C, if such a branch exists.
   procedure Add_Branch
               (C : in Character;
                S : in out State);
      -- adds a branch to the tree from state S, labeled
      -- C, and changes S to the resulting new state.
   procedure Make_Matched
               (S : in State;
                K : in String_Kind);
      -- marks state S as a matching state of kind K, and
      -- assigns a unique index for the matched string.
   procedure Check_Matched
               (S : in State;
                K : in String_Kind;
                Matched : out Boolean;
                Index   : out String_Index);
      -- sets Matched to True if S is a matching state of kind K,
      -- and sets Index to the index of the matched string.
```

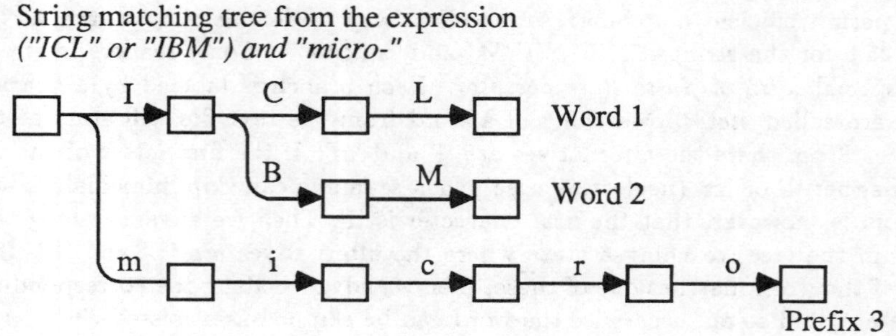

Fig. 25.9 String matching trees

```
    private
        implementation details
    end String_Matching;
```

We now describe a possible representation for the string matching tree. Each state is represented by (a pointer to) a record, in which the components have the following significance. `First_Branch` is a pointer to a linked list of the branches that lead out of this state. `Match(Word)` is *either* the index of a word matched at this state, *or* zero (indicating that no complete word is matched here). Similarly, `Match(Prefix)` is either the index of a prefix matched at this state or zero.

```
        type Branch_Record;
        type Branch_Ptr is access Branch_Record;
        type Branch_Record is
              record
                  Label       : Character;
                  Destination : State;
                  Alternative : Branch_Ptr;
              end record;
        type State_Node;
        type State is access State_Node;
        type Match_Array is array (String_Kind) of Natural;
           -- nonzero => the index of the matching string
           -- zero    => no match
        type State_Node is
              record
                  First_Branch : Branch_Ptr;
                  Match        : Match_Array;
              end record;
```

And here is the corresponding package body:

```
    package body String_Matching is
        String_Count  : Natural := 0;
        Initial_State : State := new State_Node' (null, (0, 0));
        procedure Initial
                    (S : out State) is
        begin
           S := Initial_State;
        end Initial;
        procedure Next
                    (C : in Character;
                     S : in out State;
                     Failed : out Boolean) is
           B : Branch_Ptr := S.First_Branch;
        begin
           loop
              if B = null then
                 Failed := True;
                 return;
```

```
            elsif B.Label = C then
               Failed := False;
               S := B.Destination;
               return;
            else
               B := B.Alternative;
            end if;
         end loop;
      end Next;

      procedure Add_Branch
                  (C : in Character;
                   S : in out State) is
         New_State : constant State
                   := new State_Node' (null, (0, 0));
      begin
         S.First_Branch := new Branch_Record'
                              (C, New_State, S.First_Branch);
         S := New_State;
      end Add_Branch;

      procedure Make_Matched
                  (S : in State;
                   K : in String_Kind) is
      begin
         String_Count := String_Count + 1;
         S.Match(K) := String_Count;
      end Make_Matched;

      procedure Check_Matched
                  (S : in State;
                   K : in String_Kind;
                   Matched : out Boolean;
                   Index   : out String_Index) is
      begin
         if S.Match(K) = 0 then
            Matched := False;
         else
            Matched := True;
            Index := S.Match(K);
         end if;
      end Check_Matched;

   end String_Matching;
```

The string matching tree is initially empty. **Analyze_String** checks each input string for legality and also grafts it on to the string matching tree. After the input scan-expression has been completely analyzed, therefore, the string matching tree will have been completely constructed. To avoid excessive detail, the **Analyze_String** procedure below omits one or two of the legality checks.

```
   procedure Analyze_String is
```

```
    use String_Matching;
    Current_State : State;
    No_Branch     : Boolean;
begin
    Initial (Current_State);
    Get_Symbol;
    loop
        if Current_Symbol = '"' then
            Make_Matched (Current_State, Word);
            exit;
        elsif Current_Symbol = '-' then
            Get_Symbol;
            if Current_Symbol = '"' then
                Make_Matched (Current_State, Prefix);
                exit;
            else
                Fail ("misplaced hyphen in string");
                raise Break_in;
            end if;
        elsif Alphabetic (Current_Symbol) then
            convert Current_Symbol to upper case;
            Next (Current_Symbol, Current_State, No_Branch);
            if No_Branch then
                Add_Branch (Current_Symbol, Current_State);
            end if;
            Get_Symbol;
        else
            Fail ("invalid character in string");
            raise Break_in;
        end if;
    end loop;
end Analyze_String;
```

All letters are converted to a single case, in order to facilitate case-independent comparisons.

(*Exercise*: Complete the procedure `Scan_File`. The matching is performed by a single scan of the text file, stopping as soon as the value of the scan-expression is known.)

25.9. Diagram drawing

The basic WP subsystem is not presented here. It could be based upon `Editing_Service` (Example 17.8) and `Format_Text` (Case Study III, Section 16.5). The latter text formatter was exceedingly simple, however, and a much more powerful facility would be provided in our OIS. In particular, the ability to embed simple diagrams within the text is a substantial advantage. With high-resolution displays and printers, the display and printing of diagrams is not difficult.

The diagram system is to work by defining a rectangle of white space within which lines and text can be placed. For simplicity, we shall consider only straight lines and textual annotation. Such diagrams are to be input using a pointing mechanism (light-pen or mouse), so that the operator can, in effect, draw within the rectangle. It must also be possible to control the functions performed, by means of buttons on the mouse, or perhaps by pointing the light-pen to control points on the screen outside the rectangle. Clearly the implementation details are device-dependent, so our aim should be to encapsulate them within a package whose interface describes the control mechanism at an abstract (device-independent) level.

Each diagram has a textual description embedded within the text formatter's source file, presumably bracketed by a pair of special tokens to distinguish it from the ordinary text. Our package must provide a procedure to create such a description automatically from a diagram 'drawn' by the operator, as well as a procedure to redraw a diagram from its description. So we can start to sketch our package:

```
package Graphical_Service is
   type Diagram is limited private;
      -- abstract representation of a diagram.
   procedure Read_Description
               (File : in File_Type;
                Diag : out Diagram);
      -- reads a diagram's textual description from File,
      -- and stores in Diag the corresponding abstract diagram.
   procedure Write_Description
               (File : in File_Type;
                Diag : in Diagram);
      -- takes an abstract diagram Diag and writes its textual
      -- description to File.

   ...
end Graphical_Service;
```

A value of type Diagram will contain the size of the diagram, together with the lines and annotation that make up the diagram. The primitive operations on diagrams are clearly insertion and deletion of lines and annotation. To insert a line or annotation the operator will point to its starting and finishing positions, but to delete a line or annotation the operator need only point to a position near its midpoint. So we add the following declarations to our package:

```
   type X_Coordinate is ...;
   type Y_Coordinate is ...;
   type Position is
         record
            X : X_Coordinate;
            Y : Y_Coordinate;
         end record;
   procedure Insert
               (Diag : in out Diagram;
                Start, Finish : in Position);
      -- inserts a straight line in Diag, between Start and Finish.
   procedure Insert
               (Diag : in out Diagram;
                Start, Finish : in Position;
```

```
                    Annotation : in String);
         -- inserts Annotation in Diag, between Start and Finish.
      procedure Delete
                   (Diag : in out Diagram;
                    Midpoint : in Position);
         -- deletes a line or annotation in Diag
         -- whose midpoint is near Midpoint.
```

On any change, the revised diagram should be displayed to allow the operator to check that the result is satisfactory.

The remaining provisions of the package are the control of the available graphic functions and the input of command information. Here we must have procedures to fix the diagram rectangle, to choose a graphic function, and to choose a diagram position. Thus we complete our package declaration by adding:

```
      type Graphic_Function is
            (Insert_Line, Insert_Annotation, Delete, Set_Size);
      procedure Fix_Rectangle
                   (Diag : in out Diagram;
                    Bottom_Left, Top_Right : Position);
         -- initializes the rectangle for diagram Diag.
      procedure Get_Function
                   (Func : out Graphic_Function);
         -- allows operator to select a graphic function.
      procedure Get_Position
                   (P : out Position);
         -- allows operator to select a diagram position.
```

25.10. Final words

This case study concludes our presentation of the Ada language and of a methodology for program design and implementation. We believe that the methodology is of value even when it is necessary to code programs in other languages. In fact we advocate the use of Ada as a design notation. In particular, the decomposition of a program into loosely-coupled packages and tasks provides a discipline to counter the anarchic tendencies of languages such as BASIC, COBOL and FORTRAN. Whether you are forced to use obsolete software technology of this kind, or are fortunate enough to have the use of an Ada compiler and APSE, we wish you success in the collective effort to raise programming from the status of a black art to that of an engineering discipline!

Exercises 25

25.1. Comment on the degree of coupling introduced into the OIS by the use of the `Break_in` exception, and consider possible alternatives.

25.2. **What difficulties arise from a more precise specification of the graphic function `Delete` specified in the diagram drawing system of Section 25.9?**

Bibliography

Ada 1979 — J. D. Ichbiah *et al.*: Rationale for the design of the Ada programming language. *ACM SIGPLAN Notices 14*, 6 (June 1979).

Ada 1983 — J. D. Ichbiah *et al.*: Ada Programming Language. ANSI/MIL-STD 1815A, U. S. Department of Defense (January 1983).

Ben-Ari 1982 — M. Ben-Ari: *Principles of Concurrent Programming*. Prentice-Hall, Englewood Cliffs, New Jersey (1982).

Brooks 1975 — F. P. Brooks: *The Mythical Man Month*. Addison-Wesley, Reading, Massachusetts (1975).

Brown 1977 — P. J. Brown (editor): *Software Portability — an Advanced Course*. Cambridge University Press, Cambridge, England (1977).

DeMarco 1979 — T. DeMarco: *Structured Analysis and System Specification*. Prentice-Hall, Englewood Cliffs, New Jersey (1979).

Dijkstra 1976 — E. W. Dijkstra: *A Discipline of Programming*. Prentice-Hall, Englewood Cliffs, New Jersey (1976).

Findlay 1985 — W. Findlay and D. A. Watt: *Pascal — an Introduction to Methodical Programming*. Pitman, London—Boston (1985).

Gane 1979 — C. Gane and T. Sarson: *Structured Systems Analysis*. Prentice-Hall, Englewood Cliffs, New Jersey (1979).

Gries 1981 — D. Gries: *The Science of Programming*. Springer-Verlag, New York—Heidelberg—Berlin (1981).

Hansen 1973 — Per Brinch Hansen: *Operating System Principles*. Prentice-Hall, Englewood Cliffs, New Jersey (1973).

Jackson 1974 — M. Jackson: *Principles of Program Design*. Academic Press, New York (1974).

Knuth 1968 — D. E. Knuth: *The Art of Computer Programming*, Vol. 1 (*Fundamental Algorithms*). Addison-Wesley, Reading, Massachusetts (1968).

Knuth 1973 — D. E. Knuth: *The Art of Computer Programming*, Vol. 3 (*Sorting and Searching*). Addison-Wesley, Reading, Massachusetts (1973).

Myers 1976 — G. J. Myers: *Software Reliability*. Wiley-Interscience, New York (1976).

Myers 1979 — G. J. Myers: *The Art of Software Testing*. Wiley-Interscience, New York (1979).

Nissen 1983 — J. C. D. Nissen and P. L. Wallis: *Portability and Style in Ada*. Cambridge University Press, Cambridge, England (1983).

Wichmann 1976 B. A. Wichmann: Ackermann's function — a study in the efficiency of calling procedures. *BIT 16*, 103–110 (1976).

Yourdon 1978 E. Yourdon and L. Constantine: *Structured Design*. Prentice-Hall, Englewood Cliffs, New Jersey (1978).

Answers to Selected Exercises

Answers 2

2.1.

```
Change : Integer := Payment - Price;  -- assumed >= 0
Quarters, Dimes, Nickels, Cents : Integer;
...
Quarters := Change / 25;  Change  := Change mod 25;
Dimes    := Change / 10;  Change  := Change mod 10;
Nickels  := Change / 5;
Cents    := Change mod 5;
```

2.2.

```
with Text_IO;  use Text_IO;
procedure Show_International_Times is
   package Int_IO is new Integer_IO (Integer);  use Int_IO;
   New_York_GMT : constant Integer := -5;
   Tokyo_GMT    : constant Integer := +9;
   H : Integer range 0 .. 23;
   M : Integer range 0 .. 59;
begin
   Get (H);  Get (M);  -- get GMT time
   Put ("Time in New York: ");
   Put ((H + New_York_GMT) mod 24, Width => 2);
   Put (':');  Put (M, Width => 2);
   Put ("Time in Tokyo: ");
   Put ((H + Tokyo_GMT) mod 24, Width => 2);
   Put (':');  Put (M, Width => 2);
end Show_International_Times;
```

Answers 4

4.1. Add the declaration:

```
PM : Boolean;
```

After the statements computing H, M and S insert:

```
PM := H >= 12;
if PM then H := H - 12; end if;
if H = 0 then H := 12; end if;
```

and after 'Put(S);' insert:

```
if PM then Put (" PM"); else Put (" AM"); end if;
```

Answers 6

6.2.

```
with Text_IO;  use Text_IO;
procedure Calculate is
   package Int_IO is new Integer_IO (Integer);  use Int_IO;
   Accumulator, Operand : Integer;
   Operation : Character;
begin
   Get (Accumulator);  Get (Operation);
   while Operation /= '=' loop
      Get (Operand);
      if Operation = '+' then
         Accumulator := Accumulator + Operand;
      elsif Operation = '-' then
         Accumulator := Accumulator - Operand;
      elsif Operation = '*' then
         Accumulator := Accumulator * Operand;
      elsif Operation = '/' then
         Accumulator := Accumulator / Operand;
      end if;
      Get (Operation);
   end loop;
   Put (Accumulator);  New_Line;
end Calculate;
```

6.3. (a) Similar to Example 6.2, but set `Power` to `10**(D-1)` and `Nr_Digits` to `D`, and remove the if statement that writes each comma.

(b) Add the declaration:

```
Leading_Zero : Boolean := True;
```

Replace the statement that writes each digit by:

```
if Next_Digit = 0 and Leading_Zero then
   Put ('*');
else
   Leading_Zero := False;
   Put (Character'Val (Next_Digit + Zero_Pos));
end if;
```

(c)

```
Ch       : Character := ' ';
Negative : Boolean := False;
...
while Character = ' ' loop
   Get (Ch);
end loop;
if Character = '-' then
   Negative := True;  Get (Ch);
elsif Character = '+' then
   Get (Ch);
```

```
   end if;
   N := 0;
   while Ch in '0' .. '9' loop
      N := 10 * N + Character'Pos (Ch) - Character'Pos ('0');
      Get (Ch);
   end loop;
   if Negative then
      N := - N;
   end if;
```

(Unlike 'Get(N);', this reads the character following the literal.)

Answers 7

7.1. (a)

```
package Month_IO is new Enumeration_IO (Months);  use Month_IO;
...
Put (Year, Width => 4);  Put (' ');
Put (Month);  Put (' ');  Put (Day, Width => 1);
```

(b)

```
Put (Day, Width => 1);  Put ('/');
Put (Months'Pos (Month) + 1, Width => 1);
Put ('/');  Put (Year mod 100, Width => 2);
```

7.2.

```
with Text_IO;  use Text_IO;
procedure Identify_Chemical_Elements is
   type Symbols is (H,He,Li,Be,...);
   type Names   is (Hydrogen,Helium,Lithium,Beryllium,...);
   package Symbol_IO is Enumeration_IO (Symbols);  use Symbol_IO;
   package Name_IO   is Enumeration_IO (Names);    use Name_IO;
   subtype Atomic_Numbers is
         Positive range 1 .. Symbols'Pos (Symbols'Last) + 1;
   Name   : Names;
   Number : Atomic_Numbers;
begin
   while not End_of_File loop
      Get (Name);
      Number := Names'Pos (Name) + 1;
      Put (Name, Width => 12, Set => Lower_Case);  Put ("  ");
      Put (Number, Width => 3);  Put ("  ");
      Put (Symbols'Val (Number - 1), Set => Upper_Case);
      New_Line;
      Skip_Line;
   end loop;
end Identify_Chemical_Elements;
```

(This writes the atomic symbol in upper case, such as 'HE' for helium. Enumeration_IO does not provide for upper-and-lower-case output, such as 'He'.)

Answers 8

8.1.

```
with Text_IO;  use Text_IO;
procedure Count_Characters is
   Ch : Character;
   Nr_Letters, Nr_Digits, Nr_Punctuations : Natural := 0;
begin
   while not End_of_File loop
      Get (Ch);
      case Ch is
         when 'A'..'Z' | 'a'..'z' =>
            Nr_Letters := Nr_Letters + 1;
         when '0'..'9' =>
            Nr_Digits := Nr_Digits + 1;
         when '.' | '!' | '?' | ':' | ';' | ',' =>
            Nr_Punctuations := Nr_Punctuations + 1;
         when others =>
            null;
      end case;
   end loop;
   write Nr_Letters, Nr_Digits and Nr_Punctuations;
end Count_Characters;
```

8.3.

```
with Text_IO;  use Text_IO;
procedure Make_Arithmetic_Table is
   type Operations is (Addition,Subtraction,Multiplication);
   package Op_IO  is new Enumeration_IO (Operations);  use Op_IO;
   package Int_IO is new Integer_IO (Integer);  use Int_IO;
   N  : Integer;
   Op : Operations;
begin
   Get (N);  Get (Op);
   Put (Op, Set => Upper_Case);  Put (" TABLE FOR 1 .. ");
   Put (N, Width => 1);  New_Line (2);
   for L in 1 .. N loop
      for R in 1 .. N loop
         Put ("  ");
         case Op is
            when Addition =>
               Put (L + R);
            when Subtraction =>
               Put (L - R);
            when Multiplication =>
               Put (L * R);
         end case;
      end loop;
      New_Line;
   end loop;
end Make_Arithmetic_Table;
```

Answers 9

9.1. See Example 16.2.

9.3. For the sake of simplicity, the following program uses the default format for floating-point numbers. It could easily be improved in this respect.

```
with Text_IO;  use Text_IO;
procedure Plot_Polynomial is
   package Real_IO is new Float_IO (Float);  use Real_IO;
   C3, C2, C1, C0 : Float;  -- polynomial coefficients
   First_X, Last_X, X_Interval, Y_Interval : Float;
   Plot_Width : Positive := 70;
begin
   Get (C3);  Get (C2);  Get (C1);  Get (C0);
   Get (First_X);  Get (Last_X);
   Get (X_Interval);  Get (Y_Interval);
   Put ("Graph of  y = ");
   Put (C3);  Put ("*x**3 + ");  Put (C2);  Put ("*x**2 + ");
   Put (C1);  Put ("*x + ");     Put (C0);  New_Line;
   Put ("y interval: ");  Put (Y_Interval);  New_Line(2);
   for I in 0 .. Integer ((Last_X - First_X) / X_Interval) loop
      declare
         X : Float := First_X + Float(I) * X_Interval;
         Y : Float := ((C3 * X + C2) * X + C1) * X + C0;
         Scaled_Y : Integer := Integer (Y / Y_Interval);
      begin
         Put (X);
         if Scaled_Y in 0 .. Plot_Width then
            if Scaled_Y > 0 then
               Put ('|');
               for Column in 1 .. Scaled_Y - 1 loop
                  Put (' ');
               end loop;
            end if;
            Put ('+');
         else
            Put ('|');
         end if;
         New_Line;
      end;
   end loop;
end Plot_Polynomial;
```

Answers 10

10.1.

```
with Text_IO;  use Text_IO;
procedure Count_Letters is
   package Int_IO is new Integer_IO (Integer);  use Int_IO;
   subtype Letters is Character range 'A' .. 'Z';
   Count : array (Letters) of Natural := (Letters => 0);
   Total : Natural := 0;
   Ch    : Character;
begin
   while not End_of_File loop
      Get (Ch);
      case Ch is
         when 'A'..'Z' | 'a'..'z' =>
            if Ch in 'a' ..'z' then
               Ch := Character'Val (Character'Pos (Ch) -
                                    Character'Pos ('a') +
                                    Character'Pos ('A'));
            end if;
            Count(Ch) := Count(Ch) + 1;
            Total := Total + 1;
         when others =>
            null;
      end case;
   end loop;
   for Letter in Letters loop
      Put (Letter);
      Put (100 * Count(Letter) / Total, Width => 4);
      New_Line;
   end loop;
end Count_Letters;
```

10.4.

```
with Text_IO;  use Text_IO;
procedure Filter_Car_Data is
   License   : String (1 .. 8);
   Make      : String (1 .. 12);
   Sale_Date : String (1 .. 8);
   Date1     : constant String := "80/08/01";
   Date2     : constant String := "82/01/31";
begin
   while not End_of_File loop
      Get (License);  Get (Make);  Get (Sale_Date);
      if Sale_Date >= Date1 and Sale_Date <= Date2 then
         Put (License);  Put (Make);  Put (Sale_Date);
         New_Line;
      end if;
      Skip_Line;
   end loop;
end Filter_Car_Data;
```

Answers 11

11.2.

```
with Text_IO;  use Text_IO;
procedure Paginate_Directory is
   Max_Row, Max_Col : Positive;
begin
   Get (Max_Row);  Get (Max_Col);  Skip_Line;
   declare
      Max_Entry : constant Positive := Max_Row * Max_Col;
      type Directory_Entries is
            record
               Name   : String (1 .. 20);
               Number : String (1 .. 12);
            end record;
      Page : array (1 .. Max_Entry) of Directory_Entries;
      Last_Entry : Natural range 0 .. Max_Entry;
      Last_Row   : Positive range 1 .. Max_Row;
      Last_Col_in_Last_Row,
      Last_Col_in_This_Row : Positive range 1 .. Max_Col;
      Index : Positive;
   begin
      while not End_of_File loop
         -- read and store one page of entries --
         Last_Entry := 0;
         while Last_Entry < Max_Entry and not End_of_File loop
            Last_Entry := Last_Entry + 1;
            Get (Page(Last_Entry).Name);
            Get (Page(Last_Entry).Number);
            Skip_Line;
         end loop;
         -- write one page of entries --
         if Last_Entry mod Max_Col = 0 then
            Last_Row := Last_Entry / Max_Col;
            Last_Col_in_Last_Row := Max_Col;
         else
            Last_Row := Last_Entry / Max_Col + 1;
            Last_Col_in_Last_Row := Last_Entry mod Max_Col;
         end if;
         Put (Page(1).Name);  Put (" - ");
         Put (Page(Last_Entry).Name);  New_Line (2);
         for Row in 1 .. Last_Row loop
            -- write one row --
            if Row = Last_Row then
               Last_Col_in_This_Row := Last_Col_in_Last_Row;
            else
               Last_Col_in_This_Row := Max_Col;
            end if;
            Index := Row;
```

```
                for Col in 1 .. Last_Col_in_This_Row loop
                   Put (Page(Index).Name);
                   Put (Page(Index).Number);
                   Put ("    ");
                   Index := Index + Last_Row;
                   if Col > Last_Col_in_Last_Row then
                      Index := Index - 1;
                   end if;
                end loop;
                New_Line;
             end loop;
             New_Page;
          end loop;
       end;
    end Paginate_Directory;
```

Answers 12

12.1. See Example 16.2.

12.5.

```
function Reverse (S : String) return String is
   R : String (S'Range);
begin
   for Offset in 0 .. S'Length - 1 loop
      R(R'First+Offset) := S(S'Last-Offset);
   end loop;
   return R;
end Reverse;

function Stripped (S : String) return String is
   First, Last : Positive range S'Range;
begin
   First := S'First;
   while S(First) = ' ' loop
      if First = S'Last then
         return "";
      end if;
      First := First + 1;
   end loop;
   Last := S'Last;
   while S(Last) = ' ' loop
      Last := Last - 1;
   end loop;
   return S(First..Last);
end Stripped;
```

12.8.

```
procedure Put_in_Words (N : Sub_Million) is
begin
```

```
   if N < 20 then
      case N is
         when  1        =>  Put ("one");
         when  2        =>  Put ("two");
         ...
         when 19        =>  Put ("nineteen");
         when others    =>  null;
      end case;
   elsif N < 100 then
      case N / 10 is
         when  2        =>  Put ("twenty");
         when  3        =>  Put ("thirty");
         ...
         when  9        =>  Put ("ninety");
         when others    =>  null;
      end case;
      if N mod 10 /= 0 then
         Put (" ");  Put_in_Words (N mod 10);
      end if;
   elsif N < 1000 then
      Put_in_Words (N / 100);  Put (" hundred");
      if N mod 100 /= 0 then
         Put (" ");  Put_in_Words (N mod 100);
      end if;
   else
      Put_in_Words (N / 1000);  Put (" thousand");
      if N mod 1000 /= 0 then
         Put (" ");  Put_in_Words (N mod 1000);
      end if;
   end if;
end Put_in_Words;
```

12.10.

```
procedure Print_Banner (Headline : in String) is
   subtype Image_Rows is String (1 .. 5);
   type Letter_Images is array (1 .. 5) of Image_Rows;
   Image : constant array ('A' .. 'Z') of Letter_Images
           := ( ...,
                 'C' => (" CCCC",
                         "C    ",
                         "C    ",
                         "C    ",
                         " CCCC"),
                 ...
              );
   Blank_Row : constant Image_Rows := "     ";
   Gap       : constant String     := "  ";
begin
   for Row in Letter_Images'Range loop
      for I in Headline'Range loop
```

```
            if Headline(I) in Image'Range then
               Put (Image(Headline(I))(Row));
            else
               Put (Blank_Row);
            end if;
            Put (Gap);
         end loop;
         New_Line;
      end loop;
   end Print_Banner;
```

Answers 13

13.1.

```
package Earth is
   Diameter   : constant Float := 12.757e3;  -- Km.
   Population : Natural;
   type Continents is (Africa, Antarctica, Asia, Australasia,
                       Europe, North_America, South_America);
   Area : constant array (Continents) of Float
        :=   (30.3e6, 13.0e6, 44.5e6, 8.9e6,
               9.9e6, 24.4e6, 17.8e6);  -- sq.Km.
end Earth;
...
Earth.Population := 5e9;
...
use Earth;  ...  Population := 5e9;
```

13.2.

```
package Statistical_Functions is
   function Mean    (R : List_of_Reals) return Float;
   function Std_Dev (R : List_of_Reals) return Float;
   function Median  (R : List_of_Reals) return Float;
end Statistical_Functions;

package body Statistical_Functions is
   function Mean (R : List_of_Reals) return Float is
      Sum : Float := 0.0;
   begin
      for I in R'Range loop
         Sum := Sum + R(I);
      end loop;
      return Sum / R'Length;
   end Mean;
   ...
end Statistical_Functions;
```

13.4. (a)

```
package Matrix_Algebra is
```

```
   type Matrix is array (Integer range <>,
                         Integer range <>) of Float;
   procedure Add_Matrices
               (M1, M2  : in Matrix;
                Sum     : out Matrix);
   procedure Multiply_Matrices
               (M1, M2  : in Matrix;
                Product : out Matrix);
   procedure Invert_Matrix
               (M       : in Matrix;
                Inv     : out Matrix);
end Matrix_Algebra;
package body Matrix_Algebra is
   procedure Add_Matrices
               (M1, M2  : in Matrix;
                Sum     : out Matrix) is
   begin
      -- Assume M1'Range(1) = M2'Range(1) = Sum'Range(1)
      --    and M1'Range(2) = M2'Range(2) = Sum'Range(2).
      for I in Sum'Range loop
         for J in Sum'Range(2) loop
            Sum(I,J) := M1(I,J) + M2(I,J);
         end loop;
      end loop;
   end Add_Matrices;
   ...
end Matrix_Algebra;
```

(b)

```
package Matrix_Algebra is
   type Matrix is private;
   procedure Add_Matrices
               (M1, M2  : in Matrix;
                Sum     : out Matrix);
   procedure Multiply_Matrices
               (M1, M2  : in Matrix;
                Product : out Matrix);
   procedure Invert_Matrix
               (M       : in Matrix;
                Inv     : out Matrix);
private
   type Matrix is array (Integer range <>,
                         Integer range <>) of Float;
end Matrix_Algebra;
```

The package body is not affected.

13.5.

```
package Flex_String_Handler is
   Max_Length : constant Positive := 100;
   type Flex_String is limited private;
```

```
      function Length  (X : Flex_String) return Natural;
      function Flex    (S : String) return Flex_String;
      procedure Append (X1 : in Flex_String;
                        X2 : in out Flex_String);
   private
      type Flex_String is
           record
              Length : Natural range 0 .. Max_Length;
              Ch     : String (1 .. Max_Length);
           end record;
   end Flex_String_Handler;

   package body Flex_String_Handler is
      function Length (X : Flex_String) return Natural is
      begin
         return X.Length;
      end Length;

      function Flex (S : String) return Flex_String is
         X : Flex_String;
      begin
         X.Length := S'Length;
         X.Ch(1..S'Length) := S;
         return X;
      end Flex;

      procedure Append (X1 : in Flex_String;
                        X2 : in out Flex_String) is
      begin
         for I in X1'Range loop
            X2.Length := X2.Length + 1;
            X2.Ch(X2.Length) := X1.Ch(I);
         end loop;
      end Append;
   end Flex_String_Handler;
```

If Flex_String were made private, Flex would have to pad its result with spaces to ensure that = and /= produce correct results.

Answers 14

14.1. Replace the body of the for loop by a block containing a handler for Data_Error:

```
      for State in USA loop
         begin
            Get (State_Pop);  Get (State_Area);  Skip_Line;
            write State, State_Pop, State_Area, etc.;
            update Total_Pop and Total_Area;
         exception
```

```
         when Data_Error =>
            Put ("WARNING: data for ");  Put (State);
            Put (" is invalid");  New_Line;
            Skip_Line;
      end;
   end loop;
```

14.2. The same exception part cannot be executed again. So if the subprogram Reboot_System propagates Transmission_Error, the exception will be propagated out of the unit shown.

14.3.

```
procedure Search
            (List     : in Lists;
             Target   : in Items;
             Matched  : out Boolean;
             Pos      : out Integer) is
   Mid  : Integer;
   Low  : Integer := List'First;
   High : Integer := List'Last;
begin
   loop
      if Low > High then
         Matched := False;
         exit;
      end if;
      Mid := (Low + High)/2;
      if List(Mid) not in List(Low) .. List(High) then
         raise Not_Sorted;
      end if;
      if Target < List(Mid) then
         High := Mid - 1;
      elsif Target > List(Mid) then
         Low := Mid + 1;
      else  -- Target = List(Mid)
         Matched := True;  Pos := Mid;
         exit;
      end if;
   end loop;
end Search;
```

Note that the test on the ordering of the array is very incomplete. A complete test would nullify the efficiency advantage of binary search.

14.4. No: the information lost by raising the exception is just the information that could be useful for a diagnostic message or good error recovery. Moreover, the presence of syntactically incorrect programs can be reasonably anticipated.

Answers 15

15.1.

```
procedure Copy (Source_Filename, Dest_Filename : in String) is
   package Item_IO is new Sequential_IO (Items);  use Item_IO;
   Source_File, Dest_File : File_Type;
   Item : Items;
begin
   Open (Source_File, In_File, Source_Filename);
   Create (Dest_File, Out_File, Dest_Filename);
   while not End_of_File (Source_File) loop
      Read (Source_File, Item);
      Write (Dest_File, Item);
   end loop;
   Close (Source_File);
   Close (Dest_File);
end Copy;
```

15.4.

```
with Direct_IO;
procedure Update_Accounts_Interactively
            (Accounts_Filename_1,
             Accounts_Filename_2 : in String) is
   declarations of Account_Numbers, Money, Dates,
      Accounts, Transactions as before;
   package A1IO is new Direct_IO (Accounts);
   type Pairs is
         record
            Acc_No : Account_Numbers;
            Index  : A1IO.Positive_Count;
         end record;
   package A2IO is new Direct_IO (Pairs);
   Acc_File_1 : A1IO.File_Type;
   Acc_File_2 : A2IO.File_Type;
   A_Trans : Transactions;
   ...
   procedure Update_Account
               (Trans       : in Transactions;
                Acc_File_1 : in A1IO.File_Type;
                Acc_File_2 : in A2IO.File_Type) is
      Index_1   : A1IO.Positive_Count;
      Index_2   : A2IO.Positive_Count;
      Bottom_2 : A2IO.Positive_Count := 1;
      Top_2     : A2IO.Count := A2IO.Size (Acc_File_2);
      Pair      : Pairs;
      Account   : Accounts;
   begin
      -- search Acc_File_2 for the index into Acc_File_1 --
      loop
```

```
         if Bottom_2 > Top_2 then
            raise Data_Error;
         end if;
         Index_2 := (Bottom_2 + Top_2) / 2;
         A2IO.Read (Acc_File_2, Pair, Index_2);
         if Trans.Acc_No < Pair.Acc_No then
            Top_2 := Index_2 - 1;
         elsif Trans.Acc_No > Pair.Acc_No then
            Bottom_2 := Index_2 + 1;
         else  -- Trans.Acc_No = Pair.Acc_No
            Index_1 := Pair.Index;  exit;
         end if;
      end loop;
      -- update the account record in Acc_File_1 --
      A1IO.Read (Acc_File_1, Account, Index_1);
      if Trans.Credit then
         Account.Balance := Account.Balance + Trans.Amount;
      else
         Account.Balance := Account.Balance - Trans.Amount;
      end if;
      A1IO.Write (Acc_File_1, Account, Index_1);
   end Update_Account;

begin
   A1IO.Open (Acc_File_1, A1IO.InOut_File, Accounts_Filename_1);
   A2IO.Open (Acc_File_2, A1IO.In_File, Accounts_Filename_2);
   loop
      ...
      Get_Transaction (A_Trans);
      Update_Account (A_Trans, Acc_File_1, Acc_File_2);
      ...
   end loop;
   A1IO.Close (Acc_File_1);
   A2IO.Close (Acc_File_1);
end Update_Accounts_Interactively;
```

Answers 17

17.1.

```
function List_Length (List_Head : Item_Ptr) return Natural is
begin
   if List_Head = null then
      return 0;
   else
      return 1 + List_Length (List_Head.Next);
   end if;
end List_Length;
```

17.2. (a)

```
procedure Delete_Node
      (Del_Ptr : in Item_Ptr;  Head : in out Item_Ptr) is
   Prev_Ptr : Item_Ptr;
begin
   if Del_Ptr = Head then
      Head := Del_Ptr.Next;
   else
      Prev_Ptr := Head;
      while Prev_Ptr.Next /= Del_Ptr loop
         Prev_Ptr := Prev_Ptr.Next;
      end loop;
      Prev_Ptr.Next := Del_Ptr.Next;
   end if;
end Delete_Node;
```

This operation is awkward when the node to be deleted is not the first in the list. In that case it is necessary to update the Next component of the *previous* node, and therefore to set an access variable (Prev_Ptr) to point to that previous node, which can be done only by searching the list from its head.

(b)

```
type Item_Node;
type Item_Ptr is access Item_Node;
type Item_Node is
   record
      Item       : Items;
      Prev, Next : Item_Ptr;
   end record;

procedure Delete_Node
      (Del_Ptr : in Item_Ptr;  Head : in out Item_Ptr) is
begin
   if Del_Ptr = Head then
      Head := Del_Ptr.Next;
   else
      Del_Ptr.Prev.Next := Del_Ptr.Next;
   end if;
   if Del_Ptr.Next /= null then
      Del_Ptr.Next.Prev := Del_Ptr.Prev;
   end if;
end Delete_Node;
```

17.5. The package declaration would be:

```
package Multi_Directory_Service is
   subtype Names   is String (1 .. 20);
   subtype Numbers is String (1 .. 12);
   type Directories is limited private;

   procedure Insert_Entry
```

```
                    (New_Name   : in Names;
                     New_Number : in Numbers;
                     Directory  : in out Directories);
   procedure Lookup_Entry
                    (Given_Name  : in Names;
                     Name_Found  : out Boolean;
                     Corr_Number : out Numbers;
                     Directory   : in Directories);
   procedure Copy_Directory
                    (From : in Directories;
                     To   : out Directories);
private
   type Directory_Node;
   type Directory_Ptr is access Directory_Node;
   type Directory_Node is
         record
            Name   : Names;
            Number : Numbers;
            Left, Right : Directory_Ptr;
         end record;
   type Directories is
         record
            Root : Directory_Ptr := null;
         end record;
end Multi_Directory_Service;
```

Answers 18

18.1.

```
type Tokens (Kind : Token_Kinds := Word_Token) is
      record
         case Kind is
            when Word_Token =>
               Size : Token_Sizes;
               Text : String (1 .. Max_Token_Size);
            when others =>
               null;
         end case;
      end record;
```

18.2. The critical step is the design of a suitable dynamic data structure with one node for each person, the nodes being connected by pointers representing family relationships. If each married person (or rather the node representing that person) has a pointer to his/her spouse, then parent-child relationships can be represented by a single pointer from each person to his/her mother. Sibling relationships can be represented by a pointer from a father to his oldest offspring, and also from each offspring to his/her next oldest sibling. A record type to describe this, with nearly minimal storage requirements, is as follows:

```
type Sex is (Male, Female);
type Person_Node (Gender : Sex;  Married, Youngest : Boolean);
type Person is access Person_Node;
type Person_Node (Gender : Sex;  Married, Youngest : Boolean);
   record
      Name   : String (1 .. 10);
      Mother : Person;
      case Married is
         when True =>
            Spouse : Person;
            case Gender is
               when Male =>
                  Oldest_Offspring : Person;
               when Female =>
                  null;
            end case;
         when False =>
            null;
      end case;
      case Youngest is
         when True =>
            null;
         when False =>
            Next_Oldest_Sibling : Person;
      end case;
   end record;
```

To manipulate such a complicated variant record is awkward. There is a real danger of referring to a non-existent component, e.g. `P.Oldest_Offspring` when `P.Gender` is `Female`. A more modular and robust solution is to make `Person` a private type, and provide functions such as:

```
function Father (P : Person) return Person;
function Mother (P : Person) return Person;
function Oldest_Sibling (P : Person) return Person;
```

for moving over the tree. These functions can include the necessary checks on the discriminant values, and raise a suitable exception on misuse.

Answers 19

19.1. The accuracy is unlikely to be critical, even 4 digits would be adequate:

```
type Celsius    is digits 4 range -40.0 .. +100.0;
type Fahrenheit is digits 4 range -40.0 .. +212.0;
```

The conversion functions are simpler than with integers:

```
function F_to_C (F: Fahrenheit) return Celsius is
begin
   return Celsius ((F - 32.0) * (5.0/9.0));
end F_to_C;
function C_to_F (C: Celsius) return Fahrenheit is
begin
   return Fahrenheit ((9.0/5.0) * C) + 32.0;
end C_to_F;
```

The disadvantages of floating point are that it would be very slow on computers without floating-point hardware, and that the numbers are likely to occupy more space. Also, input-output of floating-point numbers is slower. The advantage is that programming is easier and fractions of degrees can be handled without difficulty.

19.2. The accuracy of the two scales should be parameterized by a number declaration:

```
Small: constant := 0.01;
type Celsius    is delta 5*Small range -40.0 .. +100.0;
type Fahrenheit is delta 9*Small range -40.0 .. +212.0;
```

The conversion functions are textually similar to those for floating point. The ratio 5.0/9.0 and its inverse must be converted to an explicit fixed-point type. For this conversion, the types `Fahrenheit` and `Celsius` are not suitable because of the limited accuracy that would give to the ratios.

Fixed point is likely to be the most satisfactory for this application. The space and time requirements are similar to those for integers, but fractions of a degree can be handled. Input-output is likely to be fast, even direct digital input from a sensor is possible.

19.3. This is a difficult problem. Briefly, because the conversions involve only small integers, rounding errors do not accumulate. In the fixed-point case, rounding errors can be minimized by choosing the `Small` value for each scale to correspond to the same temperature difference.

19.4.

```
type Mass    is digits 6;  -- Kg.
type Volume  is digits 6;  -- cu.m.
type Density is digits 6;  -- Kg./cu.m.
function Density_of (M : Mass;  V : Volume) return Density is
begin
   return Density (M) / Density (V);
end Density_of;
```

For `Mass` and `Volume`, addition, subtraction and comparisons would be sensible. For `Density`, only comparisons would be sensible. Note that division of two `Density` values would yield a number that could sensibly be interpreted as a ratio, but the Ada type rules would nevertheless treat it as a `Density` value.

19.5.

```
type Mass    is delta 0.001 range 0.0 .. Max_Mass;
type Volume  is delta 1.0e-6 range 0.0 .. Max_Volume;
type Density is delta 0.001 range 0.0 .. Max_Density;
function Density_of (M : Mass;  V : Volume) return Density is
begin
   return Density (M / V);
```

```
end Density_of;
```

19.6. The first version overflows. The second version yields the result 20.0!

Answers 20

20.1. Prototype package private part:

```
private
   type Component_Store is
         array (Positive range <>, Positive range <>) of Real;
   type Matrix_Store (Last_Row, Last_Col : Natural) is
         record
            Component : Component_Store
                              (1 .. Last_Row, 1 .. Last_Col);
         end record;
   type Sparse_Matrix is access Matrix_Store;
```

Prototype package body (in part):

```
package body Sparse_Matrix_Handler is
   ...
   procedure Store
               (A : in out Sparse_Matrix;
                Row, Col : in Positive;
                Component : in Real) is
   begin
      A.Component(Row,Col) := Component;
   end Store;

   procedure Zero
               (A : out Sparse_Matrix;
                Last_Row, Last_Col : in Natural) is
   begin
      A := new Matrix_Store' (Last_Row, Last_Col,
                  (1..Last_Row => (1..Last_Col => 0.0)));
   end Zero;

   ...
end Sparse_Matrix_Handler;
```

These facilities differ from those of conventional 2-dimensional arrays in that the bounds of a Sparse_Matrix object can be changed at any time, by calling Zero.

20.2. The package declaration is:

```
package Contract_Bridge is
   type and subtype declarations as in the text;
   type Deal is array (Position) of Hand;
   function Next (P : Position) return Position;
   function Points_in_Hand (H : Hand) return Natural;
```

```
   procedure Sort (H : in out Hand);
   procedure Display (H : in Deal);
   procedure Deal_Cards (D : out Deal);
end Contract_Bridge;
```

Answers 21

21.1. Add the following function to the body of `Rational_Arithmetic`:

```
function Reduced (R : Rational) return Rational;
   -- returns R with common factors in Num and Den canceled
```

and add the following exception handler to the body of `"+"`:

```
exception
   when Numeric_Error =>
      declare
         XR : Rational := Reduced (X);
         YR : Rational := Reduced (Y);
      begin
         return (XR.Num * YR.Den + YR.Num * XR.Den,
                           XR.Den * YR.Den);
      end;
```

The simple implementation of `Rational_Arithmetic` is very likely to overflow. To avoid this completely is quite hard and would make the code much longer, and so should not be undertaken unless there is a clear need for this. The probability of overflow could be reduced simply by applying `Reduce` to the result of every operation.

21.2. Using subtraction is simple but will raise `Numeric_Error` in many cases, see above. Another simple method is to calculate the rational value approximately using floating point. If the floating-point type is accurate enough, then comparison of the floating-point values will suffice. Lastly, the correct method of evaluating $p/q > r/s$ is to evaluate $ps > qr$, provided that $q > 0$ and $s > 0$.

21.4.

```
package Days_of_Week is
   type Day is private;
   Monday, Tuesday, Wednesday, Thursday,
      Friday, Saturday, Sunday : constant Day;
   function "+" (D : Day; I : Integer) return Day;
   function "-" (D : Day; I : Integer) return Day;
private
   type Day is range 0 .. 6;
   Monday    : constant Day := 0;
   Tuesday   : constant Day := 1;
   Wednesday : constant Day := 2;
   Thursday  : constant Day := 3;
   Friday    : constant Day := 4;
   Saturday  : constant Day := 5;
   Sunday    : constant Day := 6;
```

```
end Days_of_Week;

package body Days_of_Week is
   function "+" (D : Day; I : Integer) return Day is
   begin
      return Day ((Integer (D) + I) mod 7);
   end "+";
   function "-" (D : Day; I : Integer) return Day;
   begin
      return Day ((Integer (D) - I) mod 7);
   end "-";
end Days_of_Week;
```

An alternative solution would be to declare **Day** visibly as an enumeration type. This would imply that the expression **Monday<Sunday** is **True**, which does not accurately model the properties of days of the week. Another difference is that, in the solution above, **Monday**, **Tuesday** and so on are ***objects*** and therefore cannot be overloaded.

21.5.

```
procedure Put (T : Time) is
   Y  : Year_Number;
   M  : Month_Number;
   D  : Day_Number;
   DD : Day_Duration;
   H  : Integer range 0 .. 23;
   M  : Integer range 0 .. 59;
   S  : Integer range 0 .. 86399;
begin
   Split (T, Y, M, D, DD);
   S := Integer (DD);
   H := S / 3600;  S := S mod 3600;
   M := S / 60;    S := S mod 60;
   Put (Y, Width => 1);  Put (':');
   Put (M, Width => 1);  Put (':');
   Put (D, Width => 1);  Put (':');
   Put (H, Width => 1);  Put (':');
   Put (M, Width => 1);  Put (':');
   Put (S, Width => 1);
end Put;
...
Put (Clock);
```

This body assumes that **Put** is available for types **Integer** and **Character**. The procedure **Split** is from package **Calendar**.

Answers 22

22.2.

```
generic
   type Element is private;
   type Index   is (<>);
   type Row     is array (Index range <>) of Element;
   with function ">" (L, R: Element) return Boolean is <>;
function Maximum (V : Row) return Element;

function Maximum (V : Row) return Element is
   Max : Element := V(V'First);
begin
   for I in Index'Succ (V'First) .. V'Last loop
      if V(I) > Max then
         Max := V(I);
      end if;
   end loop;
   return Max;
end Maximum;

type Vector is array (Integer range <>) of Float;
function Maximum_of_Vector is
      new Maximum (Float, Integer, Vector);
function Minimum_of_Vector is
      new Maximum (Float, Integer, Vector, "<");
```

22.5.

```
generic
   type Element is private;
   Q_Size : in Positive;
package Queue_Service is
   procedure Make_Queue_Empty;
   procedure Add (E : in Element);
   procedure Remove (E : out Element);
   function Queue_is_Empty return Boolean;
   Queue_Empty, Queue_Full : exception;
end Queue_Service;

package body Queue_Service is
   type Index is range 1 .. Q_Size;
   Buffer       : array (Index) of Element;
   Front, Rear  : Index;
   Length       : Natural range 0 .. Q_Size;

   procedure Make_Queue_Empty is
   begin
      Length := 0;
      Front := 1;  Rear := Q_Size;
   end Make_Queue_Empty;

   procedure Add (E : in Element) is
   begin
      if Length = Q_Size then
```

```
            raise Queue_Full;
         end if;
         Length := Length + 1;
         Rear := Rear mod Q_Size + 1;
         Buffer(Rear) := E;
      end Add;
      ...
   end Queue_Service;
```

22.6. (a)

```
package Directory_Service is
   subtype Names   is String (1 .. 20);
   subtype Numbers is String (1 .. 12);
   type Directory_Entries is
         record
            Name   : Names;
            Number : Numbers;
         end record;
   procedure Insert_Entry ( ... );
   procedure Lookup_Entry ( ... );
   generic
      with procedure P (E : in out Directory_Entries);
   procedure Traverse;
end Directory_Service;
```

Note that this version must export the type Directory_Entries (which was previously hidden) in order that a procedure can be written and used to instantiate Traverse.

(b)

```
procedure List_One_Entry (E : in out Directory_Entries) is
begin
   Put (E.Name);  Put ("  ");  Put (E.Number);  New_Line;
end List_One_Entry;
procedure List_All_Entries is new Traverse (List_One_Entry);
```

Answers 23

23.1. Shared variables induce common-environment coupling. Rendezvous induces normal coupling.

23.2. The following attempts to keep a balance between insertions and removals when producer and consumer are operating at about the same speed, thus maximizing system throughput.

```
select
   when (Length <= Q_Size/2)  =>
      accept Insert (...) do
```

```
         ...
or
   when (Length >= Q_Size/2)  =>
      accept Remove (...) do
         ...
else
   select
      when (Length < Q_Size)  =>
         accept Insert (...) do
            ...
   or
      when (Length > 0)  =>
         accept Remove (...) do
            ...
   end select;
end select;
```

23.4. The basic idea is to identify each lease and ignore relinquish operations that do not carry the correct identification. The following is a sketch of the solution.

```
type Keys is range 1 .. Max_Key;
...
task Database_Mutex is
   entry Acquire (Lease : in Duration;  Key : out Keys);
   entry Relinquish (Keys);
end Database_Mutex;

task body Database_Mutex is
   Time_Out : Duration;
   This_Key : Keys := Keys'First;
   function Next_Key return Keys is ...;
begin
   loop
      select
         accept Acquire (Lease : in Duration;
                         Key : out Keys) do
            Time_Out := Lease;
            This_Key := Next_Key;
            Key := This_Key;
            dismiss any calls on Relinquish (This_Key);
         end Acquire;
         select
            accept Relinquish (This_Key);
         or
            delay Time_Out;
         end select;
      or
         terminate;
      end select;
   end loop;
```

```
end Database_Mutex;
```

Since leases are not identified *uniquely* this version is not foolproof. Investigate the problem of unique identification yourself. See also [Welsh 1981] (which uses an earlier version of Ada).

23.5.

```
select
   Matrix_Multiplier.Take (Raw_Data, Transform);
   select
      Matrix_Multiplier.Give (Cooked_Data);
      ...
   or
      delay 1.0;
      Log_Error (...);
   end select;
else
   Log_Error ("Matrix_Multiplier cannot take raw data.");
end select;
```

23.6.

```
   Go_Ahead : Event;

   task Multi_Phase;

   task body Multi_Phase is
      ...
   begin
      perform first phase;
      Go_Ahead.Wait;
      perform second phase;
      Go_Ahead.Wait;
      perform third phase;
      ...
   end Multi_Phase;

begin -- parent task
   prepare for second phase;
   Go_Ahead.Signal;
   prepare for third phase;
   Go_Ahead.Signal;
   ...
end;
```

What happens if the parent task signals the event before the `Multi_Phase` task has reached the corresponding call on the `Wait` entry?

23.7.

```
task body Semaphore is
   Tally : Integer;
begin
   accept Initialize (V : in Integer) do
      Tally := V;
   end Initialize;
   loop
```

```
      select
         when Tally > 0 =>
            accept Wait;
            Tally := Tally - 1;
      or
         accept Signal;
         Tally := Tally + 1;
      or
         terminate;
      end select;
   end loop;
end Semaphore;
```

(Semaphores would be a better solution than events for the Multi_Phase task.)

Answers 24

24.1.

```
package Washing_Machine_Control is
   type Speed_Setting   is (Low, High);
   type Program_Setting is range 1 .. 4;  -- for example
   procedure Get_Hot_Water;
   procedure Get_Cold_Water;
   procedure Eject_Waste;
   procedure Heat_Water;
   procedure Spin (Speed : in Speed_Setting);
   procedure Lock_Door;
   procedure Select_Program (Choice : in Program_Setting);
end Washing_Machine_Control;
```

24.2. If the Random_Numbers package is used by two or more tasks concurrently (which is likely in a simulation program), problems will arise because the seed encapsulated by the package will be a shared variable. If any two tasks call Random 'simultaneously', the seed could end up with an indeterminate value. (This is *not* the same as a random value!)

APPENDICES

A

Lexicon and Syntax

A.1. Lexicon

Outside a string literal, the double hyphen '`--`' followed by the text to the end of the line is a *comment.*

Spaces, ends of lines and comments are *separators.*

No separator may appear within a numeric literal, identifier, reserved word or delimiter.

At least one separator must appear between consecutive numeric literals, identifiers and reserved words.

Outside character literals and string literals, the following transliterations have no effect on the meaning of a program:

- Any lower-case letter may be replaced by the corresponding upper-case letter, or *vice versa.*
- The character '`|`' may be replaced by '`!`'.
- The character '`#`' may be replaced *consistently* by '`:`' in a based literal.
- The character '`"`' may be replaced *consistently* by '`%`' in a string literal.

There are 63 reserved words, none of which may be chosen as an identifier:

```
abort     declare   generic  of         select
abs       delay     goto     or         separate
accept    delta              others     subtype
access    digits    if       out
all       do        in                  task
and                 is       package    terminate
array                        pragma     then
at        else               private    type
          elsif     limited  procedure
          end       loop
begin     entry              raise      use
body      exception          range
          exit      mod      record     when
                             rem        while
                    new      renames    with
case      for       not      return
constant  function  null     reverse    xor
```

A.2. Syntax

Some ninety syntax diagrams completely describing the syntax of Ada are collected here. Each syntax diagram defines one syntactic construct of the language; the lines in the diagram must be followed in the direction of the arrows, round the smooth curves, and each path through the diagram describes one possible form of the construct.

Within the diagrams, words and symbols set in bold are the reserved words and symbols of Ada. Lower-case words (e.g. 'expression', 'if_statement') are the names of syntactic constructs.

Some of the construct names have italic prefixes when used within syntax diagrams. These are 'semantic clues' and are not strictly part of the syntax. For example, the syntax diagram 'if_statement' refers to the construct '*boolean_*expression' — this actually represents the syntactic construct 'expression', and the prefix '*boolean_*' is just a reminder that the type of the expression must be `Boolean`.

The following syntactic constructs have their syntax diagrams omitted:

letter	an upper-case or lower-case letter
digit	one of the digits `0` through `9`
graphic_character	an ISO printable character or a space
operator	an operator of the language, namely one of:

****** **abs** **not**
***** **/** **mod** **rem**
+ **-** **&**
= **/=** **<** **<=** **>=** **>**
and **or** **xor**

The syntax of a pragma is given by a normal syntax diagram. In the other syntax diagrams, each circled P indicates a position where (any number of) pragmas may be placed.

The alphabetical list of syntax diagrams follows, starting on the next page. The following notes refer to the syntax diagrams 'expression' and 'simple_expression':

1. In each use of the syntax diagram 'expression', only one of **and**, **or**, **xor**, **and then**, or **or else** may actually be chosen. Therefore `A and B and C` is a legal expression, but `A or B and C` is not. Additional brackets must be inserted to avoid the illegal cases, for example `(A or B) and C` or `A or (B and C)`.
2. In each use of the syntax diagram 'simple_expression', at most one of the operators **abs**, **not** and ****** may actually be chosen. Therefore `X ** Y ** Z` is illegal, and must be written as either `(X ** Y) ** Z` or `X ** (Y ** Z)`.
3. In the syntax diagram 'simple_expression', the precedence of the operators is indicated by the order in which the branches divide — the highest-precedence dividing first.

abort_statement

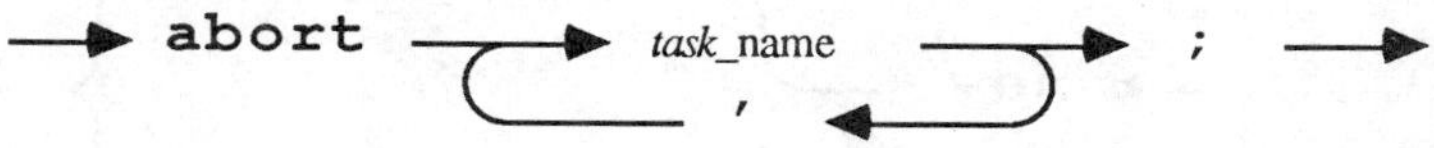

accept_statement

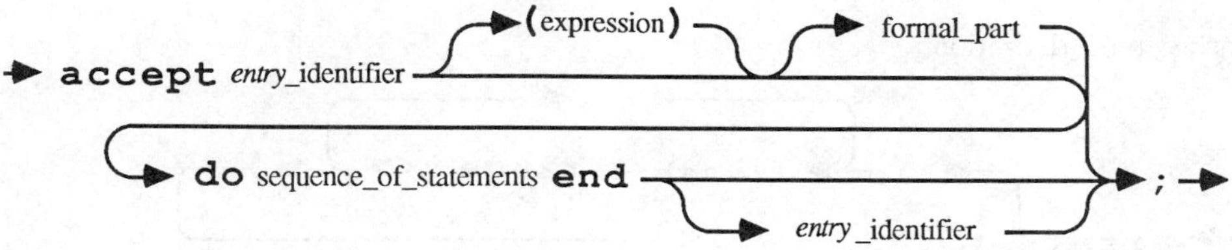

access_type_definition

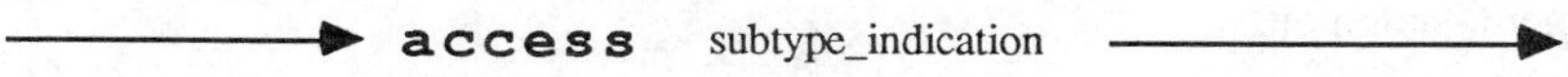

actual_parameter_part

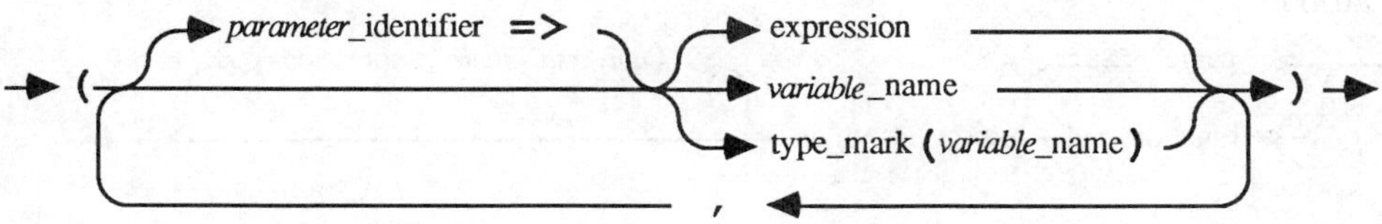

aggregate

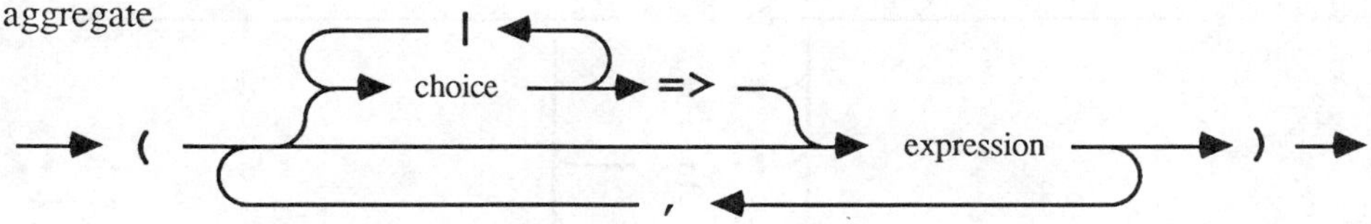

allocator

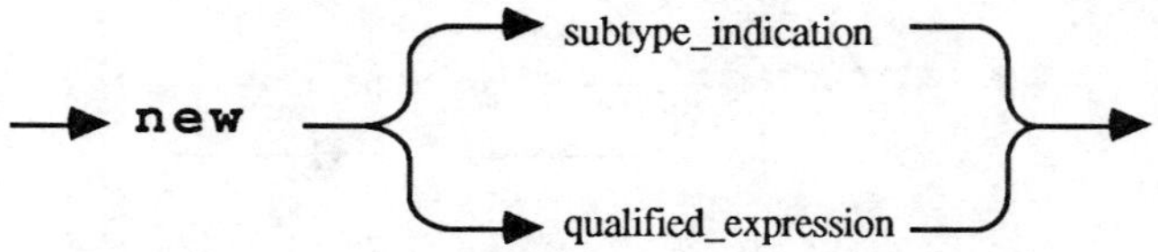

array_type_definition

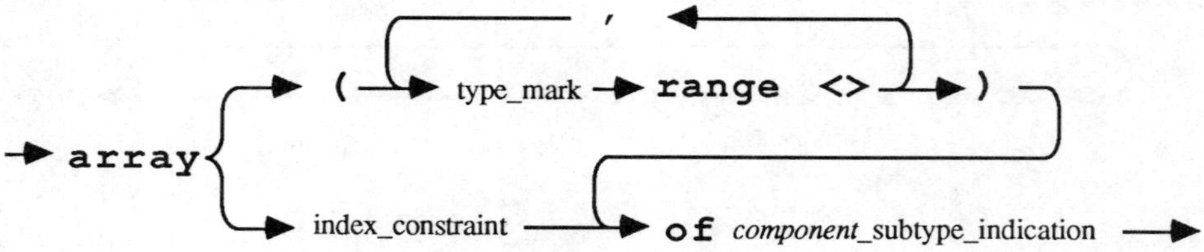

assignment_statement

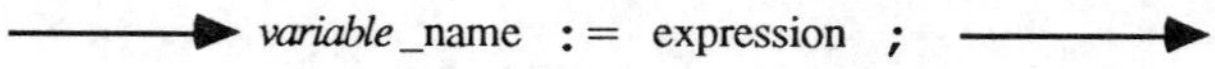

attribute

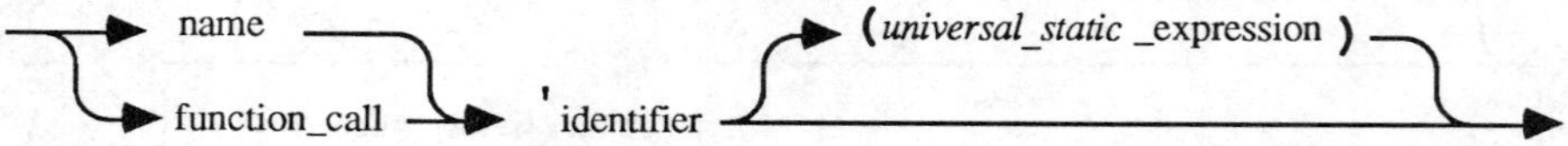

based_integer

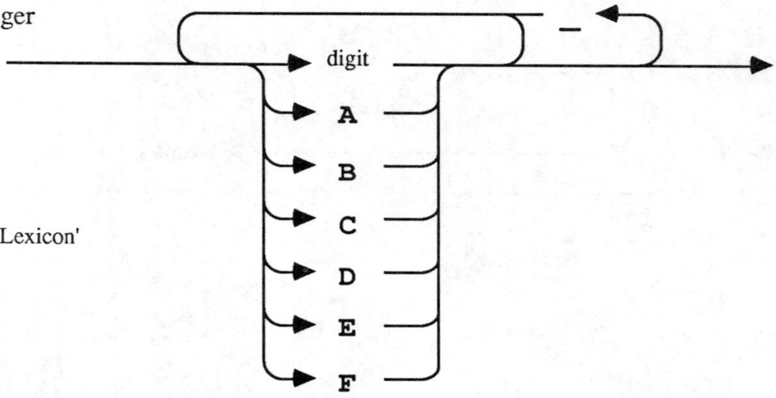

Note: See 'Lexicon'

basic_declaration

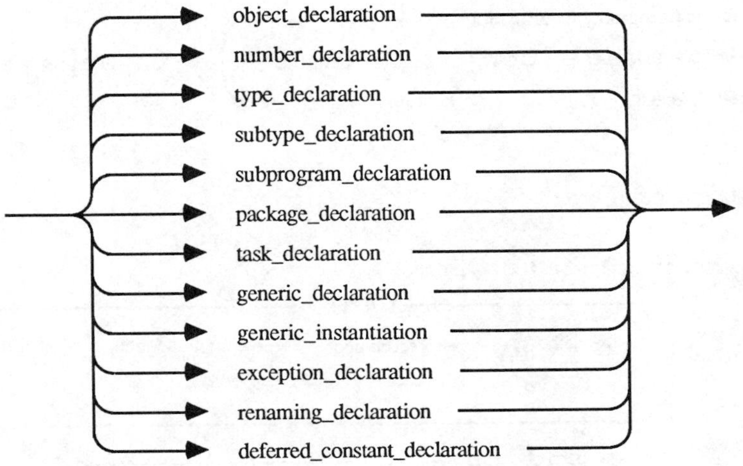

block_statement

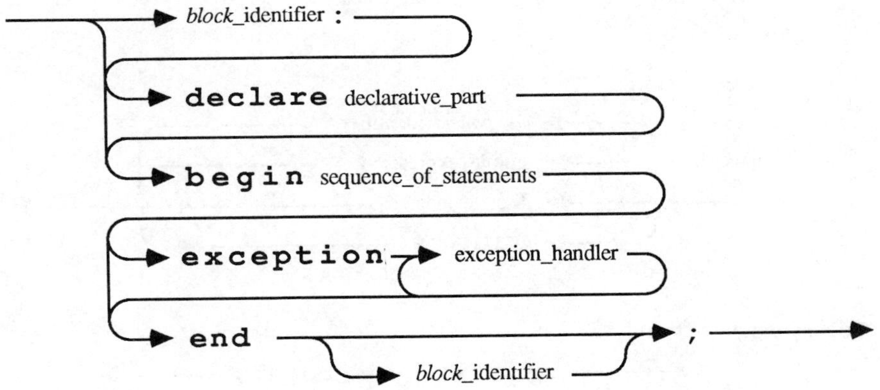

body_stub

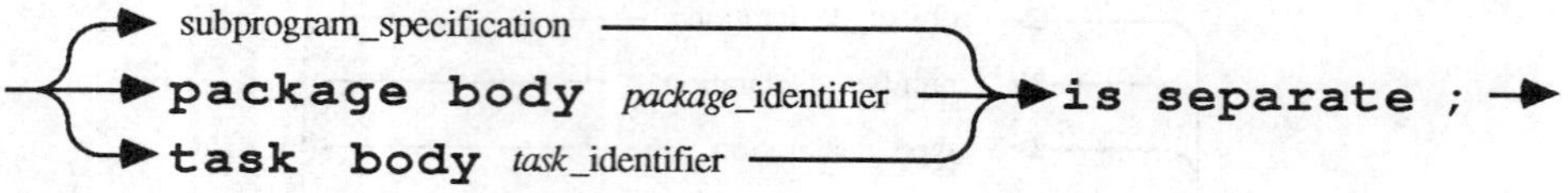

case_statement

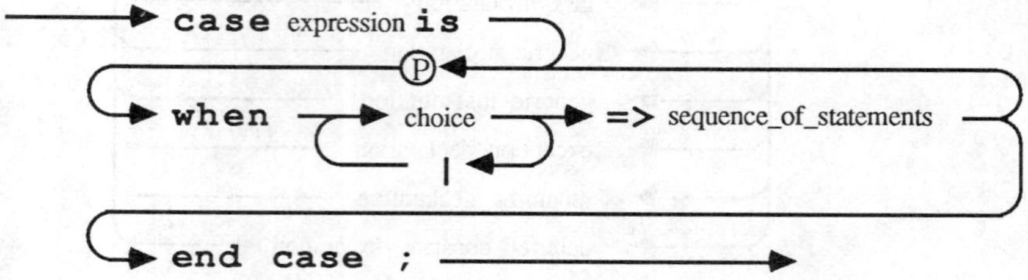

character_literal

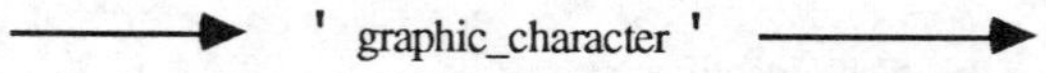

choice

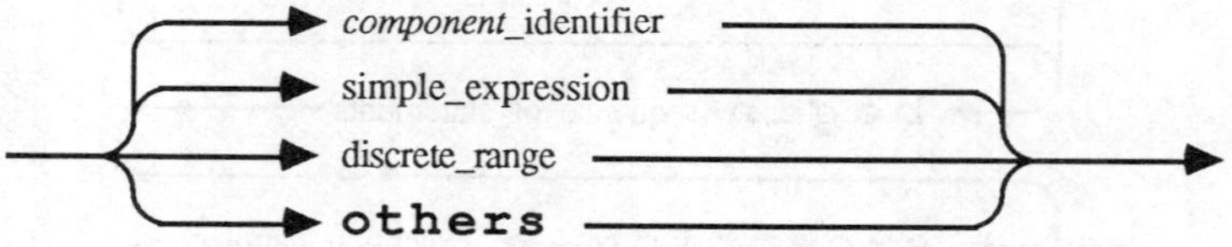

code_statement

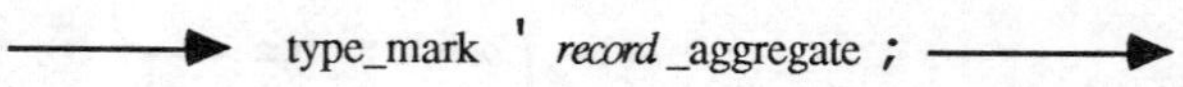

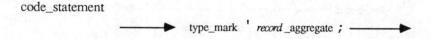

compilation

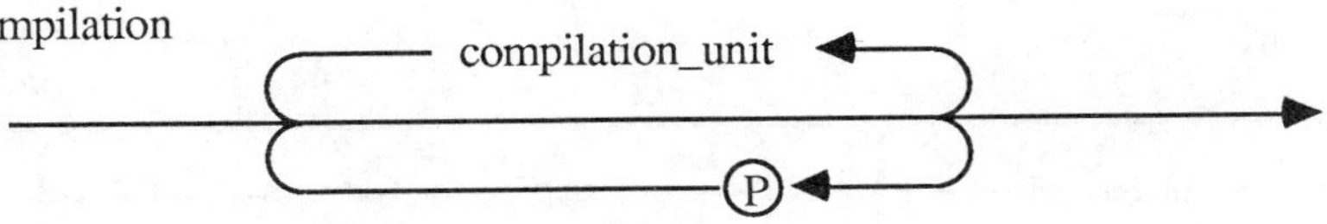

compilation_unit

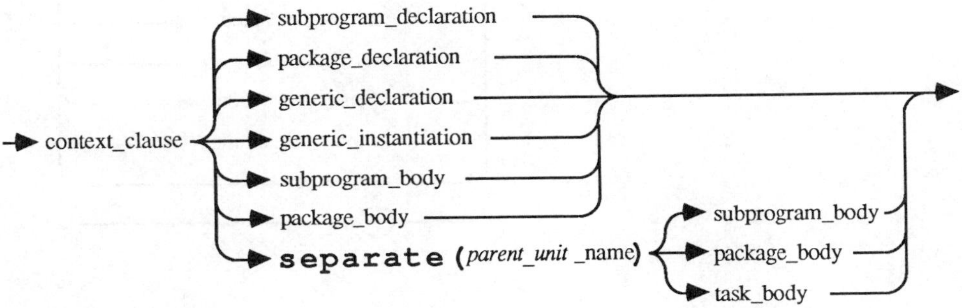

component_declaration

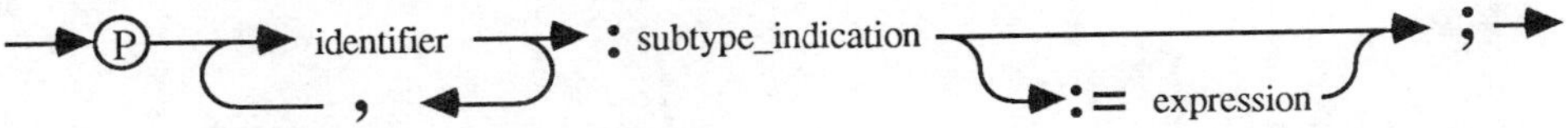

conditional_entry_call

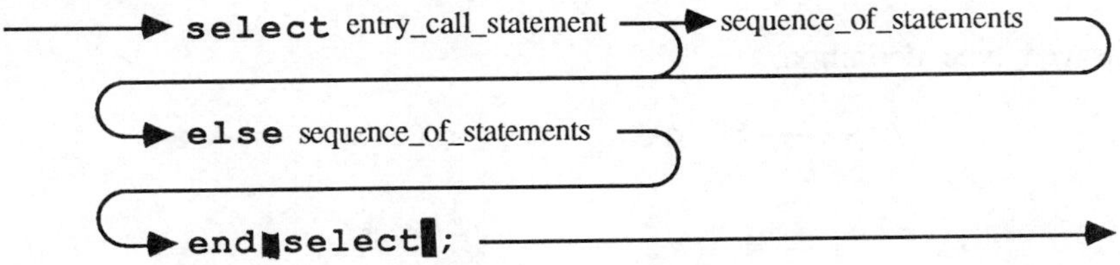

context_clause

declarative_part

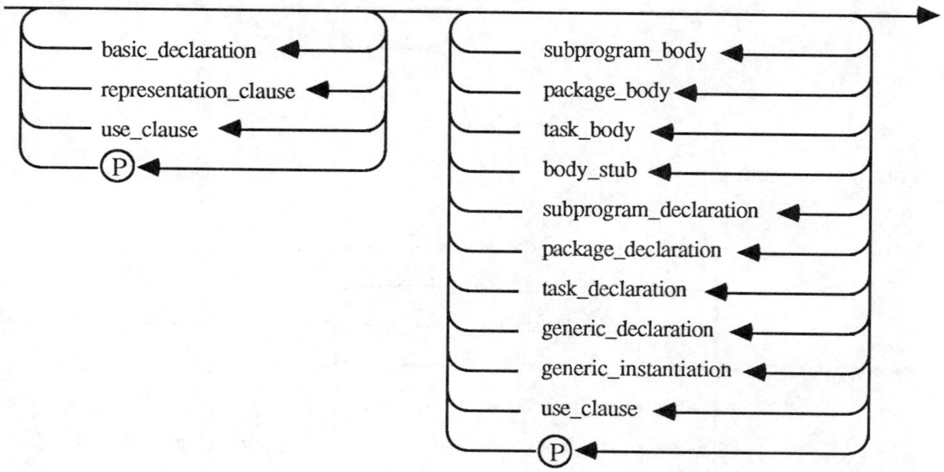

deferred_constant_declaration

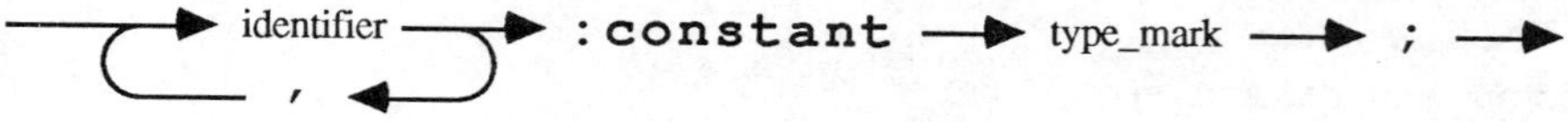

delay_statement

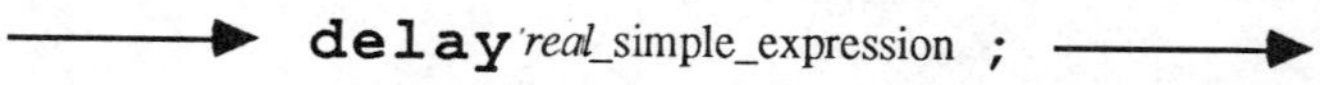

derived_type_definition

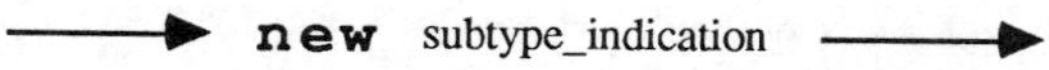

discrete_range

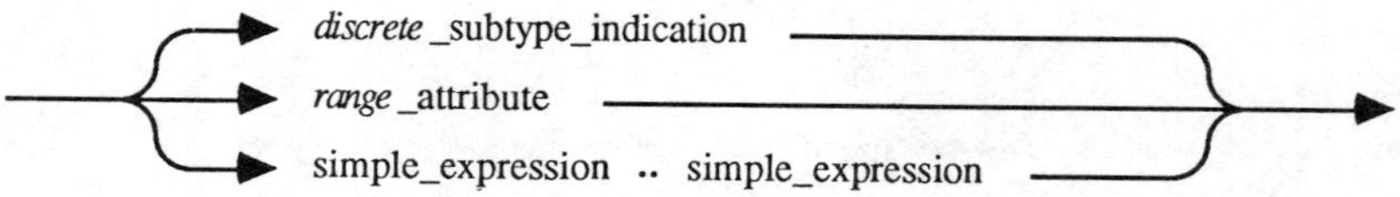

discriminant_contraint

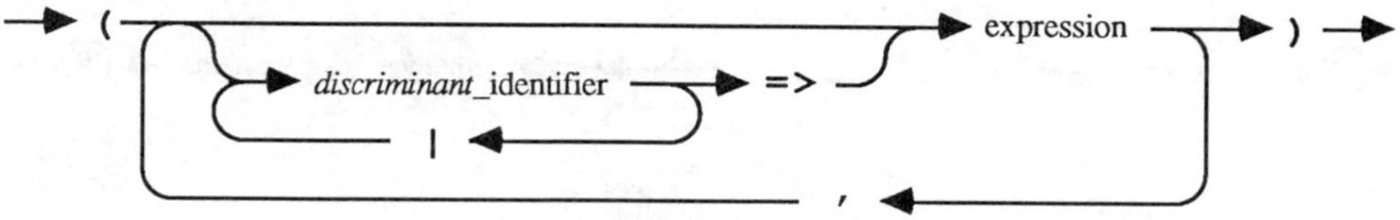

discriminant_part

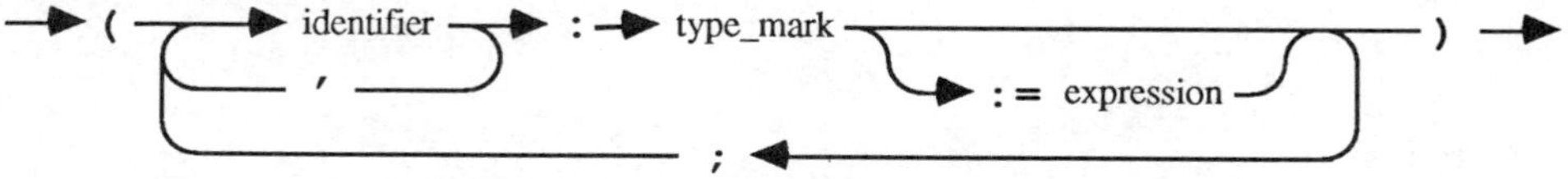

entry_call_statement

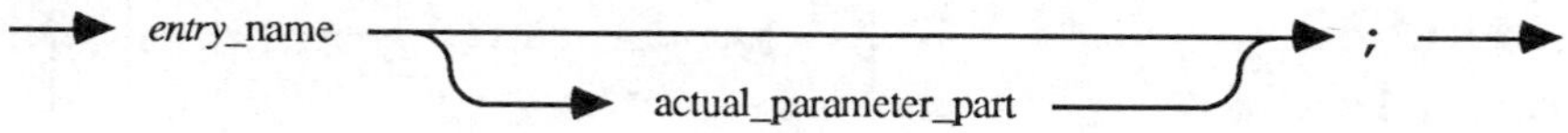

entry_declaration

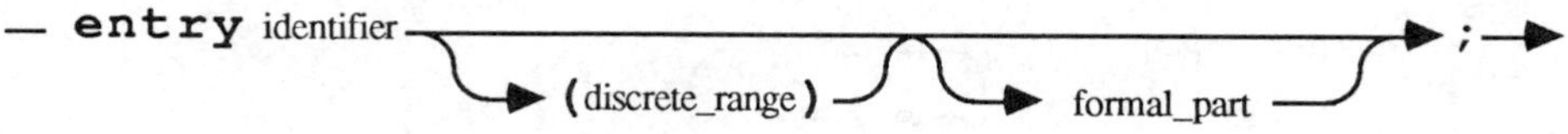

enumeration_type_definition

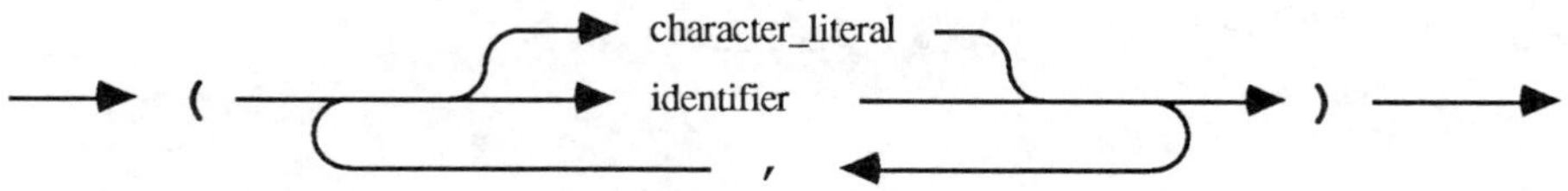

exception_declaration

exception_handler

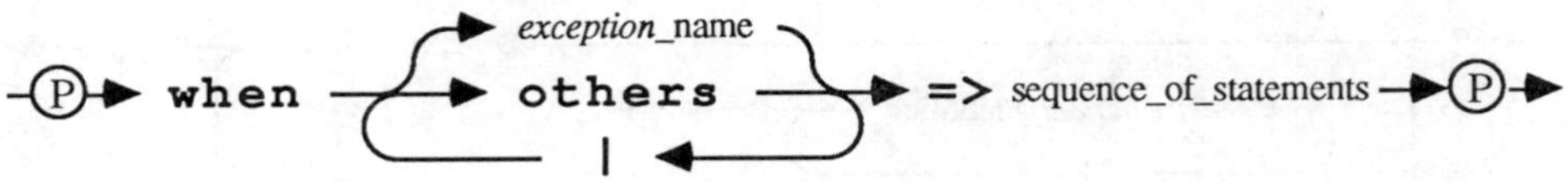

exit_statement

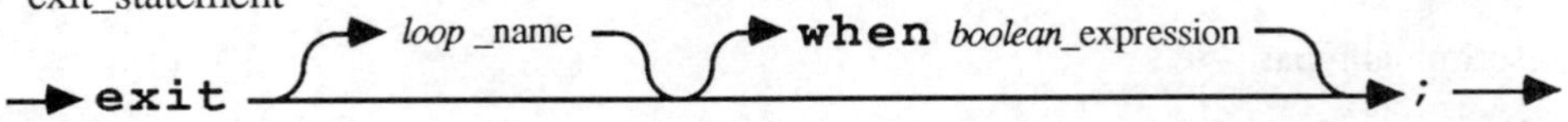

expression

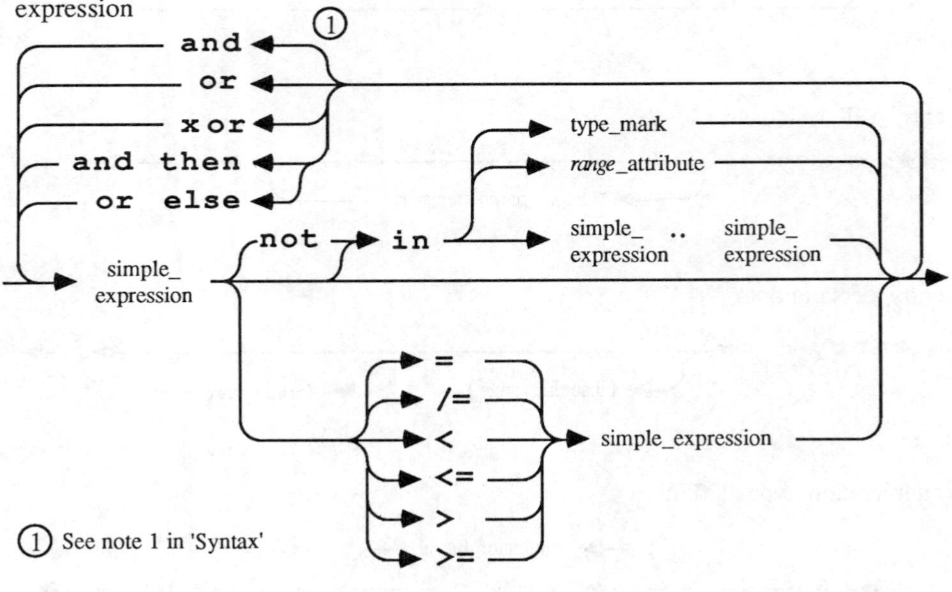

① See note 1 in 'Syntax'

fixed_point_constraint

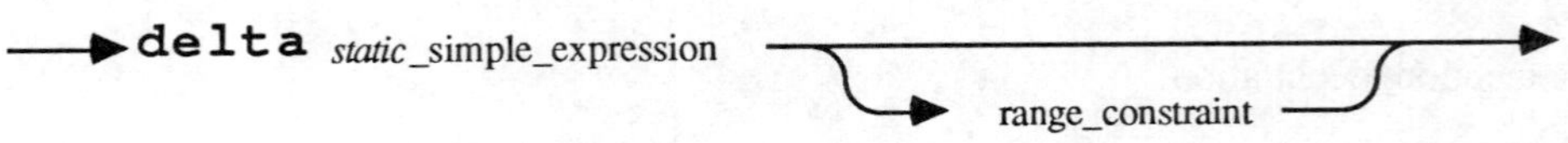

floating_point_constraint

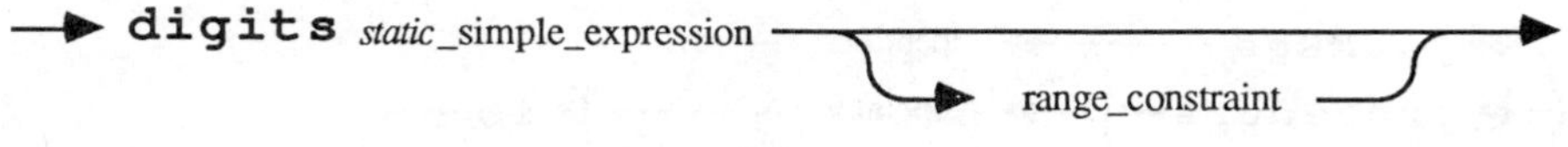

formal-part

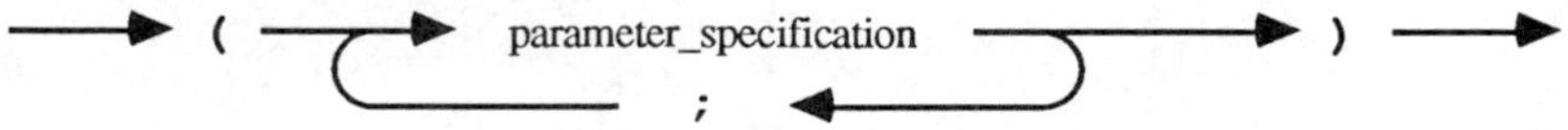

function_call

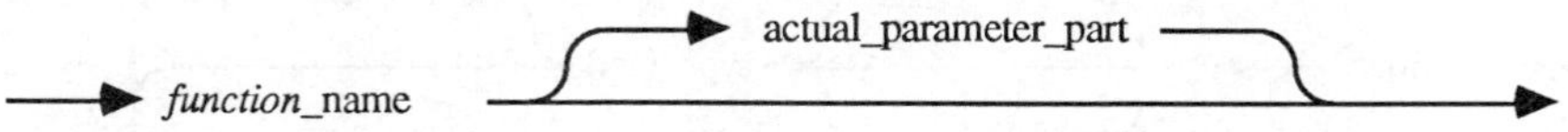

generic_actual_part

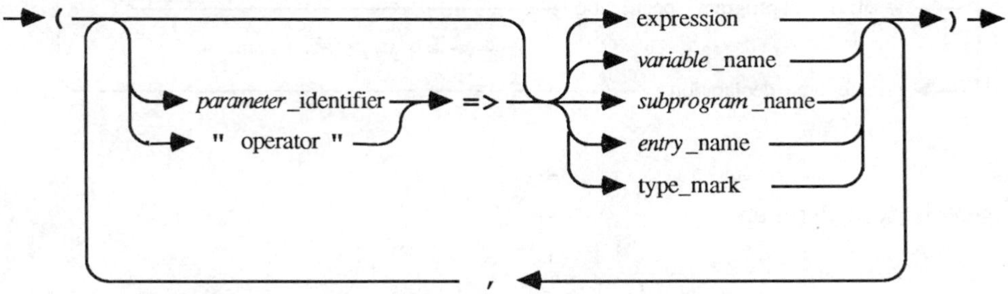

generic_declaration

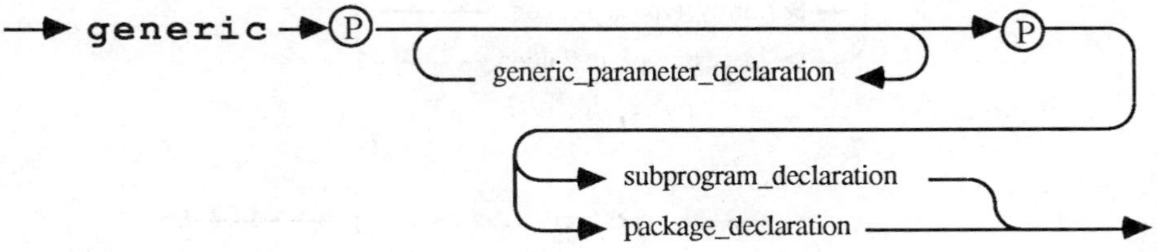

generic_instantiation

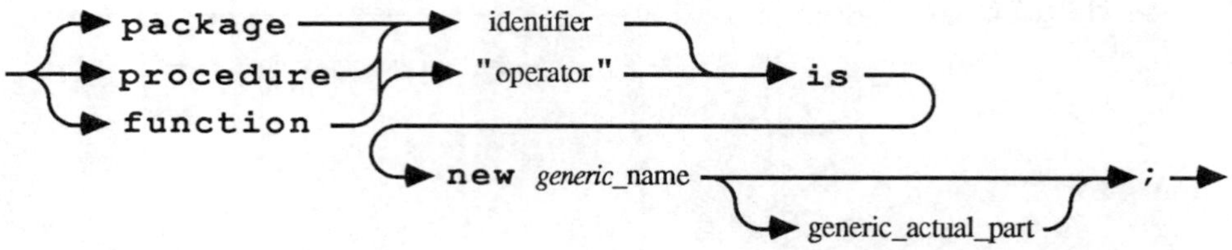

generic_parameter_declaration

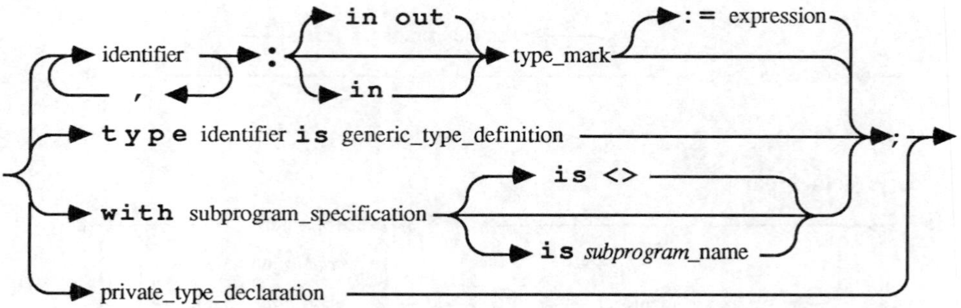

generic_type_definition

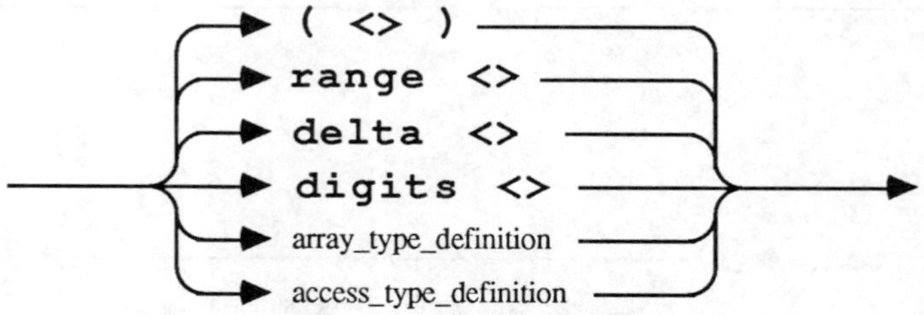

goto_statement

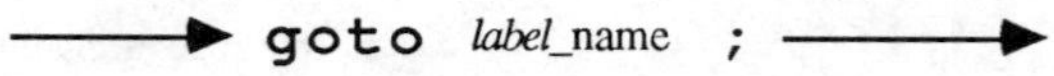

identifier

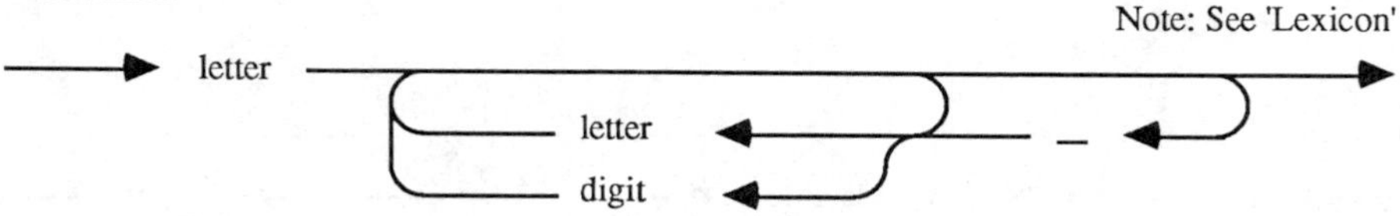

if_statement

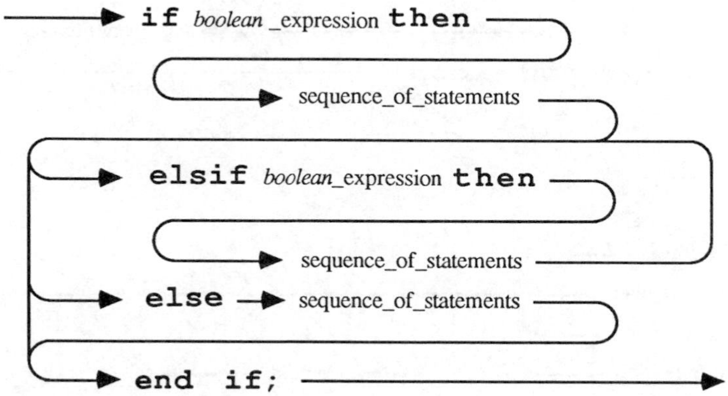

index_constraint

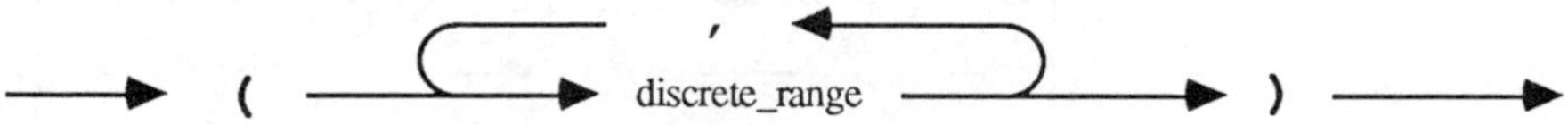

integer

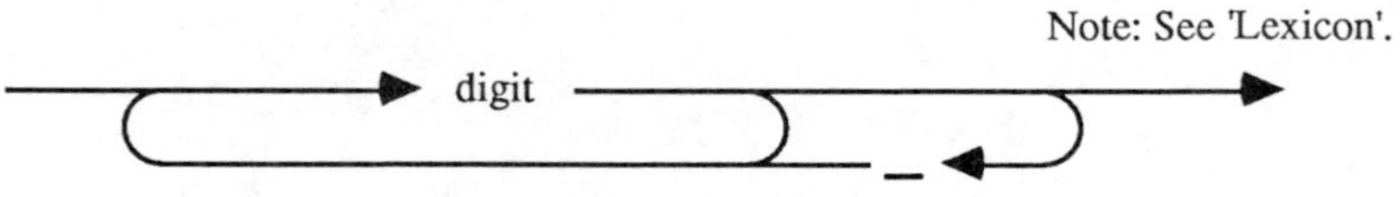

integer_type_definition

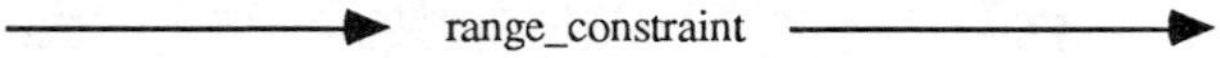

loop_statement

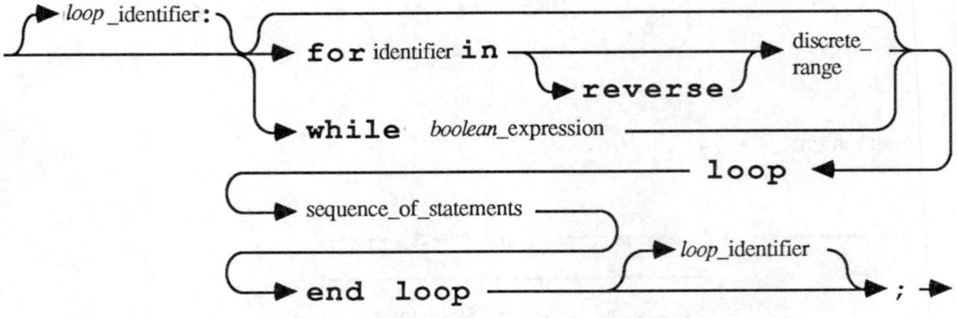

name

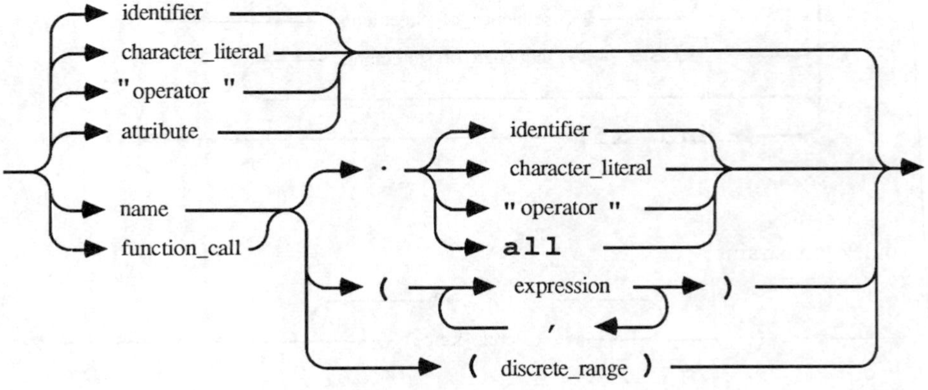

number_declaration

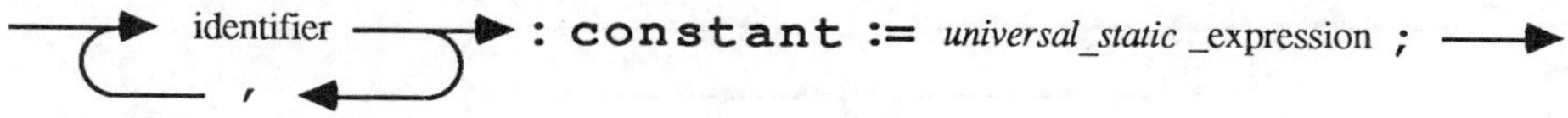

numeric_literal

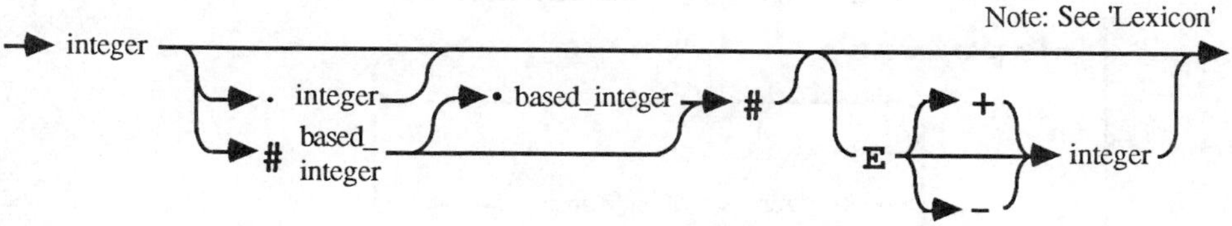

object_declaration

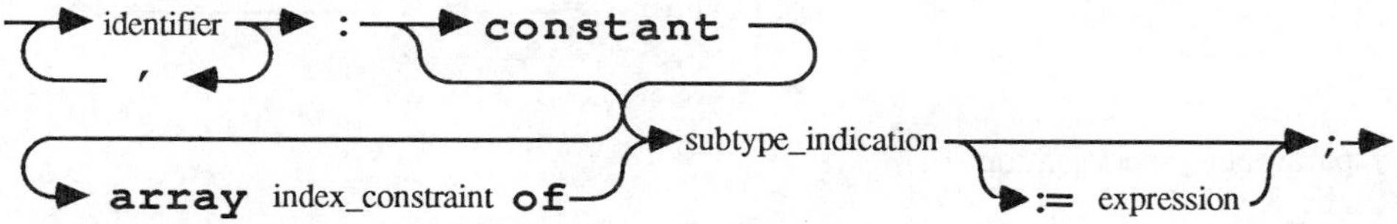

package_body

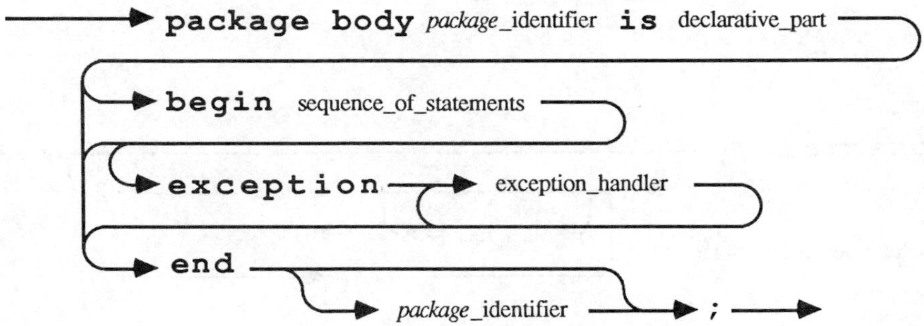

package_declaration

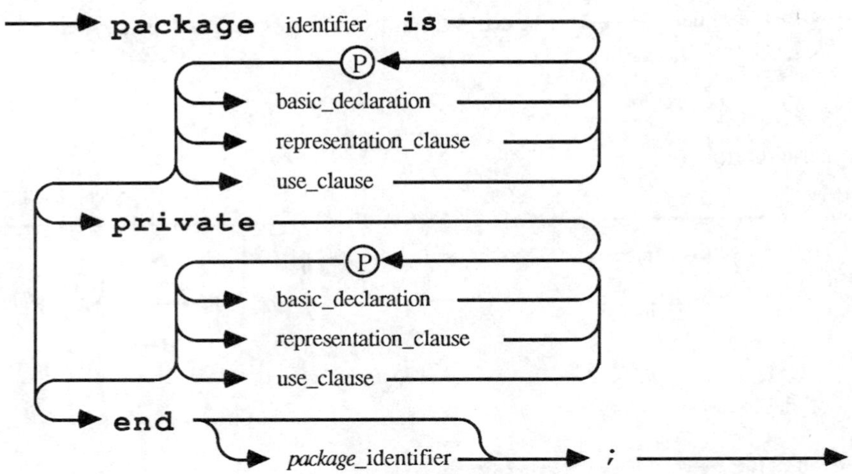

parameter_specification

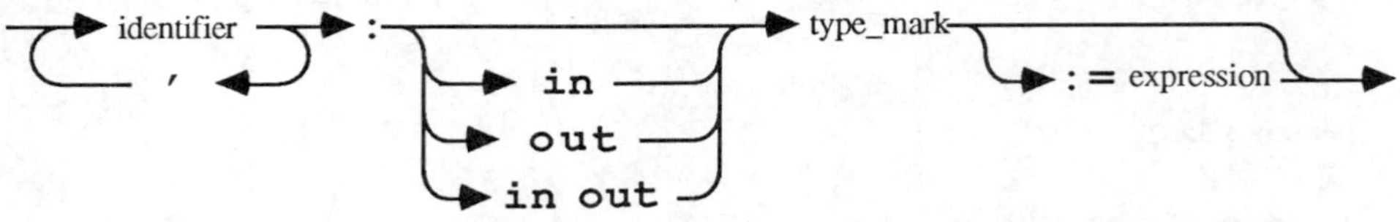

pragma

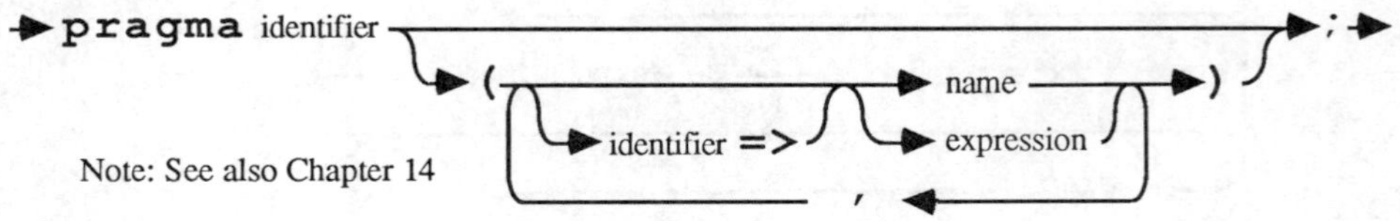

Note: See also Chapter 14

private_type_declaration

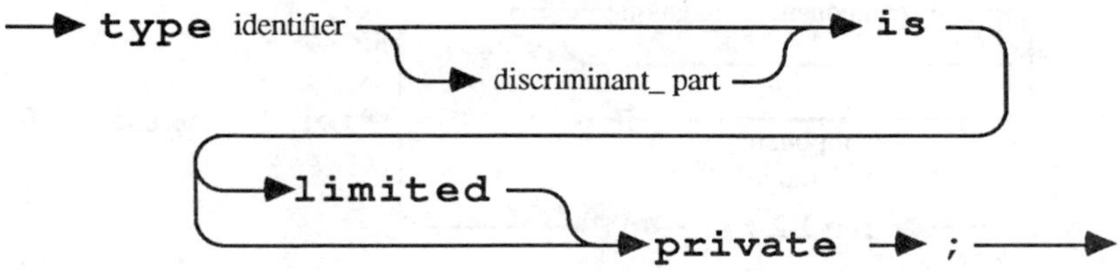

procedure_call_statement

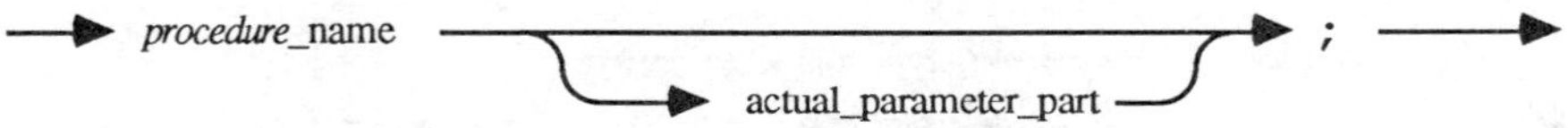

qualified_expression

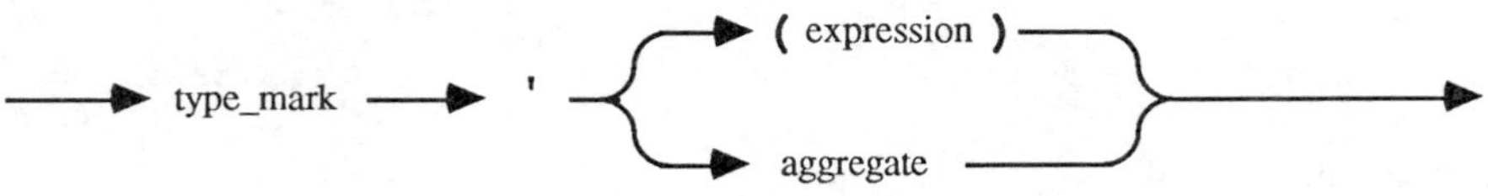

raise_ statement

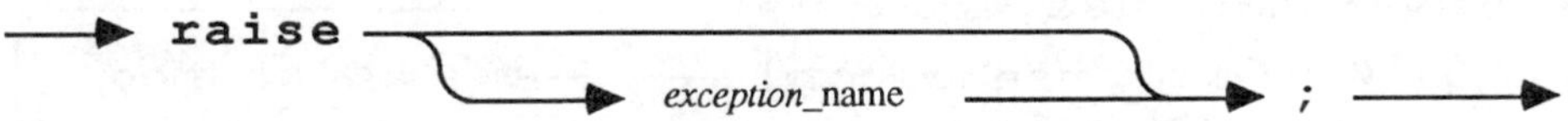

range_constraint

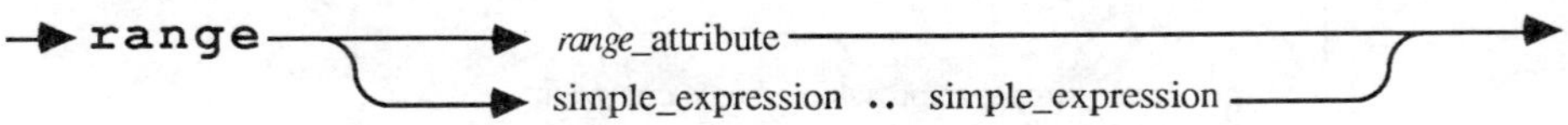

real_type_definition

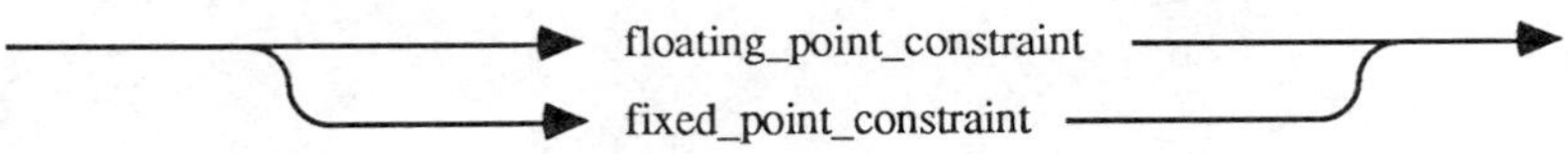

record_type_definition

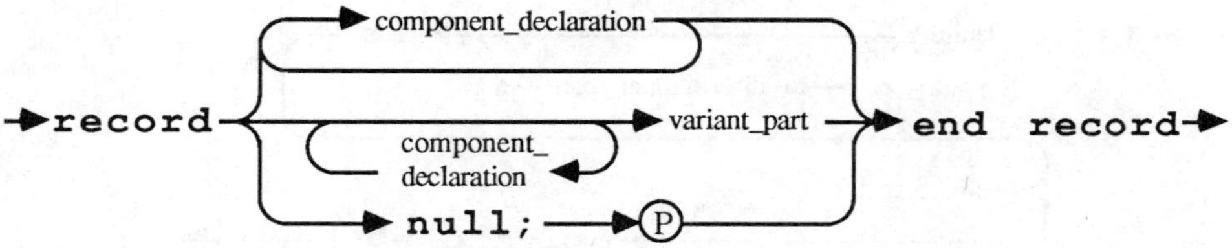

renaming_declaration

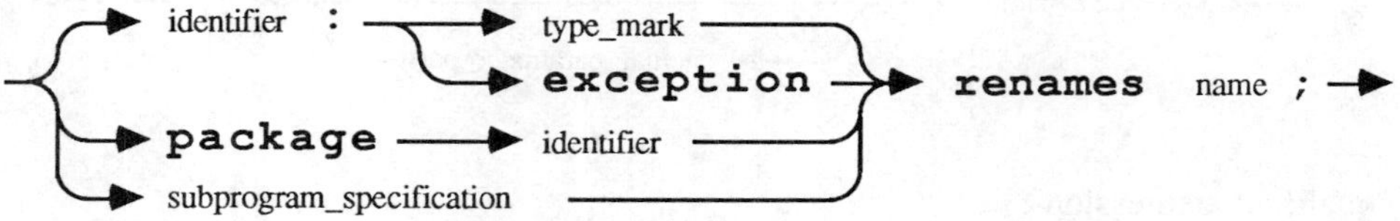

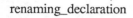

representation_clause

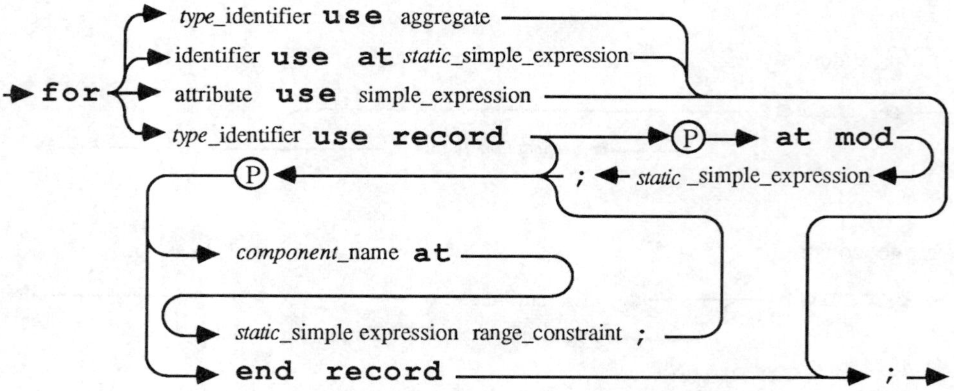

return_statement

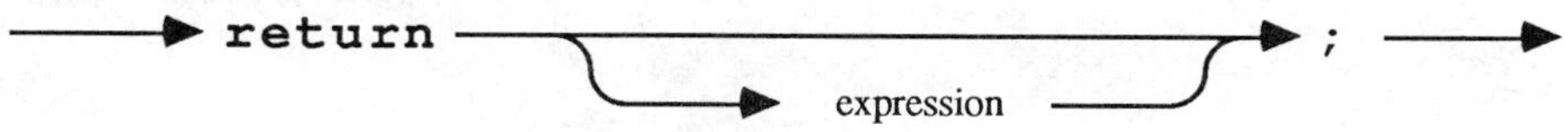

select_statement

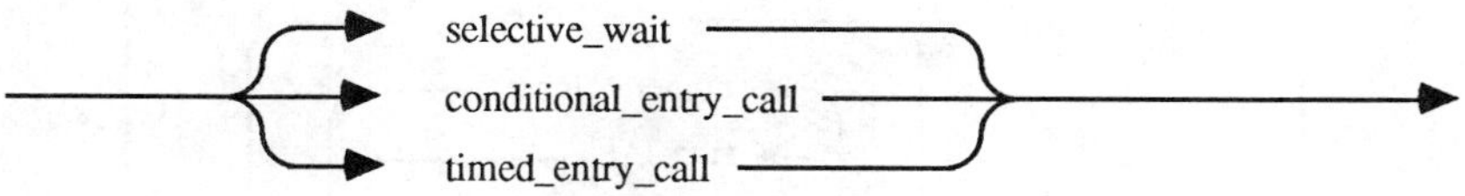

selective_wait

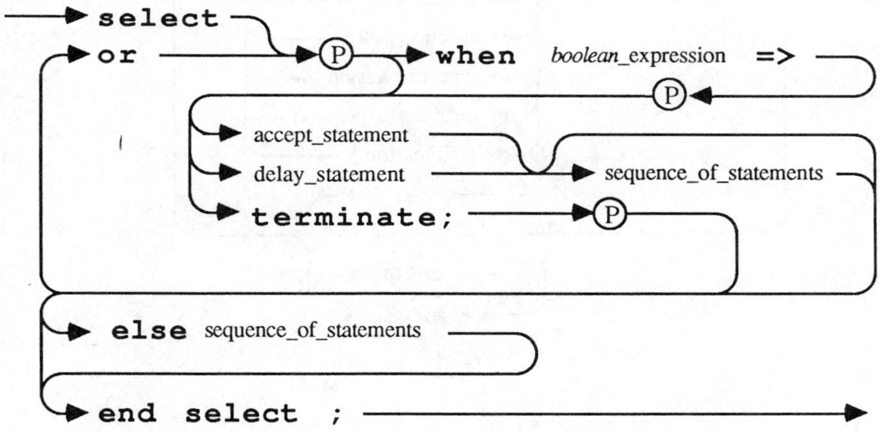

sequence_of_statements

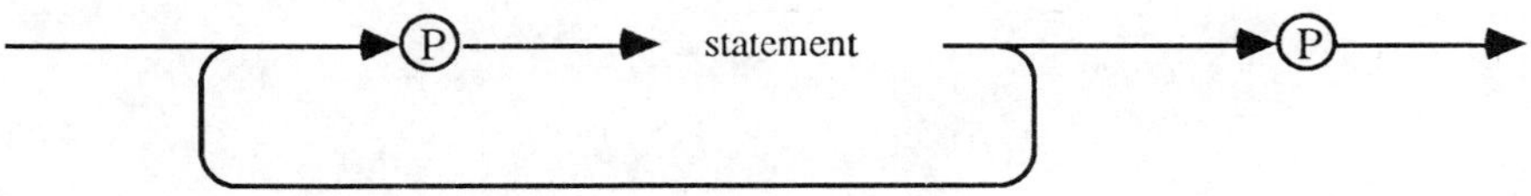

simple_expression

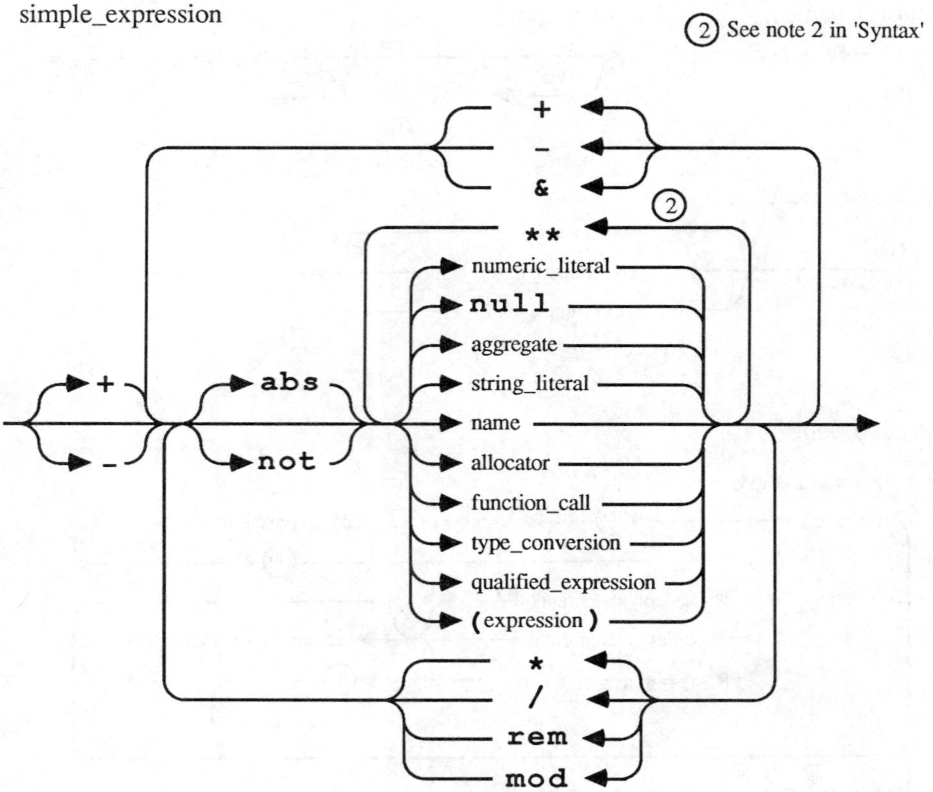

statement

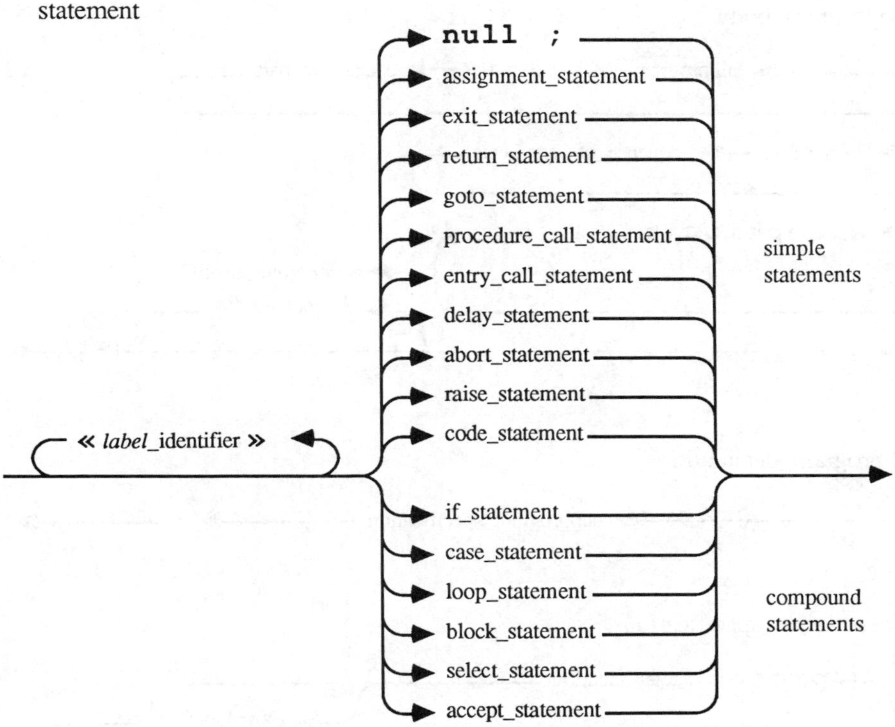

string_literal

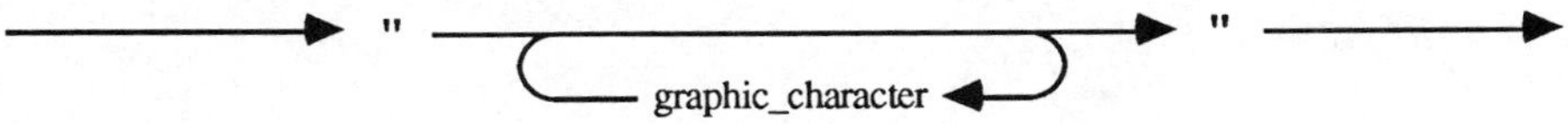

subprogram_body

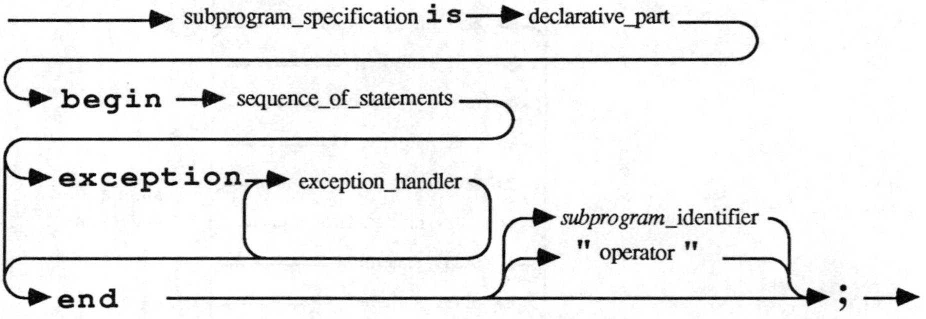

subprogram_declaration

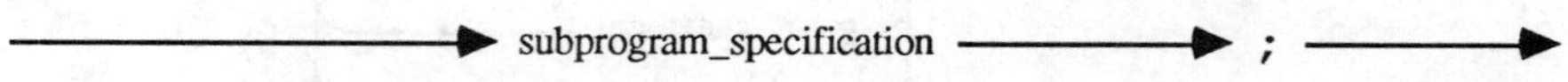

subprogram_specification

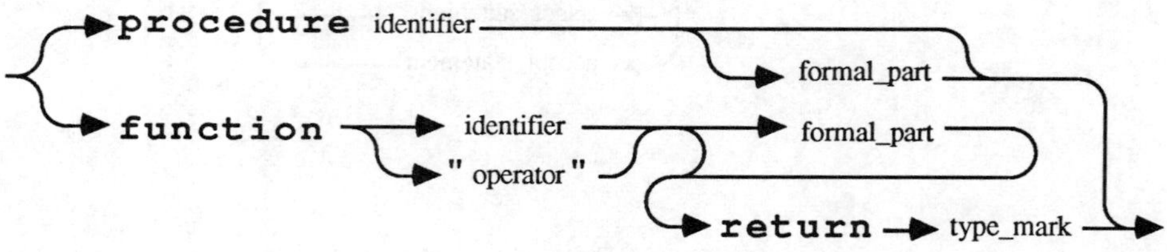

subtype_declaration

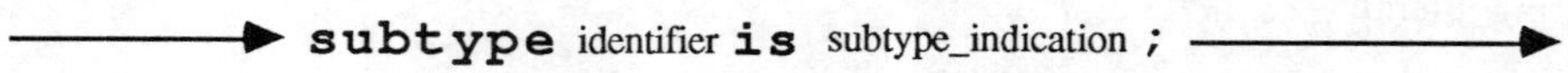

subtype_indication

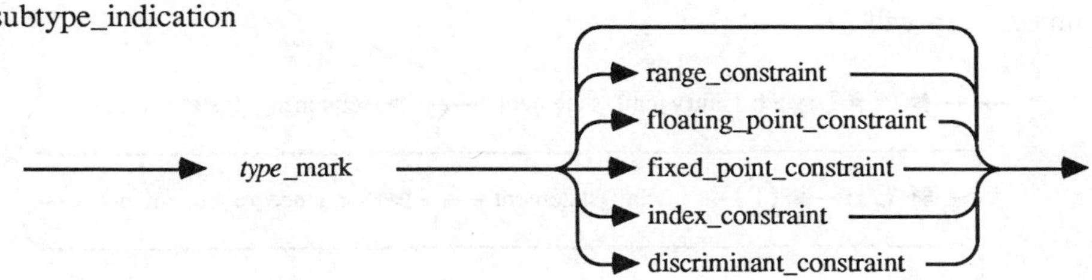

task_body

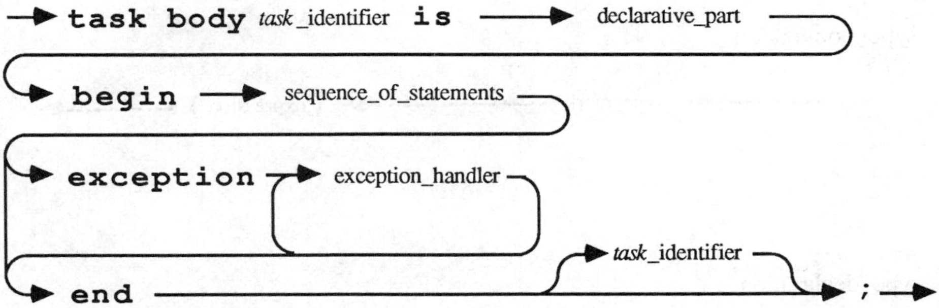

task_declaration

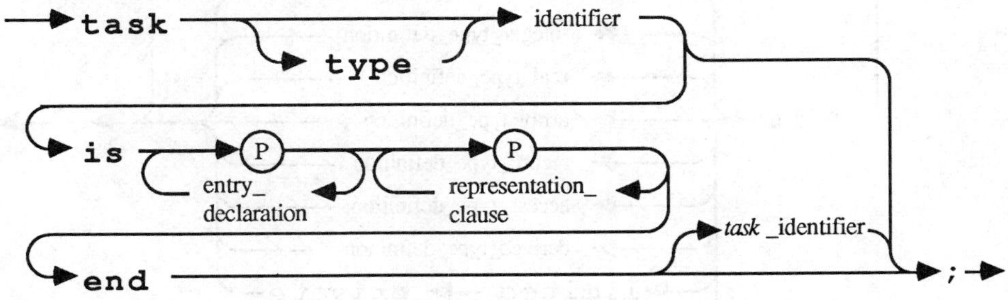

timed_entry_call

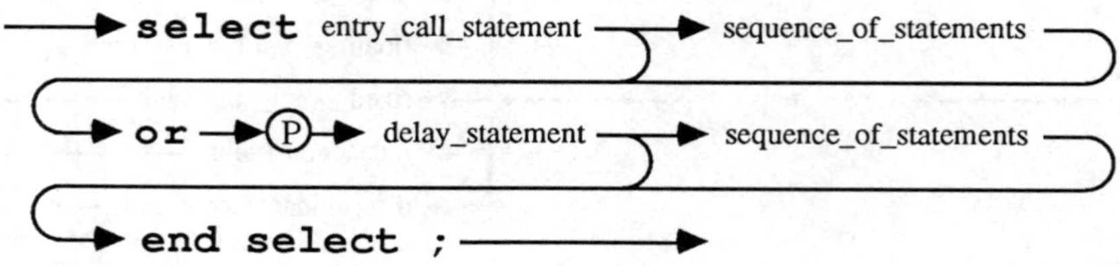

type_conversion

type_declaration

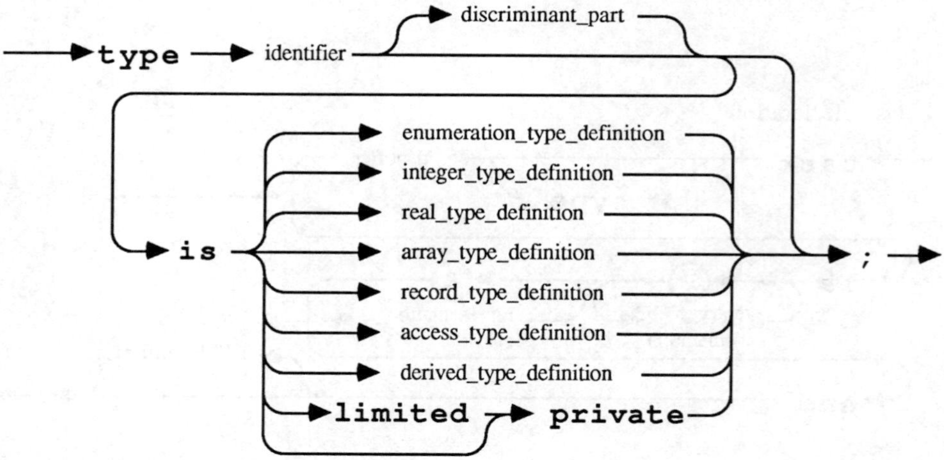

type_mark

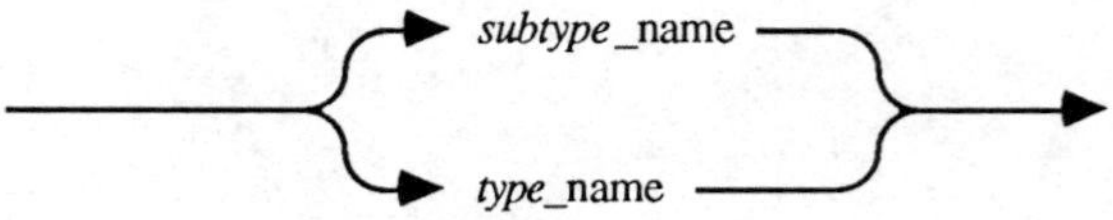

use_clause

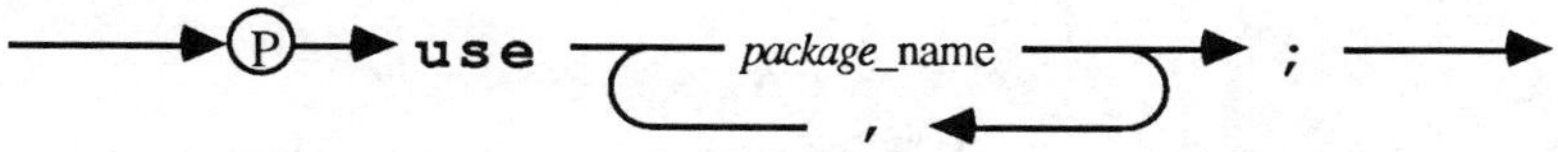

variant_part

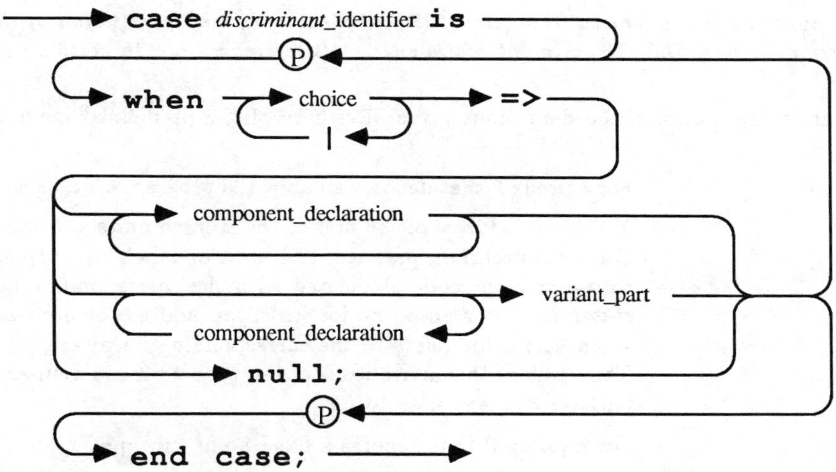

with_clause

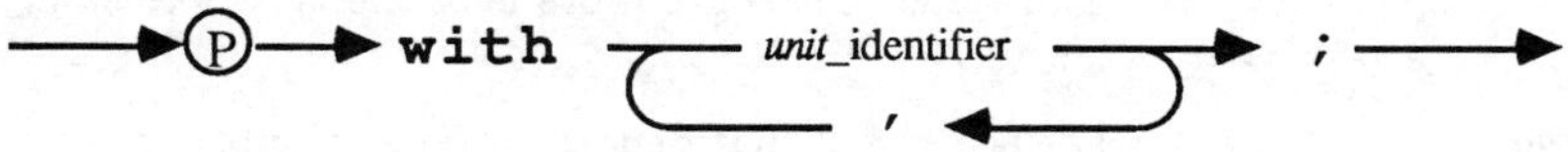

B

Predefined Language Attributes

(This appendix is reproduced from [Ada 1983], Appendix A, with permission of the Ada Joint Program Office, U.S. Department of Defense. All references are to sections of [Ada 1983].)

This annex summarizes the definitions given elsewhere of the predefined language attributes.

`P'Address` For a prefix P that denotes an object, a program unit, or an entry:

Yields the address of the first of the storage units allocated to P. For a subprogram, package, task unit or label, this value refers to the machine code associated with the corresponding body or statement. For an entry for which an address clause has been given, the value refers to the corresponding hardware interrupt. The value of this attribute is of the type `Address` defined in the package `System`. (See 13.7.2.)

`P'Aft` For a prefix P that denotes a fixed point subtype:

Yields the number of decimal digits needed after the point to accommodate the precision of the subtype P, unless the delta of the subtype P is greater than 0.1, in which case the attribute yields the value one. (`P'Aft` is the smallest positive integer N for which `(10**N)*P'Delta` is greater than or equal to one.) The value of this attribute is of the type *universal_integer*. (See 3.5.10.)

`P'Base` For a prefix P that denotes a type or subtype:

This attribute denotes the base type of P. It is only allowed as the prefix of the name of another attribute : for example, `P'Base'First`. (See 3.3.3.)

`P'Callable` For a prefix P that is appropriate for a task type:

Yields the value `False` when the execution of the task P is either completed or terminated, or when the task is abnormal; yields the value `True` otherwise. The value of this attribute is of the predefined type `Boolean`. (See 9.9.)

`P'Constrained` For a prefix P that denotes an object of a type with discriminants:

Yields the value `True` if a discriminant constraint applies to the object P, or if the object is a constant (including a formal parameter or generic formal parameter of mode `in`); yields the value

False otherwise. If P is a generic formal parameter of mode **in out**, or if P is a formal parameter of mode **in out** or **out** and the type mark given in the corresponding parameter specification denotes an unconstrained type with discriminants, then the value of this attribute is obtained from that of the corresponding actual parameter. The value of this attribute is of the predefined type Boolean. (See 3.7.4.)

P'Constrained — For a prefix P that denotes a private type or subtype:

Yields the value False if P denotes an unconstrained nonformal private type with discriminants; also yields the value False if P denotes a generic formal type and the associated actual subtype is either an unconstrained type with discriminants or an unconstrained array type; yields the value True otherwise. The value of this attribute is of the type Boolean. (See 7.4.2.)

P'Count — For a prefix P that denotes an entry of a task unit:

Yields the number of entry calls presently queued on the entry (if the attribute is evaluated within an accept statement for the entry P, the count does not include the calling task). The value of this attribute is of the type *universal_integer*. (See 9.9.)

P'Delta — For a prefix P that denotes a fixed point subtype:

Yields the value of the delta specified in the fixed accuracy definition for the subtype P. The value of this attribute is of the type *universal_real*. (See 3.5.10.)

P'Digits — For a prefix P that denotes a floating point subtype:

Yields the number of decimal digits in the decimal mantissa of model numbers of the subtype P. (This attribute yields the number D of section 3.5.7.) The value of this attribute is of the type *universal_integer*. (See 3.5.8.)

P'Emax — For a prefix P that denotes a floating point subtype:

Yields the largest exponent value in the binary canonical form of model numbers of the subtype P. (This attribute yields the product 4*D of section 3.5.7.) The value of this attribute is of the type *universal_integer*. (See 3.5.8.)

P'Epsilon — For a prefix P that denotes a floating point subtype:

Yields the absolute value of the difference between the model number 1.0 and the next model number above, for the subtype P. The value of this attribute is of the type *universal_real*. (See 3.5.8.)

P'First — For a prefix P that denotes a scalar type, or a subtype of a scalar type:

Yields the lower bound of P. The value of this attribute has the same type as P. (See 3.5.)

`P'First` For a prefix `P` that is appropriate for an array type, or that denotes a constrained array subtype:

Yields the lower bound of the first index range. The value of this attribute has the same type as this lower bound. (See 3.6.2 and 3.8.2.)

`P'First(N)` For a prefix `P` that is appropriate for an array type, or that denotes a constrained array subtype:

Yields the lower bound of the `N`-th index range. The value of this attribute has the same type as this lower bound. The argument `N` must be a static expression of type *universal_integer*. The value of `N` must be positive (nonzero) and no greater than the dimensionality of the array. (See 3.6.2 and 3.8.2.)

`P'First_Bit` For a prefix `P` that denotes a component of a record object:

Yields the offset, from the start of the first of the storage units occupied by the component, of the first bit occupied by the component. This offset is measured in bits. The value of this attribute is of the type *universal_integer*. (See 13.7.2.)

`P'Fore` For a prefix `P` that denotes a fixed point subtype:

Yields the minimum number of characters needed for the integer part of the decimal representation of any value of the subtype `P`, assuming that the representation does not include an exponent, but includes a one-character prefix that is either a minus sign or a space. (This minimum number does not include superfluous zeros or underlines, and is at least two.) The value of this attribute is of the type *universal_integer*. (See 3.5.10.)

`P'Image` For a prefix `P` that denotes a discrete type or subtype:

This attribute is a function with a single parameter. The actual parameter `X` must be a value of the base type of `P`. The result type is the predefined type `String`. The result is the *image* of the value of `X`, that is, a sequence of characters representing the value in display form. The image of an integer value is the corresponding decimal literal; without underlines, leading zeros, exponent, or trailing spaces; but with a one character prefix that is either a minus sign or a space.

The image of an enumeration value is either the corresponding identifier in upper case or the corresponding character literal (including the two apostrophes); neither leading nor trailing spaces are included. The image of a character literal other than a graphic character is implementation-defined. (See 3.5.5.)

`P'Large` For a prefix `P` that denotes a real subtype:

The attribute yields the largest possible model number of the subtype `P`. The value of this attribute is of the type *universal_real*. (See 3.5.8 and 3.5.10.)

`P'Last`	For a prefix `P` that denotes a scalar type, or a subtype of a scalar type: Yields the upper bound of `P`. The value of this attribute has the same type as `P`. (See 3.5.)
`P'Last`	For a prefix `P` that is appropriate for an array type, or that denotes a constrained array subtype: Yields the upper bound of the first index range. The value of this attribute has the same type as this upper bound. (See 3.6.2 and 3.8.2.)
`P'Last(N)`	For a prefix `P` that is appropriate for an array type, or that denotes a constrained array subtype: Yields the upper bound of the `N`-th index range. The value of this attribute has the same type as this upper bound. The argument `N` must be a static expression of type ***universal_integer***. The value of `N` must be positive (nonzero) and no greater than the dimensionality of the array. (See 3.6.2 and 3.8.2.)
`P'Last_Bit`	For a prefix `P` that denotes a component of a record object: Yields the offset, from the start of the first of the storage units occupied by the component, of the last bit occupied by the component. This offset is measured in bits. The value of this attribute is of the type ***universal_integer***. (See 13.7.2.)
`P'Length`	For a prefix `P` that is appropriate for an array type, or that denotes a constrained array subtype: Yields the number of values of the first index range (zero for a null range). The value of this attribute is of the type ***universal_integer***. (See 3.6.2.)
`P'Length(N)`	For a prefix `P` that is appropriate for an array type, or that denotes a constrained array subtype: Yields the number of values of the `N`-th index range (zero for a null range). The value of this attribute is of the type ***universal_integer***. The argument `N` must be a static expression of the type ***universal_integer***. The value of `N` must be positive (nonzero) and not grater than the dimensionality of the array. (See 3.6.2 and 3.8.2.)
`P'Machine_Emax`	For a prefix `P` that denotes a floating point type or subtype: Yields the largest value of ***exponent*** for the machine representation of the base type of `P`. The value of this attribute is of the type ***universal_integer***. (See 13.7.3.)
`P'Machine_Emin`	For a prefix `P` that denotes a floating point type or subtype: Yields the smallest (most negative) value of ***exponent*** for the machine representation of the base type of `P`. The value of this attribute is of the type ***universal_integer***. (See 13.7.3.)

`P'Machine_Mantissa` For a prefix `P` that denotes a floating point type or subtype:

Yields the number of digits in the ***mantissa*** for the machine representation of the base type of `P` (the digits are extended digits in the range `0` to `P'Machine_Radix - 1`). The value of this attribute is of the type ***universal_integer***. (See 13.7.3.)

`P'Machine_Overflows` For a prefix `P` that denotes a real type or subtype:

Yields the value `True` if every predefined operation on values of the base type of `P` either provides a correct result, or raises the exception `Numeric_Error` in overflow situations; yields the value `False` otherwise. The value of this attribute is of the predefined type `Boolean`. (See 13.7.3.)

`P'Machine_Radix` For a prefix `P` that denotes a floating point type or subtype:

Yields the value of the ***radix*** used by the machine representation of the base type of `P`. The value of this attribute is of the type ***universal_integer***. (See 13.7.3.)

`P'Machine_Rounds` For a prefix `P` that denotes a real type or subtype:

Yields the value `True` if every predefined arithmetic operation on values of the base type of `P` either returns an exact result or performs rounding; yields the value `False` otherwise. The value of this attribute is of the predefined type `Boolean`. (See 13.7.3.)

`P'Mantissa` For a prefix `P` that denotes a real subtype:

Yields the number of binary digits in the binary mantissa of model numbers of the subtype `P`. (This attribute yields the number `B` of section 3.5.7 for a floating point type, or of section 3.5.9 for a fixed point type.) The value of this attribute is of the type ***universal_integer***. (See 3.5.8 and 3.5.10.)

`P'Pos` For a prefix `P` that denotes a discrete type or subtype:

This attribute is a function with a single parameter. The actual parameter `X` must be a value of the base type of `P`. The result type is the type ***universal_integer***. The result is the position number of the value of the actual parameter. (See 3.5.5.)

`P'Position` For a prefix `P` that denotes a component of a record object:

Yields the offset, from the start of the first storage unit occupied by the record, of the first of the storage units occupied by the component. This offset is measured in storage units. The value of this attribute is of the type ***universal_integer***. (See 13.7.2.)

`P'Pred` For a prefix `P` that denotes a discrete type or subtype:

This attribute is a function with a single parameter. The actual parameter `X` must be a value of the base type of `P`. The result type is the base type of `P`. The result is the value whose position number is one less than that of `X`. The exception `Constraint'Error` is raised if `X` equals `P'Base'First`. (See 3.5.5.)

P'Range — For a prefix P that is appropriate for an array type, or that denotes a constrained array subtype:

Yields the first index range of P, that is, the range P'First .. P'Last. (See 3.6.2.)

P'Range(N) — For a prefix P that is appropriate for an array type, or that denotes a constrained array subtype:

Yields the N-th index range of P, that is, the range P'First(N) .. P'Last(N). (See 3.6.2.)

P'Safe_Emax — For a prefix P that denotes a floating point type or subtype:

Yields the largest exponent value in the binary canonical form of safe numbers of the base type of P. (This attribute yields the number E of section 3.5.7.) The value of this attribute is of the type *universal_integer*. (See 3.5.8.)

P'Safe_Large — For a prefix P that denotes a real type or subtype:

Yields the largest positive safe number of the base type of P. The value of this attribute is of the type *universal_real*. (See 3.5.8 and 3.5.10.)

P'Safe_Small — For a prefix P that denotes a real type or subtype:

Yields the smallest positive (nonzero) safe number of the base type of P. The value of this attribute is of the type *universal_real*. (See 3.5.8 and 3.5.10.)

P'Size — For a prefix P that denotes an object:

Yields the number of bits allocated to hold the object. The value of this attribute is of the type *universal_integer*. (See 13.7.2.)

P'Size — For a prefix P that denotes any type or subtype:

Yields the minimum number of bits that is needed by the implementation to hold any possible object of the type or subtype P. The value of this attribute is of the type *universal_integer*.

P'Small — For a prefix P that denotes a real subtype:

Yields the smallest positive (nonzero) model number of the subtype P. The value of this attribute is of the type *universal_real*. (See 3.5.8 and 3.5.10.)

P'Storage_Size — For a prefix P that denotes an access type or subtype:

Yields the total number of storage units reserved for the collection associated with the base type of P. The value of this attribute is of the type *universal_integer*. (See 13.7.2.)

P'Storage_Size — For a prefix P that denotes a task type or a task object:

Yields the number of storage units reserved for each activation of a task of the type P or for the activation of the task object P. The value of this attribute is of the type *universal_integer*. (See 13.7.2.)

`P'Succ`

For a prefix P that denotes a discrete type or subtype:

This attribute is a function with a single parameter. The actual parameter X must be a value of the base type of P. The result type is the base type of P. The result is the value whose position number is one greater than that of X. The exception Constraint'Error is raised if X equals P'Base'Last. (See 3.5.5.)

`P'Terminated`

For a prefix P that is appropriate for a task type:

Yields the value True if the task P is terminated; yields the value False otherwise. The value of this attribute is of the predefined type Boolean. (See 9.9.)

`P'Val`

For a prefix P that denotes a discrete type or subtype:

This attribute is a special function with a single parameter X which can be of any integer type. The result type is the base type of P. The result is the value whose position number is the *universal_integer* value corresponding to X. The exception Constraint_Error is raised if the *universal_integer* value corresponding to X is not in the range P'Pos (P'Base'First) .. P'Pos (P'Base'Last). (See 3.5.5.)

`P'Value`

For a prefix P that denotes a discrete type or subtype:

This attribute is a function with a single parameter. The actual parameter X must be a value of the predefined type String. The result type is the base type of P. Any leading and any trailing spaces of the sequence of characters that corresponds to X are ignored.

For an enumeration type, if the sequence of characters has the syntax of an enumeration literal and if this literal exists for the base type of P, the result is the corresponding enumeration value. For an integer type, if the sequence of characters has the syntax of an integer literal, with an optional single leading character that is a plus or minus sign, and if there is a corresponding value in the base type of P, the result is this value. In any other case, the exception Constraint_Error is raised. (See 3.5.5.)

`P'Width`

For a prefix P that denotes a discrete subtype:

Yields the maximum image length over all values of the subtype P (the *image* is the sequence of characters returned by the attribute Image). The value of the attribute is of the type *universal_integer*. (See 3.5.5.)

C

Predefined Language Pragmas

(This appendix is reproduced from [Ada 1983], Appendix B, with permission of the Ada Joint Program Office, U.S. Department of Defense. All references are to sections of [Ada 1983].)

This annex defines the pragmas `List`, `Page`, and `Optimize`, and summarizes the definitions given elsewhere of the remaining language-defined pragmas.

Pragma	*Meaning*
`Controlled`	Takes the simple name of an access type as the single argument. This pragma is only allowed immediately within the declarative part or package specification that contains the declaration of the access type; the declarations must occur before the pragma. This pragma is not allowed for a derived type. This pragma specifies that automatic storage reclamation must not be performed for objects designated by values of the access type, except upon leaving the innermost block statement, subprogram body, or task body that encloses the access type declaration, or after leaving the main program (see 4.8).
`Elaborate`	Takes one or more simple names denoting library units as arguments. This pragma is only allowed immediately after the context clause of a compilation unit (before the subsequent library unit or secondary unit). Each argument must be the simple name of a library unit mentioned by the context clause. This pragma specifies that the corresponding library unit body must be elaborated before the given compilation unit. If the given compilation unit is a subunit, the library unit body must be elaborated before the body of the ancestor library unit of the subunit (see 10.5).
`Inline`	Takes one or more names as arguments; each name is either the name of a subprogram or the name of a generic subprogram. This pragma is only allowed at the place of a declarative item in a declarative part or package specification, or after a library unit in a compilation, but before any subsequent compilation unit. This pragma specifies that the subprogram bodies should be expanded inline at each call whenever possible; in the case of a generic subprogram, the pragma applies to calls of its instantiations (see 6.3.2).
`Interface`	Takes a language name and a subprogram name as arguments. This pragma is allowed at the place of a declarative item, and must apply in this case to a subprogram declared by an earlier declarative item of the same declarative part or package specification. This pragma is also allowed for a library unit; in this case the pragma must appear after the

subprogram declaration, and before any subsequent compilation unit. This pragma specifies the other language (and thereby the calling conventions) and informs the compiler that an object module will be supplied for the corresponding subprogram (see 13.9).

`List` Takes one of the identifiers `On` or `Off` as the single argument. This pragma is allowed anywhere a pragma is allowed. It specifies that listing of the compilation is to be continued or suspended until a `List` pragma with the opposite argument is given within the same compilation. The pragma itself is always listed if the compiler is producing a listing.

`Memory_Size` Takes a numeric literal as the single argument. This pragma is only allowed at the start of a compilation, before the first compilation unit (if any) of the compilation. The effect of this pragma is to use the value of the specified numeric literal for the definition of the named number `Memory_Size` (see 13.7).

`Optimize` Takes one of the identifiers `Time` or `Space` as the single argument. This pragma is only allowed withing a declarative part and it applies to the block or body enclosing the declarative part. It specifies whether time or space is the primary optimization criterion.

`Pack` Takes the simple name of a record or array type as the single argument. The allowed positions for this pragma, and the restrictions on the named type, are governed by the same rules as for a representation clause. The pragma specifies that storage minimization should be the main criterion when selecting the representation of the given type (see 13.1).

`Page` This pragma has no argument, and is allowed anywhere a pragma is allowed. It specifies that the program text which follows the pragma should start on a new page (if the compiler is currently producing a listing).

`Priority` Takes a static expression of the predefined integer type `Priority` as the single argument. This pragma is only allowed within the specification of a task unit or immediately within the outermost declaration part of a main program. It specifies the priority of the task (or tasks of the task type) or the priority of the main program (see 9.8).

`Shared` Takes the simple name of a variable as the single argument. This pragma is allowed only for a variable declared by an object declaration and whose type is a scalar or access type; the variable declaration and the pragma must both occur (in this order) immediately within the same declarative part or package specification. This pragma specifies that every read or update of the variable is a synchronization point for that variable. An implementation must restrict the objects for which this pragma is allowed to objects for which each of direct reading and direct updating is implemented as an indivisible operation (see 9.11).

`Storage_Unit` Takes a numeric literal as the single argument. This pragma is only allowed at the start of a compilation, before the first compilation unit (if any) of the compilation. The effect of this pragma is to use the value of the specified numeric literal for the definition of the named number `Storage_Unit` (see 13.7).

`Suppress` Takes as arguments the identifier of a check and optionally also the name of either an object, a type or subtype, a subprogram, a task unit, or a generic unit. This pragma is only allowed either immediately within a declarative part or immediately within a package specification. In the latter case, the only allowed form is with a name that denotes an entity (or several overloaded subprograms) declared immediately within the package specification. The permission to omit the given check extends from the place of the pragma to the end of the declarative region associated with the innermost enclosing block statement or program unit. For a pragma given in a package specification, the permission extends to the end of the scope of the named entity.

If the pragma includes a name, the permission to omit the given check is further restricted: it is given only for operations on the named object or on all objects of the base type of a named type or subtype; for calls of a named subprogram; for activations of tasks of the named task type; or for instantiations of the given generic unit (see 11.7).

`System_Name` Takes an enumeration literal as the single argument. This pragma is only allowed at the start of a compilation, before the first compilation unit (if any) of the compilation. The effect of this pragma is to use the enumeration literal with the specified identifier for the definition of the constant `System_Name`. This pragma is only allowed if the specified identifier corresponds to one of the literals of the type `Name` declared in the package `System` (see 13.7).

D

Predefined Language Environment

D.1. The package Standard

The package **Standard** contains declarations of all predefined identifiers of Ada. Its declaration cannot be given entirely in Ada, but is suggested by the following:

```
package Standard is

   type Boolean is (False, True);

-- The following operators are implicitly declared:

-- function "="   (Left, Right : Boolean) return Boolean;
-- function "/="  (Left, Right : Boolean) return Boolean;
-- function "<"   (Left, Right : Boolean) return Boolean;
-- function "<="  (Left, Right : Boolean) return Boolean;
-- function ">"   (Left, Right : Boolean) return Boolean;
-- function ">="  (Left, Right : Boolean) return Boolean;

-- function "and" (Left, Right : Boolean) return Boolean;
-- function "or"  (Left, Right : Boolean) return Boolean;
-- function "xor" (Left, Right : Boolean) return Boolean;

-- function "not" (Right : Boolean) return Boolean;

-- type universal integer is 'all' whole numbers;

   type Integer       is implementation-defined;
   type Short_Integer is implementation-defined; -- optional
   type Long_Integer  is implementation-defined; -- optional

-- The following operators are implicitly declared
-- for every predefined integer type INT:

-- function "="   (Left, Right : INT) return Boolean;
-- function "/="  (Left, Right : INT) return Boolean;
-- function "<"   (Left, Right : INT) return Boolean;
-- function "<="  (Left, Right : INT) return Boolean;
-- function ">"   (Left, Right : INT) return Boolean;
-- function ">="  (Left, Right : INT) return Boolean;

-- function "+"   (Right : INT) return INT;
-- function "-"   (Right : INT) return INT;
-- function "abs" (Right : INT) return INT;

-- function "+"   (Left, Right : INT) return INT;
-- function "-"   (Left, Right : INT) return INT;
```

```
-- function "*"   (Left, Right : INT) return INT;
-- function "/"   (Left, Right : INT) return INT;
-- function "rem" (Left, Right : INT) return INT;
-- function "mod" (Left, Right : INT) return INT;

-- function "**"  (Left : INT; Right : Integer) return INT;

   subtype Natural   is Integer range 0 .. Integer'Last;
   subtype Positive  is Integer range 1 .. Integer'Last;

-- type universal real is 'all' real numbers;

   type Float       is implementation-defined;
   type Short_Float is implementation-defined; -- optional
   type Long_Float  is implementation-defined; -- optional

-- The following operators are implicitly declared
-- for every predefined floating-point type FLT:

-- function "="   (Left, Right : FLT) return Boolean;
-- function "/="  (Left, Right : FLT) return Boolean;
-- function "<"   (Left, Right : FLT) return Boolean;
-- function "<="  (Left, Right : FLT) return Boolean;
-- function ">"   (Left, Right : FLT) return Boolean;
-- function ">="  (Left, Right : FLT) return Boolean;

-- function "+"   (Right : FLT) return FLT;
-- function "-"   (Right : FLT) return FLT;
-- function "abs" (Right : FLT) return FLT;

-- function "+"   (Left, Right : FLT) return FLT;
-- function "-"   (Left, Right : FLT) return FLT;
-- function "*"   (Left, Right : FLT) return FLT;
-- function "/"   (Left, Right : FLT) return FLT;

-- function "**"  (Left : FLT; Right : Integer) return FLT;

-- The following operators are also predefined:

-- function "*"   (Left  : universal integer; Right : universal real)
--                 return universal real;
-- function "*"   (Left  : universal real; Right : universal integer)
--                 return universal real;
-- function "/"   (Left  : universal real; Right : universal integer)
--                 return universal real;

-- type universal fixed is 'all' real numbers;

-- The following operators are implicitly declared
-- for all fixed-point types FIX1 and FIX2:

-- function "*"   (Left : FIX1; Right : FIX2) return universal fixed;
-- function "/"   (Left : FIX1; Right : FIX2) return universal fixed;

   type Duration is delta implementation-defined
                    range implementation-defined;

   type Character is
```

```
        (NUL, SOH, STX, ETX, EOT, ENQ, ACK, BEL,
         BS, HT, LF, VT, FF, CR, SO, SI,
         DLE, DC1, DC2, DC3, DC4, NAK, SYN, ETB,
         CAN, EM, SUB, ESC, FS, GS, RS, US,
         ' ', '!', '"', '#', '$', '%', '&', ''',
         '(', ')', '*', '+', ',', '-', '.', '/',
         '0', '1', '2', '3', '4', '5', '6', '7',
         '8', '9', ':', ';', '<', '=', '>', '?',
         '@', 'A', 'B', 'C', 'D', 'E', 'F', 'G',
         'H', 'I', 'J', 'K', 'L', 'M', 'N', 'O',
         'P', 'Q', 'R', 'S', 'T', 'U', 'V', 'W',
         'X', 'Y', 'Z', '[', '\', ']', '^', '_',
         '`', 'a', 'b', 'c', 'd', 'e', 'f', 'g',
         'h', 'i', 'j', 'k', 'l', 'm', 'n', 'o',
         'p', 'q', 'r', 's', 't', 'u', 'v', 'w',
         'x', 'y', 'z', '{', '|', '}', '~', DEL);

   package ASCII is
      NUL : constant Character := NUL;
      SOH : constant Character := SOH;
      ...
      US  : constant Character := US;
      DEL : constant Character := DEL;
      ...
   end ASCII;

   type String is array (Positive range <>) of Character;
   pragma Pack (String);
-- The following operators are implicitly declared:

-- function "="   (Left, Right : String) return Boolean;
-- function "/="  (Left, Right : String) return Boolean;
-- function "<"   (Left, Right : String) return Boolean;
-- function "<="  (Left, Right : String) return Boolean;
-- function ">"   (Left, Right : String) return Boolean;
-- function ">="  (Left, Right : String) return Boolean;

-- function "&"   (Left : String;    Right : String)    return String;
-- function "&"   (Left : Character; Right : String)    return String;
-- function "&"   (Left : String;    Right : Character) return String;
-- function "&"   (Left : Character; Right : Character) return String;


   Constraint_Error  : exception;
   Numeric_Error     : exception;
   Program_Error     : exception;
   Storage_Error     : exception;
   Tasking_Error     : exception;

end Standard;
```

D.2. The package Calendar

The package **Calendar** declares types and functions for times and time intervals, measured in (fractional) seconds.

```
package Calendar is

   type Time is private;

   subtype Year_Number  is Integer  range 1901 .. 2099;
   subtype Month_Number is Integer  range 1 .. 12;
   subtype Day_Number   is Integer  range 1 .. 31;
   subtype Day_Duration is Duration range 0.0 .. 86400.0;

   function Clock return Time;

   function Year     (Date : Time) return Year_Number;
   function Month    (Date : Time) return Month_Number;
   function Day      (Date : Time) return Day_Number;
   function Seconds  (Date : Time) return Day_Duration;

   procedure Split   (Date    : in  Time;
                      Year    : out Year_Number;
                      Month   : out Month_Number;
                      Day     : out Day_Number;
                      Seconds : out Day_Duration);

   function Time_of  (Year    : Year_Number;
                      Month   : Month_Number;
                      Day     : Day_Number;
                      Seconds : Day_Duration := 0.0)
         return Time;

   function "+"   (Left : Duration; Right : Time) return Time;
   function "+"   (Left : Time; Right : Duration) return Time;
   function "-"   (Left : Time; Right : Duration) return Time;
   function "-"   (Left : Time; Right : Time) return Duration;

   function "<"   (Left, Right : Time) return Boolean;
   function "<="  (Left, Right : Time) return Boolean;
   function ">"   (Left, Right : Time) return Boolean;
   function ">="  (Left, Right : Time) return Boolean;

   Time_Error : exception;

private
   implementation details
end Calendar;
```

D.3. Other predefined library units

The following library units are included in every Ada program library:

Name of unit	*Kind of unit*	*Purpose*	*Reference*
`System`	package	machine properties	Section 24.2
`Machine_Code`	package	machine code insertion	Section 24.2
`Unchecked_Deallocation`	generic procedure	explicit deallocation	Section 24.3
`Unchecked_Conversion`	generic function	subverting type rules	Section 24.3
`Sequential_IO`	generic package	sequential input-output	Section 15.3
`Direct_IO`	generic package	direct input-output	Section 15.4
`Text_IO`	package	text input-output	Section 15.5
`IO_Exceptions`	package	input-output exceptions	Section 15.6
`Low_Level_IO`	package	low-level input-output	—

Index